Footprint story

It was 1921

Ireland had just been partitioned, the British miners were striking for more pay and the federation of British industry had an idea. Exports were booming in South America – how about a handbook for businessmen trading in that far away continent? The Anglo-South American Handbook was born that year, written by W Koebel, the most prolific writer on Latin America of his day.

1924

Two editions later the book was 'privatized' and in 1924, in the hands of Royal Mail, the steamship company for South America, it became The South American Handbook, subtitled 'South America in a nutshell'. This annual publication became the 'bible' for generations of travellers to South America and remains so to this day. In the early days travel was by sea and the Handbook gave all the details needed for the long voyage from Europe. What to wear for dinner; how to arrange a cricket match with the Cable & Wireless staff on the Cape Verde Islands and a full account of the journey from Liverpool up the Amazon to Manaus: 5898 miles without changing cabin!

1939

As the continent opened up, the South American Handbook reported the new Pan Am flying boat services, and the fortnightly airship service from Rio to Europe on the Graf Zeppelin. For reasons still unclear but with extraordinary determination, the annual editions continued through the Second World War.

1970s

Many more people discovered South America and the backpacking trail started to develop. All the while the Handbook was gathering fans, including literary vagabonds such as Paul Theroux and Graham Greene (who once sent some updates addressed to "The publishers of the best travel guide in the world, Bath, England").

1990s

During the 1990s the company set about developing a new travel guide series using this legendary title as the flagship. By 1997 there were over a dozen guides in the series and the Footprint imprint was launched.

2000s

The series grew quickly and there were soon Footprint travel guides covering more than 150 countries. In 2004, Footprint launched its first thematic guide: *Surfing Europe*, packed with colour photographs, maps and charts. This was followed by further thematic guides such as *Diving the World*, *Snowboarding the World*, *Body and Soul escapes*, *Travel with Kids* and *European City Breaks*.

2010

Today we continue the traditions of the last 89 years that have served legions of travellers so well. We believe that these help to make Footprint guides different. Our policy is to use authors who are genuine experts who write for independent travellers; people possessing a spirit of adventure, looking to get off the beaten track.

Laos Handbook

Claire Boobbyer

Laos is fast becoming the darling of Southeast Asia, satisfying all the romantic images of perfumed frangipani trees, saffron-robed monks, rusty old bicycles and golden temples, all set amongst a rich tapestry of tropical river islands, ethnic minority villages, cascading waterfalls and vivid, green rice paddies, and bound together by the mighty Mekong River, the country's lifeline. The vernacular architecture that other countries have swept away in a maelstrom of redevelopment survives in Laos. Simple wooden village homes, colonial-era brick-and-stucco shophouses and gently mouldering monasteries mark Laos out as different. Traditional customs are also firmly intact: incense wafts out of streetside wats, monks collect alms at daybreak and the clickety-clack of looms weaving richly coloured silk can be heard in most villages.

As compelling as these sights and sounds are, the lasting impression for most visitors is of the people and their overwhelming friendliness. Many believe the best thing about Laos is the constant chimes of *sabaidee* ringing out from schoolchildren, monks and other passers-by, extending an invitation to join their meal. This is a land that endures the terrible legacy of being the most bombed country per capita in the world, yet its people transform bomb casings into flower pots and bomb craters into fish ponds. Regardless of their history and their poverty, people here radiate a sunny, happy disposition.

Life is simple in Laos but the people share with their former French colonists an infectious joie de vivre that ensures that good food and great company are the pinnacle of enjoyment. If you're seeking a relaxed lifestyle and a warm welcome, you've come to the right place.

This page Monks at the Mekong River.
Previous page Statue at temple, Vientiane.

CHINA

Muang Uthai

Phongsali

VIETNAM

Muang Khua

Muang Sing

Luang Namtha

Udomxai

5 Muang Ngoi Neua

Sop Bao

Xam Neua **6** Muang Poun

Ou

4 Houei Xai

Tha

Het

Sam

Mekong

3 Luang Prabang

Phonsavanh **2**

Nong Het

Sayaboury

Plain of Jars

Luang Prabang Range

Vang Vieng

Khone Xa Na

Annamite Range

San

Nam Ngum Reservoir

Paksan

Phonhong

7 *Khammouane Plateau*

1 VIENTIANE

Mahaxai

Thakhek

Na Phao

THAILAND

8 Savannakhet

Lamphoy

Done

Paks

Champasak

Wat Phou

9

Mekong

10

N

100 km
100 miles

CAMBODIA

CHINA

Gulf of
Tonkin

avanh

van

kong

ven
eau

°Attapeu

Laos highlights

See colour maps in centre of book

1 Explore That Luang, Vientiane, symbol of Lao nationhood and the country's holiest site. ▶▶ page 49.

2 See the bomb legacy and perplexing giant stone jars littered over US-bombed grasslands at Phonsavanh and the Plain of Jars. ▶▶ page 168.

3 Luang Prabang is a bijou city of golden temples with UNESCO World Heritage status. ▶▶ page 96.

4 Zipline through the Bokeo forest at the Gibbon Experience, Houei Xai, in search of singing gibbons. ▶▶ page 150.

5 Muang Ngoi Neua is a laid-back town amid limestone karsts and paddies on a bend in the river. ▶▶ page 133.

6 The caves at Vieng Xai were the Communist Pathet Lao bolthole and command centre. ▶▶ page 184.

7 Take a boat through Kong Lor Cave, a spectacular river cave. ▶▶ page 196.

8 Stroll around the crumbling colonial core of Savannakhet and go trekking in the nearby Sacred Forest. ▶▶ page 212.

9 Visit the tiered 12th-century Khmer archaeological site of Wat Phou and the charming riverside town of Champasak. ▶▶ page 231.

10 The Four Thousand Islands (Don Deth, Don Khone and Don Khong) make up Laos' very own tropical archipelago. ▶▶ page 261.

Monks beside Wat Pho

Contents

Contents

Footprint features

Essentials

Planning your trip

Where to go

Laos may not be on the travel itineraries of most international tourists or in the brochures of many tour companies, but it is a beautiful country with a great deal to offer. Notwithstanding the country's poverty and lack of development, it is civilized and refined, with elegant towns, sophisticated cuisine, a leisurely pace of life and a population which is probably the most welcoming and relaxed in Asia. Laos has style.

Certainly the former royal capital of Luang Prabang – designated a World Heritage Site by UNESCO – is a charming little city. Today's capital Vientiane, along with the other Mekong towns of Pakse, Savannakhet and Thakhek, is also elegant with its French architectural heritage largely intact. Wat Phou, an outlier of the former Cambodian kingdom of Angkor, is beguiling too, and some visitors will be interested in the war history and enigmatic stone urns that litter the Plain of Jars and the caves used by the Pathet Lao for their HQ at Vieng Xai. The Mekong islands in the far south are a great place to relax, swinging in a hammock, watching dolphins and wandering the disused railway track. Laos has also firmly established itself as the region's premier ecotourism destination, with a wide range of eco-activities available, ranging from treks to kayaking. But what visitors tend to remember best of all is the warmth of the people and the pleasure that comes from visiting a country which has so far managed to keep the more lurid and crass aspects of the modern world at bay.

Timetabling a visit Because travelling in Laos can be a bit of a lottery, it is strongly recommended that you allow some leeway in your schedule. Assuming, for example, that it will be possible to catch a flight from Phonsavanh to Vientiane to connect with another from Vientiane to Bangkok, and from there to the US or Europe, is – to say the least – risky. The same goes for road transport, especially during the wet season. Those on organized tours have some distinct advantages in this regard as they will have a local tour guide who can apply pressure and secure seats on overbooked planes. Local guides are also much more aware of when problems are likely to arise. A lone traveller, with no Lao, may be left floundering on the tarmac.

Nonetheless, a three- to four-week visit to Laos is sufficient to see much of the country – or at least that fraction of the country that it is possible to see. The main issue, perhaps, is how to couple a visit to the north with a trip to the south where Pakse, Champasak, Wat Phou and the Mekong islands are to be found. Vientiane to Pakse is a journey of around 750 km and many people (because they have booked a flight into and out of Vientiane) have then to retrace those 750 km to catch their plane out. By air this is bearable; by public bus it may test your patience, although now air-conditioned overnight buses make the journey in about 10 hours and are increasingly popular and hassle free. The alternative is to enter and exit at different ends of the country. It's possible to enter at Chiang Khong/ Houei Xai in the far north, travel south, and then exit at Pakse/Chongmek. Alternatively, you can enter from Cambodia through the Siphandon area at Don Kralor (where Lao visas are now available at the border) and exit to Vietnam via Vieng Xai at Na Maew or at Sop Hun for Dien Bien Phu (though Vietnam visas will be required in advance). *See the box on border crossings on page 19.*

Packing for Laos

It is possible to buy most toiletries, as well as things like medicines and peanut butter, in Vientiane. Luang Prabang, Savannakhet and Pakse also stock most basic items. Outside these cities little is available beyond such items as soap, washing powder, batteries, shampoo, and the like. Suitcases are not ideal if you are intending to travel overland by bus. A backpack, or even better a travel pack (where the straps can be zipped out of sight), is recommended.

In terms of clothing, most people in Laos dress tidily and modestly. Strappy T-shirts and tiny shorts are not appropriate; they are considered disrespectful. Laos is relatively casual and suits are not necessary. Don't pack too many clothes; laundry services are cheap, and the turnaround is rapid.

You may want to pack antacid tablets for indigestion; antibiotics for travellers diarrhoea (eg Ciprofloxacin); antiseptic ointment (eg Cetrimide); anti-malarials (see page 34); mosquito repellents; travel sickness tablets; painkillers; condoms/ contraceptives; tampons/ sanitary towels; high-factor sun screen and a sun hat, and a blow-up pillow.

For longer trips involving jungle treks take a clean needle pack, clean dental pack and water filtration devices. However, be wary of carrying disposable needles as customs officials may find them suspicious. If you are a popular target for insect bites or develop lumps quite soon after being bitten, carry an Aspivenin kit. This syringe suction device is available from many chemists and draws out some of the allergic materials and provides quick relief.

Make sure your passport is valid for at least six months and take photocopies of essential documents, passport ID and visa pages and student ID card. Spare passport photos are needed for each entry into Laos and useful in case of loss or theft. Other useful items include spare digital camera memory cards; bumbag/money belt; cotton or silk sheet sleeping bag; earplugs; mosquito net; padlock; sun glasses; Swiss Army knife; torch; travel wash; umbrella; wet wipes; plastic bags; and bandana for dusty *songthaew* rides.

One to two weeks

A one-week trip will require careful planning and prioritizing. If you fly into **Vientiane**, head north to wonderfully preserved **Luang Prabang** via **Vang Vieng**. Or fly from Vientiane to **Luang Namtha** to access the interesting and developed trekking region in the north before overlanding it back to Luang Prabang. Alternatively, after visiting Luang Prabang, fly back to Vientiane and on to Pakse for a trip to the tranquil, laid-back **Siphandon** (4000 islands) in the south.

With an extra week, you could build on the one-week options and fly to **Pakse** for **Wat Phou**, the sublime **Tad Lo** and **Tad Fan falls** and **Siphandon**, or to **Vientiane** to access northern Laos.

Three to four weeks

With one month it is better to start at the extreme north or the south of Laos to cover as much territory as possible. You could travel overland to **Siphandon** in southern Laos via Don Kralor from Cambodia. Before heading north take a side trip to the interesting **Bolaven Plateau** with its stunning coffee plantations and ubiquitous falls and or glide across the river to charming Champasak for the UNESCO World Heritage site of **Wat Phou**. As alternatives, visit the Xe Pian wetlands or the historic crumbling core of Savannakhet and nearby National Protected Areas for their newly opened up trekking opportunities. Overland it to **Thakhek** and do the motorcycle loop around the limestone scenery of central Laos, visiting the **Kong Lor** river cave en route. Or fly direct to **Vientiane** in order to catch a flight to **Phonsavanh** and explore the mysterious **Plain of Jars**, then continue to **Xam Neua** and the Pathet Lao caves at **Vieng Xai**. A long but interesting overland route will take you west from here via increasingly popular **Nong Khiaw** (with its boat access to the nearby riverside village of Muang Ngoi Neua) to **Luang Prabang**, from where you can head north to the trekking areas of **Luang Namtha**, **Muang Sing** and **Phongsali**, or the newly opened up trekking areas in this region such as **Vieng Phouka** or catch a boat up the Mekong towards the Thai border and stop at **Houei Xai** for the unbeatable Gibbon Experience in the forest of **Bokeo**. A flight from Vientiane or Luang Prabang to Xam Neua will save two days' travel and from Vientiane to Udomxai, in order to reach Phongsali, will also save two days' travel.

When to go

The best time to travel is during the relatively cool and dry winter months from October-November to March. Not only is the weather more pleasant at this time of year but roads are also in better shape. However, temperatures in upland areas like the Plain of Jars, the Bolaven Plateau and some towns in the north of the country can be extraordinarily cold. From April onwards, temperatures can exceed 40°C in many lowland areas, although it remains dry through to May. From June or July, as the wet season wears on, so unsurfaced roads begin to deteriorate and overland transport in some areas becomes difficult. In the north, the months from March through to the first rains in May or June can be very hazy as smoke from burning off the secondary forest hangs in the air. This can cause itchiness of the eyes. What's more, it means that views are restricted and sometimes flights are cancelled. See page 328 for more details on climate. For daily weather reports for various cities, see www.wunderground.com.

If you like festivals, consult the calendar of festivals and events on page 27.

What to do

Laos is starting to garner a reputation as one of the prime adventure and ecotourism destinations in the region. The pleasure of floating lazily down the Nam Song, stopping every so often to get out of your inner tube and explore a cave or two, is indisputable, and people come back for more time and again. Kayaking is also an option, but gear yourself up for a pleasant, rather tame day out rather than a foam-flecked white-knuckle ride. There are also wonderful trekking opportunities through stunning mountainous landscape, home to a variety of ethnic groups. Other activities, such as rafting, rock climbing, ziplining and cycling, are fairly recently established or slowly emerging and are not as developed as they are in Thailand. Elephant-related activities are also possible and there is the excellent Gibbon Experience in Bokeo. Safety is always an issue when participating in adventurous sports in Laos: make sure you are fully covered by your travel insurance; check the credentials of operators offering adventure activities; and make sure that vehicles and safety equipment are in a good condition. Note that medical care in Laos is still very limited, see page 35.

The best wildlife experiences

• Look out for wild elephants while trekking through the stunning wilderness of Phou Khao Khouay National Park, www.trekkingcentrallaos.com, page 80.

• Visit a camp, 15 km out of Luang Prabang, for the rehabilitation of elephants previously employed in the logging trade, www.elephantvillage-laos.com, page 128. Or elephant trek the wetlands of Xe Pian, page 235, and be sure not to miss the annual elephant festival in February, page 239.

• Catch a glimpse of the rare, black-cheeked crested gibbons chortling out soprano tunes from the jungle's canopy, with the Gibbon Experience, T084-212021, www.gibbonexperience.org, page 160.

• See the beautiful, rare, freshwater dolphins in Siphandon, page 261.

• Watch the space around the Nakai Nam Theun National Protected Area, one of the most important eco regions in Laos, with rare and endangered wildlife. Sustainable ecotourism and wildlife viewing options are under development. See page 208.

Caving

Laos has some of the most extensive caves in the region. Some of the best are around Vang Vieng, where caving tourism has been developed. Another highlight is the amazing Kong Lor river cave in the centre of the country. There are hundreds of caves around Vieng Xai but only a few open to tourists; for those interested in history, these caves should be a first stop. Operators include **Green Discovery**, www.greendiscoverylaos.com. Also see www.visit-viengxay.com.

Cycling and mountain biking

New cycling opportunities have opened up in Udomxai and in Xieng Khouang Province, the latter with the expertise of a German NGO. Many cyclists bring their own all-terrain or racing bikes but it's possible to rent them from tour operators. Most cities and towns have guesthouses that rent bicycles (for US$1-2 per day), though these aren't suitable for riding around the country. You will also need to bring a proper helmet as they aren't available in Laos. Traffic is quite light but often speeds along the highways, particularly the southern roads. Most major roads are sealed and for the most part traverse quite hilly areas. Cycling is offered by several tour agencies; Luang Namtha is a popular place to start, and **Green Discovery**, www.greendiscoverylaos.com, runs excellent cycling tours. Also contact **Saamlan Cycling**, in Udomxai, T030-513 0184, T020-5560 9790 (mob); **Symbiosis**, www.symbiosis-travel.com; and tour operators in Phonsavanh, see page 178.

Kayaking and rafting

Laos is crisscrossed by rivers, which carve their way through stunning scenery. Kayaking and rafting are offered around the country. Before undertaking a trip ensure that the boats are in good condition and that you are supplied with safety equipment, such as helmets and life-jackets. Most kayaking and rafting trips must be organized from a provincial capital or Vientiane. Nam Song, at Vang Vieng, page 85, offers water-borne tours for most tastes. See also Luang Prabang, page 129, Luang Namtha, page 159, Nong Khiaw, page 132, Muang Ngoi Neua, page 140, and Pakse, page 240. There is also good kayaking around the Bolaven Plateau, page 245. Contact **Green Discovery**, www.greendiscoverylaos.com, **Xplore-Asia**, www.xplore-asia.com; and www.laoyouthtravel.com.

Wildlife conservation

The opportunity to buy or consume wildlife will probably present itself throughout your travels in Laos . However, while the Government of Lao PDR permits subsistence hunting for rural villagers, the sale and purchase of any wildlife is illegal in the country, and is damaging to biodiversity and local livelihoods.

You may see live wild animals for sale as meat or pets in rural areas and cities. Some travellers buy these live animals out of pity, and then release them. Please do not be tempted to do this, as the vendors do not know your motivation and the sale simply increases the demand for wildlife. Also, by this stage the animal could be sick, and could infect other wild animals.

You may also encounter rat snakes, soft-shelled turtles, mouse deer, sambar deer, squirrel, bamboo rat, muntjac and pangolins as food in markets and on the menus of Lao and Chinese restaurants in Vientiane, Luang Prabang and in the provinces. Some French restaurants in Vientiane and Luang Prabang serve deer – usually this is muntjac, a wild animal from the forest. Many of these species are either endangered themselves or are a prey source for endangered species, such as the Indochinese tiger.

Nor should travellers be tempted to purchase stuffed wild animals, animal products such as bags and wallets or insects in framed boxes (eg butterflies and beetles). Also to be avoided are animal teeth sold as rings and necklaces – sellers often state this is buffalo bone but it may be bear or wild pig bone. Do not buy bottles of alcohol with snakes, birds or insects inside. These items are illegal in Laos, and most travellers will find that their purchases are confiscated by customs in their home country (particularly in Australia and America). Only products with a CITES-certified label are legal to buy and take home.

As a part of many festivals and temple visits in Laos, Buddhists release small birds to gain merit. You are likely to see these tiny birds, frequently native munias and swallows, in small rattan cages outside temples. The Wildlife Conservation Society-Lao PDR Program is working with the Lao Buddhist Association to discourage this practice. The birds, weakened by being caged, probably perish shortly after release. Please don't participate in buying and releasing birds.

For many species of wildlife in Laos, populations are at critically low levels. The Wildlife Conservation Society-Lao PDR Program is collaborating with the Vientiane Capital City government to monitor and control wildlife trade. Government staff patrol restaurants, markets and households with suspected trade or captured species, and confiscate the wildlife. Live wildlife is released or euthanized; dead wildlife is periodically burnt in ceremonial public fires (for project transparency and to raise awareness). The Wildlife Conservation Society (WCS) appreciates the support of all visitors and residents in Laos to help conserve wildlife. For more information, visit www.wcs.org/international/Asia/laos.

Dr Renae Stenhouse, Wildlife Conservation Society.

Rock climbing

Laos has stunning karst rock formations, caves and cliffs and is an ideal destination for rock climbers. However, rock climbing is still relatively new to Laos and the only area which has developed facilities is Vang Vieng. It is expected that over the next few years this adventure sport will be established in other areas. You can pick up a copy of the *Rock Climbing – Vang Vieng Guide*, by Dr Volker Schoeffl (2005) at all **Green Discovery** offices (see also www. greendiscoverylaos.com/downloads/rockclimbing/vangvieng.pdf).

Spas
There are only a handful of authentic spas in Laos. Luang Prabang is the place to go for a range of wonderful spas. For extreme indulgence try the spa at **La Résidence Phou Vao**, page 128. For a cheaper luxury alternative try the **Spa Garden**, page 128, which offers a wide selection of massage and beauty treatments.

Trekking
Treks are offered in abundance and the most northerly parts of the country are especially geared up for this sort of activity. New centres of trekking are now based out of Vieng Phouka and Muang Long, Nong Khiaw and Muang Ngoi Neua. In other parts of the country, treks have been launched in Savannakhet (to the sacred forest of the Dong Phou Vieng National Protected Area, page 218, Phongsali (to remote ethnic minority areas), page 135, and Champasak provinces (in and around the Xe Pian National Protected Area, page 235) and a more responsible trek has been launched in the Akha-sensitive area of Muang Sing, page 148. New trekking opportunities are on the cards in the Bolaven Plateau. Other destinations include Phou Hin Poun National Protected Area, page 211; Vang Vieng, page 83; Luang Prabang, page 96; Luang Namtha, page 144; Bokeo Nature Reserve, page 150; Vieng Phouka, page 146; Savannakhet, page 221; and Tad Lo, page 247.

When trekking in Laos, it is imperative to abide by local customs in order to support efforts to keep tourism sustainable and low impact. For a different perspective on the landscape, try **elephant trekking** around Luang Prabang, Xe Pian Wetlands and Tad Lo.

For more information, contact the **National Tourism Administration** of Lao PDR, www.trekkingcentrallaos.com. In Phongsali, contact the **Provincial Tourism Office**, T088-210098, www.phongsali.net and

Northern Traveling and Information Service Center, T088-210594, northerntraveletr@ yahoo.com. In Thakhek, see the **Tourism Information Centre**, T052-212512, somkiad@ yahoo.com; in Udomxai, the **Provincial Tourism Office**, T081-212482, www.oudomxay. info; in Savannakhet, the **Eco Guide Unit**, T041-214203, www.savannakhet-trekking.com; and in Champasak, the **Provincial Tourism Office**, Pakse, T031-212021, www.xepian.org.

Tour operators include **Green Discovery**, www.greendiscoverylaos.com; **Exotissimo**, Muang Sing, www.exotissimo.com, T086-400016, akhaexp@gmail.com; **Luang Namtha Eco Guide Unit**, T086-211534; **Muang Long Tourism Office**, T020-5519 5561 (mob), tui-fat@hotmail.com; **Lao Youth Travel**, in Nong Khiaw and Muang Ngoi Neua, www. laoyouthtravel.com; **Tiger Trails**, in Nong Khiaw, www.laos-adventure.com; and **Vieng Phouka Eco Guide Service**, T081-212400, T020-5598 5289 mob, mpvpk@laotel.com. See also all tour operators in Phonsavanh, page 178.

Getting there

Air

The easiest – and cheapest – way to access the region is via **Bangkok**, **Hong Kong** or **Kuala Lumpur**. Most major airlines as well as the budget airline **AirAsia** have direct flights from Europe, North America and Australasia to these hubs. Laos is only accessible from within Asia.

There are international flights to Vientiane from the following countries: **Cambodia** (Phnom Penh and Siem Reap), **China** (Kunming and Nanning), **Thailand** (Bangkok and Chiang Mai) and **Vietnam** (Hanoi and Ho Chi Minh City), **Malaysia** (Kuala Lumpur). There are also international flights to Luang Prabang and Pakse. Most people visiting Laos from outside the region, travel via Bangkok. There are also flights from Bangkok and Chiang Mai to **Luang Prabang**. A cheaper option for getting to Laos from Bangkok is to fly to **Udon Thani**, Thailand, about 50 km south of the border at the Friendship Bridge and travel overland from there. For full details, see page 77. An alternative route is to fly from Bangkok to **Chiang Rai**, Thailand, before overlanding it to **Chiang Khong** and crossing into northern Laos at **Houei Xai**. From Houei Xai there are flights to Vientiane and boats to Luang Prabang via Pak Beng.

From Thailand **Bangkok (BKK)** is the main gateway to Vientiane. If you want to visit Bangkok as well as Laos, the best way is to include the Bangkok–Vientiane sector on your long-haul ticket. This is a cheaper option than purchasing tickets separately in Bangkok. There are daily flights between Bangkok (Suvarnabhumi) and Vientiane operated by **THAI** (www.thaiairways.com) and **Lao Airlines** (www.laoairlines.com). Lao Airlines also flies from Bangkok to Savannakhet and Pakse. **Bangkok Airways** (www.bangkokair.com) flies from Bangkok to Luang Prabang. Bangkok Airways offers the highly useful, user-friendly and competitive Discovery Air Pass for those exploring the region. A minimum of three flight routes and a maximum of six must be purchased. Reservations can be changed free of charge and rerouting is permitted for US$30 per transaction.

Chiang Mai (CNX) Lao Airlines (www.laoairlines.com) runs a four-weekly service between Chiang Mai (northern Thailand) and Luang Prabang.

Udon Thani (UTH) While most visitors to Laos fly directly into Vientiane, the preferred route in and out of Laos for many expats is via Udon Thani in northeast Thailand, situated about 50 km south of the Friendship Bridge border. This is because the single domestic airfare between Bangkok and Udon is around a third of the international fare between Bangkok and Vientiane, while a domestic return costs half the price of the international ticket. Discount airlines **AirAsia** (www.airasia.com) and **Nok Air** (www.nokair.com) fly this route. **Lao Airlines** also flies from Udon Thani to Luang Prabang. The service works very efficiently and is fairly hassle-free. From Udon Thani, you can catch a minibus or taxi to the Friendship Bridge or a bus to the Talaat Sao bus terminal in Vientiane. (You could also travel by overland from Udon Thani to Pakse in southern Laos, see below.) Taking the Udon/Friendship Bridge option between Bangkok and Vientiane will probably add only one hour to your journey, since immigration at Vientiane's Wattay Airport tends to be slow.

Another possibility for crossing into Laos from Thailand is to take a budget flight from Bangkok to Ubon Ratchathani in northeast Thailand and then cross the border into

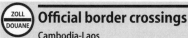

Official border crossings

Cambodia-Laos
Don Kralor-Voen Kham (Laos visas now available at the border), page 19.

China-Laos
Mohan-Boten, page 19.

Myanmar (Burma)-Laos
Foreigners are not permitted to enter or leave Laos through Myanmar (Burma).

Thailand-Laos
Mittaphab (Friendship) Bridge, Nong Khai-Vientiane, page 19.
Chiang Khong-Houei Xai, page 19.
Mouang Mon/Vangpung, Bokeo province (Lao visa required in advance).
Beung Kan-Paksan, page 19 (Lao visa required in advance).
Nakhon Phanom-Thakhek, pages 19.
Mukdahan-Savannakhet, page 19.
Chongmek-Vang Tao (near Pakse), page 19.

Vietnam-Laos
Tay Trang-Sop Hun, page 19.
Nam Xoi-Na Maew, page 19 (Lao visa required in advance).
Nam Khan-Nong Het, page 19.
Cau Treo-Nam Phao, page 19.
Cha Lo-Na Phao.
Lao Bao-Dansavanh, page 19.
Bo Y-Yalakhuntum, page 19.

southern Laos at Chongmek, see box page 228. Or you could to take a flight to Sakhon Nakhon, also in northeast Thailand, and then cross the boder at Nakhon Phanom to Thakhek in central Laos.

From Cambodia There are regular flights between Phnom Penh (PNH) and Vientiane with **Vietnam Airlines** (www.vietnamairlines.com) and **Lao Airlines** (www.laoairlines. com). **Lao Airlines** also runs flights between Siem Reap and Vientiane; between Siem Reap and Pakse; and Siem Reap and Luang Prabang.

From China **Lao Airlines** (www.laoairlines.com) runs flights between Kunming (KMG), Nanning and Vientiane.

From Vietnam **Lao Airlines** (www.laoairlines.com) operates flights between Vientiane, Luang Prabang and Hanoi and between Pakse and Ho Chi Minh City. **Vietnam Airlines** (www.vietnamairlines.com) flies between Hanoi, Ho Chi Minh City and Vientiane.

Airport departure tax The departure tax is incorporated into the air ticket price ▸▸ *For airport information, see Ins and outs sections throughout the guide.*

Road and river

Laos is a landlocked country and hopes to establish itself as a regional transit point, with international highways dissecting the country at 100 km intervals. There are more than a handful of crossings between Laos and its neighbouring countries making cross-regional travel much easier. Laos 30-day visas are also available on arrival at nearly all of these border crossings (see box, page 19). For much of its length, the Lao-Thai border is defined by the Mekong, with bridges and ferries to link the two countries. To the east, the Annamite mountain range forms a spine separating Laos from Vietnam, with a few cross-border buses running from Vientiane and Savannakhet. However, borders with Vietnam have opened up across the length of the country. There is only one official border crossing between Laos and Cambodia in the south and between Laos and China in the north. Foreigners are not permitted to cross between Laos and Myanmar (Burma).

Getting around

Air

Lao Airlines runs domestic flights from Vientiane to Luang Prabang, daily, to Phonsavanh (Xieng Khouang) and Pakse four times a week, three times a week to Houei Xai, Udomxai, Luang Namtha and Savannakhet. There are also flights twice a week from Luang Prabang to Pakse and from Pakse to Savannakhet three times a week. **Lao Airlines** now flies modern aircraft. **Phongsavanh Airlines** (T021-513 0000) has taken over the **Lao Capricorn Air Company** and operates flights to Xam Neua, Phongsali and Sayaboury province. ▸▸ *For further details, see Ins and outs sections throughout the guide.*

River

It is possible to take riverboats up and down the Mekong and its main tributaries. Boats stop at Luang Prabang, Pak Beng, Houei Xai in the northwest and around Don Deth and Don Khong in the south as well as other towns and villages, such as Nong Khiaw and north to Phongsali on the Nam Ou River in the north. Luxury services operate between Houei Xai and Luang Prabang and between Pakse and Wat Phou, Champasak. Aside from the route down from Houei Xai to Luang Prabang, often there are no scheduled services, and departures may be limited in the dry season. Take food and drink and expect crowded conditions on the Houei Xai-Luang Prabang route. The most common boats are the *hua houa leim*, with no decks, the hold being enclosed by side panels and a flat roof (metal boats get very hot). Speedboats chart some routes, but are dangerous and uncomfortable.

Road

Roads have greatly improved in recent years, making journeys much faster. Quite a few bus, truck, tuk-tuk, *songthaew* (see below) and taxi drivers understand basic English, French or Thai, although some (especially tuk-tuk drivers) aren't above forgetting the price you negotiated before hopping aboard! It is an advantage to have the name written out in Lao. Many people will not know road names, but will know all the sights of interest.

Bus/truck/minivan

It is possible to travel to most areas by bus, truck or *songthaew* (converted pickup truck) in the dry season, although road travel in the rainy season can be tricky if not impossible in some areas. VIP buses are comfortable night buses, usually allowing you to sleep – but watch out for karaoke on board. In the south, a sleeping bus plies the route from Pakse to Vientiane. Book a double bed if you don't want to sleep next to a stranger. Robberies have been reported on the night buses so keep you valuables secure.

On some long-distance routes, such as Vientiane/Luang Prabang to Xam Neua, big Langjian (Chinese) trucks are used. These have been converted into buses with divided wooden seats and glassless windows. In more remote places (Xam Neua to Vieng Xai, for instance), ancient jeeps are common. In the south, Japanese-donated buses are used although you may see the occasional shiny Volvo bus. Most roads are sealed, but breakdowns are still common. For some connections you may need to wait a day.

A decent network of minivans transport foreigners from one main tourist destination to another; for example, Luang Prabang to Vang Vieng. Costs are higher than public buses but journey times are shorter and pickups from guesthouses are usually part of the service.

Car hire

This costs from US$60-100 per day, depending on the vehicle, with petrol and kilometre usage included. The price includes a driver. Insurance is generally included (you will need an international driver's permit) but check the fine print. A general rule: if you are involved in a crash, you, the foreigner, will be liable for costs as you have more money. One car hire company is **Europcar Laos** (Asia Vehicle Rental), 354-356 Samsenthai Road, Vientiane, T021-223867, www.europcarlaos.com.

Motorbike and bicycle hire

There are an increasing number of motorcycles available from guesthouses and other shops in major towns. 110cc bikes go for around US$5-10 per day. Bicycles are a cheap way to see the sights. Many guesthouses have bikes for rent at US$1-2 per day. Mountain bikes can be rented from specialist outlets.

Tuk-tuk

The motorized three-wheelers known as 'jumbos' or tuk-tuks are large motorbike taxis with two bench seats in the back. You'll find them in most cities and metropolitan areas;

expect to pay around 10,000-20,000 kip for a short ride. They can also be hired by the hour or the day to reach destinations out of town.

In city centres make sure you have the correct money for your tuk-tuk as drivers are often conveniently short of change. Also opt to flag down a moving tuk-tuk rather than selecting one of the more expensive ones that shark around outside tourist destinations.

Maps

The **GT Rider** Lao map (www.gt-rider.com) found in bookstores and other shops in Vientiane is probably the most accurate map of the country. The National Tourism Authority has also put together pretty good provincial maps of Laos, using the GT Rider Map as a base. These are available at provincial tourism offices. There are numerous glossy maps of Vientiane and Luang Prabang, including 3D maps, and a series of locally produced town maps of Vientiane, Luang Prabang, Thakhek, Savannakhet and Pakse. **Hobo Maps** (www.hobomaps.com) produces some highly detailed and recommended maps of certain towns and areas. The best selection of maps in the UK is available from **Stanfords**, 12-14 Long Acre, London WC2E 9LP, T020-7836 1321, www.stanfords.co.uk.

Sleeping

Rooms in Laos are rarely luxurious and standards vary enormously. You can end up paying double what you would pay in Bangkok for similar facilities and service. At higher end hotels, rates are subject to 10% government tax and 10% service charge.

However, the hotel industry is expanding rapidly. There is a reasonable choice of hotels of different standards and prices in Vientiane, Luang Prabang and Pakse and an expanding number of budget options in many towns on the fast-developing tourist trail. First-class and boutique hotels exist in Vientiane and Luang Prabang. Vientiane, however, still lacks sufficient good budget choices. The majority of guesthouses and hotels have fans and attached bathrooms, although more and more are providing air conditioning where there is a stable electricity supply, while others are installing their own generators to cater for the needs of the growing tourist trade. Smaller provincial towns, having previously had only a handful of hotels and guesthouses – some of them French colonial villas – now have a growing number of rival concerns as tourism takes off. In rural villages, people's homes are transformed into bed-and-breakfasts on demand. While Vientiane may still have little budget accommodation, many towns in the north, such as Vang Vieng, Muang Ngoi Neua, Muang Sing and Luang Namtha, have a large choice of very cheap, and in some cases good accommodation, including dorm beds. In the southern provinces, upmarket and boutique accommodation has cropped up in Champasak province. There are several good eco-lodges in the country, most notably the **Boat Landing** at Luang Namtha (page 154) and the **Kingfisher Ecolodge** at Ban Kiet Ngong (page 238). Many tour companies offer homestay in ethnic minority villages and camping as part of a package tour.

General camping is not available but possible as part of booked tours. Treehouse accommodation is available in Bokeo and a luxury boat with accommodation sails between Pakse and Wat Phou.

Countrywide online reservations are now possible through www.whl.travel. The franchise is run by a team in Vientiane who support the respsonsible travel ethos. The service is very efficient and all budget ranges are covered.

Sleeping price codes

LL **Over US$200** **Luxury:** Only a couple of hotels – in Vientiane and Luang Prabang – fall into this category.

LL-AL **US$151-200** **First class plus:** Business services, sports facilities, Asian and Western restaurants, bars and discos. Most of Laos' top hotels fall into this category.

A **US$66-100** **First class:** Hotels in this category should be comfortable and offer reasonable business services, a range of recreational facilities, restaurants and bars. They may well make up in terms of personal service and friendliness what they lack in size and grandeur. A number of boutique hotels fall into this category. Toilets should be Western-style. Bed linen will be provided, and towels perhaps. There may be a restaurant.

B **US$46-65** **Tourist class:** All rooms will have air conditioning, TV and an attached bathroom with hot water. Other services should include one or more restaurants, a coffee shop/room service and, occasionally, a pool.

C **US$31-45** **Economy:** Rooms will be air conditioned and will have attached bathrooms with hot water and Western toilets. A restaurant and room service will probably be available. Wi-Fi should be available from this category up.

D **US$21-30** **Medium budget:** Probably air conditioned rooms with en suite bathroom. Toilets should be Western-style. Bed linen and towels will be provided. There may be a restaurant. Wi-Fi may also be provided.

E **US$12-20** **Budget/guesthouse:** Quite possibly air conditioned but more usually fan-cooled rooms and possibly shared bathrooms. Bed linen and towels provided. Rooms are small and facilities few.

F-G **Less than US11** **Dorm/guesthouse-type accommodation:** Shared bathroom facilities, possibly squat toilets, fans and probably cold-water showers at the very cheap end. Cleanliness will vary but will not necessarily be an issue.

Unless otherwise stated, the prices and codes in this guide are based on the cost of a double room for one night including service charges.

Eating

Food

Lao food is similar to that of Thailand, although the Chinese influence is slightly less noticeable. Lao dishes are distinguished by the use of aromatic herbs and spices such as lemon grass, chillies, ginger and tamarind. The best place to try Lao food is often from roadside stalls or in the markets. The staple Lao foods are *kao niao* (glutinous rice), which is eaten with your hands and fermented fish or *pa dek* (distinguishable by its distinctive smell), often laced with liberal spoons of *nam pa*, fish sauce. Being a landlocked country, most of the fish is fresh from the Mekong. One of the delicacies that shouldn't be missed is Mok Pa steamed fish in banana leaf.

Most dishes on most menus are variations on two themes: fish and bird. *Laap*, also meaning 'luck' in Lao, is a traditional ceremonial dish made from (traditionally) raw fish or meat crushed into a paste, marinated in lemon juice and then mixed with chopped

Eating price codes

mint. It is called *laap sin* if it has a meat base and *laap paa* if it's fish based. Beware of *laap* in cheap street restaurants, however. It is sometimes concocted from raw offal and served cold and should be consumed with extreme caution. Overall though, *laap* is cooked well for the *falang* palate.

Phanaeng kai is stuffed chicken with pork, peanuts and coconut milk with a dash of cinnamon. *Kai ping* is grilled chicken eaten with sticky rice. Another popular Lao dish is *tam som* – often called *som tam* – a spicy green shredded papaya salad served with chilli peppers, spices and fish sauce. This dish can be fiery hot at times, so you should stipulate how hot (*phet*) you want it! There are several different types of **soup** – include *keng no mai* (bamboo shoot), *keng khi lek* (vegetable and buffalo skin), *ken chut* (without pimentos) *keng kalami* (cabbage with fish or pork), *kenghet bot* (mushroom), *tom khaa kai* (chicken with coconut milk).

The most commonly used **vegetables** are aubergines, tomatoes, cabbage, corn, cucumbers and lettuce, often cooked together, pureed and eaten with sticky rice. Soups usually accompany meals – they are invariably a mixture of fish and meat infused with aromatic herbs.

The Lao are partial to **sweets**: sticky rice with coconut milk and black beans (which can be bought in bamboo tubes in the markets) and grilled bananas are favourites. Fruit is available but not as widely available as you might expect.

There is a well-ingrained **Vietnamese** culinary tradition and **Chinese** food is never hard to find. *Feu*, Vietnamese noodle soup, is itself an import from China but often masquerades in Laos as a Lao dish. It is usually served with a plate of raw vegetables. Most restaurants outside the main towns do not have menus but will nearly always serve *feu* and *laap* or local specialities. Indeed, their generic name is *raan khai feu* – restaurants that sell *feu*. Vietnamese spring rolls are also common – you can either have *yaw jeun* (deep-fried spring rolls) or *yaw dip* (fresh spring rolls) and both are usually served with fresh herbs and rice noodles.

The French left a legacy of sophisticated cuisine in Laos. **French** food is widely available in restaurants, and street cafés usually serve delectable fresh croissants, crusty baguettes, *pain au chocolat* and a selection of sticky pastries, which can be washed down with a powerful cup of Lao coffee. Bread or *khao jii* is baked daily and often served with vegetables, pâté, fried eggs or an omelette. The Lao however have a habit of eating baguette sandwiches with fish sauce sprinkled on top (these are widely available in Vientiane, Savannakhet and Pakse). Menus in many of Vientiane's restaurants still have a distinctly French flavour to them. Vintage Bordeaux and Burgundies occasionally emerge from the cellars of restaurants too – although most of the fine vintages have now been consumed. Hotels in the larger towns often provide international menus and continental breakfasts. Even in small towns it is easy enough to create a continental breakfast: baguettes are widely available, wild honey can usually be tracked down, and fresh Bolaven coffee is abundant.

Nam pa

No meal would be complete without a small dish of *nam pa* to spoon onto almost any savoury dish. Like *nam plaa* in Thailand, *nuoc mam* in Vietnam and *ngan-pyaye* in Myanmar (Burma), *nam pa* is an essential element of Laotian gastronomic life. To make the sauce, freshwater fish is packed into containers and steeped in brine. (Elsewhere in the region, it is made from saltwater fish, but because Laos is landlocked, freshwater fish is used instead.) The resulting brown liquid – essentially the by-products of slowly putrifying fish – is drained off and bottled. A variation is *pa dek, nam pa* with small chunks of fermented fish added, often with rice husks too. This variation tends to be used in cooking and is kept in an earthenware pot – often outside as the aroma is so strong!

Drink

Urban areas have access to safe water, but all water should be boiled or sterilized before drinking. Less than a third of rural areas have safe drinking water. Bottled water is widely available, however, and produced locally, so it is cheap (about 2000 kip for a litre). Soft drinks are expensive as they are imported from Thailand; a can of Coca-Cola from a stall, for example, costs about 5000-7000 kip. *Nam saa*, weak Chinese tea, is also served. There is now local fresh milk production, so milk and yoghurt can be found, but fresh milk is not widely available and coffee with milk (*cafe nam hawn*) is more often served with condensed milk.

The local brew is rice wine which is traditionally drunk from a clay jug with long straws. The white variety is called *lau-lao* (Lao alcohol) and is made from fermented sticky rice; *fanthong*, or red *lao-lao* is fermented with herbs. Bottled *lao-lao* is also widely available. Imported beers, wines and spirits can be found in hotels, restaurants, bars and nightclubs but are not particularly cheap. Beer Lao is available as a light lager (although the alcohol content is 5%) and is best served ice-cold or as a dark ale. In towns without electricity it is normal to add ice although most places are now on the grid. Beer Lao also has the advantage of being reasonably priced (about US$1 for a large bottle, depending on the restaurant or bar). Chinese beer is cheaper still and can be found in the northern provinces. French wines can be purchased (at a price) in some supermarkets and quite a few restaurants.

Eating out

Restaurant food is, on the whole, hygienically prepared, and as long as street stall snacks have been well cooked, they are usually safe. Such stalls are a great place to sample regional specialities. Expect to pay between US$2-8 per head for a meal in main towns and less outside. By ordering only Lao food in local restaurants it is possible to pay US$1 or less for a meal.

Really classy restaurants are only to be found in Vientiane and Luang Prabang (especially the former). Good French cuisine is available in both cities. Salads, steaks, pizzas and more are all on offer. Expect to pay anywhere over US$5 for a reasonable meal. Lao restaurants are better value for money. Indian restaurants are starting to find their way around the country.

The universal stimulant – the betel nut

Throughout the countryside in Southeast Asia, and in more remote towns, it is common to meet men and women whose teeth are stained black, and gums red, by continuous chewing of the 'betel nut'. This, though, is a misnomer. The betel 'nut' is not chewed at all: the three crucial ingredients that make up a betel 'wad' are the nut of the areca palm (*Areca catechu*), the leaf or catkin of the betel vine (*Piper betel*), and lime. When these three ingredients are combined with saliva they act as a mild stimulant. Other ingredients (people have their own recipes) are tobacco, gambier, various spices and the gum of *Acacia catechu*. The habit, though also common in South Asia and parts of China, seems to have evolved in Southeast Asia and it is mentioned in the very earliest chronicles. The lacquer betel boxes of Myanmar and Thailand, and the brass and silver ones of Indonesia, illustrate the importance of chewing betel in social intercourse. Galvao in his journal of 1544 noted: "They use it so continuously that they never take it from their mouths; therefore these people can be said to go around always ruminating."

Among Westernized Southeast Asians the habit is frowned upon: the disfigurement and ageing that it causes, and the stained walls and floors that result from the constant spitting, are regarded as distasteful products of an earlier age. But beyond the elite it is still widely practised.

Far more prevalent are lower-end Lao and Chinese-Lao restaurants which can be found in every town. Food in these places is usually good and excellent value for money. You'll find a cold beer and a good range of vegetarian and meat-based dishes for between US$3 and US$5. In towns on the tourist trail these local restaurants are complemented by places geared to the vicarious demands of tourists. Here you'll find fruit smoothies, Indian food, burgers and more for anywhere between US$21.50 and US$5. Finally, right at the bottom end – in terms of price if not necessarily in terms of quality – are stalls that charge a US$1-2 for filled baguettes or simple single-dish meals.

Entertainment

If you are looking for evenings out at cultural events, or are keen to dance the night away, Laos is not the place for you, and anywhere outside the capital is unlikely to provide much in the way of night-time revelry. Excepting perhaps the odd lock-in in a Luang Prabang pub or at a bar in Vientiane, a quiet evening sipping Lao beer by the Mekong is as good as it gets. Today, even in towns, a 2200 curfew exists; sometimes bars and clubs will push it and stay open to 2300 or 2400.

Most larger towns have bars and 'discos'. But a Lao disco is usually a place where live rather than recorded music is played. There are a growing number of bars and clubs in Vientiane, and a handful in the other major centres (mostly geared to locals rather than the foreign/expat markets).

Festivals and events

Being of festive inclination, the Lao celebrate New Year four times a year: the international New Year in January, Chinese New Year in January/February, Lao New Year (Pi Mai) in April and Hmong New Year in December. The Lao Buddhist year follows the lunar calendar, so many of the festivals are movable. The first month begins around the time of the full moon in December. There are also local festivals (see under individual regions). **Note** The list below is not exhaustive, but does include the most important festivals. Many Chinese, Vietnamese and ethnic minority festivals are also celebrated in Laos.

January

New Year's Day (1 Jan) Public holiday celebrated by *baci* throughout the country.
Pathet Lao Day (6 Jan) Public holiday, parades in main towns.
Army Day (20 Jan) Public holiday.
Boun Pha Vet (movable) To celebrate King Vessanthara's reincarnation as a Buddha. Sermons, processions, dance, theatre. This is a popular occasion for the ordination of young monks.

February

Magha Puja (movable) This celebrates the end of Buddha's time in the monastery and the prediction of his death. It is principally celebrated in Vientiane and at Wat Phou, near Champasak.
Chinese New Year (movable, Jan/Feb) Celebrated by Chinese and Vietnamese communities in Laos. Many Chinese and Vietnamese businesses shut for 3 days.

March

Women's Day (8 Mar) Public holiday.
People's Party Day (22 Mar) Public holiday.
Boun Khoun Khao (movable) Harvest festival centred on the wats.

April

Pi Mai (13-15 Apr) Public holiday to celebrate Lao New Year. The first month

of the Lao New Year is actually Dec but festivities are delayed until Apr when days are longer than nights. By Apr it's also heating up, so having hose pipes levelled at you and buckets of water dumped on you is more pleasurable. The festival also serves to invite the rains. Pi Mai is one of the most important annual festivals, particularly in Luang Prabang (see page 126). Statues of the Buddha (in the 'calling for rain' posture) are ceremonially doused in water, which is poured along an intricately decorated trench (*hang song nam pha*). The small stupas of sand, decorated with streamers, in wat compounds are symbolic requests for health and happiness over the next year. It is celebrated with traditional Lao folk singing (*mor lam*) and the circle dance (*ramwong*). There is usually a 3-day holiday to celebrate Lao New Year. Similar festivals are held in Thailand, Cambodia and Burma. If you attend the festival, keep your money, cameras, etc, in plastic to save them from getting wet. 'Sok Dee Pi Mai' – good luck for the New Year – is usually said to one another during this period.

May

Labour Day (1 May) Public holiday with parades in Vientiane.
Visakha Puja (movable) To celebrate the birth, enlightenment and death of the Buddha, celebrated in local wats.
Boun Bang Fai movable) The rocket festival, is a Buddhist rain-making festival. Large bamboo rockets are built and by

Baci

The *baci ceremony* is a uniquely Lao *boun* (festival) and celebrates any auspicious occasion – marriage, birth, achievement or the end of an arduous journey, for instance. It dates from pre-Buddhist times and is animist in origin. It is centred on the *phakhouan*, a designer tree made from banana leaves and flowers (or, today, some artificial concoction of plastic) and surrounded by symbolic foods. The most common symbolic foods are eggs and rice – symbolizing fertility. The *mophone* hosts the ceremony and recites memorized prayers, usually in Pali, and ties cotton threads (*sai sin*) around the wrists of guests symbolizing good health, prosperity and happiness. For maximum effect, these strings must have three knots in them. It is unlucky to take them off until at least three days have elapsed, and custom dictates that they never be cut. Many people wear them until, frayed and worn, they fall off through sheer decrepitude. All this is accompanied by a *ramvong* (traditional circle dance), in turn accompanied by traditional instruments – flutes, clarinets, xylophones with bamboo crosspieces, drums, cymbals and the *kaen*, a hand-held pipe organ that is to Laos what the bagpipes are to Scotland.

monks and carried in procession before being blasted skywards. The higher a rocket goes, the bigger its builder's ego gets. Designers of failed rockets are thrown in the mud. The festival lasts 2 days.

June/July

Children's Day (1 Jun) Public holiday.
Khao Phansa (movable) The start of Buddhist Lent and a time of retreat and fasting for monks. The festival starts with the full moon in Jun/Jul and continues until the full moon in Oct. It all ends with the *Kathin* ceremony in Oct when monks receive gifts.

August

Lao Issara (13 Aug) Public holiday, Free Lao Day.
Liberation Day (23 Aug) Public holiday.
Ho Khao Padap Dinh (movable) The celebration of the dead.

September/October

Boun Ok Phansa (movable) This is the end of Buddhist Lent when the faithful take offerings to the temple. It is held in the '9th month' in Luang Prabang and the '11th month' in Vientiane, and marks the end of the rainy season. Boat races take place on the Mekong River, with crews of 50 or more men and women participating. On the night before the race small rafts are set afloat on the river.

October

Freedom from the French Day (12 Oct) Public holiday which is only really celebrated in Vientiane.
Lai Heua Fai (Fireboat Festival) See Luang Prabang, page 126.

November

Boun That Luang (movable) Celebrated in all Laos' *thats*, most enthusiastically in Vientiane (see page 67). Includes religious rituals, local fairs, processions, beauty pageants and other festivities.

December

Hmong New Year (movable).
Independence Day (2 Dec) Public holiday, military parades, dancing and music.

Living in sinh

A lovely experience is to wear the *sinh*, the Lao traditional banded sarong. It isn't at all necessary to wear one but the Lao love the fact that you are taking an interest in their culture and are likely to shower you with compliments. If you are attending a wedding, funeral or plan to visit a government office, it is a sign of respect to wear one. Depending on the fabric, a *sinh* can be whipped up in most markets in a day and can be bought for around US$10.

Shopping

Popular souvenirs from Laos include handicrafts and textiles, which are sold pretty much everywhere. The market is usually a good starting point as are some of the minority villages. Boutique shops are now available predominantly in Luang Prabang, with a handful in Vientiane. The smaller, less touristy towns sell silk at the cheapest price (at about 40,000 kip a length). The best place to buy naturally dyed silk in Laos is in Xam Neua (see page 181). Much of this high-quality silk makes its way to Luang Prabang and Vientiane, where it is sold at much higher prices. Most markets offer a wide selection of patterns and embroidery, but two of the best places to go in Vientiane are **Talaat Sao** (Vientiane Morning Market) or, behind it, the cheaper **Talaat Kudin**, which has a textile section in the covered area.

If you wish to have something made, most tailors can whip up a simple *sinh* (Lao sarong) in a day but you might want to allow longer for adjustments or other items. **OckPopTok** in Luang Prabang also has a fantastic reputation for producing top-shelf, naturally dyed silk. Vientiane and Luang Prabang offer the most sophisticated line in boutiques, where you can get all sorts of clothes from the utterly exquisite to the frankly bizarre. Those on a more frugal budget will find some tailors who can churn out a decent pair of trousers on Sisavangvong in Luang Prabang and around Nam Phou in Vientiane. If you get the right tailor, they can be much better than those found in Thailand, both in terms of price and quality but you do need to be patient and allow time for multiple fittings. It is also a good idea to bring a pattern/picture of what you want, and keep an eye on small details. You should, for example, ensure that the same coloured thread is used in any alterations that need to be made.

Silverware, most of it in the form of jewellery and small pots (though some of the ones you see may not be made of real silver), is traditional in Laos. The finest silversmiths have always worked out of Vientiane and Luang Prabang. Chunky antique ethnic-minority jewellery, including bangles, pendants, belts and earrings, is usually found in markets in the main towns, or antique shops in Vientiane, particularly around Nam Phou. Xam Neua market also offers a good range of ethnic minority-style silver jewellery. Look for traditional necklaces that consist of wide silver bands, held together with a spirit lock (a padlock to lock in your scores of souls). Though silver is common, gold jewellery is the preference of the Lao Loum (lowland Laos) and its bright yellow colour is associated with Buddhist luck (often it is further dyed to enhance its orange goldness); the best quality gold is bought in Vientiane.

Craftsmen in Laos are still producing **wood carvings** for temples and coffins. Designs are usually traditional, with a religious theme.

Responsible travel

Since the early 1990s there has been a phenomenal growth in 'ecotourism', which promotes and supports the conservation of natural environments and is also fair and equitable to local communities. While the authenticity of some ecotourism operators needs to be interpreted with care, there is clearly both a huge demand for this type of activity and also significant opportunities to support worthwhile conservation and social development initiatives by this means.

The **International EcoTourism Society** ⓘ *www.ecotourism.org*, **Tourism Concern** ⓘ *T020-7133 3800, www.tourismconcern.org.uk*, and **Planeta** ⓘ *www.planeta.com*, develop and promote ecotourism projects in destinations all over the world and their websites provide details for interesting initiatives throughout Southeast Asia.

For opportunities to participate in an environmentally responsible and ethical manner, consult www.responsibletravel.com.

Visiting minority villages It is becoming increasingly popular for travellers to Laos to visit minority villages. This raises a whole series of questions about conduct which cannot be covered in a general discussion, because of cultural differences between the many different ethnic peoples. There is certainly a case for advising visitors, where possible, to employ the services of a local guide. As was the case in northern Thailand when trekking became popular, the actions of a few are tarring the reputation of the many. In more than a few cases, visitors have no idea how to behave with minority people. Many seek to buy drugs, female travellers are scantily clad, some have little notion of local customs, where not to go, what not to bring (many bring sweets), and so on. Because the numbers of travellers visiting minority villages has exploded in recent years this has become quite a serious problem.

In the culturally sensitive Akha area of Muang Sing, please do not trek without a guide. See page 149.

Local customs and law

Bargaining/haggling

While bargaining is common in Laos – in the market or in negotiating a trip on a tuk-tuk, for example – it is not heavy-duty haggling. The Lao are extremely laid back and it is rare to be fleeced; don't bargain hard with them, it may force them to lose face and reduce prices well below their profit margin. For most things, you won't even really need to bargain. Having said that, beware of the tuk-tuk drivers (where possible, try to flag down tuk-tuks rather than taking those waiting on street corners). Approach bargaining with a sense of fun; a smile or joke always helps.

Clothing

Informal, lightweight clothing is all that is needed, although a sweater and a few layers is vital for the highlands in the winter months (November to March). An umbrella is useful during the rainy season (June and July) or during the intense heat as a parasol. Sleeveless shirts and singlets, very short shorts and skirts are considered disrespectful. Please respect this even though many tourists do not. When visiting monasteries (wats) women should keep their shoulders covered and take their shoes off. One of the main reasons for the tight

How big is your footprint?

The point of a holiday is, of course, to have a good time, but if it's relatively guilt-free as well, that's even better. Perfect ecotourism would ensure a good living for local inhabitants, while not detracting from their traditional lifestyles, encroaching on their customs or spoiling their environment. Perfect ecotourism probably doesn't exist, but everyone can play their part. Here are a few points worth bearing in mind:

· Think about where your money goes and be fair and realistic about how cheaply you travel. Try to put money into local people's hands as far as possible; drink local beer or fruit juice rather than imported brands and stay in locally owned accommodation wherever you can.

· Haggle appropriately and with humour. Remember that you want a fair price, not the lowest one.

· Think about what happens to your rubbish. Take biodegradable products and a water filter to avoid using lots of plastic bottles. Be sensitive to limited resources such as water, fuel and electricity.

· Help preserve local wildlife and habitats by respecting rules and regulations, such as sticking to footpaths, not standing on coral and not buying products made from endangered plants or animals.

· Don't treat people as part of the landscape; they may not want their picture taken. Ask first and respect their wishes.

· Learn the local language and be mindful of local customs and norms. It can enhance your travel experience and you'll earn respect and be more readily welcomed by local people.

· And finally, use your guidebook as a starting point, not the only source of information. Talk to local people, then discover your own adventure.

controls on tourism in Laos is because of the perceived corrosive effects that badly dressed tourists were having on Lao culture. The assumption was that scruffy dress was a reflection of character. Today, 'scruffy' travellers are still frowned upon and officials are getting fed up with people wandering around skimpily clad, particularly in Vang Vieng and Siphandon. If you are bathing in public, particularly in rural areas, wear a sarong. It is expected that people will take their shoes off before entering a Lao home.

Conduct

Wats Monks are revered, don't touch their robes. If talking to a monk your head should be lower than his. Avoid visiting a wat around 1100 as this is when the monks have their morning meal. It is considerate to ask the abbot's permission to enter the *sim* and shoes should be removed before entry. When sitting down, feet should point away from the altar and main image. Arms and legs should be fully covered when visiting wats. A small donation is often appropriate (kneel when putting it into the box).

Forms of address Lao people are addressed by their first name, not their family name, even when a title is used.

Greeting The *nop* or *wai* – with palms together below your chin and head bowed, as if in prayer – remains the traditional form of greeting. Shaking hands, though, is very widespread – more so than in Thailand. This can be put down to the influence of the

French during the colonial period. '*Sabaidee*' (hello) is also a good way to greet. Avoid hugging and kissing to greet Lao people, as they tend to get embarrassed.

In private homes Remove your shoes. When seated on the floor you should tuck your feet behind you.

Eating etiquette In Laos, who eats when is important. At a meal, a guest should not begin eating until the host has invited him or her to do so. Nor should the guest continue eating after everyone else has finished. It is also customary for guests to leave a small amount of food on their plate; to do otherwise would imply that the guest was still hungry and that the host had not provided sufficient food. Sharing is a big thing at meal times, where plates of food are ordered and shared amongst everyone. Lao people often invite tourists to eat with them or share on buses, and it is a nice gesture if this is reciprocated (though Lao people tend to be shy so don't take any refusal as a rejection). Most Lao are tolerant of other cultures and don't expect things such as eating etiquette to be strictly adhered to.

General Pointing with the index finger is considered rude. If you want to call someone over, gesture with your palm facing the ground and fingers waving towards you (as opposed to the other direction). In Lao your head is considered 'high' and feet are considered 'low'. So try to keep your feet low, don't point them at people or touch people with your feet. Don't pat children on the head (or touch people's heads in general), as it is the considered the most sacred part of the body.

Lao people have a passive nature. Yelling or boisterous people tend to send them into panic mode. If a dispute arises, a smile and a joke will do the trick. Likewise when bargaining, keep a sense of humour– the funnier you are, the more successful you will be.

The Lao are proud people and begging is just not the done thing, so don't hand out money (or medicine) to local villagers. If you want to give a gift or a donation to someone, it is best to channel it through the village elder.

Essentials

Accident and emergency

Contact the relevant emergency service and your embassy. Make sure you obtain police/medical records in order to file insurance claims. If you need to report a crime, visit the local police station and take a local with you who speaks English.
Ambulance T195, **Fire** T190, **Police** T191.

Children

Lao people love small children and it is not uncommon for waiters and waitresses to spend the whole evening looking after and entertaining your offspring.

Food and drink
Stir-fried vegetables and rice or noodles go down well with children. Fruit can be bought cheaply: papaya and banana are excellent sources of nutrition, and can be self-peeled, ensuring cleanliness. Powdered milk is available in provincial centres, although most brands have added sugar. Powdered food can also be bought in some towns – the quality may not be the same as equivalent foods bought in the West, but it is perfectly adequate for short periods. Avoid letting your child drink tap water as it may carry parasites. Bottled water and fizzy drinks are sold widely. A damp cloth and some antiseptic liquid (such as Dettol) are useful for wiping hands and tabletops and can help to minimize the chance of infection.

Disposable nappies
These can be bought in Vientiane and other larger provincial capitals, but are expensive.

Sleeping
At the hottest time of year, a/c may be essential for a baby or young child's comfort. This rules out many of the cheaper hotels, but a/c accommodation is available in all larger towns.

Transport
Public transport may be a problem; long bus journeys are restrictive and uncomfortable. Chartering a car is undoubtedly the most convenient way to travel overland but rear seatbelts are scarce, although becoming more common, and child seats even rarer.

Customs and duty free

Duty-free allowance is 500 cigarettes, 2 bottles of wine and a bottle of liquor. Laos has a strictly enforced ban on the export of antiquities and all Buddha images.

Disabled travellers

Considering the proportion of the region's population that are seriously disabled, foreigners might expect better facilities and allowances for the immobile. But in Laos, pavements are often uneven, there are potholes and missing drain covers galore, pedestrian crossings are ignored, ramps are unheard of, lifts are few and far between and escalators are seen only in magazines and high-end hotels and a sprinkling of shopping complexes.
RADAR, 12 City Forum, 250 City Rd, London, EC1V 8AF, T020-72503222, www.radar.org.uk.
SATH, 347 Fifth Av, Suite 610, New York City, NY 10016, T212-447-7284, www.sath.org.

Drugs

Drug use is illegal and there are harsh penalites ranging from fines through to imprisonment or worse. Police have been known to levy heavy fines on people in Vang Vieng for eating so-called 'happy' foods, or for being caught in possession of drugs. Note that 'happy' food can make some people extremely sick. Though opium has in theory been eradicated, it is still for sale in northern areas and people have died from overdosing. *Yaa baa* is also available here and should be avoided at all costs.

Electricity

Voltage 220, 50 cycles in the main towns. 110 volts in the country; 2-pin sockets are common. Blackouts are now less common outside Vientiane than before; many smaller towns are not connected to the national grid and only have power during the evening although being wired up is eventually reaching more remote spots.

Embassies and consulates

Australia, 1 Dalman Cres, O' Malley, Canberra, ACT 2606, T02-62864595, www.laosembassy.net.
Cambodia, 15-17 Mao Tse Toung Blvd, Phnom Penh, T023-982632.
France, 74 Ave Raymonde-Poincaré 75116 Paris, T01-4553 0298, www.laoparis.com.
Thailand, 502/1-3 Soi Sahakarnpramoon 39, Thanon Pracha Uthit, Wangthonglang, Bangkok 10310, T02-539 6667, www.bkklaoembassy.com.
Vietnam, 22 Tran Binh Trong, Hanoi, T04-42854576; 181 Hai Ba Trung, Ho Chi Minh City, T08-38297667.

Gay and lesbian

Gay and lesbian travellers should have no problems in Laos. However, it does not have a hot gay scene as such and the Lao government is intent on avoiding the mushrooming of the gay and straight sex industry. Openly gay behaviour is contrary to local culture and custom and visitors, whether straight or gay, should not flaunt their sexuality. Any overt display of passion or even affection in public is taboo. In

Vientiane there aren't any gay bars per se although there are some bars and clubs where gays congregate. Luang Prabang has a few more gay-orientated options and is fast become one of South-east Asia's most gay-friendly destinations.

Officially, it is illegal for any foreigner to have a sexual relationship with a Lao person they aren't married to.

Health

See your GP or travel clinic at least 6 weeks before departure for general advice on travel risks and vaccinations. Try phoning a specialist travel clinic if your own doctor is unfamiliar with health conditions in Laos. Make sure you have sufficient medical travel insurance, get a dental check, know your own blood group and if you suffer a long-term condition such as diabetes or epilepsy, obtain a Medic Alert bracelet/necklace (www.medicalert.co.uk). If you wear glasses, take a copy of your prescription.

It is risky to buy medicine, and in particular anti-malarials, in developing countries, as they may be substandard or part of a trade in counterfeit drugs.

Vaccinations
It is advisable to vaccinate against polio, tetanus, typhoid, hepatitis A, and rabies if going to more remote areas. Japanese encephalitis may be advised for some areas, depending on the duration of the trip and proximity to rice-growing and pig-farming areas. Yellow fever does not exist in Laos. However, the authorities may wish to see a certificate if you have recently arrived from an endemic area in Africa or South America.

Health risks
Malaria is prevalent in Laos and remains a serious disease; about a third of the population contracts malaria at some stage during their lives. Most people will need to consider a malaria prophylaxis other than chloroquine, since there is such a high level

of resistance to it. Always check with your doctor or travel clinic for the most up-to-date advice before going to Laos.

The most serious viral disease is **dengue fever**, which is hard to protect against as the mosquitos bite throughout the day as well as at night.

Bacterial diseases include **tuberculosis** (TB) and some causes of the more common traveller's **diarrhoea**. Each year there is the possibility that **avian flu** or SARS might rear their ugly heads. Check news reports. just before you go to Laos. If there is a problem in an area you are due to visit you may be advised to have an ordinary flu shot or to seek expert advice. There are high rates of **HIV** in the region, especially among sex workers. **Rabies** and **schistosomiasis** (bilharzia, a water-borne parasite) may be a problem in Laos.

Medical services

Hospitals are few and far between and medical facilities are poor in Laos. Emergency treatment is available at the **Mahosot Hospital** and **Clinique Setthathirath** in Vientiane. The Australian embassy also has a clinic for Commonwealth citizens with minor ailments (see page 77). Better facilities are available in Thailand and emergency evacuation to Nong Khai or Udon Thani (Thailand) can usually be arranged at short notice. In cases of emergency where a medical evacuation is required, contact **Lao West Coast Helicopter**, Hangar 703, Wattay International Airport, T021-512023, www.laowestcoast. com. A charter to Udon Thani costs from around US$1550, subject to availability and government approval.

Contact your embassy or consulate for a list of doctors and dentists who speak your language, or at least some English. Doctors and health facilities in major cities are also listed in the Directory sections of this book. Healthcare can be expensive, especially hospitalization. Make sure you have adequate insurance (see below).

Thailand

Aek Udon Hospital, Udon Thani, Thailand, T+66 42-342555, www.aekudon.com. A 2½-hr trip from Vientiane.
Bumrungrad Hospital, 33 Sukhumvit 3, Bangkok, T+66 2-667 1000, www.bumrungrad. com. The best option: a world-class hospital with brilliant medical facilities.
Wattana Hospital Group, at Udon Thani T+66 42-325999, and Nong Khai, T+66 42-465201, www.wattanahospital.net. The latter in particular is a better alternative to the hospitals in Vientiane and only a 40-min trip from the capital.

Useful websites

www.btha.org British Travel Health Association.
www.cdc.gov US government site that gives excellent advice on travel health and details of disease outbreaks.
www.fco.gov.uk British Foreign and Commonwealth Office travel site has useful information on each country, people, climate and a list of UK embassies/consulates.
www.fitfortravel.scot.nhs.uk A-Z of vaccine/health advice for each country.
www.numberonehealth.co.uk Offers travel screening services, vaccine and travel health advice, email/SMS text vaccine reminders and screens returned travellers for tropical diseases.

Insurance

Always take out travel insurance before you set off and read the small print carefully. Check that the policy covers the activities you intend or may end up doing. Also check exactly what your medical cover includes, ie ambulance, helicopter rescue or emergency flights back home. Also check the payment protocol. You may have to cough up first before the insurance company reimburses you. It is always best to dig out all the receipts for expensive personal effects like jewellery or cameras. Take photos of these items and note down all serial numbers.

You are advised to shop around. **STA Travel** and other reputable student travel organizations offer good value policies. Young travellers from North America can try the **International Student Insurance Service** (ISIS), which is available through **STA Travel**, T1-800-777 0112, www.sta-travel.com. Other recommended travel insurance companies in North America include: **Travel Guard**, T1-800-826 1300, www.noelgroup.com; **Access America**, T1-800-284 8300; **Travel Insurance Services**, T1-800-937 1387; and **Travel Assistance International**, T1-800-821 2828. Older travellers should note that some companies will not cover people over 65 years old, or may charge higher premiums. The best policies for older travellers (UK) are offered by **Age UK**, www.ageuk.org.uk.

Internet

Internet cafés have been popping up all over Laos over the last few years. The connections are surprisingly good in major centres. Fast, cheap internet is available in Vientiane, Luang Prabang, Vang Vieng and Savannakhet for around 100-200 kip per min. Less reliable and more expensive internet (due to long-distance calls) can be found in Phonsavanh, Don Khone, Don Deth, Luang Namtha, Thakhek, Savannakhet and Udomxai. Many internet cafés also offer international phone services. Wi-Fi is on the increase and can be found in a few places in major tourist centres.

Language

Lao is the national language but there are many local dialects, not to mention the languages of the minority groups. Lao is closely related to Thai and, in a sense, is becoming more so as the years pass. Though there are important differences between the languages, they are mutually intelligible – just about. French is spoken, though only by government officials, hotel staff and many educated people over 40. However, most government officials and many shopkeepers have some command of English. See also Useful words and phrases, page 334, and Glossary, page 336.

Media

The *Vientiane Times*, www.vientianetimes. org.la, is published 5 days a week and provides quirky pieces of information and some interesting cultural and tourist-based features, as well as eye-catching stories translated from the local press and wire service. Television is becoming increasingly popular as more towns and villages get electricity. The national TV station broadcasts in Lao. In Vientiane **CNN**, **BBC**, **ABC** and a range of other channels are broadcast. Thailand's **Channel 5** gives English subtitles to news. The **Lao National Radio** broadcasts news in English. The **BBC World Service** can be picked up on shortwave.

Money

The kip is the official currency. At the time of going to press the exchange rate was US$1 = 8200 kip, £1 = 12,566 kip, €1 = 680 kip. The lowest commonly used note is the 500 kip and the highest, the recently introduced 50,000 kip. Kip tends to shadow the Thai baht but with a rather quaint one week delay. It is getting much easier to change currency and traveller's cheques. Banks are generally reluctant to give anything but kip in exchange for hard currency. US$ and sometimes Thai baht can be used as cash in most shops, restaurants and hotels and the Chinese Yuan is starting to be more widely accepted in northern parts of Laos (closer to the Chinese border). A certain amount of cash (in US$ or Thai baht) can also be useful in an emergency.

Banks include the **Lao Development Bank** and **Le Banque pour Commerce Exterieur Lao (BCEL)**, which change most major international currencies (cash) and traveller's cheques denominated in US$ and pounds sterling. BCEL branches offer cash advances on Visa/MasterCard and thankfully they have rolled out Visa and MasterCard ATMs in all tourist centres. ATMs will only dispense 700,000 kip at one time but apparently you can withdraw this amount 7 times a day. Note that some banks charge a hefty commission of US$2 per TC. While banks will change traveller's cheques and cash denominated in most major currencies into kip, some will only change US$ into Thai baht, or into US dollars cash.

Payment by credit card is becoming steadily easier – although beyond the more upmarket hotels and restaurants in Vientiane and Luang Prabang, you should not expect to be able to get by on plastic in Laos. American Express, Visa, MasterCard/ Access cards are accepted in a limited number of more upmarket establishments. Note that commission will be charged on credit card transactions.

Cost of travelling

The variety of domestic flights means that the bruised bottoms, dust-soaked clothes and stiff limbs that go hand-in-hand with some of the longer bus/boat rides can often be avoided by those who can afford to pay more. As roads gradually improve and journey times diminish in Laos though, buses and minivans have emerged above both planes and boats as the preferred (not to mention most reasonably priced) transportation option. The overnight VIP Pakse-Vientiane bus journey costs around 150,000 kip. Disproportionately, short tuk-tuk journeys in towns from bus stations to town centres cost more than a single journey on the London Underground! Budget accommodation costs US$3-10, a mid-range hotel from around US$20-30. Local food is very cheap and it is possible to eat well for under US$2 a meal. Even most Western-style restaurants will charge only between US$2-5 for a meal although it's possible to splurge in upmarket restaurants in Luang Prabang and Vientiane.

Opening hours

Banks Mon-Fri 0830-1600 (some close at 1500).
Bars and **nightclubs** Usually close around 2200-2300 depending on how strictly the curfew is being reinforced. In smaller towns, most restaurants and bars close by 2200.
Offices Mon-Fri 0900-1700; those that deal with tourists open a bit later and also over the weekend. Government offices close at 1600 and take a 1-2 hr lunch break.
Shops These keep regular business hours but those catering to tourists stay open longer into the evening.

Photography

Sensitivity pays when taking photographs. Be very wary in areas that have (or could have) military importance – such as airports, where photography is prohibited. Also exercise caution when photographing official functions and parades. Always ask permission before taking photographs in a monastery and before photographing groups of people or individuals.

Police

If you are robbed, your insurer will need you to obtain a police report. You may find the police will try to solicit a bribe for this service. Although not ideal, you will probably have to pay this fee to obtain your report. Laws aren't strictly enforced but when the authorities do prosecute people the penalties can be harsh, ranging from deportation through to prison sentences. If you are arrested, seek embassy and consular support. People are routinely fined for possessing drugs, having sexual relations with locals (when unmarried) and proselytizing. If you are arrested or encounter police, try to remain calm and friendly. Although drugs are available throughout the country, the police levy hefty fines and punishments if caught.

Post

The postal service is inexpensive and reliable but delays are common. As the National Tourism Authority assures: in Laos the stamps will stay on the envelope. Contents of outgoing parcels must be examined by an official before being sealed. Incoming mail should use the official title, Lao PDR. There is no mail to home addresses or guesthouses, so mail must be addressed to a PO Box. The post office in Vientiane has a Poste restante service. EMS (Express Mail Service) is available from main post offices in larger towns. In general, post offices open 0800-1200 and 1300-1600. In provincial areas, **Lao Telecom** is usually attached to the post office. **DHL**, **Fedex** and **TNT** have offices in Vientiane.

Public holidays

1 Jan New Year's Day.
6 Jan Pathet Lao Day.
20 Jan Army Day.
8 Mar Women's Day.
22 Mar People's Party Day.
14-16 Apr Lao New Year.
1 May Labour Day
1 Jun Children's Day
2 Dec Independence Day.

Safety

Travel advisories
The US State Department's travel advisories: **Travel Warnings & Consular Information Sheets**, www.travel.state.gov.
The UK **Foreign and Commonwealth Office**'s travel warning section, www.fco.gov.uk/en/travel-and-living-abroad.

Crime rates are very low but it is advisable to take the usual precautions. Most areas of the country are now safe – a very different state of affairs from only a few years ago when foreign embassies advised tourists not to travel along certain roads and in certain areas (in particular Route 13 between

Vientiane and Luang Prabang, and Route 7 between Phonsavanh and Route 13). Today these risks have effectively disappeared. However, the government will sometimes make areas provisionally off-limits if they think there is a security risk – take heed!

There has been a reported increase in motorcycle drive-by thefts in Vientiane, but these and other similar crimes are still at a low level compared with most countries. If riding on a motorbike or bicycle, don't carry your bag strap over your shoulder – as you could get pulled off the bike if someone goes to snatch your bag and end up seriously hurt. In the Siphandon and Vang Vieng areas, theft seems to be more common. It's advisable to use a hotel security box if available.

Road accidents are on the increase. The hiring of motorbikes is becoming more popular and consequently there are more tourist injuries. Wear a helmet.

Be careful around waterways, as drowning is one of the primary causes of tourist deaths. Be particularly careful during the rainy season (May-Sep) as rivers have a tendency to flood and can have extremely strong currents. Make sure if you are kayaking, tubing, canoeing, travelling by fast-boat, etc, that proper safety gear, such as life jackets, is provided. 'Fast-boat' river travel can be dangerous due to excessive speed and the risk of hitting something in the river and capsizing. Low Mekong River levels in the dry season in 2010 – the lowest for more than 50 years – have also caused damage and capsizing to boats. Seek advice before setting out.

Xieng Khouang Province, the Bolaven Plateau, Xam Neua and areas along the Ho Chi Minh Trail are littered with bombies (small anti-personnel mines and bomblets from cluster bomb units). There are also numerous, large, unexploded bombs; in many villages they have been left lying around. They are very unstable so DO NOT TOUCH. Only walk on clearly marked or newly trodden paths. Consult the Mines

Advisory Group (www.maginternational. org), which works in Laos.

Student travellers

There are few specific student discounts in Laos. Anyone in full-time education is entitled to an International Student Identity Card (www.isic.org). These are issued by student travel offices and travel agencies and offer special rates on all forms of transport and other concessions and services. They sometimes permit free admission to museums and sights, at other times a discount on the admission.

Telephone

International dialling code for Laos: T+856.
International operator: T170
Directory enquiries: T16 (national), T171 (international).

Public phones are available in Vientiane and other major cities. You can also go to **Lao Telecom** offices to call overseas. Phone cards are widely available in most convenient stores. Call 178 in Vientiane for town codes. Most towns in Laos have at least 1 telephone box with IDD facility. The one drawback is that you must buy a phonecard. Because these are denominated in such small units, even the highest-value card will only get you a handful of minutes talk time with Europe. Most call are charged between $0.80 and $2 a min. All post offices, telecoms offices and many shops sell phone cards. **Note** If ringing Laos from Thailand, dial 007 before the country code for Laos.

Mobile telephone coverage is now good across the country. Pay-as-you-go sim cards are available for 30,000 kip to 50,000 kip and calls and SMS are very cheap.

In summer 2010, the National Authority of Post and Telecommunications added an extra digit to all 7-digit mobile phone numbers. Depending on mobile phone providers, a 5, 9, 7 or 2 will need to be added to the front of phone numbers. Footprint has added these extra digits in this guide.

Many internet cafés have set up call facilities that charge US$0.20 and under per min to make a call. In Vientiane, Pakse, Luang Prabang and Vang Vieng most internet cafés are equipped with Skype, including headphones and webcam, which costs a fraction of the price for international calls (as long as you have an account already established).

Time

Laos is 7 hrs ahead of Greenwich Mean Time.

Tipping

Tipping is rare, even in hotels. However, it is a kind gesture to tip guides, and in some of the more expensive restaurants a 10% tip is appreciated if service charge is not included on the bill. If someone offers you a lift, it is a courtesy to give them some money to help cover the cost of fuel.

Tourist information

Contact details for tourist offices and other information resources are given in the relevant Ins and Outs sections throughout the text. Many provincial tourist offices now have an Eco Guide Unit attached or operating from a separate office. The best in the country is the one in Savannakhet. The **Laos National Tourism Authority**, Lane Xang, Vientiane, T021-212248, www.tourismlaos.org, provides a range of maps and brochures.

Some provincial tourist offices are excellent and staffed with helpful, knowledgeable and willing people. Others are woeful. The German NGO DED are doing an excellent job in many provinces to assist with providing tourist information and providing information about and creating new activities. Be patient in the less good ones and eventually they may come through with the information you need. There are particularly good tourism offices in Thakhek, Vieng Xai, Xam Neua, Udomxai and Phongsali. Unfortunately the front desk operation in Vientiane is pretty useless. You may be lucky enough to extract a bus timetable out of them, if you can raise them from their slumber.

The authority has teamed up with local tour operators to provide a number of ecotourism opportunities, such as trekking and village homestays, www. ecotourismlaos.com.

Websites

Up-to-date information on Laos is not easy to obtain. The best bet is to browse Lao-related or Lao-dedicated websites. The best sites, in our experience, are:
www.travelfish.org
www.visit-mekong.com/laos/
www.ecotourismlaos.com
www.laohotelgroup.org
www.asean-tourism.com
www.muonglao.com
www.stdplaos.com
www.visit-mekong.com
www.mekongtourism.org
http://exploremekong.org/responsible/laos
www.southeastasia.org

Tour operators

Numerous tour operators offer organized trips to this region of southeast Asia, ranging from a whistle-stop tour of the highlights of Laos to specialist trips that focus on a specific destination or activity. The main advantage of travelling with a reputable operator is that your transport, accommodation and any activities are all arranged for you in advance, which is particularly valuable if you have only limited time in the region. By travelling independently, however, you can be much more flexible and spontaneous. Although things will take a little longer, you will probably save money, if you manage your budget carefully.

UK

Adventure Company, Cross & Pillory House, Cross & Pillory Lane, Alton, Hampshire GU34 1HL, T0845-4505316, www.adventurecompany.co.uk.
Audley Travel, New Mill, New Mill Lane, Witney, Oxfordshire OX29 9SX, T01993-838000, www.audleytravel.com.
Buffalo Tours UK, The Old Church, 89B Quicks Rd, Wimbledon, London, SW19 1EX, T020-8545 2830, www.buffalotours.com.
Exodus, Grange Mills, Weir Rd, London, SW12 0NE, T020-8772 3936, www.exodus.co.uk.
Explore, Nelson House, 55 Victoria Rd, Farnborough, Hampshire, GU14 7PA, T0845-013 1537, www.explore.co.uk.
Guerba Adventure & Discovery Holidays, Wessex House, 40 Station Rd, Westbury, Wiltshire BA13 3JN, T01373-826611, www.guerba.co.uk.
Magic of the Orient, 14 Frederick Pl, Clifton, Bristol BS8 1AS, T0117-3116050, www.magicoftheorient.com. Tailor-made holidays to the Far East.
Silk Steps, Odyssey Lodge, Holywell Rd, Edington, Bridgwater, Somerset TA7 9JH, T01278-722460, www.silksteps.co.uk.
Steppes Travel, 51 Castle St, Cirencester, Glos GL7 1QD, T01285-880980, www.steppestravel.co.uk.
Symbiosis Expedition Planning, 1 Frenchies View, Denmead, Waterlooville, Hampshire, T0845-1232844, www.symbiosis-travel.com.
Trans Indus, 75 St Mary's Road and the Old Fire Station, Ealing, London, W5 5RH, T020-8566 3729, www.transindus.co.uk.
Travel Indochina Ltd, 2nd Floor, Chester House, George St, Oxford OX1 2AY, T01865-268940, www.travelindochina.co.uk.
Visit Asia (Tennyson Travel), 30-32 Fulham High St, London SW6 3LQ, T020-77364347, www.visitasia.co.uk.
W&O Travel, Welby House, 96 Wilton Rd, London, SW1V 1DW, T0845-277 3399, www.wandotravel.com.

In North America

Adventure Center, 1311 63rd St, Suite 200, Emeryville, CA, T1-800 2278747, www.adventurecenter.com.

Global Spectrum, 3907 Laro Court, Fairfax, VA 22031, T1-800 4194446, www.globalspectrumtravel.com. Travel specialists to Southeast Asia.

Hidden Treasure Tours, 509 Lincoln Boulevard, Long Beach, NY 11561, T877-761-7276 (USA toll free), www.hiddentreasuretours.com.

Journeys, 107 April Drive, Suite 3, Ann Arbor, MI 48103-1903, T734-665-4407, www.journeys./travel.

Myths & Mountains, 976 Tree Court, Incline Village, NV 89451, T001-775 832 5454 (T800-670-MYTH), www.mythsandmountains.com.

In Australia and New Zealand

Buffalo Tours, L9/69 Reservoir St, Surry Hills, Sydney, Australia 2010, T61-2-8218 2198, www.buffalotours.com.

Intrepid Travel, 360 Bourke St, Melbourne, Victoria 3000, T03-8602 0500, www.intrepidtravel.com.

Travel Indochina, Level 10, HCS House, 403 George St, Sydney, NSW 2000, T1300-138755 (toll free), www.travelindochina.com.au.

In Southeast Asia

Buffalo Tours, No 8/40 Ban Nongkham, Luang Prabang, Laos, T071-254395, www.buffalotours.com.

Exotissimo, 4666 - 06/044 Pangkham St, Vientiane, Laos, T021-241861, 44/3 Ban Vat Nong, Khemkong Rd, Luang Prabang, Laos, T071-252879, www.exotissimo.com

Discovery Indochina, 63A Cua Bac St, Hanoi, Vietnam, T+84 4 3716, www.discoveryindochina.com.

Luxury Travel Company, 5 Nguyen Truong To St, Ba Dinh District, Hanoi, Vietnam, T+84 4 3817, www.luxurytravelvietnam.com.

Vietnam Birding, 3rd floor, 71-75 Hai Ba Trung St, District 1, Ho Chi Minh City, Vietnam, T+84 8 3827 3766, www.vietnambirding.com.

Visas

A 30-day tourist visa can be obtained at most (but not all) borders. See Official border crossings, page 19. Visa prices are based on reciprocity with countries and range from US$30-42. 'Overtime fees' are often charged if you enter after 1600 or on a weekend. To get a visa you need a passport photograph and the name of a hotel you plan on staying in.

The Lao government also issues business visas that are available for 30-days with the possibility of extending for months beyond. This is a more complicated process and usually requires a note from an employer or hefty fees from a visa broker. These visas are best organized from your home country and can take a long time to process.

Tourist visa extensions can be obtained from the **Lao Immigration Office** in the

Ministry of the Interior opposite the Morning Market in Vientiane, on Phai Nam Rd, T021-212529. They can be extended for up to 1 month at the cost of US$2 per day (if you want to extend for a month it works out cheaper to cross the border); you will need 1 passport photo. It takes a day to process the extension and if you drop off early in the morning it will often be ready by the afternoon. Travel agencies in Vientiane and other major centres can also handle this service for you for a fee (ie an additional US$1-2 per day). Visitors who overstay are charged US$10 for each day beyond the visa's date of expiry on departure.

Women travellers

While women travelling alone can face more problems than men or couples, these are far less pronounced in Laos than in most countries, and it is rare for women to be harassed. Nonetheless, women should take care to dress modestly, especially in more provincial towns, and also take the usual precautions. It is illegal for a foreigner to be in a sexual relationship with a local, unless married. You may often get asked if you are married; just a friendly conversation starter.

Affection in public is frowned upon, especially in rural areas. What may be considered in the West as friendly affection, such as putting your arm around someone, could be misconstrued as romantic love in Laos, so try not to be too tactile with men.

If you are bathing in a waterfall or river, wear a sarong, as the locals are embarrassed by the sight of bare flesh. Tampons and sanitary towels can be purchased in major towns but are in short supply elsewhere.

Working in Laos

Work is not easily available in Laos and is in great demand. Laos has one of the highest retention rates of foreign workers in the region, as once they get there they don't want to leave. There is a vibrant expat community, mostly of aid workers (with NGOs or bilateral/multilateral agencies; see www.directoryofngos.org) as well as the usual diplomatic corps. But, unlike in Thailand, there is little scope for foreigners to teach English. Jobs are advertised in the *Vientiane Times*. The *Vientiane Guide*, published by the Women's International Group and available from bookshops, is useful if you are planning to live in Laos. Courses available to foreigners tend to focus on cultural activities. Details of cooking, weaving, language and meditation courses are provided.

Voluntary work

This can take the shape of long-term professional posts for humanitarian specialists and aid workers or short-, medium- and long-term positions, lasting from 2 weeks up to 9 months, for those taking sabbaticals and gap years, or young people looking for hands-on practical field experience. All these can be undertaken at a grassroots level. As a general rule, social work and environmental work are the largest sectors in the programmes offered by local NGOs in Laos.

There are several umbrella groups offering useful information and links to vetted organizations. Working Abroad (www. workingabroad.com) offers information on opportunities (paid and voluntary) in over 150 countries worldwide, including Laos. A good one-stop shop is www.yearoutgroup. org, a not-for-profit group representing, among others, SWP, i-to-i, Outreach International, Bunac, Greenforce and Raleigh International. Also worth checking out is World Wide Volunteering (www.wwv. org.uk), which organizes projects in more than 200 countries.

Other worthwhile organizations include VSO (www.vso.org.uk) in the UK; the Youth Ambassador Program (www.ausaid.gov. au/youtham) in Australia; CUSO, (www.cuso-vso.org) in Canada, and the United Nations Volunteers website, www.unv.org.

Contents

Footprint features

Border crossings

Vientiane

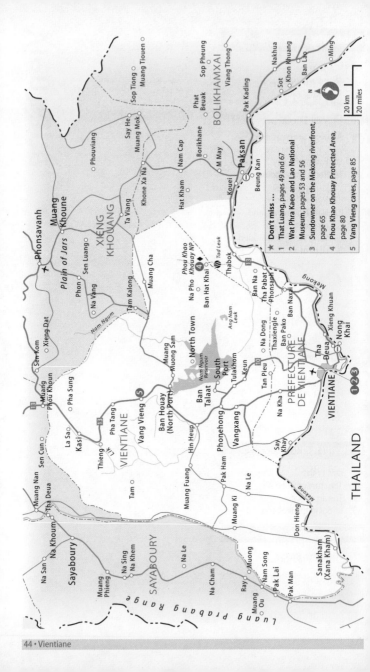

Don't miss ...

1 That Luang, pages 49 and 67
2 Wat Phra Kaeo and Lao National Museum, pages 53 and 56
3 Sundowner on the Mekong riverfront, page 65
4 Phou Khao Khouay Protected Area, page 80
5 Vang Vieng caves, page 85

Introduction

In 1563, King Setthathirat made the riverine city of Vientiane the capital of Laos. Or, to be more historically accurate, Wiang Chan, the 'City of the Moon', became the capital of Lane Xang. In those days it was a small fortified city on the banks of the Mekong with a palace and two wats, That Luang and Wat Phra Kaeo (built to house the Emerald Buddha). The city had grown prosperous from the surrounding fertile plains and the taxes levied from trade going upriver.

Today Vientiane is, perhaps, the most charming of all Southeast Asia's capital cities. Cut off from the outside world and foreign investment for much of the modern period, its colonial heritage remains largely intact. While the last few years have brought greater bustle and activity, it is still a quiet city of tree-lined boulevards, where the image of the past is reflected in the present.

Snuggled in a curve of the Mekong, Vientiane is also the region's most modest capital. It is much more than a town, but it doesn't quite cut it as a conventional city. Here, colourless concrete Communist edifices sit alongside chicken farmers; outdoor aerobics fanatics are juxtaposed against locals making merit at the city's wats; and a couple of traffic lights command a few SUVs, bikes, tuk-tuks and buses on the city's streets. During 2010, a large river reclamation and park development programme was underway, the US$31 million Mekong River Integrated Management Project, which is expected to be completed in 2013. Riverfront restaurants have already been removed as land is reclaimed and prettified.

Around Vientiane are several places of interest, some of which, including Ban Pako and Nam Ngum, make worthwhile stopovers or weekend retreats. Vang Vieng is on the road north to Luang Prabang and is a popular stop for the adventure and young crowd.

Vientiane

Vientiane's appeal lies in its largely preserved fusion of Southeast Asian and French colonial culture. Baguettes, plunged coffee and Bordeaux wines coexist with spring rolls, pho soup and papaya salad. Colourful tuk-tuks scuttle along tree-lined boulevards, past old Buddhist temples and cosmopolitan cafés. Hammer-and-sickle flags hang at 10-pin bowling discos and green and pink chickens wander the streets. But, as in the rest of Laos, the best thing about Vientiane, is its people. Take the opportunity to stroll around some of the outlying bans (villages) and meet the wonderful characters who make this city what it is. ▶▶ For listings, see pages 58-78.

Ins and outs → *Phone code: 021. Colour map 2, B2.*

Getting there

Air Most visitors arrive in Vientiane by air, the great bulk on one of the daily connections from Bangkok, with **Thai Air** (www.thaiair.com) or **Lao Airlines** (www.laoairlines.com), which also runs international flights from Thailand, Cambodia, Vietnam and China. **Vietnam Airlines** (www.vietnamairlines.com) runs flights from Hanoi and Ho Chi Minh City. **AirAsia** (www.airasia.com) flies from Kuala Lumpur.

Wattay International Airport ⓘ *T021-512012,* lies 6 km west of the town centre. Vientiane is the hub of Laos' domestic airline system, and to travel from the north to the south or vice versa it is necessary to change planes here. The international terminal is the bigger building on the west side. Both terminals have restaurants, telephone, taxi service and information booth. Both airports have taxi desks and the price is fixed at 54,000 kip to the centre (15-20 minutes). The international terminal has ATMs, a post office, hotel desk, internet (upstairs) and a branch of Lao Airlines. Only taxis are allowed to pick up passengers at the airport, although tuk-tuks can drop passengers here. Tuk-tuks can be picked up on the main road and sometimes lurk at the far side of the airport parking area, near the exit (40,000 kip to the centre). The dual carriageway into town is one of only a handful of such stretches of road in the country.

A cheaper way of getting to Vientiane from Thailand is to fly from Bangkok to **Udon Thani** on the budget airline **AirAsia** (www.airasia.com). There are several flights a day to and from Bangkok. Continue by road to Vientiane via the Friendship Bridge (see Official Border crossings, page 77), which lies just 25 km downstream from the capital (allow three hours). Shuttle buses from Udon Thani, 80 baht, four a day in each direction, run between the bus station and Vientiane. Airport shuttles are also available to the border. ▶▶ *See Essentials, page 18.*

Bus There are three public bus terminals in Vientiane. The **Southern bus station** ⓘ *T021-740521,* for destinations in the south of the country, is 9 km north of the city centre on Route 13. Most international buses bound for Vietnam depart from here as well as buses to southern and eastern Laos. The station has a VIP room, restaurants, a few shops, mini-mart and there's a guesthouse nearby.

The **Northern bus station** ⓘ*T021-261905,* is on Route T2, about 3 km northwest of the centre before the airport, and serves destinations in northern Laos. Most tuk-tuks will take you there from the city for 10,000-20,000 kip; ask for *Bai Thay Song*. There are English-speaking staff at the help desk.

A third **bus station** ①T021-216507, is across the road from the Morning Market, in front of Talaat Kudin, on the eastern edge of the city centre. This station serves destinations within Vientiane Province, buses to and from the Thai border and international buses to Nong Khai and Udon Thani in Thailand. It is also a good place to pick up a tuk-tuk.

Lak Sao, on the border with Vietnam, can be reached by a single 350-km public bus journey from Vientiane. There are also international connections with the private company **SDT Transport** ①T020-2220 5352. All these services depart from the Southern bus station. For destinations beyond Vientiane, most people either travel by bus (slow but cheap), tuk-tuk (even slower and cheaper) or plane (quick and still inexpensive by Western standards). ▶▶ *See Transport, page 73.*

Getting around

Although Vientiane is the capital of Laos, it is no Bangkok. It is small and manageable and is one of the most laid-back capital cities in the world. The local catchphrase '*bopenyang*' (no worries) has permeated through every sector of the city, so much so that even the mangy street dogs look completely chilled out, often found asleep in the middle of major intersections. The core of the city is negotiable on foot and even outlying hotels and places of interest are accessible by bicycle. Although traffic has increased substantially over the last five years or so, cycling remains the best and most flexible way to tour the city. It can be debilitatingly hot at certain times of the year but there are no great hills to struggle up. If cycling doesn't appeal to you, a combination of foot and tuk-tuk or small 110-125cc scooters take the effort out of sightseeing. There is a limited city bus service but it really serves outlying destinations on the Vientiane Plain rather than the city itself. Larger motorbikes, cars and taxis can also be hired, although these are mainly used for longer journeys and day trips.

Orientation The capital is divided into *bans* or villages, mainly centred on their local wats, and larger *muang* or districts: **Muang Sikhottabong** lies to the west, **Muang Chanthabouli** to the north, **Muang Xaisettha** to the east and **Muang Sisattanak** to the south. Vientiane can be rather confusing for the first-time visitor as there are few street signs and most streets have two names, pre- and post-revolutionary, but because the city is so small and compact it doesn't take long to get to grips with the layout. The names of major streets or *thanon* usually correspond to the nearest wat, while traffic lights, wats, monuments and large hotels serve as directional landmarks. When giving directions to a tuk-tuk it is better to use these landmarks when explaining where you want to go, as street names leave locals a little bewildered. Luang Prabang Road, which led out past the Novotel, has been renamed Souphanavong Road and That Luang Road is now 23 Singha Road. However, both names will be in use.

Maps Government-produced tourist/town maps are available from many hotels. The most common map of Vientiane in wide circulation is a well-produced 3-D map available free at the airport and at various places around town. Rather large, and not particularly useful from a tourist viewpoint, it makes a nice souvenir. (It is also sold in some places with the 'free' cunningly blanked out.) The Hobo Map of Vientiane centre is available in Phimphone Market and at the Vientiane Book Centre for 25,000 kip. The **National Geographic Office** ① *west of the Victory Monument, Mon-Fri 0900-1200 and 1300-1600*, provides plenty of maps at reasonable prices, although these may not be up to date. ▶▶ *For alternatives, see Shopping, page 68.*

Tourist information

Lao National Tourism Authority ① *Lane Xang (towards Patuxai), T021-212251, www.tourismlaos.org, Mon-Fri 0830-1200 and 1300-1600,* can provide information regarding ecotourism operators and brilliant trekking opportunities in provincial areas. This is a good starting point if you want to organize a trip to Phou Khao Khouay. For other information, it's a painful experience. The **Tourist Police** ① *0830-1200, 1300-1600,* are upstairs.

There's a listings magazine found in bars and restaurants. *Paisi* has a useful monthly cultural events calendar.

Background

Vientiane is an ancient city. There was probably a settlement here, on a bend on the left bank of the Mekong, in the 10th century but knowledge of the city before the 16th century is thin and dubious. Scholars do know, from the chronicles, that King Setthathirat decided to relocate his capital here in the early 1560s. It seems that it took him four years to build the city, constructing a defensive wall (hence 'Wiang', meaning a walled or fortified city), along with Wat Phra Kaeo and a much-enlarged That Luang.

Vieng Chan, as it was called, remained intact until 1827 when it was ransacked by the Siamese; this is why many of its wats are of recent construction. Francis Garnier in 1860 wrote of "a heap of ruins" and having surveyed the "relics of antiquity" decided that the "absolute silence reigning within the precincts of a city formerly so rich and populous, was … much more impressive than any of its monuments". A few years later, Louis de Carné wrote of the vegetation that it was like "a veil drawn by nature over the weakness of man and the vanity of his works".

The city was abandoned for decades and erased from the maps of the region. It was only conjured back into existence by the French, who commenced reconstruction at the end of the 19th century. They built rambling colonial villas and wide tree-lined boulevards, befitting their new administrative capital, Vientiane. At the height of American influence in the 1960s, it was renowned for its opium dens and sex shows.

Today Vientiane is a quiet capital with an urban population of perhaps 460,000 (up from 70,000 in 1960). There are around 695,500 inhabitants (about 10% of the population of Laos) in the Vientiane municipality but this extends far beyond the physical limits of the city. Before 1970 there was only one set of traffic lights in the whole city and, even with the arrival of cars and motorbikes from Thailand in recent years, the streets are a far cry from the congestion of Bangkok. Unlike Phnom Penh and Ho Chi Minh City, there are only scattered traces of French town planning; architecture is a mixture of east and west, with French colonial villas and traditional wooden Lao buildings intermingled with Chinese shophouses and more contemporary buildings. Some locals worry that foreign investment and redevelopment will ruin the city – already some remarkably grotesque buildings are going up – but officials seem to be aware that there is little to be gained from creating Bangkok in microcosm.

For the moment, the city retains its unique innocence: DJs are officially outlawed (although this is not enforced); there is a 2330 curfew; a certain percentage of music played at restaurants and bars every day is supposed to be Lao (overcome by banging out the Lao tune quota at 0800 in the morning) and women are urged to wear the national dress, the *sinh*, in government offices. However, to describe the Lao government as autocratic is unfairly negative. Vientiane's citizens are proud of their cultural heritage and are usually very supportive of the government's attempts to promote it. The government has tried, by and large, to maintain the national identity and protect its citizens from harmful outside influences. This is already starting to change; with the government reshuffle in 2006 came a gradual loosening of the cultural stranglehold.

Sights

Most of the interesting buildings in Vientiane are of religious significance. All tour companies and many hotels and guesthouses will arrange city tours and excursions to surrounding sights but it is just as easy to arrange a tour independently with a local tuk-tuk driver; the best English speakers (and thus the most expensive tuk-tuks) can be found in the parking lot beside Nam Phou. Those at the Morning Market (Talaat Sao) are cheaper. Most tuk-tuk drivers pretend not to carry small change, so make sure you have the exact fare with you before taking a ride.

That Luang

ⓘ *That Luang Rd, 3.5 km northeast of the city centre; daily 0800-1200 and 1300-1600 (except 'special' holidays); admission 5000 kip. A booklet about the wat is on sale at the entrance.*
That Luang is Vientiane's most important site and the holiest Buddhist monument in the country. The golden spire looks impressive at the top of the hill, northeast of the city.

According to legend, a stupa was first built here in the third century AD by emissaries of the Moghul Emperor Asoka; it is supposed to have contained the breast bone of the Buddha. Excavations on the site, however, have located only the remains of an 11th- to 13th-century Khmer temple, making the earlier provenance doubtful in the extreme. The present monument, encompassing the previous buildings, was built in 1566 by King Setthathirat, whose statue stands outside. Plundered by the Thais and the Chinese Haw in the 18th century, it was restored by King (Chao) Anou at the beginning of the 19th century. He added the cloister and the Burmese-style pavilion containing the That Sithamma Hay Sok. The stupa was restored by l'École Française d'Extrême-Orient (whose conservators were also responsible for the restoration of parts of Angkor Wat at the start of the 20th century) but was rebuilt in 1930 because many Lao disapproved of the French restoration.

The reliquary is surrounded by a square cloister, with an entrance on each side, the most famous on the east. There is a small collection of statues in the cloisters, including one of the Khmer king Jayavarman VII. The cloisters are used as lodgings by monks who travel to Vientiane for religious reasons and especially for the annual **That Luang festival** (see page 67). The base of the stupa is a mixture of styles, Khmer, Indian and Lao – and each side has a *hor vay* or small offering temple. This lowest level represents the material world, while the second tier is surrounded by a lotus wall and 30 smaller stupas, representing the 30 Buddhist perfections. Each of these originally contained smaller golden stupas but they were stolen by Chinese raiders in the 19th century. The 30-m-high spire dominates the skyline and resembles an elongated lotus bud, crowned by a banana flower and parasol. It was designed so that pilgrims could climb up to the stupa via the walkways around each level. It is believed that originally over 450 kg of gold leaf was used on the spire.

There used to be a wat on each side of the stupa but only two remain: **Wat Luang Nua** to the north and **Wat Luang Tai** to the south. The large new wat-like structure is the headquarters of a Buddhist organization. The outer walls are used to stage art exhibitions.

Although That Luang is considered to be the most important historical site in Vientiane, most visitors to the *that* will feel that it is not the most interesting, impressive or beautiful, largely because it seems to have been constructed out of concrete. Wat Sisaket and

Wat Phra Kaeo (see pages 52 and 53) are certainly more memorable buildings. Nonetheless, it is important to appreciate the reverence in which That Luang is held by most Lao, including the many millions of Lao who live across the border in Thailand. The *that* is the prototype for the distinctive Lao-style angular *chedi*, which can be seen in northeast Thailand, as well as across Laos.

1 Vientiane

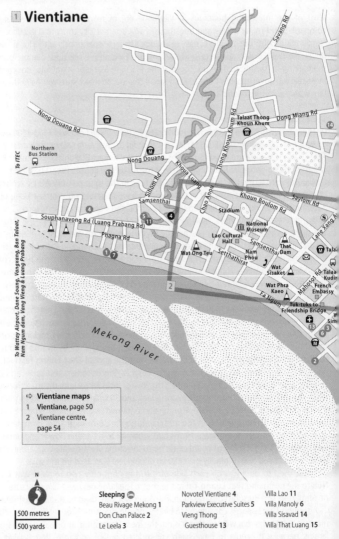

⇨ **Vientiane maps**
1 **Vientiane**, page 50
2 **Vientiane centre,**
   page 54

N

| 500 metres |
| 500 yards |

Sleeping
Beau Rivage Mekong **1**
Don Chan Palace **2**
Le Leela **3**

Novotel Vientiane **4**
Parkview Executive Suites **5**
Vieng Thong
  Guesthouse **13**

Villa Lao **11**
Villa Manoly **6**
Villa Sisavad **14**
Villa That Luang **15**

Revolutionary Monument

Also known as the **Unknown Soldier's Memorial**, this hilltop landmark is located just off Phon Kheng Road and is visible from the parade ground (which resembles a disused parking lot) in front of That Luang. Echoing a *that* in design, it is a spectacularly dull monument, built in memory of those who died during the revolution in 1975. The **Pathet**

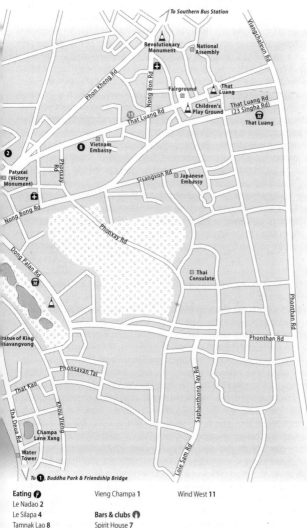

Eating 🍴
Le Nadao **2**
Le Silapa **4**
Tamnak Lao **8**

Vieng Champa **1**

Bars & clubs 🍸
Spirit House **7**

Wind West **11**

Lao Museum, to the northwest of That Luang, is only open to VIPs and never to the public but there are a few tanks, trucks, guns and aircraft used in the war lying in the grounds: these can be seen from the other side of the fence.

Patuxai

ⓘ *Junction of That Luang Rd and Lane Xang Av. Daily 0800-1200 and 1300-1630, 3000 kip.*

At the end of That Luang is the Oriental answer to Paris's Arc de Triomphe and Vientiane's best-known landmark, the monstrous Victory Monument or Patuxai. It was originally called Anou Savali, officially renamed the Patuxai or Victory Monument, but is affectionately known by locals as 'the vertical runway'. It was built by the former regime in memory of those who died in the wars before the Communist takeover, but the cement ran out before its completion. Refusing to be beaten, the regime diverted hundreds of tonnes of cement, part of a US aid package to help with the construction of runways at Wattay Airport, to finish off the monument in 1969. In 2004 the Chinese funded a big concrete park area surrounding the site, including a musical fountain; it's a pity they didn't stretch the budget to finance the beautification of the park's centrepiece.

A small sign explains that, although Patuxai might look grand from a distance, on closer inspection "it appears like a monster of concrete". The top affords a bird's eye view of the leafy capital, including the distant glittering, golden dome of the old Russian circus, now the rarely used National Circus. The interior of the monument is reminiscent of a multi-storey car park (presumably as a counterpoint to the parade ground next to the Revolutionary Monument), with graffiti sporadically daubed on top of unfinished Buddhist bas-reliefs in reinforced concrete. The frescoes under the arches at the bottom represent mythological stories from the Lao version of the *Ramayana*, the *Phra Lak Pralam*. Until 1990 there was a bar on the bottom floor; today Vientiane's youth hang out on the parapet.

Wat Sisaket

ⓘ *Junction of Lane Xang Av and Setthathirat Rd. Daily 0800-1200 and 1300-1600, 5000 kip. No photographs in the sim.*

Further down Lane Xang is the **Morning Market** or Talaat Sao (see page 70). A major waterpark has been constructed in the park just behind Talaat Sao. Beyond the market, where Setthathirat meets Lane Xang, is one of Vientiane's two national museums, Wat Sisaket. Home of the head of the Buddhist community in Laos, **Phra Sangka Nagnok**, it is one of the most important buildings in the capital and houses over 7000 Buddha images. Wat Sisaket was built in 1818 during the reign of King Anou. A traditional Lao monastery, it was the only temple that survived the Thai sacking of the town in 1827-1828 (possibly out of respect for the fact that it had been completed only 10 years before the invasion), which now makes it the oldest building in Vientiane. Sadly, it is seriously in need of restoration.

The main sanctuary, or **sim**, with its sweeping roof, shares many stylistic similarities with Wat Phra Kaeo (see below): window surrounds, lotus-shaped pillars and carvings of deities held up by giants on the rear door. The *sim* contains 2052 Buddha statues (mainly terracotta, bronze and wood) in small niches in the top half of the wall. There is little left of the Thai-style *jataka* murals on the lower walls but the depth and colour of the originals can be seen from the few remaining pieces. The ceiling was copied from temples King Anou had seen on a visit to Bangkok. The standing image to the left of the altar is believed to have been cast in the same proportions as King Anou. Around the *sim*, set into the ground, are small *bai sema* or boundary stones. The *sim* is surrounded by a large courtyard, which originally had four entrance gates (three are now blocked). Behind the *sim* is a large trough, in the shape of a *naga*, used for washing the Buddha images during the water festival (see page 67).

The **cloisters** were built during the 1800s and were the first of their kind in Vientiane. They shelter 120 large Buddhas in the attitude of subduing Mara (see page 324), plus a number of other images in assorted *mudras*, and thousands of small figures in niches, although many of the most interesting Buddha figures are now in Wat Phra Kaeo. Most of the statues date from the 16th to 19th centuries but there are some earlier images. Quite a number were taken from local monasteries during the French period.

The whole ensemble of *sim* plus cloisters is washed in a rather attractive shade of caramel, and combined with the terracotta floor tiles and weathered roof presents a most satisfying sight. An attractive Burmese-style library, or *hau tai*, stands on Lane Xang outside the courtyard. The large casket inside used to contain important Buddhist manuscripts.

Just behind Wat Sisaket is a complex of colonial houses in a well-maintained garden.

Wat Phra Kaeo

ⓘ *Setthathirat Rd; daily 0800-1200 and 1300-1600 (closed public holidays); admission 5000 kip. No photographs in the sim.*

Almost opposite Wat Sisaket is the other national museum, **Wat Phra Kaeo**, also known as **Hor Phra Kaeo**. It was built by King Setthathirat in 1565 to house the Emerald Buddha (or Phra Kaeo), now in Bangkok, which he had brought from his royal residence in Chiang Mai. It was never a monastery but was kept instead for royal worship. The Emerald Buddha was removed by the Thais in 1779 and Wat Phra Kaeo was destroyed by them in the sacking of Vientiane in 1827. (The Thais now claim the Emerald Buddha as the most important icon in their country.) The whole building was in a bad state of repair after the sackings, with only the floor remaining fully intact. Francis Garnier, the French explorer who wandered through the ruins of Vieng Chan in 1860, describes Wat Phra Kaeo "shin[ing] forth in the midst of the forest, gracefully framed with blooming lianas, and profusely garlanded with foliage". Louis de Carné in his journal, *Travels in Indochina and the Chinese Empire* (1872), was also enchanted, writing when he came upon the vegetation-choked ruin that it "made one feel something of that awe which filled men of old at the threshold of a sacred wood".

The building was expertly reconstructed in the 1940s and 1950s and is now surrounded by a garden. During renovations, the interior walls were restored using a plaster made of sugar, sand, buffalo skin and tree oil.

The **sim** stands on three tiers of galleries, the top one surrounded by majestic. lotus-shaped columns. The tiers are joined by several flights of steps and guarded by *nagas*. The main, central (southern) door is an exquisite example of Lao wood sculpture with carved angels surrounded by flowers and birds; it is the only notable remnant of the original wat. (The central door at the northern end, with the larger carved angels, is new.)

The *sim* now houses a superb assortment of Lao and Khmer art and some pieces of Burmese and Khmer influence, mostly collected from other wats in Vientiane.

Notable exhibits in Wat Phra Kaeo

A short description of each exhibit is given in French and Lao.

Nos 3, 4 and 17: Bronze Buddhas in typical Lao style.

Nos 294 and 295: Buddhas influenced by Sukhothai style (Thailand), where the attitude of the walking Buddha was first created (see page 324).

No 354: Buddha meditating made of lacquered wood, shows Burmese influence, dates from the 18th century.

No 372: Wooden, Indian-style door with erotic sculpture, dating back to the 16th century, originally from the Savannakhet region.
No 388: Copy of the Pra Bang, the revered statue associated with the origins of Buddhism in Laos (see page 102).
Nos 412, 414 and 450: Khmer pieces.
No 415: A hybrid of Vishnu and Buddha.
No 416: A Khmer deity with four arms.

2 Vientiane centre

Chanta Guesthouse **7** *B2*
Chanthapanya **40** *B2*
Day Inn **4** *B4*
Douang Deuane **5** *C2*
Dragon Lodge **39** *B2*
Green Park **38** *C6*
Inter City **8** *C1*
Lane Xang **22** *C3*
Lani **9** *B2*
Lao Orchid **37** *B1*

Lao Plaza **25** *B3*
LV City Riverine **11** *C2*
Mali Namphu Guesthouse
29 *B3*
Mixok Guesthouse **30** *B2*
Orchid Guesthouse **15** *C2*
Phonepaseuth Guesthouse
32 *B3*
Phornthip Guesthouse
16 *B1*

Sabaidy Guesthouse **33** *B2*
Saysouly Guesthouse **34** *C*
Settha Palace **23** *A4*
Soukchaleun
 Guesthouse **24** *B2*
Syri II Guesthouse **36** *B1*
Tai-Pan **26** *C2*
Vayakorn Guesthouse **28** *B*
Vongkhamsene **6** *C2*
Youth Inn **10** *C2*

200 metres
200 yards

N

Sleeping
Asian Pavilion **2** *B4*
Auberge Sala Inpeng **1** *B1*

Nos 430 and 431: 18th-century copies of the famous Khmer apsaras, the celestial nymphs of Angkor in Cambodia.

No 698: This stone Buddha is the oldest piece of Buddhist art in Laos, dating from the sixth to ninth century.

Also look out for a collection of **stelae**, inscribed in Lao and Thai script, including one with a treaty delineating a 16th-century agreement between Siam and Lane Xang. There is also an 'Atom-struck Tile', found on the site of Sairenji Temple, Hiroshima.

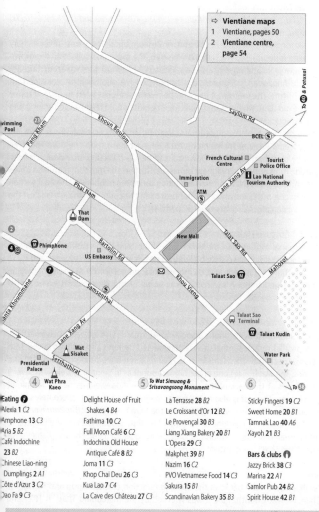

⇨ **Vientiane maps**
1 Vientiane, pages 50
2 Vientiane centre, page 54

Eating 🍴
Alexia **1** *C2*
Amphone **13** *C3*
Aria **5** *B2*
Café Indochine **23** *B2*
Chinese Liao-ning Dumplings **2** *A1*
Côte d'Azur **3** *C2*
Dao Fa **9** *C3*
Delight House of Fruit Shakes **4** *B4*
Fathima **10** *C2*
Full Moon Café **6** *C2*
Indochina Old House Antique Café **8** *B2*
Joma **11** *C3*
Khop Chai Deu **26** *C3*
Kua Lao **7** *C4*
La Cave des Château **27** *C3*
La Terrasse **28** *B2*
Le Croissant d'Or **12** *B2*
Le Provençal **30** *B3*
Liang Xiang Bakery **20** *B1*
L'Opera **29** *C3*
Makphet **39** *B1*
Nazim **16** *C2*
PVO Vietnamese Food **14** *C3*
Sakura **15** *B1*
Scandinavian Bakery **35** *B3*
Sticky Fingers **19** *C2*
Sweet Home **20** *B1*
Tamnak Lao **40** *A6*
Xayoh **21** *B3*

Bars & clubs 🍸
Jazzy Brick **38** *C3*
Marina **22** *A1*
Samlor Pub **24** *B2*
Spirit House **42** *B1*

That Dam

Travelling north on Chanta Koummane, look out for the distinctive brick That Dam, or **Black Stupa**. It is renowned for the legend of the seven-headed *naga*, which is supposed to have helped protect the Vientiane from Thai invaders (conveniently forgetting that the city was comprehensively sacked by the Thais in 1827). The *naga* now lies dormant inside the stupa, waiting to seize upon another chance. The stupa was renovated in 1995 but still has an air of neglect.

Lao National Museum

ⓘ *Samsenthai Rd, opposite the National Culture Hall. Daily 0800-1200 and 1300-1600, 10,000 kip. No photographs allowed.*

This place was formerly called the Revolutionary Museum but in these post-revolutionary days it has been redesignated the National Museum. The museum's collection has grown over the last few years and now includes a selection of historical artefacts from dinosaur bones and pre-Angkorian sculptures to a comprehensive photographic collection on Laos' modern history. The rhetoric of these modern collections has been somewhat toned down from the old days, when photographic descriptions would refer to the 'running dog imperialists' (Americans).

One of the highlights of the museum is a dazzling array of personal effects from the revolutionary leader Kaysone including his exercise machine, a spoon he used and even the coconut he once had a sip from. Downstairs there is a collection of ancient artefacts, including stone tools and quite poignant burial jars. Upstairs the museum features a range of artefacts and busts as well as a small exhibition on ethnic minorities. The final section of the museum comprises mostly photographs tracing the country's struggle against the 'brutal' French colonialists and American 'imperialists'.

Lao National Culture Hall

Facing the National Museum on the other side of the road is the Lao National Culture Hall. The hideous wedding cake-style building was a gift in kind by the Chinese and sticks out like a sore thumb. It is built in such monumental proportions that you can imagine tumbleweed blowing through the corridors at some of the ill-promoted events. ▸▸ *For further details, see page 67.*

Wat Ong Teu

Wat Ong Teu (identified by its bright orange monks' quarters) is located on Setthathirat, which runs parallel to Samsenthai. It was constructed by King Setthathirat in the 16th century, was ransacked by the Siamese in 1827 and then rebuilt during the late 19th and 20th centuries. The wat houses one of the biggest Buddhas in Vientiane, weighing several tonnes, which sits at the back of the *sim* and gives the monastery its name: Temple of the Heavy Buddha. The wat is also noted for its magnificent sofa and its ornately carved wooden doors and windows, with motifs from the *Phra Lak Pralam* (the *Ramayana*, see page 321). The monastery runs one of the larger Buddhist schools in Laos and is home to the Deputy Patriarch of the Lao monastic order, Hawng Sangkharat. The wat comes alive every year for the That Luang festival (see page 67).

Wat Chan

A short walk away, on the banks of the Mekong (junction of Chao Anou and Fa Ngum), is Wat Chan, or **Wat Chanthabuli**. It was wrecked by the marauding Thais in 1827 and

The Story of Quan Am

Turned onto the streets by her husband for some unspecified wrong doing, Quan Am dressed as a monk and took refuge in a monastery. There, a woman accused her of fathering and then abandoning her child. Accepting the blame (why, no one knows), she was again turned out onto the streets, only to return to the monastery much later when, on the point of death, she confessed her true identity. When the Emperor of China heard the tale, he made Quan Am the Guardian Spirit of Mother and Child, and couples without a son now pray to her. Quan Am's husband is sometimes depicted as a parakeet, with the goddess holding her adopted son in one arm and standing on a lotus leaf, the symbol of purity.

now only the base of a single stupa remains in front of the *sim*. The stupa originally had Buddha images in the 'Calling for Rain' attitude on each side (see page 324) but only one remains. Inside the reconstructed *sim* is a remarkable bronze Buddha from the original temple on this site. The wat is also renowned for its panels of sculpted wood on the doors and windows.

Chua Bang-Long

For those who have had their fill of Theravada Buddhist wats, there is a fine Mahayana Buddhist *chua* (pagoda) tucked away down a narrow lane off Khoun Boulom, near Chao Anou. The Chua Bang-Long was established by Vientiane's large and active Vietnamese population, who are said to have outnumbered Lao in the city before the outbreak of the Second World War. A statue of the Chinese goddess Quan Am (see box, above) stands in front of a Lao-style *that* which, in turn, fronts a large pagoda, almost Cao Dai in style. The pagoda has been extensively renovated and embellished over the last few years. Not far away, at the intersection of Samsenthai and Khoun Boulom is another, much smaller and more intimate pagoda.

Wat Simuang

ⓘ *Setthathirat Rd, east of town; daily 0600-2000; during celebrations the temple stays open until 2200.*

Wat Simuang contains the town foundation pillar (*lak muang*), which was erected in 1563 when King Setthathirat established Vientiane as the capital of the kingdom of Lane Xang. It is believed to be an ancient Khmer boundary stone, which marked the edge of the old Lao capital. Although the temple means 'Holy City Monastery', many locals vouch that it's named after pregnant Madame Simuang, who sacrificed herself, her baby and her horse by jumping in the hole dug for the foundation pillar before the consecrated stone was erected. The *sim* was reconstructed in 1915 around the foundation pillar, which forms the centre of the altar. In front of the altar is a stone Buddha thought to have magical powers because it survived the temple's razing. It is believed that if you lift the Buddha off the pillow three times and make a wish then you are indebted to return an offering of fruit and flowers. Wat Simuang may not be charming, refined or architecturally significant but for many locals it is the most important monastery in the capital and is considered the luckiest. Hawkers selling offerings of fruit, flowers, candles and incense line the surrounding streets, supplying the scores of people who come here hoping for good fortune. In the grounds of the wat are the ruins of what appears to be a Khmer laterite *chedi*.

Statue of King Sisavangvong

Just beyond Wat Simaung, where Setthathirat and Samsenthai meet, is the statue of King Sisavangvong. The original statue, carved by a Lao sculptor, apparently made the king look like a dwarf so it was destroyed. The present statue (there's a copy of it in Luang Prabang) was, peculiarly, donated by the Russians and, just as strangely, it survived the revolution.

⦿ Vientiane listings

Hotel and guesthouse prices
LL over US$200   **LL-AL** US$151-200
AL US$101-150   **A** US$66-100   **B** US$46-65
C US$31-45   **D** US$21-30   **E** US$12-20
F-G less than US$11

Restaurant prices
▼▼▼ over US$12   ▼▼ US$6-12   ▼ under US$6

⊜ Sleeping

Vientiane *p46, maps p50 and p54*
There is very little quality accommodation in Vientiane under US$10 a night. There is a big difference in the quality of rooms between the US$10 and US$20-30 brackets and the extra US$10 is a worthwhile investment. Cheaper guesthouses offer discounts in the wet season. Higher end hotels offer better rates on the internet than the rack rate if you walk in off the street. Guesthouses and boutique hotels tend to get booked up, so it is highly advisable to reserve in advance As a rule, hotels over US$50 accept major credit cards.

LL-L Don Chan Palace, Piawat Village (off Fa Ngum Quay), T021-244288, www. donchanpalacelaopdr.com. This 14-storey hotel is the largest hotel in Vientiane and probably the ugliest. It was specially built for the ASEAN summit and is so close to the river that locals joke that it may sink in. However, once you get past the unattractive exterior the 230 rooms and facilities are outstanding and afford a very comfortable stay, with the best views of both the river and the city in town. Offers a wide range of facilities including restaurant, private karaoke rooms, bar, poolside massage, gym, Wi-Fi and 24-hr room service.

LL-AL Green Park Hotel, www. greenparkvientiane.com, 248 Khouvieng Rd, T021-264097. Designed in a modern East-meets-West style, this hotel is set alongside Vientiane's primary park. Beautiful rooms with all the mod-cons, Wi-Fi and super-duper bathtubs. Beautiful garden and excellent pool. The only drawback is it is set a little further out from the city centre and river but is still within walking distance and makes a fantastic luxury option. Recommended.

LL-AL Lao Plaza Hotel, 63 Samsenthai Rd, T021-218800, www.laoplazahotel.com. Centrally located, this Thai-managed, 140-room hotel is no doubt useful for business visitors but seems rather incongruous in Vientiane. Non-guests may use the hotel's facilities for a set fee. These include 3 restaurants, a fitness centre, pool, conference centre, satellite TV, IDD telephones, karaoke bar and shopping arcade. Most major credit cards accepted. Outside guests can use the pool for 100,000 kip.

LL-AL Settha Palace Hotel, 6 Pang Kham Rd, T021-217581, www.setthapalace.com. The stunning **Settha Palace** was built in 1936 and opened as a hotel in 1999. Its French architecture, period furniture, plush rooms complete with black marble sinks and bathtubs and tropical gardens and pool sit more easily with the essence of Vientiane than the other top-level hotels. It is considered by many to be the best hotel in town. Recommended.

L-B Novotel Vientiane, Samsenthai Rd, near the junction with Luang Prabang, T021-213570, www.novotel.com. Large international-style hotel with good facilities including restaurant, pool, gym, tennis court, sauna, Lao massage, nightclub, business centre and games room. A/c throughout. The hotel often holds art exhibitions and concerts but the building itself is completely characterless and suffers from a poor location on the edge of town towards Wattay Airport (free airport transfer). Room rates include breakfast, but tax is extra; most major credit cards accepted.

A Tai-Pan, 2-12 François Ngin Rd, T021-216906, www.taipanhotel-vientiane.com. The service here is hard to fault and facilities are good: restaurant, bar, basic gym, small pool and free airport pickup. The lobby is more impressive than the 36 rooms, but they are reasonably well equipped with a/c, IDD telephones, satellite TV and flowers and fruit on arrival. Room rates include a good breakfast. Most major credit cards accepted. Non-guests can use the pool for US$7.50.

A-B Le Leela, Ban Phiawat 33, Unit 10, T021-214493, www.leleela.com. This beautiful white modernist home has been converted into a hip hotel. It's all zen-like and minimalist with a library, beautiful staircase, black lacquered wooden floors and doors and attractive furniture. Opt for a room with a 4-poster bed. Only one of the suites has a bathtub. Next to **Villa Manoly** in a quiet road just off-centre.

A-C Lane Xang Hotel, Fa Ngum Rd, T021-214100, www.lanexanghotel.com.This was the original 'luxury' hotel in Vientiane, built by the French in 1964. It has an indefinable charm, despite the fact that some of its retro-hip Soviet fittings and furniture have been ripped out to make way for a more contemporary look. One floor of the hotel has been remodelled (38 rooms) and the difference is remarkable compared with the rest of the rooms, which are shoddy. Go for a junior suite de luxe room, with its own bar and plastic carved ivory tusk decor. The service here is unmatched. The international restaurant has traditional Lao dancing shows every night 1900-2100. Other facilities include a pool and bar. Major credit cards accepted. Wi-Fi available. Recommended.

B Chanthapanya, Nokeo Khoummane Rd, T021-244284, www.chanthapanyahotel.com. Fantastic modern Asian building. The rooms are new and very comfortable. Beautifully furnished with modern Lao wooden furniture, comfy beds, fridge, TV, hot water, phone, a/c. Includes breakfast.

B Hotel Day Inn, 059/3 Pang Kham Rd, T021-222985, dayinn@laopdr.com. Run by a friendly Cambodian, this renovated villa (the former Indian embassy) is in a good position in a quiet part of town, just to the north of the main concentration of bars and restaurants. Attractive, airy, clean, large rooms, with a/c and excellent bathrooms; breakfast and complimentary airport transfer included. Wi-Fi available. Recommended.

B Lao Orchid Hotel, Chao Anou, T021-264134, www.lao-orchid.com. Beautiful spacious rooms with stunning modern furnishings, polished floorboards and large showers. Outstanding value for the price and popular with business travellers. 4½-star accommodation for a 3-star price. Advanced bookings imperative. Includes breakfast and Wi-Fi. Café and zen fish pond. Visa and MasterCard accepted. Recommended.

B-C Beau Rivage Mekong, Fa Ngum Rd, T021-243350, www.hbrm.com. One of the first Western-style boutique hotels in Vientiane is beautifully furnished with quirky decoration and fantastic baths. The pink exterior does not sit well with its surroundings but nonetheless this is a great boutique hotel with superb Mekong River views. Its location, just out of the centre of town on the river, ensures peace and quiet but it's still only a 5-min walk to the hustle and bustle. Garden view rooms are cheaper. Includes breakfast. Recommended.

B-C Inter City Hotel, 24-25 Fa Ngum Rd, T021-242842, www.ramayana-laos.com. This hotel is one of the oldest in Vientiane, now operating for over 30 years. Recent renovations have made it sparkle: mosaics, relief sculptures and murals adorn the walls, and traditional shutters, silk hangings and furniture feature in every room. The a/c rooms are light and spacious, with slick bathrooms and fantastic balconies overlooking the Mekong. Lovely atrium and excellent gift shop with beautiful antique costumes. Recommended. Wi-Fi available.

B-C LV City Riverine Hotel, 48 Fa Ngum Road, Mixay, T021-214643, www.lvcitylaos. com. A good central choice. The suite is sweet and cosy with a 4-poster bed, textile decor and a good-sized bathroom and stand-alone sink. The de luxe rooms have beds raised on small platforms but with smaller bathrooms; standard rooms are very good with thoughtful extras like a clothes stand. Wi-Fi and breakfast is included.

C Lani Guesthouse, 281 Setthathirath Rd, T021-214919, www.lanigh.laotel.com. This lovely place is in a charming location and is run by pleasant staff. Rooms are tad more expensive in the main house.

C Villa Manoly, Ban Phyavat, T021-218907, manoly20@hotmail.com. This is a wonderful ramshackle French colonial villa crowded with objet d'art, curios, books and ancient TV sets. It's like a rambling private house. There's a pool in the garden. 12 rooms are in the main building and 8 rooms in a new block with small patios out front overlooking the pool. Monthly rates are US$650. Recommended.

C VongKhamSene Hotel, 17/01 Manthaturath Rd, T021-219922, www.vongkhamsenehotel.com. Smart rooms, firm mattresses and dark wood accents. An appealing choice.

C-D Auberge Sala Inpeng, 063 Unit 06, Inpeng St, T021-242021, www.salalao.com. Nine very attractive bungalows set in a small garden in a quiet street. The economy rooms don't come with TV. Opt for a standard or superior if available for the space and superior decor. Breakfast is included.

C-D Mali Namphu Guesthouse, 114 Pang Kham Rd, T021-215093, www.malinamphu. com. Difficult to spot as it looks like a small shopfront but the façade is deceiving, as the foyer opens onto a beautifully manicured courtyard surrounded by quaint terraced rooms. The clean, bright rooms are traditionally decorated with a modern twist and come with a/c, hot water, cable TV and a fantastic breakfast. The twin rooms are much nicer than the doubles. Friendly staff. Highly recommended. One of the best guesthouses in Laos in this price range.

D Asian Pavilion, 379 Samsenthai Rd, T021-213430, www.asianpavilionlaos.com. Currently being renovated so this historic, overpriced hotel should soon be launching a new and improved version. It used to be the **Hotel Constellation,** made famous by John Le Carré in The Honourable Schoolboy. Currently, the rooms are very dark with peeling paint, ancient decor and antiquated bathrooms. Breakfast included.

D Douang Deuane, Nokeo Khoummane Rd, T021-222301, dd_hotel@hotmail.com. From the exterior, this dilapidated building looks like a classic Communist edifice, but the a/c rooms have charm and character: parquet wood floors, art deco furniture, excellent bathrooms with bathtubs (showers in single rooms), satellite TV and are a decent size. Try to get a balcony room for lovely views over the rooftops of the city. Although the room rates are no longer competitive, it is a good 'option B' if other central hotels in this price range are fully booked. Good-value motorbike rentals at 70,000 kip per day.

D Vayakorn House, 91 Nokeo Khoummane Rd, T021-241911, www.vayakorn@yahoo. com. Central and clean, with friendly staff. Wonderful airy rooms, tastefully decorated with modern furniture. Polished floors, with hot water, a/c and TV. Breakfast is no longer included, but it is still excellent value. Recommended. The new **Vayakorn Inn** has opened around the corner. Wi-Fi.

D-E Dragon Lodge, 311-313 Samsenthai Rd, T021-250114, dragonlodge2002@yahoo. com. Somewhere between a guesthouse and a hotel. Fun, colourful downstairs restaurant area, which is good for a party; if you're looking for peace and quiet this isn't the best choice, but it offers simply decorated comfortable rooms with hot water, TV and a/c. 5-star service. Visa accepted. Fan rooms are cheaper.

D-E Villa Lao (formerly Thongbay Guesthouse), off Luang Prabang Rd, turn right before the Novotel, Ban Nong Douang, T021-242292, www.villalao.com. Lovely traditional Lao house set in a lush tropical garden. Rooms have traditional-style fittings, mosquito nets and fan or a/c. Rooms with shared bathroom are cheapest. The guesthouse also runs cooking classes on request (150,000 kip), including purchasing ingredients at the local market. The only drawback is its distance from the city centre. Perfect if you wish to relax.

E Orchid Guesthouse, 33 Fa Ngum Rd, T021-252825. Friendly staff, and spotlessly clean rooms with fan or a/c, and breakfast included. Cheaper rooms have shared bathroom. Take a table and chairs onto the tiled roof for a lovely view of sunset on the river. Slap bang on the noisy Fa Ngum Rd, so only recommended for deep sleepers.

E Vieng Thong Guesthouse, Ban Phiawat, opposite Wat Phiavat in a side street, T021-212095. Family-style house, plus modern extension, in a nice garden with a café. Super friendly staff. Large rooms with thick duvets, rattan furniture, TV, china tea-sets and hot water showers. Pleasant but a little expensive, especially for the older rooms. The newer rooms are much more attractive.

E Villa Sisavad, 117/12 Ban Sisavad Neua, T021-212719, www.villasisavad.com. Set a little way out of the centre and so not convenient for sightseeing, but those on a longer stay will appreciate the small pool. It's in a quiet area, and the rooms are huge and comfortable. Don't bother with breakfast.

E Youth Inn, 29 Fa Ngum Road and on Francois Ngin Rd, T21-217130, youthinn@hotmail.com. A Vietnamese-run operation with 2 locations in the heart of town. The standard-sized rooms are spotlessly clean and are compact with a/c. The owners are sometimes friendly and sometimes not!

E-F Chanta Guesthouse, Setthathirat Rd (opposite Mixay Temple), T021-243204.

The shabby foyer doesn't do this place justice. Rooms are homely, with polished floorboards, TV, good bathrooms, wooden furniture and great cotton bedclothes. Cheaper rooms have shared facilities; more expensive ones are en suite with a/c.

E-F Phonpaseuth Guesthouse, 97 Pang Kham Rd, T021-212263, www.phonpaseuth-gh.com. Popular, clean guesthouse with cable TV, hot water and good bathroom. Rooms without a/c are cheaper. Good location.

E-F Phornthip Guesthouse, 72 Inpeng Rd, T021-217239. A quiet, family-run and very friendly guesthouse, but perhaps a little overpriced. Large rooms, with en suite bathrooms, some have a/c. There's a courtyard at the back of the guesthouse, but no garden. Bicycle hire available. Some room deals include breakfast.

E-F Saysouly, 23 Manthathurath Rd, T021-218384, saysouly@hotmail.com. A variety of rooms, a bit on the musty side. Parquet floors, cheaper single fan rooms with shared bathroom. On the upside, the shared bathrooms are excellent with powerful showers. Extra for a/c. The more expensive en suite rooms are quite good value.

E-F Soukchaleun Guesthouse, 121 Setthathirat Rd (opposite Mixay temple), T021-218723, soukchaleun_gh@yahoo.com. Quaint guesthouse with a range of rooms, from fan rooms with shared bathroom through to a/c en suite. Comfortable and homely. Clean, friendly and good value.

E-F Syri II Guesthouse, 63/6-7 Setthathirat Rd, T021-241345, syri2@hotmail.com. One of the best budget options. 3-storey guesthouse with a range of rooms including fan rooms with shared bathroom and some with own bathroom. Clean with wooden furniture. Has lounges and shared common areas decorated with curios from around Asia. Helpful staff. Recommended.

G Mixok Guesthouse, 188 Setthathirat Rd (opposite Mixay Temple), T021-215606, bucnong@hotmail.com. This ain't the Ritz but you get what you pay for as the rooms are among the cheapest in town. The very basic, pokey rooms are not for the claustrophobic, but they cost the same as a hamburger and beer. Shared hot-water bath. 11 rooms, which are frequently booked up. Excellent location.

G Sabaidy Guesthouse, 110 Setthathirat Rd, T021-213929, p_vily@hotmail.com. The cheap price reflects the facilities. Turquoise, swimming pool-esque rooms with fans. Dorms also available (20,000 kip per person). Chaotic reception. Three communal washrooms, and always a queue.

Serviced apartments

LL-AL Parkview Executive Suites, Av Souphanouvong (near the **Novotel**), T021-250888, www.parkviewexecutive.com. Serviced residence complex of 116 units, catering for both long- and short-term stays. Fitness centre, pool, sauna, jacuzzi, tennis court, office space and secretarial support. A bit off the beaten track.

🍴 Eating

Vientiane p46, maps p50 and p54
The absolutely best place to get **Lao food** is from the open-air stalls that line the banks of the Mekong along **Fa Ngum**. The restaurants are ridiculously low on price and high on atmosphere, particularly at night with their flickering candles. From time to time the government kicks all the eateries off the patch but they usually return with a vengeance. By the time this book goes to press they might all be gone, as the project to redesign the riverfront is well underway. The **Dong Palane Night Market**, on Dong Palane, and the **night markets** near the corner of **Chao Anou** and **Khoun Boulom Rd** are also good for stall food. There are other congregations of foodstalls around town, most of which set up shop at about 1730 and close by 2100. Be sure to sample Lao ice cream with coconut sticky rice.

The **Chinese quarter** is around **Chao Anou**, **Heng Boun** and **Khoun Boulom** and

is a lively spot in the evenings. There are a number of noodle shops here, all of which serve a palatable array of vermicelli, *muu daeng* (red pork), duck and chicken.

The **Korean-style barbecue**, *sindat*, is extremely popular, especially among younger Lao, as it is a social event and very cheap. It involves cooking finely sliced meat on a hot plate in the middle of the table, whilst making a broth with vegetables around the sides of the tray; reminiscent of a 1970s fondue evening. **Seendat** (see page 64) is a favourite among older Lao diners.

For cheap **Vietnamese** food, there's a good selection of stalls on **Sisangvong Rd** (Ban Sisangvong) and around **Heng Boun St** in **China Town**, where there is a dazzling array of fresh spring rolls and *feu* shops.

Restaurants that do good **vegetarian** dishes include the **Full Moon Café** and **Nazim** (see below).

🍴-🍴 Côte d'Azur, 62/63 Fa Ngum Rd, T021-217252, jmdazur@laotel.com. Daily 1100-1400, 1800-2230. Closed Sun lunch. Fine selection of dishes from the south of France, plus excellent wood-fired pizzas and delicious seafood dishes. Recommended.

🍴-🍴 Kua Lao, 111 Samsenthai Rd, T021-215777. Daily 1000-1400 and 1700-2230. A tastefully refurbished colonial house-turned-restaurant provides a sophisticated atmosphere for quality Lao and Thai food. Avoid the set menu. Good Lao music and traditional dancing. Some locals believe that Kua Lao has sold its Lao culinary credentials to the tourist dollar but most visitors to Laos will enjoy their meal here. Pricey for Laos.

🍴-🍴 La Cave des Châteaux, Nam Phou Circle, T030-514 1647. Mon-Sat 0730-1400, 1800-2200, Sun 1800-2200. This restaurant around the Nam Phou Fountain is supposed to look like a grotto. Pretty good set menu, with delicious grilled squid and steaks. Dine on the upstairs balcony.

🍴-🍴 Le Nadao, Ban Donmieng (on the right-hand side of the Patuxai roundabout), T021-213174 Mon-Fri 1200-1330, 1900-2230, Sat and Sun 1900-2230. This place is difficult to find as it is hidden by a lot of shrubbery but definitely worth every second spent searching the back streets of Vientiane in the dark. Sayavouth, who trained in Paris and New York, produces delectable French cuisine: soups, venison, lamb, puddings. Fantastic. The set menu is one of the best lunches you will get in town.

₸₸₸-₸₸ Le Provençal, Nam Phou Circle, T021- 219685. Daily 1130-1400, 1730-2200. Long-standing quaint French and Italian restaurant that generally gets dwarfed by its partners on the other side of the fountain. Serves a good plate of pasta.

₸₸₸-₸₸ Le Silapa, 17/1 Sihom Rd, T021-219689. Daily 1130-1400, 1800-2200; closed for 1 month a year in the rainy season and for a week over Lao New Year. Anthony and Frederick provide a fantastic French-inspired menu (*tilapia* with a vegetable marmalade, lime and black olives sauce) and intimate atmosphere for fine dining without blowing the budget. Innovative modern meals that would be as at home in the fine dining establishments of New York and London as they are here. Great value set lunch menu. Part of the profits (5,000 kip per bottle of wine) are donated to disadvantaged families, usually for expensive life-saving surgical procedures. Wine degustation evenings are occasionally held, US$75.

₸₸₸-₸₸ L'Opera, Nam Phou Circle, T021-215099. Daily 1130-1400, 1830-2200. A/c Italian restaurant, pompous, cold and overpriced but with delicious ice cream, a wide range of pizza and pasta dishes, and barbecue steaks.

₸₸₸-₸ Sakura, 117-119 Chao Anou Rd, T021-261922. Mon 1730-2200, Tue-Sun 1030-1400 and 1730-2200. Said to provide the best Japanese food in town. Expensive for Vientiane but good value by international standards.

₸₸ Tamnak Lao Restaurant, That Luang Rd, T021-413562. 1200-2200. It's well worth deviating from the main Nam Phou area for a bite to eat here. This restaurant and its sister branch in Luang Prabang have a reputation for delivering outstanding Lao and Thai food, usually with a modern twist.

₸₸-₸ Alexia, 7 Fa Ngum Rd, T021-241349. Daily 1100-2300. Popular with tourists, **Alexia** specializes in Mexican cuisine. The food is a bit overpriced and fairly standard. On the up side there is live music after 2000.

₸₸-₸ Amphone, opposite the Jazzy Brick, Setthathirat Rd, T020-7771 1138, and part of the same establishment. Offers Lao and international food in a lovely alfresco garden setting just off the main drag.

₸₸-₸ Aria, 8 Rue Francois Ngin, T021-222589. An outstanding addition to the Vientiane dining scene. Divine ice cream, a 16-page wine list, and a long mouthwatering menu of homemade pastas, ravioli, risottos and pizzas with real buffalo mozarella. Mountain hunter's ravioli stuffed with slow fire-braised deer and mountain cheeses, barbera red wine and herbs sauce. Service is ultra efficient; the very welcoming owner is an Italian returnee to Vientiane.

₸₸-₸ Café Indochine,199 Setthathirat Rd, T021-216758. Daily 1030-2230. Intimate restaurant with delectable cuisine, including zucchini flower salad and grilled chicken.

₸₸-₸ Chinese Liao-ning Dumpling Restaurant, Chao Anou Rd, T021-240811. Daily 1100-2230. This restaurant is a firm favourite with the expat population and it isn't hard to see why: fabulous steamed or fried dumplings and wide range of vegetarian dishes. The place is spotlessly clean, though you may find the birds in cages outside a bit off-putting. No one is ever disappointed with the meals here. Highly recommended.

₸₸-₸ Dao Fa, Setthathirat Rd, T021-215651, www.daofa-bistro.com. Daily 0800-2200. Modern European restaurant offering home-made pasta, crêpes and wood-fired pizza. Great atmosphere with a miscellany of pop-art adorning the white walls.

₸₸-₸ La Terrasse, 55/4 Nokeo Khoummane Rd, T021-218550. Mon-Sat 1100-1400 and 1800-2200. This is the best European restaurant in terms of variety and price.

Large fail-safe menu offering French, European, Lao and Mexican food. Good desserts, especially the chocolate mousse, and a good selection of French wine. Fantastic service. Great 1970s-style comfort food, including an excellent 'plat du jour' each day. Recommended.

¶¶-¶ Nazim, 39 Fa Ngum Rd, T021-223480. Daily 1000-2230. Authentic Indian (north and south) and Halal food, very popular with backpackers. Indoor and outdoor seating. They have another restaurant in Vang Vieng as well as a branch in Luang Prabang.

¶¶-¶ Seendat, Sihom Rd, T021-213855. Daily 1730-2200. This restaurant has been going for well over 20 years and is a favourite amongst the older Lao for its good food (*sindat*) and atmosphere. About US$1 per person more than most places but this is reflected in the quality. Recommended.

¶¶-¶ Seendat Somphouthong, Luang Prabang Rd, T021-250540. Daily 1030-2200. Distinguishes itself from many other barbecue (*sindat*) restaurants by using a delicious prawn sauce instead of the standard peanut. A bit far from the centre of town but worth the trip.

¶¶-¶ West Coast Airport Restaurant, Wattay International Airport. Open 0800-2130; buffet 1100-1400. The buffet is a favourite with senior-ranking Lao government officials and local VIPs who make the long hike out during their lunch hour. It represents unparalleled value: 64,000 kip for as much Lao food (curries, fried dishes, etc), Japanese food (sushi), dessert, coffee and tea as you can stomach. Highly recommended.

¶¶-¶ Xayoh, Nokeo Khoummane Rd, T021-262111, www.xayohgroup.com. Daily 0800-2330. Attractive bar and restaurant next to the hideous Lao National Cultural Hall. Salads, pizzas, burgers plus Lao/Thai food. The restaurant's speciality is a Sunday roast of beef and Yorkshire pud, etc, for homesick Brits. Double-check your order as the staff have a tendency to serve the wrong thing. Deliveries available. Wi-Fi.

¶ Fathima, Th Fa Gnum, T021-219097. Without a doubt, this is the best-value Indian in town. Ultra-friendly service and a large menu, including good curries.

¶ Full Moon Café, François Ngin Rd, T021-243373. Daily 1000-2300. Delectable Asian fusion cuisine and Western favourites. Huge pillows, good lighting and great music make this place very relaxing. Fantastic chicken wrap and good Asian tapas. The Ladybug shake is a winner. Also offers a book exchange and music and movie shop for iPods. Free Wi-Fi available.

¶ Khop Chai Deu, Setthathirat Rd, on the corner of Nam Phou Rd, T020-251564, www.khopchaideu.com. Daily 0800-2330. This lively place housed in a colonial building is one of the city's most popular venues. Garden seating, good atmosphere at night with soft lanterns, and an eclectic menu of Indian, Italian, Korean and international dishes (many of which come from nearby restaurants). The best value are the local Lao dishes, made on site and toned down for the *falang* palate. Also serves draught or bottled beer at a pleasant a/c bar. Excellent lunch buffet. Live performances.

¶ Makphet, in a new location behind Wat Ong Teu, T021-260587, www.friends-international.org. Fantastic Lao non-profit restaurant that helps raise money for street kids and is run by former street kids. Modern Lao cuisine with a twist. Selection of delectable drinks such as the iced hibiscus with lime juice. Beautifully decorated with modern furniture and painting by the kids. Also sells handicrafts and toys produced by the parents from vulnerable communities.

¶ PVO Vietnamese Food, T021-214444, Ban Phiavat. A firm favourite that had to move from its previous location on the Mekong due to the riverbank redevelopment. Full menu of freshly prepared Vietnamese food but best known for baguettes stuffed with your choice of pâté, salad, cheese, coleslaw, vegetables and ham. Bikes and motorbikes for rent too. Keep an eye out for the miniature dog wearing the Hannibal

Lector-style dog-mask – a popular doggy accessory with Vientiane citizens paranoid about rabies. Brilliant cheap food makes this a fantastic choice.

♥ **Sticky Fingers**, François Ngin Rd, T021-215972. Tue-Sun 1000-2300. Very popular small restaurant and bar serving Lao and international dishes including fantastic salads, pasta, burgers and suchlike. Everything from Middle Eastern through to modern Asian on offer, with lots of great comfort food and the best breakfast in town. Excellent cocktails, lively atmosphere, nice setting. **Stickies** should be the first pit-stop for every visitor needing to get grounded quickly as, food aside, the expats who frequent the joint are full to the brim with local knowledge. Deliveries available.

Cafés, cakeshops and juice bars

Pavement cafés are ten a penny in Vientiane. You need not walk more than half a block for hot coffee or a cold fruit shake. On Chao Anou you'll find **Liang Xiang Bakery**, **Sweet Home** and **Nai Xiang Chai** (for good juices and shakes).

Delight House of Fruit Shakes, Samsenthai Rd, opposite the **Asian Pavilion Hotel**, T021-212200. Daily 0700-2000. A wonderful selection of fresh shakes and fruit salads for next to nothing.

Indochina Old House Antique Café, 86/11 Setthathirat Rd, T021-223528. A delightful curio store with an upstairs café where you can sip wholesome juices or coffee amid the artful clutter of antiques, propaganda work and knick-knacks. A real treat.

Joma (aka **Healthy and Fresh Bakery**), Setthathirat Rd, T021-215265. Mon-Sat 0700-2100. Hugely popular. A very modern, chic bakery with a good selection of tasty pastries, bagels, sandwiches, pastas, salads, pizzas, yoghurts and coffee. Efficient service, Wi-Fi and Arctic-style a/c. However, it is starting to get a bit pricey and the iced coffee is better next door at **Dao Fa**.

Le Croissant d'Or, top of Nokeo Khoummane Rd, T021-223741. Daily 0700-

2100. French bakery, selling small selection of pastries including good cheap croissants.

Scandinavian Bakery, 71/1 Pang Kham Rd, Nam Phou Circle, T021-215199. Daily 0700-2100. Delicious pastries, bread, sandwiches and cakes. Friendly *falang* chef/ baker, who made the President of Tanzania's daughter's wedding cake – and has the photo to prove it. Great place for a leisurely coffee and pastries. Pricey for Laos but a necessary European fix for many expats. Recommended.

🔊 Bars and clubs

Vientiane *p46, maps p50 and p54*
Bars

A number of bar-stalls set up along **Quai Fa Ngum** (the river road) in the evening (though they may be cleared away when the new park opens), and are a good place for a cold beer as the sun sets. Most bars close at 2300 in accordance with the local curfew laws, though some places seem able to stay open past this time. Government officials go through phases of shutting down clubs and bars and imposing curfews.

Jazzy Brick, Setthathirat Rd, near Phimphone Market (brown building on the corner of the lane that leads to Wat Xieng Khoune). Very sophisticated, modern den, serving delectable cocktails, with jazz cooing in the background. Decorated with an eclectic range of quirky and kitsch artefacts. Very upmarket but a bit pretentious. Garish shirts are banned. Has become the place for well-heeled Lao. Head here towards the end of the night.

Khop Chai Deu, Setthathirat Rd (near the corner with Nam Phou). Probably the most popular bar for tourists in Vientiane. Casual setting and nightly band. Also serves food (see Eating, above).

Samlor Pub, Setthathirat Rd. Snooker, darts, pizza and the only place in town where you can play table-football.

Spirit House, follow Fa Ngum Rd until it turns into a dirt track, past the Mekong

River Commission, T021-243795, www.
thespirithouselaos.com. Beautiful wooden
bar in perfect river location. Good range
of snacks and burgers but salads are
overpriced. Good for those wanting to catch
the sunset in style with some of the best
cocktails in the city. Wi-fi.

Sticky Fingers, François Ngin Rd, opposite
the **Tai Pan Hotel**. This has long been a
favourite drinking hole among the city's
expats. The small and intimate bar and
restaurant are run by two Australian women.
It serves exceptional cocktails, especially the
Tom Yum. Very atmospheric and a lot of fun.
Also serves food (see Eating, above). Highly
recommended.

Sunset Bar, end of Fa Ngum Rd. Although
this run-down wooden construction isn't
much to look at, it is a firm favourite with
locals and tourists hoping to have a quiet
ale and take in the magnificent sunset
overlooking the Mekong. Recommended.

Wind West, by traffic lights, Luang Prabang
Rd. Usually stays open after 2300. Seedier
than most; many wild nights take place here.

Clubs

Many of the discos in town, both those in
hotels and independent set-ups, sometimes
feature live bands usually playing a mixture
of Lao and Thai music and cover versions
of Western rock classics. Vientiane lacks
good places to dance, since the most
popular Western-style clubs were closed
down in late 2004. Some Lao places are still
running, but you are strongly advised to take
earplugs with you – they like to play the
music very loudly.

Don Chan Palace (see Sleeping). For late
night owls looking for a party. Entrance fee,
terrible music but the best bet for boogie
late at night.

D'Tech, at the **Novotel** (see Sleeping).
T021-213570. Quite happening. DJs and
hip-hop acts from around Asia. Popular with
the locals.

Marina, Luang Prabang Rd, behind the
Marina Bowling Centre. Popular with

wealthy young Lao. Drinks of choice are
either Beer Lao or Johnny Walker Black. The
music is extremely loud so you might want
to bring earplugs.

● Entertainment

Vientiane *p46, maps p50 and p54*
Cinema
Blue Sky Café, on the corner of Setthathirat
and Chao Anou roads. Movies are shown on
a 29-inch TV on the 2nd floor.
French Cultural Centre, Lang Xang Rd,
T021-215764, www.centredelangue.org.
Shows exhibitions, screens French films and
also hosts the Southeast Asian Film Festival.
Check the *Vientiane Times* for up-to-date
details or pick up its quarterly programme.
**Lao-International Trade Exhibition &
Convention Center** (ITECC), T4 Rd – Ban
Phonethane Neua, T021-416002, www.
laoitecc.info. Shows international films.

Circus
The National Circus, known as **Hong
Kanyasin**, holds infrequent performances in
an old Russian tent, usually in conjunction
with the French Cultural Centre. The
performances usually include acrobatics and
clowns and are worthwhile if you're in town
at the right time.

Exhibitions
Keep an eye on the *Vientiane Times* for
upcoming international performances at the
Lao Cultural Centre (the building that looks
like a big cake opposite the museum).
COPE Visitors' Centre, National
Rehabilitation Centre, Khou Vieng Rd
(signposted), www.copelaos.org. Open
0900-1800, free. COPE (Cooperative Orthotic
and Prosthetic Enterprise) has set up an
interesting exhibition on UXO (unexploded
ordnance) and its effects on the people
of Laos. It includes a small movie room,
photography, UXO and a range of prosthetic
limbs (some, which are crafted out of
UXO). The exhibition helps raise money

for the work of COPE, which includes the production of prosthetic limbs and the rehabilitation of patients.

T'Shop Lai, Vat Inpeng St (behind Wat Inpeng), T021-223178, www.artisanslao. com. Mon-Sat 0800-2000, Sun 0800-1500. Exhibitions of crafts made by disadvantaged people, as well as a shop.

Fairs and amusements
There's often a ferris wheel and bouncy castle at **That Luang** in the evenings, particularly if it is a public holiday. But a more reliable option is to travel out to the **ITECC Centre** (see above), where there is a collection of fairground rides, including a ferris wheel, merry-go-rounds and dodgem cars. Popular at weekends.

Karaoke
This could almost be the Lao national sport, and there's nothing like bonding with the locals over a heavy-duty karaoke session. Karaoke places are everywhere – just keep your ears out for the off-key bellowing. Good spots include the **Blue Note** in the Lao Plaza Hotel or the more expensive, upmarket **Don Chan Palace** (see page 58).

Live music
Bands will perform almost every night at **Khop Chai Deu** and **Alexia** (see Eating, above) and at the **Music House**, on Fa Ngum, T021-212123. The **French Cultural Centre**, on Lang Xang, hosts a variety of musical performances, from local bands through to hip-hop ensembles.

Occasionally, music concerts and beauty pageants are held at the **Lao National Culture Hall**, opposite the National Museum. No official notice is given of forthcoming events but announcements sometimes appear in the *Vientiane Times* and large banners will flank the building.

Traditional dance
Lao National Theatre, Manthathurath Rd, T020-550 1773. Daily shows of traditional

Lao dancing, from 1730. Tickets, US$7, available at the theatre. Performances are less regular in the low season. Temporarily closed at publication time.

⊛ Festivals and events

Vientiane *p46, maps p50 and p54*
1st weekend in Apr Pi Mai (Lao New Year) is celebrated with a 3-day festival and a huge water fight. It is advisable to put your wallet in a plastic bag and invest in a turbo water pistol. There are numerous *bacis* (good luck celebrations) and the traditional greeting at this time of year is 'Sok Dee Pi Mai' (good luck for the New Year).
Sep/Oct Boun Ok Phansa is a beautiful event on the night of the full moon at the end of Buddhist Lent. Candles are lit in all homes and candlelit processions take place around the city's wats and through the streets. Then, thousands of banana-leaf boats holding flowers, tapers and candles are floated out onto the river. The boats represent your bad luck floating away.
Sep/Oct Boun Souang Heua, the boat-racing festival, is held towards the end of the rainy season. Boat races (*souang heua*) take place with 50 or so men in each boat; they power up the river in perfect unison. An exuberant event, with plenty of merrymaking.
12 Oct Freedom of the French Day is a public holiday.
Nov (date varies each year) Boun That Luang is celebrated in all of Vientiane's *thats* but most notably at That Luang (the national shrine). Originally a ceremony in which nobles swore allegiance to the king and constitution, it amazingly survived the Communist era. On the festival's most important day, **Thak Baat**, thousands of Lao people pour into the temple at 0600 and again at 1700 to pay homage. Monks travel from across the country to collect offerings and alms from the pilgrims. It is a really beautiful ceremony, with monks chanting and thousands of people praying. Women

who attend should invest in a traditional *sinh* (traditional skirt). A week-long carnival surrounds the festival with fireworks, music and dancing. Recommended.

O Shopping

Vientiane *p46, maps p50 and p54*

Books

A selection of maps and books on Laos can be found in **Phimphone Market**. The **Full Moon Café** has a book exchange.

Kosila Books, Nokeo Khoummane Rd, T021-241352. A good selection of English, Lao, German and French books, maps and guides and a small selection of second-hand books.

Monument Books, 124/1 Nokeo Khoummane Rd, T021-243708, www.monument-books.com. The largest selection of new books in Vientiane, **Monument** stocks a range of books on Southeast Asia as well as coffee-table books. Good place to pick up Lao-language children's books to distribute to villages on your travels.

Vientiane Book Center, 32/05 Fa Ngum Rd, T021-212031, vientianebookcenter@yahoo.com. The first English-language bookshop in Laos, this still has a good selection. Coffee-table books, glossy magazines and maps as well as specialist Lao PDR publications. There is a book exchange and a limited but interesting selection of used books in a multitude of languages.

Clothing, fashion and textiles

Every hue and design is available in the **Morning Market**. For cheaper (but still good quality) fabric, pop across the road to **Talaat Kudin**; the fabric section is in the covered area at the back of the market. A *sinh*, the traditional Lao skirt, can be made within the day for US$1-2 extra; just pick the length of fabric and the patterned band for the bottom of the skirt. See also **Tailors**.

Cama Craft, Mixay Rd, T021-501271. Handmade clothes in Hmong styles.

Couleur d'Asie, Nam Phou Circle. Modern-style Asian clothing, very well known and

a favourite of locals and expats. Pricey but high-quality fusion fashion.

Lao Cotton, Luang Prabang Rd, out towards Wattay Airport, approximately 400 m on right from **Novotel**, T021-215840. Sells a good range of material, shirts and handbags; ask to have a look at the looms. Another branch on Samsenthai.

Lao Textiles by Carol Cassidy, Nokeo Khoummane Rd, T021-212123, www.laotextiles.com. Mon-Fri 0800-1200 and 1400-1700, Sat 0800-1200. Exquisite silk fabrics, including *ikat* and traditional Lao designs, made by an American in a beautifully renovated colonial property. Dyeing, spinning, designing and weaving all done on site. It's pricey, but many of the weavings are real works of art; custom-made pieces available on request.

Mixay Boutique, Nokeo Khoummane, T021-214534, contact@mixay.com. Exquisite Lao silk in rich colours, clothing as well as fantastic photographs and artefacts.

True Colour, Setthathirat, T021-214410. Ready-made clothes from the Hoay Women's Centre. Also good tailoring, though they will need a couple of weeks to finish.

Tailors There are many Vietnamese tailors along Samsenthai and Pang Kham roads (north of Nam Phou fountain). **Queen's Beauty Tailor**, by the fountain, is quite good for women's clothes, but allow at least a week. Also try **Adam Tailleurs**, 72 Pang Kham Rd, and **TV Chuong**, 395 Samsenthai Rd. There are also a few tailors in the **Morning Market**.

Department stores

Satri Laos, Setthathirat, T021-244387. If Vientiane had a Harrods this would be it. Upmarket boutique retailing everything from jewellery, shoes, clothes, furnishings and homeware. Beautiful stuff, though most is from China, Vietnam and Thailand.

Food

baràvin (formerly **Vinotheque La Cave**), 354 Samsenthai Rd, with the big wine barrel

The art of ikat

In the handicraft shops and at the Morning Market in Vientiane, it is possible to buy distinctively patterned cotton and silk *ikat*. A technique of patterning cloth characteristic of Southeast Asia, *ikat* is produced all over the region, from the hills of Burma to the islands of Eastern Indonesia. The word comes from the Malay word *mengikat*, which means to bind or tie. Very simply, bundles of warp or weft fibres (or, in one Balinese case, both) are tied with material or fibre (or more often plastic string these days), so that they resist the action of the dye. Hence the technique's name: resist dyeing. By dyeing, re-tying and dyeing again through a number of cycles it is possible to build up complex patterns.

This initial pre-weaving process can take anything from two to 10 days, depending on the complexity of the design. *Ikat* is distinguishable by the bleeding of the dye which inevitably occurs no matter how carefully the threads are tied; this gives the finished cloth a blurred finish. The earliest *ikats* date from the 14th-15th centuries.

To prepare the cloth for dyeing, the warp or weft is strung tight on a frame. Individual threads, or groups of threads, are then tied together with fibre and leaves. In some areas wax is then smeared on top to help in the resist process. The main colour is usually dyed first, secondary colours later. With complex patterns (which are done from memory; plans are only required for new designs) and using natural dyes, it may take up to six months to produce a piece of cloth. Today, the pressures of the marketplace mean that it is more likely that cloth is produced using chemical dyes (which need only one short soaking, not multiple long ones – six hours or so – that some natural dyes require), and motifs have generally become larger and less complex. Traditionally, warp *ikat* used cotton while weft *ikat* used silk. Silk in many areas has given way to cotton, and cotton sometimes to synthetic yarns.

out front, T021-217700. French wine shop with a large range of wine, run by Claude Monnier, who serves aperitifs with cheese.
Phimphone Market, Setthathirat Rd, opposite Khop Chai Deu Restaurant. This supermarket has everything a foreigner could ask for in terms of imported food and drink, magazines and newspapers, translated books, personal hygiene products, household items and much more (and the high prices to go with them).
Simuang Minimarket, Samsenthai Rd, opposite Wat Simuang. Supermarket with a very good selection of produce, including a great array of Western products. It is also a great place to pick up wine at good prices but double-check that it is not past its use-by date.

Udom Pathana, Dong Palane Rd, T021-214256. Range of cheap food imports.

Galleries
T'Shop Lai, Wat Inpeng Soi. Funky studio exhibiting local sculptures and art. Artists can be seen at work Mon-Sat. Media include coconut shells, wood and metal. Proceeds from sales are donated to Lao Youth projects. Upstairs there is an exhibition on Asian elephants.

Hair and beauty
There are several hairdressers dotted around the city. Men should be careful not to wind up with a bowl cut.
Barber Jam, just off Khou Vieng Rd. Cute Lao barbershop (and youth centre) where

you can get a haircut for under US$1 while someone plays the guitar to you. Don't ask for anything too complex. Also has an 'ear coning' service.

Elly Boutique, Setthathirat Rd near the Kodak shop, T021-243675. Women's and men's fashion cuts, dyeing, facials and waxing, plus reportedly the best manicure and pedicure in Vientiane.

New Wave Hair Studio, 73/4 Pang Kham Rd, T021-216542. Soukanh Chantarath, the proprietor, trained at Vidal Sassoon and Toni and Guy in London. Great place to get a reasonably cheap hairdo from an internationally acclaimed hairdresser. Cutting, colouring, straightening, manicures, pedicures, waxing and eyelash tinting.

Handicrafts and antiques

The main shops are along Setthathirat, Samsenthai and Pang Kham. The **Talaat Sao** (Morning Market) is also worth a browse, with artefacts, such as appliquéd panels, decorated hats and sashes, basketwork both old and new, small and large wooden tobacco boxes, sticky-rice lidded baskets, axe pillows, embroidered cushions and a wide range of silverwork. The likelihood of finding authentic antiques is pretty low. **Talaat Kudin** offers cheaper artefacts and silks but not as great a selection as Talaat Sao.

Camacraft, Nokeo Khoummane, T020-556 1660. NGO which retails handicrafts produced by the Hmong people. Beautiful embroidery, mulberry tea, Lao silk.

Ekhor Boutique, Pang Kham Rd. Textiles, clothes and handicrafts.

Indochine Handicrafts, Samsenthai Rd next to the big wine barrel, T021-263619, maiphone@hotmail.com. Larger size collectibles, not really suitable for the suitcase shopper.

MaiChan Fine Arts & Handicrafts, Samsenthai Rd, T021-263619, maiphone@hotmail.com. This is a neat little shop with lots of treasures.

Mixay Boutique, Setthathirat Rd, Ban Mixay. Wooden and textile products.

Namsin Handicrafts, Setthathirat Rd. Wooden objects.

Oot-Ni Art Gallery, Samsenthai Rd, T021-214359. This is an Aladdin's Cave of serious objets d'art.

Jewellery and silverware

Many of the stones sold in Vientiane are of dubious quality, but silver and gold are more reliable. Gold is always 24 carat and is good value. Silver is cheap but not necessarily pure silver; nevertheless, the selection is interesting, with amusing animals, decorated boxes, old coins, earrings and silver belts. There's a wide selection in the Morning Market (**Talaat Sao**). Silver, gold and gem shops on Samsenthai are concentrated along the stretch opposite the Asian Pavilion Hotel; there are also gold shops further west towards the Chinese quarter. The Inter City hotel has a lovely but pricey shop too.

Doris Jewelry, 2 shops in Lao Plaza Shopping Centre. Sells range of silverware, gems and antiques.

Tamarind, T021-243564, Manthathurath. Great innovative jewellery designs, nice pieces. Also stocks a range of beautiful clothes made in stunning silk and organza.

Markets and shopping malls

Vientiane has several excellent markets.

Morning Market (Talaat Sao) off Lane Xang Av, is busiest in the mornings (from around 1000), but operates all day. There are money exchanges here (quite a good rate), and a good selection of foodstalls selling Western food, soft drinks and ice cream sundaes. It sells imported Thai goods, electrical appliances, watches, DVDs and CDs, stationery, cosmetics, a selection of handicrafts (see above), an enormous choice of Lao fabrics, and upstairs there is a large clothing section, silverware, gems and gold and a few handicraft stalls.

There is also a modern shopping-centre addition to the Morning Market. It is pricier and less popular, and stocked with mostly Thai products sold in baht. On the second floor, there is a reasonable food court. Next to it, the most enormous shopping mall should be open by the time you read this. **Talaat Kudin**, on the other side of the bus stop. This is a ramshackle market with an interesting produce section. It offers many of the same handicrafts and silks as the Morning Market but is a lot cheaper.

Talaat Thong Khoun Khum, on the corner of Khoun Khum and Dong Miang roads. The largest produce market. It is sometimes known as the **Evening Market** but it's busiest in the mornings.

Talat Sao Mall, www.talatsaomall.com. This will be 8 storeys of shops, restaurants, cinema, gym, disco and hotel.

Other markets include **Talaat That** Luang, south of the parade ground; **Talaat Dong Palane**, Dong Palane Rd (there's a sign near the temple, pointing down a lane, as the bulk of the market has been moved away from the main road); and **Talaat Chin**, which is good for electrical goods, CDs, DVDs, toys, clothes, furniture and cheap imported tat.

Music and film

Cheap DVDs and VCDs can be bought from the **Morning Market**. Walkman Village, Fa Ngum Rd, T021-213609, also stocks a selection of good-quality DVDs and CDs, along with goods geared towards foreigners, from handbags to binoculars.

Photo processing

Konica Plaza, 110/5 Samsenthai Rd. The best film developer in Vientiane and also offers cheap CD-burning and photocopying.

▲ Activities and tours

Vientiane *p46, maps p50 and p54*
Aerobics
At **Sengdara Gym** (see below).

Cooking

Villa Lao (formerly Thongbay Guesthouse) (see Sleeping), T021-242292. Cooking classes, covering all aspects of meal preparation, from purchasing the ingredients to eating the meal. Must be arranged in advance.

Cycling

Bicycles can be hired from several places in town, see Transport, page 73. A good outing is to cycle downstream along the banks of the Mekong. Cycle south on Tha Deua Rd until Km 5 (watch the traffic) and then turn right down one of the tracks towards the river. A path, suitable for bicycles, follows the river from Km 4.5. There are monasteries and drink sellers en route.

Football

Regular national league matches are held at the **National Stadium** in Vientiane. One of the few places in the world where you can see World Cup qualifying matches for under US$1.

Kickboxing

Held intermittently at the **Soxai Boxing Stadium** and every Sat 1400-1600, about 200 m past the old circus in Baan Dong Paleb; 20,000 kip.

Language courses

Vientiane College, Singha Rd, T021-414873, www.vientianecollege.com. The best Lao courses. Ask for Seng.

Massage, saunas and spas

The best massage in town is given by the blind masseuses in a street off Samsenthai Rd, 2 blocks down from Simuang Minimart (across from Wat Simuang). There are 2 blind masseuse businesses side-by-side and either one is fantastic: **Traditional Clinic**, T020-5565 9177 and **Porm Clinic**, T020-562 7633 (no English spoken). They are indicated by blue signs off both Khou Vieng and Samsenthai roads. Recommended.

Mandarina, 74 Pang Kham, T021-218703. A range of upmarket treatments between US$5-30. Massage, facials, body scrubs, mini-saunas, oils, jacuzzi.

Oasis Spa Massage & Beauty, 18/01 Francois Ngin Rd, T021-243579. Provides very good, strong massages (*keng* – means strong in Lao).

Papaya Spa, opposite Wat Xieng Veh, T020-561 0565, www.papayaspa.com. Papaya is a favourite among locals looking to spoil themselves. You feel more relaxed the minute you walk through the gates. Offers massage, sauna, facials. Lovely gardens. Recommended.

Wat Sok Paluang, Sok Paluang. Peaceful leafy setting in the compound of Wat Sok Paluang. Herbal sauna, followed by herb tea (2000 kip) and massage by 2 young male masseurs (4000 kip); very relaxing but some women have reported groping. Vipassana meditation is held every Sat 1600-1730, free, T021-216214. To get there, walk through the small stupas to the left of the wat; the sauna is a rickety building on stilts on the right-hand side, recognizable by the blackened store underneath.

Rugby

There are 4 club teams (2 men and 2 women's) in the city (www.laorugby.com). Training sessions are held twice a week and visitors are welcome to watch. Lao Rugby folk teach rugby in schools and also work with street children and a drugs rehabilitation centre.

Shooting

There is a shooting range in the Southern corner of the national stadium US$1-2 for a few rounds.

Sports clubs and fitness centres

Several hotels in town permit non-residents to use their fitness facilities for a small fee, including the **Tai Pan** (rather basic), **Lao Plaza**, **Lane Xang**, **Don Chan** and **Novotel** (for all, see Sleeping).

Australia Club Recreation Centre, Km 3, Tha Deua Rd, T021-314921. A beautiful setting, with one of the nicest pools in Vientiane. It's a lovely place for a swim followed by a glass of wine as the sun sets. Also a small restaurant and a squash court. Short-term membership available. It is cheaper if you get a member to sign you in; loiter around some of the expat drinking holes and you might find someone willing. A tuk-tuk to the centre is 20,000-30,000 kip.

Sengdara, 77/5 Phonthan Rd, T021-414058. Daily 0500-2200. Modern fitness centre with gym, pool and sauna. US$5 for use of all the facilities for a day, massage extra.

Swimming

The **Australia Club Recreation Centre** (see Sports clubs, above) has a fantastic saltwater pool with superb Mekong views. Several hotels in town permit non-residents to use their fitness facilities for a small fee.

Lane Xang Hotel (see Sleeping). Not the loveliest of settings but secluded and conveniently located. 30,000 kip.

Lao Plaza Hotel (see Sleeping). A very clean pool on the 3rd floor, with a great view of the city, open to non-guests for US$5.

Nongchan Water Park, Khou Vieng St T021-219386. Open 1000-1800. 30,000 kip, children 20,000 kip.

Settha Palace Hotel, 6 Pang Kham Rd (see Sleeping). Lovely royal blue pool with matching sun loungers in landscaped gardens. The most luxurious (with a hefty US$7.50 entrance fee).

Sokpaluang Swimming Pool, Sok Paluang Rd, south of centre. Daily 0800-2000. Good-sized pool for serious swimmers, paddling pool for children, costumes for hire, restaurant and bar.

Tai-Pan Hotel (see Sleeping). Open to non-guests. Rather basic.

Vientiane Swimming Pool, close to the Settha Palace Hotel. This is the 1950s retro trip with communist-red decor. Daily 0800-2000. 10,000 kip.

Tennis

Vientiane Parkview, Luang Prabang Rd, T021-250888. Expensive but easily the best court in town. Book in advance.

Vientiane Tennis Club, National Stadium. Equipment for hire. Floodlit courts stay open until 2100. Bar.

Ten-pin bowling
Bowling is very popular, particularly as the bars in the bowling centres are often the only ones open after curfew. The **Lao Bowling Center**, behind the Lao Plaza Hotel, T021-218661, is good value; shoe hire is included but bring your own socks. On the way out to the airport (Luang Prabang Rd) you'll find **Marina Bowling** , T021-216978, aimed at a younger clientele, with retro lighting and fluorescent balls and pins. Not a great selection of larger shoe sizes for hire, though, so if your feet are over a size 9 you'll be bowling barefoot.

Tour operators
For general travel information on getting to Phou Khao Khouay, visit the **National Tourism Authority** (see page 48). Most tour operators will include 'eco' somewhere in their name but this doesn't necessarily mean very much.
Asian Trails Laos, Unit 10, Ban Khounta Thong, Sikhottabong District, T021-263936, www.asiantrails.travel. This company is a Southeast Asia specialist.
Christophe Kittirath, No 15, Unit 01, Ban Savang, Chanthaboury District, Vientiane, T020-5504604, laowheels@yahoo.co.uk. Christophe runs tours all over the country with or without employing public transport, speaks English and French and is always very helpful.
Diethelm Travel, Nam Phou Circle, Setthathirat Rd, T021-215129, www.diethelmtravel.com. Flight agent only.
Exotissimo, 6/44 Pang Kham Rd, T021-241861, www.exotissimo.com. Various tours and travel services. Excellent but pricey.
Green Discovery, Setthathirat Rd, next to Kop Chai Deu, T021-223022, www.greendiscoverylaos.com. Specializes in ecotours and adventure travel. Recommended.

Yoga
Vientiane Yoga Studio, Sokpaluang Rd, Soi 1 (first *soi* on the right after you turn onto Sokpaluang from Kuvieng Rd), www.vientianeyoga.com. Yoga and Pilates classes, 50,000 kip.

⊖ Transport

Vientiane *p46, maps p50 and p54*
See also Ins and outs, page 46.

Air
Prices and schedules are always changing, so check in advance. See also Getting there, page 46, for international operators.
Lao Airlines to **Bangkok** (80 mins) and **Chiang Mai** in Thailand; to **Siem Reap** and **Phnom Penh** (1½ hrs); **Kunming** and **Nanning** in China. In Vietnam, to **Hanoi** and **Ho Chi Minh City**. Domestic services include **Luang Prabang** (40 mins); to **Pakse** (50 mins), **Oudomxay**, **Luang Nam Tha**, **Xieng Khouang** (Phonsavan), **Savannakhet** and **Sayaboury**. Phongsavanh Airlines (021-513 0000) has taken over the Lao Capricorn Air company and flies to **Xam Neua**, **Phongsali** and **Sayaboury province**.
    Airline offices Lao Airlines, 2 Pang Kham Rd, T021-212054, www.laoairlines.com, also at Wattay Airport; T021-212051. Mon-Fri 0800-1200 and 1300-1600, Sat 0800-1200. Thai Airways, Head Office, Luang Prabang Rd, not far past the Novotel, T021-222527, www.thaiairways.com, Mon-Fri 0830-1200, 1300-1500, Sat 0830-1200; and at Wattay Airport, T021-512024. Vietnam Airlines, Lao Plaza Hotel, T021-217562, www.vietnamairlines.com.vn, Mon-Fri 0800-1200, 1330-1630. **Bicycle and motorbike**
For those energetic enough in the hot season, **bikes** are the best way to get around town. Many hotels and guesthouses have bikes available, including **Lani I**, **Syri**, and **Douang Deuane** (see Sleeping). Expect to pay about 10,000 kip per day. There are also bike hire shops dotted around town. Markets, post offices and government offices

usually have 'bike parks' where it is advisable to leave your bike. A small minding fee is charged.

Motorbikes are available for hire from many guesthouses and shops within the city centre. Expect to pay around US$5-10 per day and leave your passport as security. Trail bikes can be hired for around US$20 per day, although the price goes down to around US$15 per day if you hire the bike for a longer period. Most places will hire out helmets (a necessity) but insurance for motorbikes is seldom available in Laos. Check your insurance policy before you venture out, as most companies include a clause excluding cover for motorbike accidents. **Jules classic rental**, Setthathirat Rd, T020-7600813, www.bike-rental-laos.com, offers a range of motorbikes including classics for hire. **PVO** also has a reliable selection of motorbikes from 70,000-250,000 kip per day. Often a driving licence can be used in lieu of a motorbike licence if the police pull you over.

Boat

Improved roads means the old boat transport system has disappeared. The only pier offering transport out of Vientiane is at **Tha Hua Kao Liaw**, 8 km west of the Novotel in Ban Kao Liaw. Departures are intermittent so you may need to charter a boat if you're determined to travel by river; this will need to be organized at least a day in advance. Public boats make the trip to **Pak Lai** (115 km, 120,000 kip per person) stopping at Xanakham and Kenthao on Mon and Wed, 8-9 hrs. If you have 5 or 6 people you can charter speed boats to **Luang Prabang** (8 hrs) for US$45 per person but it isn't the most comfortable journey.

Bus

There is no city bus service but buses, trucks and pickups to destinations around Vientiane all leave from the station next to the **Talaat Sao bus station**, next to the Morning Market (see below). Many private tour operators also run buses to popular locations like Vang Vieng and will pick up/drop off around Nam Phou or pick up passengers from their guesthouse.

Vientiane has 3 main public bus terminals: **Southern**, **Northern** and **Talaat Sao** (Morning Market).

VIP buses are very comfortable night buses, allowing you to sleep during the trip – but watch out that they don't swap the normal bus for a karaoke one! – with snacks served by waitresses. Book a double if you don't want to be stuck with a strange bed partner. Robberies have been reported on the night buses so keep valuables secure.

Southern bus station Route 13, 9 km north of the city centre (T021-740521). Public buses depart daily for destinations in southern Laos. Prices change around every 3 months and also fluctuate (yes, they go down!) in accordance with gas prices, so these prices are just a guide. The southern bus station has a range of stores, pharmacy and massage. To **Paksan**, at 0730, 1030, 1100, 1200, 1330, 150 km, 1 hr 30 mins, 25,000-40,000 kip. To **Lak Sao** (for the Vietnamese border), 335 km, 8 hrs, 50,000 kip, 3 daily at 0500, 0600, 0700. To **Thakhek**, 3 daily, 360 km, 5-6 hrs, 50,000 kip; 1 VIP bus at 1300, 75,000 kip or take any southbound bus. To **Savannakhet**, 8 daily (early morning), 483 km, 8 hrs, 65,000 kip. To **Pakse**, 8 daily, 736 km, 13 hrs, 100,000 kip; express buses, 5 buses, 130,000 kip; there are also overnight express buses to Pakse, 11 hrs, 150,000 kip at 2030. **Thongli**, T021-242657, operates an overnight VIP service daily at 2030, which takes about the same length of time but has beds, water, snacks, etc, 135,000 kip. **KVT**, T021-213043, also runs VIP bus to Pakse at 2030.

Banag Saigon, T021-720175, runs buses to **Hanoi**, 24 hrs, 130,000 kip, **Vinh**, 1900, 160,000 kip, **Thanh Hoa**, 1900, 180,000 kip, **Hué**, 1900-1930, 150,000 kip, and **Danang**, 1900-1930, 200,000 kip. These services run on odd days so be sure to check bus schedules in advance.

Northern bus station Route 2, towards the airport 3.5 km from the centre of town, T021-261905. Northbound buses are regular and have a/c. For the more popular routes, there are also VIP buses which offer snacks and service. To **Luang Prabang** (400 km), standard buses, 8 daily, 10 hrs, 95,000 kip; VIP buses daily at 0800 and 0900, 8 hrs, 115,000 kip. To **Udomxai** (550 km), standard buses 0645 and 1345, 13 hrs, 110,000 kip; a/c bus at 1700 daily, 130,000 kip; VIP bus at 1600, 155,000 kip. To **Luang Namtha**, 0830 daily, 698 km, 19 hrs, 140,000 kip. To **Phongsali**, 0715 daily, 815 km, 26 hrs, 160,000 kip. To **Houei Xai**, daily 1730, 895 km, 25-30 hrs, 180,000 kip. To **Sayaboury** (485 km), standard at 0900 and 1630 daily, 12-15 hrs, 90,000 kip; a/c at 1830 daily, 110,000 kip. To **Xam Neua**, at 0700, 0945, 1245, 850 km, 30 hrs (it may go via Phonsavanh), 150,000 kip. To **Phonsavanh** (365 km), standard at 0630, 0930, 1600, 10 hrs, 80,000 kip; a/c at 0800 and 1840 daily, 95,000 kip; VIP bus at 2000 daily, 115,000 kip.

Talaat Sao bus station (T021-216507) Across the road from Talaat Sao, in front of Talaat Kudin, on the eastern edge of the city centre. Destinations, distances and fares are listed on a board in English and Lao. Most departures are in the morning and can leave as early as 0400, so travellers on a tight schedule should check departure times the night before. There is a useful map at the station, and bus times and fares are listed in Lao and English. Staff at the ticket office speak only a little English so ask in the planning office if you need help. T021-216506. The times listed below depend on the weather and number of stops.

To the **Southern Bus Station**, 0600-1800 every 30 mins, 2000 kip. To the **Northern Bus Station**, catch the Nongping bus (5 daily) and ask to get off at 'Thay Song', 1500 kip. To **Wattay Airport**, every 30 mins 0640-1800, 3000 kip. To **Vang Vieng**, 5 daily, 15,000 kip, 3½ hrs.

Numerous buses criss-cross the province; most aren't very useful for tourists. To **Barksarp** (via Som Sa Mai for the boat to **Ban Pako**), 6 daily, 5000 kip. To **Ban Keun** (via Ban Thabok for **Phou Khao Khouay**), 9 daily, 7000 kip. To **Xieng Khuan**, bus No 14 every 15 mins 0530-2030, 1 hr, 4000 kip. To **Nam Ngum**, direct bus 0700 daily, 3 hrs, or catch a bus to **Ban Talaat**, every hr 0630-1630, 2½ hrs, 8000 kip, and then get a *songthaew* to the lake. To **Vang Vieng**, 20,000 kip (but unless you're dead broke, there are much better ways of getting to Vang Vieng), 0700, 0930, 1300 daily. To **Thakek**, three daily. To **Savannakhet**, 3 daily. To the **Friendship Bridge** (Lao side), every 15 mins 0650-1710, 4000 kip (bus no.14). To **Nong Khai** (Thai side of the Friendship Bridge), 6 daily 0730-1800, about 1 hr including immigration, 15,000-80,000 kip. To **Udon Than**i, 6 daily 0800-1800, 22,000 kip.

Other private bus services To **Vang Vieng**, Green Discovery, from their office on Setthathirat, www.greendiscoverylaos. com (it also runs to **Luang Prabang** and **Pakse**); also Sabaidee Bus for the same price. Both services will pick you up from your guesthouse if you arrange this with them in advance. Other tour companies also offer this service. Sabaidee Bus to **Luang Prabang**, Tue and Thu, 130,000 kip, with a stopover in Vang Vieng on the way. Sabaidee also runs international buses to **Bangkok**, 800 baht at 1700 with a change at Nong Khai leaving at 2000, arriving Bangkok 0600. Green Discovery, www.greendiscoverylaos.com, also runs international buses to **Udon Thani**, **Bangkok**, **Nong Khai**, **Chiang Mai** and **Pattaya** in Thailand and **Hanoi**, **Vinh**, **Hue**, **Danang** and **Ho Chi Minh City** in Vietnam.

Car

It is not essential to hire a driver but in the event of an accident a foreigner is likely to shoulder the responsibility and costs. Rates vary according to the vehicle and whether out-of-town trips are planned. Expect to pay about US$50-90 per day. Europcar (Asia Vehicle Rental), 354-356 Samsenthai Rd,

T021-223867, www.avr.laopdr.com. There is also a Europcar office at the airport.

Taxi
These are mostly found at the Morning Market (Talaat Sao) or around the main hotels. Newer vehicles have meters; flag fall is 8000-12000 kip. A taxi from the Morning Market to the **airport**, US$5-6; to **Tha Deua** (for the Friendship Bridge and Thailand), US$10-12 – you can usually get the trip much cheaper but the taxis offering bargain fares are usually so decrepit that you may as well take a less expensive tuk-tuk, 95,000 kip (see below). To hire a taxi for trips outside the city costs around US$20-30 per day. To **Nam Ngum**, US$40-60.

Lavi Taxi, T021-350000, is the only reliable call-up service in town, but after 2000 you may find it difficult to get someone to answer your call.

Train
In 2009 a new train station opened in Laos –Thanaleng, beyond the Friendship Bridge, where trains cross into Thailand and run to Bangkok, thus avoiding the need to change trains to cross the border (though you will still need to change trains in Nong Khai). See box on the Friendship Bridge border, above.

Tuk-tuks
Tuk-tuks usually congregate around tourist destinations: **Nam Phou**, **Talaat Sao** and **Talaat Kudin**. Tuk-tuks can be chartered for longer out-of-town trips (maximum 25 km) or for short journeys of 2-3 km within the city (From 100,000-40,000 kip per person). Printed official prices are 55,000 kip to the **airport**; 40,000 kip to **That Luang** and Northern Bus Station; 60,000 kip to the **Southern Bus Station**; 95,000 kip to the **Friendship Bridge**; 150,000 kip return to the **Beer Lao Factory**; 195,000 kip return to the **Buddha Park** and 80,000 kip per hr sightseeing. An 8-hr charter is officially quoted at US$30. There are also shared tuk-tuks, on regular routes on main streets.

For shared tuk-tuks to the **Friendship Bridge**, see border box, right.

Tuk-tuks are available around the fountain area until 2330 but are often difficult to hire after dark in other areas of town. The tuk-tuks that congregate on the city corners are generally part of a quasi cartel and are best avoided; it is much cheaper to travel on one that is passing through. To stop a tuk-tuk, flag it down. A reliable driver is Mr Souk, T020-7712220, who speaks good English and goes beyond the call of duty. **Saamlors** are as rare as hen's teeth.

⊙ Directory

Vientiane *p46, maps p50 and p54*
Banks
See Money, page 36, for details on changing money. There are around a dozen multicard ATMs in the city. The **Banque Pour le Commerce Exterieur** (BCEL), corner of Fa Ngum and Pang Kham roads, takes all the usual credit cards (maximum withdrawal 700,000 kip; much less on Sun). Other multicard ATMs can be found in front of the Novotel, and next to Green Discovery and beside the petrol station near Wat Simuang. BCEL, 1 Pang Kham Rd, offers the lowest commission (1.5%) on changing US$ TCs into US$ cash; there is no commission on changing US$ into kip. **Joint Development Bank**, 33 Lane Xang Av (opposite market), T021-213535, offers good rates on cash advances. ATM.

Embassies and consulates
Australia, Km4 Thadeua Rd, T021-353800, www.laos.embassy.gov.au. Britain, no embassy; served by the Australian Embassy. Cambodia, Tha Deua Rd, Km 3, T021-314952, visas daily 0730-1030. Cambodian visas US$20. Canada, no embassy; served by the Australian Embassy. China, Thanon Wat Nak Nyai T021-315105. Visas take 4-days. France, Setthathirat Rd, T021-21267400, www.ambafrance-laos.org. Germany, 26 Sok Paluang Rd, T021-312110. Japan,

Border essentials: Friendship Bridge

The bridge is 20 km southeast of Vientiane; catch the Thai–Lao International bus from the Talaat Sao terminal (15,000 kip), 90 minutes at 0730, 0930, 1240, 1430, 1530 and 1800 to Nong Khai bus station (see page 77). Or take one of the Friendship Bridge tuk-tuks from the corner of Setthathirat and Gallieni (close to the French embassy), which run 0700-1800, 30 minutes, 5000 kip to the border The border is open daily 0730-1800. Shuttle minibuses cross the bridge every 20 minutes, stopping at the Thai and Lao immigration posts, where an overtime fee is charged at weekends and on public holidays.

There are good facilities at the Lao border, including a telephone box, a couple of duty-free shops, snack stalls and a post office. Allow up to 1½ hours to get to the bridge and through formalities on the Lao side. The paperwork is pretty swift, unless you are arriving in Lao and require a visa or are leaving the country and have overstayed your visa. Thirty-day visas are processed in about 15 minutes and cost US$30-42 depending on your nationality. You will require a passport-sized photograph and the name of your guesthouse or hotel. Bargain hard, but in a friendly way, for a good price on private transport from the border. Coming into Lao, the taxi drivers can charge up to US$15 into the centre of Vientiane; it should be no more than US$7-10. The Thai side is über-efficient but not nearly as friendly. Tuk-tuks wait to take punters to Nong Khai (10 minutes), 50 baht per person; Udon Thani is another hour further on; taxis from the Thai side of the border charge about 700 baht to get you there; add another 300 baht if you organize the Thai taxi from the Lao side. If you get stuck in Nong Khai, Mut Mee Guesthouse (www.mutmee.com) is recommended. From Udon Thani you can get to Bangkok easily by budget airline; AirAsia and Nok Air fly several times daily. From Udon Thani, you can catch a minibus or a taxi to the Lao border or a bus directly to the border for 200 baht. Taking the Udon/Friendship Bridge option between Bangkok and Vientiane will probably only add one hour to your journey, since immigration at Wattay Airport tends to be slow.

Sisavangvong Rd, T021-414400, www.la.emb-japan.go.jp. **Malaysia**, 23 Singha Rd, T021-414205. **Myanmar (Burma)**, Lao Thai St, Watnak, T021-314910, daily 0800-1200, 1300-1630. **Sweden**, Sok Paluang Rd, T021-315003, www.swedenabroad.se/vientiane. **Thailand**, Kaysone Phomvivane Rd, T021-214581 (consular section has moved to Unit 15, Ban Phonsinaun, T021-415335 ext 605, www.consular.go.th; open 0830-1200 for visa extensions), Mon-Fri 0830-1200. If crossing by land, 30-day visas are also issued at the Friendship Bridge, see above. **USA**, Bartolonies St, Xieng Nyuen, T021-267000, www.laos.usembassy.gov. **Vietnam**, 85, 23 Singha Rd, T021-413401, www.mofa.gov.vn/vnemb.la, visas 0800-1045, 1415-1615. One-

month visa costs US$45 and you must wait 3 days. An extra US$5 for the visa in 1 day.

Emergencies

Ambulance, T195 but note that you will be taking a significant risk by placing your life in the hands of the emergency services; in cases of medical emergency, your best bet is to see Dr Ben at the **Australian Clinic** (see Medical services, below). **Police Tourist Office**, Lang Xang Av (in the same office as the National Tourism Authority of Laos), T021-251128.

Immigration

Immigration office, Phai Nam Rd (near Morning Market), Mon-Thu 0800-1200,

1300-1800. Visa extensions can be organized for US$2 per day. Overstay, US$10 per day. For visa information, see page 41.

Internet

Internet cafés are plentiful on Setthathirat and Samsenthai roads. Most open daily 0800-2200/2300, and charge about 100 kip per min. Most also offer internet phones for under US$1 per min, as well as Skype. **Apollo Internet**, Setthathirat Rd, Mon-Fri 0830-2300, Sat and Sun 0900-2300, is a good bet.

Laundry

Laundrettes can be found all over Samsenthai Rd and the streets around Nam Phou. Try **Delight House of Fruit Shakes** (see Cafés, cakeshops and juice bars, page 65).

Media

The English-language *Vientiane Times*, 3000 kip, runs items of Lao news, plus snippets translated from the local newspapers and listings. The French-language *Le Renovateur*, 10,000 kip, takes a more serious approach and includes lots of news on France.

Medical services

There are 2 good pharmacies close to the Talaat Sao Bus Station. **Australian Embassy Clinic**, Australian Embassy, KM 4 Thadeua Rd, T021-353800/840, Mon-Fri 0830-1230, 1330-1700. **Mahosot Hospital**, Fa Gnum, T021-214018, is suitable for minor ailments only. For anything major, cross the border to Nong Khai and visit **AEK Udon International Hospital**, T+66-4234 2555. For other hospitals in Thailand, see page 35. When a medical evacuation is required, contact **Lao West Coast Helicopter**, Hangar 703, Wattay International Airport, T021-512023, www.laowestcoast.com. A charter to Udon Thani costs from US$1550, subject to availability and government approval.

Post

Post Office, Khou Vieng Rd/Lane Xang Av (opposite market), T021-216425, offers poste restante (Counter 13), local and international telephone calls and fax services. To send packages, use **DHL**, Nong No Rd, near the airport, T021-214868, or **TNT Express**, in the Thai Airways Building, Luang Prabang Rd, T021-261918.

Telephone

Area code: 021 for landlines and 020 for mobile phones. Dial 170 for international operator. The international telephone office is on Setthathirat Rd, near Nam Phou Rd, 24 hrs daily; fax service daily 0730-2130.

Around Vientiane

There are plenty of short trips from Vientiane, ranging from the popular backpacker hotspot of Vang Vieng, through to the stunning Phou Khao Khouay National Park. Vang Vieng has become very popular with action sports enthusiasts, with kayaking, caving and rock climbing all on offer. For years the Nam Ngum dam has been a popular weekend escape for Vientiane residents and is starting to gain appeal with the tourist set. ▶▶ *For listings, see pages 87-92.*

South of the city

Bus No 14 from the Talaat Sao bus station follows Route 2 southeast towards Tha Deua, the Friendship Bridge, to Thailand and Xieng Khuan (Garden of the Buddhas). ▶▶ *For immigration formalities at the bridge, see Border essentials, page 77.*

Along Thanon Tha Deua (Route 2)
Although it isn't officially recognized as a tourist sight, the **Beer Lao factory** *Km 12, Thanon Tha Deua (Route 2), T021-812000, www.beer-lao.com (free tours 0900-1130, 1300-1600)*, is surprisingly interesting and worth the trip. People who visit are welcomed warmly then taken on a mini tour and plied with the award-winning ale. Beer Lao has become something of a national symbol and the locals swell with pride if you share their enthusiasm for their amber liquid. Two kilometres further on is **555 Park (Saam Haa Yai)**. These extensive but rather uninspiring gardens encompass Chinese pavilions, a lake and a small zoo. In the 1980s, a white elephant was captured in southern Laos. Revered for its religious significance, it had to be painted to ensure it was not stolen on the way to the capital. It was originally kept in the Saam Haa gardens but has since been moved to the zoo, where it is paraded in front of the crowds during the That Luang festival. White elephants are not really white, but pink.

Xieng Khuan
ⓘ *Route 2 (25 km south of Vientiane); daily 0800-1630; admission 5000 kip, plus 5000 kip for cameras. Food vendors sell drinks and snacks. Getting there: 1 hr by bus No 14 from the Talaat Sao bus station, charter a tuk-tuk for approximately US$15, hire a private vehicle for up to US$15, or take a motorbike or cycle because the road follows the river and is reasonably level.*
Otherwise known as the **Garden of the Buddhas** or **Buddha Park**, Xieng Khuan is a few kilometres beyond **Tha Deua** on Route 2, close to the border with Thailand. It has been described as a Laotian Tiger Balm Gardens, with reinforced concrete Buddhist and Hindu sculptures of Vishnu, Buddha, Siva and other assorted deities and near-deities. There's also a bulbous-style building with three levels containing smaller sculptures of the same gods.

The garden was built in the late 1950s by a priest-monk-guru-sage-artist called Luang Pu Bunleua Sulihat, who studied under a Hindu *rishi* in Vietnam and then combined the Buddhist and Hindu philosophies in his own view of the world. He left Laos because his anti-Communist views were incompatible with the ideology of the Pathet Lao (or perhaps because he was just too weird) and settled across the Mekong near the Thai town of Nong Khai, where he built a bizarre concrete theme park for religious schizophrenics, called Wat Khaek. With Luang Pu's forced departure from Laos, his garden came under state control and it is now a public park. Luang Pu died in 1996 at the age of 72 and remains popular in Laos and northeastern Thailand.

Bridging the Mekong

In April 1994, King Bhumibol of Thailand and the President of Laos, accompanied by prime ministers Chuan Leekpai of Thailand and Keating of Australia, opened the first bridge to span the lower reaches of the Mekong River, linking Nong Khai in northeast Thailand with Vientiane in Laos. The bridge had taken a long time to materialize. It was initially mooted during the 1950s but war in Indochina and hostility between Laos and Thailand scuppered plans until the late 1980s. Then, with the Cold War drawing to an end, and growing rapprochement between the countries of Indochina and

ASEAN, the bridge, as they say, became an idea whose time had come.

The 1200-m-long Friendship Bridge, or Mittaphab, was financed with US$30 million of aid from Australia. It is a key link in a planned road network that will eventually stretch from Singapore to Beijing. For landlocked Laos, it offers an easier route to Thailand and through Thailand to the sea. For Thailand, it offers an entry into one of the least-developed countries in the world, rich in natural resources and potential, while, for Australia, it demonstrated the country's Asian credentials.

East of the city → For listings, see pages 87-92.

Kaysone Phomvihane Museum
ⓘ *Km 6, Route 13 south, T021-911215. Bus from the Morning Market or cycle. 5,000 kip. Camera 10,000 kip. Daily 0800-1600.*
This museum, mostly visited by schoolchildren, commemorates the exploits and leadership of the Lao PDR equivalent of Vietnam's Ho Chi Minh. Kaysone was the critical character in Laos' recent history: revolutionary fighter, inspired leader and statesman (see page 296).

Ban Pako → *Colour map 2, B2.*
Ban Pako lies 50 km northeast of Vientiane, on the banks of the Nam Ngum river (off Route 13). There is a quiet and secluded 'nature lodge' here, established by an Austrian couple a few years back. It's a lovely place to retreat to, for swimming, boating, trekking, rafting, walks to local Lao villages and relaxing in the herbal sauna. To reach Ban Pako, take the Paksan bus from Vientiane's Morning Market and get off at Som Sa Mai (one hour). From here, take a boat to Lao Pako (another 25 minutes). Alternatively, the route makes a great trail bike ride; the last 20 km are on dirt and can get quite wild, especially in the wet season.

Tha Pabat Phonsanh
About 80 km down the Paksan road, is Pabat Phonsanh, built on a plug of volcanic rock in the middle of a coconut plantation. It is known for its footprint of the Buddha and has a statue of a reclining Buddha (*mudra*) rarely seen in Laos.

Phou Khao Khouay National Protected Area → *For listings, see pages 87-92.*

Phou Khao Khouay NPA (pronounced *poo cow kway*) is one of Laos' premier national protected areas. The area extends across 2000 sq km and incorporates an attractive sandstone mountain range. It is crossed by three large rivers, smaller tributaries and two waterfalls at **Tad Leuk** and **Tad Sae**, which weave their way into the **Ang Nam Leuk**

reservoir, a stunning man-made dam and lake on the outskirts of the park. Within the protected area is an array of wildlife, including wild elephants, gibbons, tigers, clouded leopards and Asiatic black bears.

Ins and outs

Getting there The park is a two-hour drive northeast from Vientiane, along Route 13 South; a good vehicle is recommended as the roads are terrible. To get to Ban Na you need to stop at Tha Pabat Phonsanh, 80 km northeast of Vientiane (see above); the village is a further 2 km from here. For Ban Hat Khai, 100 km northeast of Vientiane, continue on Route 13 to Ban Thabok, where a *songthaew* can usually take you the extra 7 km to the village. Buses to Paksan from the Talaat Sao bus station and That Luang market in Vientiane stop at Thabok. Most people, however, take a tour.

Tourist information Although treks can be organized in Ban Na (T020-2220 8286/62) and Ban Hat Khai (T020-2224 0303), advance notice is required so it's advisable to go with a tour operator from Vientiane instead. Visit www.trekkingcentrallaos.com and contact the **National Tourism Authority** in Vientiane (see page 48) for advice or **Green Discovery Laos** (see page 73), or the project advisor, Klaus Schwettman (kschwett@laopdr.com).

It costs 2000 kip per person to enter the park and 5000 kip per vehicle.

Tad Leuk

Accessed by dirt track (one hour) or boat from Ban Thabok (the waterfall sign is easily seen on the left), these are the most visited falls in the park and contain several large, undulating tiers. It is a good picnic spot, with swimming possible in the lake behind the waterfall although it is sometimes too rough. Tad Leuk has a visitor information centre which has toilets and washing facilities and also rents camping equipment. There's also a good little snack stand on a platform, offering a view of the falls. Mr Khamsavay Kingmanolath, the supervisor at Tad Leuk, organizes cheap treks from Tad Leuk (about US$7-10 per group).

Tad Sae

These are the most stunning falls in the park but don't boast the facilities of Tad Leuk. The falls tumble down seven tiers, flowing for about 800 m before plummeting 40 m into a magnificent river gorge. There is a small, clear pool that's perfect for swimming. To get to the waterfall, take the road from Ban Thabok and turn right at the fork – it's signposted.

Ban Na

These days the principal draw-cards for Phou Khao Khouay are the organized treks and the elephant observation tower, both of which are based on the small farming village of Ban Na (meaning rice field). The village's sugar cane plantations and river salt deposits attract a herd of wild elephants (around 30), which have, in the past, destroyed the villagers' homes and even killed a resident. This has limited the villagers' ability to undertake normal tasks, such as collecting bamboo. To help compensate, the village, in conjunction with some NGOs, has constructed an **elephant observation tower** 4 km from Ban Na and has started running trekking tours to see the elephants in their natural habitat. It is possible to stay overnight at the elephant tower, to try and catch a glimpse of the giant pachyderms lapping up salt from the nearby salt lick in the early evening. One- to three-day treks through the national park cross waterfalls, pass through pristine jungle and, with luck, offer the opportunity to hear or spot the odd wild elephant.

This is an important ecotour that contributes to the livelihood of the Ban Na villagers and helps conserve the elephant population. Unfortunately, the project suffered a large loss in 2009 when five elephants were killed by unknown people. Advance notice is required, so it's advisable to book with a tour operator in Vientiane (see page 73). If you are travelling independently you will need to organize permits, trekking and accommodation with the village directly. To do this, contact Mr Bounthanam (T020-220 8286). Visit www.trekkingcentrallaos.com and contact the National Tourism Authority in Vientiane (see page 48) or **Green Discovery Laos** (see page 73). Visitors will need to bring drinking water and basic snacks. Do not try to feed the elephants, they are very dangerous.

Ban Hat Khai

This village is home to 90 families from the Lao Loum and Lao Soung ethnic groups and is a starting point for organized treks crossing the Nam Mang river and the Phay Xay cliffs. Most treks take in the Tad Sae falls. Homestay accommodation is available in the village.

North of the city → *For listings, see pages 87-92.*

Route 13 North

About 30 km from Vientiane, on the Luang Prabang road, is **Dane Soung**, an area where large fallen rocks have formed a cave. There are Buddhist sculptures inside and a footprint of the Buddha on the left of the entrance. Too steep for tuk-tuks, it tends to be only private cars and motorbikes that make it here. Turn left at the 22 km mark towards Ban Houa Khoua. Dane Soung is 6 km down the track and is only accessible in the dry season.

Vangxang

Located 80 km north of Vientiane on Route 13, Vangxang, which means elephant drinking hole, is a lovely place to stop on the way to Vang Vieng. Worth a look are the amazing Buddha sculptures carved into a cliff face 2 km from the Vangxang Resort. The 10 Angkorian relief sculptures are believed to be over 500 years old, with two of them hovering at about 4 m. Aside from the carvings, walks through the jungle are the only diversion.

Phonehong

Near Phonehong, 17 km from Hin-Heup and 10 km from Route 13 is Green Discovery's **Jungle Fly**, a new series of zip lines up to 180 m long and 37 m high in the Nam Lik forest. Contact www.greendiscoverylaos.com for more information and kayak and camping combination tours.

Nam Ngum dam and reservoir → *For listings, see pages 87-92.*

The Nam Ngum dam, 90 km from Vientiane, is the pride of Laos. It provides electricity for much of the country and its energy exports to Thailand are Laos's second biggest foreign exchange earner. Dotted with hundreds of small islands, the lake is very picturesque.

Background

Many people believe that the dam was built with Soviet aid following the victory of the Communists in 1975. In fact construction began in the 1960s under the auspices of the Mekong Development Committee and was funded by the World Bank and Western nations. Indeed a large slice of the country's aid budget went into the construction of the dam, which was officially opened in the early 1970s. After the Communist victory, two of the lake's islands became open prisons for the most 'culturally polluted' of Vientiane's population. Two thousand drug addicts, prostitutes and other 'low lifers' were rounded up and shipped out here. One island was allocated for men and the other for women. Semi-submerged tree-trunks pose a navigational hazard, as no one had the foresight to log the area before it was flooded. The underwater cache of timber has now been spotted by the Thais; sub-aqua chainsaws are used to take out the 'treasure'.

Exploring the lake
Access to the Nam Ngum reservoir is via Phonhong on Route 13: turn right at the strategically placed concrete post in the middle of the road, then head left to the village of **Ban Talaat** on the southwest shores of the reservoir. The market here is worth a browse (the word '*talaat*' means market), as minority groups from the surrounding area come to the village to sell their wares and produce. From Ban Talaat, turn right across the narrow bridge to reach the dam, about 4 km up the road. An alternative route to the dam is via Route 10 out of Vientiane, which passes through much prettier countryside and traverses the Nam Ngum by ferry. Turn right at the end of the road for the dam. Hourly buses leave the Morning Market in Vientiane daily for Ban Talaat and from there take a bus or organize a *songthaew* to Nam Ngum. There are boats from the dam to **Ban Pao Mo** on the other side of the reservoir. The trip should take around two hours and cost about US$10 per hour but it will be necessary to bargain hard with the boatmen before crossing the lake. Boats can also be hired out; again, barter hard to get a good hourly rate. Vang Vieng is two hours' ride from the dam.

Vang Vieng and around → *For listings, see pages 87-92.*

The drive to Vang Vieng, on the much improved Route 13, follows the valley of the Nam Ngum north to Phonhong and then climbs steeply onto the plateau where Vang Vieng is located, 160 km north of Vientiane. The surrounding area is inhabited by the Hmong and Yao hill peoples and is particularly picturesque: craggy karst limestone scenery, riddled with caves, crystal-clear pools and waterfalls. In the early morning the views are reminiscent of a Chinese Sung Dynasty painting.

The town itself is nestled in a valley on the bank of the Nam Song river, amid a misty jungle. It enjoys cooler weather and offers breathtaking views of the mountains of Pha Tang and Phatto Nokham. There are a number of 16th- and 17th-century **monasteries** in town; the most notable are **Wat That** at the northern edge of the settlement and **Wat Kang**, 100 m or so to the south.

The town's laid-back feel has made it a haunt for backpackers, while the surrounding landscape has helped to establish Vang Vieng as a centre for rock climbing, caving, and kayaking. (It is also a stop-off point on the journey to Luang Prabang.) Its popularity has also become its downfall: neon lights, pancake stands, and 'happy' this, 'happy' that now pollute this former oasis. Nevertheless, the area is still full of things to do and see.

Ins and outs
Getting there and around Vang Vieng is on Route 13 between Vientiane and Luang Prabang so a bus between Vientiane and anywhere up north (or vice versa) will pass Vang Vieng even if it is not on the itinerary. The journey to/from the capital takes about three to four hours and from Luang Prabang around five to seven hours.

Vang Vieng

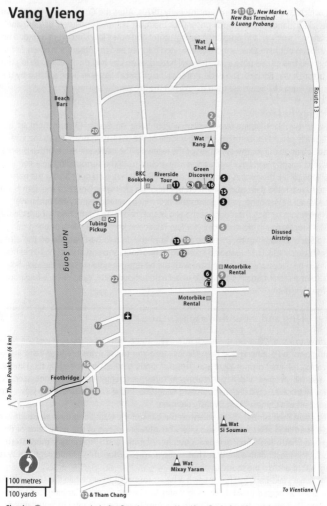

Sleeping 🛏
Ban Sabai Bungalow **17**
Chanthala **3**
Chillao Hostel **2**
Dokkhoun & Dokboua
  Guesthouse **4**
Elephant Crossing **1**
Grandview **6**
Inthira
  Vangvieng **9**

Le Jardine Organique
  Guesthouse **18**
Malany Guesthouse **5**
Malany Villa **10**
Maylyn Guesthouse **7**
Organic Farm **11**
Saysong Guesthouse &
  Riverhills Bungalows **14**
Thavonsouk Resort **16**
Thavisouk **19**

Vang Vieng Eco-Lodge **15**
Vang Vieng Orchid **20**
Vang Vieng Resort **12**
Vansana **22**
Villa Nam Song **8**

Eating 🍴
Luang Prabang Bakery **11**
Nangbot **3**
Nazim **4**

Nisha **5**
Organic Farm Café **6**
Rising Sun **13**
Vieng Champa **15**
Xayoh **16**

Bars & clubs 🍸
Oh La La **1**
Q Bar **2**
Sakura **12**

Tourist information   There is no official tourist information. Hobo Maps produces a remarkably detailed map of the town and surrounding area with caves, paths and walks all marked. It sells for 25,000 kip from Maylyn Guesthouse and the Elephant Crossing Hotel. It is well worth the purchase, especially if you want to explore much of the surrounding area that is not marketed by tour operators.

Safety   Laos is a very safe country for tourists but a disproportionate number of accidents and crimes seem to happen in Vang Vieng. **Theft** is routinely reported here, ranging from robberies by packs of kids targeting tubers on the river to the opportunist theft of items from guests' rooms. It is usually advisable to hand in any valuables to the management of your guesthouse or to padlock your bag and leave cash stashed in a very good hiding spot. Another major problem is the sale of illegal **drugs**. Police often go on sting operations and charge fines of up to US$600. There have even been some unsubstantiated reports of the police planting drugs on tourists. Legal issues aside, numerous travellers have become seriously ill from indulging in the 'happy' supplements that are supplied by some of the town's restaurants. ▸▸ *For details of the significant safety risks involved in adventure activities, see Tour operators, page 91.*

Nam Song River

Vang Vieng has become synonymous with tubing down the Nam Song. Tubes can be picked up from the Old Market area where the tubing company has formed a cartel. Without stops the 3-km tubing from the **Organic Farm** back to town can take one to two hours if done quickly, but most people do it in three to four hours or take all day, choosing to stop along the way to drink, play volleyball or use the flying fox swings at the many bars dotted along the river on the way into town. ▸▸ *See also Tubing, page 91.*

Many tour operators offer kayaking trips as well. Popular routes include kayaking down the Nam Song to the caves (especially Tham Nam – water cave), or the trip back to Vientiane via the drop-off point at Nam Lik. If you want to break the journey there are several nice guesthouses at Nam Lik including the Nam Lik eco-village, south of the town. ▸▸ *See also Kayaking and rafting, page 90.*

Caves

Vang Vieng is best known for its limestone caves, sheltered in the mountains flanking the town. Pretty much every guesthouse and tour operator offers tours to the caves (the best of these is **Green Discovery**) and, although some caves can be accessed independently, it is advisable to take a guide to a few as they are dark and difficult to navigate. Often children from surrounding villages will take tourists through the caves for a small fee. Don't forget to bring a torch, or even better a head-lamp, which can be picked up cheaply at the market both in Vang Vieng and Vientiane. Each cave has an entrance fee of 10,000 kip and many have stalls where you can buy drinks and snacks. You can buy hand-drawn maps from the town but all the caves are clearly signposted in English from the main road so these are not really necessary. ▸▸ *See Activities and tours, page 90.*

Of Vang Vieng's myriad caves, **Tham Chang** ① *access via the Vang Vieng Resort south of town (see Sleeping)*, is the most renowned. It passes right under a mountain and is fed by a natural spring, perfect for an early morning dip. From the spring, it is possible to swim into the cave for quite a distance (bring a waterproof torch, if possible). The cave is said to have been used as a refuge from Chinese Haw bandits during the 19th century and this explains its name: *chang* meaning 'loyal'. The entrance fee includes electric illumination of the cave. Although the cave is not the most magnificent of Vieng Vang's caves, it serves as a superb lookout point.

Another popular cavern is **Tham Poukham** ⓘ *7 km from Vang Vieng, 10,000 kip*. The cave is often referred to as the Cave of the Golden Crab and is highly auspicious. It's believed that if you catch a golden crab you will have a lifetime of fortune. To get there, cross the footbridge near the **Villa Nam Song**, and then follow the road for a further 6 km until you reach the village of Ban Nathong. From the village, the cave is a short climb up a steep hill. Mossy rocks lead the way into the main cavern where a large bronze reclining Buddha is housed. Here there is an idyllic lagoon with glassy green-blue waters, perfect for a dip.

Tham None ⓘ *4 km north of Vang Vieng, 10,000 kip*, is known locally known as the 'Sleeping Cave' because 2000 villagers took refuge there during the war. The large cave is dotted with stalagmites and stalactites, including the 'magic stone of Vang Vieng', which reflects light. There are also lots of bats residing in the grotto. This cave is very popular with tour groups and rock climbers.

Tham Xang ⓘ *14 km north of Vang Vieng on the banks of the Nam Song, 10,000 kip*, also known as the 'Elephant Cave', is named after the stalagmites and stalactites that have created an elephant formation on a ledge. The cave also contains some Buddha images, including the footprint of Buddha. Although the cave itself is relatively nondescript the bell used by monks is made of a former bomb.

From this cave there is a signposted path that leads to **Tham Nam** (water cave) ⓘ *15 km from town, 10,000 kip*, a long spindly cave that is believed to stretch for at least 7 km. It takes about two hours to explore the cavern and at the entrance there is a crystal-clear pool, perfect for a dip. This is one of Vang Vieng's most interesting caves and in the wet season needs to be explored with an inner tube or by wading, while pulling yourself along a rope, although tour operators will take you beyond the roped area too. It's not easy and should not be attempted alone. At times the cavern is an extremely tight fit and commando-type crawling is required; a hard helmet with lamp attached is necessary. In spite of the difficulties, it is an incredible caving experience. To get to these two caves follow Route 13 north and turn left at Km 14, then follow this dirt road for 1 km until you reach the river. Boats charge 10,000 kip to cross the river to see Tham Xang, from which you can walk to Tham Nam.

There are many more caves in the vicinity of Vang Vieng, most to the west and north. It is possible to hire a bicycle in Vang Vieng (around 10,000 kip per day), take it across the river and cycle to the caves and villages on the other side of the Nam Song as all the sites are between 2 km and 15 km from Vang Vieng. See the Hobo Map for all routes.

Kasi → *Colour map 2, A2.*

A trucking stop on Route 13, and only 60 km north of the much more attractive town of Vang Vieng, Kasi entices few people to stay longer than necessary. The surrounding countryside is said to have the second largest cave in the world, Khoun Lang. This hasn't popped up on the tourism radar yet and no official tours have been established. Delightfully, the introduction of tourists to the area looks set to be done in a traditional Lao style, incorporating local food and homestay accommodation, including showers in the river and suchlike.

The 45-km stretch of hilly road north of Kasi, up towards Muang Phou Khoun, was notorious for Hmong rebel attacks, although it has calmed down in the last few years. **Muang Phou Khoun** is an old colonial garrison at the junction of Route 13 and Route 7. Its strategic position was heavily fought over during the second Indochina war.

For Sleeping and Eating price codes and other relevant information, see pages 23-24.

● Sleeping

Ban Pako *p80*

D-G Ban Pako eco-lodge, T030-5257937, www.banpako.com. Accommodation is in a Lao-style longhouse or in single bungalows overlooking the river. Dorm beds are also available. Can be crowded at weekends. The restaurant (†) serves good Lao and European food. Breakfast included for the bungalow rooms. Pickups arranged at Nam Phou for 140,000 kip one way. Call in advance to arrange.

Phou Khao Khouay Protected Area *p80*

The visitor centre at Tad Leuk rents out tents, mattresses, mosquito nets and sleeping bags. It costs 40,000 kip per night to rent a tent and 15,000 kip a night to hire a sleeping bag. Toilets and washing facilities on site. It is also possible to organize a homestay in one of the surrounding villages or stay overnight in the Elephant Observation Tower near Ban Na. Ban Hatkai and Ban Na also offer homestay accommodation.

Vangxang *p82*

E Vangxang Resort, 13 Neau Rd, Ban Phonengerun, T023-21526, T020-545 4076 (mob). The resort has cute little cottage-style bungalows, with hot water. Great Lao restaurant and scenic man-made lake.

Nam Ngum dam and reservoir *p82*

C Nam Lik Eco-Village, Ban Vang Mong, about 8 km from Ang Nam Ngum, turn off Route 13 at Km 75, T020-550 8719, www.namlik.com. A complex of ovely bungalow rooms with brilliant views and situated equidistant (1½ hrs) from Vientiane and Vang Vieng. Lots of adventure sports are on offer, from kayaking to rock climbing. The price includes breakfast, transfer from Vang Vieng or Vientiane plus activities.

C-D Nam Ngum Resort, southern end of Nam Ngum, T021-217595, www.dansavanh.com. A Malaysian and Lao government joint-venture hotel with 209 rooms, Chinese and Thai restaurant, health centre, video games. Future plans include adding marine sports facilities, a funfair and golf course. Rates include breakfast and a shuttle bus from Vientiane.

C-D Vansana Nam Ngum Resort, T023-241162, www.vansanahotel-group.com. 20 tasteful rooms overlooking the water. There's a pool too.

Vang Vieng and around *p83, map p84*

The town's popularity has ensured a uniformity among almost all places catering to budget tourists. However, in the last 2 years a couple of higher-end hotels have opened. Accommodation in the centre of town is usually cheaper, but try to get a room with a view of the river, as it is stunning. A couple of bamboo bridges have been built across the river to new bungalow developments; note that in the rainy season the only bridges in operation are the Namsong bridge (4000 kip return, 6000 kip for bikes, 10,000 kip for motorbikes) and the high bridge leading past the **Vang Vieng Orchid** to the island bars.

In town

A-B Villa Nam Song, T023-511637, www.villanamsong.com. Quaint terracotta villas set in manicured gardens overlooking the Nam Song with parquet floors, hot water and separate shower compartments. Fan-cooled restaurant attached; breakfast included. Although this is an attractive hotel there is better value for money in town. Cheaper rooms lack river view; 2 rooms have wheelchair access.

A-D Thavonsouk Resort, on the river, T023-511096, www.thavonsouk.com. Offers

5 different styles of accommodation across sprawling riverfront premises. Unfortunately, the rooms are more attractive on the outside than in; standard rooms come with tacky wood-imitation tiles. But some mid-range bungalows are great value, with massive balconies complete with sunbeds. There is also a traditional Lao house which is ideal for groups, plus suites (equipped with TV, fridge, bath, a/c) and standard accommodation. Fantastic restaurant. Look out for local pop star, Aluna, and her father, Alom, who run the place.

B-D Elephant Crossing, on the Nam Song River, T023-511232, www.theelephantcrossinghotel.com. An attractive mid-range option. Australian-owned riverfront hotel with modern wooden furnishings. The big bathtub and sliding window between the bedroom and bathroom will be a big hit with romantics. All rooms, bar 6, have view, fridge, Wi-Fi and a/c. Breakfast included.

C Ban Sabai Bungalow, on the banks of the river, T023-511088, www.xayohgroup.com. This is a lovely complex of bungalows with balconies, in a spectacular location. However, it doesn't entirely live up to its promise. The rooms are not well lit, the water is insufficiently hot, the bathroom is badly designed (with the sink in the shower compartment), and the breakfast service is pretty unpolished. Rooms 1-4 are near the laundry room and light sleepers will be disturbed. Bungalows closer to the river are a bit more expensive.

C Vansana, by the river, T023-511598, www.vansanahotel-group.com. Despite its soulless exterior this hotel has some of the best facilities in town. The large bedrooms are fitted with all mod cons and there are mountain and river views. Modern wooden furniture and handicrafts decorate the rooms. Other attractions are the beautiful pool and bar by the river (with deckchairs). Ask for a room with a view; breakfast is included. Recommended. Non-guests can use the pool for 20,000 kip per day.

C-D Inthira Vangvieng, T023-511070, www.inthirahotel.com. Opened in November 2009 with 28 rooms in a rather narrow slot on the main street. Well-furnished rooms with medium-sized bathrooms and small balconies.

E-F Grandview, on the river, T023-511474, grandviewguesthouse@gmail.com. Opened in 2007, this place has spotless rooms with attached hot-water bathroom. There are beautiful balcony views and cheaper rooms without view and a/c. Excellent value. Highly recommended.

E-F Le Jardine Organique Guesthouse, on the river, about 900 m from the centre of town, T023-511420. This set of bungalows and a guesthouse is surrounded by 2 other properties owned by family members. The raised bungalows are smart with balconies; the guesthouse rooms are plain and clean. The **Bansuan Riverview** with rattan bungalows hogs the view while the **Vilayvong**, which faces Le Jardine's bungalows, offers smart wooden bungalows with balconies. Cheaper rooms have fan only. The owners are delightful.

E-F Malany Guesthouse, on the main road, T023-511083. In the centre of town, this big concrete building has large clean rooms that are surprisingly nice, with en suite bathrooms, hot water and fan. Hardish beds, though.

E-F Vang Vieng Orchid, on the river road, T023-511172. Comfortable fan or more expensive a/c rooms. Hot water in the bathrooms, clean tiled floors, very comfortable rooms. The rooms with the private balconies are well worth the few extra dollars because you will have your own personal piece of the phenomenal view.

E-F Vang Vieng Resort, close to Tham Chang, T021-219380, www.vangvieng-resort.com. A Chinese-owned resort, with bar and noodle restaurant. Some chalets have bathrooms; not all have a/c.

E-G Saysong Guesthouse & Riverhills Bungalows, by the river, T023-511130, www.saysong-guesthouse-riverhillbungalows.com. The cheaper rooms have en suite bathrooms but are a bit mouldy. The doubles are much better, cleaner and bigger and there is a fantastic communal balcony overlooking the river. New bungalows with views (more expensive) have been built on the river island. A new restaurant with riverside huts specializes in fish.

F-G Chanthala, next to Wat Kang, T023-511146. One of Vang Vieng's older cheap guesthouses, with shared facilities. Clean. A newer building has opened next door.

F-G Chillao Hostel (formerly **Bountang**), near Wat Kang, T023-511328, chilllao@ yahoo.com. This is a large 3-storey villa with 2 dorms and spotless bathrooms plus private rooms supplied with clean towels. Free Wi-Fi; call or email for free pick up from bus station. It's 5000 kip less if you have a YHA card.

F-G Dokboua Guesthouse, T020-614 4933. This newcomer, close to **Dokkhoun**, offers some of the best budget rooms in town. Sparklingly clean rooms with taut white linens and good mattresses, and huge attached bathrooms. A/c rooms are more expensive; older rooms are cheaper. Friendly family owners. Highly recommended.

F-G Dokkhoun 1 Guesthouse, T023-511032. Villa with 2 storeys and balcony area, clean rooms with en suite bathrooms with hot water. A/c rooms are available for a few dollars extra.

F-G Maylyn Guesthouse, T020-5604095. Atmospheric setting on the far side of the river. Basic rattan-style bungalows, with shared facilities, rooms with and without bathrooms, and a new concrete building with rooms. It is situated a bit far from town but ideal if you're looking for peace and quiet. Trail bike and bike hire. Accessed by the Namsong bridge.

G Thavisouk, in the centre of town, T023-511658. No frills but very clean, though sometime there's an ant problem. Rooms with hot water bath attached US$3-4. While the rooms are good value, their tours and tickets aren't.

Out of town

Out of town, the lack of facilities and transport ensures tranquillity but also makes it quite difficult to get to town.

D-E Vang Vieng Eco-Lodge, 7 km north of town, T021-413370, www.vangvieng-eco-lodge.com. Although this isn't an eco-lodge it is still a beautiful place to stay. Set on the banks of the river with stunning gardens and beautiful rock formations, it has 4 well-decorated chalet-style bungalows with balconies, comfortable furnishings and a big hot-water bathtub, a bungalow of four rooms with sliding doors with great riverside views but small double bed and shower room, and a rattan longhouse (cheaper still, **G**) with 8 rooms and shared bath; breakfast is included. Good Lao restaurant. Will also arrange activities.

G Vang Vieng Organic Farm, 3 km north of town in Ban Sisavang, T023-511174, www.laofarm.org. This mulberry farm has basic rooms with mosquito net, dorm accommodation and full board. If you volunteer (say, building a mudhouse, teaching English, working on the farm) you get a 20,000 kip per night discount. A new guesthouse with very overpriced rooms with hard mattresses has opened (**E**), and there is a popular restaurant, serving great starfruit wine and mulberry pancakes (open 0600-2130). It's a popular drop-off spot for tubers. The farm supports the Equal Education for All project (www.eefaproject.com).

Kasi *p86*

Rooms are available at several guesthouses in town.

F Somchith, Route 13 Main Rd. The most popular place is this small guesthouse above a restaurant in the centre of town.

🍴 Eating

Nam Ngum dam and reservoir *p82*
¶¶-¶ **Lao Food Rafts**, there are several floating restaurants lining the shore. Atmospheric.

Vang Vieng and around *p83, map p84*
There is a string of eating places on the main road through town, with the same menu in almost every establishment – generally hamburgers, pasta, sandwiches and basic Asian. Most of the restaurants offer 'happy' upgrades – marijuana or mushrooms in your pizza, cake or lassi, or opium tea. Although many people choose the 'happy' offerings, some wind up ill. The police have also been known to go on drug-busting sprees.

¶ **Luang Prabang Bakery Restaurant**, just off the main road. Excellent pastries, cakes and shakes and delicious breakfasts. Make sure you ask for the freshest batch as they have a tendency to leave cakes on the shelf well past their use-by date. Recommended.

¶ **Nangbot**, on the main road, T023-511018. This is one of the oldest tourist diners in town and serves a few traditional dishes, such as bamboo shoot soup and *laap* with sticky rice, alongside the usual Western fare.

¶ **Nazim**, on the main road, T023-511214. Largest and most popular Indian joint in town. Good range of South Indian and *biriyani* specialities, plus vegetarian meals.

¶ **Nisha Restaurant**, on the main road, T020-5571015. Good-value Indian food and Lao dishes.

¶ **Organic Farm Café**, further down the main road. Small café offering over 15 fruit shakes and a fantastic variety of food. Mulberry shakes and pancakes are a must and the harvest curry stew is delicious. Try the fresh spring rolls, with pineapple dipping sauce as a starter. There is a sister branch at the **Organic Mulberry Farm** (see Sleeping).

¶ **Rising Sun**, T020-5397535, just off the main road. The decor is brightly coloured and the menu features good comfort food such as cottage pie.

¶ **Vieng Champa Restaurant**, on the main road, T023-511370. Family-run restaurant with a good selection of Lao food. The only drawback is the green fluorescent lighting.

¶ **Xayoh**, on the main Luang Prabang Rd, T023-511088. Restaurant with branches in Vientiane and Luang Prabang offering good

Western food in a comfy environment. Pizza, soups and roast dinners. **Xayoh** may have moved location by the time you read this.

⊙ Bars and clubs

Vang Vieng and around *p83, map p84*
The latest hotspot in Vang Vieng changes week to week.
Oh La La Bar, off the main street. Very popular, open bar with pool table.
Q Bar, on the main road diagonally opposite Xayo. A new addition to the night scene.
Sakura Bar, between the main road and the river. A big open bar, often with live music. .

⊙ Shopping

Vang Vieng and around *p83, map p84*
BKC Bookshop, T023-5118694. A reasonable range of second-hand books and guides to buy and exchange.
New Market, 2 km north of town, has the greatest selection of goods.

▲ Activities and tours

Phou Khao Khouay National Protected Area *p80*
Trips organized by the LNTA in Vientiane. Prices to Ban Na, including transport, guides, and accommodation in the elephant tower, start at US$50.

Vang Vieng and around *p83, map p84*
Kayaking and rafting
See also Tour operators, below. Kayaking is very popular around Vang Vieng and competition between operators has become fierce. Options range from day trips (with a visit to the caves and surrounding villages) to kayaking all the way to Vientiane via the stop-off point at Nam Lik, US$33-87, about 6 hrs, including a 40-min drive at the start and finish. Any valuables can be kept in a car, which meets kayakers at the end of their paddle. Be wary of intensive kayaking trips through risky areas during the wet season

as this can be extremely dangerous. It is also important to check equipment thoroughly.

Rock climbing

Vang Vieng is the only properly established rock-climbing area in the country, with over 50 sites in the locality, ranging from grade 5 to 8A+. Almost all of these climbs have been 'bolted'. There are climbing sites suitable for beginners through to more experienced climbers. **Green Discovery** (see Tour operators, below) runs climbing courses almost every day in high season (US$20-45 per day, including equipment rental). The best climbing sites include:

Sleeping Cave (Tham None, see page 86 85). A popular destination, accessed by dug-out canoe across the Nam Song river. The cave offers 14 separate routes, after which you can jump into the water on one of the rope swings to cool off.

Sleeping Wall, near Sleeping Cave. A tough 20-m crag, which features 19 separate climbs, including a few ascents requiring some tricky manoeuvring and steep overhangs. Boatmen offer climbers a lift along the Nam Song river (5000 kip) to get to the wall. There are refreshment stalls at both Sleeping Wall and Sleeping Cave.

Tham Nam Them, 7 km from town. Fantastic clambers around the entrance of the cave. There are 19 bolted tracks here, both inside and outside the cave.

Tour operators

Tour guides are available for hiking, rafting, and visiting the caves and minority villages, from most travel agents and guesthouses. Safety issues need to be considered when taking part in any adventure activity. There have been fatalities in Vang Vieng from boating, trekking and caving accidents. The Nam Xong river can flow very quickly during the wet season (Jul and Aug) and tourists have drowned here. Make sure you wear a life-jacket and ensure you are not on the river after dark. Make sure all equipment is in a good state of repair. A price war between

operators has led to cost cutting, resulting in equipment that is not well maintained or non-existent. The more expensive companies are usually the best (see also Tour operators, page 73).

Green Discovery, attached to Xayoh Café, T023-511440, www.greendiscoverylaos.com. Caving, kayaking, hiking and rock climbing plus motorbike tours and mountain bike tours from US$22-40 for one day. Very professional and helpful. Recommended. Also rents motorbikes from US$25-30 for one day. The office may have moved location by the time you read this.

Riverside Tour, T020-2254137, www. riversidetourlaos.com. Kayaking and adventure tours. Also tour agency; friendly.

VLT Natural Tours, T023-511369, T020-5208283, www.vangviengtour.com. As well as the usual tours, offers cookery tours, fishing, camping, a slow boat to Vientiane and a sunset barbecue on the river. Combined trekking, caving, tubing, kayaking is around 150,000 kip; a similar trip with **Green Discovery** is from $52.

Trekking

Almost all guesthouses and agents in town offer hiking trips, usually with a visit to caves and minority villages and, possibly, some kayaking or tubing. The major tour operators who will provide an English-speaking guide, all transport and lunch for US$10-15 per day.

Tubing

Floating slowly along the Nam Song is an ideal way to take in the stunning surroundings of misty limestone karsts, jungle and rice paddies. The drop-off point is 3 km from Vang Vieng, near the **Organic Farm**, where bars and restaurants have set up along the river. Start early in the day as it's dangerous to tube after dark, when the water temperature drops sharply. Take a sarong with you, and do not walk through town in a bikini as it is offensive to the locals.

Since July 2009, tube operators have formed a cartel to benefit the 1555 families in town who have a stake in this activity. Thus there is only 1 place where you can pick up the tubes (marked on map). Tube collection is from 0830-1530 and costs 55,000 kip including the tuk-tuk ride to the drop-off point and a life jacket. A deposit of 60,000 kip is required. A rented dry bag costs 20,000 kip. For a lost tube the fine is US$7, a lost life jacket US$20 and a lost dry bag US$15. The tube must be returned by 1800 or a fine of 20,000 kip is imposed (people may offer to return the tubes for you; it is best to decline this offer). It is essential that you wear a life jacket while tubing as people have drowned on the river, particularly during the wet season (Jul and Aug). Without stopping expect the journey to take 2 hrs in the dry season and 1 hr in the wet season. Most people stop on the way and make a day of it.

⊖Transport

See also Vientiane Transport, page 73.

Vang Vieng and around *p83, map p84*
Bicycle and motorbike hire
There are many bicycles for rent in town (10,000 kip per day). There are also a few motorbike rental places (60,000 kip per day); the best of these is diagonally opposite the **Organic Farm Café** in town.

Bus
Buses leave from the bus terminal at the New Market, 2 km north of town, T023-511657. Ticket office open daily 0530-1630; staff speak English. There are toilets, shops and cafés. A tuk-tuk into town costs 5000-10,000 kip per person. Minibuses leave from most guesthouses to both **Vientiane** and **Luang Prabang**. To **Vientiane** on local bus at 0530-0600, 0630, 0700, 1230 and 1400, 30,000 kip, 4 hrs; express bus at 1000, 1300, 60,000 kip, 3½ hrs; pickups every 20 mins, 30,000 kip, 4 hrs. To **Luang Prabang** express bus at 1000, 80,000 kip. To **Phonsovan** at 0930, 90,000 kip, 7 hrs.

Private minivan transport and VIP buses
Tickets are usually sold by guesthouses and include pickup to the bus. Minivan to **Vientiane** at 0900, 80,000 kip, 3½-4 hrs; drop off at Mekong riverside restaurants. Minibus to **Luang Prabang** at 0900 and 1400, 90,000 kip (5-6 hrs). Every guesthouse and travel agent can book the VIP/minivans.

Tour companies sell through tickets to **Pakse** and international tickets to **Vietnam** and **Bangkok** but there are more efficient ways to get to the Thai capital.

Tuk-tuk
A day trip to the caves should cost US$10 but there have been reports of some drivers offering trips to the caves for 10,000 kip per person and then demanding an outrageous fee for the return leg. Make sure all prices are set in stone before leaving town.

Kasi *p89*
Bus/truck
There are connections south to **Vang Vieng** (2 hrs) and north to **Luang Prabang** (4 hrs).

❶Directory

Vang Vieng and around *p83, map p84*
Banks BCEL, T021-511480, exchanges cash and TCs and will also do cash advances on Visa and MasterCard, daily 0830-1530. Visa and MasterCard ATM. There are a number of ATMs in town. **Internet** There are internet cafés along the main drag; most offer international net calls from 3000 kip per min. **Magnet** is the best of these; as well as internet it offers music/movie transfer to iPod and cash advances from the EFTPOS facility for 3% commission. **Medical services** Vang Vieng Hospital, on the road parallel to the river; is woefully under-equipped; in most cases it is much better to go to Vientiane or into Thailand, see pages 35 and 78.
Post The post office is next to the old market, daily 0830-1600.

Contents

The North

CHINA

VIETNAM

MYANMAR
(BURMA)

Lan Toui
Muang
Uthai
Ngay Neua
Hat Xa
Phongsali
PHONGSALI

Muang
Sing
Mohan
Boten
Nateui
Muang Khua
Luang
Namtha
Xieng Kok
Muang La
Muang
Ngoi Neua
Muang Et
Sop Bao
Sop Hao

Muang
Moeng
LUANG
NAMTHA
Vieng
Phouka
Udomxai
Pakmong
Nam
Bak
Nong Khiaw &
Ban Saphoun
Xam Neua
Vieng
Xai
Na
Maew

BOKEO
UDOMXAI
Nam Et/
Phou Loei NPA
HUA
PHAN
Caves

Houei Xai
Muang Houn
Pak Ou Caves
Muang
Muoi
Sao Hintang
Nam Nouan
Xam
Tai

Chiang
Khong
Pak Beng
Tha Suang
LUANG
PRABANG
Vieng
Thong
Muang
Na
Pung
Thac

Muang
Ngeun
Hongsa
Luang
Prabang
Tham
Phiu
Muang Kham
Nam Khan

Mep
Tad
Kuong Si
Nong Tang
Phonsavanh
Muang
Khoune
Nong Het
VIETNAM

SAYABOURY
Kasi
Plain of Jars
XIENG
KHOUANG
Muang
Mok

Na Vang
Sayaboury
VIENTIANE
Tam
Kalong

THAILAND
Na Sing
Vang Vieng
BOLIKHAMXAI

Na Le
Viang Thong
Paksan
Pak Kading

Na Cham
Keun
Khamkeut
Lak
Sao

Pak Lai
Tha Pabat
Phonsanh
Ban Lao

Nakok
VIENTIANE
Muang
Hin Boun

Kene Thao
Botene
Pak Hin Boun
Thakhek

THAILAND
Nong Bok

N

50 km
50 miles

Introduction

Much of Laos' northern region is rugged and mountainous, a remote borderland with a significant minority population of hill peoples. Until recently, in some areas at least, the only way to travel was by boat, along one of the rivers – many fast-flowing – which have cut their way through this impressive landscape. Today road travel is much improved, though still not easy.

The key centre of the north is the old royal capital of Luang Prabang, one of the world's most beautiful cities. To the east is the Plain of Jars and Vieng Xai, a former stronghold of the Pathet Lao, while to the north is a string of small towns that are becoming increasingly popular places to visit. Eco-resorts in peaceful forest settings, treks to upland villages, dips in icy mountain streams and rafting trips down innumerable rivers are among the highlights of this region. And, as tourist numbers rise, local people are learning to cater for the peculiar demands of foreigner visitors.

Luang Prabang and around

In terms of size, Luang Prabang hardly deserves the title 'city' – the district capital has a population of around 40,000. But in terms of grandeur the appellation is more than deserved. Luang Prabang is the town that visitors often remember with the greatest affection. Its rich history, incomparable architecture, easygoing atmosphere, good choice of restaurants, friendly population and stunning position, surrounded by a crown of mountains, mark it out as exceptional.

Anchored at the junction of the Mekong and Nam Khan rivers, the former royal capital is home to a spellbinding array of gilded temples, weathered French colonial shopfronts and art deco shophouses. Luang Prabang was founded on Mount Phousi – a small rocky hill with leafy slopes – and has been a mountain kingdom for over 1000 years. Despite a few welcome concessions to modern life, including great food, internet cafés, electricity and the occasional car, Luang Prabang still oozes the magic of bygone days. In the 18th century there were more than 65 wats in the city; many have been destroyed over the years but over 30 remain intact, including the former royal Wat Xieng Thong; Wat Visoun, built in 1513 and the oldest operational temple in Luang Prabang); That Pathum (Lotus Stupa), noted for its odd watermelon-like shape, and Wat Aham, formerly the seat of the Lao Supreme Patriarch. The continuing splendour and historical significance of the town led UNESCO to designate Luang Prabang a World Heritage Site in 1995 and declare it the best-preserved traditional city in Southeast Asia.

Yet for all its magnificent temples, this royal 'city' feels more like an easy-going provincial town: in the early evening children play in the streets, while women cook, old men lounge in wicker chairs and young boys play takraw. *The town's timelessness can be observed by simply walking the ancient cobbled paths.* ▶▶ *For listings, see pages 118-131.*

Ins and outs → *Phone code: 071. Colour map 2, A2.*

Getting there Visitors to Luang Prabang used to be advised by Vientiane's foreign consular staff to fly rather than risk the road journey. This was because vehicles on the stretch of Route 13 between Vientiane and Luang Prabang, particularly north of Kasi, were periodically attacked by Hmong bandits. Although there have been no attacks on this stretch for several years now, flying is still the easiest option, with daily connections from Vientiane, plus flights from Hanoi, Siem Reap, Bangkok and Chiang Mai to **Luang Prabang International Airport** (LPQ) ① *4 km northeast of town, T071-212172/3.* Don't expect anything too jazzy, but the airport does have a phone box, a couple of restaurants, foreign exchange desk, ATMs and handicraft shops. There is a standard US$6 (50,000 kip) charge for a tuk-tuk/van ride from the airport into the centre; on the way back you can probably negotiate a cheaper price.

Route 13 is now safe, with no recent attacks reported, and the road has been upgraded, shortening the journey from Vientiane to a relatively painless eight or nine hours. There are also overland connections with other destinations in northern Laos including Sayaboury, Nong Khiaw, Xieng Khouang (Phonsavanh), Xam Neua, Luang Namtha, Udomxai, Muang Ngoi and Pak Mong. Luang Prabang has two main bus stations: **Kiew Lot Sai Neua** (northern bus station), on the northeast side of Sisavangvong Bridge, for traffic to and from the north; and **Naluang** (southern bus station) for traffic to and from the south. Occasionally buses will pass through the opposite station to what you would expect, so be sure to double-check. The standard tuk-tuk fare to/from either bus station is about 10,000 kip. If there are only a few passengers, it's late at night or you are travelling to/from an out-of-town hotel, expect to pay 20,000 kip. These prices tend to fluctuate with the international cost of petroleum.

A third option is to travel by river: a firm favourite is the two-day trip between Houei Xai (close to the Thai border) and Luang Prabang, via Pak Beng. Less frequent are the boats between Luang Prabang and Vientiane, via Pak Lai, and to Muang Khoua, via Muang Ngoi and Nong Khiaw. ▶▶ See Transport, page 129.

Getting around Luang Prabang is a small town and the best way to explore is either on foot or by bicycle. Bicycles can be hired from most guesthouses for US$1 per day. Strolling about this beautiful town is a real pleasure but there are also tuk-tuks and saamlors available for hire. Depending on the prevailing mood of the local government, motorbikes may or may not be available for hire. As of this printing, motorbikes can be rented for about US$15-20 per day. Note that road names are not widely used and there seems to be some confusion over precisely what some of the roads are called. Buses provide links with out-of-town destinations (although the service is limited and intermittent), and there are also boats and minibuses for charter.

Best time to visit Luang Prabang lies 300 m above sea level on the upper Mekong, at its confluence with the Nam Khan. The most popular time to visit is during the cooler months of November and December but the best time to visit is from December to February. After this, the weather is warming up and the views are often shrouded in a haze, produced by shifting cultivators using fire to clear the forest for agriculture. This does not really clear until May or even June. During the months of March and April, when visibility is at its worst, the smoke can cause soreness of the eyes, as well as preventing planes from landing.

In terms of festivals, on the October full moon, the delightful Lai Heua Fai, fireboat festival takes place, see page 126.

Tourist information **Luang Prabang Tourist Information Centre** ① *Sisavangvong Rd, T071-212487.* Aside from provincial information, it offers a couple of good ecotourism treks (which support local communities), including one to Tad Kuang Si and one in Chompet district. The Chompet trek receives quite good reviews and includes visits to hot springs, villages and the chance to watch a traditional performance from Hmong performers.

The best city map is one produced by **Lao National Tourism Authority**, with support from the Asian Development Bank and GT Rider; the tourist office have copies available for sale. Other maps are increasingly available, including a detailed one by Hobo maps.

History

According to legend, the site of Luang Prabang was chosen by two resident hermits. Buddha was believed to have glanced in Luang Prabang's direction, saying a great city would be built there. The discovery of large, stone container-like artefacts nearby allude to an ancient history yet to be unravelled by archaeologists. Some believe the artefacts are linked with the Vietnamese Dong Son period (500 BC-AD 100), while others suggest a prehistoric connection to the Plain of Jars. Details are sketchy regarding the earliest inhabitants of Luang Prabang but historians imply the ethnic Khmu and Lao Theung groups were the initial settlers. They named Luang Prabang, 'Muang Sawa', which literally translates as Java, hinting at some kind of cross-border support. By the end of the 13th century, Muang Sawa had developed into a regional hub.

A major turning point in the city's history came about in 1353, when the mighty Fa Ngum travelled up the Mekong, backed by a feisty Khmer army, and captured Muang Sawa. Here, the warrior king founded Lane Xang Hom Khao, the Kingdom of a Million Elephants, White Parasol and established a new Lao royal lineage, which was to last another 600 years. The name of the city refers to the holy Pra Bang, Laos' most sacred image of the Buddha which was given to Fa Ngum by his father-in-law the King of Cambodia.

Fa Ngum imported Khmer traditions including Theravada Buddhism and great architecture, but his constituents and army, wary of his warmongering ways, exiled him in 1373, and his son, Oun Heuan, then assumed the throne. Oun Heuan was known as Samsenthai a name that indicated the size of his army – a man-force of 300,000 – and, during his reign, the city was renamed Muang Xieng Thong, the City of Gold.

In 1478 the city was invaded by Vietnamese. After several years occupying and ransacking the place, they were driven out and the Kingdom embarked upon a massive reconstruction campaign. During this period some of Luang Prabang's finest monuments were built, including Wat Xieng Thong. The city had been significantly built up by the time King Visunarat came to power in 1512 and remained the capital until King Setthathirat, fearing a Burmese invasion, moved the capital to Vieng Chan (Vientiane) in 1563.

Luang Prabang was a religious as well as a trading centre. To begin with, it seems that Theravada Buddhism was creatively combined with ritualistic elements from the Hinduist and animist past. Mendez Pinto, in his account of 1578, describes Luang Prabang (or what historians take to be Luang Prabang) as having 24 religious sects and writes that there is "so great a variety and confusion of diabolical errors and precepts, principally in the blood sacrifices they employ, that it is frightful to hear them". The royal chronicles of the 16th century describe successive attempts to erase these sects from the kingdom.

Luang Prabang's importance diminished in the 18th century, following the death of King Souligna Vongsa and the break-up of Lane Xang, but it remained a royal centre until the Communist takeover in 1975. During the low point of Laos' fortunes in the mid-19th century, when virtually the whole country had become tributary to Bangkok (Siam), only Luang Prabang retained a semblance of independence. The tiny kingdom, shorn of most of its hinterland, paid tribute to Siam, Hué and Peking, hoping to play one off against the other. What the king did not envisage, however, was the arrival of the French.

The French and the British competed diligently for control of mainland Southeast Asia. France's piece of the cake became French Indochina and their attempt to wrest control of Laos from Siamese suzerainty was linked to the energy, perseverance and force of will of one man: Auguste Pavie. Contemporary accounts describe Pavie as "thin and weak-looking" but this physical demeanour disguised a man of extraordinary abilities. He was appointed French vice-consul in Luang Prabang in May 1886, after accumulating 17 years' experience in Cambodia and Cochin China (south Vietnam). According to Martin Stuart-Fox in *A History of Laos* (1997), Pavie had not only acquired a comprehensive knowledge of the people, cultures and languages of the area, but also developed a deep dislike of the Siamese. His part in securing Laos for France was achieved when he rescued King Ounkham from marauding Haw and Tai bandits in 1887. The protecting Siamese and their Lao soldiers had departed from Luang Prabang, leaving Pavie with the opportunity to save the day. He plucked the aged king from a burning palace, escaped downstream and was rewarded when the king requested France's protection. The events marked the dispossession of the Siamese by the French.

Mekong monsters, real and imagined

It is said that the *pa beuk*, the giant catfish of the Mekong, was only described by Western science in 1930.

That may be so, but the English explorer and surveyor, James McCarthy, goes into considerable detail about the fish in his book *Surveying and exploring in Siam*, which was first published in 1900 and draws upon his travels in Siam and Laos between 1881 and 1893. He writes: "The month of June in Luang Prabang is a very busy one for fishermen. Nearly all the boats are employed on fishing, each paying a large fish for the privilege. Two kinds of large fish, *pa beuk* and *pa lerm*, are principally sought after... A *pa beuk* that I helped to take weighed 130 lbs; it was 7 ft long and 4 ft 2 in round the body; the tail measured 1ft 9 in. The

fish had neither scales nor teeth, and was sold for 10 rupees. The roe of this fish is considered a great delicacy. The fish is taken in June, July and August, when on its upward journey. Returning in November, it keeps low in the river, and a few stray ones only are caught."

McCarthy also recounts a story he had heard of a mythical river serpent of the Mekong: "It lives only at the rapids, and my informant said he had seen it. It is 53 ft long and 20 in thick. When a man is drowned it snaps off the tuft of hair on the head [men wore their hair in this manner], extracts the teeth, and sucks the blood; and when a body is found thus disfigured, it is known that the man has fallen victim to the *ngeuak*, or river serpent, at Luang Prabang."

The city had been ransacked and set ablaze by the bandits but the French helped to rebuild the city, using indentured labour from Vietnam and giving Luang Prabang much of the look it has today.

James McCarthy, an otherwise rather plodding recorder of events and sights, wrote of Luang Prabang at the end of the 19th century: "In a clear afternoon, Luang Prabang stood out distinctly. At evening the pagoda spires and the gilded mouldings of the wats, glancing in the light of the setting sun, added their effect to that of the natural features of the landscape – and caused in me a feeling of irresistible melancholy. Since my visit in February 1887, Luang Prabang had passed through much suffering. It had been ravaged by the Haw; its people had been pillaged and murdered or driven from their homes, and the old chief had only been rescued by his sons forcing him to a place of safety. The town seemed doomed to suffer, for within two months past it had again been burned, and, more recently still, about 500 of its inhabitants had died of an epidemic sickness." Yet, by 1926 American Harry Franck could find paradise in Luang Prabang, as recorded in his book, *East of Siam*: "It is not a city at all, in the crowded, noisy, Western sense, but a leisurely congregation of dwellings of simple lines, each ... with sufficient ground so that its opinions or doings need not interfere with its neighbours. In short, Luang Prabang town is in many ways what idealists picture the cities of Utopia to be".

Luang Prabang didn't suffer as much as other provincial capitals during the Indochina wars, narrowly escaping a Viet Minh capture in 1953. Rumour has it that as the Vietnamese troops approached Luang Prabang, the citizens stayed calm because a blind monk had prophesized that the city wouldn't be taken. During the Second Indochina War, however, the Pathet Lao cut short the royal lineage, forcing King Sisavang Vatthana to abdicate and sending him to a re-education camp in northeastern Laos where he, his wife and his son died from starvation.

Luang Prabang's streets have retained the aura of old Lane Xang. In the early 1990s it was proposed that a highway be built through the city to the Chinese border. Fortunately, UNESCO's designation of Luang Prabang as a World Heritage Site restricted redevelopment. The old town – essentially the promontory – is protected while elsewhere only limited building is permitted (no building, can be higher than three storeys). Although the new road went ahead, the authorities built a bypass to ensure that the town wasn't disrupted.

Sights

The sights are conveniently close together in Luang Prabang, the majority dotted along the main Sakkaline, Sisavangvong and Souvanna Khampong roads. Most are walkable – the important ones can be covered within two leisurely days – but a bike is the best way to get around. To begin with it may be worth climbing Phousi or taking a stroll along the

1 Luang Prabang

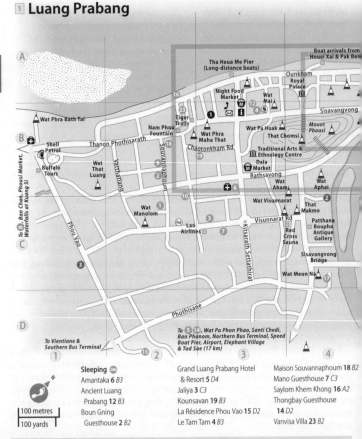

Sleeping		
Amantaka **6** *B3*	Grand Luang Prabang Hotel	Maison Souvannaphoum **18** *B2*
Ancient Luang	& Resort **5** *D4*	Mano Guesthouse **7** *C3*
Prabang **12** *B3*	Jaliya **3** *C3*	Saylom Khem Khong **16** *A2*
Boun Gning	Kounsavan **19** *B3*	Thongbay Guesthouse
Guesthouse **2** *B2*	La Résidence Phou Vao **15** *D2*	**14** *D2*
	Le Tam Tam **4** *B3*	Vanvisa Villa **23** *B2*

Mekong and Nam Khan river roads to get a better idea of the layout of the town. Most of Luang Prabang's important wats are dotted along the main road, Phothisarath. When visiting the wats it is helpful to take a guide to obtain entry to all the buildings, which are often locked for security reasons. Without a guide, your best chance of finding them open is early in the morning. ▸▸ *For a walking tour of the town, see page 110* .

Royal Palace

ⓘ *Sisavangvong Rd, daily 0800-1100 and 1330-1600 (closed Tue), admission 30,000 kip or 80,000 kip including a new audio tour and map. Shorts, short-sleeved shirts and strappy dresses are prohibited; shoes should be removed and bags must be put in lockers. No photography.*

Also called the **National Museum**, the Royal Palace is right in the centre of the city on the main road, Sisavangvong, which runs along the promontory and allowed royal guests ready access from the Mekong. Unlike its former occupants, the palace survived the 1975 revolution and was converted into a museum the following year. It replaced a smaller wooden palace on the same site.

Construction of the palace started in 1904, during the reign of Sisavang Vong, and took 20 years. It was built by the French for the Lao king, in an attempt to bind him and his family more tightly to the colonial system of government. Although most of the construction was completed by 1909, the two front wings were extended in the 1920s and a new, more Lao-style roof was added. These later changes were accompanied by the planting of the avenue of palms and the filling in of one of two fish ponds. Local residents regarded the ponds as the 'eyes' of the capital, so the blinding of one eye was taken as inviting bad fortune by leaving the city unprotected.

The subsequent civil war seemed to vindicate these fears. The palace is Khmer in style, cruciform in plan and mounted on a small platform of four tiers. The only indication of French involvement can be seen in the two French lilies represented in stucco on the entrance, beneath the symbols of Lao royalty. There are a few Lao motifs but, in many respects, the palace is more foreign than Lao: it was designed by a French architect, with steps made from Italian marble; built by masons from Vietnam; embellished by carpenters from Bangkok; and funded by the largesse of the colonial authorities. While the palace itself is modest, its contents are spectacular.

Mekong River
Tourist Boats to Pak Ou
Souvanna Khampong
Sakkaline
Nam Khan

To Pak Ou Northern Bus Terminal & Xang Hai

To Airport, Ban Hat Hien & Ban Phanom (6 km)

Wat Tao Hai

The museum now contains a collection of 15th- to 17th-century Buddha statues and artefacts from wats in Luang Prabang such as the ancient bronze drums from Wat Visoun. Notable pieces include an ancient Buddha head, an offering from Indian dignitaries, and a reclining Buddha with the unusual addition of mourners. The most important piece is the **Golden Buddha**, from which the city derives its name. The Buddha is in the attitude of Abhayamudra or 'dispelling fear' (see page 324). Some believe that the original is kept in a bank vault in Vientiane or Moscow, although most dispel this as rumour. It is 90% solid gold, stands 83 cm high and weighs around 53 kg. Reputed to have come from Ceylon, and to date from between the first and ninth centuries, the statue was brought to Cambodia in the 11th century, given to King Phaya Sirichanta, and then taken to Lane Xang by King Fa Ngum, who had spent time in the courts of Angkor and married into Khmer royalty.

An alternative story has the Pra Bang following Fa Ngum to the city. It is said that he asked his father-in-law, the King of Angkor, to send a delegation of holy men to assist him in spreading the Theravada Buddhist faith in Lane Xang. The delegation arrived bringing with them the Pra Bang as a gift from the Cambodian King. The Pra Bang's arrival heralded the capital's change of name, from Xieng Thong to Nakhon Luang Prabang – 'The city of the great Buddha'. In 1563 King Setthathirat took the statue to Lane Xang's new capital at Vientiane. Two centuries later in 1779 the Thais captured it but it was returned to Laos in 1839. The Pra Bang is revered in Laos as its arrival marked the beginnings of Buddhism in Lane Xang. The Pra Bang is currently kept in a small enclosure to the right of the entrance but is expected to be moved to the Haw Prabang some time in the future.

Entrance Hall The main entrance hall of the palace was used for royal religious ceremonies, when the Supreme Patriarch of Lao Buddhism would oversee proceedings from his gold-painted lotus throne.

King's Reception Room The room to the immediate right of the entrance was the King's Reception Room, also called the **Ambassadors' Room**. It contains French-made busts of the last three Lao monarchs, a model of the royal hearse (which is kept in Wat Xieng Thong) and a mural by French artist Alex de Fontereau, depicting a day in the life of Luang Prabang in the 1930s.

Coronation Room (Throne Room) To the rear of the entrance hall, the Coronation Room was decorated between 1960 and 1970 for Sisavang Vatthana's coronation, an event which was interrupted because of the war. The walls are a brilliant red with Japanese glass mosaics embedded in a red lacquer base with gilded woodwork. They depict scenes from Lao festivals, such as boat racing. The carved throne has a gold three-headed elephant insignia; on one side is a tall pot to hold the crown. To the right of the throne, as you face it, are the ceremonial coronation swords and a glass case containing 15th- and 16th-century crystal and gold Buddhas, many from inside the 'melon stupa' of Wat Visoun. Because Luang Prabang was constantly raided, many of these religious artefacts were presented to the king for safekeeping. At the back, to the right of the entrance, is the royal *howdah*, a portable throne was used during battle. The throne is covered with shields to protect it.

Private Apartments In comparison to the state rooms, the royal family's private apartments are modestly decorated. They have been left virtually untouched since Sisavang Vatthana and family left for exile in Xam Neua Province. The **King's Library** backs onto the Coronation Room: Sisavang Vatthana was a well-read monarch, having studied at the École de Science Politique in Paris. Behind the library, built around a small inner courtyard are the queen's modest bedroom, the king's bedchamber and the royal yellow bathroom, with its two regal porcelain thrones standing side by side. These rooms are cordoned off but you can still see them. The king's bed is a marvellous construction with a three-headed elephant insignia. The remaining rooms include a small portrait gallery, dining room and the children's bedroom, which is decorated with musical instruments and headdresses for *Ramayana* actors. In the hallway linking the rooms is a miscellany of interesting objects, including a an intricately patterned *sinh*, worn by the queen, and a royal palanquin, which would have been tied to an elephant. Domestic rooms, offices and library are located on the ground floor beneath the state apartments.

Other reception rooms To the left of the entrance hall is the reception room of the **King's Secretary**, and beyond it, the **Queen's Reception Room**, which together house an eccentric miscellany of state gifts from just about every country except the UK. Of particular note is the moon rock presented to Laos by the USA following the Apollo 11 and 17 lunar missions. Also in this room are portraits of the last King Sisavang Vatthana, Queen Kham Phouy and Crown Prince Vongsavang, painted by a Soviet artist in 1967.

King's Chapel On the right wing of the palace, next to the King's Reception Room, is the king's private chapel, which houses the Pra Bang. It also contains four Khmer Buddhas, ivories mounted in gold, bronze drums used in religious ceremonies and about 30 smaller Buddha images from temples all over the city.

Haw Prabang This small ornate pavilion is located in the northeast corner of the palace compound, to the right of the entrance to the Royal Palace. It was designed by the Royal Architect of the time to house the Pra Bang and was paid for by small donations sent in from across the country. The Pra Bang should move here some time in the future.

Other buildings In the left-hand corner (south) of the compound, is the **Luang Prabang Conference Hall**, built for the official coronation of Savang Vatthana, which was terminally interrupted by the 1975 revolution. The southwestern corner of the compound is now used as the **Royal Theatre**, where traditional performances are held.

Wat Mai
ⓘ *Sisavangvong Rd, daily 0800-1700, admission 10,000 kip.*

Next to the Royal Palace is Wat Mai. This royal temple, inaugurated in 1788, has a five-tiered roof and is one of the jewels of Luang Prabang. It took more than 70 years to complete. It was officially called Wat Mai Souvanna Phommaram and was the home of the Buddhist leader in Laos, Phra Sangkharath, until he moved to That Luang in Vientiane. Auguste Pavie and his crew took up residence here while trying to win Luang Prabang over from the Siamese who controlled the Lao court at the time. The Siamese thought that detaining Pavie in the compound would keep him out of their way but the Frenchman struck up a friendship with a local abbot, who acted as a runner between the king and Pavie. The temple housed the Pra Bang from 1894 until 1947 and, during Pi Mai (New Year), the Pra Bang is taken from the Royal Palace and installed at Wat Mai for its annual ritual cleansing, before being returned to the palace on the third day.

Today, Wat Mai is probably the most popular temple after Wat Xieng Thong. The façade is particularly interesting: a large golden bas-relief tells the story of Phravet (one of the last reincarnations of the Gautama or historic Buddha), with village scenes, including wild animals, women pounding rice, and people at play. The interior is an exquisite amalgam of red and gold, with pillars similar to those in Wat Xieng Thong and Wat Visoun. The temple is indicative of Luang Prabang architecture, aside from the roofed veranda, whose gables face the sides rather than the front. The central beam at Wat Mai is carved with figures from the Hindu story of the birth of Ravanna and Hanuman. Behind the temple is a new construction where two classical racing boats are kept, ready to be brought out for Pi Mai (Lao New Year) and the August boat racing festival. ▸▸ *See Festivals and events, page 126.*

Mount Phousi

ⓘ *The western steps lead up from Sisavangvong Rd, daily 0700-1800, admission at western steps 20,000 kip. If you want to watch the sun go down, get there early and jostle for position.*
Directly opposite the Royal Palace is the start of the climb up Mount Phousi, the spiritual and geographical heart of the city and a popular place to watch the sunset over the Mekong. Luang Prabang was probably sited at this point on the Mekong, in part at least, because of the presence of Phousi. Many capitals in the region are founded near sacred hills or mountains, which could become local symbols of the Hindu Mount Mahameru or Mount Meru, the abode of the gods and also the abode of local tutelary spirits.

As you start the ascent, to the right is **Wat Pa Huak** ⓘ *daily 0800-1800, admission 10,000 kip*, a disused wat suffering from years of neglect, daily 0800-1800, admission 10,000 kip. It is worth visiting because the monastery has some fine 19th-century murals, depicting classic scenes along the Mekong. There are a few Buddha images here that date from the

2 Luang Prabang detail

Mekong

Ounkham — Fibre2Fabric
@ Luang Prabang 13
OckPop Tok 18
Khem Kong

Wat Chom Khong 21 · Wat Xieng Mouan
Green Discovery · Elephant Village · All Laos Service 13 · BCEL (S)
Wat Pa Phai 8
Wat Nong
Spa Garden
Wat Sibou Heung · Wat Sop

Naga Creations
1930s Chinese / French Shophouses
Sisavangvong
Wat Sene
Wat Siphouttabath
Wat Tham Phousi 26
Kingkitsarath

Nam Khan

100 metres
100 yards

Sleeping 🛏
3 Nagas **14** *B3*
Ammata
  Guesthouse **20** *A3*
Apsara Rive Droite **15** *B4*

Apsara **1** *B4*
Belle Rive **3** *A3*
Bougnasouk
  Guesthouse **2** *A2*
Kongsavath **18** *A3*
Le Calao Inn **5** *A4*
Merry Lao Swiss **6** *B1*
Oui's Guesthouse **21** *B5*
Pa Phai **8** *A2*
Pack Luck **7** *A3*
Riverside **4** *B4*

Sala Luang Prabang **9** *A1*
Say Nam Khan **10** *B2*
Sayo Guesthouse **11** *A1*
Silichit Guesthouse **12** *A2*
Sokdee Residence **13** *A2*
Villa Santi **16** *B3*
Villa Santi Annexe **22** *B3*
Villa Savanh **17** *B3*

Eating 🍴
Blue Lagoon **21** *A1*

Café Ban Vat
  Sene **1** *B3*
Café des Arts **2** *B1*
Coconut Garden **13** *B1*
Couleur Café **6** *A2*
Dao Fa **3** *B2*
Dyen Sabai **12** *B2*
Khemkhan Food
  Garden **5** *B2*
L'Éléphant **7** *A3*
L'Étranger **8** *B1*

same period and a fine carved wooden mosaic on the temple's exterior, depicting Buddha riding Airavata, the three-headed elephant from Hindu mythology.

From Wat Pa Huak, 328 steps wind up Phousi, a gigantic rock with sheer forested sides, surmounted by a 25-m-tall *chedi*, **That Chomsi**. The *chedi* was constructed in 1804, restored in 1914 and is the starting point for the colourful Pi Mai (New Year) celebrations in April (see Festivals and events, page 126). Its shimmering gold-spired stupa rests on a rectangular base, ornamented by small metal Bodhi trees. Next to the stupa is a little sanctuary, from which the candlelit procession descends at New Year, accompanied by effigies of Nang Sang Khan, the guardian of the New Year, and naga, protector of the city. The drum, kept in the small *haw kong* on the east side of the hill, is used on ceremonial occasions. The summit of Phousi affords a panoramic view of Luang Prabang and the mountains. The Mekong lies to the north and west, with the city laid out to the southeast.

A path next to the *ack-ack* cannon leads down to **Wat Tham Phousi**, which is more like a car port than a temple, but which is home to a rotund Buddha, Kaccayana (also called Phra Ka Tiay). At the top of the steps leading out of the wat are two tall cacti, planted defiantly in the empty shell casings of two large US bombs – the monks' answer to decades of war.

Wat Siphouttabath (Wat Pha Phoutthabat)
Located down a path to the north of Wat Tham Phousi, just off the central road running along the promontory, is a compound containing three monasteries. Of them, **Wat Pa Khe** is most notable, predominantly for its carvings of 17th-century Dutch and Italian traders. Why these traders are depicted in a Buddhist temple in Luang Prabang remains a mystery, although many suspect it may have been influenced by trading merchants from the East India Company, who travelled through the area in the late 16th century. Behind the *sim* is a shrine housing a 3-m-long footprint of the Buddha. The shrine is normally only open during festive occasions, so you will need to ask someone for a key. Flanking the shrine is a small pavilion where Cambodia's former King Sihanouk entertained the press (in his usual publicity-centric fashion) during King Sisavang Vong's cremation ceremony.

Wat Xieng Mouan and Wat Pa Phai
A block back from Sisavangvong Road is the old monastery site of **Wat Xieng Mouan**. The *sim* here was constructed in 1879, although work is believed to have started decades earlier. The temple features a few impressive sculptures and an imposing fresco of *nagas* on the ceiling. UNESCO has funded an artistic training centre for monks here to ensure that skills are available to continue restoration work in the future. The novices are being taught the crafts of wood-carving, painting and Buddha-making.

⇨ **Luang Prabang maps**
1 Luang Prabang, page 100
2 **Luang Prabang detail**, page 104
3 Luang Prabang walking tour, page 112

rist Boats
Pak Ou

Peninsula
Massage

Souvanna Khampong

Wat
Xieng
Thong

kkaline

Wat
Pak Khan

Wat
ni Li

⑤

⑥

uang Prabang Bakery **9** *B1*
uang Prabang Pizza **10** *B1*
Morning Glory **23** *B3*
lazim's Indian **11** *A1*
amarind **22** *A3*
amnak Lao **15** *B3*
um Tum Cheng **16** *B4*
Jn Petit Nid **27** *B3*
iew Khaem Khong **4** *A1*

Bars & clubs 🍸
Arisai **20** *B3*
Hive **18** *B1*
Ikon Club **14** *B2*
Khily Wine Bar **24** *B5*
Lao Lao Garden **26** *B1*
Lao Lao Sports Bar **19** *B1*
Lusine **17** *A2*
Pack Luck **25** *B2*

Also in the same block is **Wat Pa Phai**, called the Bamboo Monastery, although there isn't an overwhelming amount of bamboo in evidence. The *sim*, however, is decorated with colourful serpents and peacocks.

Wat Sene (Wat Saen)

Further up the promontory, Wat Sene was built in 1718 and was the first *sim* in Luang Prabang to be constructed in Thai style, with a yellow and red roof. The exterior may lack subtlety, but the interior is delicate and refined, painted red, with gold patterning on every conceivable surface. *Sene* means 100,000 and the wat was built with a local donation of 100,000 kip from someone who discovered 'treasure' in the Nam Khan river. At the far end of the wat compound is a building containing a large, gold, albeit rather crudely modelled, image of the Buddha in the 'calling for rain' *mudra* (standing, arms held stiffly down). Note the torments of hell depicted on the façade of the building (top, left). The temple was restored in 1932, with further renovations in 1957. One of Laos' most sacrosanct abbots, the recently deceased Ajahn Khamchan, was ordained at the temple in 1940.

Wat Xieng Thong

ⓘ *Xiengthong Rd, daily 0800-1700, admission 20,000 kip.*

Wat Xieng Thong Ratsavoraviharn, usually known as just Wat Xieng Thong, is set back from the road, at the top of a flight of steps leading down to the Mekong. It is arguably the finest example of a Lao monastery, with graceful, low-sweeping eaves, beautiful stone mosaics and intricate carvings. The wat has several striking chapels, including one that houses a rare bronze reclining Buddha and another sheltering a gilded wooden funeral chariot. The back of the temple is encrusted with a stunning glass mosaic depicting a bodhi tree, while inside, resplendent gold-stencilled pillars support a ceiling with *dharma* wheels. The temple's tranquility is further enhanced by beautiful gardens of bougainvillea, frangipani and hibiscus, shaded by banyan and palm trees.

This monastery was a key element in Luang Prabang's successful submission to UNESCO for recognition as a World Heritage Site. The striking buildings in the tranquil compound are decorated in gold and post-box red, with imposing tiled roofs, intricate carvings, paintings and mosaics, making this the most important and finest royal wat in Luang Prabang. It was built by King Setthathirat in 1559, and is one of the few buildings to have survived the successive Chinese raids that marked the end of the 19th century. It retained its royal patronage until 1975 and has been embellished and well cared for over the years: even the crown princess of Thailand, Mahachakri Sirindhorn, has donated funds for its upkeep.

The sim The *sim* is a perfect example of the Luang Prabang style, with its low, sweeping roof in complex overlapping sections. The roof is one of the temple's most outstanding features and is best viewed at a distance. Locals believe that the roof has been styled to resemble a bird, with its wings stretched out to protect her young. The eight central wooden pillars have stenciled motifs in gold and the façade is finely decorated. The beautiful gold-leaf inlay is predominantly floral in design but a few of the images illustrate Ramayana-type themes and the interior stencils depict *dharma* wheels and the enigmatic King Chantaphanit.

In an ancient form of the modern-day Mousetrap game, a serpent-like aqueduct sits above the right-hand side of the main entrance. During Lao New Year water is poured into the serpent's tail, causing it to gush along to its mouth and tip onto the Buddha image below. The water then filters down a drain, flowing under the floor and eventually spouting out of the mouth of the mirrored elephant on the exterior wall.

At the rear of the *sim* is a mosaic representation of the thong copper 'Tree of Life' in glass inlay. This traditional technique can also be seen on the 17th-century doors of That Ingheng, near Savannakhet in central Laos (see page 215).

Side chapels Behind the *sim* are two red *haw song phra* (side chapels): the one on the left is referred to as **La Chapelle Rouge** (the Red Chapel) and houses a rare Lao reclining Buddha in bronze, dating from the 16th century, which was shown at the 1931 Paris Exhibition. The image was kept in Vientiane and only returned to Luang Prabang in 1964. Several other Buddha images, of varying styles, dates, and materials, surround the altar. The exterior mosaics on the *haw song phra*, which relate local tales, were added in 1957 to honour the 2500th anniversary of the Buddha's birth, death and enlightenment. Somewhat unusually, the fresco features a heroic character from local Lao folklore, Siaw Sawat. The other *haw song phra*, to the right of the *sim*, houses a standing image of the Buddha which is paraded through the streets of the city each New Year and doused in water. A small stone chapel with an ornate roof stands to the left of the *sim*.

Chapel of the Funeral Chariot The **haw latsalot** (chapel of the funeral chariot) is diagonally across from the *sim* and was built in 1962. The centrepiece is the grand 12-m-high gilded wooden hearse, with its seven-headed serpent, which was built for King Sisavang Vong, father of the last sovereign, and used to carry his urn to the stadium next to Wat That Luang (see below) where he was cremated in 1959. It was built on the chassis of a six-wheel truck by the sculptor Thid Tan. On top of the carriage sit several sandalwood urns, none of which contain royal ashes. Originally the urns would have held the bodies of the deceased in a foetal position until cremation. The mosaics inside the chapel were never finished but the exterior is decorated with some almost erotic scenes from the *Ramayana* (or local *Phalak Phalam*), sculpted in enormous panels of teak wood and covered with gold leaf. Glass cabinets feature several puppets that were once used in royal performances.

Other structures The **Tripitaka Library**, near the boat shelter, was added in 1828. The **haw kong** at the back of the garden was constructed in the 1960s and near it is the site of the copper tree, from which Wat Xieng Thong took its name.

Wat Pak Khan

At the far northeast end of Phothisarath Road is Wat Pak Khan, which is not particularly noteworthy other than for its scenic location overlooking the confluence of the two rivers.

Wat Visounnarat (Wat Wisunarat)
ⓘ *Daily 0800-1700, admission 20,000 kip.*
This is better known as Wat Visoun and is on the south side of Mount Phousi. It is a replica of the original wooden building, constructed in 1513, which had been the oldest building in Luang Prabang, until it was destroyed by marauding Chinese tribes. Louis Delaporte's sketches from the 1860s show the original temple as boat- or coffin-shaped. The wat was rebuilt in 1898 and, in keeping with the original style, renovators tried to ensure that the brick and stucco construction resembled the original medieval shapes of the lathed wood. The arch on the northwest side of the *sim* is original and the only remaining piece of the 16th-century building.

The *sim* is virtually a museum of religious art, with numerous 'Calling to the Rain' Buddha statues: most are more than 400 years old and have been donated by locals. One of the biggest philanthropists was Prince Phetsarat who donated them in order to redeem the temple after the Haw invasion. Wat Visoun also contains the largest Buddha in the city and old stelae engraved with Pali scriptures (called *hin chaleuk*).

The big stupa, commonly known as **That Makmo** ('melon stupa'), was built by Queen Visunarat in 1504. It is of Sinhalese influence with a smaller stupa at each corner, representing the four elements. The stupa originally contained hundreds of small Buddha images, many of which were pilfered by the Haw. The remaining images were relocated to the Royal Museum for safe-keeping.

Wat Aham
① *Next door to Wat Visoun, daily 0800-1700, admission 20,000 kip.*
Wat Aham was built by a relative of the king in 1823 and, before Wat Mai took over the function, was the residence of the Supreme Patriarch of Lao Buddhism, Sangkharat. The interior has beautiful pillars and roof and overbearing modern murals of the torments of hell, and has a panoramic view of Luang Prabang. The two banyan trees outside are important spirit shrines.

Wat Phra Maha That
Close to the **Hotel Phousi** on Phothisarath Road, this is a typical Luang Prabang wat, built in the 1500s and restored at the beginning of this century. The ornamentation of the doors and windows of the *sim* merit attention, with their graceful golden figures from the *Phalak Phalam* (the *Ramayana*). The pillars, ornamented with massive *nagas*, are also in traditional Luang Prabang style and reminiscent of certain styles adopted in Thailand. The front of the *sim* was renovated in 1991. The monastery contains a stupa, holding the ashes of Prince Phetsarath and his younger brother Prince Souvanna Phouma.

Wat Phra Bath
Behind the market at the far northwest end of Phothisarath Road is Wat Phra Bath (or Phraphoutthabat Tha Phralak). The original wooden temple on this site dated back to the 17th century but most of the present structure was built in 1959 by the local Chinese and Vietnamese community. It doesn't evoke the grandeur of other temples in town but is worth a visit for its picturesque position above the Mekong. It is renowned for its huge Buddha footprint – 'bath' is the Pali word for footprint.

Wat That Luang
Close by, behind the sports field, on Phou Vao Rd, is Wat That Luang. Rumour suggests that the original structure was built by Indian missionaries, although evidence suggests that the royal wat was built in 1818 by King Manthaturat. Note the bars on the windows of the *sim* in wood and gold leaf, typical of Luang Prabang. The gold stupa, in front of the compound, was built in 1910 and contains the ashes of King Sisavang Vong and his brother. King Sisavang Vong is remembered fondly in the city and many offerings are left here. The stone stupa contains relics of the Buddha and is the site of the Vien Thien (candlelit) festival in May (see Festivals and events, page 126). There are also some traditional *kuti*, or monks' quarters, with carved windows and low roofs.

When James McCarthy visited Wat That Luang at the end of the 19th century, he was told of the ceremonies that were performed here on the accession of a new 'chief'. In his book *Surveying and exploring in Siam* (1900) he writes that the "Kamus assembled and took the oath of allegiance, swearing to die before their chief; shot arrows over the throne to show how they would fight any of its enemies, and holding a lighted candle, prayed that their bodies might be run through with hot iron and that the sky might fall and crush them if they proved unfaithful to their oaths".

Wat Manolom

South of Wat That Luang (between Phou Vao and Kisarath Settathirat), Wat Manolom was built by the nobles of Luang Prabang to entomb the ashes of King Samsenthai (1373-1416) and is notable for its large armless bronze Buddha statue, one of the oldest Lao images of the Buddha, which dates back to 1372 and weighs two tonnes. Locals maintain that the arm was removed during a skirmish between Siamese and French forces during the latter part of the 19th century. The Lao have replaced the missing appendage with an unsuccessful concrete prosthetic. The monastery has an attractive weathered look and the usual carved doors and painted ceilings. While it is not artistically significant, the temple – or at least the site – is thought to be the oldest in the city, dating back, it is said, to 1375 and the reign of Fa Ngum. Close by are the ruins of an even older temple, **Wat Xieng Kang**, dating from 1363.

Wat Pa Phon Phao and Santi Chedi

① *3 km out of town to the northeast, near Ban Phanom, daily 0800-1000 and 1300-1630, donation expected.*

Outside town, **Wat Pa Phon Phao** is a forest meditation centre renowned for the teachings of its famous abbot, Ajahn Saisamut, one of the most popular monks in Lao history. Better known to tourists, though, is **Santi Chedi**, known as the Peace Pagoda. It looks as though it is made of pure gold from a distance and it occupies a fantastic position. The wat's construction, funded by donations from Lao living abroad and from overseas Buddhist federations, was started in 1959 but was only completed in 1988; the names of donors are inscribed on pillars inside. It is modelled on the octagonal Shwedagon Pagoda in Yangon (Rangoon) and its inner walls are festooned with gaily painted frescoes of macabre allegories. The lurid illustrations depict the fate awaiting murderers, adulterers, thieves, drunks and liars who break the five golden rules of Buddhism. Less grotesque paintings, extending up to the fifth floor, document the life of the Buddha. On the second level, it is possible to duck through a tiny opening to admire the Blue Indra statues and the view of Luang Prabang.

Traditional Arts and Ethnology Centre

① *Ban Khamyong, T071-253364, www.taeclaos.org, Tue-Sun 0900-1800, 20,000 kip.*

This fantastic museum is dedicated to the various ethnic groups that inhabit Laos. It is a non-profit centre with a permanent exhibition featuring interesting photographs, religious artefacts, clothing, traditional household objects and the various handicrafts practised by the different groups. Within the exhibition there is a focus on the Hmong and their New Year celebrations; the Khmu, their baskets and the art of backstrap looms; the Mien Yao embroidery and Lanten Taoist religious ceremonies; the Tai Dam bedding and Tai Lue culture. This museum is well worth a visit – particularly for anyone who is planning to venture further north to go trekking.

Attached to the centre is a handicraft shop that directly supports ethnic artisan communities. There's also a café and a small library.

A guide to Luang Prabang's secular buildings

Traditional Lao The traditional Lao house is rectangular, supported on timber stilts, with a two-sided steep roof and built of bamboo, wood or daub. The stilts help to protect the occupants against wild animals at night and also help to keep the living area dry, especially during the rainy season. The underside also provides a shaded spot for working during the day, as well as area for storage. Living above ground is said to be a characteristic of the Lao and a 16th-century Lao text, the *Nithan Khun Borom*, records that the Lao and Vietnamese Kingdoms of Lane Xang and Dai Viet agreed to demarcate their respective zones of influence according to house style: people living in houses raised on stilts would owe allegiance to Lane Xang, those on the ground, to Dai Viet. The traditional Lao house is divided into three principal sections, recognizable from the exterior: the sleeping room, the veranda, and the kitchen. Under the main roof is the sleeping area and the very characteristic veranda is contiguous to it. The kitchen is linked to the main building by an open deck commonly used for bathing and washing. Roof, gables, rafters and balustrade are ornamented with lots of savoir-faire. All aspects of the building process of traditional Lao houses were governed by strict rules: the orientation of the building, the date when building could commence, the setting of the wooden piles, and so on, all had to conform to spiritual guidelines.

French colonial The French introduced new technologies and materials into house construction, in particular the fired brick and the ceramic roof tile. Traditionally, these materials were reserved for wat construction – explaining why almost all buildings of pre-colonial vintage that you see in Laos today are religious. The main characteristics of French colonial architecture are: extensive roof area to protect against the onslaught of sun and rain; large window openings, paned and shuttered; verandas; arcades; a monumental entrance; a fireplace and chimney breast; brick and wooden decorative details expressing different construction systems (for instance, columns, capitals, rafters and lintels) and ceramic roof tiles.

Architectural tour

→ *Numbers in the text are marked on the map, see page 112.*

In a town as small as Luang Prabang, it is easy enough just to set out and find your own route. However, we have provided a walking tour that takes in Luang Prabang's architectural highlights (secular as well as religious). It concentrates on the peninsula and the streets that form the original core of the city. The route and the most interesting buildings are shown on the map below. ▶▶ *For a guide to the secular architectural styles described in this tour, see above.*

The start of the tour is on Thanon Phothisarath in front of the **Royal Palace** (**1**; see page 101). Historically, the area to the west of the palace was considered the noble quarter of town, the east was inhabited by the middle classes, while the working class lived around the foot of Phousi. Walking from the Royal Palace along Phothisarath Road southwest towards the post office, look out for the **traditional Lao house** (**2**) in front of Wat Mai. This is a construction on stilts with a closed veranda. Continuing along Phothisarath Road, the former French colonial **Gendarmerie** (**3**) – now the Children's Cultural Centre – is on your

Lao-French colonial As French influences gathered momentum through Lao society, so Laos' indigenous builders began to incorporate some aspects of French architectural design into their constructions. For example, some houses which in most other respects conform to the traditional Lao house style, have French openings and a grandiose doorway leading to an impressive staircase.

Lao-French colonial-Lao In the same way as Lao builders adopted some French elements, so French architects and builders embraced Lao stylistic features. This is particularly evident in the use of temple-style ornamentation, on the roof for example.

International-modern Many houses are now built of concrete and the bungalow has become common throughout the country. In many cases, traditional Lao architectural motifs and designs are merely made from concrete rather than the traditional wood. But concrete has also allowed some innovations in design: cantilevers, flat roofing, pre-fabricated elements and geometric ornamentation are all linked in part to this change in building medium from wood and bamboo to concrete. 'International modern' is used for both domestic buildings and compartments (shophouses).

Lao contemporary Modern homes fall into two categories. Either they are very much in keeping with traditional Lao style, or they embrace modern design and construction materials wholesale. Houses in the first category are part of an evolution of the traditional Lao house: the main entrance has shifted to the gable side, the veranda is smaller, while the open area between the piles below the main house is enclosed with brick or concrete walls and has become part of the house. Wood is still used for exterior facing for the first floor, but the walls of the ground floor are now made from stone and bricks. This is the most common form of house built in Laos today.

The second category of Lao contemporary house is built entirely of brick and concrete and most Lao consider it to be more luxurious.

left, with gables on the façade. There's another example of a French colonial building, the **Central Bank of Laos** (**4**), on your right.

Turn right onto Kittsarath Setthathirat Road and walk down towards the Mekong. Just past the post office, on the right, is a **Lao house showing French colonial influences** (**5**). Take the first road on your right to see more examples of traditional Lao houses. In some cases the ground level area, which was once open, has been enclosed to increase the habitable space, using a variety of materials, such as bricks, wood and bamboo (this practice is also very common in Thailand). Traditionally, the under-house area was used for weaving and lounging during the hottest hours of the day. At night, animals were corralled under the house to keep them safe. Fires were also lit here at night during the coldest months of the year.

At the very end of this street, just beside the Royal Palace, are two opulent **Lao-French colonial-style houses** (**6**), one of which is now a hotel. Turn left to reach the Mekong River road and then right to walk along the riverbank. The **Royal Taxes office** (**7**), now operating as a tourism company, lies behind the Royal Palace. It is decorated with the classic three-headed elephant insignia. To see some truly beautiful examples of traditional

Lao architecture, enter **Wat Xieng Mouan** (8; see page 105) and take the exit into the alley running behind the temple. Opposite the wat is a **traditional Lao house** (9).

Continue up to Phothisarath Road, turn left and take a look at the **compartment buildings** (10) on both sides of the street. These skilfully combine commercial and residential functions under the same roof, much like the Chinese 'shophouse' found throughout Southeast Asia, in which the ground floor serves as a business, shop or workshop. The Lao traditionally never lived and worked in the same building; they always ran their businesses from some other location, even if it was a street-side stall just a few yards away from their home. It is therefore safe to assume that these 'compartments' were used by Chinese and Vietnamese immigrants. They are built in a variety of styles, mainly French colonial and Lao-French colonial.

Walking on towards the tip of the peninsula, there are several other notable buildings, including the **French colonial school** (11) and the **Villa Santi Hotel** (12), on the left-hand side of the road, and **Villa Savanh** (13), a traditional Lao compartment building on the right. At **Wat Xieng Thong** (14; see page 106) take the exit from the monastery on the east side to look at the modest **bamboo house** (15) down the alley.

At the tip of the peninsula, turn back along the Mekong River road. On the left is the **Calao Inn** (16), an example of a renovated colonial building and the only Portuguese building on the peninsula. Immediately after the inn, take the first road on your left and then turn right. Along this road, at the first intersection, are two very fine **Lao houses** showing **French colonial influences** (17). Past the intersection further along the same street, the **School of Fine Arts** (18) is one of few Lao traditional-style buildings in Luang Prabang, with two adjoining roofs. Return to the Mekong River road along which are a number of buildings showing various degrees of international influence.

3 **Luang Prabang walking tour**

⇨	**Luang Prabang maps**
1	Luang Prabang, page 100
2	Luang Prabang detail, page 104
3	**Luang Prabang walking tour**, page 112

Royal Palace **1**
Traditional Lao house **2**
Gendarmerie **3**
Central Bank of Laos **4**
Lao-French colonial house **5**
Lao-French colonial house **6**
Royal Taxes office **7**

Wat Xieng Mouan **8**
Traditional Lao house **9**
Compartment buildings **10**
French colonial school **11**
Villa Santi Hotel **12**
Villa Savanh **13**
Wat Xieng Thong **14**
Bamboo house **15**

Calao Inn **16**
Lao houses with French colonial influence **17**
School of Fine Arts **18**
French colonial hospital (Amantaka) **19**
Lao-French colonial buildings **20**
Maison Souvannaphoum **21**

100 metres
100 yards

Cross the peninsula to the Nam Khan river road and then follow the road south around Phousi. Along the road are a number of examples of Lao traditional and Lao-French colonial buildings. On Rathsavong Street is the **French colonial hospital (19)**, now the most expensive hotel in Laos, the Amantaka, see Sleeping page 119. Further along, turn right towards Nam Phou. This street has a number of **Lao-French colonial buildings (20)**, showing French influences on Lao architecture. Follow the road until it reaches the **Maison Souvannaphoum (21)** on the left. Take a minute to have a look at the main building (not the new annexes), which was built in 1962 in a modern French-colonial style. The tour ends north of here at the post office.

West bank of the Mekong → *For listings, see pages 118-131.*

The monasteries and villages on the right bank of the Mekong are accessible by boat from Luang Prabang. For anyone who does not fancy spending three hours on a boat travelling to and from the Pak Ou caves, this makes for an enchanting alternative excursion. Also on the right bank are two hills, **Phou Thao** and **Phou Nang**, named after Luang Prabang's very own Romeo and Juliet. Thao Phouthasene and Nang Kang Hi were two lovers who died in tragic but romantic circumstances only to find themselves transformed into rock and incorporated in the local landscape. The hills are said to look like a man and woman sleeping next to each other.

Ins and outs
It is simpler to explore sights outside the city with a tour operator, as roads are unmarked and rural communities are less used to tourists. Many hotels organize trips. Boats run from the boat pier downstream from the Royal Palace to the other side of the river, near Wat Long Khoun or Ban Xiang Men, 70,000 kip return. If you can't find a boat here, you should try the pier behind the Royal Palace. Remember to fix a return time with the ferryman. Public ferries also run regularly across the river for 5000 kip. See Tour operators and Transport, page 129.

Wat Long Khoun
ⓘ *Daily 0800-1700, admission 5000 kip for foreigners.*
The first stop is usually Wat Long Khoun at the top of a flight of steps leading up from the riverbank, almost opposite Wat Xieng Thong. This wat was built in two stages and was renovated by the École Française de l'Extrême-Orient in 1994 at a cost of FF400,000. The oldest section of the wat is at the back and dates from the 18th century. The beautifully sculpted door was made in 1937. The *sim* on the river side of the compound is a delightful building, small, well-proportioned and intimate. It has some vibrant but fading Jataka murals. On the exterior, either side of the main doorway, are two bearded warriors, with swords slung over their backs, that seem to be representations of Chinese Haw soldiers. The kings of Lane Xang are said to have come on three-day retreats to this spot, to prepare for their coronation.

Wat Tham
ⓘ *100 m upstream from Wat Long Khoun, daily 0800-1700, admission 5000 kip.*
A well-trodden path leads upstream to Wat Tham, literally 'cave monastery', nestled in Sakkarin Savannakuha cave, above a dilapidated sala. The wat is a limestone cave temple with stairs and balustrades cut out of the stone. The interior is very dark but is worth

The North Luang Prabang & around • 113

exploring, as it is stacked with ancient, rotting Buddha images. During Pi Mai celebrations the cave temple comes alive with pilgrims and candles. Resident children, with the aid of dim torches, will lead visitors down into the airless cavern, pointing out notable rock formations and the Buddha images. Fearful that the torches may not be powered by long-life batteries, visitors may emerge into the light with a degree of relief. This is not an experience for the claustrophobic. If the cave is locked ask someone at Wat Long Khoun to let you in.

Wat Chom Phet and Wat Xiang Men

Leading from Wat Long Khoun downstream is another well-trodden track. Before reaching the small community of Ban Xiang Men, a stairway leads up to **Wat Chom Phet** ① *entry 5000 kip*, a hilltop *sim* offering fine views over the Mekong river and Luang Prabang. The site has been apparently abandoned as a religious site, although the mouldering *sim*, kiltering *chedis* and profusion of apricot-coloured lilies give the place a rather attractive 'lost wat in the forest' feel. It is worth coming up for the view of Luang Prabang alone–a perfect panorama of the city.

Continuing downstream, the track passes through **Ban Xiang Men**, a peaceful village where households cultivate the exposed riverbanks during the dry season, taking advantage of the annual deposition of silt, which is especially fertile. **Wat Xiang Men** was originally built in 1592 by Chau Naw Kaewkumman, son of Setthathirat, and has undergone extensive renovations since. The doors date from the original construction, as do several artefacts within the wat. This temple is particularly sacred to local residents because the Pra Bang was located here for a week when it returned to Luang Prabang from Vientiane in 1867. About 1 km downstream, in a clearing in the middle of the forest, is the **royal cemetery**. There are sculptures depicting those members of the royal family who could not be cremated for religious reasons, such as children who died as infants and victims of contagious diseases. It is hard to find a local guide willing to take you there as most are terrified of ghosts.

Ban Chan

Ban Chan is on the northern bank of the Mekong, 5 km downstream from Luang Prabang (about 15 minutes by boat; US$6) or 4 km on the road beyond the evening market to Ban Sangkhalok and a short crossing by boat (villagers will paddle you across). The village is known for its local pottery industry and mostly produces thongs (large water storage jars) and salt pots. Boats regularly cross the river – although the fare varies depending on the number of passengers. You can charter a boat from the main pier on the Mekong for a couple of hours (about 100,000 kip). It is possible to cross over to Wat Long Khoun, walk downstream and catch another boat back to the Luang Prabang bank of the river either at Ban Xiang Men or Ban Chan. Or the circuit can be completed in the reverse direction. There are a couple of foodstalls in Ban Xiang Men.

Tad Hoy Khoua

Hoy Khoua Waterfall is 14 km west of Luang Prabang in Ban Pakleung. The beautiful two-tiered cascades plummet 50 m, with a deep pool at the bottom. There are several Hmong and Khmu villages in the vicinity. To get to the falls cross the Mekong by boat at Tha Heua (boat station) in Luang Prabang to Xiang Men Village and then travel the rest by road. If you want to stay the night, there are three bungalows here at **Tad Hoy Khoua Guesthouse** (T020-5557 0825).

Ban Phanom and around

Ban Phanom, or Milk Cliff Village, is 6 km east of Luang Prabang. This is a 300-year-old weaving village, where shawls (*pha biang*) and sarongs (*pha sin*) are made from silk and cotton. Although best known for its weaving, the village's main economic activity is rice cultivation. The 100 or so families in Ban Phanom are members of the Lue minority, who originated from Yunnan in southern China. They were traditionally the king's weavers, soldiers and palace servants. King Sisavang Vong's dancers were traditionally hand-picked from this village at the age of six or seven and were required to undergo intensive training aimed at increasing their flexibility.

A few years ago cloth was sold from a street market in the middle of the village. However, some of the larger producers have turned their houses into small shops and it is now possible to buy lengths of cloth at any time. Tourists are more than welcome to wander around and look at the process of silk manufacture, from the silk worm's inception to finish, with the weavers clacking away at their looms. The village has turned into a bit of a tourist trap and those looking for a bargain might be disappointed to find that the silk is almost the same price as in town.

The French explorer Henri Mouhot stumbled across Angkor Wat in 1860 but succumbed to a malarial attack in Luang Prabang on 10 November the following year: his last journal entry read, "Have pity on me, O my God". Resident foreign aid workers spent months searching for his grave before rediscovering it in 1990, 2 km beyond Ban Phanom, at the top of a bank looking down into the Nam Khan, a tributary of the Mekong. **Henri Mouhot's tomb**, 3 km from Ban Phanom, was constructed six years after his death, in 1867, and was designed by another French explorer, Doudart de Lagrée. The town of Mouhot's birth, Montbéliard, donated a plaque inscribed simply, 'Proud of Our Son', and the French government has granted an allowance for the tomb's upkeep. When going to the tomb on foot, bicycle or motorbike, follow the road along the river until you see the sign and turn left; follow this path for a further 300 m. It is also possible to get a boatman to take you the extra kilometres for a couple of dollars. If you are unsure ask villagers in Ban Phanom for directions; children will sometimes show visitors the way.

Ban Hat Hien

This village is on the airport road; fork right before the terminal and at the end of the road is Luang Prabang's knife-making village. Residents beat scrap metal over hot stoves to make blades and tools. The flames are fanned by bellows, originally made from teak tubes and operated with plungers; several craftsmen use old 155-mm Howitzer propellants and say their "little presents from the US come in very handy". One shed is stacked with hundreds of old car batteries from which the lead is extracted and poured into moulds for ball bearings and gunshot. The results of their labours can be seen in the markets in town. From the nearby Nam Khan, villagers harvest 'seaweed', which is dried, fried and eaten with sesame in a dish known as *khai pehn*; it is sold all over the country.

Pak Ou caves

The Pak Ou caves are perhaps the most popular excursion from Luang Prabang and are located 25 km upstream from the city, set in a limestone cliff opposite the mouth of the Nam Ou tributary (Pak Ou means 'Mouth of the Ou'). The two caves are studded with thousands of wood-and-gold Buddha images – 2500 in the lower cave and 1500 in the upper – and are one of the main venues for Pi Mai in April, when hundreds make the pilgrimage upriver from Luang Prabang. During the dry season the river shrinks, exposing huge sandbanks, which are improbable gold fields. Families camp out on the banks of the Mekong and pan for gold, most of which is sold to Thailand.

Ins and outs

Many restaurants, hotels, guesthouses and tour companies in Luang Prabang will arrange this boat trip, which is the best way to reach the caves. Otherwise, boats can be chartered from Tha Heua Me or from one of the stairways leading down to the river along Manthatourath, where boatmen wait for business. The going rate for the journey – about two hours upstream and one hour down with stops en route – is US$10-15. Boats vary in size but the larger ones can take up to eight people. Long-tailed boats also depart from the pier in Luang Prabang and charge US$25 for up to five people. Boats will often stop at Xang Hai (see below) and Ban Pak Ou, across the water from the caves, where enterprising villages have set up thatched stalls serving sticky rice, barbecued Mekong fish and *Tam Maak Houng*, plus cold drinks and snacks. Although rest houses, tables and a basic toilet have been built below the upper cave, there is no restaurant and no drinks stall at the caves themselves.

Background

The two sacred caves were supposedly discovered by King Setthathirat in the 16th century but it is likely that the caverns were associated with spirit (*phi*) worship before the arrival of Buddhism in Laos. For years the caves, which locals still believe to be the home of guardian spirits, were inhabited by monks. The king visited them every New Year, staying at Ban Pak Ou on the opposite bank of the Mekong, where there is a royal wat with beautiful old murals on the front gable. The famous French traveller, Francis Garnier, also visited the caves on his travels in the 1860s.

Some of the Buddha images in the caves are thought to be more than 300 years old, although most date from the 18th and 19th centuries. In the past, gold and silver images were in abundance but these have all been stolen; now the Buddha images are crafted from wood, copper or stone. Both the caves and the many Buddhas they contain were restored with Australian funds but since the Australian government completed its conservation project in 1998, theft has been a chronic problem, particularly between 2001 and 2002, when hundreds of statues were stolen and sold to Thai antique dealers and tourists in Luang Prabang.

Exploring the caves

① *Admission 20,000 kip, free for children.* Torches are available but candles make it possible to see reasonably well after your eyes have become accustomed to the dark. The lower cave, really a deep overhang, is named **Tham Ting**, while the upper, an enervating climb up 100 or so slippery steps, is called **Tham Phum**. A carved wooden frieze, supporting two massive wooden doors flanks the entrance of the cave. Aside from the numerous Buddha images, the cave features a statue of one of Buddha's disciples and a carved wooden water channel for the ceremonial washing of the sculptures. The cave is around 54 m long and the sculptures range from 10 cm to 1.5 m in height. Many of the images are in the distinctive attitude of the Buddha calling for rain (the arms held by the side, with palms turned inwards).

Xang Hai

Xang Hai is 20 km upstream from Luang Prabang, on the way to Pak Ou caves and a popular stop-off. The name of this village translates as 'making wine pots'. In the rainy season the villages grow glutinous or 'sticky' rice and in the dry season they ferment it in water and yeast to brew *lao-lao*, a moonshine whisky, which is sold illegally in Luang Prabang. The village has now become rather touristy, with scores of stalls selling textiles, ceramics, souvenirs from Thailand and China, opium pipes and weights, ethnic clothes, and some *lao-lao* too. Villagers are delighted to give visitors a tasting session.

South of the city → *For listings, see pages 118-131.*

Tad Sae

Seventeen kilometres (30 minutes) south of Luang Prabang are the beautiful multi-tiered, limestone cascades of Tad Sae, which make for a great half-day trip during the rainy season. (In the dry season, the waterfall is reduced to a mere trickle.) The falls sit at the confluence of the Huay Say and Nam Khan rivers and feature a multitude of crystal-clear swimming holes, similar to Kuang Si but on a smaller scale. They are not as touristy as Kuang Si and offer greater privacy. To get there, head south along Route 13 for 17 km and turn off for Ban En (signposted); follow this track for 2 km. From the village you must buy a boat ticket for around US$1 to take you to the falls, admission 10,000 kip. Foodstalls and facilities are also available. A tuk-tuk from Luang Prabang will cost about US$15.

Tad Kuang Si

ⓘ *30 km south Luang Prabang; admission 20,000 kip, parking 2500 kip.*

These waterfalls are 30 km south of Luang Prabang on a tributary of the Mekong. The trip to the falls is almost as scenic as the cascades themselves, passing through small Hmong and Khmu villages and vivid green, terraced rice paddies. Travel agents run tours to the falls or you can charter a tuk-tuk for about US$15 return (make sure you agree how long you want to spend at the falls). Slow boats take one hour down and two hours back up river, via **Ban Ou** (a pretty little village), where it is necessary to take a tuk-tuk (or walk) the last 6 km or so to the waterfalls. A third possibility is to take a speedboat from either Tha Heua Xieng Keo (about 3 km downstream from Luang Prabang) or Ban Don, a few kilometres upstream.

The falls are stunningly beautiful, misty cascades flowing over limestone formations, which eventually collect in several tiered, turquoise pools. In 2003 a large section of the limestone cliff collapsed, so the falls are a little shorter these days but just as scenic. Originally the waterfall's surroundings were inhabited by numerous animals, including the deer that give the falls their name, Kuang Si. However, the only wildlife you're likely to see today are some Asiatic black bears, rescued from poachers, in enclosures halfway between the entrance and the falls. The United Nations Development Programme (UNDP) has cleared a path to the falls which winds right up to the top. The bottom level of the falls has been turned into a park and viewing area, with a small platform that affords good photo opportunities. The local village's economy seems increasingly to depend on the tourist business, so you'll find a large number of vendors selling snacks and drinks and some souvenirs. The site also has public toilets and changing rooms.

Although the waterfall is impressive year round, in the summer, the water cascades so gently over the various tiers of the falls that it's possible to scramble behind the curtains of water without getting wet. In the rainy season, the gallons of water roaring down the mountain catch the imagination and could form the backdrop for any Indiana Jones or James Bond adventure. Best of all, and despite appearances, it's still possible to take the left-hand path halfway up the falls and strike out through the pouring torrents and dripping caves to the heart of the waterfall. The pools above the falls are sheltered and comparatively private and make a wonderful spot for a swim; the second tier is best for a dip. If you follow the water either upstream or downstream there are plenty of other shady swimming spots. Note that swimming is only permitted in designated pools and, as the Lao swim fully clothed, you should wear modest swimwear and bring a sarong.

Hmong villages

There are numerous Hmong villages within a shortish distance of Luang Prabang and on the way to Kuang Si falls. Hmong children will usually come out on the road and stop your vehicle to sell you wristbands or embroidery. It is better to buy something from them than to give them cash or lollies. ▸▸ *For more information about the Hmong, see page 314.*

Ban Longlan is east of town. To get there, take the main road upstream. At Ban Pak Xuang, just before the bridge over the river Xuang, turn right to follow this tributary of the Mekong. Just before reaching Ban Kokvan turn right onto a track to Ban Natan. From here an even smaller track leads off to the left. It follows the Houei Hia, a small stream, between two mountains and works its way upwards to the mountain village of Ban Longlan. Allow about two hours to get there. Few tourists visit this village so dress modestly and be especially sensitive to local sensibilities. In the rainy season you will need a trail bike or 4WD to get there.

Another Hmong village downstream from Luang Prabang is **Ban Long Lao** (one hour by tuk-tuk, US$20). Take the road southwest from town and after about 8 km turn left (after Ban Lak Pet and before Ban Naxao). At the radio transmitter, continue straight ahead (rather than turning right to a waterfall). The road climbs steeply, passing a small dam and ends at the village of Long Lao. Again this is a village rarely visited by tourists. ▸▸ *For more details of how to get to the villages, see page 117.*

⊙ Luang Prabang and around listings

For Sleeping and Eating price codes and other relevant information, see pages 23-24.

⊙ Sleeping

Luang Prabang *p96, maps p100 and p104*
Accommodation in Luang Prabang continues to expand at the rate of knots. There are a few new places in development worth keeping an eye out for, in particular a new luxury riverfront hotel built in a former palace next to Wat Xieng Thong that will probably be completed in late 2011. The restored colonial villas on the peninsula and along Phou Vao Road tend to get booked up, particularly during national holidays, so, if you are thinking of plumping for an upper-range hotel, it is advisable to arrange accommodation in advance. Around Lao New Year, hotels and guesthouses can almost charge what they like but during the wet season prices tend to be a lot lower, with most smaller establishments quoting half the price given here and more expensive hotels knocking off about 20%. It is well worth checking the websites of the more upmarket hotels, as internet rates are usually cheaper than rack rates. Also contact **Lao Airlines**, as they sometimes offer deals with the top-notch hotels, which can also bring down the price. Advance bookings

are recommended at all times except in the wet season.

There are plenty of hastily constructed budget guesthouses springing up all the time in Luang Prabang, particularly in the narrow streets between the post office and the river and also inland from Phothisarath Rd. However, many of these are of mediocre standard while the older ones among them tend to be fairly run down. New establishments can be found on the tip of the peninsula, on the way towards Wat Xieng Thong, and also among the quiet streets around Phou Vao.

LL Amantaka, Kingkitsarath Rd, T071-860333, www.amanresorts.com.
A wonderfully luxurious option for those on a splurge. Slip into one of the Pool Villas (complete with private plunge pool) in this latest addition to the Aman Resort chain. Minimalist decor and top-notch gym and spa now grace the old buildings of the French colonial hospital at the foot of Phousi hill. Try the Four Hands Massage for a supremely relaxing experience.

LL La Résidence Phou Vao, T071-212 5303, www.residencephouvao.com. This is the best hotel in town by a mile. Every little detail in this plush hotel is perfect, from the fragrance of frangipani that wafts through the foyer to the beautiful, carefully-lit infinity pool with lines of lamps. Massive, beautiful rooms with lounge area, a selection of fresh fruit and a simply divine bathroom. This is a luxury hotel through and through. In the

low season they drop their rates by as much as US$200.

LL-L Villa Maly, T071-253903, www.villa-maly.com. This is a gorgeous boutique hotel set around a beautiful pool with ivory-coloured umbrellas in a leafy garden. A former royal residence, it is stylish and petite, and the rooms are suitably plush. The bathrooms, however, are a little on the small side, with some practical flaws. The service here is impeccable.

LL-AL Maison Souvannaphoum, Phothisarath, T071-212200, www.angsana.com. Formerly Prince Souvannaphouma's residence, this place really is fit for royalty. There are 4 spacious suites and 23 rooms, with a/c, aromatherapy burners and special treats left in the rooms. The service here is top notch.

L 3 Nagas by Alila Sakkaline Rd, T071-253888, www.alilahotels.com/3nagas. Housed in a beautifully restored building, with an annexe across the road, this boutique hotel is a running contender for best room in town. Attention to detail is what sets it apart from the rest: from the 4-poster bed covered with local fabrics to the large deep-set bathtub with natural handmade beauty products. Private balconies or rooms lead onto a stunning courtyard. There's a lovely sitting area in each room, plus traditional *torchis* walls and teak floors. Breakfast (included) is served in the fantastic café downstairs. There is Wi-Fi in each room.

L-AL The Belle Rive, Souvannakhamphong Rd, T071-260733, www.thebellerive.com. Sumptuous well-equipped rooms occupy elegant colonial-style buildings facing the Mekong on a quiet part of the peninsula. Watch boats drifting past from the garden patio of the hotel's restaurant. The attraction of this hotel lies in its nostalgic charm; you almost expect to find Graham Greene or Noel Coward staying here.

AL-A Villa Maydou, set very close to the grounds of Wat Meun Na, T071-254601, www.villamaydou.com. The French-owned hotel is set in restored government buildings, originally built in 1925. Spacious airy a/c rooms simply decorated in a modern style with modern bathtub, minibar. Slightly on the expensive side but beautiful nonetheless, and right on the doorstep of Wat Meun Na.

AL-A Villa Santi Hotel, Sisavangvong Rd, T071-252157, www.villasantihotel.com. Almost an institution in Luang Prabang, this is a restored house from the early 20th century that served as the private residence of the first King Sisavangvong's wife and then Princess Manilai. It's a charming place, full of character and efficiently run, and it has recently received a facelift. There are 6 heavenly suites in the old building, and 14 newer rooms, with baths and showers, in a stylish annexe. The daughter of the official royal cook rustles up mouthwatering French cuisine in the **Princess Restaurant** and there are attractive seating areas in the garden, lobby and on the balcony.

A Ancient Luang Prabang, Sisavangvong Rd, T071-212264, www. ancientluangprabang.com. 12 fantastically designed open-plan rooms featuring lovely wooden furnishings and a big modern tub (separate toilet). The perfect romantic retreat for couples but not the place to bunk down with your mother. Rooms represent good value, though those facing the road can be a bit noisy as the night market carries on down below. Café downstairs with Wi-Fi and a good range of coffees including frappés.

A Le Calao Inn, river road, T071-212100, www.calaoinn.laopdr.com. Enclosed by yellow walls, this Portuguese/French colonial (1902) building boasts beautiful rooms in an incomparable position overlooking the Mekong. The balcony view is a real plus, so ensure you ask for a room with water views.

A-B Sala Luang Prabang, 102/6 Ounkham Rd, T071-252460, www.salalao.com. Very chic, renovated 100-year-old buildings, several of which overlook the Mekong. Nice use of beams and stone inlay in communal areas. Rooms can be quite small, but have a minimalist edge with a/c and modern bathrooms and doors either opening onto a small courtyard or river balcony (more expensive). Bus, car, bicycle hire available.

A-C The Apsara, Kingkitsarath, T071-254670, www.theapsara.com. Ivan Scholte, wine connoisseur and antique collector, has done a perfect job on this establishment. It oozes style. The stunningly beautiful rooms are themed by colour, with 4-poster beds, changing screen, big bathtub and lovely balcony. Very romantic with a modern twist. The rooms in the second building are also magnificent with terrazzo showers you could fit an elephant in. The foyer and lovely restaurant (see Eating) are decorated with Vietnamese lanterns, Burmese offering boxes and modern art. Room rate includes breakfast. Get in early as it is popular and gets booked up in advance. Recommended.

A-C The Apsara Rive Droite, Ban Phanluang, T071-254670, www.theapsara. com. The Apsara's 9-room cousin across the Khan River is accessible by boat from the other Apsara. Spacious, well-appointed rooms sport a unique French-Lao vibe and have balconies that have striking views of the city. This hotel also has the first saltwater pool in Luang Prabang, if not the country.

A-C Sayo Guesthouse, Sotikoumman Rd, T071-252614, sayo@laotel.com. A lovely hotel set in a colonial mansion. The front rooms are beautifully and tastefully decorated with local fabrics and woodwork, polished wooden floors and furniture, and they have a fantastic view over Wat Xieng Mouan – you can watch the monks painting and woodworking. The back rooms aren't as good value but are still recommended. This hotel also has branches on the Mekong and near the post office.

B Pack Luck, opposite L'Éléphant, Ban Vat Nong, T071-253373, packluck@hotmail.com. This boutique hotel has 5 rooms that you couldn't swing a cat in but they are very tastefully decorated with beautiful fabrics and the luxurious bathrooms have deep slate bathtubs.

B-C Merry Lao Swiss, Kingkitsarath Rd, T071-260211, samoraphouma@hotmail.com. Clean rooms with traditional-style furniture. Funky chequered floor. All rooms have a/c, TV. Prices include breakfast.

B-C Say Nam Khan, overlooking the river, T071-212976, saynamkhan_lp@hotmail.com. Attractive renovated building with a homely feel. White paint and wooden furnishings, and clean a/c rooms, although the inner ones are quite dark. Private bathrooms and hot water. Sitting on the terrace overlooking the Nam Kham emphasizes the lovely setting. Friendly and helpful staff. Often gets booked up.

B-C Villa Ban Lao, Souvannaphoum Rd, T071-252078. An impressive white mansion with polished wooden floors. Large double rooms have en suite bathrooms and a/c; others have shared facilities. 2 new annexes have reasonable, clean rooms with showers, hot water and satellite TV. Good value. Excellent restaurant.

B-D Sokdee Residence, just off Ounkham Rd, www.sokdeeresidence.com, T071-252555. Down a quiet, pleasant side street. Clean rooms with TV, a/c and hot water baths in this newly upgraded boutique-style hotel. Small restaurant attached that offers a limited breakfast menu. Bicycle rental. Pretty good value. Recommended.

C Ammata Guesthouse, T071-212175, phetmanyp@yahoo.com.au. Very popular guesthouse with largish rooms decorated simply and stylishly with wooden furniture

and polished floorboards. Hot water and en suite bathroom.

C Oui's Guesthouse, at the end of the peninsula in Ban Khili on Sukkaserm, ouisguesthouse@gmail.com, T071-252374. Charming little guesthouse with sparkling new rooms and polished floorboards, hot water, TV and fridge. Nicely decorated with local artefacts. Great wine bar next door.

C Riverside Guesthouse, T071-212664, www.villariverside.com. Attractive guesthouse in a quiet area. There are 5 rooms on the first floor (one with a great balcony) but their walls are thin, so the concrete ground-floor rooms are a better option. The owner is helpful. Wi-Fi available.

C-D Kongsavath Guesthouse, Ounkham Rd, T071-212994, khongsavath@hotmail.com. Nice clean guesthouse overlooking the Mekong, with comfy beds, a/c, hot water, teak doors throughout and lovely views. Restaurant attached with good breakfast selection, stir-fry and drinks (US$2-3).

D-E Silichit Guesthouse, just off Ounkham Rd, T071-212758. This clean guesthouse is excellent value and well located. The rooms are comfortable with fan, en suite bathroom and hot water. Friendly owners can speak English and French, and often invite guests to sit down for a family dinner or a Beer Lao. Prices drop dramatically in low season.

E Bougnasouk Guesthouse, Ounkham Rd, T071-212749. This riverfront guesthouse has rather cramped, fan-cooled rooms and en suite bathrooms with hot water. The Lao restaurant serves an exceptionally cheap Asian breakfast.

E Boun Gning Guesthouse, 109/4 Ban That Luang, T071-212274. Rooms are quite bare, but there is an attractive balcony, and triples available. Friendly and helpful English-speaking management.

E Jaliya, Phamahapasaman Rd, T071-252154. The ever-popular Jaliya has a range of bungalow-type rooms, with varied facilities, from shared bathrooms and fan through to a/c and TV. Relaxing garden. Bicycle and motorbike rental.

E Le Tam Tam, Sisavangvong Rd, T071-253300, chantavong@hotmail.com. You're paying for the great location here. The big rooms are reasonably good, with bathroom, hot water and a/c. Large restaurant with outdoor seating, serving a wide selection of drinks, big breakfast menu, burgers, salads, spaghetti and some Lao food.

E Vanvisa Villa, T071-212925, vandara1@hotmail.com. Brightly coloured guesthouse down a quaint street. A little gem, with teak floors, large rooms and friendly owners. The downstairs has handicrafts and antiques. It's a bit run down but with a homely feel.

E-F Kounsavan, Chaotonkham Rd, T071-212297. This beautifully situated guesthouse is easy to miss because it's halfway down a sleepy-looking street but it's an oasis of tranquillity, with grass, flowers, balconies and showers with hot water; some rooms are en suite, others share facilities. Very friendly, and within easy striking distance of the town centre. Recommended.

E-F Mano Guesthouse, Phamahapasaman Rd, T071-253112. A clean guesthouse, with a tiled ground floor and wood upstairs, this is a charming, family-run option, with some a/c. A large chess board is carved into a stone table outside. The owners speak English and some French.

E-F Pa Phai, opposite Wat Pa Phai. This guesthouse is run by an elderly lady who speaks good English and French. It is a bit run down but classic Laos: an attractive wooden building with a garden and a veranda on the first floor. 10 clean rooms (separated only by rattan walls, which don't leave much to the imagination), very clean bathrooms, bikes for rent and same day laundry service. Recommended.

F-G Saylom Khem Khong, T071-212304, wonmany2001@yahoo.com. Basic rooms on the river with fan and shared facilities. A bit cramped. Not much English spoken.

Self-catering

A Villa Savanh, Sisavangvong Rd, T071-212420, contact@villasavanh.com. A fully restored wooden house in beautiful gardens, with 3 double bedrooms and bathrooms. Good use of Lao fabrics and furniture. The steep stairs could pose a difficulty for some.

West bank of the Mekong *p113*

LL-L Chanthavinh Resort, Ban Chan Neua 4 km from town, then across the Mekong by their own ferry in Ban Sankaloke, T071-253851/7, www.chanthavinhresortandspa.com. Stunning gardens surround the free-standing rooms, replete with all mod cons. The restaurant and bar are recommended too, even if just for cocktails at sunset. A bit of a hike from town to the ferry pier.

East of the city *p115*

AL Zen Nam Khan Resort, 15 km east of Luang Prabang, T020-5557 1120, www.zennamkhanresort.com. Set along the bank of the Khan River, these fan-cooled bungalows are perfect for lazy afternoons on the veranda, and are also close to the Elephant Village. Rooms also have open-air showers. The resort has Wi-Fi, a stream-fed ecological swimming pool and a Japanese-style spa.

D Thongbay Guesthouse, Ban Vieng May, 3 km southeast of the centre of Luang Prabang, T071-253234, www.thongbay-guesthouses.com. Stunning set-up of 12 modern bungalows including 2 family-sized ones, overlooking the Nam Khan. Beautiful tropical garden with a small pond in the centre. The rooms overlooking the river are the best, affording fantastic views of rural life. Bungalows have a fridge, 4-poster bed and hot water. Popular with tour groups so booking is necessary. Recommended.

South of the city *p117*

AL-A Grand Luang Prabang Hotel & Resort, Ban Xiengkeo, 4 km from town, T071-253851, www.grandluangprabang.com. Beautifully restored hotel in the former Prince Phetsarath's residence. Simple, classically decorated rooms set in lovely gardens. Try to get a room with a view of

the river. The 80 rooms have all mod cons including IDD telephone, minibar, TV and marble bathroom. A bit of a hike from town.
AL-A Villa Santi Resort, Ban Na Deuai, T071-252157, www.villasantihotel.com. This new 55-room resort, under the same management as **Villa Santi Hotel** (see page 120), could hardly be more dreamy. It's set in 10 ha of ground 6 km from town on the road to Kuang Si falls. The foyer is decorated with art deco-style furniture and the rooms are very comfortable. There is a good pool. If you can get on one of the **Laos Airlines** deals, this hotel is very good value. Shuttle buses into town are scheduled to leave every 30 mins throughout the day. Recommended.

🍴 Eating

Luang Prabang *p96, maps p100 and p104*

Note that Luang Prabang has a curfew; most places won't stay open past 2200.

Luang Prabang produces a number of culinary specialities that make interesting souvenirs. The market is a good starting point for buying these, although restaurants have also latched onto their popularity. The most famous is *khai pehn*, dried river weed, from the Nam Khan, mixed with sesame and fried. *Cheo bong*, a spicy, smoky purée made with buffalo hide, is also popular. Other delicacies include: *phak nam*, a watercress that grows around waterfalls and used in soups and salads; *mak kham kuan*, tamarind jam, and *mak nat kuan*, pineapple jam.

One of the best local culinary experiences is to grab some Lao takeaway food from the night market that runs off **Sisavangvon Rd**, 1600-2200. Here you can pick up fresh spring rolls (*nem dip*) papaya salad (*tam som*), sticky rice (*khao niao*), the local delicacy Luang Prabang sausage (*Sai Oua*), barbecue chicken on a stick (*gai*) or fish (*pa*), dried buffalo (*sin savanh*) and dried seaweed. There are also a number of cheap buffets where you can get a selection of

local curries and dishes. If you don't want your food too spicy ask for '*bo pet*'.

🍴🍴-🍴🍴 **Arisai**, 49-3 Sakkaline Rd, T071-255000, www.thearisai.com. In a stylish converted 2-storey shop house, Arisai has been wooing the tourists. The menu is principally Mediterranean and varied. While tasty, dishes are not outstanding; service can also be erratic. The alfresco pavement seats are a top spot for people watching.

🍴🍴-🍴🍴 **L'Éléphant**, Ban Vat Nong, T071-252482, contact@elephant-restau. com. About as fine as dining gets in Luang Prabang. Very upmarket and utterly delectable cuisine. Pan-fried fillet of snapper, with capers and basil-flavoured mash is delicious, as are the simmered scallops. Also offers Lao dishes. There are 3 set menus and an extensive wine list. A good place to treat yourself. Highly recommended.

🍴🍴-🍴🍴 **Un Petit Nid**, 98/5 Sakkaline Rd, T071-260686. This stylish sunken bistro in a restored 1854 building offers small street-view alfresco tables or interior dining on crisp white linens. Service is attentive and the fish dishes are winners.

🍴🍴 **Café des Arts**, Sisavangvong Rd, T071-252162. Pleasant and reasonably priced French restaurant with artwork for sale on the walls, and a veranda perfect for people-watching. Good salads, pizzas, scrumptious crème caramel. Steak dishes are a bit expensive, US$10, but the chicken dishes are delicious and reasonable

🍴🍴-🍴 **3 Nagas**, Sakkaline Rd, T071-253888. In the hotel of the same name, the food here is both Lao and Western and highly recommended. The restaurant also has an exemplary wine list and its own unique concoctions of cocktails.

🍴🍴-🍴 **The Apsara**, see Sleeping. Lao/Thai/Western fusion restaurant offering dishes such as braised pork belly and pumpkin, and great fish cakes. Try their delicious red curry cream soup with lentils and smoked duck or braised beef shin Chinese style. Good value.

🍴🍴-🍴 **Blue Lagoon**, beside the Royal Palace, T071-253698, www.blue-lagoon-cafe.com.

This restaurant offers a great selection of delicious hearty European meals – especially Swiss-inspired dishes such as the fondue chinoise. Great steaks, beef stroganoff and pasta and ice creams to die for. Indoor and outdoor seating in candlelit garden setting.

Café Ban Vat Sene, Sakkaline Rd, opposite Wat Sene. A very pleasant option, with a breezy, colonial air. White walls and polished dark wooden floors, tables and chairs. Great for breakfast. The food (French) is a treat. Good place for coffee or tea.

Coconut Garden, Sakkaline Rd, T071-252482. A hip spin-off of the L'Elephant and centrally located on main street. Similar French and Lao menu but affordable prices. The chic bar and excellent service make this a place not to miss.

Couleur Café/Restaurant, Ban Vat Nong, T020-55621064. The French expats in town have nothing but praise for this place with its French and Lao meals and ambient setting. Good wine. It is particularly renowned for its steaks.

Dyen Sabai, Ban Phan Luang, T020-55104817. In the dry season, this cosy, prettily-lit spot is accessible via a bamboo bridge (4000 kip 0800-1700; 1700-2330 free) across the Khan river (around mid-Nov to late May). From late May to mid-Nov the restaurant offers free paddle boat rides across the river. The unusual cocktails (happy hour 1200-1900) and Lao food are not to be missed, nor the amazing sunset views. This is a highly recommended spot.

Luang Prabang Pizza, Sisavangvong Rd. No surprises for guessing its signature dish. Pizzas and pasta are cheap and passable.

Nazim's Indian Restaurant, Sisavangvong Rd. Luang Prabang's first Indian restaurant appears to be a roaring success. The menu offers a huge selection of authentic Indian food from both north and south of the country, plus halal dishes. The management and the chefs are all Indian which ensures that the food is traditionally prepared. The servings are huge, and the service is efficient; the interior remains dodgy, but the cheap delicious grub more than makes up for it.

Tamnak Lao, Sisavangvong Rd, opposite **Villa Santi**, T071-252525. Brilliant restaurant, serving modern Lao cuisine, with a strong Thai influence. Very popular with tour groups. The freshest ingredients are used: try fish and coconut wrapped in banana leaf or pork-stuffed celery soup. Atmospheric surroundings, particularly upstairs, yet service can be a bit erratic. Best for dinner.

Tum Tum Cheng, just off Sakkaline Rd, T071-252019. Lao food prepared by a Hungarian returnee. Tasty fusion-style meals. Very comfortable outdoor seating. Also offers classes in Lao cooking and classical Lao dancing.

Dao Fa, Sisavangvong Rd, T071-215651, www.daofa-bistro.com. Great selection of teas and coffees, fab ice creams and tasty homemade pasta. The latter is the real draw and is recommended. Brightly decorated space with pavement seating.

Khemkhan Food Garden, Nam Khan Rd, T071-212447. A reasonable line in spicy foods but it's better for a beer than a feed. Pleasant terrace overlooking the Nam Khan. Popular with government groups.

Morning Glory, Sakkaline Rd. Open 0800-1600. Small but cosy Thai restaurant decorated with the proprietor's photographs and paintings. Intimate open-style kitchen serving up fantastic home-style meals – great juices, breakfasts and curries. Try the *Tom Kha Gai* and zesty juice.

Tamarind, facing Wat Nong, T020-7777 0484, www.tamarindlaos.com. Mon-Sat 1100-1800. Brilliant restaurant offering modern Lao cuisine. Try the five-bites (the Lao equivalent to tapas) or the 'dining experiences', such as the traditional Lao celebration meal 'Pun Pa', which includes succulent marinated fish and a purple sticky rice dessert, or the Adventurous Lao Gourmet degustation menu. They also do market tours with explanations of Lao delicacies (advance booking is essential) and can organize picnics. The owners Joy and Caroline have received many accolades.

¶ View Khaem Khong, Ounkham Rd, T071-212726. The most popular of the dining establishments along the river with consistently excellent food. Good for a beer at sunset. Tasty Luang Prabang sausage and *laap* and curry spaghetti. Recommended.

Foodstalls

A tempting choice of early evening stalls is to be found on Kittsarath Setthathirat, towards the river, and on the sidestreet down towards the river near the night market on Sisavangvong Rd. Very cheap and usually pretty good food.

Cafés and bakeries

Joma, Sisavangvong Rd near Nam Phou fountain, T071-252292. Utterly delicious array of comfort foods: shakes, coffee, sandwiches, lasagne, quiche and more. Nice and cool a/c interior.

L'Étranger, Kingkitsarath Rd, near **Hive Bar**, T020-5547 1736. Great little bookshop-cum-café. The upstairs is exceptionally comfortable with cushions and low tables. This is the perfect place to wind down, grab a book and have a cuppa. Outstanding breakfasts. Books are rented here for 5000 kip per day. A movie is shown daily at 1900.

Luang Prabang Bakery, Sisavangvong Rd, T071-252499. Croissants, lemon bars, raisin slices, brownies, muffins, coffee, rolls, to eat on premises or take away. Also sells muesli, making it a good place for breakfast. Great selection of chocolate cakes.

See also **Café Ban Vat Sene**, page 124.

❼ Bars and clubs

Luang Prabang *p96, maps p100 and p104*

L'Éléphant, **La Résidence Phou Vao** and **Apsara** provide attractive settings for a drink. A sunset beer at one of the restaurants overlooking the river is divine. After every-

thing closes between 2200 and 2300 most locals head to Dao Fa or to Phou Vao Rd to have a bowl of soup and a cold beverage at one of the many *pho* noodle shops.

Dao Fa nightclub, on the way to the South Bus Station. Extremely popular with locals and plays Asian dance music.

Hive Bar, Kingkitsarath Rd, next to L'Étranger. Luang Prabang's most happening bar-club is good for a dance, though it has become quieter now that the competition around it has started to grow.

Icon Klub, Just off of Sisavangvong Rd near the Khan River. For bohemians, poets and lovers, this Hungarian-owned bar is perfect for a drink. Signature cocktails and a worldly clientele make for interesting conversation. Open from 1730 until the bar runs dry!

Khily Wine Bar, tucked away next door to **Oui's Guesthouse** at the end of the peninsula. The secret hotspot for locals. This intimate bar has high chairs with a long bar stocked with an extensive selection of Lao wines. Great for a quiet drink.

Lao Lao Garden, Kingkitsarath Rd. A tiered landscaped terrace, with low lighting and cheap, delicious cocktails, that's become a favourite backpacker haunt. A bonfire keeps you cosy in the winter months. The Lao-style barbecue is the best in town.

Lao Lao Sports Bar, Kingkitsarath Rd, opposite **Hive Bar** (formerly known as **Khob Jai**). This bar fills up during football matches, televised on a big screen.

Lusine, Souvannakhamphong Rd. Well stocked bar includes Belgian beers, as well as the local tipple Beer Lao. Happy hour specials are unbeatable, as well as river views in the shady garden.

Muang Swa, Phouvao Rd. Local style nightclub decked out with low couches, with Thai pop, Lao traditional music and western oldies. Practice your Lamvong (circle dance) moves. Highly recommended.

Pack Luck, Sisavangvong Rd. For a more upmarket drink, this cosy wine bar has a great selection of tipples and well-selected wines. This modern establishment is high

on atmosphere, with beanbags, modern art adorning its walls, and candlelit tables.
Utopia, on the Khan River in Ban Aphay. Landscaped gardens, a sand volleyball court and a long wooden deck overlook the Khan. Great for a drink at sunset, but there are better places in town for food.

☺Entertainment

Luang Prabang *p96, maps p100 and p104*
Cinema
There isn't a cinema in Luang Prabang anymore. **L'Étranger** (see Cafés and bakeries, above) shows arthouse and other well-reviewed movies every evening.

Theatre and dance
Traditional dance performances, influenced by the *Ramayana*, are held at the **Theatre Phalak Phalam** in the Royal Palace compound, T071-253705, Mon, Wed and Sat at 1800, US$6-15. The traditional dance of Luang Prabang, which is incorporated into most shows, is over 600 years old.

☺Festivals and events

Luang Prabang *p96, maps p100 and p104*
April
Pi Mai (Lao New Year; movable) is the time when the tutelary spirits of the old year are replaced by those of the new. It has special significance in Luang Prabang, with some traditions that are no longer observed in Vientiane. In the past, the King and Queen would clean the principal Buddha images in the city's main wats, while masked dancers pranced through the streets re-enacting the founding of the city by 2 mythical beasts. People from all over the province descend on the city. The newly crowned Miss New Year (Nang Sang Khan) is paraded through town, riding on the back of the auspicious animal of the year. Certain customs are observed on each day of the festival:

Day 1 Bazaar is held in the streets around the post office; sprinkling of Buddha statues with water; release of small fish into Mekong from pier behind Royal Palace – a symbolic gesture, hoping for good luck in the New Year; construction of sand stupas on western bank of Mekong, next to Wat Xiang Men; fireworks in the evening.
Day 2 1st procession from Wat That to Wat Xieng Thong; dance of the masks of Pou Nheu Nha Nheu and Sing Kaeo Sing Kham; fireworks and festivities in the evening.
Day 3 2nd procession from Wat Xieng Thong to Wat That; procession of monks; *baci* celebrations; fireworks in evening.
Day 4 Pra Bang is moved from the Royal Palace to Wat Mai.
Day 5/6 All-day traditional washing of Pra Bang at Wat Mai.
Day 7 Pra Bang Buddha is returned to Royal Palace.
Days 9-11 Wat Xieng Thong Phraman image brought outside for ritual washing.

May
Vien Thiene (movable), the candlelit festival.

August
Boat races (movable). Boats are raced by the people living in the vicinity of each wat.

October
Lai Heua Fai (Fireboat Festival). Each village creates a large boat made of bamboo and paper and decorated with candles and offerings. These are paraded down the main street to Wat Xieng Thong where they are judged and sent down into the Mekong river to bring atonement for sins. Temples and houses are decorated with paper lanterns and candles. People also make their own small floats to release in the Mekong.

December
Luang Prabang Film Festival is the country's first and only major film festival, this new annual event held in early December showcases Southeast Asian cinema. The

project also produces educational activities for young Lao, www.lpfilmfest.org.

OShopping

Luang Prabang *p96, maps p100 and p104*

Antiques

Authentic antiques are almost impossible to find as the Thai dealers have got there first. Real antiques are immensely valuable and will usually be priced accordingly.

Patthana Boupha Antique Gallery, Ban Visoun, T071-212262. Lttle gem in a fantastic colonial building. Antique silverware and jewellery, Buddhas, old photos and textiles. Reasonable prices. Often closed, so ring first.

Baskets

The best baskets can be found in several shops on **Sisavangvong Rd**, near Villa Santi.

Books

A selection of second-hand books is available at **Luang Prabang Bakery Restaurant**, Sisavangvong Rd (not to be confused with the Luang Prabang Bakery Restaurant, see Cafés). A wider selection of books can be found at **L'Étranger** (see Cafés), the best bookshop in the country.

Fashion and textiles

Mulberries, on the Mekong near Wat Nong, sells a range of silk homewares and clothes, as well as local teas.

Ock Pop Tok, near L'Éléphant restaurant, T071-253219. **Ock Pop Tok**, which translates as 'East meets West', incorporates the best of both worlds in beautiful fabrics. It specializes in naturally dyed silk. Clothes, furnishings and hangings, plus custom-made (order well in advance). Check out the **Fibre2Fabric** gallery next door (see Galleries, below). Recommended.

Satri Lao Silk, Sisavangvong Rd, T071-219295. Beautiful silks and handicrafts. The quality is reflected in high prices, but still well worth a look.

Galleries

Fibre2Fabric, 71 Ban Vat Nong (next door to Ock Pop Tok), T071-254761, www.fibre 2fabric.org. A fantastic gallery exhibiting textiles of different ethnic groups. Local weavers are often on hand to explain the weaving processes.

Kinnaly Gallery, Sakkaline Rd, T020-55557737. Black and white photography.

Kop Noi, Ban Aphay, www.kopnoi.com. This little shop has a rotating exhibition on the second floor. It also exhibits work by renowned Lao photographer Sam Sisombat.

Handicrafts

There is a handicraft market, geared to tourists, close to the intersection of Phou Vao Rd and the river road. A row of shops lines Phothisarath Rd.

Jewellery

Naga Creations, Sisavangvong Rd, T071-212775. Lao silver with semi-precious stones. Contemporary and classic pieces available, including innovative work by the jeweller **Fabrice**.

Markets

The **night market** sprawls down several blocks of Sisavangvong Rd. Daily 1700-2230. Hundreds of villagers flock to the market to sell their handicrafts, ranging from silk scarves to embroidered quilt covers and paper albums. It shouldn't be missed.

Phousi market, 1.5 km from the centre of town. A fantastic place to pick up quality silk garments. Pre-made silk clothes are sold here for a fraction of the price in town. .

Talat Dala, housed in market building in the middle of town on the corner of Setthathirat and Chao Sisophon roads. A major market for artisans and jewellers.

Silver

One of Luang Prabang's traditional crafts is silversmithing. Most tourists buy silver from the main market in Luang Prabang. However, most of these pieces are made in Vientiane and trucked to the royal capital. Expert silversmiths like Thith Peng Maniphone maintain that Vientiane-made pieces are inferior. Signposted almost opposite Wat That, his workshop and shop has jewellery and pots.

The silversmith along the river, near the rear of the Royal Palace, produces good workmanship; his father made one of the King's crowns. There are others around the Nam Phou area (fountain). **Woodcarving Caruso Gallery**, Sisavangvong Rd (towards the Three Nagas Hotel) has stunning but expensive wooden furniture and artefacts.

Woodcarving
Caruso Gallery, Sisavangvong Rd (towards the 3 Nagas Hotel. Stunning but expensive wooden furniture and artefacts.

⊖Activities and tours

Luang Prabang *p96, maps p100 and p104*
Cookery classes
There are a number of classes offered in Luang Prabang. The cooking classes are ordered in preference.
Tamarind, www.tamarindlaos.com, facing Wat Nong, T020-7777 0484. This successful restaurant runs specialized classes for groups in their enchanting jungle garden school outside of town. Recommended.
Tamnak Lao, T071-252525, www. laocookingcourse.com, US$25 per person for 1-day class, including shopping for ingredients at the markets.
Tum Tum Cheng, Sakkaline Rd, T071-253388, www.tumtumcheng.com. Mon-Sat. Popular cooking classes operating since 2001. 1 day, US$25; 2 day, US$45; 3 day US$60. Advance bookings are required.

Elephant tours and activities
Elephant Village, 15 km from Luang Prabang (visits and activities can be organized through their office on Sisavangvong Rd, www.elephantvillage-laos.com, T071-252417). Established in conjunction with Tiger Trails in Luang Prabang, they have bought up old working elephants. To keep the elephants active, the operators run up to 25 activities for tourists, including experiencing life as a *mahout* (elephant keeper).

Sauna and massage
Aroma Spa, Sisavangvong Rd, T020-7761 1255. Another mid-priced spa offering aromatherapy, facials, body scrubs, etc.
Khmu Spa, Sisavangvong Rd, T071-2212092. A range of inexpensive massages including the Khmu massage (gentler, lighter strokes) Lao massage (stretching, cracking and pressure points) and foot massage. Also has herbal sauna. Open until 2200.
Maison Souvannaphoum (see Sleeping). A spa with a range of luxurious and expensive treatments. For sheer indulgence.
Red Cross Sauna, opposite Wat Visunnarat, reservations T071-212303. Daily 0900-2100 (1700-2100 for sauna). Massage 30,000 kip per hr, traditional Lao herbal sauna 10,000 kip. Bring your own towel/sarong. Profits go to the Lao Red Cross.
The Spa at La Résidence Phou (see Sleeping), T071-21253, www. residencephouvao.com. Offers very expensive 3-hr massage courses, US$190 for 2 people. This includes a 1-hr massage for each person, the class, a handbook and oils. .
Spa Garden, Ban Phonheauang, T071-212325, spagardenlpb@hotmail.com. More upmarket. Offers many massage and beauty treatments including aromatherapy massage US$12 per hr, sports body massage, facials, skin detox US$25 per hr. Packages between US$5 and US$38.
Peninsula Massage, near Wat Xieng Thong on Souvanna Khampong Rd. Daily 1600-2030. An entrepreneurial family have set up a sauna and massage in their home.

Tour operators
All Laos Service, Sisavangvong Rd. Large agency organizing ticketing and services.

Asia Pacific, 88/07 Ban Phonpheng Phou Vao Rd, T013-224473, www.laosvoyage.com.
Asian Trails, Unit 06, Baan Vat That, Khaem Khong Rd, PO Box 779, T071-252764, www.asiantrails.com. Also has tours to Cambodia and Vietanm
Buffalo Tours, 8/40 Ban Nongkham, T071-254395, www.buffalotours.com. New player on the block organizes tours that delve into local culture. Very helpful.
Green Discovery, T071-212093, www.greendiscoverylaos.com. Rafting and kayaking trips that pass through grade 1 and 2 rapids. Also cycling trips around Luang Prabang, homestays, trips to Pak Ou caves.
Tiger Trail, Sisavangvong Rd, T071-252655, www.laos-adventures.com. Adventure specialists: elephant treks, biking, rafting, etc.

Weaving classes
Weaving Centre, 2 km out of town on the river (bookings at **Ban Vat Nong Gallery**, T071-253219. info@ockpoptok.com). Run by the team behind the creations at **Ock Pop Tok** (see page 127) Half-day dyeing classes US$35. A variety of 1- to 3-day weaving classes are offered at US$35 per day. Classes are run by weavers and their English-speaking assistants.

⊖ Transport

Luang Prabang *p96, maps p100 and p104*
See also Ins and outs, page 96.

Air
Luang Prabang International Airport (LPQ) about 4 km from town, T071-212172/3. **Lao Airlines**, Phamahapasaman Rd, T071-212172, has 3 daily connections with **Vientiane**, 40 mins, and a service to **Chiang Mai**, **Pakse**, **Siem Reap** and **Hanoi**. It also runs daily flights between **Bangkok** and Luang Prabang. These flights are prone to change so check schedules in advance. **Bangkok Airways** runs daily flights to **Bangkok**.

In the rainy and cool seasons, dense cloud can sometimes make Luang Prabang airport inoperable until about 1100. Tickets are often cheaper from travel agents than from the airline. Confirm bookings a day in advance and arrive at the airport early as flights may depart as soon as they're full.

Bicycle hire
Bikes can be rented for US$1 per day from most guesthouses.

Boat
With the development of overland links, river transport has languished, but a few passengers take the route upstream to Houei Xai via Pak Beng, on the border with Thailand, remains popular. There are 3 departure areas, with most boats leaving from the 2 docks behind the Royal Palace. **Tha Heua Me Pier** is the most popular departure point and lists all the destinations and prices available (daily 0730-1130, 1300-1600). Prices are dependent on the cost of

gasoline. There is also a dock at **Ban Don** (15 mins north of town and accessible by tuk-tuk, US$1-2).

To Houei Xai/Pak Beng The 2-day boat trip down the Mekong between Houei Xai and Pak Beng has become a rite of passage for travellers in Southeast Asia. There are options to suit all budgets.

The slow boat to Houei Xai leaves from the boat pier on Khem Khong Rd called the Tha Heua Mea pier, 2 days, with a break in Pak Beng after 6-7 hrs on the 1st day. It costs US$25 for each leg of the trip and almost all travel agents sell tickets. It's often packed, so wear something comfortable, and the seats are usually wooden benches, so bring padding to sit on. The trip from Luang Prabang to Houei Xai (via Pak Beng overnight) is usually less busy than in the other direction. (If the boat to Pak Beng is full, you can charter your own for about US$400-500.) Tickets for the onward trip to Houei Xai, can be purchased in Pak Beng. Take a good book and food. Most boats have a drinks vendor. The boat usually leaves between 0800 and 0900 (changeable so check) but arrive early to secure a good seat.

The most luxurious way to make the trip is on the **Luangsay Cruise**, office on Sisavangvong Rd, T071-252553, www.luangsay.com, which makes the trip in 2 days and 1 night, stopping over at Pak Ou Caves en route and staying overnight at their lodge in Pak Beng (page 156). The boat is comfortable with lounges, a well-stocked bar and library; food and drinks are more than ample. It needs to be booked 6 months in advance in high season. In low season, the boat runs from Houei Xai to Luang Prabang on Mon and Fri and in the opposite direction on Wed and Sat (US$348 twin/US$427 single). In the high season the boat runs from Houei Xai to Luang Prabang on Mon, Thu and Fri, and Luang Prabang to Houei Xai on Tue, Wed and Sat (US$546 twin/US$630 single). In the low season, it may be possible to get a standby ticket. The Luangsay Lodge, off Phouvao, in the

southwest of town should be open by the time you read this.

Speedboats depart from Ban Don to **Houei Xai** (on the Thai border; see page 151), US$30, around 6 hrs, with a break in **Pak Beng**. Tickets are available from travel agents. The boats are noisy and dangerous. Ensure that you get a helmet and life jacket.

To Vientiane via Pak Lai The passenger service between Vientiane and Luang Prabang has ceased but you may be able to get on a southbound cargo boat (use a translator to negotiate the price). The stretch of river from Luang Prabang to Pak Lai is quite hazardous, with rapids, so an alternative may be to take the bus to **Sayaboury** (see Bus, below) and on to **Pak Lai**, where there is a basic guesthouse, then catch the boat to Vientiane from there. Slow boats depart Pak Lai for Vientiane at 0730 and take all day (US$15). Or you can hire a speed boat, 5-6 hrs, US$150 for up to 6 people. It is possible to see working elephants between Pak Lai and **Sanakham** (Xana Kham). The next settlement downstream, Sanakham has 3 wats, one with a ruined stupa and another with an unusual Buddha image. There is a river crossing here to Chiang Khan in Thailand, but officially foreigners are not permitted to cross (however, boats ply the river and it is said no-one checks your passport). Boats from Sanakham to Vientiane take 8 hrs.

To Nong Khiaw and Muang Khoua A few boats travel up the Nam Ou to Nong Khiaw and Muang Ngoi, but these are infrequent, especially when the river is low. The journey takes 6 hrs to Nong Khiaw, 150,000 kip, and a further 1 hr to Muang Ngoi Neua. The Nam Ou joins the Mekong near the Pak Ou caves, so you can combine a journey with a visit to the caves. Departures to Nong Khiaw are posted outside the pier. It is possible to charter a boat for 1-6 people for US$200. Speedboats to Nong Khiaw sometimes leave from Ban Don (5 km from Luang Prabang); expect to pay 200,000 kip. However, these are hazardous.

Bus/truck

The northern bus terminal is for northbound traffic and the southern one for traffic to the south. Check which terminal your bus is using, as unscheduled changes are possible.

From the northern terminal To **Luang Namtha**, daily 0900 and 1730, 10 hrs, usually via Udomxai, 80,000 kip. The 1730 bus comes from Vientiane and is often full. An alternative is to catch the bus to **Udomxai**, 0900 and 1130 daily, 5 hrs, 50,000 kip, and then continue to Luang Namtha in the afternoon. There are daily departures (usually in the morning) to **Houei Xai** on the Thai/Lao border, 110,000 kip, 11-12 hrs. A VIP bus to Houei Xai passes through daily, 1000, 10 hrs, 155,000 kip. There is a bus to **Xam Neua**, 1630 (officially 14 hrs but it can be up to 20 hrs), 120,000 kip. **Phongsali**, 1600, 13-15 hrs 110,000 kip. To **Nong Khiaw**, by *songthaew*, regular departures in the morning, 35,000 kip.

From the southern terminal There are up to 8 daily buses to **Vientiane**, although departures tend to be fewer in the low season, 10-11 hrs, 950,000 kip; most of these services stop in **Vang Vieng**, 6 hrs, 80,000 kip. VIP buses to Vientiane depart 0800 and 0900, 9 hrs, 115,000 kip; both services stop in Vang Vieng, 115,000 kip.

To **Phonsavanh**, daily 0830, 8-9 hrs, 75,000 kip. It should cost 10,000-15,000 kip to get to the centre of town from the station.

To Sayaboury *Songthaew* for **Pak Khon**, on the Mekong, depart several times a day, when full, 3 hrs. From Pak Khon there is a Mekong ferry to **Tha Deua**, from where buses continue to **Sayaboury**, 1 hr. This is the route to take if you want to catch a boat from Pak Lai to Vientiane (see above).

Minibus

Minibuses with driver can be hired for US$50 per day for excursions around Luang Prabang, US$60 per day further afield. Check noticeboards for services to **Vang Vieng**, 5 hrs, and **Vientiane**, 7 hrs. Big groups can organize independent minivan rental.

Saamlor and tuk-tuk

These can be hired to see the sights or to go to nearby villages. A short stint across town costs about 10,000 kip per person, but expect to pay 20,000 kip for more than 1 km. Trips to nearby excursions cost US$10-15.

ⓘ Directory

Luang Prabang *p96, maps p100 and p104*

Banks There's a healthy scattering of ATMs around Luang Prabang. **Lao Development Bank**, Ban Visoun, Mon-Sat 0830-1200 and 1330-1530, will change US$/Thai baht into US$ or kip, and accepts credit cards. **Banque pour le Commerce Exterieur Lao** (BCEL), Sisavangvong Rd, Mon-Sat 0830-1200 and 1330-1530; all transactions in kip, will exchange Thai baht, US$, AU$, UK£, € and TCs, also cash advances on Visa cards; they also have an ATM. Some tourist shops and restaurants change US$ and Thai baht. Travel agencies may give credit card advances, but charge 6-8% commission.
Internet There is a concentration of internet cafés on Sisavangvong Rd. **Luang Prabang Internet**, opposite Silichit Guesthouse, is good value. Wi-Fi is available in many guesthouses and cafés. Non-guests can often access Wi-Fi for a fee.
Medical services Facilities in Luang Prabang are limited. The **main hospital**, about 3 km outside of town, T071-252049, is only useful for minor ailments. For anything major you're better off flying to Bangkok. There are a few pharmacies towards Villa Santi on Sisavangvong Rd.
Post, telephone and internet Post and telephone office on the corner of Chau Fa Ngum and Setthathirat streets, Mon-Fri 0830-1730, Sat 0830-1200, express mail service, fax and international telephone facilities. There are IDD call boxes around the post office and on Sisavangvong Rd. Hotels allow international calls from their reception (about US$5 a min), but it is cheaper to make international calls from internet cafés.

North of Luang Prabang

In recent years the settlements of Nong Khiaw and Muang Ngoi Neua in the north of Luang Prabang Province have become firm favourites with the backpacker set. In fact, idyllic Muang Ngoi Neua is often heralded as the new Vang Vieng, surrounded by stunning scenery and the fantastic ebb and flow of life on the river. It is far more pleasant to travel between Luang Prabang and Nong Khiaw/Ban Saphoun by long boat, than by bus. The Nam Ou passes mountains, teak plantations, dry rice fields and a movable water wheel mounted on a boat, which moves from village to village and is used for milling. But with the improvements that have been made to Route 13, road travel has now become the preferred option for many – partly because it is cheaper, and partly because it is quicker. Route 13 north runs parallel with the river for most of the journey to Nam Bak. There is trekking around Nong Khiaw and Muang Khua further north upriver. ▸▸ *For listings, see pages 136-142.*

Nam Bak → *Colour map 1, B3.*

The town of Nam Bak lies on the banks of the Nam Bak. It is a rather beautiful place and is worth an overnight stop. The market is interesting in the very early morning, when hill people including Blue Hmong converge to sell a miscellany of pickings from the forest. There is a small wat on the right, at the end of town as you come from Luang Prabang, called **Wat Tiom Tian**. From here there are good views of the surrounding countryside. There is a small children's graveyard behind the wat.

Nong Khiaw and Ban Saphoun → *For listings, see pages 136-142. Colour map 1, B4.*

Nong Khiaw lies 22 km to the northeast of Nam Bak and is a delightful little village on the banks of the Nam Ou, surrounded by limestone peaks and flanked by misty mountains, the largest the aptly named Princess Mountain. The remote little town is one of Laos' prettiest destinations. There are, in fact, two settlements here: Ban Saphoun on the east bank of the Nam Ou and Nong Khiaw on the west. Of the two, Ban Saphoun offers the best views and has the best riverside accommodation. Confusingly, the combined village is sometimes called one name, sometimes the other and sometimes **Muang Ngoi** which is actually another town to the north (see opposite) and also the name of the district.

One reason why Nong Khiaw/Ban Saphoun has become such a popular stopping place for travellers is because of its pivotal position on the Nam Ou, affording river travel up from Luang Prabang north. It also makes for a more scenic route to Xam Neua/Udomxai. The road trip between Udomxai and Xam Neua that Nong Khiaw sits upon is one of the most spectacular in Laos, moving through remote villages. Despite its convenience as a staging post this town is a destination in its own right. It is a beautiful spot, the sort of place where time stands still, journals are written, books read and stress is a deeply foreign concept.

It is possible to swim in the river (women should wear sarongs) or walk around the town or up the cliffs. The bridge across the Nam Ou offers fine views and photo opportunities.

Around Nong Khiaw

The most obvious attractions in the area are the caves used by locals when the US bombed the area. **Tham Pha Thok** ① *2.5 km southeast of the bridge, entry 10,000 kip*, was a Pathet Lao regional base during the civil war. It was divided into sections – a hospital section, a police section and a military section. Old remnants exist like campfires and ruined beds but other than that there is little evidence of it being the PT headquarters until you see the bomb crater at the front. To get there you walk through beautiful rice paddies. There is a second cave, **Tham Pha Kwong**, about 300 m further down on the left, which was the Pathet Lao's former banking cave. The cave is a tight squeeze and is easier to access with help from a local guide. It splits into two caves, one of which is the financial office and the accountant's office.

To walk to the caves, turn left out of the village heading towards Nam Bak and the Tham Pha Kwong caves are about 30 minutes' walk, up on the right. There is a shrine to the Buddha, various relics, and a pile of old ammunition and bombshells inside. Take a strong torch to explore the tunnel at the back. It's a 30-minute trek to Tham Pha Thok: go over the bridge and follow the main road. The caves are signposted.

A further 2 km along the road, at Ban Nokien, is the **Than Mok** waterfall. To get there, you can either walk for about 3 km or charter a boat (around 500,000 kip per boat for the return trip); remember to agree a return time. There's a 10,000 kip fee to see the waterfall, and some cheeky little child will likely charge you a further 10,000 kip to guide you there (40 minutes each way). It's difficult to find on your own. It's best to go in the morning, so as not to have to rush the climb up to the falls or cut short your time there before dark.

If you go to the boat landing it is also possible to organize a fishing trip with one of the local fishermen for very little money. You might need someone to translate for you.

Muang Ngoi Neua → For listings, see pages 136-142. Colour map 1, B4.

The town of Muang Ngoi Neua lies 40 km (one hour) north of Nong Khiaw, along the Nam Ou. This small town surrounded by ethnic villages has become very popular with the backpacker set over the last few years, with many calling it the new Vang Vieng. The town is a small slice of utopia, set on a peninsula at the foot of Mount Phaboom, shaded by coconut trees, with the languid river breeze wafting through the town's small paths. Most commonly known as **Muang Ngoi**, the settlement has had to embellish its name to distinguish it from Nong Khiaw, which is also often referred to as Muang Ngoi (see above). It's the perfect place to go for a trek to surrounding villages, or bask the day away swinging in your hammock. A market is held every 10 days to which the villagers come to sell their produce and handicrafts.

If journeying downriver from Muang Khua, the scenery only becomes really beautiful about 20 minutes before Muang Ngoi Neua. The limestone equivalent of the NYC Flatiron building rears up followed by soaring sharply pinnacled mountains; this leg of the journey is truly breathtaking.

Around Muang Ngoi Neua

Tham Kang cave, a large limestone cave, with a glassy river running through it, is a pleasant 30-minute walk south of town. Follow the road out of town, turn left where the morning market is held and head through the school grounds and along a narrow path through vegetation. Follow the path on the left to avoid wading through very deep and very cold water. Just past the school, villagers will collect the entrance fee of 2000 kip. The cave is over 30 m high and exceptionally dark inside, so bring a torch. There's a swimming hole at ground level. **Tham Pa Kaew** is a further five minutes' walk along the trail. Inside the cave is a small Buddha image and there's also a crystal-clear pool that's great for a dip. On the other side of the path are sticky rice paddies, where you can catch a glimpse of locals planting or harvesting the rice by hand. Another 30 minutes' walk along the same path leads to some friendly Khmu and Lao villages; the people of **Ban Ha** are exceptionally friendly. Here there is the OB Guesthouse with four rustic bungalows (10,000 kip per person) and a restaurant at the other end of the village. Both guesthouse and restaurant have incomparable views. Another 30 minutes' walk leads to **Ban Huay Baw**, from where you can reach the **Than Mok** waterfall by boat (see page 133). It is a 20-minute trip downstream to **Ban Sopkhong** (60,000 kip per boat), where you disembark for a one-hour walk to the waterfall. Villagers are more than obliging to assist in directions.

Muang Khua → *For listings, see pages 136-142. Colour map 1, B3. Phone code: 081.*

Muang Khua is nestled into the banks of the Nam Ou, close to the mouth of the Nam Phak, in the south of Phongsali Province. Hardly a destination in itself, it's usually just a stopover between Nong Khiaw and Phongsali. But Muang Khua is a great place to kick back for a few days, if you want to take a break from the well-worn travellers' path.

Located at the junction of two rivers and on Route 4 to Vietnam, Muang Khua has long been a crossroads between Vietnam and Laos. A French garrison was based in Muang Khua until 1954, when it was ousted by Vietnamese troops in the aftermath of the battle at Dien Bien Phu. For a brief period from 1958, Polish and Canadian officials of the Comité International de Contrôle were quartered in the town to monitor the ceasefire between the Pathet Lao and the Royal Lao government. Nowadays, Muang Khua is home to a burgeoning market in Vietnamese goods, trucked in from Dien Bien Phu. The border with Vietnam has now opened to tourists but the road is still under construction on the Lao side; a steady and increasing trickle of tourists seem to be making their way through on this route.

Muang Khua is a small, tidy-ish settlement with a line in buffalo and deer head trophies in nearly all the buildings' foyers and where the main focus seems to be on the car ferry that is towed by a ginormous metal line across the river. The morning market, which sometimes attracts Akha women, sells fresh vegetables and meat, while the goldsmith, off the main square, is usually surrounded by a small group watching his very delicate work.

There is a small tourist office at the top of the hill ① *Mon-Fri 0800-1130 and 1400-1600.* If it's closed, call T020-2284 8020 for trekking opportunities.

Around Muang Khua

The Akha, Khmu and Tai Dam are the main hilltribes in the area. The nearest villages are 20 km out of town and you will need a guide if you want to visit them. Trekking around Muang Khua is fantastic and still a very authentic experience, as this region remains largely unexplored by backpackers. The friendly villagers are very welcoming to foreigners, as they don't see as many here as in somewhere like Muang Sing. For these very reasons, it is important to tread lightly and adopt the most culturally sensitive principles: don't hand out sweets and always ask before taking a photograph. Treks usually run for one to three days and involve a homestay at a villager's house (usually the Village Chief). ▶▶ *See Activities and tours, page 139.*

Towards Phongsali

You can travel from Muang Khua to Phongsali either by truck, bus or boat. Trucks, on their way from Udomxai, depart from the nearby village of **Pak Nam Noi**; buy lunch from the market there before departure. The ride is a long one, made more difficult when the pickup is full. However, it's a great experience and the hilltribes you come across along the way are very interesting and the scenery toward the Phongsali end of the trip is

Border essentials: Sop-Hun-Tay Trang (Vietnam)

The border linking Vietnam's Dien Bien Phu with this part of Laos is now open daily 0800-1700. A Laos visa can be obtained on arrival, but Vietnamese visas cannot. There is limited transport on the Laos side to Muang Khua, and the road may still be under construction, so expect delays. There is a direct bus from Muang Khua to Dien Bien Phu, costing 50,000 kip, which lets you off for border formalities. It leaves from the opposite side of the river bank to Muang Khua at 0600.

utterly breathtaking. The road is also due to be paved which will reduce the travel time considerably. Alternatively, catch a boat direct from Muang Khua. It's also a beautiful trip, especially for birdwatching, with kingfishers everywhere. The river is quite shallow in places and there is a fair amount of white water, so take a blanket. Boats stop at **Hat Xa**, 20 km or so to the northeast of Phongsali, where you may find yourselves stuck, as there are no buses to Phongsali after mid-afternoon. ▸▸ *See Transport, page 141.*

Phongsali → *For listings, see pages 136-142. Colour map 1, A3. Phone code: 088.*

High up in the mountains at an altitude of about 1628 m, this northern provincial capital provides beautiful views and an invigorating climate. It is especially stunning from January to March, when wildflowers bloom in the surrounding hills. The town can be cold at any time of the year, so take some warm clothes. Mornings tend to be foggy and it can also be very wet. There is an end-of-the-earth feel in the areas surrounding the main centre, with dense pristine jungle surrounded by misty mountains.

Phongsali was one of the first areas to be liberated by the Pathet Lao in the late 1940s. The old post office (situated just in front of the new one) is the sole physical reminder of French rule. The town's architecture is a strange mix of Chinese post-revolutionary concrete blocks, Lao wood-and-brick houses with tin roofs, and bamboo or mud huts with straw roofs. The most attractive part of town is a series of shophouses that wind away from the Phongsaly hotel towards Hat Xa. The town itself is home to about 20,000 people, mostly Lao, Phou Noi and Chinese, while the wider district is a potpourri of ethnicities, with around 25 different minorities inhabiting the area. At the time of Footprint's visit there was talk of changing the district capital from Phongsali to Boun Neua, the site of the provincial airport.

The **Provincial Tourism Office** ① *signposted as 60 m off the main road, T088-210098, www. phongsali.net, Oct-Apr Mon-Fri 0800-1200 and 1330-1630, May-Sep Mon-Fri 0730-1130 and 1300-1600,* can arrange a variety of guided eco-treks, including village homestays, for up to five nights.

Around Phongsali

Many paths lead out of town over the hills; the walking is easy and the views are spectacular. It is not possible to hire bikes, tuk-tuks or even ponies here so walking is the only way to explore the fantastic landscapes of this region. Climb the 413 steps to the top of **Mount Phoufa** ① *4000 kip*, for views of the surrounding hills. There is also a **Museum of Tribes** ① *5000 kip*, with sketchy exhibits relating to some of the 25 ethnic minorities in the province. If you can hire transport, or walk, visit the rice wine-making and corn whisky (*lao-lao*)-making village of Ban Khounsouk Noi, 4.5 km north of town. The alcohol is not made on a daily basis but you may be lucky. Some people trek north from Phongsali to **Muang Uthai**, staying in Akha villages. Muang Uthai is as unspoilt as it gets. During the rainy season, it may be possible to take a boat back downriver from Uthai to Luang Prabang. The tourism office also runs one- and two-day treks including homestays in Akha villages. The Phu Den Din NPA is not yet open but the tourist office is exploring adventure tours in the area. ▸▸ *See Activities and tours, page139*.

Towards Udomxai
The road from Phongsali to Udomxai has been upgraded, but it remains only partially sealed for around 60 km; it is in good condition but the ride is bumpy. The surroundings and scenery are incredible. Break the journey at **Pak Nam Noi**, which lies at the intersection of the two roads going either to Muang Khua or Udomxai.

⊙ North of Luang Prabang listings

For Sleeping and Eating price codes and other relevant information, see pages 23-24.

⊜ Sleeping

Nam Bak *p132*
F-G Bounthiem, canary yellow building opposite the wat at the opposite end of town to the market, T071-253640. Friendly place with 5 double or twin rooms, clean, Comfortable mattresses, fans and mosquito nets. Balcony area, Western-style toilet downstairs and shower with hot water. Recommended.
F-G Khounvilay Guesthouse, next door to Bounthiem, T071-253647. Basic doubles, triples and twins. Quite scruffy with a squat toilet and shower out the back. Mosquito nets, cold drinks available. The friendly family owners are likely to invite you to share their evening meal – an extravaganza of spices that will blow your mouth away!
F-G Viengthong Guesthouse, 100 m past the bridge on the right. 9 very clean and comfortable rooms, singles, twins and doubles, with fan and mosquito nets. Separate Western-style toilet and scoop showers located downstairs. Free bottle of water on check-in.

Nong Khiaw and Ban Saphoun *p132*
D Riverside, turn off right beside the bridge in Ban Saphoun, T020-5570 5000,

www.nongkiau.com. Stunning modern bungalows and restaurant. The upscale rooms are beautifully decorated in modern Asian East-meets-West style, with 4-poster beds, mosquito nets and tiled hot-water bathrooms.. For those looking for something a little more upmarket than the average guesthouse, this exquisite place fits the bill perfectly. The restaurant has a great selection of wines, and internet is available. Book in advance as it is a favourite of the tour groups. Recommended.
E Sunset Guesthouse, down a lane about 100 m past the bridge, Ban Saphoun, T071-810033, sunsetgh2@hotmail.com. This guesthouse is slap bang on the bank of the river, and you couldn't ask for a better setting from which to watch the sunset. The charming, sprawling bamboo structure looks out onto various levels of decking that serve as a popular restaurant in the evenings. There are 13 wood and brick bungalows with decent bathrooms, including a Western toilet, and there are hot water showers outside. The twin-bedded rooms are more attractive than the doubles; breakfast included. Internet access.
F Bamboo Paradise, T071-810066. This friendly family has 6 rooms set back from the river. The beds, with mosquito nets, are extremely comfortable and the rooms seem, remarkably, impenetrable to bugs. Tepid water in the bathroom.

F-G Delilah (formerly Manipoon Guesthouse), near the post office, Nong Khiaw, T071-5632167. Four small stuffy upstairs rooms with fans and sunken mattresses. The shared bathrooms with squat toilets and tepid water are downstairs behind reception. It's a bit of a traipse. Restaurant attached with cluster bomb seating outside.

F-G Meexay Guesthouse, T020-5517 2304, in Ban Saphoun, just before **Sunset Guesthouse**. 5 spartan but clean rooms with modern and clean bathrooms, mosi nets and ceiling fans.

G CT Guesthouse (formerly Phanoy Guesthouse), just past the bridge, Ban Saphoun, T071-253919. Guesthouse has 7 basic but clean and comfortable thatched bungalows with mosquito nets and squat toilets. Inside bathroom. Fantastic verandas overlooking the river. Very nice family-owned business with a great atmosphere.

Muang Ngoi Neua *p133*

All accommodation in town is dirt cheap and the same standard: bungalows with hammocks on their balconies. Most offer a laundry service, clothes repair service and all have electricity 1800-2200 only. Theft has become a bit of a problem in Muang Ngoi Neua. Secure all windows and doors and do not leave any valuables in your room. Bring earplugs for the cockerels from 0400 and the wat gong at 0500.

E Ning Ning Guesthouse, T030-514 0863, behind the boat landing with a restaurant with a great ringside view for sunset. Double and twin bungalows, with separate Western-style toilet and hot shower; the smarter rooms have large comfy double beds and super-white linens and mosi nets; breakfast included. The food in the adjoining restaurant is great and the owner speaks good English. A popular spot.

F Aloune Mai, 100 m off the main road, T030-513 0290. This complex of 10 bungalows is set in a well-tended garden with mountain views. The rooms are quite

dark but there's a decent-sized bathroom (no hot water). There's an adjoining pizza restaurant (pizzas must be ordered by 1500 on the day for an evening pizza) and **Sky Bar**, see page 139.

F Lattanavongsa Guesthouse 1, T030-514 0770. Two cluster bombs line the steps leading up to these attractive bungalows, which front a garden on the northern side of the main road. There are polished floorboards, large beds and reasonably lit rooms with bathroom.

F Rainbow Guesthouse, T030-514 2296, muangngoi@yahoo.com. Just behind **Saylom** is this tasteful (but out of keeping with the area's character) concrete building with 10 doubles and twins; there's no hot water in the bathroom, but breakfast is included in the price.

F Veranda. The 5 rooms are lovely with slatted doors, hammocks, textiled counterpanes and mosquito nets. However, there is no hot water in bathrooms and, as the notice says, theft from the rooms has been a problem.

G Lattanavongsa Guesthouse 2, T030-514 0770. Situated closer to the river than its sister guesthouse, these 4 bungalows are fenced in around a garden, cluster bomb and picnic table, just beyond the main Lattanvongsa restaurant and near the dock. Decent-sized bathrooms.

G Phet Davanh Guesthouse, T020-2214 8777, on the main road, near the boat landing. Concrete guesthouse, with 7 double and twin rooms. Comfy mattresses on the floor; three shared Western toilets and shower. There's a well-positioned balcony on the second floor complete with hammocks. By the time you read this, **Penny's Place**, run by the same owner, will be open by the wat, with bungalows, an 8-room house and a dorm room facing the river.

G Saylom Guesthouse, T020-2243 0931. 6 bungalows right next to the boat dock overlooking the river with medium-sized rooms, bathrooms with Western toilet; no hot water.

Muang Khua p134

Electricity is only available from around 1800-2200.

E Sernnaly Hotel, in the middle of town, near the top of the hill, T021-414214. By far the most luxurious lodging in town. 18 rooms with large double and twin beds, hot water showers and Western-style toilets, immaculately clean. Some balconies overlook the Nam Ou. Chinese, Vietnamese and Lao food served in the restaurant. Breakfast included. You'll be fined 100,000 'kippers' if you don't obey the hotel rules says the notice in reception!

F Daosavan Guesthouse, turn left out of the bus station and walk for 5 mins, T081-210820. A nice, family-run 8-room guesthouse where some of the rooms are right over the river. The bright rooms, with firm beds, mosquito nets and fan, have squat toilet and cold-water shower.

G Keophila Guesthouse, almost at the top of the hill, T081-210807. A reasonably new building with 14 clean and tidy double and twin rooms, with hard beds and en suite hot-water shower rooms; rooms with shared shower room and squat toilets are along the corridor. There's a table on a balcony on the top floor overlooking the street.

G Nam Ou Guesthouse & Restaurant, follow the signs at the top of the hill, T081-210844. Looking out across the river, this guesthouse is the pick of the ultra-budget bunch in Muang Khua. Singles, twins and doubles, some with hot water en suites, and 3 newer rooms with river views. Rooms with en suite squat toilets are the same price as en suite with Western toilets. Good food (see Eating, below). A popular spot. Go for an upstairs room. Electricity 1745-2145.

G Singsavanh Guesthouse, on the top of the hill next to the market and bus station, T088-210812. Clean concrete structure. 6 basic twins and doubles, with mosquito net, and mattresses too thin for the beds; some have squat toilet and shower attached (no hot water). With or without bathroom, the price of the rooms is the same.

Towards Phongsali p134

F Hat Xa has 2 unsigned homestays for 30,000 and 40,000 kip a night.

Phongsali p135

E-F Phongsaly Hotel, around the corner from the Kaysone Monument, T088-210042. This 4-storey monstrosity has large and airy double and twin rooms with hot-water bathrooms. Views from the roof and a good restaurant. More expensive rooms have a/c.

F Viphaphone Hotel, next to the post office, T088-210111. This 3-storey building has 24 very clean, large and airy twin and double rooms, with excellent hot water bathrooms, some with Western flush toilets, some with squats but the building is very run down. There is a coffee table with chairs in most rooms as well as Laos tea. Good value.

F-G Sensaly Guesthouse, up the hill and around the bend from the market, T088-210165. A new building houses comfortable rooms with hot water showers, TV and fan. There are also worn but comfortable rooms in a concrete building, with squat toilets and scoop showers. The friendly owners will bring you hot water in the evening for the Lao tea provided in your room. If you end up in the cheaper rooms, opt for the first floor as the floorboards are paper thin.

G Yu Houa Guesthouse, across the road from the market, T088-210186. A 3-storey building with 6 clean twin and double rooms with hard beds, bathrooms and Western toilets. It's a little scruffy around the edges, but there are sweeping views of the valley from the rooms at the back. Restaurant downstairs.

Towards Udomxai p136

G Sinsay Guesthouse, Pak Nam Noi. Simple rooms.

❶ Eating

Nam Bak p132

Ψ Han Nang Nit, opposite the market. The best of 2 or 3 noodle shops. No English spoken but very friendly service – good place to wait for onward transport as the trucks stop outside.

Nong Khiaw and Ban Saphoun *p132*

Most of the guesthouses have cafés attached. For fine dining the restaurant at the **Riverside** (see Sleeping) is absolutely fantastic, with an extensive wine list to boot. For those on a budget the **CT Guesthouse** does reasonably good food; the pizzas are passable. Ask for dishes to be served with *jeow* (chilli jam) – delicious.

Muang Ngoi Neua *p133*

Aside from the many guesthouse restaurants, which serve good quality Lao food, there are also a number of places to eat along the main road. Most have exactly the same food on offer; in fact, many of them just copy their competitors' menus. The fruit shake stands in the centre of town are good value.

¶-¶ Sainamgoi Restaurant & Bar, in the centre of town. Tasty Lao food in a pleasant atmosphere, with good background music. There's a bar, the only one in town, in the next room.

¶ Nang Phone Keo Restaurant, on the main road. All the usual Lao food plus some extras: try the 'falang roll' for breakfast (a combination of peanut butter, sticky rice and vegetables).

¶ Sengdala Restaurant & Bakery, along the main road. Very good, cheap Lao food, terrific pancakes and freshly baked baguettes.

¶ Sky Bar & Restaurant is ambient in the evening although the food is not great (see Sleeping above).

Muang Khua *p134*

This is a small town with very few eateries, although what it lacks in restaurants, it makes up for in pool tables; very small children show a frightening aptitude and you should be prepared to have an instant audience if you try your hand; there is

usually a box in which you are expected to make a donation.

Noodles and baguettes are available in the market.

¶-¶ Nam Ou Guesthouse & Restaurant (see Sleeping), up the mud slope from the beach. An incomparable location for a morning coffee overlooking the river; it has an English menu and friendly staff.

¶-¶ Restaurant opposite the Singsavanh Guesthouse. Tasty fried noodles and rice dishes and an English menu.

¶ Restaurant next door to **Keophila Guesthouse**. Serves nice and cheap Vietnamese-style *feu*.

Towards Phongsali *p134*

¶ Hat Xa. There is a noodle shop on the hill towards Phongsali, above the dock, which serves noodle soup and sells biscuits, etc.

Phongsali *p135*

The rice here is steamed rather than sticky. There are *feu* stalls opposite the market.

¶ Phongsaly Hotel (see Sleeping). A good bet, with a variety of dishes including Thai, Chinese and Lao.

¶ Yu Houa Guesthouse (see Sleeping). A short Lao and Chinese section on an English menu. Cheap and good.

▲ Activities and tours

Nong Khiaw and Ban Saphoun *p132*

Bicycles can be rented from Tiger Trails, next to Delilah's for 35,000 kip per day. There's a movie house on the main road marked 'Cinema'. Check out www.nongkiauclimbing.com in association with **Green Discovery**.
Lao Youth Travel, at the boat landing, www.laoyouthtravel.com. It offers trekking, fishing, tubing, boat trips and kayaking.
Tiger Trails, www.laos-adventure.com. Runs trips to the 100 waterfalls, 3 hrs, 260,000 kip per person; 1-day Payong trail trek, 240,000 kip per person; half-day local trek, 130,000 kip per person; 2-day Phatup Nai-trek, 560,000 kip per person; day trip to

Hat Sao (with boat), 220,000 kip per person. Office open daily 0800-1130, 1330-1600 and 1830-2100.

Muang Ngoi Neua p133

Trekking, hiking, fishing, kayaking, trips to the waterfalls and boat trips can be organized through most guesthouses. Tubing can be arranged for 1000 kip though Lao Youth Travel does not recommend tubing here because of the dangers.
Lao Youth Travel, T030-514 0046, www. laoyouthtravel.com. Daily 0730-2000. Half-day, day, overnight or 2- and 3-night treks, starting from US$34 per person. Also kayaking (US$43 for two) and fishing trips (US$47 for two). Some 85% of funds goes back into the community and KYT has partnered with the Bamboo School Foundation (www.die-bambussschule.de) to build a school in Ban Houay Lor. To Ba Na (a Lao Lum village), Ban Houay Lor (a Lao Loum and Khmu village) and Tham Ka (US$38). Ask for the excellent Peeng, who has a good command of English; he is a rice farmer and part-time guide who can show you his plot.

Phongsali p135
Trekking

The **tourism office** can arrange guided treks around Boun Neua and Phongsali with homestays for 400,00 kip for 1 day for 2 people or 800,000 for 2 days. It will also arrange visits to 400-year old tea trees at a plantation at Ban Komaen, where a homestay is also possible.
Northern Traveling and Information Service Center, on the main road, not far from Yu Houa restaurant, T088-210594, northerntraveletr@yahoo.com. Offers 15 treks ranging from 1-5 days with prices starting at 300,000 kip for 1 person. Also offers internet and phone calls, and motorbike rental is available for 150,000-180,000 kip per day.

Most of the tour agencies in Luang Prabang and Luang Namtha run group treks around Phongsali.

⊖ Transport

Nam Bak p132

There are regular trucks/buses to **Luang Prabang**. To **Nong Khiaw**, 1 hr by truck on a good road. In theory, the trucks wait for the boats to arrive from Luang Prabang and Muang Khua. To **Muang Ngoi Neua**, 0700 and throughout the day as soon as they're full, 7000 kip; be prepared to wait around for a few hours, tuk-tuks are more frequent for the same price. To **Udomxai** (94 km), you need to take a *songthaew* to **Pak Mong**, 10 km west of Nam Bak, 8000 kip, and change there for a bus to Udomxai, 3 hrs, 15,000 kip. To **Nam Nouan**, flag down one of the vehicles from Vientiane travelling east along Route 1, which usually pass the market at around 2000, 60,000 kip.

Nong Khiaw and Ban Saphoun p132
Boat

Boat services have become irregular following road improvements, although you may find a service to **Muang Ngoi Neua**, 1 hr, 20,000 kip, from the boat landing. Boats to Luang Prabang only run if enough people want to make the trip, so you need to wait a couple of days, 100,000 kip per person, minimum 10 people or charter the whole boat, 7-8 hrs. Some vessels head upriver to **Muang Khua**, 5 hrs, 100,000 kip per person, minimum 10 people. The river trips from Nong Khiaw are spectacular.

Bus/truck

Buses en route from surrounding destinations stop in Nong Khiaw briefly. Basic time-tables are offered but buses can be hours early or late, so check details on the day. It is often a matter of waiting at the bus station for hours and hoping to catch the bus on its way through. Plonking yourself in a restaurant on the main road usually suffices but you will need to flag down the bus as it passes through town. To **Luang Prabang**, 3-4 hrs, by *songthaew* at 0900 and 1100, 35,000 kip; minibus at 1300, 50,000 kip. Also several departures daily to **Nam Bak**, 30 mins, 10,000 kip and on to **Udomxai**, 1100, 4 hrs, 40,000 kip.

Alternatively, you could take one of the more regular *songthaew* to **Pak Mong**, 1 hr, 20,000 kip, where there is a small noodle shop-cum-bus station on the west side of the bridge, and then catch another vehicle on to Udomxai/ Vientiane (see Nam Bak Transport, above).

Travelling east on Route 1, there are buses to **Vieng Kham**, 0900, 2 hrs, 25,000 kip, and a village 10 km from **Nam Nouan**, where you can change and head south on Route 6 to **Phonsavanh** and the **Plain of Jars**. There are direct buses north to **Xam Neua** and the village near Nam Nouan, which can be caught from the toll gate on the Ban Saphoun side of the river when it comes through from Vientiane at around 2000-2200, 100,000 kip; it's usually quite crowded. If you miss a bus to or from Nong Khiaw you can always head to **Pak Mong** which is a junction town sitting at the crossroads to Luang Prabang, Nong Khiaw and Udomxai. You should aim to arrive here early in the day in order to catch through traffic; if you don't, you may find yourself stranded and need to stay overnight. (If this does happen, try the **Pak Mong Guesthouse Restaurant**, T020-5579 5860, or any of the other 6 places in town.)

Muang Ngoi Neua *p133*
Boat
From the landing at the northern end of town, slow boats travel north along the beautiful Nam Ou river, surrounded by mountainous scenery, to **Muang Khua**, 5 hrs, 100,000 kip per person, minimum 10 people. Slow boats also go south (irregularly) to **Nong Khiaw**, 1 hr, 25,000 kip per person (minimum 10 people), and **Luang Prabang**, 8 hrs, US$100 per boat. Departure times vary and depends on there being sufficient passengers. For more information and to buy tickets, consult the booth at the landing.

Towards Phongsali *p134*
Hat Xa. A bus transports travellers on from Hat Xa to Phongsali, 20 km, 1.5-2 hrs along a very bad road at 1000 and 1430, 10,000 kip. Alternatively, charter whatever transport is available which might not be much; the sand trucks go back and forth though.

Muang Khua *p134*
Boat
Road travel is now more popular but irregular boats still travel south on the Nam Ou to **Muang Ngoi Neua/Nong Khiaw**, 3 hrs to Muang Ngoi Neua, 100,000 kip, if there is enough demand at 0900 and 1000. Also north to **Phongsali** via **Hat Xa**, 4-6 hrs, 90,000-100,000 kip per person, minimum 10 people at 0900 and 1000. Boats can be charted to Phongsali for around US$110. From Hat Xa to Phongsali, see the section Towards Phongsali above. From Muang Khua to **Nong Khiaw**, 120,000 kip per person, 4 hrs at 0900 and 1000 but only if there are 10 people. To **Luang Prabang** also leaving at 0900 and 1000, 8 hrs, 230,000 kip per person (minimum 10 people); more expensive by speed boat (4 hrs).

You can travel from Muang Khua to **Phongsali** either by truck or by boat. Trucks also depart from **Pak Nam Noi** (near Muang Khua); buy lunch from the market before departure, 20,000 kip. The ride is long and difficult when the pickup is full, but it's a great experience: the hill tribes along the way are interesting and the scenery towards Phongsali is breathtaking. Alternatively, catch a boat from Muang Khua to **Hat Xa**, 20 km or so to the northeast of Phongsali, 3-5 hrs, 90,000 kip per person, minimum 10 people for a slow boat; a speed boat is cheaper (850,000 kip minimum) but not recommended. Boats are scheduled at 0900 and 1000 but won't leave without enough passengers. In the low season, there may not be any scheduled boats but you could gather up a few more interested tourists and charter a boat for around US$110. Depending on the season, the river is shallow in places, with a fair amount of whitewater. It can be cold and wet so wear waterproofs and take a blanket. Tatty life jackets are available but you will need to request them before setting out as they are not stashed on the boats.

Hat Xa *p135*
Songthaew/truck
The bus station is next to the Singsavanh guesthouse. To get to **Phongsali**, take a *songthaew* to the nearby village **Pak Nam Noi**, daily 0800, 1 hr, 10,000 kip, then take the *songthaew* or bus that passes through from Udomxai at around 1000, 9 hrs, 50,000 kip.

To **Udomxai**, buses leave daily 0800, 1200, 1530, from the bus station alongside the market, 3 hrs, 30,000 kip, and to **Luang Prabang**, 8 hrs, US$7. Buses also now travel to **Sop Hun** for the border crossing to Vietnam at **Tay Trang**. See box, page135.

Phongsali *p135*
Air
Phongsavanh Airlines Group (T021-513 0000) now operates to and from **Vientiane**. Boun Neua airport (PSL), is 1½-hr bus ride from Phongsali.

Bus/truck and boat
Buses to **Hat Xa** leave at 0730-0800 and 1300, 10,000 kip from the bus station, about 500 m from the centre of Phongsali on the road to Hat Xa (If walking, leave 30 mins' walking time). To **Udomxai**, 0740, 65,000 kip; to **Pak Nam Noi** 50,000 kip; to **Luang Prabang**, 0800; to **Boun Neua** at 0715.

If you want to charter a minivan to Udomxai, this is possible through the tourist office for around 1,700,000 kip. The road is sealed for around 60 km south of Phongsali to Ban Yo and from then it is unsealed but in good condition. The journey to Udomxai is around 8½ hrs.

For boat information see under **Muang Khua**, Transport, page 141. For motorbike hire see Activities and Tours above. For

information on getting to the Vietnamese border, see box page 135.

ⓘ Directory

Nam Bak *p132*
Bank There's an exchange by the market.
Post The post office is 100 m west of the market.

Nong Khiaw and Ban Saphoun *p132*
Internet Sunset and Riverside guesthouses (see Sleeping) offer internet access. **Post** The post office is located on the Nong Khiaw side of the bridge.

Muang Ngoi Neua *p133*
Bank Lattanavongsa Money Exchange.

Muang Khua *p134*
Bank Lao Development Bank, near the truck stop, Mon-Fri 0800-1130 and 1300-1630, can change US$, Thai baht and Chinese ¥ for kip at quite poor rates. They won't change TCs or do cash advances on credit cards, so make sure you have plenty of cash before you come here. **Electricity** Daily 1830-2200. **Post** The post office is opposite the wat; turn right at the top of the hill. **Telephone** International calls can be made from the Telecom office, a small unmarked hut with a huge satellite, halfway up the winding road, behind the bank, daily 0700-1130, 1300-1630.

Phongsali *p135*
Banks There is a branch of the Lao Development Bank, 20 m along from Phonsaly Hotel. It will only change US$, Thai baht and Chinese ¥. There is a branch of Western Union too. **Internet** is available at the Northern Traveling Center for 300 kip/min. **Post** The post office is just along the road from the Viphahone. **Telephone** Calls can be made from Lao Telecom Office, next door to the post office, or international calls can be made from the Northern Traveling Center.

Northwest Laos

Northwestern Laos comprises dramatic, misty mountainous scenery, clad with thick forests and peppered with small villages. This area is home to a variety of ethnic minority groups including the Akha, Hmong, Khmu and Yao and is a firm favourite with trekkers. The mighty Mekong forges its way through picturesque towns, such as Pak Beng and Houei Xai, affording visitors a wonderful glimpse of riverine life. ▸▸ *For listings, see pages 153-164.*

Udomxai (Oudom Xai) and around → *For listings, see pages 153-164.*

Colour map 1, B3. Phone code: 081.

Udomxai, the capital of Udomxai Province, is a hot and dusty town that is used as a pit-stop and a brothel stop but the local tourist board, with the help of a German NGO, is keen to promote the area's other attractions, see below. Udomxai was razed during the war and the inhabitants fled to live in the surrounding hills; what is here now has been built since 1975, which explains why it is such an ugly settlement. Since the early 1990s, the town has been experiencing an economic boom – as a result of its position at the intersection of roads linking China, Vietnam, Luang Prabang and Pak Beng – and commerce and construction are thriving. It also means that Udomxai has a large Chinese and Vietnamese population, a fact that appears to rile the locals.

The town's truck-stop atmosphere doesn't enamour it to tourists and, unfortunately, the other bad elements which come with major transport thoroughfares seem to be raising their heads here too, such as prostitution and increased HIV/AIDS. However, the town does make a decent stop-off point at a convenient junction; it's one of the biggest settlements in northern Laos and has excellent facilities. The **Provincial Tourism Office** ① *near the river on the main road in the centre of town, T081-212482, www.oudomxay.info, Oct-Mar Mon-Fri 0800-1200 and 1330-1600, Apr-Sep Mon-Fri 0730-1200 and 1330-1600*, can offer helpful advice.

Udomxai

Udomxai Province is populated by 23 different ethnic minority groups, with strong contingents of Hmong, Akha and Khmu. The village of **Ban Ting**, behind Udomxai is interesting to wander through. Its wat, just the other side of the stream, has a ruined monastery and a bizarre life-size tree made of concrete, with tin leaves, concrete animals in the foliage and two reclining Buddhas mounted on the topmost branches. The wat also includes a Buddhist high school for monks and offers a good view of the town and surrounding mountains.

The local tourism authorities have teamed up with **Udomxai Travel** to offer treks in the **Houay Nam Kat Nature Reserve** and to the **Nam Kat** waterfall. A few tourists who have gone on the trip have reported only a trickle of water from the falls.

Biking and trekking tours to ethnic minority villages are also available from the friendly Mr Ken of Saamlan cycling. ▸▸ *See Activities and tours, page 159.*

Muang La

Muang La is located 28 km north of Udomxai, off Route 4 to Phongsali, and makes a lovely stop en route. **Wat Ban Pakkla** is considered one of the most sacred temples in the area, due to the presence of a 400-year-old, gold-plated Buddha image, known as the Pra Xaek

Visiting an Akha village

Many people have complained that visiting tribal villages is similar to visiting a human zoo. Here are some tips on how to avoid this experience:
• Always visit an Akha village with an Akha or locally endorsed guide rather than on your own.
• Never touch the spirit symbol, spirit gate, spirit house or swing and do not walk through the Akha entrance gate.

Touching any of these things is believed to bring bad luck to the village.
• If you wish to give gifts, such as money, to the Akha people, these should be offered only to the village chief.
• Accept food and drink if it is offered to you. The Akha may also offer you a massage; it's OK to accept.
• Rather than watching people go about their work, ask if you can help them.

Kham. Steeped in superstition and highly auspicious, the temple is the place to go if you want to make your dreams come true.

Muang La has gained popularity with travellers for its hot springs. Set in beautiful surroundings, the springs are a favourite spot for locals, who come for a dip in the very hot waters. If you bathe here, wear a sarong or something discreet. The other section of the springs has been cordoned off and is part of the Muang La Resort, see Sleeping.

Muang Houn → *Colour map 1, B2.*

This is a new town (although it looks as old as any other), built in 1986 by the government to entice people down from the hills, in an attempt to stop them growing opium. There are quite a number of Blue Hmong in town.

Luang Namtha and around → *For listings, see pages 153 -164. Colour map 1, B2.*

→ Phone code: 086.

The provincial capital was obliterated during the war and the concrete structures erected since 1975 have little charm. As in other towns in the north of Laos, the improvement in transport links with China and Thailand has led to burgeoning trade. The main attraction is the food market, where members of the many minorities who inhabit the area can be found selling exotic species. Despite the presence of this dubious trade, the area has established itself as a major player in Laos' ecotourism industry, primarily due to the Nam Ha National Protected Area (see page 147) and the environmentally friendly **Boat Landing Guesthouse** (see page 154).

Getting there and around

There are three flights a week from Vientiane. The airport is 6 km from the city centre; a tuk-tuk costs 20,000 kip per person into town. Buses arrive from Houey Xai at the Thai border, from the Chinese border at Boten and from Udomxai and Luang Prabang. The new intra-provincial bus station is 10 km from town; a tuk-tuk to town should cost about 10,000 kip per person, 15-10 minutes. Inter-provincial buses arrive 100 m south of the town strip.

Tourist information

The **Luang Namtha Provincial Tourism Office and Eco Guide Unit** ① *T086-211534, www. luangnamtha-tourism.org, Mon-Fri 0800-1200 and 1330-2030, Sat-Sun 0815-1200 and 1330-*

2000, is a bit of a shambles with a can't-quite-be-bothered-attitude. You'll get warmer and better service from Green Discovery.

Sights

The **Luang Namtha Museum** ① *near the Kaysone Monument, Mon-Fri 0800-1130, 1300-1600, 10,000 kip*, is worth a visit. The museum houses a collection of indigenous clothing and artefacts, agricultural tools, weapons, textiles and a collection of Buddha images, drums and gongs.

In the centre of town is the fledgling **night market** with a range of foodstalls. Only in its infancy, the local authorities have aspirations to expand the market to include ethnic handicrafts like the one in Luang Prabang.

The old **That Poum Pouk** ① *3 km west of the airfield, 5000 kip entrance*, sits in a ruinous state on a hill. Local sources suggest that the stupa was built as part of a competition between the Lanna Kingdom (in northern Thailand) and the Lane Xang Kingdom to prove which of the two kingdoms had the most merit. Severe damage due to bombing in 1964 led local villagers and monks to reconstruct the stupa but this proved a fruitless exercise as further bombing in 1966 dislodged the stupa, parts of which can still be seen lying on the ground. Incredibly, much of the original stucco and an incripted stelae survived the attacks. A new stupa has been built behind the ruined one.

The trip to That Poum Pouk is most pleasant in the afternoon; tuk-tuks will do the return trip from Luang Namtha's market for 60,000 kip.

Villages around Luang Namtha

Luang Namtha Province has witnessed the rise and decline of various Tai Kingdoms and now over 30 ethnic groups reside in the province, making it the most ethnically diverse province in the country. Principal minorities residing here include Tai Lue, Tai Dam, Lanten, Hmong and Khamu. There are a number of friendly villages around the town of Luang Namtha. As with all other minority areas, you should only visit the villages with a local guide or endorsed tourism organization.

Ban Nam Chang is a Lanten village 3 km walk along a footpath outside Luang Namtha; ask the way. Lanten women are easily recognized: they wear their hair back and pluck their eyebrows from the age of 15. Their clothes are black, with coloured borders, and they wear a lot of delicate silver jewellery.

Ban Lak Khamay is quite a large Akha village 27 km from Luang Namtha on the

Luang Namtha

To Muang Sing & Udomxai

Luang Namtha Museum
Kaysone Monument
Luang Namtha Provincial Tourism Office & Eco Guide Unit
NIT @
Lao Telecom ♪
Bike Rental
Night Market
Green Discovery
@ KNT
Intra-Provincial Bus Station

To ⑩⑫, Boat Landing, Airport, Lao Airlines, That Poum Park, Inter-Provincial Bus Station & Houei Xai

N

100 metres
100 yards

Sleeping ⬭
Adounsiri 1
Boat Landing Guesthouse & Restaurant 12
Luang Namtha Guesthouse 7
Manychan Guesthouse 4
Thoulasith Guesthouse 3
Vila Guesthouse 10
Zuela Guesthouse 5

Eating ⊙
Bakery 1
Banana 3
Coffee House 6
Panda 4
Yamuna 4

road to Muang Sing. It was resettled from a nearby location higher in the hills in 1994 as part of a government programme to protect upland forests. The community now grows teak and rubber trees. The village chief speaks Lao. The settlement features a traditional Akha entrance; if you pass through this entrance you must visit a house in the village, or you will be considered an enemy. Otherwise you can simply pass to one side of the gate, but be careful not to touch it. Other features of interest in Akha villages are the swing, which is located at the highest point in the village and used in the annual swing festival (you must not touch the swing), and the meeting house, where unmarried couples go to court and where newly married couples live until they have their own house. There is another, smaller Akha village a few kilometres on towards Muang Sing. ▶▶ *See also Visiting an Akha village, page 144.*

Ban Nam Dee is a small bamboo paper-making Lanten village located about 6 km northeast of Luang Namtha. The name of the village means 'good water' and, not surprisingly, if you continue on from Ban Nam Dee for 1 km, you will come to a waterfall. The trip to the village is particularly scenic, passing through verdant green rice paddies dotted with huts. A motorbike rather than a bicycle will be necessary to navigate these villages and sights as the road is very rocky in places and unsuitable for cyclists. Villagers usually charge 5000 kip for access to the waterfall.

The small Tai Lue village of **Ban Khone Kam** is also worth a visit. The settlement is based on the banks of the Nam Tha, halfway between Luang Namtha and Houei Xai, and is only accessible by boat or by foot. The friendly villagers offer **homestays** here (30,000 kip per night, includes meals), for one or two nights, providing an interesting cultural insight into the daily lives of the region's boatmen and rice farmers.

Ban Vieng Nua, 3 km from the centre of town, is a Tai Kolom village famous for its traditional house where groups can experience local dancing and a good luck baci ceremony (150,000 kip per person). Contact the tourist information office (see page 144) for further information and to make bookings. Dinner can also be organized here at a cost of 42,000 kip per head.

Vieng Phouka and around

Before the roads in the region were upgraded, Vieng Phouka was the place to stay overnight when travelling between Luang Namtha or Muang Sing and the Mekong. Located south of Luang Namtha (and 125 km north of Houei Xai), the town is surrounded by a variety of minority villages – Akha, Hmong, Lahu and Khmu, with the Khmu comprising about 90% of the population. The local tourism authority ① *Vieng Phouka Eco Guide Service, T081-212400 (T020-5598 5289 mob), www.luangnamtha-tourism.org*, organizes treks in the surrounding area, which is not as busy as Luang Namtha and is recommended by trekkers. By the end of 2010 there should be a canopy walk in the Nam Ha Protected Area close to Vieng Phouka. ▶▶ *See Activities and tours, page 159.*

The 5-km-long **Nam Aeng cave**, located 12 km north of Vieng Phouka, is famous locally for an annual ceremony held on 13 January, when elders call up the large fish that inhabit part of the cave. The **Nom Cave**, a four-hour walk from the town, was once home to a famous sacred Buddha, but this has now been pilfered. During the revolution the Nom Cave served as a hideout. Around the area are a few scattered remains of the wall from the ancient city of Kuvieng, much of which has been dismantled by local villagers at the government's insistence.

Both Luang Namtha and Vieng Phouka make great bases from which to venture into the **Nam Ha National Protected Area** (NPA), one of a few remaining places on earth

The border between Boten (Laos) and Mohan (China) is open to international traffic daily 0800-1600. There have been reports of some citizens getting Chinese visas here but it depends on your nationality, so if you plan to do this be sure to check in advance (it is less risky to organize a visa in advance in Vientiane). Tourist visas cost US$70-150, depending on nationality. US citizens are unable to obtain visas at this crossing (the nearest Chinese embassy is in Vientiane).

After crossing into China, the first town you come to is Mengla (two hours from Boten). But Mengla is a nasty introduction to China, reverberating with the tiresome sounds of karaoke and prostitutes until the early hours. It is better to try to get to the much better town of Jinghong or Chieng Houng (five hours from Mengla).

Coming into Laos from China, you can pick up a 30-day Lao visa at the border or in advance from the Lao consulate in Kunming, which is located inside the Camelia Hotel (T0871-317 6624); the latter usually takes three working days to process or 24 hours on payment of a surcharge.

You can change remaining yuan into Lao kip at the border. The bus station is a walk down the hill. There is only limited accommodation in Boten so if you want to make it to Luang Namtha, you should aim to cross the border in the morning when there are a lot of buses, rather than in the afternoon when there are fewer and you could find yourself stranded. If there isn't a direct bus, take the first bus to Udomxai and change at Natuei. If you want to go to Vientiane and there isn't a direct bus, your best bet is to catch a bus to Udomxai and transfer there to Vientiane/Luang Prabang. .

where the rare black-cheeked crested gibbon can be found (see below). If you're lucky, you can hear the wonderful singing of the gibbons in the morning.

Nam Ha National Protected Area

This area has firmly established itself as a major player in Laos' ecotourism industry, primarily due to the **Nam Ha Ecotourism Project**, which was established in 1993 by NTA Lao and UNESCO to help preserve Luang Namtha's cultural and environmental heritage in the Nam Ha National Protected Area. The Nam Ha NPA is one of the largest protected areas in Laos and consists of mountainous areas dissected by several rivers. It is home to at least 38 species of large mammal, including the black-cheeked crested gibbon, tiger and clouded leopard, and over 300 bird species, including the Blythe's kingfisher. The Nam Ha project has won a UN development award for its outstanding achievements in the area.

The organization currently leads two- and three-day treks in the area for small groups of four to eight. The treks offer the chance to visit traditional villages, explore various forest habitats, take river trips and support local conservation efforts. A relatively new trek to **Phu Sam Yord**, Three Peak Mountain, has recently been unveiled. The trek is a fantastic way to witness a variety of cultures, partake in local village activities and see stunning landscapes. New, longer routes to other villages are also being explored. Treks leave three to four times a week; check with the **Luang Namtha Eco Guide Unit** (see 144) or **Green Discovery** (see Tour operators, page 159) for departures; an information session about the trek is given at the Guide's Office. Prices cover the cost of food, water, transportation, guides, lodging and the trekking permit. All the treks utilize local guides who have been trained to help generate income for their villages. Income for conservation purposes is also garnered from the fees for trekking permits into the area. A new Information Centre is due to open at Chalensouk, the access point to the Nam Ha NPA, south of Luang Namtha. ▸▸ *See Activities and tours, page 159.*

Boten → *Colour map 1, B2.*
Boten lies on the border with China and, until recently, was nothing more than a trucking stop for drivers, with a couple of guesthouses here and a handful of noodle shops. However, the town is set for dramatic change, with the construction of the massive Chinese-funded 'Golden Boten City' project. The 10-year project aims to build warehouses, several marketplaces, 2000 hotel rooms and 500 guesthouses, entertainment venues and a golf course. The first foundation stone was laid in 2005 but whether these grandiose plans actually come to fruition remains to be seen. The city project is hoping to capitalize on the upgrading of Highway R3, which will eventually run from Kunming, China, through Luang Namtha and Bokeo provinces to Bangkok, Thailand (see also box, page 147).

Muang Sing → *For listings, see page 153-164. Colour map 1, B2.*

Many visitors consider this peaceful valley to be one of the highlights of the north. Lying at the terminus of the highway in the far northwest corner of Laos, it is a natural point to stop and spend a few days recovering from the rigours of the road, before either heading south or moving on to China. This area is a border region that has been contested by the Chinese, Lao and Thai at various points in the last few centuries. While it is now firmly Lao territory, there is a gnawing sense that the Chinese have again invaded by stealth; their economic presence is all too evident. There are also several NGOs, as well as bilateral and multilateral development operations in the area. The only way to get to Muang Sing is by bus or pickup from Luang Namtha. The road is asphalt and the terrain on this route is mountainous with dense forest.

Tourist information
Muang Sing Tourism Office ① *T086-400015, www.luangnamtha-tourism.org, Mon-Fri 0800-1130 and 1330-1700, Sat-Sun 0800-1000 and 1500-1700,* offers one-, two- and three-day treks from 300,000 kip per person (minimum two people). Tuk-tuk tours are also offered of Muang Sing and Xieng Kok.

Sights
Muang Sing itself is little more than a supremely picturesque village, situated on an upland plateau, where golden rattan huts glow among misty blue-green peaks. The town features some interesting old wooden and brick buildings and, unlike nearby Luang Namtha and several other towns in the north, it wasn't bombed close to oblivion during the struggle for Laos. The **old French fort**, built in the 1920s, is off limits to visitors, as it is occupied by the Lao army, but the relocated market is certainly worth a look if you're up very early in the morning; it starts about 0600 and begins to wind down after 0800. Along with the usual array of plastic objects, clothes and pieces of hardware, local silk and cotton textiles can be purchased. Numerous hill peoples come to the market to trade, including Akha and Hmong tribespeople, along with Yunnanese, Tai Dam and Tai Lue.

The **Muang Sing Ethnic Museum** ① *in the centre of town, daily 0800-1200 and 1300-1600, 5000 kip; Akha documentary, 5,000 kip,* is a beautiful building housing a range of traditional tools, ethnic clothes, jewellery, instruments, religious artefacts and household

Opium

Most ethnic groups in Muang Sing still live traditionally and practise slash-and-burn agriculture, growing rice, corn and even some cotton. Many of the local Akha villages were originally built on slopes as high as 600-1500 m but the government relocated villages down to 400-600 m in an attempt to eradicate opium farming in the hills. For a long time Muang Sing was highly reliant on the opium trade, with the drug used for medicinal purposes for over a hundred years. The government crackdown (in the face of international pressure) has impoverished many farmers, but despite the government's best efforts opium is still readily available to buy in the town. Needless to say, don't buy it under any circumstances.

One tourist who had taken too much opium ran naked into an ethnic minority village in the middle of the night, only to be beaten up by local villagers who thought an evil ghost (*pii*) had come to attack their village. There are two morals to this story: never take opium and always dress modestly in Laos.

items, like the loom. The building was once the royal residence of the Cao Fa (Prince), Phaya Sekong. Most Buddhist monasteries in the vicinity are Tai Lue in style. The most accessible is **Wat Sing Chai**, on the main road.

Around Muang Sing

The area around Muang Sing is home to many minorities who have been resettled, either from refugee camps in Thailand or from highland areas of Laos. The town is predominantly Tai Lue but the district is 50% Akha, with a further 10% Tai Neua. The population of the district is said to have trebled between 1992 and 1996 and, as a result, it is one of the few places in northern Laos where hilltribe villages are readily accessible. The main activity for visitors is to hire bicycles and visit the villages that surround the town in all directions; several guesthouses have maps of the surrounding area and trekking is becoming increasingly popular. However, please do not undertake treks independently as it undermines the government's attempts to make tourism sustainable and minimize the impact on the culture of local villages.

From Muang Sing, trek uphill past **Stupa Mountain Lodge** for 1 km to reach **That Xieng Tung**, the most sacred site in the area. The stupa was built in 1256 and is believed to contain the Buddha's adam's apple. It attracts lots of pilgrims in November for the annual full moon festival. Originally a city was built around the stupa but everyone migrated down to lower lands. There is a small pond near the stupa, which is believed to be auspicious: if it dries up it is considered bad luck for Muang Sing. It is said that the pond once dried up and the whole village had no rice and starved. Most tourism operators will run treks up to the stupa and a stop at Nam Keo waterfall, a large cascade with a 10-m drop, 7 km from the guesthouse. It's a nice place for a picnic. The local tourism authority runs treks to the falls for US$42 per person including guide and transport. Bring good shoes.

Muang Long is being developed as a trekking centre. There is a tourism office that will arrange six treks from one to five days. The office is run by Mr Bounbang, T020-5519 5561 (mob), www.luangnamtha-tourism.org. There are a few guesthouses (30,000-50,000 kip).

On the 13-14 and 28-29 of each month at Xieng Kok a market is held to which all the local minorities come. The Muang Sing tourism office organizes tuk-tuk tours. ▶▶ *See Activities and tours, page 160.*

Houei Xai (Houay Xai) → *Phone code: 084. Colour map 1, B1.*

This town is in the heart of the Golden Triangle and used to derive its wealth from the narcotics trade on the heroin route to Chiang Mai in Thailand. Today trade still brings the town considerable affluence, although it is rather less illicit: timber is ferried across the Mekong from Laos to the Thai town of Chiang Khong and, in exchange, consumer goods are shipped back. Sapphires are mined in the area and, doubtless, there is also still some undercover heroin smuggling.

Houei Xai is a popular crossing point for tourists travelling to and from Thailand and a considerable amount of money flows in from the numerous guesthouses and restaurants that have been built here. However, few people spend more than one night in the town. Most passengers arrive at the passenger ferry pier, close to the centre. The vehicle ferry pier is 750 m further north (upstream), while the post office is about 500 m south, on the edge of town. Although the petite, picturesque town is growing rapidly as links with Thailand intensify, it is still small and easy enough to get around on foot. **Lao National Tourism State Bokeo** ① *on the main street up from immigration, T084-211162, Mon-Fri 0800-1130 and 1330-1600*, can offer limited advice.

Wat Chom Kha Out Manirath, in the centre of town, is worth a visit for its views. The monastery was built at the end of the 19th century but, because it is comparatively well endowed, there has been a fair amount of re-building and renovation since then. There is also a large former French fort here called Fort Carnot, currently used by the Lao army (and consequently out of bounds), which is to be redeveloped as a tourist spot by the LNTA.

The **Morning Market** can be entertaining, particularly for first-time visitors who have entered from Thailand, as this will be their first experience of a Lao market. There is little of note about the products on display but local tribespeople come from their villages to sell things here. To get there, take a tuk-tuk (3000 kip). There is a **sapphire mine** south of the town, near the fast boat terminal. The miners pan in the morning and clean the stones in the afternoon, so the afternoon is the best time to visit.

Most visitors who stick around Houei Xai do so to visit the **Gibbon Experience** ① *T084-212021, www.gibbonx.org, from €180 for 2 nights including treehouse accommodation, transport, food, access to Bokeo Nature Reserve and well-trained guides*, a thrilling, exciting and unmissable three-day trip into **Bokeo Nature Reserve** where a number of treehouses have been built high in the jungle canopy and linked with a course of interconnected zip-lines. The experience of staying in one of these treehouses and being awoken by singing soprano gibbons is truly awe-inspiring, as is zip-lining through the mist high above the jungle canopy. In the morning well-trained guides take visitors for hikes to see if they can spot the elusive gibbons and other animal and plant species. Such species include the giant squirrel, one of the largest rodents in the world, and the Asiatic black bear, whose numbers are in decline due to hunting for their bile and gall bladders. First and foremost this is a very well-run conservation project. It was started to help reduce poaching, logging, slash-and-burn farming and the destruction of primary forest by working with villagers to transform the local economy by making a non-destructive living from their unique environment. Already the Gibbon Experience has started to pay dividends: the forest conservation and canopy visits can generate as much income year on year as a local logging company could do only once. **Ban Nam Chan** is a pleasant Chinese-speaking village, about 17 km from Houei Xai. The Lanten tribespeople who live here are famous for their textiles: the women wear black, kaftan-style dresses and shave their eyebrows and wear a headpiece once they

Border essentials: Houei Xai-Chiang Khong (Thailand)

Small boats ferry passengers across the Mekong between Houei Xai (Laos) and Chiang Khong (Thailand) every 10-20 minutes 0800-2000, 10,000 kip, five minutes. Thai immigration is open daily 0800-1800. A one-month Thai visa is available at the border. Buses and taxis travel from Chiang Kong to Chiang Rai Airport where there are connections to Bangkok. From Chaing Khong there are regular buses to Chiang Rai, 0600-1700, and Chiang Mai, 0630, 350 baht.

Crossing into Laos, immigration is open daily 0730-1730, but expect to pay a US$1 overtime fee at the weekend or after 1600. Tourist visas (30 days) are available at the border for US$30-42. There is also a bank at the Lao border (daily 0830-1600). A fourth Thai-Lao Friendship Bridge is due for completion in 2012 and may make the river crossing redundant.

are married; the men wear black shirts and blue trousers. Along the way, the road passes Hmong villages (15 km in). **Ban Nam Keun**, a small traditional village on the high plateau not far from the main town, is worth a visit for its natural beauty.

Pak Beng → Colour map 1, C2.

This long thin strip of a village is perched halfway up a hill, with fine views over the Mekong. Its importance lies in its location at the confluence of the Mekong and the Nam Beng. There is not much to do here but it's a good place to stop (and is the obligatory stop) on the slow boat between Houei Xai and Luang Prabang (or vice versa). The village is worth a visit for its traditional atmosphere and the friendliness of the locals, including various minorities. Just downstream from the port is a good spot for swimming in the dry season, but be careful as the current is strong. There are also a couple of monasteries in town. The locals are now organizing guided treks to nearby villages; check with Bounmy Guesthouse (see page 156). Electricity is now available 24 hours.

Hongsa and around

From Pak Beng you can take a boat downriver to the small town of **Tha Suang** and then catch a *songthaew* (one hour), through beautiful jungled hills, to the valley of Hongsa. Hongsa district is renowned for its 70 working elephants, which are used as all-purpose heavy 'machinery' for the timber trade and other agricultural purposes. There is a plan to insta an elephant exhibit in Hongsa. Hongsa town is usually just a jump-off point for excursions to nearby **Vieng Ghiaw**, whose men have a long tradition as *mahouts* (elephant handlers), training elephants specifically for use in the local timber trade. Hongsa Tourism office, T020-5577 8142 mob (Mr Siphouvong) ▶▶ *For details of elephant treks, see Activities and tours, page 160.*

Vieng Ghiaw is surrounded by overgrown, ruined city walls, believed to be hundreds of years old, and an extensive moat system that spans several kilometres. The predominantly Tai Lue village features traditional stilt houses, made of solid Mai Du (an Asian rosewood) and designed to house both elephants and humans, with a large spacious area underneath so that the *mahout* can step straight off his veranda onto the elephant's back. Locals are actively involved in the preservation of these unique houses and are hoping, through sponsorship, to keep their village homes rather than replacing them with ugly concrete equivalents. Displayed beneath the veranda are miscellaneous items, usually weaving looms or elephant saddles, which symbolize the family's social status. The Tai Lue use a variety of saddles, separate ones for training, hunting, weddings or religious celebrations. The village is also well known for its textiles, which are woven by the Tai Lue women.

Sayaboury (Xayaboury) → For listings, see pages 153-164. Colour map 1, C2.

→ *Phone code: 074.*

Sayaboury is not on many visitors' agendas. This is partly because it is a difficult place to get to and partly because there doesn't seem any obvious reason to make the effort, although the annual elephant festival is staged in this province, see page 159. There is no direct road between Vientiane and Sayaboury so the only way to get here from the capital is to take a boat upriver to Pak Lai and then to catch a bus – if the road isn't washed away. Rather easier is to catch a bus from Luang Prabang through Muang Nan, cross the Mekong by ferry, and then take a bus to Sayaboury – a comparatively painless four- to seven-hour journey. Having reached Sayaboury and sampled its limited enticements, it is then necessary to retrace your steps or set out for Pak Lai and hope for a downstream boat to Vientiane – wishful thinking for the most part.

These transport difficulties have given Sayaboury a charming forgotten atmosphere. It may be the capital of a province covering over 16,000 sq km – equivalent to the area of Hawaii or Northern Ireland – with 300,000 inhabitants, but it doesn't feel like it. The town has an attractive setting on the Nam Houn – a tributary of the Mekong – and a number of monasteries; those of note are **Wat Thin**, **Wat Pha Phoun**, **Wat Natonoy** and **Wat Sisavang Vong**, named after the king who reigned during the de facto Japanese occupation of French Indochina. The province is mountainous with Phu Khao Mieng, Laos' ninth highest peak, just exceeding 2000 m.

Gluttons for punishment or very adventurous travellers may want to take the seven- to 10-hour *songthaew* trip from Sayaboury to Hongsa (see page 151). The trip passes through stunning scenery and sometimes includes the chance to see working elephants en route but it is a bone-jarringly bumpy trip on unsealed roads, which, in the rainy season, are often flooded.

Sayaboury Provincial Tourism Department, ① *T074-213107, kham_ph@hotmail.com.*

Pak Lai → *Colour map 2, B1.*

Pak Lai is not very much more than a convenient place to stop on the long river journey between Vientiane and Luang Prabang and it grew up as a boating equivalent to a truck stop. There are a sprinkling of colonial shopfronts and old wooden Lao houses, a couple of guesthouses, a few restaurants and shops, and a branch of the Lao Development Bank.

Pak Lai does, however, enjoy a footnote in Laos' colonial history which is worth recounting. In 1887 Luang Prabang was attacked by a band of Chinese Haw and northern Tai bandits. Auguste Pavie, the newly appointed French vice consul, rescued King Unkham from his burning palace and escaped downstream to Pak Lai. Here they remained while the old and frail king recovered from the journey and Pavie researched the early history of Lane Xang. This piece of quick-thinking indebted the king to Pavie and therefore also to the French. Within five years of this heroic rescue Laos was French and the Siamese had lost control of the country.

For Sleeping and Eating price codes and other relevant information, see pages 23-24.

ⓢ Sleeping

Udomxai *p143*

E-F Litthavixay Guesthouse, about 100 m before the turning onto the airport road, 081-212175, litthavixay@yahoo.com. Large clean single, double and triple rooms. Hot water shower attached. Opt for the nicer upstairs rooms if possible; fan rooms are cheaper. Wi-Fi available. Restaurant serves selection of foreign breakfast dishes. Car hire also possible.

E-F Surinphone, T081-212789. 29 comfortable and clean a/c rooms with TV and decent beds, and hot-water shower rooms. All in all, this is a reasonable choice, though the furnishings are starting to look a little dated now.

E-F Villa Keoseumsack, 2 doors down from the *Sinphet Restaurant*, T081-312170, seumsack@hotmail.com. The classiest place to stay in town and good value. 17 rooms with polished floors, large double beds, desks, wardrobes and hot-water showers. Fan rooms are cheaper. Recommended.

F Dokbouadeng, T081-312142. Rooms with en suite shower and Western-style toilet; small restaurant downstairs.

F Saylomyen Guesthouse, about 200 m from the airport, T081-211377. Offers comfortable clean rooms, some with bathrooms with hot water. Friendly owners. Fan rooms are cheaper.

G Phuxay, downhill on the main street from the market and across the bridge, turn right after the petrol station (there is a sign at the petrol station), T081-312140. This is a rather forlorn place which should be a last resort only. The rooms are clean but worn with en suite hot shower and toilet. Plus points are the massive double beds and garden.

Kamu lodge

L-AL Kamu Lodge, Ban Nyong Hay, Udomxai Province; book via the office in Luang Prabang at 44/3 Ban Wat Nong, Kham Kong Rd, T071-260319, T020-5603 2365 (mob), www.kamulodge.com. On the banks of the Mekong, 3 hrs upstream from Luang Prabang. Visitors stay here en route from Houei Xai, when booking an ecotour with Exotissimo (see page 160), but you can stay here independently. Accommodation is in modern canvas tents, decorated with local furnishings. The Lao restaurant serves excellent fish. Also runs treks and activities, such as gold panning. The price includes boat transfer.

Muang La *p143*

L-AL Muang La Resort, www.muangla. com. This small newish resort with eight rooms is set amid well-attended gardens.

The smart rooms feature French fans, silk lanterns and rain showers in the bathroom. The resort faces the river and hot springs. A jacuzzi, overlooking the river, is filled with pumped up hot spring water.

Muang Houn *p144*

F-G Bounnam Guesthouse, T081-212289. Basic no-frills guesthouse, with reasonable facilities for a short stay.

F-G Miss Manyvane. A 2-storey concrete house, with a little balcony upstairs. Basic facilities, 4 rather mouldy twin rooms, with tattered mosquito nets, shared toilet and scoop shower. The family lives on the ground floor.

Luang Namtha *p144, map p145*

There has been a sudden rush of guesthouses popping up here over the last few years but the **Boat Landing**, the best ecotourism venture in the country is still the stand-out choice in the area.

B-C Boat Landing Guesthouse & Restaurant, T086-312398, www.theboatlanding.com. Further out of town than most other guesthouses, this place is located right on the river. Time stands still here. It's an eco-resort that has got everything just right: pristine surroundings, environmentally friendly rooms, helpful service and a brilliant restaurant serving northern Lao cuisine. The rooms combine modern design with traditional materials and decoration; breakfast included. The gardens brim with butterflies and birds; the best time weatherwise is Oct and Nov. Great restaurant attached serving local dishes. Recommended.

D Vila Guesthouse, on the southern side of town, T086-312425, vilaguesthouse@yahoo. com. This 2-storey building has 18 of the smartest rooms in town, with sparkling en suite bathrooms with hot water.

F Manychan Guesthouse, on the main road in the centre of town, T086-312209, ath. phongsavanh@yahoo.com. This is one of the most popular places in town, probably due to its central location and its good restaurant. It offers decent, clean rooms with fan and hot water bathrooms. The staff are pleasant and friendly.

F Thoulasith Guesthouse, T086-212166, thoulasithguesthouse@gmail.com. This is one of the newbies in town, set off the main road in a compound with a garden, tables and chairs. Rooms come with TV, desk, hot-water bathroom (3 rooms have bathtubs) and free Wi-Fi. Friendly management. There's a restaurant too.

F Zuela Guesthouse, T020-5588 6694. This family-run guesthouse represents fantastic value. The beautiful modern wooden buildings have immaculate rooms with comfortable beds, good linen, fans and en suite hot-water bathrooms. The attached restaurant serves great breakfasts, though breakfast service could be better. It is a league apart from the other budget options in town. Highly recommended.

G Adounsiri Guesthouse, T020-2299 1898. A new spacious guesthouse, with tourist information, situated 1 block back from the main road, making it reasonably quiet. Clean rooms; the ones at the front are smarter and the same price.

G Luang Namtha Guesthouse, 2 blocks west of the main centre, T086-312087. Run by 2 friendly Hmong brothers, one of whom speaks English. The house is an impressive building for Luang Namtha, with a grand staircase. But the accommodation is not what it used to be. All rooms are now in less-than-welcoming rattan bungalows by a fishpond. A last resort these days.

Vieng Phouka *p146*

There are 6 very basic guesthouses in town, try the **G Don Vieng**, T084-212394, or the **G Bo Kung**.

Boten *p148*

At present there is a small, unmarked guesthouse right on the border (**E**). Basic doubles, clean enough, geared to Chinese, Vietnamese and Lao truckers. Expect a few more to crop up soon as the major construction work begins on the 'Golden Boten City' project. Boten also has a couple of *feu* stalls but little else.

Muang Sing *p148*

E Phou lu Bungalows, at the southern end of town, T030-5511 0326, www.muang-sing. com. This is the nicest accommodation in town by a long way. There are great spacious double ground-floor bungalows with four-poster beds, small balconies with bamboo seats, set around a grassy compound with restaurant and massage service.

E Stupa Mountain Lodge, 6 km out of Muang Sing on the main road towards Luang Namtha, T020-5568 6555, stupalodge@yahoo.com. 10 wooden bungalows are perched on the side of a hill, looking over the small town, mountains and rice paddies. Quaint gardens, home to an abundance of butterflies, link the bungalows via a small paved path. Solar-powered hot water, fan, Western toilet and balcony. Stunningly beautiful. There is also a decent restaurant with views stretching all the way to China. Very good value. Recommended.

F-G Adima Guesthouse, near Ban Oudomsin, 8 km north of Muang Sing towards the Chinese border, 600 m off the main road, T020-22393398. A little hard to get to but the location is scenic. Peaceful bungalows constructed in traditional Yao and Akha style (some with shared bathroom), bathrooms with squat toilets, plus a lovely open-air restaurant. Paddy field views for some of the rooms will be marred by new fish pond constructions. Minority villages are literally on the doorstep. Footprint does not endorse DIY treks using the guesthouse map; these are having a very negative impact on the nearby Akha villages. If you wish to trek, visit the local tourism office or contact **Exotissimo**, see page160, to organize a bonafide eco-trek. To get there, take a tuk-tuk (20,000 kip) or hire a bike.

F-G Singchalern Hotel, T020-9966 3913, singchalern_hotel@yahoo.com. An ugly

orange construction but you won't see that from the inside. The new, decent but Spartan rooms are good value.

G Daenneua Guesthouse, on the main road, T030-511 0966. Friendly staff and renovated guesthouse with hot water bathrooms and laundry service.

G Sengdeuane Guesthouse, at the far end of town, T020-5508 6611. Sengdeuane's helpful owners have built large clean bungalow rooms out the back, which have adjoining bathrooms, hot water and enormous double beds.

G Taileu Guesthouse, on the main road, T030-5110354. Above the restaurant there are 8 very basic rattan rooms with bamboo-style, 4-poster beds (the rickety backpacker version not the romantic type), squat toilets and temperamental hot water heated by solar power. The guesthouse owners are lovely people.

Additional guesthouses (**G**) in the centre of town include **Viengsing**, **Viengxai** (see Eating; run by the same people as **Adima**). There's nothing much to distinguish between them: basic, cramped double rooms, with shared squat toilets and shower and paper-thin walls, although the **Viengxai** now has some en suite bathrooms.

Houei Xai *p150*

There is a cluster of hotels on Sekhong Rd, which is the main street running through the town.

E-F BAP Guesthouse, on the main Sekhong Rd, T084-211083, bapbiz@live.com. One of the oldest guesthouses in town consisting of a labyrinth of additions and add-ons as their business has grown over the years. A range of rooms, though the newer tiled ones with hot-water bathrooms are the best. Rooms with TV are more expensive; rooms with shared bath are cheaper. The female proprietor here is a tough cookie but has loads of charisma and a wily sense of humour. She's also super helpful.

E-F Taveensinh Guesthouse, northwest end of the town, T084-211502. The best value in town with fan, TV hot water bathrooms; a/c costs more. Great communal balconies overlooking the river and friendly family in charge.

F Sabaydee, T020-5692 9458. Big, tiled rooms, with en suite hot showers and Western toilets. Recommended.

F Thanormsub Guesthouse, on the main Sekhong Rd, T084-211095. Double rooms, clean, hot water, fan and satin curtains to boot. Nice, helpful staff.

Pak Beng *p151*

During peak season, when the slow boat arrives from Luang Prabang, about 60 people descend on Pak Beng at the same time. As the town doesn't have an endless supply of great budget guesthouses, it is advisable to get someone you trust to mind your bags, while you make a mad dash to get the best room in town. There are a number of shack-like bamboo lodgings running up the hill.

A Pakbeng Lodge, T081-212304, www.pakbenglodge.com. A wooden and concrete construction, built in traditional Lao style, this stunning guesthouse perches on a hillside above the Mekong and includes 20 rooms with fan, toilet and hot water. Good restaurant and wonderful views. Breakfast is included. 10 new de luxe rooms were due to open. Wi-Fi available. Elephant activities can be arranged.

A-B Luangsay Lodge, about 1 km from the centre of town, www.mekong-cruises.com. This is the most beautiful accommodation available in Pak Beng. An attractive wooden pathway curves through luscious tropical gardens to several wooden bungalows with fantastic balconies and large windows overlooking the river and misty mountains. Hot water bathrooms and romantic rooms make this a winner. Great restaurant. Book in advance as it tends to get booked up by customers on the Luangsay Cruise especially in high season but Sun and last-minutes are possible. Breakfast and dinner is included. Highly recommended.

C Phetsoxkai Hotel, T081-212299. Large Lao-owned hotel which looks grand but doesn't live up to expectations. Nonetheless, the 29 rooms are beautifully decorated, if on the smallish side. Smart hot-water bathrooms and DVD player. Restaurant with Western, Lao and Thai cuisine. Welcoming owners. Breakfast included in the price.

F Dockhoun Guesthouse, T081-212540. Good, basic and clean rooms with a fast laundry. Opposite **Monsavan**.

F Donevilisack Guesthouse, T081-212315. This popular guesthouse offers a pretty reasonable choice of rooms. In the older, wooden building are basic budget rooms, with fan, mosquito net and shared hot-water showers. More expensive rooms in the newer concrete building have private hot water bathrooms.

F Salika, T081-212306. This is an elegant structure on the steep cliff overlooking the Mekong river. Offers 15 big, clean rooms with toilet and en suite shower (mostly cold water) and tiled floors. There is a great restaurant, serving reasonably priced meals. Fantastic service.

F-G Bounmy Guesthouse, T081-212294 Smallish bamboo rooms, with bed, fan and good, clean, bathrooms with hot water (some shared facilities with cold water are cheaper). Although it occupies a quiet location, the walls are paper thin, which can be a bit annoying. Lovely family. Also runs the new (**F**) Duang Pasert with 9 rooms (T081-212624).

Hongsa *p151*

F Jumbo Guesthouse, T020-5685 6488, www.lotuselephant.com. The nicest place to stay, with 5 rooms and lots of elephant-focused activities arranged. Run by the helpful Monica.

There are several other guesthouses.

Sayaboury *p152*

F New Sayaboury Hotel. Large, 3-storey hotel with clean, fair-sized rooms boasting fan, en suite bathroom and hot water.

For a few extra dollars you can get a/c. Recommended.

F-G Hongvilay Guesthouse, south of the centre on the banks of the Nam Houn, T074-211068. This place has a good outlook but the rooms are a bit squalid – shared cold-water bathrooms and not quite clean. Even so, it makes a nice spot to stay.

Pak Lai *p152*

F Lamdouan Guesthouse, to the west of the boat landing, along the river road, T020-9980 3451. Very friendly, family-run guesthouse offering basic rooms with shared facilities.

F-G Banna Guesthouse, along the river road, east of the boat landing, T074-211995. Very clean, 3-storey guesthouse, 17 rooms with fan and shared facilities.

There is a good little restaurant beside the boat landing that serves *feu* and *pad gow*.

🍴 Eating

Udomxai *p143*

As well as those listed below, **Litthavixay Guesthouse** (see Sleeping) can whip up some good dishes, including Western-style pancakes and breakfasts and **Dokbouadeng** guesthouses (see Sleeping) also have small cafés on the ground floor. There are a number of restaurants on the first left turn after the bridge; all do good Laos and Chinese food. Noodle soup shops are scattered throughout town and stalls in front of the market sell beer and tasty snacks from nightfall.

🍴 **Kanya Restaurant**, just off the main street not far from the tourist office. This is popular with Laos tour guides and has a menu in English offering the usual staples. The pork vermicelli is tasty and the iced coffees are most welcome.

🍴 **Sinphet Restaurant**, opposite **Linda Guesthouse**. One of the best options in town. English menu, delicious iced coffee with Ovaltine, great Chinese and Lao food. Try the curry chicken, *kua-mii* or yellow noodles with chicken. Also does sandwiches, fruit shakes and pancakes, and stocks some French wines.

🍴 **Thanousin**, on the corner of the road to the airport. Friendly service, menu in English, good basic Lao food.

Muang Houn *p144*

There are 2 eating places facing each other next to the market. Both serve noodles, eggs and sticky rice, no menu. Fresh baguettes are available from the market in the morning.

Luang Namtha *p144, map p145*

🍴🍴 **Boat Landing Guesthouse & Restaurant**, see Sleeping, T086-312398, Open 0700-2100. Best place to eat in town, with a beautiful dining area and exceptionally innovative cuisine: a range of northern Lao dishes made from local produce that supports local villages. Highly recommended.

🍴🍴 **Manychan**, see Sleeping. A very popular restaurant with outdoor seating and a variety of toned-down Lao dishes plus a few Western interpretations.

🍴 **Banana Restaurant**, on the main road, T020-5558 1888. This restaurant is gaining favour with locals and tourists for its good fruit shakes and Lao food. A few Western dishes, too.

🍴 **Coffee House**, off the main road around the corner from **Green Discovery**, T030-5257842. This fantastic little Thai restaurant serves a range of delicious Thai meals all under 12,000 kip. The meals are served on brown rice imported from Thailand. Massaman curry, Tom Yum soup plus a great variety of other Thai staples. Fantastic espresso coffee and cappuccinos. Mr Nithat, the owner's husband, is good for a chat. Recommended.

🍴 **Panda Restaurant**, T020-5560 6549. This is a find, serving cheap and tasty food. The curries are outstanding. The friendly owner speaks English.

🍴 **Yamuna Restaurant**, on the main road, T020-5557 1579. A delicious Indian restaurant with veg and non-veg dishes and halal cuisine. Extensive, predominantly south Indian menu.

Bakeries, cafés and street stalls

There is a **bakery** and cake shop near the market that sells mouthwatering treats; try the green tea cake. There are a few *feu* stalls by the main market. At night, food vendors gather at the night market, selling meat on a stick and waffles from pretty, candlelit stalls.

Muang Sing *p148*

It is highly recommended that you eat some of the delicious ethnic food while you're in Muang Sing as there aren't many other places where you will be able to sample these meals.

♥♥-♥ Adima Guesthouse, see Sleeping. Western offerings, such as the usual backpacker pancakes or fried eggs, as well as some Lao-inspired meals.

♥ Muang Sing View Restaurant. A bamboo walkway leads to this rustic restaurant which enjoys the best views in Muang Sing overlooking the paddy fields and the valley. All the usual Lao staples are served.

♥ Sengdeuane Guesthouse and Restaurant. Korean barbecue only (*sindat*). It opens from 1700. Popular with the locals.

♥ Taileu Guesthouse and Restaurant, see Sleeping, T081-212375. The most popular place to eat due to its indigenous Tai Lue menu. Try baked aubergine with pork, soy mash and fish soup. One of the few places in the country where you can sample northern cuisine. Try their local piña colada with *lao lao*, their *sa lo* (Muang Sing's answer to a hamburger) or one of the famous *jeow* dishes. The banana flower soup is fantastic. This is an eating experience you won't find elsewhere in Laos. Noi, the owner, is very friendly. Highly recommended.

♥ Viengphone, next door to the **Viengxai Restaurant**. This place has an English menu offering the usual fare. Excellent fried mushrooms, although the service here is a bit *bopenyang*.

♥ Viengxai Restaurant, see Sleeping. Very good food, with some of the best chips in Laos, English menu, friendly service, reasonable prices. Good selection of shakes.

Houei Xai *p150*

♥♥-♥ Riverside, just off the main road, near the **Houay Xai Guesthouse**, T084-211064. Huge waterfront restaurant on large platform. Perfect position for taking in the sunset. Great shakes. Extensive menu that's a mixture of Lao and Thai food. The curries are quite good. Usually live music is played here, some of it decidedly off-key.

♥ BAP Guesthouse, see Sleeping. Without doubt the best breakfast menu in town: wide range of dishes including pancakes, croissants and eggs.

♥ Bar How? A cute little place with fresh spring rolls, soups, sarnies, and other Western and Lao offerings. There's a warm atmosphere with paper lanterns and wooden tables. Breakfast is a little expensive.

♥ Deen Restaurant, on the main road, T020-55901871. Indian restaurant with a very extensive menu of dishes including a large selection of halal and vegetarian food. Sparkly clean with formal tablecloths and table settings. Helpful owner.

♥ Khemkhong Restaurant, across from the immigration stand. This is a good option for travellers who want a drink and a snack after the cross-border journey. Lao and Thai food.

♥ Nutpop, on the main road, T084-211037. The fluorescent lights and garish beer signs don't give a good impression. However, this is a pleasant little garden restaurant, set in an atmospheric lamp-lit building. Good Lao food – fried mushrooms and good curry. Excellent fish.

♥ Riverview Garden Restaurant. There's no river view in spite of the name, but its streetside view and tables have become a firm favourite with the backpacker set. There's a mixed menu of sandwiches, pizzas, stir fries, barbecue and noodle dishes. Conveniently, it's next to the **Gibbon Experience** office.

Pak Beng p151

Restaurants serve breakfast (baguettes, pancakes and coffee) really early. The eco-lodges have pretty upscale restaurants, and there are several more modest restaurants lining the main road towards the river; all seem to have the same English menu, basic Lao dishes, eggs and freshly made sandwiches. The local market has an array of dishes from *feu* through to frogs!

ℌ Kopchaideu Restaurant, overlooking the Mekong. This restaurant has a wide selection of Indian dishes with a few Lao favourites thrown in. Great shakes, fab naan bread and fantastic service.

Sayaboury p152

There are restaurants, along with the usual noodle shops and stalls on streets leading off the market. None are particularly noteworthy. Simple Chinese and Lao dishes.

✺ Festivals and events

Hongsa/Sayaboury *p151 and p152*
Mid-Feb Elephant Festival. Check www.elefantasia.org. The annual elephant festival is gaining momentum in this least-visited area of the country. Recommended.

✪ Shopping

Luang Namtha *p144, map p145*
Night market sells textiles woven by the women of Luang Namtha and warm clothes for travellers who've forgotten that it's cold in the mountains. Fresh and packaged foods also sold.

▲ Activities and tours

Udomxai p143
Traditional Lao herbal sauna and massage is offered by the **Red Cross Centre**, behind the main stupa past the Phuxay Hotel, T022-211477, daily 1330-1930, 30,000 kip per hr. Look out for the signs on the main road.

Po Saa paper-making courses (Feb-Apr) can be arranged in a nearby village as can a half-day cooking course. Contact the tourism office for more information.
Saamlan Cycling, on the main road near the airport junction, T030-5130184, T020-5560 9790 (mob), www.saamlancycling.com. Organizes biking and trekking tours in the area, from half a day to 10 days. Bike tours start at US$8; trekking to minority villages, from US$15-230. It's also possible to organize treks to Muang Khua and Luang Prabang. Ken who runs **Saamlan** also offers bike repairs and spare parts.
Trekking. The tourist office organizes 1- to 3-day treks, including trips to Chom Ong Cave and homestays in Khamu villages, as well as visits to a beekeeper (Apr-Jun).
Udomxai Travel, near the bus station, T081-212020, www.udomxaitravellaos.com. Offers ecotours and travel services.

Luang Namtha p144, map p145
Massage and sauna
There are a few herbal saunas in town; bring your own towels.

Tour operators

If you want to trek from Luang Namtha and you're travelling solo or as a couple, it's expensive. Try to hook up with people before you get there or at your guesthouse. Agencies also put up boards requesting more takers. The larger the group, the cheaper the price.
Green Discovery, opposite Banana Restaurant, T086-211484, www.greendiscoverylaos.com. Offers 1- to 7-day kayaking/rafting, cycling and trekking excursions into the Nam Ha NPA. Office open daily 0730-2100.
Luang Namtha Eco Guide Unit, T086-211534, www.luangnamtha-tourism.org. Information on 1-4-day treks into the Nam Ha NPA. Biking tours, boat trips and tuk-tuk tours also possible. Trek prices from 250,000 kip per person. The tourism office has also set up an Eco Guide unit at Muang Nalea.

Into the Wild, T086-212006, www.
luangnamthatravel.com. An alternative
to the main operators in town but not
necessarily cheaper.

Vieng Phouka *p146*

The local tourism office runs four 1-3 day
treks around the local villages, the Nam
Ha National Park and caves with food and
accommodation and camping with a host
family. The guides (trained by the LNTA and
the EU) are usually Khmu and Akha from
the surrounding villages. Contact the **Vieng
Phouka Eco Guide Service Unit**, T084-
212400, mpvpk@laotel.com. Open daily
0800-1200, 1330-1700.

Muang Sing *p148*
Bike tours and hire

Tiger Man, T030-5263576. Offers biking
tours from 220,000 kip per person as well as
renting bikes. Run by the helpful Mr Tong.

Trekking

Trekking has become a delicate issue around
Muang Sing as uncontrolled tourism was
beginning to have a detrimental effect on
some of the minority villages. Luckily some
sensible procedures have been put in place
to ensure low-impact tourism.
Exotissimo, www.exotissimo.com (T086-
400016; akhaexp@gmail.com) in Muang
Sing in cahoots with **GTZ**, a German aid
agency, have launched more expensive
but thoroughly enjoyable treks such as the
Akha Experience, which include tasty meals
prepared by local Akha people. Advertised
as a 3-day trek, it can be organized as a 1-
and 2-day trek too. Minimum price US$41
per person. Office closed at weekends.
Tourism office and trekking centre, in
the centre of town, see page 148, can also
organize treks for 1, 2 or 3 days, including
accommodation and food. Guides are from
local villages and speak the native tongue,
Akha or Tai Lue. Treks have received glowing
reports, particularly the **Laosee Trek**. Prices
of treks are reduced for larger groups.

Houei Xai *p150*
Tour operators

Gibbon Experience, T084-212021, www.
gibbonx.org. This unique ecotourism
operation provides the rare opportunity to
see or hear the soprano-singing, black-
cheeked crested gibbons (once thought
to be extinct) from a network of canopy
treehouses and zip lines. Sightings are
seasonal. Accommodation is in a treehouse,
affording sensational views of the
surrounding Bokeo Forest Reserve. Some
of the treehouses are more luxurious than
others but the most luxurious ones aren't
always in the best location to access the
best zip lines.

Pak Beng *p151*
Elephant trekking

Contact **Pakbeng Lodge**, see Sleeping.

Massage

Next door to **Bounmy Guesthouse** is an
understated but fantastic massage place.

Hongsa *p151*
Elephant trekking

Elephant treks can also be organized
through **Jumbo Guesthouse**. See Sleeping.

⊖ Transport

Udomxai *p143*
Air

There are flights to **Vientiane**, 3 times
a week. **Lao Airlines** has an office at the
airport, T081-312047. A tuk-tuk to town
costs 5000-10,000 kip.

Bus/truck/songthaew

Udomxai is the epicentre of northern
travel. If arriving in Udomxai to catch a
connecting bus, it's better to leave earlier
in the day as transport tends to peter out in
the afternoon. The prices quoted below are
subject to change.
   One of the nicest ways to get to Udomxai
from either Luang Prabang or Houei Xai is to

catch the boat to Pak Beng (see page 151) and then take a bus from there.

The bus station is 1 km east of the town centre (tuk-tuk to the centre, 5000 kip). Departures east to **Nong Khiaw**, 3 hrs, trucks are fairly frequent, most departing in the morning. If you get stuck on the way to Nong Khiaw it is possible to stay overnight in **Pak Mong** where there are numerous rustic guesthouses. The bus to **Nong Khiaw** leaves at 0900, 114 km. **Pak Mong**, 1400 and 1600, 2 hrs, 82 km, 22,000 kip. To **Luang Prabang**, 3 daily, 194 km, direct, 5 hrs, 48,000 kip. Direct bus to **Vientiane**, 1530 and 1800, 15 hrs, 100,000 kip. Vientiane VIP bus, 1600 and 1800, 121,000 kip (also runs via **Luang Prabang**). **Xam Neua**, Tue-Sat 1230, 100,000 kip. **Luang Namtha**, 3 daily, 115 km, 4 hrs, 32,000 kip. **Boten** (the Chinese border) 0800, 82 km, 28,000 kip. It is possible for some nationalities to obtain Chinese visas at the border (see box, page 147). However, you will need to check if you are eligible (at the time of publication UK citizens could but US citizens could not get a Chinese visa at the Boten border).

There are services north on Route 4 to **Phongsali**, 0800, 232 km, 9-12 hrs, 60,000 kip; this trip is long so bring something soft to sit on and try to get a seat with a view.

There are plenty of *songthaew* on standby waiting to make smaller trips to destinations like **Pak Mong** and **Nong Khiaw**; if you miss one of the earlier buses, it may be worthwhile bargaining with the drivers; if they can get enough money, or can round up enough passengers, they will make the extra trip.

At the bus station there is a range of foodstalls, a Chinese restaurant and an internet café (temperamental internet), 10,000 kip per hr.

Muang Houn *p144*
Regular buses south to **Pak Beng**, 2 hrs, 15,000 kip, and north to **Udomxai**, 4-5 hrs, 25,000 kip.

Luang Namtha *p144, map p145*
Air
Luang Namtha's airport is 6 km south of town. There are flights 3 times a week to Vientiane. **Lao Airlines**, T086-212072, has an office south of town on the main road.

Bicycle/motorbike
Bicycles for hire from **Namtha Vehicle Rental Service**, next door to the Manychan Guesthouse, T086-312172, for 8000-20,000 kip a day. Motorbikes for hire for 30-50 a day. Also from **Zuela Guesthouse**, see Sleeping. Discounts for guests.

Boat
Officially, fast boats are not allowed on the Nam Tha. Slow boats are the best and most scenic travel option but their reliability will depend on the tide and, in the dry season (Jan–May) they often won't run at all as the water level is too low. There isn't really a regular boat service from Luang Namtha, so you will have to charter a whole boat or hitch a ride on a boat making the trip already. If you manage to organize a boat it should cost around 1,900,000 kip to **Houei Xai**; it is cheaper to go from Luang Namtha to Houei Xai than vice versa. The **Boat Landing Guesthouse** is a good source of information about boats; if arrangements are made for you, a courtesy tip is appreciated.

Bus/truck/songthaew
The inter-provincial bus station and its ticket office have moved to 10 km south of town. A new intra-provincial bus station is close to the **Panda Restaurant**, on the main road.

From the intra-provincial (unsigned) bus station: to **Muang Sing**, 3 daily, 1½ hrs, 20,000 kip, additional pickups may depart throughout the rest of the day, depending on demand. To **Boten** (Chinese border) 0800, 0930, 1100, 1230, 1400, 1530, 2 hrs, 20,000 kip.

From the inter-provincial bus station: to **Udomxai**, 0830, 1200, 1430, 100 km, 4 hrs, 32,000 kip, additional services will leave in the early afternoon if there is demand, otherwise jump on a bus to Luang Prabang.

To **Houei Xai**, 0900 and 1330, 55,000 kip, 4 hrs. Take this service for Vieng Phouka. To **Luang Prabang**, 0930 daily, 8 hrs, 65,000 kip. To **Vientiane**, 0830, 1430, 21 hrs, 140,000 kip. To get to **Nong Khiaw**, you need to go via Udomxai (leave early). To **Mengla, China**, 0800, 4-5 hrs, 45,000 kip; to **Chieng Houng** (China), 0900, 7 hrs, 88,000 kip. To **Muang Long**, 0830, 40,000 kip, 4 hrs.

Vieng Phouka p146

Buses and *songthaew* depart for **Houei Xai**, a few times daily from the market, usually in the morning, 5 hrs, US$5. It is also possible to catch buses to **Luang Namtha**, 4 hrs, and **Udomxai**.

Boten p148

Pickups to **Luang Namtha**, 0800, 0930, 1100, 1230, 1400, 1530, 2 hrs, 20,000 kip. To **Udomxai**, 0930, 1200 and 1400 daily, 23,000 kip. For international connections with China, see Border essentials, page 147.

Muang Sing p148
Bicycle

Available for rent from **Tiger Man** trekking agency (see Activities and tours above) on the main road. Rents city bikes for 20,000 kip per day and mountain bikes for 25,000 kip.

Boat

It is sometimes possible to charter boats from **Xieng Kok** downstream on the Mekong to **Houei Xai**, 3-4 hrs. This is expensive – around US$150-200.

Bus/truck/songthaew

The bus station is across from the new morning market, 500 m from the main road. To **Luang Namtha**, by bus or pickup, 0800, 0930, 1100, 1300, 1400, 1500, 2 hrs, 20,000 kip. To charter a *songthaew* or tuk-tuk to Luang Namtha costs at least 250,000 kip. *Songthaew* to **Xieng Kok**, 0830, 30,000 kip, 3 hrs. Officially **Xieng Kok**, on the Mekong

at the Myanmar/Burma border, does not allow foreigners to cross into Myanmar (Burma) here, but there have been reports of travellers being granted a visa and entering.

To **Muang Long**, 0800 and 1100, 48 km, 2 hrs, 20,000 kip.

Houei Xai p150

Lao National Tourism State Bokeo, on the main street up from immigration, T084-211162, can advise on the sale of boat, bus, pickup and other tickets but limited English is spoken. You are better off approaching the travel agencies around the immigration centre, offering bus and boat ticket sales. See page 129 for information on boat travel between Houei Xai and **Luang Prabang**.

Air

The airport is located 2 km south of town and has flights to **Vientiane** 3 times a week; book in advance as it is a small plane and tends to fill up quickly. Lao Airlines, T084-211026. Open Mon-Sat.

Boat

The BAP Guesthouse is a good place to find out about boat services. For services across the Mekong to Thailand, see Border essentials, page 151.

The 2-day trip down the Mekong to Luang Prabang is a Southeast Asian rite of package. The slow boat to **Pak Beng** is raved about by many travellers. However, in peak season it can be packed. Bring something soft to sit on, a good book to read and a packed lunch. The boat leaves from a jetty 1½ km north of town, 1100 daily, 6-7 hrs, 250,000 kip for the 2-day trip (usually you buy the ongoing ticket at Pak Beng; just to Pak Beng is 120,000 kip). If you can get enough people you can charter your own boat for 1,765,000 kip, although ask for advice at the tourist office as they quote much cheaper. The trip in reverse usually has fewer passengers.

For a luxury option there is the lovely Luangsay Cruise, T084-212092, www.

luangsay.com, opposite Laos immigration, which makes a 2-day/1-night cruise down the river in comfort with cushioned deckchairs, a bar, wooden interior, and plenty of food. Stops are made to visit riverside villages. Guests stay at the beautiful **Luangsay Lodge** in Pak Beng. Accommodation and meals are included. **Speedboats** are a noisy, dangerous alternative to the slow boats; they leave from the jetty south of town, to **Pak Beng**, 0900, 3 hrs, 180,000 kip, and to **Luang Prabang**, 360,000-400,000 kip. There have been reports of boatmen claiming there are no slow boats in the dry season, so that travellers will take their fast boats.

To **Xieng Kok**, see above, 1,500,000 kip, 4 hrs from the northern pier. To **Luang Namtha** by longtail boat, 1,750,000 kip, maximum 5 people, 2 days.

Bus/truck/songthaew
The bus station is at the Morning Market, 3 km out of central Houei Xai; a tuk-tuk to the centre costs 10,000 kip. To **Nam Chan** by taxi, 1 hr, 80,000 kip, for the whole vehicle.

Trucks, buses and minivans run to **Vieng Phouka**, daily 0830, 1230, 5 hrs, 35,000 kip; to **Luang Namtha**, daily 0830, 1230, 1700, 170 km, 7 hrs, 55,000 kip (there are also more regular minivans to Luang Namtha); to **Udomxai**, daily 0900, 1200, 1700, 12 hrs, 120,000 kip; to **Luang Prabang**, 0900, 1200, 1700, 12 hrs, 120,000 kip; to **Vientiane**, daily 1130, 20 hrs, 200,000 kip.

Pak Beng *p151*
Boat
Times and prices are always changing so it's best to check before you travel. The slow boat to **Houei Xai** leaves at around 0900 from the port and takes all day, 110,000 kip. The slow boat to **Luang Prabang** leaves around the same time, also 110,000 kip. Speedboats to Luang Prabang (2-3 hrs) and Houei Xai leave in the morning, when full, 3500 baht for both journeys. You can also take a boat downriver to **Tha Suang**, 2 hrs,

80,000 kip, and then catch a *songthaew* from here to **Hongsa**, US$3 or arrange a private pickup through the **Jumbo Guesthouse** in Hongsa, see Sleeping. A speedboat to Tha Suang will cost about 1,000,000 kip.

Bus/truck/songthaew
Buses and *songthaew* leave about 2 km from town in the morning for the route north to **Udomxai**, 6-7 hrs, 40,000 kip. Direct *songthaew* to Udomxai are few and far between, so take one to Muang Houn and then catch a more frequent service from there. The road to Udomxai passes through spectacular scenery. If you need private transport, **Bounmy** guesthouse (see Sleeping) can arrange transport to Nong Khiaw, Udomxai and Luang Namtha.

Sayaboury *p152*
Air
Flights to **Vientiane**, are now operated by Phongsavanh Airlines (T021-513 0000), 45 mins. On each occasion the plane makes a round trip. Tickets can be purchased at the airport, about 1 km south of town.

Bus
There are 2 bus terminals, the South Bus Station, 2 km southeast of town, and the North Bus Station, 2 km north of town.

There are no direct road links with Vientiane. The road south from Sayaboury only goes as far as Muang Ken Thao, close to the border with Thailand. This road passes through Pak Lai, on the Mekong, where it is possible to catch a boat downstream to **Vientiane**. There are buses to **Pak Lai** daily 0900, 1000, 1300, 1500, 1600, 4 hrs, US$2.50. Note that the road is in poor condition – although it is being upgraded – and transport in the wet season (Jun/Jul-Oct/Nov) is difficult and sometimes impossible.

You can catch a *songthaew* north to **Tha Deua** on the Mekong, 23 km, 1 hr, from where a ferry crosses to **Pak Khon**, 3000 kip. There are regular buses from Pak Khon to **Luang Prabang**, 4 hrs, US$1.50. Speedboats also run from Tha Deua direct to Luang Prabang, 1 hr, US$20, but you may have to rent the whole boat, which is costly.

Pak Lai *p152*
Boat
There are connections by slow boat (downriver) to **Vientiane**, daily 0730, 8 hrs, US$7. However, due to the upgrading of Route 13 between Vientiane and Luang Prabang, there are no longer scheduled boats upriver to Luang Prabang; instead you must head to Sayaboury then Tha Deua.

Songthaew
Songthaews terminate 3 km out of town; share a tuk-tuk to the centre. *Songthaews* run to **Sayaboury**, 4 hrs, US$3, twice daily.

⊙ Directory

Udomxai *p143*
Banks Lao Development Bank, just off the road on the way to Phongsali, changes US$, Chinese ¥ and Thai baht. The BCEL Bank, on the main road near the Kaysone Monument, T081-211260, is much more convenient and offers the same services and has an ATM. **Electricity** Temporary black outs seem common. **Internet** Available at Litthavixay Guesthouse (Wi-Fi, 10,000 kip/hr). **Post and telephone** Post office and Lao Telecom, opposite the Sai Xi Hotel, uphill from the Chinese market; international calls available.

Luang Namtha *p144, map p145*
Banks Banks open Mon-Fri only. Lao Development Bank, in the centre of town, T086-211398, changes US$ and Thai baht to kip, also exchanges TCs but charges a sizeable commission. Visa and MasterCard withdrawals now possible. The BCEL also changes US$ and Thai baht and does cash advances via Visa and MasterCard. ATM too. **Internet** KNT Computers, on the main road, south of Manychan Guesthouse, 200 kip per min and at NIT Computers,

100 kip/min. **Telephone** You can make international calls from Lao Telecom.

Muang Sing *p148*
Banks There is a small branch of the Lao Development Bank opposite the market which will exchange Thai baht, Chinese ¥ and US$. **Internet** Muang Sing Tourism Office offers internet, 300 kip/min.

Houei Xai *p150*
Banks BCEL, operates Mon-Fri and has an ATM. **Immigration** At the boat terminal and the airport, daily 0800-1800, a small overtime fee is charged Sat and Sun and after 1600 (see also box, page 151). **Internet** There is internet opposite Sabaydee guesthouse, 10,000 kip/hr. **Post and telephone** Post office with telephone facilities is about 500 m south (downstream) from the centre of town.

Pak Beng *p151*
Banks There is no bank in town, but most guesthouses and restaurants change Thai baht and US$ cash for a hefty commission. **Electricity** is sporadic and sometimes only available 1800-2200. **Internet** Available at the boat ferry office. **Post** The post office is up over the hill on the main road.

Sayaboury *p152*
Banks There is only one bank in town, the Lao Development Bank, just down from the Kaysone Monument, Mon-Fri 0830-1600. It does not accept TCs but will change US$ and Thai baht. The rate of exchange is poor. **Post and telephone** The post office, Mon-Fri 0800-1100 and 1300-1700, and Lao Telecom Office are in the centre of town, on the other side of the road from the market.

Pak Lai *p152*
Banks The Lao Development Bank, a block north of the boat landing, will change Thai baht and US$. **Post and telephone** There is a telephone office and post office a block west of the bank.

Xieng Khouang Province

Apart from the historic Plain of Jars, Xieng Khouang Province is best known for the pounding it took during the war. Many of the sights are battered monuments to the plateau's violent recent history. Given the cost of the return trip and the fact that the jars themselves aren't that spectacular, some travellers consider the destination oversold. However, for those interested in modern history, it's the most fascinating area of Laos and helps one appreciate the resilient nature of the Lao people. The countryside, particularly towards the Vietnam border, is very beautiful – among the country's best – and the jars, too, are interesting by dint of their very oddness: as if a band of carousing giants had been suddenly interrupted, casting the jars across the plain in their hurry to leave. The local tourist office has also just launched new culture and nature tours to woo visitors into staying longer. ▸▸ *For listings, see pages 175-179*

Ins and outs

Getting there **Phonsavanh Airport** (aka Xieng Khouang airport) is 4 km west of Phonsavanh. **Lao Airlines** flies to and from Vientiane; check www.laoairlines.com for up-to-date information. A tuk-tuk to town costs 20,000 kip per person. The most direct route by road from Luang Prabang to Xieng Khouang Province is to take Route 13 south to Muang Phou Khoun and then Route 7 east. You might want to take travel sickness tablets as it's quite a bumpy trip. An alternative, scenic, albeit convoluted, route is via Nong Khiaw (see page 140), from where there are pick-ups to Pak Xeng and Phonsavanh via Vieng Thong on Route 1 or Nam Nouan.

The bus station is 4 km west of Phonsavanh on Route 7; a tuk-tuk to/from the centre costs 10,000 kip.

Getting around Public transport is limited and sporadic. Provincial laws have occasionally banned tuk-tuks and motorbikes from ferrying customers around the area.▸▸ *See Transport, page 178.*

Tourist information **Xieng Khouang Provincial Tourism Department** ① *T061-312217, xkgtourism@yahoo.com* is 2 km from the town centre and is signposted,. Some members of staff here speak a bit of English. As well as having the largest collection of bomb paraphernalia in town, the office has interesting displays and can provide useful leaflets, as well as up-to-date bus timetables. The Xieng Khouang Discovery Guide (see page 168) should also be available at the office.

Best time to visit It is cold here from November to March. Several jumpers and a thick jacket are required.

Background

Xieng Khouang Province has had a murky, blood-tinted, war-ravaged history. The area was the most bombed province in the most bombed country, per capita, in the world, as it became a crucial strategic zone that both the US and Vietnamese wanted to control. The town of Phonsavanh has long been an important transit point between China to the north, Vietnam to the east and Thailand to the south and this status historically made the town a target for neighbouring countries. What's more, the plateau of the Plain of Jars is one of the flattest areas in northern Laos, rendering it a natural battleground for the numerous conflicts that ensued from the 19th century to 1975. As a result, the region holds immense appeal for those interested in the modern history of the country.

The earliest known settlers in this area were believed to be of the ethnic Tai origin and a Phuan kingdom was established in the region in the 14th century. The kingdom suffered numerous sackings by the Vietnamese over hundreds of years, until, in 1832, they invaded Phonsavanh, executing the Phuan king and turning the area into an Annan vassal state. The region was incorporated into the kingdom of Lane Xang by King Fa Ngum briefly in the 16th century but was more often than not ruled by the Vietnamese (who called it Tran Ninh) because of its proximity to the border. The Chinese Haw also ravaged Phonsavanh in the 19th century, an event that, along with the sacking of Luang Prabang, became a catalyst for the government's acceptance of French protection.

Under the French, Xieng Khouang supported tea plantations and many colonial settlers took to the temperate climate of the province. Like the Bolaven Plateau to the south, the French colonial administration had visions of populating the Plain of Jars with thousands of hard-working French families. Only in this way, it was reasoned, could Laos be made to pay for itself.

Once the French departed, massive conflicts were waged in 1945-1946 between the Free Lao Movement and the Viet Minh. The Pathet Lao and Viet Minh joined forces and, by 1964, had a number of bases dotted around the Plain of Jars. From then on, chaos ensued, as Xieng Khouang got caught in the middle of the war between the Royalist-American and Pathet Lao-Vietnamese (see also page 169). The extensive US bombing of this area was to ensure it did not fall under Communist control of Pathet Lao. The Vietnamese were trying to ensure that the US did not gain control of the area from which they could launch attacks on North Vietnam.

During the Secret War' (1964-1974) against the North Vietnamese Army and the Pathet Lao, tens of thousands of cluster bomb units (CBUs) were dumped on Xieng Khouang Province. Other bombs such as the anti-personnel plastic 'pineapple' bomblets were also used. As 30% of the original CBUs did not explode, these cluster bombs continue to kill and maim today. The Plain of Jars was also hit by B-52s returning from abortive bombing runs to Hanoi, which jettisoned their bomb loads before heading back to the US air base at Udon Thani in northeast Thailand. One bombing raid destroyed 1600 buildings in Xieng Khouang town alone. Suffice to say that, with over 580,944 sorties flown (one-and-a-half times the number flown in Vietnam), whole towns were obliterated and the area's geography was permanently altered. Today, as the **Lao Airlines** plane begins its descent towards the plateau, the meaning of the term 'carpet bombing' becomes clear. On the final approach to the town of Phonsavanh, the plane banks low over the cratered paddy fields, affording a T-28 fighter-bomber pilot's view of his target, which in places has been pummelled into little more than a moonscape. Some of the craters are 15 m across and 7 m deep. Testament to the Lao people's resilience, symbolically, many of these craters have been turned into tranquil fish ponds; the bombs transformed into fences and the CBU carriers serving as planter pots.

The so-called 'collateral damage' was also staggering. There is no official figure on the number of dead but, since over 80% of the population is believed to have inhabited the northern and southern provinces targeted by US bombing, some sources estimate 300,000 Lao were killed – between a ninth and a tenth of the country's total population at the time. One survivor from just outside Phonsavanh recalled his experiences of the bombing campaigns: "I was just a boy, coming home and saw a bomb hit my house. It exploded and split my home right in two! My parents and my brother were killed; my sister, killed; the family, killed; my dog was killed, the buffaloes, killed. Everything gone." He remembers how "the kids would run out to the streets and pick up these things that had fallen from the sky, like parachutes, thinking they were chocolate bars or something, and their arms would catch fire and no matter how hard you tried you couldn't put it out, these screaming children on fire. It was horrific, truly horrific."

Today, hundreds of thousands of bomblets – and equally lethal impact mines, which the Lao call *bombis* – remain buried in Xieng Khouang's grassy meadows. Because the war was 'secret', there are few records of what was dropped where, and even when the unexploded ordnance (UXO) has been uncovered their workings are often a mystery – the Americans used Laos as a testing ground for new ordnance so blueprints are unavailable. One aid worker relates how in the mid-1980s, a specially designed, armour-plated tractor was terminally disabled by *bombis*, while attempting to clear them from the fields. The UK-based **Mines Advisory Group (MAG) UXO Visitor Information Centre** ① *on the main road in the centre of town, Mon-Fri 0800-2000, Sat-Sun 1600-2000*, is currently engaged in clearing the land of Unexploded Ordnance. It has an exhibition of bombs, interesting photographs and information on the bombing campaign and ongoing plight of Laos with UXO. Usually there are members of staff on hand to explain exactly how the bombs were used. All T-shirts sold here help fund the UXO clearance of the area and are a very worthwhile souvenir. Films are shown at 1630, 1745 and 1830 but can be seen at other times; donations are welcome.

Opposite the MAG centre is the **Xieng Khuang UXO Survivors Center** ① *www.laos. worlded.org, daily 0900-2100*, detailing the work of World Education Laos in preventing UXO accidents and aiding UXO survivors.

Uncle Sam has, however, bequeathed to local people an almost unlimited supply of twisted metal. Bombshells and flare casings can frequently be seen in Xieng Khouang's villages where they are used for everything from cattle troughs and fences, to stilts for houses and water-carriers. In Phonsavanh steel runway sheets make handy walls, while plants are potted out in shell casings.

Xieng Khouang remains one of the poorest provinces in an already wretchedly poor country. The whole province has a population of only around 250,000, a mix of different ethnic groups, predominantly Hmong, Lao and a handful of Khmu. Government attempts to curtail shifting cultivation and encourage the Hmong to settle have not been very successful, largely because there are no alternative livelihoods available. Travelling through the province there is a sense not just that the American air war caused enormous suffering and destruction, but that the following decades have not provided much in the way of economic opportunities.

Phonsavanh → *For listings, see pages 175-179. Colour map 1, C4. Phone code: 061.*

Phonsavanh is the main town of the province today – old Xieng Khouang having been flattened – and its small airstrip is a crucial transport link in this mountainous region. Surrounding the town are huge mountains, among them Phu Bia, one of the country's highest. The town itself is notable mainly for its ugliness. It was established in the mid-1970s and sprawls out from a heartless centre with no sense of plan or direction. While Phonsavanh will win no beauty contests, it does have a rather attractive 'Wild West' atmosphere. As journalist Malcolm Macalister Hall wrote in 1998: "I liked this ugly, rough-hewn town: for its unlikely invitations, its mad breakfasts, and the beautiful landscapes that surrounded it". What's more, it's the only base from which to explore the Plain of Jars (see below), so it has a fair number of hotels and guesthouses. The daily market is busy but rather undistinguished, with the usual assortment of cheap Chinese bric-a-brac. The food market, behind the post office, is more lively and worth a look.

South of Phonsavanh, on two small hills, a pair of white and gold monuments can be seen. (The road to the memorials is marked Ban Yone Temple.) It is worth the short hike up, if only for the views they afford of the surrounding countryside. The **Vietnamese war memorial**, on the west side, was built to commemorate the death of over one million Vietnamese troops during the war against the anti-Communists. It contains the bones of Vietnamese soldiers and is inscribed 'Lao Vietnamese Solidarity Forever'. It is the more interesting of the two for its golden socialist statues in strident pose and socialist murals in relief. The newer **Lao war memorial** to the east, is more rounded in the Lao style and was built later in memory of 4500 Pathet Lao soldiers who died, including Hmong and Khmu fighters (often only remembered as fighting for the US).

Just before the bus station on the way into town is **Mulberries** ① *Route 7, T020-5552 1408, www.mulberries.org*, where you can visit a silk farm, see the sericulture process in action and buy a wide range of exquisite silk goods in the shop. It's open for tours Monday to Saturday 0800-1600.

The German NGO DED, along with other agencies, have done an excellent job in producing the Xieng Khouang Discovery Guide (available in the tourist office), which explains and promotes brand-new tours it has created in the area: trekking between jar sites, past waterfalls, lakes, visiting war scrap spoon factories, umbrella-making villages, Hmong villages, caves and stupas. These one- and two-day tours are possible on foot, by 4WD or by motorbike and can be arranged through local operators, see page 178. A city tour has also been drawn up.

Plain of Jars → For listings, see pages 175-179. Colour map 1, C5.

The undulating plateau of the Plain of Jars (also known as Plaine de Jarres, or **Thong Hai Hin**), stretches for about 50 km east to west, covering an area of 1000 sq km at an altitude of 1000 m. In total there are 136 archaeological sites in this area, containing thousands of jars, discs and deliberately placed stones. Of these only three are currently open to tourists. Note that the plateau can be cold from December to March.

Ins and outs
Getting there and around
Provincial laws have sporadically banned tuk-tuks and motorbikes from ferrying customers outside of town. At the time of writing, motorbikes were allowed to the sites but tuk-tuks were not. It should be possible to drive to the Plain of Jars, see Site one and return to town in two hours. Expect to pay in the region of US$30 for an English-speaking guide and vehicle for four people, or US$60 for seven people and a minivan. A tuk-tuk to Site one costs approximately US$7 per person. Alternatively, guesthouses and tour companies in Phonsavanh run set tours to the Plain of Jars. If you arrive by air, the chances are you'll be inundated with official and unofficial would-be guides as soon as you step off the plane. Note that it is not possible to walk from the airport to Site one, as there is a military base in between. It is recommended that you hire a guide, for at least a day, to get an insight into the history of the area. The cost of admission to each site is 10,000 kip. The sites are open Oct-Feb 0800-1600 and Mar-Sep 0700-1700. ▸▸ *See Activities and tours, page 178 and Transport, page 178.*

Secret war on the Plain of Jars

The Plain of Jars occupies an important place in modern Lao history as it became one of the most strategic battlegrounds of the war. For General Vang Pao's Hmong, it was the hearthstone of their mountain kingdom; for the royalist government and the Americans it was a critical piece in the Indochinese jigsaw; for Hanoi it was their back garden, which had to be secured to protect their rear flank. From the mid-1960s, neutralist forces were encamped on the Plain (dubbed 'the PDJ' during the war). They were supported by Hmong, based at the secret city of Long Tien, to the southwest. US-backed and North Vietnamese-backed forces fought a bitter war of attrition on the PDJ; each time royalist and Hmong forces were defeated on the ground, US air power was called in to pummel from above. In mid-February 1970, American Strategic Air Command, on presidential orders, directed that B-52 Stratofortress bombers should be used over the PDJ for the first time. Capable of silently dumping more than one hundred 500-lb bombs from 40,000 ft, they had a devastating effect on the towns and villages of the plain but a minimal effect on Communist morale. Even if the B-52s had managed to wipe out North Vietnamese and Pathet Lao forces, the US-backed troops were unable to reach, let alone hold, the territory. Hanoi had garrisons of reinforcements waiting in the wings.

On the plain, the B-52 proved as ineffective a weapon as it would later on the Ho Chi Minh Trail. As US bomber command turned its attention to the trail, the Pathet Lao seized the upper hand and retook the PDJ. The Communists were beaten back onto the surrounding hills by Vang Pao's forces and American bombers but they kept swarming back and, by March 1972, the North Vietnamese Army had seven divisions in Laos supporting the Pathet Lao. The so-called 'Mountain of Courage' – the hill behind the new airport to the northwest – was the scene of particularly hard fighting. It was here that the royalists, encamped on Phu Kheng, were trapped on two fronts by the Communists. When the Pathet Lao retook Xieng Khouang for the last time in 1973, they consolidated their position and bided their time.

Background

Most of the jars are generally between 1 m and 2.5 m high, around 1 m in diameter and weigh about the same as three small cars. The largest are about 3 m tall. The jars have long presented an archaeological conundrum, leaving generations of theorists nonplussed by how they got there and what they were used for. Local legend relates that King Khoon Chuong and his troops from Southern China threw a stupendous party after their victory over the wicked Chao Angka and had the jars made to brew outrageous quantities of *lao-lao*. However attractive this alcoholic thesis, it is more likely that the jars are in fact 2000-year-old stone funeral urns. The larger jars are believed to have been for the local aristocracy and the smaller jars for their minions.

Some archaeologists speculate that the cave below the main site was hewn from the rock at about the same time as the jars themselves and that the hole in the roof possibly indicates that the cave was used for cremation or that the jars were made and fired in the cave. But this is all speculation and the jars' true origins and function remain a mystery. In fact, the stone from which the jars at Site one are made doesn't seem to come from that area. Instead, using the evidence of some half-hewn jars made of the same stone found near Sites two and three, archaeologists have postulated that the jars were carved here and then transported to Site one.

Tools, bronze ornaments, ceramics and other objects have been found in the jars, indicating that a civilized society was responsible for them but no-one has a clue which one, as the artefacts bear no relation to those left behind by other ancient Indochinese civilizations. Some of the jars were once covered with round lids and there is one jar, in the group facing the entrance to the cave, which is decorated with a rough carving of a dancing figure.

Over the years, a few jars have been stolen and a number have been transported by helicopter down to Vientiane's Wat Phra Kaeo and the backyard of the National Museum (see pages 53 and 56). Local guides will claim that despite four or five B-52 bombing raids on the plain every day for five years during the Secret War (see box, page 169), the jars remained mysteriously unscathed. However, several bomb craters and damaged jars at the main site show this to be a fanciful myth. During heavy fighting on the plain in the early 1970s, the Pathet Lao set up a command centre in the cave next to the jars and then posed among the jars for photographs (which can be seen in the Revolutionary Museum in Vientiane). Around the entrance to the cave are numerous bomb craters, as the US targeted the sanctuary in a futile attempt to dislodge the Communists.

A vast aviation fuel depot was built next to the jars, early in the 1990s, to supply the huge new airbase just to the west. The base, designed by Soviet technicians, is the new

Plain of Jars

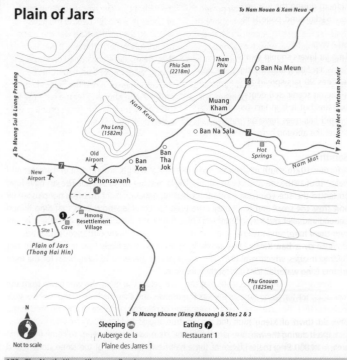

Sleeping ⊟
Auberge de la
Plaine des Jarres 1

Eating ⊙
Restaurant 1

Not to scale

headquarters for the Lao Air Force, although why the government needs a large airbase here remains a mystery and something of a political minefield. On the grasslands around the jars are stumpy little flowers, known as '*baa*' by the Hmong and '*dok waan*' by the Lao; the stems are boiled to make a soup, while the red buds are fried. Once the flower has bloomed (turning yellow), they are no longer tasty. Along with the bomb craters that scar the landscape there are also patches of bare earth that have nothing to do with the Indochina conflict. These are sparrow free-fire zones: after the first rains, local people clear the land of grass over an area of about 10 sq m and build a small hide; they then put sticky rice down on the ground and wait for the poor creatures to alight for a leisurely lunch before being blasted.

Site one

Some 334 jars survive, mainly scattered on one slope at so-called 'Site one' or **Thong Hai Hin**, 10 km southwest of Phonsavanh. This site is closest to Phonsavanh and has the largest jar – along with a small café. A path, cleared by MAG, winds through the site, with a warning not to walk away from delineated areas as UXO are still around. Each of the jars weighs about a tonne, although the biggest, called **Hai Cheaum**, is over 2 m tall and weighs over 6 tonnes. Folklore suggests that the jar is named after a Thai-Lao liberator, who overthrew Chao Angka. Further downhill is another smattering of jars, some of which feature carvings. The smallish cave in the hill to the left was used by the Pathet Lao as a hideout during the war and may have been the ancient kiln in which the jars were fired (see Background, page 169).

Site two

True jar lovers should visit Site two, known as **Hai Hin Phu Salatao** (literally 'Salato Hill Stone Jar Site'), and Site three (see below). Site two is 25 km south of Phonsavanh and features 90 jars spread across two hills. The jars are set in a rather beautiful location, affording scenic 360 degree views over the surrounding countryside. Most people miss this site, but it is in fact the most atmospheric because of the hilltop location. On the second hill, trees have grown through the centre of the jars, splitting them four ways; butterflies abound here.

Site three

A further 10 km south of Site two, Site three, also called **Hai Hin Laat Khai**, is the most peaceful of all the sites, set in verdant green rolling hills, Swiss-cheesed with bomb craters. To get to the site you have to walk through some rice paddies, past a burbling brook and cross the small bamboo bridge. There are more than 130 jars at this site, which are generally smaller and more damaged than at the other sites. There's also a very small, basic restaurant here, serving *feu*.

Close by is **Ban Xieng Dee**, a friendly village, home to a monastery featuring some Buddha images, which were badly damaged during the war. Villagers will lead treks to the nearby Lang waterfall for 10,000 kip.

Muang Khoune (old Xieng Khouang) → *Colour map 1, C4.*

The old town of Xieng Khouang – now rebuilt and renamed Muang Khoune – was destroyed during the war, between 1964 and 1969, and now the population is reduced to a mere 14,000. Prior to the bombing, the town was extremely picturesque, similar to Luang

Prabang, with over 400 old colonial buildings and 30 wats and pagodas, but today, reduced to little more than a row of wooden Lao houses and a market area, it holds nothing in the way of aesthetic charm, and a sense of impermanence pervades the town. However, while Muang Khoune itself is spectacularly unimpressive, its position, surrounded by mountains, is noteworthy.

Background

Xieng Khouang was founded by Chao Noi Muang and was a stronghold for the Xieng Khouang royal family. In 1832 the Hmong mountain state was annexed by Vietnam and renamed Tran Ninh; the king was marched off to Vietnam and publicly executed in Hué, while the population of Xieng Khouang was forced to wear Vietnamese dress.

Many important temples were built here in the distinctive Xieng Khouang style but these were completely obliterated by the American bombing. The religious architecture of the province was one of Laos' three main architectural styles (Luang Prabang and Vientiane styles being the other two). The town was also the main centre for the French in this area during the colonial period and remnants of French colonial architecture are still in evidence.

Xieng Khouang was most heavily bombed during 1969 and 1970, when US air power was called in to reverse the success of the Communists' dry season offensive on the Plain of Jars. In his book *The Ravens*, Christopher Robins interviews several former US pilots who describe the annihilation of the town in which 1500 buildings were razed, together with another 2000 across the plain. Three towns, he says, "were wiped from the map. By the end of the year (1970) there would not be a building left standing". During this time most villagers left their homes and lived in caves or in the forest, subsisting on rice from China and Vietnam. So incessant was the bombing and strafing that peasants took to planting their rice fields at night. One brave woman recalled, "I would have to get the rice at two or three in the morning so as not to be seen. I would carry it on my back, sometimes 100 kg, it was so heavy that I was doubled over, my head almost touching the ground."

The town, now not much more than a village, was rebuilt after 1975 and renamed Muang Khoune.

Sights

Those excited about the prospect of visiting a unique collection of 500-year-old wats must, for the most part, be content with piles of bricks. There is virtually nothing left of the 16th-century **Wat Phia Wat** (at the far end of town on the right-hand side by the road), except the basement and several shrapnel-pocked Buddha statues, including a large, seated Buddha which is believed to be over 600 years old. The once-picturesque wat underwent a series of renovations in 1930 only to be bombed into oblivion by the Americans. The half-hearted attempt at further renovation is barely noticeable. Walking up the hill, the remains of the French colonial Governor's house, built in the 1930s, can be seen, with some old tile floors still in place and a hospital, patched together Lao-style.

Two stupas perch on a pair of hills rising above the town. **That Chompet** is a stump of its former self and is relatively overgrown. A better alternative is the 16th-century **That Foun**, which is quite sizeable and similar to That Dam in Vientiane. It is said to contain relics of the Indian emperor Asoka but this legend should be taken with a large pinch of *nam pa*. It may, however, explain why the heart of the stupa has been hollowed out, as thieves have searched, apparently in vain, for buried treasure, in particular old Buddha images said to have been hidden here.

Wat Si Phoum (opposite the market below the main road) was also destroyed by the war and now a new inelegant wat has been built next to the ruined *that*. There is a small monastery attached.

The market in Muang Khoune sell the bare essentials. Head to the Black Tai village, about 500 m northwest of town, to buy local handicrafts and scarves.

West of Phonsavanh

Nong Tang (formerly Muang Sui)

Nong Tang lies 45 km west of Phonsavanh on Route 7. The town was formerly known for its vast array of old Buddhist temples and traditional Lao architecture but its fate was sealed once it became a primary landing site for US planes. The town was later razed by the North Vietnamese Army. It is part of a district called Phu Kut, an area known for Hmong insurgency, so don't be surprised if you see armed personnel around. The strip of road, in particular, has experienced ongoing difficulties with Hmong insurgents and, although things are settling down now, with a large group surrendering to the government in 2005, there is still a small risk of attack. There aren't many sights in the actual town and a day trip from Phonsavanh should be more than sufficient to take in the outlying caves and picturesque **Nong Tang Lake**. The lake is crowned by limestone karst formations and believed to be very deep.

The caves around Nong Tang make the trip worthwhile; a US$1 entrance fee is paid at **Buddha Cave** (Tham Pha), a large honeycomb network of labyrinthine passages, grottoes and caverns that is said to house over 1000 Buddha images, many dating back 1200 years. Another nearby cave, was used by the Vietnamese Army as a hospital and is still known as **Hospital Cave**. **Water Cave**, named after the water that falls through its roof, isn't as interesting as the other caves. Nearby is the large **Stupa Cave** (Tham That), which contains the ruins of an old stupa believed to be several hundred years old. Within walking distance is **Coffin Cave**, nestled high up in a limestone cliff. It's a bit of a climb to the cave but worth it as it contains prehistoric coffins carved out of old tree trunks. The caves have been raided but there are a few human remains and remnants scattered around the floor.

East of Phonsavanh → *For listings, see pages 175-179.*

Route 7 heads east from Phonsavanh towards Muang Kham and the border with Vietnam (see page 175). The journey is characterized by attractive rolling hills and grassy meadows in the wet season but becomes very barren in the dry season, especially where the bomb craters have pock-marked the landscape. The drive is an abject lesson in the potentially destructive nature of some forms of shifting cultivation. Some authorities estimate that up to 100,000 ha of forest were being destroyed in this area by slash-and-burn agriculture before the government implemented a policy to minimize the practice. The difficulty is that minority shifting cultivators – especially the Hmong – often farm land that has already been logged by commercial timber firms (for the simple reason that it is easier to cultivate) and then find themselves blamed for the destruction.

About 12 km east of Phonsavanh is the village of **Ban Xon**, which lays claim to two famous daughters, Baoua Kham and Baoua Xi, who are reported to have shot down a US B-52 with small arms fire. War historians are very sceptical about this claim but a Lao popular song was nonetheless written about them. The ballad is said to extol the beauty and courage of the women of Xieng Khouang.

Hmong villages

Route 7 winds its way down off the plateau along the Nam Keua, a fertile area where Hmong villagers grow rice and maize. About 25 km east of Phonsavanh is the Hmong market, held on Sundays from 0400 to 1000. Hundreds of people come in from surrounding villages to the colourful market to sell local produce, animals and handicrafts. Many of the older people wear traditional attire. Seven kilometres further east is the roadside Hmong village of **Ban Tha Jok**, where there are some old Hmong houses that use old bomb casings as stilts but you must walk away from the main road to see them; it is well worth it.

If you wish to visit a more traditional Hmong settlement, leave your vehicle at Ban Na Sala Mai on the main road and walk south for 5 km, up a pleasant valley to **Ban Na Sala**. This is a very beautiful village, perched in the hills. During the war, the Pathet Lao occupied the hills surrounding this village, so the US army was not able to go anywhere near it. Ban Na Sala is one of the best places in Laos to see the creative architectural and household application of war debris, as here, too, the people have utilized bomb casings to construct their houses.

Muang Kham

This small trading town, 53 km east of Phonsavanh, is situated in the centre of a large open valley on the route to Vietnam. It was devastated during the war but now has a thriving economy dealing in Vietnamese and Chinese goods. The valley is an important fruit- and rice-growing area. There's a market early every morning in the centre of town and there are also a couple of groups of stone jars close by.

Tham Phiu

ⓘ *East of Muang Kham, off Route 7, just after the Km 183 post, entry to caves 5000 kip. A rough track leads down to an irrigation dam, built in 1981. To get to Tham Phiu, either go the easy way and hire a vehicle and driver US$30-40 from Phonsavanh, or go the hard way, by public transport. For the latter, take the bus to Nong Het, and request to stop at the Tham Phiu turn-off. From here walk towards the towering limestone cliff and follow the small trails for the last kilometre. It is best to do this with a guide as UXOs still litter the area.*

Evidence of the dirty war can be seen in the area immediately surrounding Muang Kham. The intensity of the US bombing campaign under the command of the late General Curtis Le May was such that entire villages were forced to take refuge in caves. (Curtis Le May is infamously associated with bragging that he wanted to bomb the Communists "back into the Stone Age".) In Tham Phiu, a cave overlooking the valley, 374 villagers from nearby Ban Na Meun built a two-storey bomb shelter and concealed its entrance with a high stone wall. They lived there for a year, working in their rice fields at night and taking cover during the day from the relentless bombing raids.

On the morning of 24 November 1968 two T-28 fighter bombers took off from Udon Thani air base in neighbouring Thailand and located the cave mouth which had been exposed on previous sorties. It is likely that the US forces suspected that the cave contained a Pathet Lao hospital complex. Indeed, experts are at odds whether this was a legitimate target or an example of collateral damage. The first rocket destroyed the wall; the second, which was fired as the planes swept across the valley, carried the full length of the chamber before exploding. There were no survivors; in total 437 people died, many reportedly women and children. Local rescuers claim they were unable to enter the cave for three days, but eventually the dead were buried in a bomb crater on the hillside next to the cave mouth. Today there is an official

Nong Het is 60 km east of Muang Kham. It is deep in Hmong country and an important trading post with Vietnam, a few kilometres away at Nam Khan. Few tourists use this crossing, although trucks and *songthaew* ply between Phonsavanh and the border daily, four to five hours, US$4-5. There are also buses via Nong Het from Phonsavanh's bus station Tuesday and Friday at 0630, US$10. Lao visas (30 days) available border for US$30-42; Vietnamese visas are required in advance.

memorial halfway up the steps but nothing inside the cave, just the eerily black walls. The interior of the cave was completely dug up by rescue parties and relatives and today there is nothing but rubble inside. It makes for a poignant lesson in military history and locally it is considered a war memorial. Further up the cliff is another cave, **Tham Phiu Song**, which didn't suffer the same fate. Visitors are welcome to explore but will need to take a torch.

Bor Yai and Bor Noi

ⓘ *Hot Springs Resort, off Route 7, daily 0900-1900, 5000 kip. Taxi from Muang Kham 50,000 kip or tour from Phonsavanh; public bus from Phonsavanh, 18,000 kip.*

Not far from Muang Kham, off the Vietnam road, are two hot springs (*bor nam lawn*) on the Nam Mat, imaginatively named Bor Yai (Big Spring) and Bor Noi (Little Spring). They are locally known for their curative properties and are said to have enormous potential for geothermal power but this is hard to believe as they do not appear to be particularly active. The murky water is distinctly uninviting but it is piped to showers and wooden tubs, where a therapeutic soak can be quite pleasant. The springs are owned and operated by the government, so to bathe you have to go to the resort, which has a number of private bathrooms that tourists can use for the day. The resort was purportedly built by Kaysone Phomvihane's wife for visiting dignitaries.

⦿ Xieng Khouang Province listings

For Sleeping and Eating price codes and other relevant information, see pages 23-24.

⦿ Sleeping

Phonsavanh *p167*

None of the streets in Phonsavanh are named. Nearly all the guesthouses, restaurants and travel agents are located on a short strip of the main road or just off it. Some of the guesthouses offer free airport/bus station transfer; it's worth ringing in advance to request this. A new hilltop hotel of smart white bungalows, **Phou Vieng Kham** (T020-2215 1888), close to the

Auberge, should be open by the time you read this.

B Auberge de la Plaine des Jarres (aka Phu Pha Daeng Hotel), 1 km from the centre of Phonsavanh, T030-517 0282, www.plainedesjarres.com. In a spectacular position on a hill overlooking town are 15 attractive stone and wood chalets, each with its own living room, fireplace and shower room. The chalets are clean and comfortable, and have lovely views (from a new terrace), with roses, geraniums, wild poinsettia and petunias planted around the chalets. The restaurant, with a roaring fire, serves good food. (Anthony Bourdain stayed here for his book *Kitchen Confidential*, working with owner Sanya.)

B Vansana, on a hill about 1 km out of town, T061-213170, www.vansanahotel-group.com. Offers big, modern rooms equipped with telephone, TV, minibar, and tea/coffee-making facilities, and has phenomenal views of the countryside. The best room is the smart suite with polished wooden floors and textile decoration. Or opt for one of the rooms upstairs, which have free-form bathtub and picturesque balcony views. The restaurant offers Lao and foreign cuisine. Highly recommended.

B-C The Hillside Residence (aka Nearn Phou), T061-213300, www.thehillresidence.com. New, family-run guesthouse on the track to the Vansana Resort. Rooms are decorated with textiles and come with luggage racks and floral-tiled bathrooms; twins are larger (a couple of the doubles are tiny). The first-floor balcony is a great place to kick back.

B-C Maly Hotel, down the road from local government offices, T061-312031, www.malyht.laotel.com. All the rooms have hot water and are furnished with a hotchpotch of local artefacts, including a small (defused!) cluster bomb on the table. The more expensive, much larger rooms on the upper floors have satellite TV, internet for those who have laptops, out-of-place baths in large bathrooms, a sitting area, fireplace and hairdryers; the standard rooms are considerably smaller but have their own shower unit. There is also a restaurant. Unfortunately, the former owner, the knowledgeable Mr Sousath Phetrasy, who during the war spent his teenage years in a cave at Xam Neua, died in 2009. There is a tour desk inside the hotel.

D Phu Chan Resort, on a hill on the outskirts of town, T061-312264. Rustic set up surrounded by pine trees, this comprises cosy yet spacious wooden bungalows with 3 rooms each. The rooms have modern fittings but are a little on the dark side. Price includes breakfast.

D-E White Orchid, just off the main road in the centre of town, T061-312403. You can't miss this big green building. Guesthouse, not quite up to hotel standard but close enough to be good value. Rooms with TV, hot water, comfortable beds and bathroom. Nicely decorated; twins are spacious and have bathtubs. Breakfast is included and airport pick up can be arranged if you ring in advance.

E Dok Khoun, Route 7, main road, T061-312189. Spacious, tiled rooms with desk. The small bathrooms do not contain separate shower units. Only 2 rooms offer a/c. Reception decorated with UXO.

E Nice Guesthouse, on the main road, T020-55616246, naibhoj@hotmail.com. Has a Chinese feel about it but is owned by local Lao. Clean and decent-sized rooms with hot water and comfortable beds. Offers reasonable value.

E-F Kong Keo, just off the main road, T061-211354, www.kongkeojar.com. This popular hangout is run by the friendly Kong. It comprises 13 modern rooms, which are small and basic with tiny bathrooms, and wooden bungalows, which are darker but larger and more atmospheric but with even smaller bathrooms. The bonfire ignited inside the cluster bomb case each night is a popular draw in the restaurant.

F Sabaidee, a block back from the main road, T020-5506 7990, sabaidee2000@hotmail.com. Tiled, clean rooms with hot-water bathroom. Very low Hobbit-like doors. Central location, family atmosphere but a little run down these days, and with no exterior windows.

Plain of Jars *p168*

There is one guesthouse in the town of Muang Khoune, part of the **Manivanh** restaurant, see below.

Bor Yai and Bor Noi *p175*

F Senebot, around the corner from Hot Springs Guesthouse. Rooms are on the small side.

Parasol Renaissance

Aside from the war paraphernalia, Phonsavanh is also the best place in Laos to pick up a traditional paper parasol. The art of making paper and wood umbrellas, also known as *khan nyu*, has undergone a renaissance in the last decade. The tradition is a centuries-old practice, originally bequeathed to the domain of monkhood. Novices and monks would make the parasols to give as gifts to the villages they were visiting. After 1975, the paper umbrellas were quickly usurped by plastic and metal ones from China. The frame of the umbrella is formed from bamboo and the paper made from a pulp of mulberry trees and usually dyed with colour from fruits, such as apple. The paper is stuck to the frame with glue made from persimmon resin and the outside spokes are painted with a charcoal compound. The umbrellas sell from US$5 upwards and can be found in the market and at guesthouses, such as Seng Tava.

G Hot Springs Guesthouse, Bor Yai. 2 lovely wooden bungalows, each with 4 rooms and 1 bathroom. Recommended.

Eating

Phonsavanh p167

Maly Hotel, see Sleeping. This is a great little restaurant serving fantastic food from a very extensive menu: everything from duck curry to beef steak.

Auberge de la Plaine de Jarres, see Sleeping. Reasonable menu of Lao dishes and some delicious French food. The French menu is overpriced given the competition but the Asian menu represents much better value. The dining room with roaring fire is a welcome retreat.

Craters, main street, T020-7780 5775. Modern, Western-style restaurant offering range of burgers, pizza and sandwiches. Comfortable cane sofas, good music, attentive service. Also has delectable but pricey cocktails.

Nisha Indian, on the main road. Wins the prize for most unexpected find in Phonsavanh. Good choice of north and south Indian food – very welcome if you need a reprieve from the same Asian dishes found throughout the north of Laos. The owner, endeavouring to exhibit some marketing prowess, has handwritten his name and phone number on every single water bottle.

Phonexay, on the main road. Excellent fruit shakes and good Asian dishes – fried noodles, sweet and sour. Exceptionally friendly service.

Sangah, main street. Wide range of Thai, Lao and Vietnamese (good noodle soup) dishes, as well as some Western fare including steak and chips. Known for its enormous portions.

Simmaly, main street, T061-211013. What this place lacks in atmosphere it makes up 10-fold with food. Fantastic *feu* soup. Great service and immensely popular. Recommended.

Plain of Jars p168

There are many good restaurants in **Muang Khoune**. Manivanh, T020-2234 5396, for example, has good soup and fried rice/noodles dishes. There's also good *pho* opposite the market.

Shopping

Phonsavanh p167

There are a multitude of shops at the town's market. The dry market is beside the town bus station and sells a good selection of local handicrafts including textiles and silver. Most everyday items, from shoes to biscuits can also be purchased here. West of the centre of town is the Chinese Market, which stocks a good variety of ethnic clothes and jewellery as well as lots of cheap tacky imported products. Behind the post office is a fresh produce market with a gamut of fruit and vegetables on offer. The **Navang Craft Center**, behind the new hilltop Phou Vieng Kham hotel, specializes in crafts made of wood (Fijian cypress) (daily 0730-2000). Silk goods are sold at **Mulberries**, see page 168, a silk farm on the outskirts of Phonsavanh.

⊛ Festivals and events

Phonsavanh *p167*
Dec National Day on 2 Dec is celebrated with horse-drawn drag-cart racing. Also in Dec is **Hmong New Year** (movable), which is celebrated in a big way in this area. Festivities centre on the killing of a pig and then offering the head to the spirits. Boys give cloth balls, known as *makoi*, to girls they've taken a fancy to.

▲ Activities and tours

Phonsavanh *p167*
Tour operators
There are no shortage of tour operators in Phonsavanh and most guesthouses can also arrange tours and transport. A full-day tour for 4 people, travelling about 30 km into the countryside around Phonsavanh, should cost up to US$50-60, although you may have to bargain for it. The tourist office does not organize tours but it does offer a guide service for 60,000-70,000 kip. Most of the travel agencies are located within a block of each other on the main road.

All agencies should be able to organize the new tours featured in the Xieng Khouang Discovery Guide.
Amazing Lao Travel, on the main road, T061-312121, www.amazinglao.com. Offers tours to Xam Neua and can arrange transport to other destinations. Provides an internet service too.

Indochina Travel, on the main road, T061-312409, www.indochinatravelco.com. This is a comparatively expensive but well-regarded company offering minivan tours. These will work out a lot cheaper if you can organize a group.
Inter-Lao Travel, on the main road, T061-211729, www.interlao.laopdr.com. This company offers a range of minivan tours to the Plain of Jars and several outlying villages as well as motorbike and bicycle rental and transport to Vientiane.
Lao Youth Travel, on Route 7, T020-5576 1233, www.laoyouthtravel.com. Offers a wide range of tours to the jars and post-conflict sites.

⊖ Transport

Phonsavanh *p167*
Air
As you fly into Phonsavanh (XKH), the pock-marked landscape comes into view and the war's collateral damage becomes apparent.
Lao Airlines, T061-312027 (airport T061-312177), runs flights to **Vientiane**, daily except Sat; check www.laoairlines.com for current schedules, 660,000 kip. It flies to **Luang Prabang** on Sun.

Bus
From the main bus station outside of town (T030-517 0148): To **Luang Prabang**, 0830 daily (VIP bus), 265 km on a sealed road, 8 hrs, 75,000 kip. To **Vientiane**, 6 daily, 9-10 hrs, 95,000 kip, also a VIP bus (with a/c and TV) daily, 120,000 kip. Also north to **Vang Vieng**, six VIP buses daily, 80,000-120,000 kip. To **Xam Neua**, daily 0800, 1900, 2200, 60,000 kip, a 10-hr haul through some of the country's most beautiful scenery with very winding roads towards the end (in fact, you may want to take travel sickness medicine with you).

Buses also travel to **Vinh**, Vietnam, Tue, Thu, Fri and Sat 0630, 10 hrs, 138,000 kip. A VIP bus heads for **Hanoi** on Mon at 0630, 185,000 kip. If you want to cross the Nam

Khan border here (see box, page 175) you will need to plan ahead and organize a visa in advance, as there is no consulate in Phonsavanh or agencies that will send your passport to Vientiane.

Buses leaving from the new market (T061-312178): To **Muang Kham**, 1 hr, 18,000 kip. To **Nong Tang** in Phu Kut district, 1130, 8000 kip.

To the hot springs, 1130, 1300, 1½ hrs, 25,000 kip.

Buses from the Namngam market (near the tourist office, T020-5587 5207). To **Muang Khoun**, 8 daily, 45 mins, 15,000 kip. Also north to **Nam Nouan**, 0900, 4 hrs, 35,000 kip (change here for transport west to **Nong Khiaw**).

Car with driver/songthaew

Hiring a car with driver is the easiest way of touring the area. A full car to the **Plain of Jars** will cost US$20 (US$5 each) to Site one, or US$30-40 if you want to see all 3 sites. The tour could be combined with a trip to the hot springs, west of Muang Kham, for an additional US$20-30. To **Nong Tang**, US$60-80 return.

To hire a *songthaew* to go to **Tham Phiu** is US$30-40 for the day, a minivan here will cost you about US$60.

Motorbike

Happy Motorbike for Rent (next to Craters), T224 7131, rents bikes for 100,000 kip per day and bicycles for 40,000 kip.

Plain of Jars *p168*

Route 1D is surfaced between Muang Khoune and Phonsavanh (32 km). Buses to **Phonsavanh** depart daily from the Morning Market, 45 min, 15,000 kip.

Muang Kham *p174*

The only way to visit the minority villages en route to Muang Kham is by hiring a taxi. A taxi from Muang Kham to the hot springs costs 50,000 kip.

⊙ Directory

Phonsavanh *p167*

Banks Lao Development Bank, next to Lao Airlines Office, 2 blocks back from the dry market, changes cash and TCs and provides cash advances on MasterCard, Mon-Fri 0800-1530, no advances on Visa. There are 2 BCEL ATMs on the main road. **Indochine Travel** has an exchange booth with Visa advance but they charge a whopping 6.9% commission. Moneygram service. **Internet** There are a couple of internet cafés on the main road, charging 200 kip per min, but the service is not very reliable. **Medical services** Lao-Mongolian Hospital, T061-312166, Sufficient for minor ailments, but not for more serious problems. Pharmacies are plentiful around the market. **Post and telephone** The post office is opposite the dry market and has IDD phone boxes outside.

Hua Phan Province

Hua Phan Province has a total population of 270,000 and is one of the most isolated areas of the country. Over 20 ethnic groups, mostly mountain-dwellers, inhabit the province, whose character has been shaped over the centuries by a variety of shifting rulers: it was part of the Tai Neua Kingdom, then integrated into the Annamese state of Ai Lao and also experienced stints as a Siamese protectorate and French colonial outpost. Until recently, Hua Phan remained relatively sheltered from the free market ethos that has spilled into towns along the Thai and Chinese borders, and memories of the period when it was the base for the revolutionary struggle are still close to the surface. Traders from China and Vietnam are more common these days but Hua Phan is still known in Laos as the 'revolutionary province'.

Hua Phan is spectacularly beautiful but largely overlooked by tourists. This is a shame, as it is one of the most scenic parts of the country. It is also one of the country's poorest provinces, with over 75% of the population living below the poverty line. Local authorities hope that the area's large tourism potential will help to alleviate the plight and they have teamed up with the NGO SNV to develop infrastructure. There are plans for new guesthouses, a new runway, a visa facility at the Vietnam border and, generally, more open access. The LNTA also plan to launch the Northern Heritage Route, taking visitors from Luang Prabang in a clockwise route up to Nong Khiaw, Vieng Thong, Xam Neua, Vieng Xai, Phonsavanh and either returning to Luang Prabang at the Muang Phu Khoun turn-off or heading south to Vang Vieng. Stray Travel plan to run a hop-on, hop-off service. ▸▸ *For listings, see pages 188-190.*

Ins and outs

Getting there Tourists are often put off visiting Hua Phan by the long bus haul to get there but, considering the road passes through gorgeous mountain scenery, the trip is well worth the endeavour. There are three main sealed roads to Xam Neua: Route 6 from the south, linking Xam Neua with Phonsavanh; Route 1 from Vieng Thong and the west, and Road 6A from the Vietnamese border. Due to the upgrading of Route 6, it is now possible to make the journey between Phonsavanh and Xam Neua in a day without an overnight stop in Nam Nouan en route, but always check on road conditions before setting off. There is an airport at Xam Neua, 3 km from the centre of town on the road to Vieng Xai and Vietnam. Tuk-tuk from the airport to town, 20,000 kip. ▸▸ *See Transport, page 189.*

Getting around Tourists should exercise caution when travelling independently in the province, as some of the authorities harbour a residual suspicion of Westerners and there are very few guides that can speak English. The provincial tourism office is probably the best first port of call, and you can organize a car with driver/guide to Vieng Xai caves or Hintang Archaeological Park.

Tourist information Houa Phanh Provincial Tourist office ① *T064-312567, hp_pto@ yahoo.com, Mon-Fri 0830-1200 and 1300-1600,* is run by the helpful Kaiphet and his team in Xam Neua, . It can offer car rental.

When to visit Summer is pleasant in Xam Neua but temperatures at night reach freezing in winter and you should bring a pullover, even in summer. The area is at its most picturesque in October, when the rice is almost ripe. Mosquitoes are monstrous here, so precautions against malaria are advised (see Health, page 34).

Background

Together with Phongsali Province, Hua Phan was the base for left-wing insurgency from the late 1940s until the final victory of the Pathet Lao over the royalist forces in 1975. Members of the Lao Issara, who had fled to Vietnam after French forces smashed the movement in 1946, infiltrated areas of northeast Laos in 1947-1949 under the sponsorship of the Viet Minh. The movement coalesced when Prince Souphanouvong, who had fled to Thailand, arrived in Hanoi and organized a conference in August 1950 at which the Free Lao Front and the Lao Resistance Government were formed. Thereafter, the Pathet Lao adopted strategies developed by the Viet Minh in Vietnam, who in turn drew on the strategies of Mao Zedong and the Chinese Communists: establishment of bases in remote mountain areas; use of guerrilla tactics; exploitation of the dissatisfaction of tribal minorities, and mobilization of the entire population of liberated areas in support of the revolutionary struggle. By the time of the Geneva Agreement of 1954, following the French defeat at Dien Bien Phu, Communist forces effectively controlled Hua Phan and Phongsali provinces, a fact acknowledged in the terms of the settlement, which called for their regroupment inside these provinces pending a political settlement. The Pathet Lao used the breathing space and the succession of coalition governments during the late 1950s and early 1960s to reorganize their operations. The Lao People's Revolutionary Party was formed at Xam Neua in 1955 and the Neo Lao Hak Sat, or National Front, was established in 1956.

While Party President Prince Souphanouvong spent a good deal of time in Vientiane, participating in successive coalition governments between 1958 and 1964, Secretary-General Kaysone Phomvihane remained in Hua Phan overseeing the political and military organization of the liberated zone. The beginning of the American bombing campaign in 1964 forced the Pathet Lao leadership to find a safe haven from which to direct the war. Vieng Xai was chosen because its numerous limestone karsts contained many natural caves which could be used for quarters, while their proximity to each other inhibited attack from the air. American planes tried to dislodge the Communists from their mountain hideout but, protected in their caves, they survived the onslaught. Nevertheless, phosphorous rockets and napalm caused many casualties in the less-fortified caves. After the war, senior members of the Royal Lao Government were sent to re-education camps in the province.

Xam Neua (Sam Neua) → *For listings, see pages 188-190. Colour map 1, B5.*

→ *Phone code: 064.*

Xam Neua is one of the most intriguing provincial capitals in Laos and is buzzing with a colourful outdoor food market and the eclectic dry market. It is set against a picture-perfect mountain backdrop, amid forested hills and rice fields. The town itself was obliterated during the war and rebuilt after 1973, so it offers little in the way of historic sights. However, it has a bustling atmosphere, thanks to the many villagers who descend from the mountains to sell their wares here, and provides visitors with the increasingly rare chance to experience a culturally intact, unspoilt town. It is also a staging post for visiting the caves at Vieng Xai.

Sights

The **market** is a good place to see the province's mixture of cultures and peoples – Hmong, Yao, Tai Dam (Black Tai), Tai Khao (White Tai), Tai Neua (Northern Thai) and other ethnic groups – who can all be found buying and selling various commodities. In the adjoining

Border essentials: Na Maew-Nam Xoi (Vietnam)

Route 6A heads east from Xam Neua to the border crossing between Na Maew (Laos) and Nam Xoi (Vietnam), which was opened to tourists in 2004. You'll need to get your Laos or Vietnam visa in advance. The border is open 0730-1130 and 1330-1700. It may be necessary to pay a processing or overtime fee.

The trip to the border is two hours from Vieng Xai. *Songthaew* leave Vieng Xai at 0640 from the main Xam Neua–Na Maew road, 1 km from the centre of Vieng Xai, 20,000 kip. It is also possible to take a *songthaew* from Xam Neua station at 0630-0715 (three to four hours), 30,000 kip, or to charter one to the border from Xam Neua for about US$50.

Footprint has received several complaints about difficulties with unethical tourism operators on the Vietnamese side of this border charging a fortune for transport. A motorbike taxi to Quan Son should cost around US$10. If you get really stuck on the Vietnam side contact Mr Pham Xuan Hop in Na Maew, T0084-9923 7425, who may be able to organize minivan rental (US$42-50 to Quan Son).

There are two guesthouses in Na Maew (Phucloc Nha Tru and Minhchien); they both offer rudimentary facilities for US$3-5 per night).

A bus runs from Na Maew to Thanh Hoa Tue, Thu and Sat at 1130, US$8 but it's advisable to check all transport details in Xam Neua, at the bus station or with the provincial tourism office.

dry market, examples of the distinctive weaving of Xam Neua and Xam Tai can be found for reasonable prices, along with goods trucked in from China and Vietnam. Loudspeakers in the market area often blast music and propaganda from 0600 in the morning, and there is a strong military presence in the town. The province is known for its weaving and you will see numerous houses in Xam Neua with looms on their verandas. There are also several weaving workshops with four or five looms each; some of these still use traditional vegetable dyes rather than the aniline (chemical) dyes that have become the norm in other areas.

South of Xam Neua

South of Xam Neua are the **Houiyad** falls, located amid undulating hills in a stunning river valley, and surrounded by fields, rice paddies and ethnic minority villages. The falls themselves don't rank highly in the Lao waterfall stakes but make a nice half-day picnic trip from Xam Neua. Nearby **Ban Houaiyad** is renowned for making belts from aluminium gathered from crashed aircrafts, although these days recycled cans are used instead. A few kilometres away are the **Nameuang hot springs** ⓘ *22 km south of Xam Neua, off Route 6; at the junction follow the unpaved road for 3 km, 5000 kip*, which feature a small bathing pool and six washrooms, three of which have bathtubs. The site is currently managed by local villagers.

Continuing south on Route 6 towards Nam Nouan, the waterfall of **Nam Tok Dat Salari** is visible on the left, 3 km after the village of Ban Doan. The falls are difficult to miss as there are numerous empty houses and stalls by the road, used once a year by the people of Xam Neua for Pi Mai celebrations. A track on the right leads up through the jungle to the top of the falls, a very good swimming and picnic spot.

Sao Hintang

ⓘ *Off Route 6, at Ban Liangsat, 57 km south of Xam Neua and 36 km north of the junction with Route 1 at Phou Lao. For further information contact the tourist office in Xam Neua where cars can be rented for this trip; it might make sense as the site is not signposted and the stones are not always easy to see.*

The Hintang Archeological Park is situated about 130 km north of Phonsavanh and 56.5 km southwest of Xam Neua, on Route 6. At the faded billboard-sized sign in Ban Liang Sat, turn up the dirt road heading east. This road is quite rough in places, and you will need a 4WD car or all-terrain motorbike in order to reach the site in one piece. About 3 km up the road is a sign for the Kechintang Trail, a 90-minute walking trail that takes you to some of the sites. The first is visible from the road after a further 3 km, with Site two located another 3 km after that.

The park features hundreds of ancient upright stone pillars, menhirs and discs, gathered in Stonehenge-type patterns over a 10-km area, surrounded by jungle. The megaliths have been cut into narrow blades, up to 2 m tall, and stand one behind the other, with the tallest usually in the middle. According to local sources they are at least 1500 years old. Interspersed between the stone sites are burial chambers dug deep into the bedrock. These were originally covered with large stone discs, up to 7 m wide, and could only be accessed via a narrow vertical chimney.

The enigmatic stones are as mysterious as the Plain of Jars: no-one is quite sure who, or even which ethnic group, is responsible for erecting them and they have become steeped in legend. It is believed that the two sites are somehow linked, as they are fashioned from the same stone and share some archaeological similarities. In 1931, the sites were surveyed and partially excavated by an archaeological team, led by Madeleine Colani, although, by this time, the contents of the chambers had already been raided or simply washed away. The exploration uncovered a number of objects – funerary urns, ceremonial stones, bronze bracelets and ceramic pendants – that give credence to the theory that the stone park was an ancient burial site.

While travelling along Route 6 to the park keep your eyes peeled for the numerous roadside **fox-holes**. These small bolt-holes were used as air-raid shelters during the US bombardment of the area. A large number actually expand into large bunkers capable of accommodating 10 or 12 people.

East of Xam Neua

Xam Tai

Hua Phan is supposed to be a 'cradle' of traditional Lao weaving. The province's remoteness means that the diversity of designs produced here is second to none and techniques that have become rare elsewhere are still practised here. The premier centre for weaving is Xam Tai (local pronunciation, Xam Teua), 100 km southeast of Xam Neua, close to the Vietnamese border. You can try to charter a pickup to Xam Tai from the market, or hire a car through the tourist office but be aware that the road is in a poor state and there is no guesthouse at Xam Tai.

Sop Hao

This town, 60 km east of Xam Neua on the Vietnam border, has a trade fair each Saturday but is pretty much a no-go zone for foreigners due to the presence of one of the country's last re-education centres. The border crossing here is only open to Lao and Vietnamese.

Vieng Xai (Viengsay) → *For listings, see pages 188-190. Colour map 1, B6.*

The village of Vieng Xai lies 31 km east of Xam Neua on a road that branches off Route 6 at Km 20. The trip from Xam Neua is possibly one of the country's most picturesque journeys, passing terraces of rice, pagodas, copper- and charcoal-coloured karst formations, dense jungle with misty peaks and friendly villages dotted among the mountains' curves. The area is characterized by lush tropical gardens, a couple of smallish lakes and spectacular limestone karsts, riddled with natural caves that proved crucial in the success of the left-wing insurgency in the 1960s and 1970s. Although it takes only one day to see the caves, it is worth spending some more time exploring the area. The valley contains many other poignant reminders of the struggle, although the war debris is less obvious here than in Xieng Khouang.

Ins and outs

There are seven caves open to visitors. (By late 2010, the market cave will open with a new bakery and garden with tea trees and mulberry bushes.) Five caves were formerly occupied by senior Pathet Lao leaders (Prince Souphanouvong, Kaysone Phomvihan, Nouhak Phounsavanh, Khamtai Siphandon and Phoumi Vongvichit). All the caves are within walking distance of the village. Tickets are sold at the **Viengxay Caves Visitor Centre** ① *T064-314321, www.visit-viengxay.com, daily 0800-1200 and 1300-1600; guided tours are conducted in English at 0900 and 1300, 30,000 kip with compulsory guide.* If you pitch up out of these hours, tours are 50,000 kip. Tours are usually conducted on bikes which can be rented from the office (20,000-30,000 kip) if you don't have your own transport. Tours last between three to four hours. A new set of excellent 90-minute audio tours, including personal memories of local people, has launched (US$6.50). A taster can be heard on www.visit-Viengxay.com. The visitors' centre has historical information, photographs, Communist gifts on display and a book exchange. If you plan on coming across from Xam Neua it is advisable to stay overnight. ▸▸ *See Sleeping, page 188.*

The caves have a secretive atmosphere, with fruit trees and frangipani decorating the exteriors. Each one burrows deep into the mountainside and features 60-cm-thick concrete walls, encompassing living quarters, meeting rooms, offices, dining and storage areas. The caves are lit but you may find a torch useful.

Background

From 1964 onwards, Pathet Lao operations were directed from the cave systems at Vieng Xai, which provided an effective refuge from furious bombing attacks. The village of Vieng Xai grew from four small villages consisting of less than 10 families into a thriving hidden city concealing over 20,000 people in in the 100 plus caves in the area. The Pathet Lao leadership renamed the area Vieng Xai, meaning 'City of Victory' and it became the administrative and military hub of the revolutionary struggle.

A conservation survey of the area in 1982 identified over 95 caves of historical significance. Included in these was a former hospital complex approximately 15 km from Vieng Xai and a school for children of government officials at Ban Bac. A separate cave complex at Hang Long, 25 km from Xam Neua, housed the provincial government during the war years but is now completely abandoned. Other caves, called 'Embassy Caves', were intended for VIPs from other countries, with individual caves set aside for Russia, Vietnam, Cuba and China. Locals make unsubstantiated suggestions that King Sihanouk from Cambodia also spent a long time hiding out in Vieng Xai during the war.

Footprint Mini Atlas
Laos

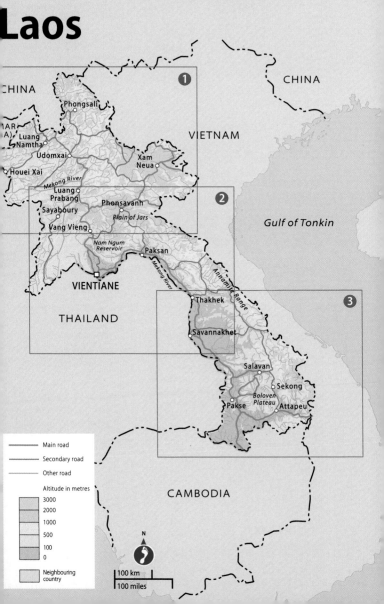

CHINA

CHINA

Phongsali

VIETNAM

MAR
(A)

Luang
Namtha

Udomxai

Houei Xai

Xam
Neua

Mekong River

Luang
Prabang

Sayaboury

Phonsavanh

Plain of Jars

Gulf of Tonkin

Vang Vieng

Nam Ngum
Reservoir

Paksan

Mekong River

VIENTIANE

Thakhek

THAILAND

Annamite Range

Savannakhet

Salavan

Sekong

Boloven
Plateau

Pakse

Attapeu

CAMBODIA

❶

❷

❸

	Main road
	Secondary road
	Other road

Altitude in metres

3000
2000
1000
500
100
0

Neighbouring
country

N

100 km

100 miles

Map 1

Map 2

Map symbols

□	Capital city	▬	Building
○	Other city, town	▪	Sight
≈	International border	♱♰	Cathedral, church
≈	Regional border	☗	Chinese temple
⊖	Customs	🛕	Hindu temple
◎	Contours (approx)	👤	Meru
▲	Mountain, volcano	☪	Mosque
⇌	Mountain pass	△	Stupa
⊔⊔⊔	Escarpment	✡	Synagogue
⌣	Glacier	ⓘ	Tourist office
▦	Salt flat	🏛	Museum
⚭	Rocks	✉	Post office
ⵉ	Seasonal marshland	Ⓟ	Police
▦	Beach, sandbank	Ⓢ	Bank
𝍖	Waterfall	@	Internet
∿	Reef	♪	Telephone
═══	National highway	☎	Market
───	Paved road	✚	Medical services
───	Unpaved or *ripio* (gravel) road	Ⓟ	Parking
∷∷∷	Track	⛽	Petrol
⋯⋯	Footpath	⛳	Golf
───	Railway	∴	Archaeological site
⊢═══	Railway with station	♦	National park,
✈	Airport		wildlife reserve
🚌	Bus station	✲	Viewing point
Ⓜ	Metro station	▲	Campsite
----	Cable car	⌂	Refuge, lodge
++++	Funicular	♜	Castle, fort
⛴	Ferry	⤵	Diving
⊐⊐⊐	Pedestrianized street	♠♣♧	Deciduous, coniferous,
⟫ ⟪	Tunnel		palm trees
⟶	One way-street	✽	Mangrove
▥▥▥	Steps	⌂	Hide
⊨	Bridge	♪	Vineyard, winery
▃▃▃	Fortified wall	△	Distillery
▦	Park, garden, stadium	⤷	Shipwreck
●	Sleeping	✕	Historic battlefield
●	Eating	⇨	Related map
●	Bars & clubs		

Vieng Xai village

The village itself was built in 1973, when the bombing finally stopped and the short-lived Provisional Government of National Union was negotiated. Today the former capital of the liberated zone is an unlikely sight: surrounded by rice fields at the dead end of a potholed road, it features street lighting, power lines, sealed and kerbed streets and substantial public buildings – all in varying stages of decay. Nonetheless it is truly one of the most beautiful towns in Laos. The Garden of Eden-type village is dotted with fruit trees and hibiscus and is flanked by amazing karst formations and dotted with man-made lakes (reputedly formed from bomb craters). Vieng Xai is Vang Vieng without the backpackers and the river, though it is possible to swim in the man-made lake, which is lined with thatched cabanas.

Just before the market and truck stop, a wonderful socialist-realist statue in gold-painted concrete pays tribute to those three pillars of the revolution: the farmer, the soldier and the worker; the worker has one boot firmly planted on a bomb inscribed 'USA'. Behind this statue is a **small museum**, which contains some interesting old photographs, many of them unlabelled. Few of the guides seem to know about the museum, so make a point of asking to visit it.

The main street divides as it reaches the top of the village to form a town 'square' which is in fact a triangle. At the apex is a war monument topped by a red star, while at the southern end is a yellow two-storey building housing government offices; the cave **tourist office** is just around the corner.

There is a spectacular **waterfall**, 8 km before Vieng Xai. About 3 km after the turn-off from Route 6, a swift stream passes under a steel and concrete bridge. A path just before the bridge leads off to the left, following the river downstream. It takes just a few minutes to reach the top of the waterfall, but the path leads all the way to the bottom, about 20 minutes' walk. Swimming is not advised.

Tham Souphanouvong

A mossy path flanked by large grapefruit trees leads to Tham Souphanouvong. This cave was home to Prince Souphanouvong, the 'Red Prince' and son of the Queen of Luang Prabang. To the right of the path stands a pink stupa, the tomb of the prince's son, who was beaten to death with a hammer by infiltrators a few kilometres away in 1967, at the age of 28. Souphanouvong's stunning garden, bursting with a rainbow of flowers and dripping with fruit, was planted in 1973-1974 and is a memorial to his son and a metaphor for the war. An old bomb crater has been ingeniously concreted into a pool, referred to as the broken heart; a head, shoulders and neck have been landscaped around the heart. The whole area is surrounded by a sea of red plants, to symbolize all the blood lost during the war. Watch the far entrance of the cave as occasionally rocks have fallen. Souphanouvong and Phoumi's caves both feature a 'garage cave' at the base of the karst, a cavity in the limestone large enough to accommodate a car.

Tham Kaysone

Kaysone Phomvihane's cave is reached by mossy steps cut into the cliff face and is over 100 m long. The cavern is surrounded by blossoming bushes and large frangipani trees. Like the other caves here, it has a suite of rooms, including a bedroom, meeting room and library. A few of Kaysone's books are on display; it's no surprise that the collection includes Lenin, Marx, Engels, Ho Chi Minh and an economic text from Vietnam. Also on display are a few gifts from foreign dignitaries, including a lacquer-ware vase from Vietnam and a bust of Lenin (a framed picture of Che Guevara given to Kaysone by Fidel Castro has been removed due to water damage).

The cave's construction started some time prior to 1963 but Kaysone and Co moved in in 1974. Kaysone rarely left the cave and allowed only the most important of visitors inside, mostly other Communist leaders. About 10 people lived in the cave, Kaysone, his children, a doctor, intelligence officer, cook and bodyguards. At the start of the war Kaysone's wife relocated to Yunnan, China, where she was head of a school. These days she lives in Vientiane. The Americans knew of Kaysone's whereabouts but were unable to attack the cave directly or infiltrate it, due to its position and to the large numbers of Pathet Lao soldiers that were mounted on the summit. The cave remained Kaysone's official residence until 1973, when he relocated to the building in front of the cave. In 1975 he left the cave and moved to Vientiane.

An interesting feature of Kaysone's cave is a long, narrow passage which connects the living quarters to a large meeting area which includes emergency accommodation for dozens of guests.

Tham Than Khamtai

Khamtai Siphandone's cave and the Military Headquarters, is slightly different from the others. The first thing you'll notice is a set of three bomb craters within metres of the entrance to the cave. The craters, now overgrown, are so close together they almost touch. Possibly inspired by their arrival, the entrance is shielded by an enormous, tapering slab of concrete, 4.5 m high and nearly 2 m wide at the base. Inside, the cave is darker and more claustrophobic than the others, with no outside areas. The attendant may or may not lead you through a thick steel door at the bottom of some stairs well inside the cave. It gives access to a staircase which descends steeply before ending in a sheer drop of several metres, and connects to a number of military caves including the army administration. There is a longish tunnel which connects to Tham Xang Lot (Elephant Cave) but this is sometimes inaccessible.

Tham Xang Lot

A small distance from Khamtai's cave and included in its entry price, is the large and obvious entrance to what is known as Tham Xang Lot, or 'cave that an elephant can walk through'. Formerly used as an enclosure to keep animals such as elephants and monkeys, during the war this natural cavern was used as a theatre, complete with stage, arch, orchestra pit and a concrete floor with space for an audience of several hundred. At the opposite end from the stage, a long passage featuring a number of stalactites and lit by daylight connects to the theatrette below Khamtai's cave. It is hard to imagine now, but this damp, dark area once entertained numerous dancers, symphonies, circuses and foreign dignitaries from Romania, Bulgaria, Vietnam and China, who would pop in for a boogie. As one local recalls: "I snuck in for a look and an orchestra was playing. I got so excited but was trying to contain myself because I was worried that the grenade in my pocket would go off." At times up to 2000 soldiers were hidden in the two caves.

Other caves

The **Artillery Cave**, set halfway up a hillside, offers phenomenal views. The cave was a military installation purposefully set up to conceal fighters who would return fire during US bombing raids. **Phoumi Vongvichid's Cave**, home to the former Minister of Education and Public Health, also houses the enclosure of Sithon Kommadam, of the Lao Theung minority, who was reputedly immune to bullets. **Nouhak Phoumsavan's Cave** has been recently opened to the public. The cave was home to the former President of Laos.

West on Route 1 → For listings, see pages 188-190

Nam Nouan

The junction of Routes 1 and 6 is known as Phou Lao; just to the south is the larger settlement of Nam Nouan, a staging post that travellers bound for Xam Neua or Nong Khiaw will invariably find themselves stopping at. The through traffic for Xam Neua is relatively frequent and most buses/songthaew from Phonsavanh stop on their way through. To get a connecting bus to Nong Khiaw is a little more complicated as Nam Noun is 7 km south of the junction between Routes 1 and 6, which is at a village called **Ban Sam Nyay**. You can get to the actual junction town by songthaew or by asking one of the locals for a lift on a motorbike. Most buses to/from Nong Khiaw stop at this junction settlement not Nam Nouan. It is a pleasant Khmu village with very little in the way of amenities. If you are coming from Nong Khiaw you will probably arrive disorientated and dishevelled at some ungodly hour. Locals may try to charge you an extortionate rate to get a pickup to Nam Nouan; if that is the case you may be able to grab a lift with someone on a motorbike for about US$5-6.

Vieng Thong

Vieng Thong, also known as Muang Hiam, lies 158 km west of Xam Neua on Route 1 and is a reasonable stopover for those journeying to or from Nong Khiaw. The town itself has little to offer but the surrounding countryside is nothing short of spectacular and improved access in the near future should enable tourists to sample its attractions. The Nam Khan flows through the town, straight from Luang Prabang, so it's a shame no tour operators have yet capitalized on what could be an amazing journey between the two areas.

North of town are the Vieng Thong **hot springs** ⓘ *5000 kip*, which offer great respite from what can be quite a tiring journey. There's a decent bathing area and washrooms are available near the road. Further back, it's way too hot to linger but interesting to see the buffaloes mooching about in the steaming field. The LNTA are to pump US$100,000 into developing the hot springs into a proper centre so it could all be glamorous by the time you get there. To get there, cross the bridge, turn right and walk for 1 km; ask locals along the way.

Nam Et/Phou Loei NPA

Just 10 km beyond Vieng Thong is Laos' largest protected area, the Nam Et/Phou Loei National Protected Area. Camera trap studies conducted in recent years by the Wildlife Conservation Society have discovered a vast array of large mammals here, including tiger; guar, bear, leopard, macaque, wild pig and deer. The NPA also contains a couple of impressive caves that have piqued archaeologists' interests. The cavern of **Tham Han** is 20 km north of Vieng Thong, towards the Vietnamese border. A swift 20-minute stroll, following the road along the Nam Neun, will bring you to this river cave, which stretches a considerable distance into the hillside and leads to a village on the far side. It can also reportedly be accessed by boat (if there are any available).

Ban Secock, a small village 40 km west of Vieng Thong, is the place to head if you want to trek to the Phou Loei waterfall; the walk should take around two hours. In the future, it is hoped that there will be organized treks to Phou Loei, the second highest peak in Laos.

For the time being this area remains undeveloped, particularly from a tourism perspective. There aren't any major ecotourism operators running tours through the NPA yet but there are concerted efforts to get something up and running in the near future. The Wildlife Conservation Society plans to open up trekking in the area.

◉ Hua Phan Province listings

For Sleeping and Eating price codes and other relevant information, see pages 23 -24.

● Sleeping

Xam Neua *p181*

D Samneua Hotel, next to the bridge just over the Nam Xam, T020-5509 444. Offers 17 smart rooms with comfortable mattresses (the beds hog most of the space in the room) and en suite bathrooms. This is the smartest place to stay in town.

F Boun Home, in the lane around the corner from **Shuliyo** in a brand-new building, T064-312223. Offers clean and pleasant rooms, with private bathrooms and hot showers. It represents one of the best deals in town. Highly recommended.

F Kheamxam Guesthouse, on the corner by the river, T064-312111. Provides a wide range of fairly well-appointed large rooms (beds with soft pillows), with attached spacious hot-water bathrooms, some with a/c and TV. This is another good choice in Xam Neua.

F Outhaithany Guesthouse, opposite the airport, a few kilometres out of town, T064-314777, snhotel_08@yahoo.com 14 shabby rooms: there are log cabins at the back that are dark and damp-smelling and white cabins at the front which don't look so nice from the outside but are a tad nicer than the log cabins on the inside. There's a decent restaurant but the menu has not been translated into English.

F Shuliyo, about 100 m from the *songthaew* station, T064-312462. This guesthouse has hard mattresses with hard pillows but it is very quiet and clean, and the rooms have a TV. Check that your bathroom appliances are in working order when you check in

(be aware that the shower water is usually tepid). Ask if the more spacious 'hong har' (Room 5) is available.

Vieng Xai *p185*

Most visitors to Vieng Xai and the caves stay in Xam Neua and make a day trip out to see the caves. However, it is advisable to stay overnight as it is difficult to fit everything into one day unless you arrive very early in the day.

F-G Naxay Guesthouse 2 , opposite Vieng Xai Cave Visitor Centre, T064-314336. The best option with 11 clean, beautiful bungalows with tepid water, comfortable beds and Western-style toilet, set in a leafy compound. Recommended.

G Khamnong Guesthouse, T020-5508 8898, on the lake. Basic with sunken beds, squat toilet and bucket shower. Restaurant overlooks the lake.

G Naxay Guesthouse, close to Prince Souphanouvong's Cave, T064-314336. Very rustic accommodation in rattan house. Beds have seen better days and are as hard as a rock. Squat toilets and shower block are facing the building. This was the first guesthouse in Vieng Xai and it's now looking a little sorry.

G Xailomyen Guesthouse, T030-516 1399. There are 13 small rooms but this is the next best option after Naxay 2. The bathrooms are tiny but with Western-style toilets and hot water. There are lovely views from the vast restaurant.

Nam Nouan *p187*

This staging post isn't the best of places to stay in the region but if you find yourself stuck here overnight, **Nam Nouan Guesthouse**, which is signposted with a small blue sign just near the row of restaurants, would suffice.

Vieng Thong *p187*
Vieng Thong has 3 below-average guesthouses, all with shared facilities, in the 20,000-30,000 kip range.
G Souksavan Guesthouse T064-314478. This is probably the pick of the bunch. Rustic, basic rooms, with mosquito nets and attached bath.

🍴 Eating

Xam Neua *p181*
The colourful fresh food market has a wonderful selection of local dishes. There is also a good *feu*/coffee shop on the corner opposite the bus station. You'll find most of the restaurants in Xam Neua display their menus in Lao script on white boards but they will usually have an English menu tucked away somewhere on the premises, so ask to see it.
¶ Chittavanh Restaurant, opposite the Nam Xam River near the end of the market. Great Lao food, particularly *feu*, with a good English menu on a white board. Sells 'whine and spy' (Sprite)!
¶ Dannaomuangxam, a block back from the river, near the bridge, T064-314126. This is a good option. The fried fish is excellent as is the *feu*, *laap* and French fries. Good service. Menu in English.

Vieng Xai *p185*
There are a few noodle shops scattered along the main street opposite the post office, and several of the guesthouses have restaurants, including **Naxay 2 Guesthouse** (see Sleeping) and the **Xailomyen**, which does a range of fish, pork, noodle and egg dishes and also offers a lovely view over the lake. You will also find a number of eating options at the market.
¶ Nang Sang Jan Restaurant, near the lake/swamp as you enter town. This

simple eaterie serves tasty *feu* and coffee. No English is spoken but the staff are helpful and friendly and will endeavour to communicate in spite of this.

Vieng Thong *p187*
Not a great deal to choose from in this stopover town, but you will find a few local restaurants and *feu* stalls.

☺ Transport

Xam Neua *p181*
Air
The airport is 2 km from the centre of town. **Phongsavanh Airlines** (T021-513 0000) now runs the route to **Vientiane**.

Bus/truck/songthaew
There are 2 bus stations. The Nathong (T030-312238) and the Phoutanou up the hill (T030-516 0974). There are regular *songthaew* from Xam Neua to **Vieng Xai**, 50 mins, 10,000 kip, from 0620-1640 from the Nathong bus station, every 50 mins.
From Nathong bus station to **Na Meo** (the Vietnam border), 0710, 3 hrs, 20,000 kip; to Xam Tai, 0900, 5 hrs, 34,000 kip. To **Thanh Hoa** (Vietnam), 0800 daily, 180,000 kip, 11 hrs. From Phoutanou bus station to **Vieng Thong**, 0710, 6 hrs, 43,000 kip; to **Phonsavanh**, 0800, 0830, 0900, 1230, 60,000-70,000 kip, 1400 (VIP bus) 165,000 kip (8 hrs); to **Luang Prabang**, 0730, 0800, 14 hrs, 120,000 kip (the Luang Prabang bus goes via **Nong Khiaw**, 12 hrs, 80,000 kip); to **Vientiane**, 0800, 0900 and 1230, 24 hrs, 150,000 kip, VIP bus at 1400, 18 hrs, 165,000 kip; to **Nam Neun** for **Sao Hintang**, 0700, 29,000 kip (get off at Natork village).

Motorbike and minivan hire
Motorbikes, 60,000 kip per day, can be rented from **Rent out Motorcycle**, diagonally across the road from the **Xam Neua Provincial Tourism Office**, T064-312255 (check tyre treads). The tourist office, rents motorbikes for US$10/day. It also

offers minivan hire to various destinations: to the **Na Meo border**, 700,000 kip; to **Sao Hintang** with guide, 700,000 kip; to **Xam Tai**, 1,500,000 return; **Phonsavan**, 2,500,000; **Nong Khiaw**, 3,000,000 kip; **Luang Prabang**, 4,000,000 kip; to **Thanh Hoa** (Vietnam), 3,000,000 kip; to **Hanoi** (Vietnam), 5,000,000 kip; to **Vientiane**, 5,000,000 kip. Call Mr Kaiphet out of hours, T020-5587 6129.

Tuk-tuk
A tuk-tuk to **Nameuang hot springs** should cost US$15 return; to **Vieng Xai**, 31 km, 50 mins, 15,000-20,000 kip per person.

Vieng Xai *p185*
Pickups and passenger trucks leave from in front of the market in Vieng Xai to **Xam Neua** 0630-1640, 50 mins, 10,000 kip. It will cost around 200,000 kip to charter a pickup if you miss the last truck back to Xam Neua. It is best to charter a vehicle in Xam Neua for a whole day trip to Vieng Xai.

Vieng Thong *p187*
The so-called public transport system is a bit hit and miss. The intersection near the market is the best place to catch a bus or truck east to **Xam Neua**, 158 km, 5-6 hrs,

30,000 kip, or west to **Nong Khiaw**, 175 km, 3-4 hrs, 20,000 kip, and **Luang Prabang**, 30,000 kip. Route 1 west from Vieng Thong is rough but work began on upgrading the road in 2005. Some tourists have reported that this trip is impossible during the rainy season but this should change once the road has been completed.

Directory

Xam Neua *p181*
Banks The Lao Development Bank will change Thai baht, US$ and Chinese yen into kip but will only accept TCs in US$. **Internet** Available from Tami.com, just past the Sam Neua hotel, over the first crossroads, 6000 kip/hr. **Post** Xam Neua has a post office, Mon-Fri 0800-1100 and 1300-1600, but it's best to wait until you are in either Phonsavanh or Luang Prabang. **Telephone** International phone calls can be made from Lao Telecom, behind the post office, daily 0800-1100 and 1300-1600.

Vieng Xai *p185*
Police The police station is situated just behind the disused department store on the town square.

Contents

Central Provinces

Footprint features

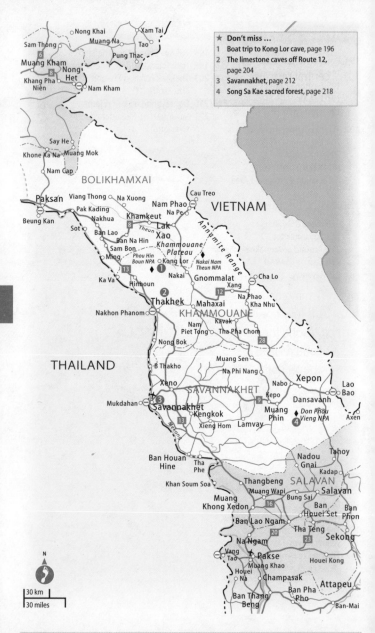

★ **Don't miss ...**
1 Boat trip to Kong Lor cave, page 196
2 The limestone caves off Route 12,
   page 204
3 Savannakhet, page 212
4 Song Sa Kae sacred forest, page 218

Nong Khai
Xam Tai
Sam Thong
Muang Na
Tao
Pung Thac
Muang Kham
Nong
Het
Khang Pha
Niên
Nam Kham

Say He
Khone Xa Na Muang Mok
Nam Cap

BOLIKHAMXAI

Viang Thong Na Xuong
Cau Treo
Paksan
Pak Kading Nam Phao
VIETNAM
Beung Kan
Nakhua Khamkeut Na Pe
Sot Ban Lao
Ban Na Hin Lak
Xao
Sam Bon *Khammouane*
Ming *Plateau*
Phou Hin
Boun NPA Kong Lor *Nakai Nam*
Theun NPA
Ka Va Nakai Cha Lo
Hinboun Gnommalat
Xang
Thakhek Na Phao
Mahaxai Kha Nhu
KHAMMOUANE
Nakhon Phanom Nam
Piet Tong Kavak
Tha Pha Chom
Nong Bok

THAILAND Muang Sen
B Thakho Na Phi Nang
Xeno Nabo Xepon Lao
Bao
Mukdahan **SAVANNAKHET** Kepo Dansavanh
Savannakhet Muang *Don Phou*
Kengkok Phin *Vieng NPA* Axen
Xieng Hom Lamvay

Ban Houan Tahoy
Hine Tha Nadou
Phe Gnai Kadap
Khan Soum Soa Thangbeng **SALAVAN**
Muang Muang Wapi Salavan
Khong Xedon Bung Sai Ban
Houei Set Ban
Ban Lao Ngam Phon
Na Ngam Tha Teng Sekong
Vang ★Pakse
Tao Muang Khao Houei Kong
Houei Champasak **Attapeu**
Na Ban Pha
Ban Thang Pho Ban-Mai
Beng

N

30 km
30 miles

Introduction

Laos' central provinces, sandwiched between the Mekong (and Thailand) to the west and the Annamite Mountains (and Vietnam) to the east, are the least visited in the country. Travellers entering Laos from Vietnam cross the border via Lak Xao or Xepon but few choose to linger for long. This is a shame because the scenery here is stunning, with dramatic limestone karsts, enormous caves, beautiful rivers and forests. In particular, the upland areas to the east, off Route 8 and Route 12, are a veritable treasure trove of attractions, mottled with scores of caves, lagoons, rivers and unusual rock formations.

Tourists will require some determination in these parts, as the infrastructure around here is still being developed. Also, the road network may change once the Nam Theun II Dam, which opened in 2010, is fully operational.

The Mekong towns of Thakhek and Savannakhet are also elegant and relaxed and, if you are short on time, Thakhek is the best stopover point for the central provinces.

Paksan to Lak Xao → *Phone code: 054.*

East of Paksan adventurous visitors will encounter some of the county's most stunning landscapes. This little-known region contains a maze of limestone karst peaks, studded with thousands of caves, and a beautiful river flanked by pristine jungle. The magical Kong Lor cave, a river cave running straight through the centre of a mountain for 6 km, and the principal tourist attraction in the region, could be straight out of The Lord of the Rings. ▸▸ *For listings, see pages 199-201.*

Paksan and around → *For listings, see pages 199-201. Colour map 2, B4.*

In the mid-1990s people used to stop in Paksan (Paxsan) to break the journey south (or north) but, now that road upgrading has shortened the journey between Vientiane and Thakhek to a bearable five to six hours, the town's one purpose in life, as far as most tourists were concerned, has been rendered obsolete. However, you might just find yourself stranded here on your way to Vientiane from the Vietnamese border at Lak Xao. There are other potential visitor draws, however, in the shape of **Wat Prah Bat**, an important pilgrimage site for Lowland Lao. Built in 1933, the stupa boasts a footprint of the Buddha as well as one of the largest drums in Laos. Overlooking the Mekong is the more modern **Phonsane Temple**, which isn't anything spectacular in itself but has become famous for its annual Naga Fireball Festival (see Festivals and events, page 200).

For those travellers who are beginning to feel all 'templed out', there are exhilarating opportunities to explore the province's natural heritage by boat, canoe or kayak 50 km east of Paksan, where the **Nam Kading** river, one of the most pristine rivers in Laos, flows into the Mekong (see below).

Pak Kading

Pak Kading is a small whistlestop of a town at the mouth of the Nam Kading. Many commentators have earmarked it as the next major ecotourism centre in Laos but it's not quite ready for the hordes yet: there aren't really any tours set up and it's very difficult to arrange transport to see things independently; the best option is to charter your own boat. The picturesque Nam Kading is known as a local fishery goldmine and is one of the most pristine rivers in the country.

A worthwhile boat trip travels upstream leads through the Nam Kading NPA to **Nam Tok Taat Wang Fong**, a pretty, undulating set of small rapids spectacularly set in a small valley flanked by jungle and steep hills. The trip takes three hours there and back and boatmen wait at the boat landing at the south end of town, US$20, bargaining required.

Alternatively, you can pick up a boat 15 km east of town to **Ban Phonsi**, where there are signposts advertising the boat trips. There are a few good restaurants on the main road through Ban Phonsi, as it has developed into a bit of a truck stop.

Ban Lao (Vieng Kham/Tham Beng)

Sitting at the junction of Route 13 and 8 is the small settlement of Ban Lao. The town's folk aren't quite sure of the official name, which creates a lot of confusion, but it seems Ban Lao is the safest bet (try Vieng Kham or Tham Beng if Ban Lao pulls a blank). The settlement is pretty nondescript and only noteworthy for its position at the western end of Route 8 to Kong Lor cave and Lak Xao.

Border essentials: Paksan-Beung Kan (Thailand)

This crossing is for the more intrepid travellers and is seldom used. If you intend to use it, check information in advance. The Thai border is 2 km from Paksan on the Mekong, where there's a small port and immigration office, open daily 0800-1200 and 1330-1630. Visas are not available at the border and need to be arranged in advance. Boats to Beung Kan on the Thai side leave when they are full, usually about every 30 minutes. You can charter a boat for 300-400 baht. From Beung Kan there are irregular buses to Udon Thani and Bangkok.

East on Route 8 → For listings, see pages 199-201.

After leaving the north-south Route 13, take Route 8 east towards Lak Xao. This road leads into the hills, with tremendous views over a karst landscape of pinnacles, cones and a patchwork of forest. Big charcoal grey, jagged rocks cut through the surrounding jungle, conjuring a somewhat daunting, Gothic fairytale image. Two-thirds of the way to Ban Na Hin, on the right-hand side, look out for **Phu Phu Man Limestone Forest**, a cluster of sharp limestone pillars, saw-toothing across the countryside. There is a a small lookout where you can stop; most *songthaew* passengers won't mind if you stop for a minute to take a picture.

Ban Na Hin (Khoun Kham)

Ban Na Hin is a real end-of-the-earth town, low on charm but redeemed by the phenomenal landscapes surrounding it. Its two *raisons d'être* are as a transit point for Nam Theun II dam operations and for visitors to Kong Lor cave to the south; the settlement is also known as Khoun Kham – the 'Gateway to Kong Lor'. Ban Na Hin has quite a big market where you can buy fresh fruit and vegetables, bread and other supplies; if you haven't got a torch, it's a good idea to pick one up here. There are also a few cheap *feu* shops dotted around the market's periphery.

There isn't a whole lot more here but just outside of town is **Namsanam waterfall**. Take the signposted path on the left-hand side of Route 8, beside a colourful monastery. The trek to the falls is roughly 3 km through quite pleasant countryside. The two-tiered, 70-m-tall falls are magnificent and flow year round. There are reputed to be wild elephants in the area around the falls but the likelihood of seeing one is next to nil. The provincial tourism office has built an information centre on Route 8, just before the turn-off to the waterfall. Apparently local guides do exist but you will probably find the waterfall before you find a guide.

Towards Tham Kong Lor

The new 40-km laterite road has made the journey much easier from Ban Na Hin to the cave. (For details of this route by motorbike, see page 206.) Despite the new road, it is still possible to hire a boat all the way from Ban Na Hin to the guesthouses for around US\$100 return. There is also one *songthaew* a day from Ban Na Hin to Kong Lor, 25,000 kip. (To charter a songthaew for this journey is US\$50. The boat will run along the Nam Hinboun to either **Ban Phonyang**, where eco-lodge **Sala Hin Boun** is located (see Sleeping, page 199), or to **Ban Kong Lor**, the closest village to the caves, where you can find a homestay for 50,000 kip, including food and the nearby new Sala Kong Lor. The boat trip from Ban

Hydropower: raid on resources

Major international scrutiny of the Nam Theun II hydropower project resulted in the World Bank's unprecedented investment in mitigating the environmental and social impacts of construction. Initially the World Bank said that if even one animal species was at risk, the project would be halted. Unfortunately these concerns are not being applied to the planning of other dams. The Lao government and foreign investors plan to exploit the Mekong and its tributaries with more than 30 other dam projects in the coming decades. These dams do not have Nam Theun II's budget, safeguards or the international pressure required to reduce the environmental impact. The International River Network refers to this as the "hydropower gold rush" and predicts "grim consequences for Lao villagers and the Mekong River ecosystem".

The cumulative impact of the dam-building frenzy will have a major impact on the region's fisheries, which over 60 million people in the Lower Mekong depend on for food, income and transport. Worth an estimated US$2 billion annually, the Lower Mekong accounts for nearly 2% of the total world catch and 20% of all fish caught from inland waters of the world. More importantly, the annual catch accounts for 80% of the region's protein needs.

Dam building has a ripple out effect. Firstly, it has a direct environmental impact on the villages, animal and plant species surrounding the proposed dam site, including the socioeconomic effect on the nearby villages. Secondly, there is a detrimental effect on the tributaries, which are the predominant breeding ground for the Mekong's fish. The dams will block migration routes and inundate the spawning grounds, poisoning tributaries with anoxic waters (water with reduced oxygen). Thirdly, there will be a negative cumulative effect on the Mekong river when scores of dams are built on the tributaries and the mainstream, particularly for those countries downstream.

Napur to Ban Phonyang is fascinating, with excellent views of impressive limestone cliffs along the way and classic riverside scenes with people fishing and bathing. Take some padding as the wooden seats, even if they are cushioned, can be uncomfortable.

Some people have reportedly trekked from Ban Na Hin to Ban Kong Lor (47 km) but there isn't much shade and you will need to bring plenty of water. The river trip is still the most scenic route. The journey varies from season to season so it is best to check on road conditions in advance. ▸ See Transport, page 200.

Tham Kong Lor (Kong Lor cave) → Do not miss this!
ⓘ *Entrance fee at cave 5000 kip; US$12 for boat from Sala Kong Lor and US$17 from Sala Hin Boun; 100,000 kip to go through the cave (max 3 people per boat).*

Tham Kong Lor cave is sensational. The Nam Hinboun River has tunnelled through the mountain, creating a giant rocky cavern, 6 km long, 90 m wide and 100 m high, which opens out into blinding bright light at Ban Natan on the other side. The cave is apparently named after the drum makers who were believed to craft their instruments here. lit is also home to the largest living cave-dwelling spiders in the world, though it is unlikely you will have a run in with the massive arachnid as they are very rare. Fisherman will often come into the cave to try their luck as it is believed that 20-kg fish lurk below the surface.

The Mlabri – spirits of the yellow leaves

The elusive Mlabri 'tribe', which occupies the forests around Lak Xao as well as parts of Thailand, represents one of the few remaining groups of hunter gatherers in Southeast Asia. They are also known as the Phi Tong Luang or 'Spirits of the Yellow Leaves'; when their shelters of rattan and banana leaves turn yellow they take this as a sign from the spirits that it is time to move on. Traditionally the Mlabri hunted using spears. If they were stalking larger game, they would brace the weapon against the ground, rather than throwing it, and allow the charging animal to impale itself on the point. In this way, the Mlabri were able to kill the great *saladang* wild buffalo (*Bos gaurus*), as well as bears and tigers. Smaller game was more common, however, and this was supplemented with tubers, nuts, honey and other forest products to provide a balanced diet.

Many of the Mlabri's traditions are already on the verge of extinction. The destruction of the forest means that the Mlabri have been forced to lead more sedentary lives, turning to settled agriculture in place of hunting and gathering, while inter-marriage with other tribes is reducing their number. As recently as the 1980s, a Mlabri was displayed in a cage in a Bangkok department store. Today, many of the few Mlabri that remain have been forced to become cheap labourers for groups such as the Hmong.

At the start of the cave, you will have to scramble over some boulders while the boatmen carry the canoe over the rapids, so wear comfortable shoes with a good grip. A torch or, better still, a head-lamp (2000 kip at Thakhek market), is also recommended. It is eerie travelling through the dark, cool cave, with water splashing and bats circulating. There are a few minuscule rapids inside and the cave's surface is riddled with nooks and crannies, crevices and holes. About two-thirds of the way through the cave is an impressive collection of stalagmites and stalactites.

For details of the journey, see Towards Tham Long Kor, page 195. Beyond Ban Phonyang the river route to Tham Kong Lor is gorgeous, with small fish skipping out of the water, languid buffalo bathing, kids taking a dip and ducks floating by – all surrounded by a Lord of the Rings fantasyland of cliffs and rocky outcrops.

It is possible to continue from Ban Natan, on the other side of Kong Lor, into the awesome Hinboun gorge. This is roughly 14 km long and, for much of the distance, vertical cliffs over 300 m high rise directly from the water on both sides. The discovery of some valuable religious documents indicates the historical significance of the gorge both during the Vietnamese War and much earlier. There is no white water but the river frequently flows quite fast. More impressive scenery then follows until the village of **Paktuk**, close to Route 13 where any journey can be continued. ►► *For further information on getting to the Kong Lor cave, see Transport, page 200. The cave can also be visited as part of the 400-km 'loop' from Thakhek, see page 206.*

Lak Xao (Lac Sao) → *For listings, see pages 199-201. Colour map 2, B5.*

Lak Xao is a relatively new town. It was established by the army's Bolisat Phathana Khet Phoudoi (BPKP or Mountainous Area Development Company) back in 1968 in a remote and sparsely populated area close to the border with Vietnam, and still retains a frontier

The border is 30 km east of Lak Xao, at Nam Phao (Laos), a legal crossing point since 1997. There are buses to the border from Vientiane (via Paksan, see page 200). *Songthaews* leave Lak Xao market every hour 20,000 kip and take about 50 minutes to the border (see also Transport, page 200). The border is open 0800-1800 and the official exit fee is 3000 kip, although the Lao border officials are quite lackadaisical. Be prepared for slow service around lunchtime and an overtime fee at weekends. You need to organize Vietnamese visas in advance (ideally in Vientiane) as they aren't issued at the border. Crossing into Vietnam can induce culture shock as you will be descended upon by a gang of 'sharks', trying to extort ridiculous sums of money for minivan/bus services to Vinh (reports of up to US$30!). Take your time to bargain for the right price (US$6-7 is reasonable), rather than rushing your travel arrangements. Arriving from Vietnam, 30-day Laos visas are issued at the border (prices vary for different nationalities but expect to pay around US$30-42.

atmosphere. It is sometimes called Muang Kham Keut, which is confusing because there is another Kham Keut, 30 km to the west of town. (This was the original settlement and is worth a visit as it is over 500 years old.) The surrounding countryside is beautiful but Lak Xao itself has little to recommend it, except that it provides a necessary break on the journey overland to Vietnam.

This part of Laos was once one of the richest in terms of wildlife. Unfortunately, you only have to look around the town to see that it's also a major logging centre, with big timber trucks rumbling through to Vietnam. It is believed that Lak Xao was once a mini fiefdom controlled by an old Lao general, who logged the town into oblivion. Another threat to the forests and fauna is the area's great hydropower potential. Many feared that the controversial **Nam Theun II** dam project would open up the region to yet more loggers and settlers. In reality, some dam pundits would suggest that logging in the surrounding region was reduced by the presence of the dam. Construction of the dam has been monitored by a hawk-eyed bunch of consultants and it was rumoured that, if even one fish species were to become extinct as a result of the dam-building, then the World Bank and other financiers would pull the funds. The **Lak Xao Wildlife Centre** used to operate in the town, trying to protect animals displaced by the logging and dam construction. Unfortunately the centre has now closed and an assortment of wildlife is now to be found for sale at the market stalls: monkeys, reptiles, frogs and basically anything else the locals can lay their hands on.

The local army of tuk-tuk drivers is also worth mentioning as a breed apart. The town's Wild West atmosphere seems to have gone to their heads, so it's a question of holding on to your hats and your wallets, too, as they will probably do their level best to fleece you.

For Sleeping and Eating price codes and other relevant information, see pages 23-24.

● Sleeping

Paksan *p194*

Accommodation seems insufficient, given the many backpackers constantly passing through Pakse.

E Paksan Hotel, T054-791333. Well appointed, Vietnamese-run hotel with clean, modern rooms.

F B&K Guesthouse, across the river, on the first road on the right, T054-212638. The friendly owners of this establishment speak very good English and, with clean rooms and en suite bathrooms, it's worth a try. Another plus is the very good restaurant that's attached.

Ban Lao *p194*

If you get stuck en route there are 2 guest-houses on Route 13, just past the Route 8 intersection, which, by and large, are better than those found at Ban Na Hin.

F Bunthieng Guesthouse, on the right-hand side of Route 13. Reasonable accommodation, with basic furnishings.

F Vieng Thong, on the left-hand side of the road. Quite big rooms with fan.

Ban Na Hin *p195*

You may need to stay either here or in Ban Lao for 1 night if you are trying to make your way back quickly from Kong Lor cave. Accommodation is mostly of a 'rustic' nature.

E-F Mithuna Guesthouse, Route 8, T020-22240182. A surprise find, modern guest-house with hot water, a/c, comfortable beds, internet and an excellent restaurant attached. Great stop-off for those wanting advice on getting to Kong Lor.

F-G SP Guesthouse, right in the centre of town. This wooden guesthouse is a little lack-lustre, but the large verandas are a distinct advantage.

Towards Tham Kong Lor *p195*

There are 2 guesthouses on Route 13 in **Ban Lao**, just past the Route 8 intersection, which are passable. Homestays are available in **Ban Kong Lor** and **Ban Natan**. The homestays generally charge about US$5 per person including breakfast.

C-E Sala Hin Boun, Ban Phonyang, 10 km from Kong Lor cave, T020-7775 5220, www.salalao.com. The best option. It enjoys a scenic location on the riverbank amongst karst rock formations and has 10 well-equipped and very pleasant rooms in 2 bungalows. The manager, will arrange for a boat to pick you up in Napua for US$25, with advance notice. A tour to Kong Lor for 2-3 people is US$30 with picnic lunch. Discounts in low season.

E-G Sala Kong Lor Lodge, 1.5 km from Kong Lor cave, near Ban Tiou, T020-7761846. Lodge with 4 small huts with twin beds and several superior rooms.

Lak Xao *p197*

There are several reasonably pleasant places to stay in Lak Xao.

F Phoutthavong Guesthouse, T054-341074. Spotless rooms with a/c or fans, tiled floor, polished wooden furniture and white paintwork at odds with the dusty atmosphere of the town. Recommended.

F Souriya Hotel , T054-341111. Another pleasant alternative with 20 spotlessly clean, simple rooms (some a/c) with TV and some baths (hot water). Friendly owner speaks quite good English.

F Vongsouda Guesthouse, T054-341035. Quite a nice guesthouse with a/c and en suite bathrooms with Western toilets and hot water. Not the most comfortable mattresses in the world but the rooms are clean and serviceable. Clean and airy lobby too, but the real selling point is the large veranda outside the main entrance where you can sit and relax with a drink. Motorbike hire also available.

🍴 Eating

Paksan p194

There are many small restaurants along the main drag. Few have English menus and most are of poor quality and not even particularly cheap.

🍴 **Saynamxam** Restaurant, at the north of the bridge. Has a fairly decent menu.

Ban Lao p194

There is a small market at the intersection, with several *feu* restaurants.

Lak Xao p197

🍴 **Only One Restaurant**, 200 m from Phoutthayong Guesthouse, on the same side of the road. Plenty of tables in a pleasant but unexceptional setting. Reasonable Vietnamese and Lao food, daily 0600-2200.

🎊 Festivals and events

Paksan p194

Jul (movable) Every year Wat Prah Bat hosts a full moon festival.
Mid-Oct (movable) The famous Naga Fireball Festival (Bang Fai Phayanuk), at the Phonsane Temple, when small, colourful fireballs shoot out of the river.

🚌 Transport

Paksan p194
Bus

The bus stop is next to the Morning Market. To **Vientiane**, 7 daily in the morning, 1-2 hrs, 25,000 kip. In the other direction, most buses from Vientiane to southern destinations ply through the town every couple of hours, so it's just a matter of waiting at the bus stop/market to pick up a lift: to **Thakhek**, 190 km, 4-5 hrs, 15,000 kip; to **Savannakhet**, 25,000 kip. To reach the Vietnam border at **Nam Phao** (see box, page 198), catch one of the border-bound buses that starts from the southern terminal in Vientiane or

travel by pickup to Lak Xao, 5-6 hrs, 50,000 kip, for onward transport (see below). These *songthaew* depart between 0500 and 0600.

Ban Lao p194

There is a small transport terminus at the intersection here. If a bus/*songthaew* happens to dump you here, your best bet is to hop on one of the northbound buses to Vientiane or a southbound bus to Thakhek, Savannakhet and Pakse. *Songthaew* generally scurry through from early in the morning to well into the afternoon, on their way to **Ban Na Hin** (for Kong Lor cave, and **Lak Xao**.

Towards Tham Kong Lor p195

The best way to get to Tham Lor is by road and boat. There is a small transport terminus at the Route 13/Route 8 intersection in **Ban Lao** (also known as Tham Beng or Vieng Kham) for north-south buses between Vientiane and Thakhek, Savannakhet or Pakse. *Songthaew* generally pass through here from early in the morning to well into the afternoon to **Ban Na Hin**, US$1-2. This trip along Route 8 is about 60 km. The drive between Ban La and Ban Na Hin is magical and passes through some truly amazing scenery; keep an eye open for the lookout point at Km 54 from Route 13. Generally, a pickup waits in Ban Na Hin to take passengers to Ban Kong Lor, where it's possible to pick up a boat to take you into the cave. There is also one public *songthaew* a day making the journey.

Alternatively, if the new road is flooded you can get a *songthaew*, as far as **Ban Napur**, or Na Phouak, and then catch a boat to **Ban Phonyang**, 2-3 hrs, or **Ban Kong Lor** (closer to the cave), and onto the cave, a further 1 hr.

If you are staying at **Sala Hin Boun**, see Sleeping, they will send a boat to Ban Napur to collect you, US$25.

Lak Xao p197

Songthaew depart for **Paksan**, every hr from 0700 daily, 5-6 hrs, 40,000 kip, and **Thakhek**, every hr 0730-noon daily, 40,000 kip. If you wish to leave after midday, go to Ban Lao and pick up a lift from there. Buses leave for **Vientiane** at 0500, 0600 and 0800, 6-8 hrs, 60,000 kip. These buses go via **Ban Lao** (Vieng Kham). There is a scheduled bus for **Thakhek** daily at 0730, 5-6 hrs, 50,000 kip.

The road up into the mountains is excellent, partly because there is a hydro-power dam here and also because of the need to establish and maintain good transport links with neighbouring countries.

Pickups depart from the Lak Xao market throughout the day to the Vietnam border 32 km away, at **Nam Phao**, 1 hr, 10,000 kip each if you can fill a whole tuk-tuk but be prepared to barter hard. Often tour buses to Vietnam leave from the **Phou Doi Hotel**, so it is worth checking if you can get on board, as it is an infinitely more comfortable mode of transport. There is also a minivan service from Lak Xao market to **Chung Thom**, near Vinh, daily 1100. Otherwise, it's sometimes cheaper to catch a ride in the mornings, as there's a better chance the drivers will be able to pick up passengers; the chances deteriorate as the day goes on.

❶ Directory

Lak Xao *p197*
Banks Lao Development Bank, open daily 0800-1500, with an hour's lunch break, quite a competitive exchange rate on major currencies. **Post** The post office is open daily 0800-1200 and 1300-1600.

Thakhek and around

→ Phone code: 052. Colour map 2, B5.

Thakhek is sometimes translated as Indian (Khek or Khaek) Port (Tha), although it probably means Guest (Khaek) Port after the large number of people who settled here from the north. During the royalist period (through to the mid-1970s) it was a popular weekend destination for Thais who came here in droves to gamble. After the Communist victory, when Laos effectively shut up shop, everything went very quiet. But the recent recovery of commercial traffic has brought some life back to this small settlement, although Thakhek remains a quiet town, set in beautiful countryside. This will inevitably change with the opening of the third Friendship Bridge to Thailand due to be completed by 2012.

The origins of Thakhek can be traced back to the Cambodia-based kingdoms of Chenla and Funan, which reached their heyday in the seventh century AD. But modern Thakhek was founded in 1911-1912, under the French, clearly evident in the architecture. Apart from Luang Prabang, this is probably the most outwardly French-looking town in Laos, particularly with the fading pastel hues of the villas around the town's fountain area.

Today Thakhek is the most popular stopover point in the central provinces, although it is still not considered a primary tourist destination. However, the region encompasses some of the most beautiful scenery in Laos: imposing jagged mountains, bottle green rivers and lakes and caves. Tourism infrastructure is still quite limited but is improving and a trip to this area will prove a highlight of most visitors' holidays to Laos, particularly the stunning karst scenery and impressive trip out to Buddha Cave, or the popular route known as 'the Loop' (see page 206).
▶▶ For listings, see pages 209-211.

Ins and outs

Getting there and around There are two bus terminals: the main terminal, which is about 4 km from town and offers inter-provincial and international buses, and the small *songthaew* station, near Soksombook market, which services local regions.

Thakhek is small enough to negotiate on foot or by bicycle. A number of places organize motorbike hire, such as the **Thakhek Travel Lodge** and the Tourism Information Centre, which acts as an agent for motorcycle dealers. ▶▶ *See Transport, page 211.*

Tourist information The **Tourism Information Centre** ⓘ *Vientiane Rd, in a signposted chalet-like building, T052-212512, Mon-Fri 0800-1130 and 1330-1630, Sat-Sun 0800-1130 and 1400-1700*, has particularly helpful staff who are champing at the bit to take tourists out on their ecotours and hikes. This is a good stop-off place for advice. Proceeds from the tours go to poor, local communities. The office is full of brochures and glossy displays of the surrounding sites. Mr Somkiad, the head of the centre, is helpful and speaks good English, T020-55751791, somkiad@yahoo.com. Motorbike hire for the loop, 100,000 kip per day; for town 70,000 kip per day. ▶▶ *For further details, see page 211.*

Sights

There are few officially designated sights in Thakhek but many visitors consider it to be a gem of a settlement. Quiet and elegant, with some remaining Franco-Chinese architecture, including a simple fountain square, it has a fine collection of colonial-era shophouses, a breezy riverside position and a relaxed ambience. What locals regard as the

Border essentials: Thakhek-Nakhon Phanom (Thailand)

Thakhek is across the Mekong from Nakhon Phanom in Thailand. There's a customs and immmigration office by the pier in Thakhek, open daily 0800-1730, and boats cross between the two towns every 30 minutes, 0800-1600 (although this tends to slow down to an hourly service around lunchtime), 15,000 kip. There are usually 'overtime service fees' at weekends, when boats are less frequent. From Nakhon Phanom, scheduled buses depart for Udon Thani and Bangkok. Arriving from Thailand, 30-day Lao visas are available at the border, US$30-42.

In 2012, a third Friendship Bridge linking Laos and Thailand will cross the Mekong around 6 km north of Thakhek.

central business district at the river end of **Kouvoravong Road** is wonderful for its faded elegance. Other visitors, in contrast, look more critically at the dusty streets, seeing pockets of squalor, dilapidated buildings and an uncharacteristic atmosphere of disinterest among the locals. ▶ *For details of the town's three markets, see Shopping, page 210.*

That Sikhot

ⓘ *6 km south of Thakhek, daily 0800-1800, admission 5000 kip, tuk-tuk 30,000 kip return.*

That Sikhot or **Sikhotaboun** is one of Laos' holiest sites. It overlooks the Mekong and the journey downstream from Thakhek, along a quiet country road, reveals bucolic Laos at its best. The *that* was restored in 1956 but is thought to have been built by Chao Anou at the beginning of the 15th century, around the same time as That Ingheng in Savannakhet Province (see page 215). The *that* houses the relics of Chao Sikhot, a local hero, who founded the old town of Thakhek.

According to local legend, Sikhot was an ordinary man who once cooked some rice which he stirred with dirty – but as it turned out, magic – sticks. When he ate the filthy rice he was bestowed with Herculean strength. At that time, the King of Vientiane had been having a major problem with elephants killing villagers and taking over the country (hard to believe now but Laos was once called Land of a Million Elephants). The king offered anyone who could save the region half his kingdom and his daughter's hand in marriage. Due to his new-found strength, Sikhot was able to take on the elephants and secure most of the surrounding area as well as Vientiane, whereupon he married the king of Vientiane's daughter. The king was unhappy about handing over his kingdom and daughter to this man, and plotted with his daughter so as to to regain control. The king asked his daughter to discover whether Sikhot had any weakness. Her husband foolishly revealed that he could be killed only through his anus, so the King of Vientiane placed an archer at the bottom of Sikhot's pit latrine and when the unfortunate Oriental Hercules came to relieve himself, he was killed by an arrow.

That Sikhot consists of a large gold stupa raised 29 m on a plinth, with a viharn upstream commissioned in 1970 by the last King of Laos. The *that* is partly surrounded by a high wall. The tip of the stupa is said to be fashioned after a banana flower and there are reliefs of the Buddha in various *mudras* along the base. Stalls selling drinks and a small range of snacks are to be found under the trees to the left. A major annual festival is held here in July and during February.

Kong Leng lake

① *33 km northeast of Thakhek.*

This stunning lake is usually incorporated into hikes as there isn't direct road access to the site. It is steeped in legend, for locals believe an underground kingdom lies beneath the surface of the 100-m-deep lake. As a result, you must request permission to swim in this lake from the local village authority and you can swim only in the designated swimming zone. Fishing is not permitted. The beautiful green waters of the lake morph into different shades season to season due to the dissolved calcium from the surrounding limestone outcrops. It is very difficult to get to the lake independently and sometimes the track is completely inaccessible except on foot. The Tourism Information Office organizes excellent treks to the lake.

Excursions off Route 12 → *For listings, see pages 209 -211.*

The caves along Route 12 can be visited on day trips from Thakhek, although some are difficult to find without a guide and access may be limited in the wet season. Some sights have no English signposts but locals will be more than obliging to confirm you are going in the right direction if you ask.

Tham Xang (Tham Pha Ban Tham)

This is the closest cave to Thakhek, around 9 km northeast of town. The cave is considered an important Buddhist shrine and contains a number of Buddhist artefacts, including some statues and a box containing religious scripts. The Buddhist component, however, pales into insignificance compared to the 'elephant head' that has formed from calcium deposits. Locals herald it as a miracle and in the Lao New Year they sprinkle water on it. Visitors will need a flashlight to find the formation along a small passage at the right-hand corner of the cave, behind the golden Buddha. To get to the cave, follow Route 12 for about 7 km until you pass the bridge, then turn right (difficulties can arise in the wet season due to flooding). Of lesser interest but in the same general direction are a few **railway bridges**, part of a project, designed by the French in the early 1900s, to connect Laos and Vietnam, but abandoned in 1920. The best remnant is the bridge crossing the Nam Don river. To get there, turn north off Route 12 at Km 8 and follow the road for 1 km until you hit the old railway bed. Then turn right and continue along the dirt track for another 1 km until you cross the bridge.

Tham Pha (Buddha Cave)

① *Ban Na Khangxang, off Route 12, 18 km from Thakhek. A tuk tuk will cost 100,000 kip, use of boat 5000 kip and entrance to the cave 2000 kip. Women will need to hire a* sinh *(sarong) at the entrance, 3000 kip.*

A trip out here is highly recommended not just for the cave itself, which is impressive in its own historical right, but for the surrounding villages, pristine waterways and wonderful karst scenery. A farmer hunting for bats accidentally stumbled across Buddha Cave (also knowns as Tham Pa Fa – Turtle Cave) in April 2004. On climbing up to the cave's mouth, he found 229 bronze Buddha statues, believed to be over 450 years old, and ancient palm leaf scripts. The Buddhas were part of the royal collection believed to have been hidden here when the Thais ransacked Vientiane. Since its discovery, the cave has become widely celebrated, attracting pilgrims from as far away as Thailand, particularly around Pi Mai (Lao New Year). In the wet season it is possible to bathe in the beautifully clear waters surrounding the cave, though women will need to bring a *sinh* (sarong). A wooden ladder and ugly concrete steps have been built to access the cave but it is still quite difficult to get to, as the road from Thakhek is in poor condition. It is recommended that you organize a guide through the Thakhek Information Centre, page 202, to escort you. In the wet season, it is necessary to catch a boat. The trip out to the cave is half the fun as it is surrounded by spectacular scenery – jagged karst formations sprawling across the landscape like giant dinosaur teeth.

Tha Falang (Vang Santiphap – Peace Pool)

This lovely emerald billabong is surrounded by pristine wilderness and breathtaking cliffs. The swimming pool, created by the Nam Don river, was a favourite French picnic spot during the colonial period and it's a nice place to spend the afternoon or break your journey if you're doing 'the Loop' (see page 206). The water is less pleasant in the dry seas, when it can become a bit stagnant. To get there, follow Route 12 for 13 km and then turn north for 2 km. In the wet season it may be necessary to catch a boat from the Xieng Liab Bridge.

Tham Xiang Liab

Turn off Route 12 at Km 14 (1 km past the turn-off for Tham Xang) and follow the track south to reach Tham Xiang Liab, the first cave in the province to be officially opened to tourists. The 200-m-long cave sits at the foot of a 300-m-high limestone cliff, with a small swimming hole (in the dry season) at the far end. It is not easy to access the interior of the cavern on your own and, in the wet season, it can only be navigated by boat, as it usually floods. This cave, called 'sneaking around cave', derived its name from a legend of an old hermit who used to meditate here with his beautiful daughter. A novice monk fell in love with the hermit's daughter and the two love birds planned sneaky trysts around this cave and Tham Nan Aen (see below). When the hermit found out he flew into a rage and did away with the novice monk; the daughter was banished to the cave for the rest of her life. There are limestone formations on the roof of the cave and experts have suggested that there may be some cave drawings hidden among the shadows.

Tham Sa Pha In

This little-visited cave contains a small lake, reputed to be 75 m long, and a couple of interesting Buddhist shrines. Swimming in the lake is strictly prohibited as the auspicious waters are believed to have magical powers. To reach the cave, follow Route 12 to Km 17; beyond the narrow pass turn to the left (north) and follow the path for 400 m.

Tham Nan Aen

① *First entrance 2,000 kip; cave dmission 5000 kip.*

Follow Route 12 until you see a sign on the right (south) at Km 18, which reads '700 metres'; follow this path to the cave entrance. The largest of the caverns hereabouts, it is said to be 1.5 km long and stands over 100 m tall. It is worth a visit, if only to catch the cool breeze, which rushes from within the rock and emanates from the cave entrance. Outside the cave is a wooded picnic area and a rather motley collection of animals, a disgrace considering this is supposed to be a protected area. The large cave is accessed by a wooden platform, purpose-built in 1987, for the visiting Princess of Thailand. The breezy cave is like a labyrinth, with multiple chambers and entrances, and also contains a small underground freshwater pool. The cave has stairs and fluorescent lighting.

Nam Don Resurgence

Close to Ban Na, off Route 12 at Km 14, 25 km northeast of Thakhek, is a beautiful lagoon, located within a cave and shaded by a sheer 300-m-tall cliff. The lagoon offers about 20 m of swimming then filters off into an underground waterway network, believed to extend for 3 km. In 1998 French surveyors found a rare species of blind cave fish 23 m below the surface here. If you follow the cave wall round, there is another entrance which offers a good vista of the turquoise pool below. A trip to Nam Don Resurgence can be done in conjunction with the 'Loop' but requires a few hours. It is also a bit tricky to find on your own so you might need to ask the locals or recruit a local guide. During the wet season, access is often only by boat. The Provincial Tourism Office runs some pretty good tours which include this sight.

Mahaxai

Mahaxai is a beautiful small town 50 km east of Thakhek on Route 12. The sunset here is renowned but even more stunning is the surrounding scenery of exquisite valleys and imposing limestone bluffs. A trip to Mahaxai should be combined with a visit to one or more of the spectacular caves along Route 12 and some river excursions to see the Xe Bang Fai gorges or to run the rapids further downstream.

The Loop

Ins and outs

ⓘ *Contact Thakhek Travel Lodge (see Sleeping, page 209) for latest information on the route posted in their log book. Mr Ku who rents the motorbikes is based at an office at the lodge daily 0700-1100, 1500-1930, T020-2220 5070. Motorbikes (100cc) cost 100,000 kip per day and come with a helmet and a good map. Mr Ku has contacts around the Loop. He recommends riders take four days. He will help out in an emergency and advises on no-go times such as Sep and Oct during the rains.*

A motorbike tour looping around Mahaxai, Lak Xao, the caves and other beautiful scenery along the way has become increasingly popular with the backpacker set. However, by doing the entire 'circuit' by motorbike you will miss some of the most beautiful landscapes in the country, many of which can only be accessed by boat, in particular the trip to Kong Lor cave (see page 195). The circuit – if done quickly – should take approximately three days but allow four or five, particularly if you want to sidetrack to Tham Kong Lor and the other caves, and also to allow for the punctures and muddy shenanigans that are par for the course in this part of the world. The weather will have a major impact on the roads, which may be impassable in the wet season; it is imperative to check in advance.

The 'loop' is mostly for motorcyclists, who pick up a bike in Thakhek and travel by road. The whole loop covers an area over 400 km (without the side-trips). This includes 50 km from Thakhek to the petrol station before the turn-off to Mahaxai; 45 km between the petrol station and Nakai; 75 km between Nakai and Lak Xao; 58 km between Lak Xao and Ban Na Hin; 41 km between Ban Na Hin and Ban Lao and then 105 km between Ban Lao and Thakhek. The trip between Ban Lao and Ban Na Hin offers some spectacular views.

It is a wild ride in parts, so pack lightly: include a waterproof jacket, a torch, a few snacks, a long-sleeved shirt, sunglasses, sun block, closed-toe shoes, a *sinh* or sarong (to use as a towel, to stop dust and – for women – to bathe along the way), a phrase book and a good map. It is a bumpy, exhausting but enjoyable ride. All of the sites are now well signposted in English. Most sites charge a parking fee for motorbikes.

Note that this whole region is susceptible to change due to the Nam Theun II dam (see box, page 196) and other developments in the area. Check for up-to-date information (and on the status of the roads) with the Tourism Information Centre, page 202, and with Mr Ku at **Thakhek Travel Lodge**. This trip is difficult in the wet season and will probably only be possible for skilled riders on larger dirt-bikes. In the dry season it is very dusty.

The route

Thakhek to Mahaxai From Thakhek take Route 12 east. The 50-km trip to Mahaxai should take two to three hours, without stops. It can be bumpy, potholed and muddy during the rainy season. Most travellers will want to stop off at some of the caves, swimming holes or the railway line en route. Close to Mahaxai there is a small village, with a large, blue-coloured factory, and a good *feu* soup restaurant. After this, turn right at the T-junction to Mahaxai, where there are a few cheap guesthouses (see Sleeping, page 210).

Mahaxai to Nakai/Ban Tha Long Alternatively you can continue on to Nakai (an additional 1½ to two hours), where there are also basic guesthouses and fuel. There is a 7-km hilly section en route to Nakai. There is a guesthouse in Nakai (40,000-80,000 kip, clean but with quite a few bugs) but this isn't the nicest of towns in which to stay so you might want to continue a further 20 km to Ban Tha Long, which has a lovely riverfront guesthouse, serving pretty good omelettes (40,000-80,000 kip).

Around Thakhek: The Loop

Nakai/Ban Tha Long to Lak Xao Lak Xao is 70 km and four to five hours from Nakai or 50 km and three to four hours from Ban Tha Long. The road is relatively bad for half the journey; the other half is smooth due to the kindly efforts of the Nam Theun dam crew. Seventeen kilometres from Nakai you hit a junction. The left fork will take you to the Nam Theun II site; the most common route, though, is to take the right fork along the forested, paved road to Lak Xao. Lak Xao offers extraordinary scenery but doesn't emanate the kind of vibe which makes you want to stay for long.

Lak Xao to Kong Lor To get to Kong Lor from Lak Xao follow the road 60 km to **Ban Na Hin** (also known as **Khoun Kham**), the last town before Kong Lor. It has a couple of small guesthouses (see page 199). A new 40-km laterite road from Ban Na Hin to Kong Lor is now open. Follow the main road through town and turn south after the hydroelectric project (now signposted in English). Follow the hydroelectric waterway and after a few kilometres turn right at the intersection marked by red painted barrels. (You'll know you have the correct turning when you can see a settlement on the other side of the waterway.) Keep following the road until you hit a rusty bridge at **Namsanam**. Sometimes in September and October the new road floods and you will need to store your motorbike at Na Phouak (negotiate bike-minding fee) or at the village just before Na Phouak, Ban Napur, and take the final leg by boat. The boat trip is recommended anyway, as it takes in stunning scenery (see page 195). The return boat trip from Na Phouak to the guesthouses is 500,000 kip return for the whole boat. (Despite the new road, it is still possible to hire a boat all the way from Ban Nahin to the guesthouses for around US$100 return.) There is also one *songthaew* a day from Ban Na Hin to Kong Lor. See also Transport, page 211. Ten kilometres from Kong Lor is **Sala Hin Boun**, which can make a pleasant stopover (see page 199). Closer still is the new **Sala Kong Lor** (also on page 199).

Ban Na Hin to Thakhek Once you get back to Ban Na Hin, check out **Namsanam waterfall** (see page 195), 3 km off the main road, then continue on Route 8 towards the intersection with Route 13. You will hit a little uphill stretch followed by a very dangerous big downhill run; don't miss out on the stunning lookout point, which is well worth a break. At the intersection is the small village of Ban Lao (also known as Vieng Kham) (see page 194), from where it is 104 km back to Thakhek; this last stretch should take two and a half hours and the scenery is pretty boring.

Nakai Nam Theun National Protected Area

The **Nakai Plateau** was once a royal hunting ground, but today it is part of a National Protected Area (NPA). Over 3700 sq km of stunning landscape have been designated for protection, making it the largest area of its type in Laos and some of the most pristine wilderness remaining in Southeast Asia. Gradually rising from the Nakai Plateau, the heavy jungle looms up into the Annamite Mountain range, bordering Vietnam. Although numbers are dwindling, there is a great wealth of rare and endangered flora and fauna in this region, including elephants, tigers, the giant muntjac, Asiatic black bears, Malayan sun bears, clouded leopards and the very rare saola (or spindlehorn).

Tourist access to the area is limited due to the **Nam Theun II Dam Project**. Nam Theun NPA was thrown into the international spotlight over the controversial dam, which now supplies electricity to nearby Thailand and will eventually be a major source of income for the Laos government. Many conservationists believe the project is an environmental minefield (see also box, page 196). The dam opened in 2010. However, it is hoped that the Nakai Plateau will soon open to tourism with a five-year sustainable tourism plan in place and plans for four community-managed ecotourism and wildlife sanctuaries. There are plans for kayaking, rafting, trekking and rock climbing and four eco-tourism tours and one ecolodge. The NPA will run tours and will have an office in Nakai. Meanwhile, contact the Thakhek tourism office for further information.

◉ Thakhek listings

For Sleeping and Eating price codes and other relevant information, see pages 23-24.

● Sleeping

Thakhek *p202*

B-C Hotel Riveria, Setthathirat Rd, T051-250000, www.hotelriveriathakhek.com. This huge white, nautical-looking building is the first structure that arrivals from Thailand will see. Situated right on the riverfront, it offers comfort at a price, although the beds are comically short and bathrooms are small. Go for the superior de luxe, which does have space. There's a restaurant, pool and gym and there's Wi-Fi in the lobby. The views of the karst landscape are beautiful from the upper floors; it's a shame the hotel owners didn't think to put in a rooftop bar.

D Inthira Sikhotabong Hotel, Chao Anou Rd, close to the fountain, T051-251237, www.inthirahotel.com. In a Lao nautical-style building, this small new hotel offers attractive rooms that are warmly decorated but twins are cramped, with a tiny toilet closet; doubles are better. Restaurant and Wi-Fi available.

E Mekong Hotel, Setthathirat Rd , T051-250777, www.truongsonnghean.com.vn. Prime location on the riverfront, this large grey 1950s hotel has 60 or so a/c rooms overlooking the Mekong. No windows facing the river but the wide balconies are perfect for the sunset vista. Large, plain but clean and newly renovated, with TV, telephone, fridge and bathtub. Since you're not exposed to the exterior from your room, the US$15 asking price represents one of the best deals in town. The Vietnamese

management is lethargic in the extreme; limited English is spoken. There's internet in the lobby.

E-F Sooksomboon Guesthouse , Setthathirat Rd, T051-212225. An immensely attractive building that was once the provincial police station. It faces the Mekong and has the most character in Thakhek, though this may not be to everyone's taste. The interior is 1970s kitsch with padded panelling and 70s glass mosaic, not to be cool but because it hasn't been renovated in the last 30 years. The a/c rooms in the main house are musty with peeling paint, but are en suite with bathtubs and have a fridge and a TV. There are cheaper rooms in the motel-esque annexe. It's in a prime location, with a view across the river to Thailand. There's a run-down restaurant.

E-F Southida Guesthouse, Chao Anou Rd (1 block back from the river), T051-212568. Very popular guesthouse in the centre of town. Clean comfortable rooms with a/c, TV, and hot water; cheaper with fan. Very helpful staff; often booked up.

E-F Thakhek Travel Lodge, 2 km from the centre of town, T030-530 0145, travell@ laotel.com. Popular guesthouse set in a beautifully restored and decorated house. Fantastic outdoor seating area and with nightly open fire. The cheaper rooms are very basic but the 9-bed dorm (not bunk beds) is extremely nice (25,000 kip per person). The a/c rooms are huge with large bathrooms and very comfortable. For details of their restaurant, see Eating below. The Danish/Lao owners can provide travel advice, when they're around, and there's an excellent log-book for those intending to travel independently around the 'Loop'. Motorcycle hire can be arranged. Ring them in advance if you're coming in on one of the midnight buses. .

F Khammuan Inter, Kouvoravong Rd, T051-212171. Military-owned hotel that has a soulless penitentiary feel. Smallish rooms without windows but some have a/c and the en suite bathrooms are good with hot water showers. Cheaper single rooms with powerful ceiling fans are also available.

F-G Phoukanna, Vientiane Rd, T051-212092. Attractive gardens with a loud bar, good food and ice cream. Rooms have TV and hot water. Popular with the NGO crowd, and good value. Rooms with a shared bath to en suite with a/c.

Mahaxai *p206*

G Mahaxai Guesthouse. Offers 10 large clean airy rooms, with en suite showers. The upstairs rooms are brighter, and have an attractive balcony overlooking the river – ideal for sitting and watching the world go by.

🍴 Eating

Thakhek *p202*

Thakhek is not a place to come to for its cuisine. But you will find the usual array of noodle stalls – try the one in the town 'square' with good fruit shakes – and warmed baguettes are also sold on the square in the morning. The best place to eat is at one of the riverside restaurants on either side of the square. Otherwise, most of the restaurants are attached to the hotels and guesthouses.

♥ Sabaidee, T051-251245. Closed 1500-1700. Serves great backpacker fare (burgers, salads, sandwiches) plus a range of Laos dishes on cheery red-checked tablecloths. Book exchange and CNN on TV.

♥ Kaysone Restaurant, in the centre of town, T051-212563. Although from the outside this looks like someone's backyard, inside is a sprawling restaurant compound.

Sindat, Korean barbecue, and fantastic ice cream. And there's karaoke on site.

♥ Lao-named restaurant, on the corner of Ounkham Rd and the east-west street leading to Wat Nabo. English menu with Lao and some Western dishes, mainly centred on seafood. Popular with local expats.

♥ Phoukanna, see Sleeping. Big choice of Western and Lao dishes plus new noisy bar.

♥ Sukiyaki, Vientiane Rd, T020-5575 1533. A pokey but exceptionally friendly restaurant where you can barbecue your on meal on the tables.

♥ Thakhek Travel Lodge, see page 209. The food in the lodge's restaurant is not all good but recommended are the Hawaii curry and barbecue (which needs to be ordered in advance); the service, on the other hand, is ridiculously and unacceptably slow and haphazard.

♥ Vanthiu Restaurant. Walk through a wine shop to get to the Vietnamese restaurant out back. Friendly owners. Some English dishes also on the menu.

Mahaxai *p206*

Food is generally of a high quality in the local noodle shops and foodstalls.

🍷 Bars

Thakhek *p202*

Boua's Place on the Mekong is great for a sunset drink. There are a lot of drinking holes strung along the front here.

🛍 Shopping

Thakhek *p202*
Markets

There are 3 markets in Thakhek. The largest (**Talaat Lak Saam**) is at the bus terminal, 4 km east of town and is a good place to pick up odds and ends, with tuk-tuks ferrying market-goers to and fro (10,000 kip). **Talaat Lak Song** is at the eastern end of Kouvoravong Rd, 1.5-2 km from the centre. It is a mixed, mainly dry goods market, although basketry and hand-crafted buffalo bells are also sold. North on Chaoanou Rd is the **Talaat Nabo**. A new night market has opened in the fountain area.

☉ Activities and tours

Thakhek *p202*
The tourism office organizes treks and excursions and is super helpful. A 3-day trip to Kong Lor, 770,000 kip per person for 2; to Phou Hin Poun for lakes and caves, 600,000 kip per person for 2; to Buddha Cave, 300,000 kip per person for 2; Route 12 trips too. A private minivan to Kong Lor, 3500 baht.

☉ Transport

Thakhek *p202*
For boats to **Thailand**, see box, page 203.

Bus/truck
Thakhek's **main bus station** is 4 km northeast of town, T051-251519. It is a large station with a mini-market and is open throughout the night. Frequent daily connections from 0400-1200 northbound to **Vientiane**, 346 km, 6 hrs, 50,000 kip; the VIP bus also dashes through town at 0915 daily, 70,000 kip. Frequent scheduled buses to **Paksan**, 0400-1200, 190 km, 4-5 hrs; it is also possible to pick up a bus to Paksan en route to Vientiane. Get off at **Ban Lao**, 15,000 kip, for connections along Route 12.

Southbound buses to **Savannakhet**, from 1030, every 30 mins daily, 139 km, 2½-3 hrs, 25,000 kip; to **Pakse**, every hr from 1030 until 2400 daily, 6-7 hrs, 50,000 kip; Pakse VIP bus leaves at 2400, 70,000 kip; also to **Sekong**, 3 daily, 70,000 kip; to **Attapeu**, 1500 and 2300 daily, 75,000 kip; to **Don Khong**, 2300 daily, 15 hrs, 75,000 kip.

Buses to Vietnam To Vinh, 0800 daily, 90,000 kip. To **Dong Hoi**, 0700 Mon, Wed, Sat and Sun, 85,000-130,000 kip; to **Hué**, 2000 Wed, Thu, Sat and Sun 90,000 kip. To **Hanoi**, 0800 Sat and Sun, 160,000 kip.

The **local bus station** is at Talaat Lak Sarm and services towns and villages within the province. From here *songthaew* depart hourly between 0900 and 1300 to **Mahaxai**, 45 km, 2-3 hrs, 15,000 kip; to **Nakai**, 0800-1600, 77 km km, 2-4 hrs, 25,000 kip; **Na Phao** (Vietnam border) 142 km, 6-7 hrs, 40,000 kip; **Na Hin**, 45,000 kip. There is also a *songthaew* to **Kong Lor** village at 0830, 65,000 kip.

Motorbike hire
Bikes can be rented from **Thakhek Travel Lodge**, 70,000 kip per day. The Provincial Tourism Office can also organize motorbike rental: 70,000 kip in town; 100,000 kip per day for The Loop.

Mahaxai *p206*
Songthaew leave from the station in the morning. The last bus back to **Thakhek** leaves Mahaxai at 1500.

☉ Directory

Thakhek *p202*
Banks BCEL, Vientiane Rd, T051-212686, will change cash and TCs and does cash advances on Visa and MasterCard. It now also has a 24-hr Visa and MasterCard ATM and there is another close to the fountain in the town centre. **Lao Development Bank**, Kouvoravong Rd (eastern end), T052-212089, exchanges cash but doesn't do cash advances. There is also a second exchange counter at the immigration pier. **Internet** Available at the Thakhek Travel Lodge (expensive), Inthira Hotel, Mekong Hotel and Mukda internet café. Wi-Fi in the lobby of the Riveria and Inthira. **Post** Post office, Kouvoravong Rd (at crossroads with Nongbuakham Rd). **Telephone** International calls can be made from the post office.

Savannakhet Province → *Phone code: 041.*

Savannakhet Province has the highest provincial population in Laos. It consists of 15 districts, with 826,000 inhabitants dispersed within its boundaries. Like most provinces in the country, it comprises a kaleidoscope of ethnicities, including the Lao, Phouthai, Thaidam, Katang, Chali, Lava, Souai, Pako, Kaleng, Mangkong and Tai. The cultural diversity is even more visible in Savannakhet city, which has large Chinese and Vietnamese populations. Vietnamese and Thai merchants sell their products throughout the city, while the ubiquitous colonial houses and fading shopfronts are an ever-present reminder of French influence. Due to its proximity to both Thailand and Vietnam, Savannakhet is considered an important economic corridor. The Province has several natural attractions, although the majority are a fair hike from the provincial capital. ▶▶ *For listings, see pages 219 -222*

Savannakhet → *For listings, see pages 219-222. Colour map 2, C5.*

Situated on the banks of the Mekong and at the start of the Route 9 to Danang in Vietnam, Savannakhet – or Savan as it is usually known – is an important river port and the gateway to the south. It is also an important trading centre with Thailand.

Across the Mekong, high-rise Mukdahan in Thailand may be cocking a snook at its poorer neighbour to the east, but Savannakhet has got a lot to offer that Mukdahan has bulldozed away in the name of modernization. It feels as though the countryside never left Savan: goats and chickens graze and wander around the urban area and a large portion of the town's French colonial buildings still stand, moulding gently in the tropical climate. With a good lick of paint, Savannakhet could scrub up well and, although it's not quite Luang Prabang, it certainly shares many of the same characteristics. In 2010, the authorities recognized the value of its historic core and planned a 30 billion kip investment to preserve its colonial-era architecture. Whether this will last long is questionable. A new Japanese-sponsored bridge across the Mekong to Mukdahan is now open, a development that may change the town's character.

Ins and outs

Getting there and around It is possible to cross into Vietnam by taking Route 9 east over the Annamite Mountains via Xepon. The border is at Dansavanh (Laos) and Lao Bao (Vietnam) (see box, page 215), 236 km east of Savannakhet, with bus connections direct from Savannakhet to Dong Ha, Hue and Danang. It is also possible to cross the border into Mukdahan via the new Friendship Bridge. The government bus terminal on the northern edge of town, near the Savan Xai market, has connections with Vientiane, Thakhek, Pakse, Lao Bao and the Friendship Bridge; a tuk-tuk to the centre should cost about 10,000 kip. Just west of the bus station is the *songthaew* terminal, where vehicles depart to provincial destinations. Tuk-tuks, locally known as 'Sakaylab' (as in Skylab), criss-cross town. A tuk-tuk from the airport is 20,000 kip. ▶▶ *See Transport, page 221.*

Tourist information The **Provincial Tourism Office** ① *Chaleun Meuang Rd, T041-212755, Mon-Fri 0800-1200 and 1300-1600,* is one of the least helpful in the country with staff slumped on desks; 'too busy to help', apparently. Much more helpful, professional and friendlier is the nearby **Eco Guide Unit** ① *see page 221,* which runs a number of excellent ecotours and treks to Dong Natad and Dong Phou Vieng National Protected Areas;

Savannakhet

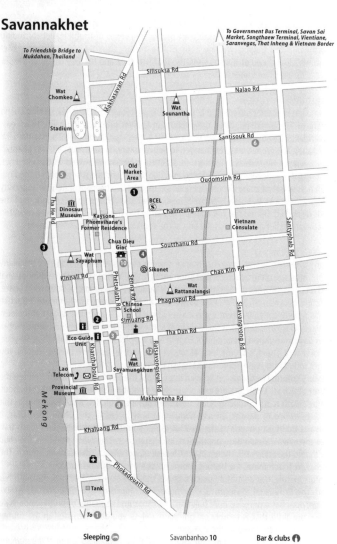

To Friendship Bridge to
Mukdahan, Thailand

To Government Bus Terminal, Savan Sai
Market, Songthaew Terminal, Vientiane,
Saranvegas, That Inheng & Vietnam Border

Silisuksa Rd

Nalao Rd

Wat
Sounantha

Wat
Chomkeo

Stadium

Santisouk Rd

Old
Market
Area

Oudomsinh Rd

BCEL

Chalmeung Rd

Dinosaur
Museum

Kaysone
Phomvihane's
Former Residence

Vietnam
Consulate

Chua Dieu
Giac

Soutthanu Rd

Wat
Sayaphum

@ Sikonet

Chao Kim Rd

Kinnali Rd

Wat
Rattanalangsi

Phagnapul Rd

Chinese
School

Simuang Rd

Tha Dan Rd

Eco Guide
Unit

Wat
Sayamungkhun

Lao
Telecom

Provincial
Museum

Makhavenha Rd

Khatuang Rd

Phokadouath Rd

Tank

To

Mekong

Makhasavran Rd

Tha He Rd

Phetsalath Rd

Senna Rd

Khanthaboul Rd

Ratsavongseuk Rd

Sisavangvong Rd

Santyphab Rd

N

200 metres
200 yards

Sleeping		Bar & clubs
Daosavanh Resort & Spa 1	Savanbanhao 10	Seven 4
Hoongthip 2	Xayamoungkhun 12	
Nongsoda 5		
Phonepasut 6	Eating	
Saisouk 8	Café Chéz Boune 1	
Sala Savanh 3	Dao Savanh 2	
	Savan Lao Deum 3	

these should be organized in advance. The office can also arrange guides and drivers for other trips. The tourism office has at least produced a series of useful leaflets including a worthwhile self-guided walking tour of the historic quarter, called Savannakhet Downtown, distributed at guesthouses, the tourism office and the Eco Guide unit ►► *See also Activities and tours, page 220.*

Background

Savannakhet was established in 1642 by Prince Thao Keosimphali, the son of King Luang of Phonsim. The Prince relocated the majority of families from Ban Phonsim, 18 km east of Savannakhet, to the modern-day town, naming the new fiefdom Ban Thahae (Mineral Port Village). The name was later changed to Souvannaphoum and, in 1883, was adapted to Savannakhet by French colonizers. In 1989 US servicemen arrived in Savannakhet, searching for the remains of men missing in action (MIAs) and the whole town turned out to watch their arrival at the airport. Not realizing that the Lao bear absolutely no animosity towards Americans, the men kept their heads down and refused to disembark until the crowds dispersed. During the war against the Pathet Lao the Royal Lao Air Force operated out of Savannakhet and, towards the end of the conflict, even headquartered here.

Sights

Like any town of this size, Savan has quite a number of wats; although none is particularly notable, most are quite beautiful. **Wat Sounantha** on Nalao Road has a three-dimensional raised relief on the front of the *sim*, showing the Buddha in the *mudra* of bestowing peace, separating two warring armies. **Wat Sayaphum** on the Mekong is rather more attractive and has several early 20th-century monastery buildings. It is both the largest and oldest monastery in town, although it was only built at the end of the 19th century. Some monks at **Wat Sayamungkhun** speak a bit of English and are pleased to talk about their 50-year-old monastery. There is a large temple school here and, if you arrive during lessons, you may get roped into some impromptu English teaching.

Savan's **colonial heritage** can be seen throughout the central part of town. Perhaps the most attractive area is the square east of the old Immigration office between Khanthabouli and Phetsalath roads. Simuang Road, near the Catholic church, is also rewarding in this regard. Evidence of Savan's diverse population is reflected in the **Chua Dieu Giac**, a Mahayana Buddhist pagoda at the intersection of Soutthanu and Phetsalath roads that serves the town's Vietnamese population. In deference to Theravada tradition, the *chua* has a *that* in the courtyard. There's also a Chinese school close to the Catholic church. The church, which dominates the historic centre, holds Mass at 0800 on Sunday.

Unfortunately, the beautiful French colonial building housing the local museum has closed. The **Provincial Museum** ① *Khanthabouli Rd, Mon-Sat 0800-1200 and 1330-1600, 5000 kip*, now has a purpose-built building. The museum has plenty of propaganda-style displays but little that is terribly enlightening, unless you are interested in the former revolutionary leader Kaysone Phomvihane.

Another attraction is the **Dinosaur Museum** ① *Khanthabouli Rd, south of the stadium, T041-212597, daily 0800-1200 and 1300-1600, 5000 kip*, which houses a collection of four different dinosaur and early mammalian remains, and some fragments of a meteorite that fell to earth over 100 million years ago. The first fossils in the region were unearthed in 1990 by a team of French and Lao scientists. All exhibits are accompanied by explanations in Lao and French; some staff speak good English and French and are happy to explain their work. A DVD in French explains the discoveries.

Border essentials: Dansavanh-Lao Bao (Vietnam)

The Vietnam border is 236 km east of Savannakhet (45 km from Xepon). Getting through customs and dealing with potential obstacles on the other side means that it's impossible to state how long it may take to get into Vietnam itself. Buses leave Savannakhhet for the border at 0630 and 0930 1200, four to five hours, 30,000 kip. There are buses that run from Savannakhet to Dong Ha, Hué and Danang, but for some you will need to change buses at the border.

The Lao border post is at Dansavanh, from where it is about 500 m to the Vietnamese immigration post and a further 3 km to Lao Bao, the first settlement across the border; motorbike taxis are available. We have received reports of long delays at this border. Don't be surprised if formalities take one hour – and keep smiling! The problem is at the Vietnamese end but those with a Vietnamese visa (required) should be OK. The closest Vietnamese consulate is in Savannakhet; see page 222 for visa application details. Lao immigration can also issue 30-day tourist visas for US$45. Expect to pay 'overtime fees' on the Lao side if you come through on a weekend.

In the near future, the local tourism authority intends to open up a few more local sights to visitors, including Kaysone Phomvihane's former residence and the Thonglahasinh factory, where you can learn about the processes of natural silk-dyeing (which are surprisingly interesting). The town's night market is also to be developed, along with a Savannakhet historic trail, so that travellers can visit the ethnic minority groups near Muang Phin (where there is a downed helicopter and a wonderful socialist-realist Lao-Vietnamese statue), the lao-lao-making village of Ban Nong Yang and the bombed out bridge at Tad Hai. At Ban Makhong, some women have embroidered American bombers into their skirts.

Savannakhet's newest attraction is the architecturally kitsch **Savan Vegas Hotel & Casino**. At the city roundabout, dominated by dinosaur statues, a sign reads 'Welcome to Lao Vegas'. If you're passing, do divert to see the mammoth white elephant statues supporting the building. If you want to play, it's Thai baht only; if you want to stay, the comfortable rooms overlook the casino hall (T041-252200, www.savanvegas.com); there's a spa and pool too.

Around Savannakhet

That Inheng

That Inheng ⓘ *12 km northeast of Savannakhet, open 0800-1800, 5000 kip*, is a holy 16th-century *that* or stupa. It was built during the reign of King Sikhottabong at the same time as That Luang in Vientiane, although local guides may try to convince you it was founded by the Indian emperor Asoka over 2000 years ago. Needless to say, there is no historical evidence to substantiate this claim. The wat is the site of an annual festival at the end of November akin to the one celebrated at Wat Phou, Champasak (see page 239). The regular tuk-tuks that ferry people between Savannakhet and Xeno will usually take you to That Inheng (100,000 kip return). Otherwise, take a shared *songthaew* to Xeno and ask to hop off at That Inheng. They will usually take you all the way, but if they drop you at the turning it is only a 3-km walk from the road.

Alternatively, hire a bicycle in town and cycle out here. Another option is to travel by the Bungva Lake, 7 km outside of Savannakhet, and stop for lunch at the lakeside restaurant.

Salt works

Located northeast of the city, the salt works in the village of Ban Nateuy make for a good excursion. About 90% of Lao salt is produced here, either in large open saltpans or in an interesting Heath-Robinson contraption where the saline solution is pumped into small metal trays over wood fires in open sheds. Visits can be arranged by prior appointment (T041-212255). You will see grilled fish encrusted in salt sold from stalls along the Mekong in Savannakhet.

Champone District

An increasingly popular excursion, particularly for nature and wildlife enthusiasts, is a day trip to Champone District, the location of Hai Suey Lake, the Monkey Forest, Hotay Pidok Library (a repository of palm leaf books written in Burmese Pali) and Don Deng Turtle Lake. A number of villages in the area provide an insight into local farming life. These include **Ban Kengok**, a typical village surrounded by beautiful countryside. A tuk-tuk will do the round trip for US$40, divided amongst passengers. Otherwise contact the local tourist office, who should be able to hook you up with a guide/driver.

Take Route 13 south towards Pakse and turn left at Km 35; follow this road for approximately 20 km until you reach **Ban Sokuan**, a friendly village that's a good place to break the journey. **Hai Suey Lake**, the largest lake in Savannakhet Province, is 4 km further on. Boats will do short trips on the lake for about 5000 kip. Another 7 km beyond Ban Sokuan is Ban Dong Meun, known as the **Monkey Forest**. If travelling independently ask locals to point you in the right direction. The monkeys reign supreme from their forested habitat, not far from Champone River, and locals have attached many superstitions to their presence, such as imminent death if you hit a monkey.

From Monkey Forest it is another 30 km south, via the Ban Nong Lan Chanh intersection, to Ban Dong Deng and **Turtle Lake** ① *open 0800-1800; admission 10,000 kip*. There are more monkeys than turtles at Dong Meun, but they are still reasonably visible. Locals revere these soft-shelled turtles (*paa faa*), and it is believed that certain residents can summon the creatures from the waters with a special call.

Ban Houan Hine

Ban Houan Hine, or Stone House, was built between the sixth and the end of the seventh centuries. It does not begin to compare with the better known Wat Phou outside Champasak but a visit here can be combined with a visit to **That Phone**, a hilly Buddhist *that* en route. It was previously possible to travel by boat down the Mekong to this lesser known Khmer site, 75 km south of Savannakhet, but, again, improvements in road conditions coupled with the usual tourist's disposition to press on elsewhere, has meant this is no longer an option. Instead, buses take Route 13 south, 60 km from Savan, and then turn right onto a track for a further 15 km (signposted 'Stone House Pillars').

East on Route 9 → *For listings, see pages 219- 222.*

Xepon (Sepon) and around → *Colour map 3, A3.*

It is possible to cross into Vietnam by taking Route 9 east over the Annamite chain of mountains to **Lao Bao** (just over the border) and from there to the Vietnamese town of

The Ho Chi Minh trail

Throughout the Vietnam War, Hanoi denied the existence of the Ho Chi Minh Trail and, for most of it, Washington denied dropping 1.1 million tonnes of bombs on it – the biggest tonnage dropped per sq km in history. The North Vietnamese Army (NVA) used the Trail, really a 7000-km network of paths and roads – some two-lane carriageways, capable of carrying tanks and truck convoys – to ferry food, fuel and ammunition to South Vietnam. Bunkers beneath the trail housed cavernous workshops and barracks. Washington tried everything in the book to stem the flow of supplies down the trail.

The Viet Minh had used it as far back as the 1950s in their war against the French. By 1966, 90,000 troops were pouring down the Trail each year, and four years later, 150,000 infiltrators were surging southwards using the jungle network. Between 1966 and 1971, the Trail was used by 630,000 communist troops. At any given time, the Trail was guarded by 25,000 NVA troops and studded with artillery positions, anti-aircraft emplacements and SAM missiles.

The Trail wound its way through the Annamite mountains, entering Laos at the northeast end of the 'Panhandle', and heading southeast, with several access points into Cambodia and south Vietnam. The US airforce started bombing the Trail as early as 1964 in Operation Steel Tiger and B-52s first hit the Mu Gia pass on the Ho Chi Minh Trail in December 1965. Carpet-bombing by B-52s was not admitted by Lao Prime Minister Prince Souvanna Phouma until 1969, by which time the US was dispatching 900 sorties a day to hit the Trail.

In an effort to monitor NVA troop movements, the US wired the Trail with tiny electronic listening devices, infra-red scopes, heat- and smell- sensitive sensors, and locational beacons to guide fighter-bombers and B-52s to their target. The NVA carefully removed these devices to unused lengths of trail, urinated on them and retreated, while preparing to shoot down the bombers.

Creative US military technicians hatched countless schemes to disrupt life on the Trail: they bombed it with everything from Agent Orange (toxic defoliant) to Budweiser beer (an intoxicating inebriant) and washing up liquid (to turn the trail into a frothing skid-track). In 1982 Washington admitted to dumping 200,000 gallons of chemical herbicides over the Trail between 1965 and 1966. The US also dropped chemical concoctions designed to turn soil into grease and plane-loads of Dragonseed – miniature bomblets which blew the feet off soldiers and the tyres off trucks. Nothing worked.

The US invasion of Cambodia in May 1970 forced Hanoi to further upgrade the Trail. This prompted the Pentagon to finally rubberstamp a ground assault on it, codenamed Lamson 719, in which south Vietnamese and US forces planned to capture the Trail-town of Tchepone, east of Savannakhet, inside Laos. The plans for the invasion were drawn up using maps without topographical features.

In February 1971, while traversing the Annamite range in heavy rain, the South Vietnamese forces were routed, despite massive air support. They retreated, leaving the Trail intact, 5000 dead and millions of dollars-worth of equipment behind. Abandoned vehicles, bomb casings and even gutted choppers and bombers can still be seen along the Trail. There is more war debris here than on the Plain of Jars as trucks cannot easily enter the area to pick it up.

Dong Ha and the cities of Hué and Danang (see box, page 215). The largest place on the Lao side of the frontier is Xepon. At first glance it might seem that there's not much to see and do in Xepon but as there is a government guesthouse here, travellers very occasionally use it as a stopping place en route to Vietnam.

The waterfall of **That Salen** is 25 km north of Xepon. The owner of Vieng Xai Guesthouse will be able to get you there and fit visitors have been known to hire bicycles. The other waterfall, **Sakoy**, is about 4 km away by river, or 15 km by main road towards Vietnam. Wide without being high, it's nevertheless a great place for a picnic, and some travellers have pitched camp here, situated as it is by the small village of Ban Sakoy, surrounded by coconut trees. There is a tourist office in the town office in Xepon, where they can organize a boat trip to a traditional Lao village, 2½ hours away. The area around Xepon, particularly Ban Dong 20 km east of the town, intersected the Ho Chi Minh Trail and was devastated during the war. It remains littered with unexploded ordnance and war remnants.

Dong Phou Vieng National Protected Area

The **Savannakhet Eco Guide Unit** (see page 221) runs excellent treks through the Dong Phou Vieng National Protected Area, south of Route 9, which is home to wildlife such as Siamese crocodiles, Asian elephants, the endangered Eld's deer, langurs and wild bison (most of which you would be incredibly lucky to see). Located within the NPA is a **Song Sa Kae** (Sacred Forest and Cemetery), revered by the local Katang ethnic group, who are known for their buffalo sacrifices. The well-trained local guides show how traditional natural produce is gathered for medicinal, fuel or other purposes. The tours are exceptionally good value and homestay is included. Most of the tours only run during the dry season.

Ho Chi Minh Trail

This is an enticing prospect for some visitors but getting here is not easy from Savannakhet and should only be attempted in the dry season, November to March being the ideal time. It is necessary to hire a jeep or 4WD in order to cross the rivers because many of the bridges are broken, so your best bet is to organize a tour from Savan, although you could also travel with a guide on public buses, staying overnight in Xepon (see Sleeping, page 219), the nearest town to the Trail. A guide, arranged through the Savannakhet Eco Guide Unit, will charge US$130 per day for two to nine people for a vehicle plus US$12 per day per guide. The easiest access point to the trail is **Ban Tapung**. On the way, stops include the downed helicopter at Muang Phin and the American-bombed bridge at Tad Hai, its fallen carcass (1967) still there to see in the river. At Ban Dong, the Lamson 719 war museum is under construction. Old weapons and tanks will be displayed.

Savannakhet listings

For Sleeping and Eating price codes and other relevant information, see pages 23-24.

Sleeping

Savannakhet *p212, map p213*
Savannakhet has a good selection of places to stay for US$5 and upwards but rock-bottom budget accommodation is scarce.
A-B Daosavanh Resort & Spa Hotel, 1 km south of the historic centre, T041-252188, www.daosavanhhtl.com. A brand-new resort with attractive rooms (rooms with Mekong views cost more), super mattresses, rain shower in bathrooms, great pool and Wi-Fi; bathrooms need much better ventilation, though. It's a little stuck out of the centre but great for the spa and pool. Let's hope they preserve the lovely French colonial building, the former provincial museum, in the grounds.
C-D Phonepasut, Santisouk Rd, 1 km from town centre in quiet street, T041-212158. Motel-like place with 2 courtyards, restaurant and pool (US$10 for non-residents to use). The rooms are clean, with hot water in the bathrooms, a/c and satellite TV. Friendly and well run with business support services.
D Sala Savanh, T041-212445, www.salalao.com. A small hotel (5 spacious rooms) in an historic building that used to be the Thai consulate. There is original tiling throughout. This is an old building with no soundproofing so you would be wise to opt for the upstairs rooms. Friendly management and excellent location.
D-E Hoongthip, Phetsarath Rd, T041-212262, hoongtip@laotel.com. A/c, satellite TV, dark rooms, big bathrooms en suite, breakfast included. New rooms are large but austere with bathtubs in the en suites. Other services include sauna, and car hire with driver. Wi-Fi in lobby.
E Nongsoda, Tha He Rd, T041-212522. If you're not put off by the oodles of white lace draped everywhere, you'll find clean rooms with a/c and en suite bathrooms with wonderfully hot water. During the low season the hotel drops its room rate. Motorbike hire (80,000 kip) and bike hire (10,000 kip) also available.
F Savanbanhao, Senna Rd, T041-212202, sbtour@laotel.com. Centrally located hotel comprising 4 colonial-styles houses set around a quiet but large concrete courtyard, with a range of rooms. There are cheaper rooms in '4th class' (not musty, contrary to appearances). The more expensive rooms have en suite showers and hot water. Some a/c. Large balcony. **Savanbanhao Tourism Co** is attached (see Activities and tours, page 221). Good choice for those who want to be in and out of Savannakhet, quickly, with relative ease.
F-G Saisouk, Makhavenha Rd, T041-212207. A real gem, this new guesthouse has good-sized twin and double rooms which are immaculately furnished and spotlessly clean, with a/c in some rooms, communal bathrooms and cold water. It's beautifully decorated with interesting *objets d'art* and what look like dinosaur bones. There are plenty of chairs and tables on the large verandas. It is efficiently run by very friendly staff who speak English. Homely.
F-G Xayamoungkhun, 85 Rasavongseuk Rd, T041-212426. An excellent little guesthouse with 16 rooms in an airy colonial-era villa. Central with a largish compound. Range of very clean rooms available, with hot water, a/c and fridge in the more expensive ones. Friendly owners. Second-hand books available. Recommended.

Xepon *p216*
E-F Vieng Xai Guesthouse, T041-214895. A big house, wooden upstairs and concrete down. The rooms are very clean, with a shared bathroom. The friendly owners speak a little English.

F-G Nangtoon Guesthouse, Route 9, 2 km from Xepon, T041-214894. Rooms with either fan or a/c and hot water in the bathrooms. Outstanding value. Recommended.

🍴 Eating

Savannakhet *p212, map p213*
Several restaurants on the riverside serve good food and beer. The market also has stalls offering decent fresh food, including excellent Mekong river fish. **Phengsy** coffee shop at the bottom of the square is a great people-watching spot and serves good coffee too.

🍴 **Bungva Lake Restaurant**. Daily 0800-2200. Stilted restaurant in the lake, with individual dining rooms. Enjoy fresh seafood washed down with Beer Lao. A lovely way to pass the afternoon.

🍴🍴-🍴 **Dao Savanh**, Simuang St, T041-260888. Open 0700-2200. A newcomer to the restaurant scene, this place occupies a restored French colonial building, and provides good but pricey food. It's worth splashing out on a set menu (65,000-95,000 kip) for the charm and central location. Sit at one of the outdoor tables for views of the central square.

🍴🍴-🍴 **Savan Lao Deum**, T041-252125. This lovely place has taken over the old ferry pier area. The attractive wooden restaurant juts out onto the river on a floating veranda. It's a particularly good venue for a sunset drink. The food is delicious too, especially steamed fish and herbs. You might like to try some of the more adventurous options: fried tree ant eggs, grilled buffalo skin and roasted cicadas. The service is exceptional.

🍴 **Café Chéz Boune**, T041-215190. Open 0700-2300. Opposite the old market, this place provides good travellers' fare in attractive surrounds.

Xepon *p216*
On the west side of the market there is a reasonable restaurant called **Bouphan**, which does good eggs, *feu* and coffee.

🍸 Bars and clubs

Savannakhet *p212, map p213*
There are several large discos/beer gardens in Savannakhet, most of which stage live bands and are open 7 days a week. **Seven** on Ratsavongseuk Rd is especially popular with young Lao.

🎉 Festivals and events

Savannakhet *p212, map p213*
Feb Than Ing Hang (movable) similar to the festival at Wat Phou, Champasak.

🛍 Shopping

Savannakhet *p212, map p213*
Talaat Savan Sai Daily 0700-1700. The central market has moved from its former location in town to a new site behind the government bus station, north of town. Though not as convenient for tourists, the spanking new building, built and managed by a Singaporean company, comes complete with parking spaces and one of the few escalators in Laos. You'll find the usual selection of meat, vegetables, fruit, dry goods, clothes, fabrics and baskets, plus an abundance of gold and silversmiths.

There is a branch of **Lao Cotton** on Ratsavongseuk Rd.
One District One Product, Km 6, T020-5554 0226, not too far from Savan Vegas. A large warehouse with all sorts of handicrafts and wares on sale.

⛰ Activities and tours

Savannakhet *p212, map p213*
Spa
Champa Savanh Spa, at the Daosavanh Resort, T041-252188 ext 402, www.daosavanhhtl.com. Open 1300-2200. This spa offers a broad range of treatments. Go for the kitsch waterfall experience and steam rooms and then make use of the large swimming pool.

Border essentials: Savannakhet-Mukdahan (Thailand)

Crossing the border into Mukdahan via the new Friendship Bridge is now straightforward. Buses leave the terminal in Savannakehet at 0815, 0900, 0945, 1030, 1115, 1230, then hourly until 1730, last bus 1900, and takes 10 minutes, 13,000 kip. The bus will pick you up on the other side of Lao immigration to take you on to the Thai authorities. There are nine buses daily to Ubon Ratchathani from Mukdahan 0800-1740, 3 hours; and 4 public buses plus six VIP buses a day to Bangkok. Lao visas (30 days) are available at the border for US$35 with one passport photo. If you are coming from Thailand and miss the connecting bus to Savannakhet at 0830, 0915, 1000, 1045, 1145, 1245, then hourly to 1745, and at 1900, *songthaew* will make the journey for 150 baht. There are ATMs at both borders.

Swimming

Non-guests can use the pool at the **Daosavanh Resort** (see above) for 50,000 kip. It has an attractive *sala* in which to lounge after your swim.

Trekking

Savanbanhao Tourism Co, at the Savanbanhao Hotel (see Sleeping), T041-212944, sbhtravel@yahoo.com. Mon-Sat 0800-1200 and 1330-1630. Provides trips to most sights in the vicinity as well as bus tickets to Vietnam.

Savannakhet Eco Guide Unit, Rasphanit Rd, 041-214203, www.savannakhet-trekking. com. Mon-Fri 0800-1130 and 1330-1700, Sat-Sun 0800-1130 and 1400-1700. This unit, run by Oudomsay Thongsavath, operates excellent ecotours and treks to the national parks in the area. There are several keen and enthusiastic English-speaking guides to take tourists out to see the local ethnic culture and sights. Highly worthwhile treks have been established, with proceeds filtering down to local communities.

Note that some treks only operate Nov-Mar. Tours include 1-5 day treks and homestay to Dong Phou Vieng NPA, Phu Xang Hae NPA, Dong Natad protected area to see the honey collection (Feb-Mar), tree oil extraction, Nom Lom Lake and the ancient ruins of Meuang Kao. A 1-day cycling trip to Dong Natad and Bungva Lake takes in That Ing Hang and village visits; a 2-day cycling trip takes in a homestay at Ban Phonsim. The minimum price for a 1-day trekking tour for 2-3 people is US$26, including transport, food, water and a guide. Highly recommended.

⊖ Transport

Savannakhet *p212, map p213*

Air

Lao Airlines (T041-212140) flies to Vientiane and Bangkok 3 times a week.

Bus/truck

From the bus station (T041-213920) on the northern edge of town, frequent northbound buses depart daily to **Vientiane**, (0600-1130), 457 km on a good road, 9 hrs, 80,000 kip. Most of the Vientiane-bound buses also stop at **Thakhek**, 125 km, 2½-3 hrs, 25,000 kip; **Paksan**, 5-6 hrs, 55,000 kip, and **Pak Kading** 7-8 hrs, 55,000 kip. There are also specially scheduled morning buses to **Thakhek**.

Southbound buses to **Pakse** depart daily at 0700, 0900, 1030, 1230, 1730, 6-7 hrs, 35,000 kip; buses in transit from Vientiane to Pakse will usually also pick up passengers here. A VIP bus leaves at 2130, 8 hrs, 95,000 kip. To **Don Khong**, 1900 daily, 9-10 hrs, 75,000 kip; to **Salavan**, 1230 daily, 8-10 hrs, 60,000 kip; to **Attapeu**, 0900 and 1900 daily,

9-12 hrs, 70,000 kip. This road is also in pretty good condition.

Eastbound buses depart daily to **Xepon** at 0700, 0800, 1000, 1100, 1230, 4 hrs, 30,000 kip and **Lao Bao** (Vietnam border, see page 215), 0630, 0900 and 1200 daily, 6 hrs, 40,000 kip. A bus also departs at 2200 daily for destinations within Vietnam, including **Hué**, 13 hrs, 90,000 kip; **Danang**, 508 km, 13 hrs, 110,000 kip, and **Hanoi**, 24 hrs, 200,000 kip on Tues and Sat; there are additional services at 1000 (VIP bus to Hue). Luxury Vietnam-bound buses can be arranged through the **Savanbanhao Hotel** (see Sleeping), 90,000 kip. Although buses claim to be direct, a bus change is required at the border. Buses leave on even days at 0800 and arrive in Hue at 1600.

For buses to the border at Mukdahan, Thailand (see Border essentials, page 221).

Car, motorbike and bicycle hire
Car and driver can be hired from the Savanbanhao Hotel (see Sleeping). Some of the guesthouses rent bicycles for 10,000 kip and motorbikes for 50,000-80,000 kip.

Tuk-tuk and saamlor
Most tuk-tuks charge around 10,000 kip per person for a local journey. There is one traditional old bicycle saamlor still operating in town. Track down the old man for a leisurely jaunt around the colonial core.

Xepon *p216*
Songthaew depart from the market to **Savannakhet** at 0800 daily, 30,000 kip. There are numerous *songthaew* from the market to **Lao Bao**, 45 km, 1 hr, 20,000 kip but you'll need to get there by 0700 to ensure a space. It's also possible to jump on the various buses from Savannakhet to Vietnam, which pass through Xepon, the cheapest option being the service to Lao Bao (see above).

Directory

Savannakhet *p212, map p213*
Banks Lao Development Bank, T041-212226, Oudomsinh Rd, Mon-Fri 0830-1600, will change most major currencies. Banque pour le Commerce Exterieur Lao (BCEL), Ratsavongseuk Rd, will exchange currency and has an ATM.
Embassies and consulates Vietnam Consulate, Sisavangvong Rd, T041-212182, Mon-Fri 0730-1100, 1330-1600. Provides Vietnamese visas in 3 days on presentation of 2 photos and US$45.
Thai Consulate, Thahae Rd, T041-212373, Mon-Fri 0830-1200, 1300-1630; visas are issued on the same day if dropped off in the morning. **Internet** Sikonet, Chalmeung Rd, and others on this road. The Hoongthip hotel offers Wi-Fi in its lobby.
Medical services Savannakhet Hospital, Khanthabouli Rd, T041-212171. Dr Kongsy, T041-212711. **Police** Makhasavanh Rd, Next to the new provincial museum, T020-2601993. **Post** Post office Khanthabouli Rd, T041-212205, daily 0800-2200.
Telephone Lao Telecom Office, next door to the post office, for domestic and international calls.

Contents

The South

Footprint features

★ **Don't miss ...**

Introduction

Laos' southern provinces offer a varied array of enticements and a different character from the north of the country. Base yourself in the region's unofficial capital, Pakse, to explore the many attractions of Champasak Province, including the romantic, pre-Angkorian ruins of Wat Phou and Ban Kiet Ngong, with its opportunities for elephant trekking. Inland from Pakse is the Bolaven Plateau, an area that was earmarked by the French for settlement and coffee production. The rivers running off the plateau have created a series of spectacular waterfalls, including towering Tad Fan and stunning Tad Lo.

A highlight of any trip down south is Siphandon, where the Mekong divides into myriad channels and 'Four Thousand Islands'. The idyllic, palm-fringed Don Khone, Don Deth and Don Khong provide perfect places to relax and absorb riverine life, as fisherman cast nets amongst lush green islets and children frolic on the sand bars.

Pakse (Pakxe) and around

Phone code: 031. Colour map 3, B2.

Pakse is the largest town in the south and is strategically located at the junction of the Mekong and Xe Don rivers. Two bridges span the Xe Don here. The single-lane bridge downstream was built by the French in 1925, while the upstream structure was erected by the Soviet Union and was not completed until about 1990. Pakse is a busy commercial town, built by the French early in the 20th century as an administrative centre for the south. The town has seen better days but the tatty colonial buildings lend an air of old-world charm. Pakse is a major staging post for destinations further afield, such as the old royal capital of Champasak, famed for its pre-Angkor, seventh-century Khmer ruins of Wat Phou (see page 231). The town's old colonial ebb is quickly succumbing to Thai and Vietnamese influences. Regardless, it is still quite a charming spot. Champasak Province used to include Champasak, Sedon and Sitandon provinces. The governor's office was located in Ban Muang in Sedon prior to French settlement in the area. Pakse's appointment as a French administrative outpost in 1905 spurred the

Pakse

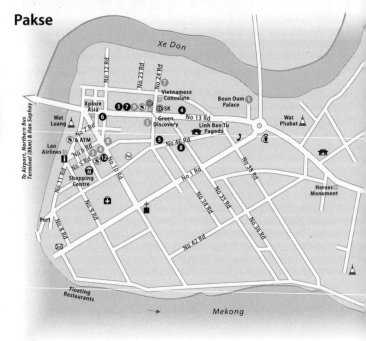

Sleeping	Daovieng 2 **3**	Sabaidy **2**	Eating
Champasak Grand **6**	Lao Chaleun **4**	Guesthouse **7**	Bakery **8**
Champasak Palace **1**	Mekong Paradise	Salachampa **8**	Delta Coffee **1**
Champa	Resort **10**	Sang Aroun **9**	Jasmine **3**
Residence **2**	Pakse **5**		Ket Many **4**

226 · The South Pakse & around

relocation of all major government offices and businesses across the three provinces to Pakse and an amalgamation of provincial authorities. Close to Pakse are various ecotourism projects where elephant treks, birdwatching and homestays can easily be arranged. ▸▸ *For listings, see pages 235-244.*

Ins and outs

Getting there Pakse is Southern Laos' transport hub: from here you can get to anywhere in the southern region, and travel between smaller towns in the region often requires a connection through Pakse. Although it is not on the **border** with Thailand, Pakse is the largest Lao town close to the border crossing at Chongmek. From the Thai side, *songthaew* continue on to Ubon Ratchathani in Thailand (there are also through buses). ▸▸ *See box, page 228.*

The **airport** is situated 2 km northwest of town; cross the bridge over the Xe Don river, next to Wat Luang, and continue straight up No 13 Road; tuk-tuks will make the airport run for around 20,000 kip. There is a small café and BCEL exchange inside the terminal building. There are international flights to Pakse from Bangkok and Siem Reap, and domestic flights to/from Vientiane run several times a week.

A passenger **boat** from Champasak to Pakse, 60,000 kip, leaves at 1500 and arrives in Pakse at 1700. But, do check on all times. Boats leave from Pakse to Champasak at 0830 and arrive at 1030.

There are three official bus terminals in Pakse: the **Northern terminal** (Km 7 on Route 13 north, T031-251508) is for buses to and from the north (a tuk-tuk from town costs 15,000 kip); the **Southern terminal** (Km 8 south on Route 13, T031-212981) is for buses to and from the south (a tuk-tuk from town costs 15,000 kip); and the **VIP, Khiang Kai** and **international terminal**, with neighbouring **Seangchaolearn terminal**, near the football stadium and Talaat Lak Song, just off Route 13, T031-212228, for VIP buses to **Ubon** (Thailand) and Vientiane. ▸▸ *See Transport, page 241.*

Getting around Tuk-tuks and **saamlors** are the main means of local transport and can be chartered for half a day for about US$5. The main tuk-tuk 'terminal' is at the Daoheung market. **Cars**, **motorbikes** and **bicycles** are available for hire from hotels and tour companies. Note that the town's roads are numbered as if they were

Korean Barbecue **5**
Mengky Noodle Shop **7**
Nao Dao **9**
Nazim's **6**
Xuan Mai **12**

Border essentials: Vang Tao-Chongmek (Thailand)

This route is an important exit point for Lao traders; timber trucks rumble their way towards the sizeable timber yard at Chongmek (Thailand).

Lao visas (30 days) are available at the border. There is a new bus service direct from Ubon Ratchathani bus station to Pakse. From Pakse the Thai-Lao international bus leaves from the VIP bus terminal 0830 and 1530, three hours, 55,000 kip.

Travelling to Thailand, *songthaew* for the border at Vang Tao (Laos) depart from the Daoheung market in Pakse, daily 0800-1600 every hour, 45 km, one hour, 25,000 kip. The border is open daily 0500-2000 but allow extra time as the *songthaew* is slow.

Once you've been dropped off at Vang Tao, walk 250 m to the building where you will receive an exit stamp; you may need to pay 'overtime fees' if you cross the border at the weekend. Walk another 50 m or so to the Thai border, where you will be automatically issued with a 30-day visa. There is a post office and duty free shop at the border. Customs formalities at this border are very relaxed.

From the Thai side, *songthaew* run to Phibun Mangsahan, one hour, 30 baht, where you can pick up another *songthaew* (30 baht) or a taxi-minibus (600 baht divided between all the passengers) to the city and airport of Ubon Ratchathani. Both airlines (AirAsia and Thai Airways) and buses operate from Ubon Ratchathani direct to Bangkok (see page 18).

highways: No 1 Road through to No 46 Road. The result is that no-one knows where they live and tuk-tuk drivers are oblivious to road names.

Tourist information Champasak Provincial Tourism Office ⓘ *No 11 Rd, T031-212021, www.xepian.org, daily 0800-11300 and 1330-1630*, have some fantastic ecotours on offer through its Eco-Guide Service Unit, see Activities and tours, page 240.

Sights

Pakse, by anyone's standards, is not a seething metropolis, which, of course, gives it much of its charm. But this is starting to change now that infrastructure has improved and Pakse is firmly linked into the Thai economy; it has become a major crossroads between the two countries. A strong Vietnamese influence is also apparent.

There's not that much to see in Pakse, so far as official sights are concerned. Locals tend to mention the shopping centre-style market slap-bang in the centre of town and the Daoheung (morning) market as the most interesting places to visit; in fact, it may seem Pakse exists for little else (see page 239). However, it's also a good place to base yourself to visit destinations further afield, including Tad Lo, Tad Fan and Wat Phou.

Champasak Historic Museum

ⓘ *No 13 Rd (the main highway) running east out of town, close to the stadium, T031-212501. Daily 0830-1130 and 1330-1600. Admission 10,000 kip.*
This museum opened in 1995 and displays pieces recovered from Wat Phou, handicrafts from the Lao Theung of the Bolaven Plateau, weaponry, musical instruments and a

seemingly endless array of photographs of plenums, congresses and assemblies and of prominent Lao dignitaries opening hydropower stations and widget factories. The charming Lao guides who show visitors around speak only limited English, and the labels are not very informative, but it's still a treat for museum aficionados. Opposite the museum is a *that*-like **Heroes Monument**.

Wat Luang

There are 40 wats in town but none figures particularly high in the wat hall of fame. Wat Luang, in the centre of town, is the oldest. It was built in 1830, but was reconstructed and redecorated in 1990 at a cost of 27 million kip. The *sim* now sports a kitsch pink and yellow exterior complete with gaudy relief work. Lots of monks can be found loitering around the premises, as this is one of the main centres where they practise English. The hefty doors were carved locally. The compound was originally much larger but, in the 1940s, the chief of Champasak Province requisitioned the land to accommodate a new road. To the right of the main entrance stands a stupa containing the remains of Khatai Loun Sasothith, a former Prime Minister who died in 1959. To the right of the *sim* is the monks' dormitory, which dates from the 1930s; the wooden building behind the *sim* is the monastic school, the biggest in southern Laos, and on the left of the entrance is the library, built in 1943. These earlier structures are, needless to say, the finest – at least for Western sensibilities. The compound backs onto the Xe Don.

There are many more Lao monasteries in town. For those who desire a change there is also a Vietnamese Mahayana Buddhist **Linh Bao Tu Pagoda** on No 46 Road, and a church on No 1 Road.

Boun Oum Palace

Situated on the road north towards Paksong, the Boun Oum Palace is now the **Champasak Palace Hotel** and by far the largest structure in town. Before Thai hotel interests bought the place, it was the half-finished palace of the late Prince Boun Oum of Champasak, the colourful overlord of southern Laos and a great collector of *objets d'art*. He began constructing the house of his dreams in 1968, with the intention of creating a monument with more than 1000 rooms. However, the Prince was exiled to France before his dream was realized. Looking at the hotel it is hard not to conclude that his exile was wholly for the best, at least architecturally.

Muang Khao

Muang Khao lies on the opposite bank of the Mekong to Pakse and, as the name suggests (it means 'Old Town'), was established before its larger sibling across the water. Once the French concentrated their attentions on Pakse, Muang Khao was neglected and fell into decline. As a consequence it has a quaintness that is largely absent from Pakse. Most people come here on their way to the Lao-Thai border at Chongmek, but it has some attractive buildings which are worth a closer look. A tuk-tuk to Muang Khao from Pakse costs around US$3.

Ban Saphay

ⓘ *5 km off Route 13, 15 km northwest of Pakse. Chartered tuk-tuks cost 200,000 kip for a full day's excursion.* This specialist silk-weaving village is 15 km north of town on the banks of the Mekong. Here a group of about 200 women weave traditional Lao textiles on hand looms. The designs, like the classic *lao mut mee*, show clear similarities with those of northeastern Thailand, where the population is also Lao. However, there are also some unique designs. Prices vary according to the quality and the intricacy of the design but a sarong length (1.5 m) costs about 50,000-70,000 kip. There is also an unusual statue of Indra, Ganesh and Parvati at the local wat.

Champasak and around → For listings, see pages 235-244.

The appealing agricultural town of Champasak, which stretches along the right bank of the Mekong for 4 km, is the nearest town to Wat Phou and a good base from which to explore the site and the surrounding area. Although the trip to Wat Phou can be done in a day from Pakse (it is about 40 km south of Pakse), the sleepy town of Champasak is quaint and charming with a plentiful supply of comfortable accommodation.

Ins and outs
Getting there Most *songthaew* run from Pakse's Southern bus terminal on Route 13 to Ban Lak Sarm Sip (which translates as 'village 30 km'), where they take a right turn to Ban Muang (2-3 km). Here, people sell tickets for the ferry to Champasak (3000 kip; person and motorbike 10,000 kip). The ferry runs from 0630 until 2000. A tuk-tuk from the ferry port into town costs 5000 kip. Public ferries operate from Pakse to Champasak at 0800 daily. It is also possible to charter a boat, albeit at quite a high price. A new road, due for construction, direct from Pakse, will make the little ferry crossing redundant. ▶ *See also Transport, page 243.*

Tourist information **Champasak District Visitor Information Centre** ⓘ *Mon-Fri (daily in high season) 0800-1230 and 1400-1630*, can arrange boats to Don Daeng, guides to Wat Phou and tours to surrounding sights.

Sights
Champasak is dotted with stunning colonial buildings. The former residence of Champasak hereditary Prince Boun Oum and former leader of the right-wing opposition, who fled the country in 1975 after the Communist takeover, is quite possibly the most magnificent colonial building in Laos. His daughter-in-law now resides there; it is not open to tourists but worth a look from the outside.

Champasak is known for its wooden handicrafts and you'll find vases and other carved ornaments for sale near the jetty. About 15 km southwest of Champasak is **Don Talaat**, which is worth a visit for its weekly market (Saturday and Sunday). It's renowned for the number of snakes on show.

Um Muang (Tomo Temple)
ⓘ *It is possible to hire a car or tuk-tuk from Pakse. If you go by bus, you need to get off at Ban Huaytomo. Chartering a boat from Champasak will cost 250,000 kip return; from Dong Daeng, 40,000-50,000 kip.*
Also known as Muang Tomo and Oup Moung, Um Muang is a lesser-known temple complex built at about the same time as Wat Phou on the opposite (left) bank of the Mekong. It lies 45 km south of Pakse off Route 13 and is accessible via the main road south from Pakse to Ban Thang Beng, Km 30, from where a track (vehicle access possible) leads 4 km to Ban Noi. From the village it is a 1-km walk to the temple. You can charter a boat from Don Daeng or Ban Muang, Champasak.

In colonial days, Um Muang was a stopping point for ships travelling upriver from Cambodia. Its main treasure is a ninth-century Khmer-era temple complex built at roughly the same time as Wat Phou. The temple is thought to have been built by Yasarvoman I and is dedicated to Shiva's companion, Rudani. The site comprises an assortment of ruins, surrounded by jungle. A seven-headed sandstone *naga* greets you as you approach the site from the Mekong.

Like Wat Phou, the main temple is built of laterite and its carvings are in similar style to those of the bigger complex upriver. It is thought, in fact, that the laterite blocks used in the construction of Wat Phou were taken from Um Muang. There are also the ruins of a second building, more dilapidated and moss-covered, making it difficult to speculate about its function, and, hidden in the jungle, are the remains of two *baray*. Um Muang is not on the same scale and nowhere near as impressive as Wat Phou but stumbling across a sixth-century Khmer temple in the middle of the jungle is nonetheless a worthwhile experience. Despite the presence of seemingly abandoned tourist facilities, it's still an atmospheric spot. With great slabs of laterite protruding from the undergrowth and ancient sandstone carvings lying around the bushes, there is no doubt that a great deal about the site remains undiscovered.

Some of the best artefacts from the temple are exhibited in the museum in Pakse (see page 228).

Don Daeng Island

This idyllic river island sits right across from Champasak. It stretches for 8 km and is the perfect place for those wishing to see quintessential village life, with basket weaving, fishing and rice farming, with little hustle and bustle. There is a path around the island that can be traversed on foot or by bicycle. A crumbling ancient brick stupa, built in the same century as Wat Phou, is in the centre of the island and there are a few ancient remnants from the construction in **Sisak village**. The inhabitants of **Pouylao village** are known for their knife-making prowess.

There is a lovely sandy beach on the Champasak side of the island, perfect for a dip. The way to get here is on an arranged ecotour; these can include treks and explorations of local villages. The island has only recently opened up for tourism purposes, so it is important to tread lightly. Contact the Provincial Tourism Office in Pakse or the Tourism Office in Champasak (which runs a two-day biking and boat trip around the island) for further information. A trip by boat from Champasak will cost around US$1. If you would like to stay overnight, there is one upmarket hotel and homestay on the island, see Sleeping, page 237.

Hao Pa Kho island

One hour downriver from Pakse is this island, where Chao Boun Oum (see page 229), had his weekend house. It was abandoned after his exile to France.

Wat Phou → *For listings, see pages 235-244.*

Wat Phou lies at the foot of the Phou Pasak, 8 km southwest of Champasak and is the most significant Khmer archaeological site in Laos. With its teetering, weathered masonry, it conforms exactly to the Western ideal of the lost city. The mountain behind Wat Phou is called **Linga Parvata**, as the Hindu Khmers thought it resembled a lingam – albeit a strangely proportioned one. Although construction of the original Hindu temple complex was begun in the fifth and sixth centuries, much of what remains today is believed to have been built in the 10th to 11th centuries. Wat Phou was a work in progress and was constructed and renovated over a period spanning several hundred years.

Ins and outs

Getting there The nearest town to Wat Phou is Champasak (see page 230), which also lies on the west (or right) bank of the Mekong River; the main road is on the east bank. Most *songthaew* run from Pakse's Southern bus terminal on Route 13 to **Ban Lak Sarm Sip** (which translates as 'village 30 km'), where they take a right turn to **Ban Muang** (2-3 km). Here, people sell tickets for the ferry to Champasak (or Ban Phaphin on the outskirts of Champasak (3000 kip; person and motorbike 10,000 kip). From Champasak you can get a tuk-tuk to Wat Phou for around 80,000 kip return. Most tourists prefer to cycle the 8 km from Champasak centre to the ruins. Bikes are available for hire (10,000 kip) at the guesthouses in Champasak town as well as motorbikes, saamlors and tuk-tuks where the return price with waiting fee is 80,000 kip. ▸▸ *See Transport, page 243.*

Tourist information The site is officially open daily 0800-1630 but the staff are happy to let you in if you get there for sunrise, even as early as 0530, and you won't get thrown out until 1800. Admission is 30,000 kip and goes towards restoration of the wat (entering the site before hours or staying after hours incurs an extra 10,000 kip fee). There is also the Wat Phu Exhibition Centre (closes 1600) at the entrance, a surprisingly good museum with a fantastic array of artefacts, such as the garuda, nandi bull and explanations from Wat Phou (entrance to the centre is included in admission to the temple). Guides to Wat Phou need to be arranged at the Champasak Tourist Information Centre, with prices starting at US$15. There are several restaurants in the vicinity of the temple. A new full moon event has been launched at Wat Phou; this is an atmospheric exploration of the site with lights from 1800-2100, 30,000 kip.

Background

Linga Parvata provides an imposing backdrop to the crumbling temple ruins, many of which date from the fifth and sixth centuries, making them at least 200 years older than Angkor Wat. At that time, the Champasak area was the centre of power on the lower Mekong. The Hindu temple only became a Buddhist shrine in later centuries. The French explorer, Francis Garnier, discovered Wat Phou in 1866 and local villagers told him the temple had been built by 'another race'. Unfortunately, not much is known about Wat Phou's history. Ruins of a palace have been found next to the Mekong at Cesthapoura (halfway between Wat Phou and Champasak – now an army camp) and it is thought the sixth-century Chenla capital was based there.

Archaeologists and historians believe most of the building at Wat Phou was the work of the Khmer king, Suryavarman II (1131-1150), who was also responsible for starting work on Angkor Wat, Cambodia. The temple remained important for Khmer kings even after they had moved their capital to Angkor. They continued to appoint priests to serve at Wat Phou and sent money to maintain the temple until the last days of the Angkor Empire.

Exploring the site

Processional causeway The king and dignitaries would originally have sat on a platform above the 'tanks' or *baray* and presided over official ceremonies or watched aquatic games. In 1959 a palace was built on the platform so the king had somewhere to stay during the annual **Wat Phou Festival** (see page 239). A smaller house had been for the

Wat Phou

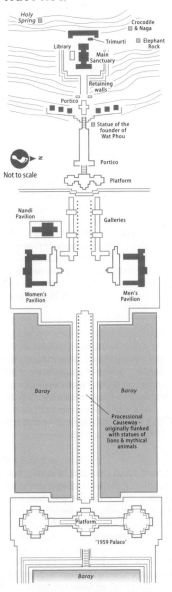

Holy Spring

Library

Trimurti

Crocodile & Naga

Elephant Rock

Main Sanctuary

Retaining walls

Portico

Statue of the founder of Wat Phou

Not to scale

Portico

Platform

Nandi Pavilion

Galleries

Women's Pavilion

Men's Pavilion

Baray

Baray

Processional Causeway - originally flanked with statues of lions & mythical animals

Platform

'1959 Palace'

Baray

king's entourage. These have now been dismantled. A long avenue leads to the pavilions. The **processional causeway** was probably built by Khmer King Jayavarman VI (1080-1107), and may have been the inspiration for a similar causeway at Angkor Wat. This grand approach to the temple would originally have been flanked by statues of lions and mythical animals, but few traces of these remain.

Pavilions The sandstone pavilions, on either side of the processional causeway, were added after the main temple and are thought to date from the 12th century (in all probability from the reign of Suryavarman II). Although crumbling, with great slabs of laterite and collapsed lintels lying aesthetically around, both pavilions are remarkably intact and, as such, are the most photographed part of the temple complex. The pavilions were probably used for segregated worship by pilgrims, one for women (left) and the other for men (right). The porticoes of the two huge buildings face each other. The roofs were thought originally to have been poorly constructed with thin stone slabs on a wooden beam-frame and later replaced by Khmer tiles.

Only the outer walls of the pavilions now remain but there is enough still standing to fire the imagination: the detailed carving around the window frames and porticoes is well-preserved. The laterite used to build the complex was brought from **Um Muang**, also called Tomo Temple, a smaller Khmer temple complex located a few kilometres downriver (see page 230), but the carving is in sandstone. The interiors were without permanent partitions, although it is thought that rush matting was used to divide areas, and furniture was limited – reliefs depict only low stools and couches. At the rear of the women's pavilion are the remains of a brick construction, which is believed to have been the queen's private quarters. Brick buildings were very costly at that time.

Nandi Pavilion and temple Above the main pavilions is the Nandi Pavilion, a small temple with entrances on two sides. It is dedicated to Nandi, the bull (Siva's vehicle), and is a common feature in Hindu temple complexes. There are three chambers, each of which would originally have contained statues – these have been stolen. As the hill begins to rise above the Nandi temple, the remains of six brick temples follow the contours, with three on each side of the pathway. All six are completely ruined and their function is unclear. Archaeologists and Khmer historians speculate that they may have been Trimurti temples. At the bottom of the steps is a portico and statue of the founder of Wat Phou, Pranga Khommatha. Many of the laterite paving stones and blocks used to build the steps have holes notched down each side; these would have been used to help transport the slabs to the site and drag them into position.

Main sanctuary The main sanctuary, 90 m up the hillside and orientated east-west, was originally dedicated to Siva. The rear section (behind the Buddha statue) is part of the original sixth-century brick building. Sacred spring water was channelled through the hole in the back wall of this section and used to wash the sacred linga. The water was then thrown out, down a chute in the right wall, where it was collected in a receptacle. Pilgrims would then wash in the holy water. The front of the temple was constructed later, probably in the eighth to ninth century, and has some fantastic carvings: apsaras, dancing Vishnu, Indra on a three-headed elephant (the former emblem of the kingdom of Lane Xang) and, above the portico of the left entrance, a carving of Siva, the destroyer, depicted tearing a woman in two.

The Hindu temple was converted into a Buddhist shrine, either in the 13th century during the reign of the Khmer king Jayavarman VII or when the Lao conquered the area in the 14th century. A large Buddha statue now presides over its interior. There is also a modern Buddhist monastery complex on the site.

Around the sanctuary To the left of the sanctuary is what is thought to be the remains of a small library. To the right and to the rear of the main sanctuary is the **Trimurti**, the Hindu statues of Vishnu (right), Siva (central) and Brahma (left). Behind the Trimurti is the holy spring, believed by the Khmers to have possessed purificatory powers. Some of the rocks beyond the monks' quarters (to the right of the temple) have been carved with the figures of an elephant, a crocodile and a *naga*. They are likely to have been associated with human sacrifices carried out at the Wat Phou Festival; it is said the sacrifice took place on the crocodile and the blood was given to the *naga*. Present-day visitors to the festival in February (see page 239) should note that this practice has now stopped!

Around Wat Phou

If you are particularly interested in archaeology, and haven't had your fill at Wat Phou, there are several other ancient sites that can be visited in the surrounding area, though they are all in a state of disrepair. **Ho Nang Sida**, just 1 km south of Wat Phou, is an understated ruined temple, overgrown with jungle and strewn with piles of rubble and rocks. The temple, called Lady Sida Hall, is believed to have sat on an ancient highway that linked Angkor Wat to Wat Phou; it was probably used as a hospital. (Accessible by saamlor and tuk-tuk.)

One kilometre south of Ho Nang Sida is **Hong Nan Tao**, another set of ancient ruins, built under Jayavarman VII and used as a shrine (not accessible by larger vehicles). Another 3 km along the route are three ancient stupas.

Xe Pian National Protected Area → For listings, see pages 235-244.

The Xe Pian National Protected Area is rich in a wide variety of birdlife, including large water birds and great hornbills, and home to sun bears, Asiatic black bears and the yellow-cheeked crested gibbon.

North of Xe Pian, the village of **Ban Kiet Ngong** is at the **Kiet Ngong Wetland**, the largest wetland in Southern Laos. Here you'll find a community-based project which offers elephant trekking and homestay accommodation. The villagers have traditionally been dependent on elephants for agricultural work for centuries and their treks to the amazing fortress of **Phu Asa**, as well as wetland walks and canoeing, can be organized either through the Xe Pian National Protected Area or the Eco-Guide Unit at the tourism office in Pakse (T031-212021), the Kingfisher Ecolodge (see Sleeping, page 238) or the Kiet Ngong Visitor Centre. Located 2 km from Kiet Ngong at the summit of a small jungle-clad hill, this ancient ruined fortress is an enigmatic site that has left archaeologists puzzled. It consists of 20 stone columns, 2 m high, arranged in a semi-circle – they look a bit like a scaled-down version of Stonehenge.

To get to Ban Kiet Ngong from Pakse takes about 1½ hours. From Pakse follow Route 13 until you get to the Km 48 junction with Route 18 at **Thang Beng village** (the Xe Pian National Protected Area office is here). Follow Route 18 east for 7 km, turn right at the signpost for the last 1.5 km to Ban Kiet Ngong.

The provincial authorities are trying to promote ecotourism in this area and have launched a new website, www.xepian.org, so please take this into consideration if you visit. (A 30,000 kip per person fee is now levied on entrance to the park.) To organize an elephant trek go to the **visitor centre** in Ban Kiet Ngong (T030-534 6547). Only guests staying at **Kingfisher Ecolodge** (see page 238) may book its treks and tours. Several other two- to three-day trekking/homestay ecotours are offered in the area; contact the Provincial Tourism Information Office in Pakse.

The Kiet Ngong Village Elephant Festival is held annually in late January or early February and is held in the village and on the curious archaeological remains at Phu Asa, which is a fascinating backdrop at this time. ►► See Activities and tours, page 241.

⦿ Pakse and around listings

For Sleeping and Eating price codes and other relevant information, see pages 23-24.

⦿ Sleeping

Pakse *p226, map p226*

AL-A Champasak Grand Hotel, Lao Nippon Bridge, T031-260211, www.champasakgrand.com. Not the most attractive of hotels, this huge cream building sits next to the bridge to the Thailand. It's thoroughly exposed and the rooms heat up like a greenhouse. But the rooms are comfortably furnished, with bathtubs, and there's a lovely pool right on the Mekong,

which is wonderful at sunset. Staff are helpful and friendly. Wi-Fi in the lobby; gym and massage available.

A-D Pakse Hotel, No 5 Rd , T031-212131, www.paksehotel.com. This is one of the best places to stay in town – and indeed in the country – with 65 rooms. The French owner, Mr Jérôme, has integrated local handicraft decorations, rosewood accents and tasteful furnishings into this slick hotel. The eco-rooms are good value and the de luxe rooms are a bonus in this part of the country. Breakfast is included, and Wi-Fi is available. There's also a good rooftop restaurant with a perfect view over the city and river; the dimly lit eatery oozes ambience. The chicken curry soup is a must, as are the lethal mojitos!

C-D Champasak Palace, No 13 Rd, T031-212263, www.champasak-palace-hotel.com. This is a massive chocolate box of a hotel with 55 rooms and lit up like a Christmas tree. It was conceived as a palace for a minor prince. There are some large rooms and 40 more modern, and very plain rooms. It is quite bizarre to see bellhops in traditional uniforms. Recent renovations have resulted in a loss of original character in favour of modernity but some classic touches remain: wooden shutters, some art deco furniture and lovely tiles. The restaurant is one of the most atmospheric places to eat in town, set on a big veranda overlooking frangipani trees. The friendly staff speak a smattering of English, there's a good terrace and the facilities include a massage centre. It's a great position above the Xe Don and the views from higher levels are stunning. If you want to kick back for a day or two, splash out on the King suite for the kitsch factor, jacuzzi and private balcony.

C-D Mekong Paradise Resort, T031-254120, mekongparadise@yahoo.com. This is an attractive resort in a rural setting on the banks of the Mekong. Although inconveniently located for town centre services, it's the perfect choice if you want to kick back for a few days. Rooms with views of the Mekong cost US$10 more but the extra cost is worth it. Newer rooms have their own private balcony; twins are more spacious than doubles. The staff are helpful and friendly.

C-E Salachampa, No 10 Rd, T031-212273, salachampa@yahoo.com. This is the most characterful place in town. Choose one of the rooms in the main 1920s building; they are huge with wooden floors, large en suite bathrooms with warm-water showers. The upstairs rooms with balconies are the best. There are also additional, quaintly rustic rooms in a 'new' extension and a pleasant garden area. A recommended choice for

those wanting a touch of colonial elegance. The rooms represent exceptionally good value for money.

D Champa Residence (Residence du Champa), No 13 Rd, east of town near the stadium and museum, T031-212120, champaresidence@yahoo.com. Modern-style rooms, with a/c, minibar, hot water and satellite TV. Very clean and with some character. Attractive terrace and lush garden; Visa accepted and tours arranged. Includes breakfast. Wi-Fi.

D-E Sang Aroun, Route 13, T031-252111, sangarounhotel@hotmail.com. The most modern hotel in town, with little character. There are 85 rooms with cable TV and a/c. More expensive rooms also have a bathtub. Wi-Fi is available.

E Daovieng 2 Hotel, No 13 & 35 Rd, T031-214331, www.daovienghotel.com. This is a comfortable hotel in the heart of the action close to all tourist services. Wi-Fi available.

E Lao Chaleun Hotel, opposite Salachampa, corner of Roads 6 and 4, T031-251333. This place has 43 simply decorated a/c and fan rooms with TV and minibar. The name of the hotel means 'Modern Lao' but the façade of newness is starting to fade and the place is in need of some maintenance. A bit of an architectural eyebrow raiser: different areas of the hotel are separated by partitions under which you can duck to get to other corridors. The outer rooms have a communal veranda. Motorbike rental (80,000 kip) and other tour services offered.

F-G Sabaidy 2 Guesthouse, No 24 Rd, T031-212992, www.sabaidy2tour.com. Offers a wide range of rooms from dorms through to rooms with private bathroom and hot water. The rooms are quite basic but the service here is quite exceptional. The proprietor, lively Mr Vong, offers tours. His grandfather, Liam Douang Vongsaa, was the first governor of Pakse and this building was the governor's residence, where Mr Vong was born in 1944. It's very popular so you may need to book in advance. Basic food is available. Motorbike rental.

Champasak p230

B Inthira Champakone Hotel, diagonally opposite Vong Pasued, T031-214059, www.inthirahotels.com. This is a lovely hotel with a friendly US manager. The twins in the courtyard outback come with outdoor rain showers and wooden-floored spacious rooms. The double de luxe is a mini apartment with mezzanine bed area, balcony, shower room and bathroom. The twins are actually more homely. The colonial building opposite is due to open with 6 more rooms.

E-G Anouxa Guesthouse, 1 km north of the roundabout, T031-213272. A wide range of accommodation from wooden bungalows through to concrete rooms with hot water and either a/c (pay extra) or fan and dingy bamboo structures with cold water. The concrete villas are the best, with a serene river vista from the balconies. The restaurant is probably one of the best in town, overlooking the river plus a shady cabana. The only drawback is that it is a little out of town (although next to the new spa) and some of the staff can't be bothered to serve customers. Bikes (10,000 kip) and motorbikes (70,000 kip) for hire.

E-G Vong Pasued Guesthouse, 450 m south of the roundabout, T020-22712402. The grimy, dingy shopfront façade is deceiving, as out the back, beside the river, are a range of pleasant rooms to suit all budgets. The owners are very pleasant. A firm favourite with the backpacker set, this small family-run guesthouse offers pretty reasonable rooms. The ones by the river are great value and are clean with hot water; the more basic rooms don't face the river and are fan only. There's a good restaurant, perfect for a natter with fellow travellers. Bike rental for 10,000 kip per day. A strange resident parrot squawks 'cow' incessantly.

F Souchitra Guesthouse, T031-212365, wtphouxay@yahoo.com, opposite former royal residences. A selection of rooms ranging from cheap cold-water rooms through to tastefully decorated clean rooms with fan, fridge and hot water. The ones in the newer annexe are better. There's a good restaurant downstairs. They have a boat you can charter: 300,000 kip to Pakse, US$150 to Siphandon and 50,000 kip to Don Daeng.

F-G Khamphouy Guesthouse, on the main road southwest of the roundabout, T031-252700. A delightful family-run place, which is clean and comfortable, with a friendly and relaxed atmosphere. Fine, bright but basic rooms in the main house with en suite shower. Newer rooms, built in the garden, will cost more. The room facing the front room has a semi-private patio with tables and chairs out front and a larger bathroom than most. Bikes for hire (10,000 kip); book exchange. Good value for those on a budget.

G Saythong Guesthouse and Restaurant, on the main road southwest of the roundabout, T020-2220 6215, bobbychampa@yahoo.com. Riverside location. 5 basic rooms upstairs with shared toilet; 6 more rooms with private showers (3 with a/c) out the back. The rooms are OK, if a little dour, but the restaurant is better, serving ample portions of good food. There's cold water only. They can organize a bus ticket to Siphandon, 60,000 kip.

Don Daeng Island p231

L-A La Folie Lodge, T030-5347603, www.lafolie-laos.com. 24 rooms housed in lovely wooden bungalows, each with its own balcony overlooking the river. The lodge has a stunning pool surrounded by landscaped tropical gardens. The restaurant serves good wine and a cocktail selection. Bicycle hire and pool use is available to non-guests for a fee. It's a luxurious base from which to explore the island. The German manager is efficient and entertaining.

G Homestays are offered in a community lodge and 17 homestays in Ban Hua Don Daeng. The wooden lodge has 2 common rooms, sleeping 5 people with shared bathrooms and dining area. Meals are 20,000 kip. The **Champasak Tourism Office** can arrange the homestay or call direct to

English-speaking Mr Khamfong, T020-5599 6609. Boat transfer 30,000 kip. The restaurant serves meals for 20,000 kip. Bicycle hire, 20,000 kip; boat to Tomo temple, 150,000 kip; guide 20,000 kip.

Xe Pian National Protected Area *p235*

A-D Kingfisher Ecolodge, 1 km east of Kiet Ngong, T030-5345016, www. kingfisherecolodge.com. A bonafide eco-lodge set facing wetlands. The set of 6 glass-fronted bungalows are lovely and romantic with 4-poster beds. There are also 4 attractive thatched rooms with nearby shared bathroom. The restaurant, set on the 2nd floor of the lodge, has stunning views over the Pha Pho wetlands. Elephant-related activities arranged; massage too. The owners Massimo and Bangon are very helpful. Highly recommended.

G Homestay, Ban Kiet Ngong, www.xepian. org/accommodation. 27 villagers offer basic homestay. Meals are 20,000 kip per person. You can book at the **Village Information Center** in Lao only, T030-534 6547. If you can't make yourself understood on arrival, ask for Mr Ho who speaks a little bit of English; he lives in the first house behind the wat.

❶ Eating

Pakse *p226, map p226*
The town has numerous international eateries. Most close at around 2100-2200; Indian restaurants stay open latest.

There are a couple of excellent *sindat* (barbecue) places near the Da Heung market; they are very popular with locals.

If the weather is fine, the **Pakse Hotel** has a superb rooftop restaurant offering a range of Lao dishes plus pretty good pizza, delicious chicken curry soup and some delectable mojitos from 1600.

₩ Champasak Palace, see page 236. Reasonable French interpretations in sublime surroundings.

₩ Na Dao, opposite the **Champasak Grand Hotel** near the bridge. A new French restaurant serving French and fusion cuisine fashioned after the Vientiane eatery of the same name.

₩-₩ Korean Barbecue, No 46 Rd (near corner with No 24 Rd), T031-212388. As you would expect, a classic Korean cook-it-yourself restaurant.

₩ Delta Coffee, Rd 13, opposite the **Champasak Palace Hotel**, T020-55345895. This place is a real find if you are craving some Western comfort food. The menu is tremendously varied and offers everything from pizza and lasagne to Thai noodles. The coffee is brilliant too, and the staff are exceptionally friendly. There is an unusual ordering system in place where you write down orders by number.

₩ Jasmine Restaurant, No 13 Rd, T031-251002. This small place has outdoor seating and has long been a firm favourite with Western travellers. It offers the standard Indian fare as well as a few Malaysian dishes, and represents reasonable value. The town's conglomerate of tuk-tuk drivers gathers here and very subtly touts for business among the diners.

₩ Ket Many Restaurant, 227 No 13 Rd, T031-212615. Chinese and Lao food from a limited menu are served in a/c restaurant. The deep-fried frog and Mekong River fish have both been recommended, or why not sample the spicy sour virgin pork uterus? Also serves a number of less adventurous European options (spaghetti, etc) for more cautious diners.

₩ Mengky Noodle Shop, No 13 Rd. Simple standby serving bowls of tasty duck and beef noodle soup.

₩ Nazim's Restaurant, in a new location, T031-252912. Serving a selection of Indian/ Malaysian dishes. The service is a little slow.

₩ Xuan Mai, near Pakse Hotel, T031-213245, Vietnamese restaurant with outdoor kitchen and eating area. Serves good shakes and fresh spring rolls, but it can be a little hit and miss.

Cafés & Bakeries
Crusty baguettes are available across town; they're great for breakfast with wild honey and fresh Bolaven coffee.

Café Sinouk. This new French-style café is charming and the staff are great. The outside view is a non-event but inside is comfortable seating, framed black and white photos, a range of patisserie and jams, honey and teas to buy in attractive packaging.

Floating restaurants
There are 4 floating restaurants: the Champa **Nava**, **Hongphay**, **Khamphong** and **Lan Xang** (T031-254411) on the Mekong with set menus around 100,000 kip for several courses. They are excellent value but the seating arrangements are not conducive to conversation for couples.

Champasak *p230*
Most restaurants are in the guesthouses; all are cheap (†).

† **Anouxa Guesthouse**, see page 237. Has a lovely restaurant set over the river, with a small but delectable menu. The fish dishes are especially good. Also offers a selection of wines.

† **Inthira Hotel**. The Inthira does Western burgers and pizzas as well as Asian dishes in handsome surroundings. The iced coffee is fabulous.

† **Vong Paseud Guesthouse**, see Sleeping. Has a cheap and extensive menu ranging from backpacker favourites like pancakes through to *tom yum* soup.

Xe Pian National Protected Area *p235*
Eating in Ban Kiet Ngong is very basic and, with the exception of nearby **Kingfisher Lodge** (see below), you will have to rely on the local food available – generally *feu* and noodle soup, rustled up on the spot.

††† **Kingfisher Ecolodge**, see page 238. This genuine ecolodge includes an excellent restaurant with lovely views. Serves a range of Western and Lao dishes. Also stocks wine.

✷ Festivals

Wat Phou *p231*
Wat Phou Festival lasts for 3 days around the full moon of the 3rd lunar month (usually **Feb**). Pilgrims come from far and wide to leave offerings at the temple. In the evening there are competitions – football, boat racing, bullfighting and cockfighting, Thai boxing, singing contests and the like. There is also some pretty extravagant imbibing of alcohol.

A *Son et Lumière* of sorts has been arranged at each full moon in the dry season with thousands of lamps lighting the archaeological site. For further information before heading to Champasak ask at the tourist office in Pakse or at the **Pakse Hotel**.
Phu Asa (**Ban Kiet Ngong**) Elephant festival held in **late Jan-early Feb**. Lots of elephants gather from all over the province and *mahouts* dressed in traditional costume. Procession to top of Phu Asa.

○ Shopping

Pakse *p226, map p226*
Markets
Central market. The closest thing to a shopping centre in town remains half-filled with vendors mostly selling clothes. The initial plans were for it to be a pan-Asian centre, stocking Thai, Japanese, Vietnamese and Lao goods but this is yet to happen.
Daoheung market, opposite Champasak Museum. Even for Southeast Asia this is a major agglomeration of stalls and traders. It is best to get here between 0730 and 0800 when the place is in full swing. Although it continues to function throughout the day, it does so in a rather detached fashion. Most people come here just to look but there are some fun things to buy: tin cans, clay pots, textiles and sarongs.

Textiles
Traditional handwoven silk cloth is available in the Daoheung Market (see above). There

is a good handicraft shop opposite the small park near Wat Luang, which sells lovely woven baskets, wooden carvings and good-quality embroidery. Many people, however, prefer to visit **Ban Saphay** where the embroidery is actually produced and buy lengths there (see page 229). The *mut mee ikat* designs are similar to those produced across the border in the northeastern or Isan region of Thailand. However, here in Laos it is more likely that the design will be produced using home-produced silk (in Thailand, silk yarn is often interwoven with imported thread) and coloured using natural rather than aniline dyes.

▲ Activities and tours

Pakse *p226, map p226*
Golf and swimming
There are two golf courses in the area and an Olympic pool under construction.

Massage and sauna
Keo Ou Don Physiotherapy, Ban Ta Ou Dome, T031-251895. Although this place is just out of the main town area, it is well worth the short trip. A wide range of massage options are offered, from oil through to foot massage, as well as the Lao favourite: the 'reduced fat massage' (be warned, this is like burning fat off). All treatments and the sauna cost under US$3.

There is also a small sauna and massage centre at the **Champasak Palace Hotel**, and a brilliant new massage place across the road from the **Pakse Hotel**.

Tour operators
Most of the hotels in town arrange day tours to Wat Phou, Tad Lo and the Khong Phapheng Falls; of these the best is Wat Phou Travels at the **Pakse Hotel**. There are also a number of tour agencies in town, all of which will arrange tours to local sites like Wat Phou, Phu Asa, Siphandon, Bolaven Plateau and Champasak. They are also the best sources of information, although it

is obviously in their interest to convince visitors that taking a tour is the best, possibly even the only, option.
Green Discovery, T031-252908, www.green discoverylaos.com, on the main road, offers a range of adventure tours and ecotourism treks around Champasak province including Ban Kiet Ngong, Bolaven waterfalls, Xe Pian trekking, Siphandon trip, Wat Phou trip and trekking in Dong Hua Sao National Protected Area. Prices from US$49-242 per person (minimum 2 people). Highly recommended.
Pakse Travel. To Champasak, 55,000 kip; to 4000 islands, 50,000 kip return. Pakse to Phnom Penh, 250,000 kip, 13 hrs; to Siem Reap with 1 night in Kampong Cham, 280,000 kip.

The provincial tourist office offers a variety of trips including a new 3-day trip to Phou Xieng Thong mountain near the Thai border, from US$150 per person for 2.
Sabaidy 2, see Sleeping, T031-212992. Mr Vong and crew offer a wide range of tours around a variety of top-notch provincial sites, very good value and recommended for visitors who are only around for 1-2 days. The 1-day Bolaven tour costs US$24 per person and is great fun. Mr Vong contributes to a school project charity in the province: www.kokphungtai-primaryschool-fund.com.
Xplore Asia, opposite **Jasmine Restaurant**, Rd 13, T031-212893, www.xplore-laos.com. Offers a variety of tours and useful tour services (including a minivan service to Siphandon). Open-tour trip to Bolaven with stops at Tad Fane, Tad Yuang, Tad Lo, Lao Ngam, 140,000 kip.

Champasak *p230*
Spas
Champasak Spa, T020-5649 9739, www. champasak-spa.com. Daily 1000-1200 and 1300-1900. This new venture, run by a French couple, is lovely. It aims to be sustainable and they plan to hand it over to local management after training is complete. The massages are simply divine (opt for coconut oil) and the service exceptional.

The foot massage is perfect after a morning at the ruins. Prices 45,000 kip-120,000 kip. Packages too and pickups can be arranged. Booking advised after 1600.

Don Daeng Island *p231*

The tourist office in Pakse organizes a 2-day biking and long-tail boat trip around Don Daeng that departs from Pakse and takes in Wat Phou. From US$100 per person for 2 people.

It is possible to hire bikes from La Folie (see page 237) to explore the island.

Xe Pian National Protected Area *p235*
Elephant treks and birdwatching

There are several 2- to 3-day trekking/homestay trips offered in the area. These include elephant treks across the Xe Pian forests, wetlands and rocky outcrops; treks from Kiet Ngong village to the top of Phu Asa (this one takes about 2 hrs; the elephant baskets can carry 2 people); and birdwatching trips. There is a 2-day canoe/trekking/homestay trip called the Ban Ta Ong Trail in the company of guides trained in wildlife and the medicinal uses of plants (from US$95 per person; minimum 2 people). A challenging 3-day camping Kiet Ngong-Ta Ong Trail is a walking/elephant back/canoeing trip in Xe Pian from US$280 per person. These tours are designed to ensure that local communities reap the rewards of tourism in a sustainable fashion; they are highly recommended. The best time for birdwatching in Xe Pian is Dec-Feb.

The Kingfisher Ecolodge (see Sleeping), T030-5345016, can arrange for you to train to be a bona fide elephant rider with a traditional *mahout* (elephant keeper).

Tour operators in Pakse can also organize trips to the Xe Pian National Protected Area. Contact the Provincial Tourism Office in Pakse for complete information, T031-676 4144, www.xepian.org. It can also offer a 1-day elephant safari from US$100 per person for 2 people.

If you wish to travel independently to this area, you need to allow enough time for the elephants to be organized by the *mahouts* once you arrive. Contact the visitor centre, T030-5346547, in advance. Although only minimal English is spoken in the village, most of the locals will understand the purpose of your visit. Elephant ride to Phu Asa, 120,000 kip; local trekking, 30,000 kip; 1-day trek, 160,000 kip per person; 2 day trek, 320,000 kip per person; half-day canoe trip 50,000 kip; 1-night camping 490,000 kip; Ta Ong 2-night camping and homestay trip; 1,060,000 kip.

⊖ Transport

Pakse *p226, map p226*

For out-of-town journeys, hotels, such as the Pakse Hotel and Champasak Palace, and tour companies such as Xplore-Asia charter cars and minibuses (with driver).

Air

The flight schedule changes frequently so it is best to check with a travel agent prior to making arrangements. There are currently domestic flights to Vientiane and Luang Prabang and internationally to Bangkok and Siem Reap, with Lao Airlines, who have offices at the airport and by the river in town, T031-212140, Mon-Fri. Bangkok Airways also runs direct flights to/from Bangkok and to Siem Reap.

Boat

A boat to Champasak leaves at 0830 daily, 80,000 kip, 2 hrs. If you have enough people and money it is possible to charter a boat to Don Khong or Champasak, contact Mr Boun My, T020-5563 1008; a charter to Champasak, US$70; to the 4000 islands, US$210. See also Ins and outs, page 230.

The Luang Say company and Mekong Islands Tours run cruises from Pakse to Wat Phou and down to the 4000 Islands. The Vat Phou (T031-251446, www.vatphou.com) offers 3-day cruises in 12 cabins from

€ 419. The **Mekong Islands** has 11 cabins (T031-410155, www.mekongislands.com). Its 4-night cruise costs from €620.

Bus/songthaew

Buses/trucks travelling north (to **Savannakhet**, **Thakhek** and **Vientiane**) leave from the Northern bus station, Km 7 on Route 13, across the Xe Don, T031-251508, 15,000 kip to the centre. The southern terminal is at Km 8 also on Route 13, heading south out of town, T031-212981; 15,000 kip to the centre. From the Kiang Kai bus station, 5000-10,000 kip. From Daoheum market, 5000-10,000 kip. Lists of bus departures can be found in many of the hotels and guesthouses. There are regular morning departures to most destinations until 1600 and journey times are decreasing as the roads improve.

You can charter a tuk-tuk to take you to the airport, northern bus station (8 km away), southern bus station (8 km away), for about 20,000 kip. To get to the VIP bus station (Kiang Kai) and neighbouring **Seangchaolearn** at the afternoon market, 2 km from the town centre, at *talaat lak song*, costs about 10,000 kip.

The Northern terminal 7 km north of town on Route 13. Hourly departures daily 0730-1630 to **Savannakhet**, 250 km, 5 hrs, 40,000 kip; to **Thakhek**, 7-8 hrs, 55,000 kip; to **Paksan**, 10 hrs, 100,000 kip; to **Vientiane**, 16-18 hrs, 100,000 kip. These buses can be painfully slow due to the number of stops they make en route. For those heading to **Vientiane** it makes more sense to fork out a couple of extra dollars and take the much quicker and comfortable VIP bus from the VIP station.

The Southern terminal 8 km south of town on Route 13. There are regular *songthaew* connections with **Champasak** 1030-1400, 20,000 kip including the ferry fare; stay on the bus if you are travelling to **Wat Phou** (see page 231). Ask for Ban Lak Sarm Sip (translates as 'village 30 km'); here there is a signpost and you turn right and

travel 4 km towards Ban Muang (5 km). In the village there are people selling tickets for the ferry. (**Dao Heung market**, the morning market, has regular *songthaew* for Champasak in the morning from 1030, 20,000 kip.)

Local buses coming through from **Vientiane** provide the main means of transport to other destinations down south, so can be slightly off kilter. Buses depart for **Salavan**, 4 departures in the morning 0630-1330 from the Southern Bus Station, 110 km, 2-3 hrs, 30,000 kip. This is a good alternative for those wishing to head to **Tad Lo**, just make sure that the bus is taking Route 20 (not Route 23) and that the driver understands you want to get off at the junction; most drivers now know to stop at the junction.

Songthaew to the **Bolaven Plateau** from the Southern Bus Station; **Paksong**, 50 km, 0930, 1000, 1230, 20,000 kip. **Tad Fan**, 5 departures in the morning, 50 km, 1 hr, 20,000 kip; to **Tha Theng**, 5 departures in the morning, 20,000 kip; A *songthaew* leaves for **Ban Kiet Ngong** and **Ban Phapho** at 1200, 2 hrs, 25,000 kip. To **Attapeu** via **Paksong** and **Sekong** at 0630, 0900, 1100, 1400, 1500, 3 hrs, 35,000 kip.

Buses/*songthaew* leave for **Siphandon** at 0830, 1030, 1130, 1300 and 1430 (Muang Khong on Don Khong) 30,000 kip, 4 hrs; for **Ban Nakasang** (the closest port to Don Deth/Don Khon) departures at 0700, 0800, 0900, 1130, 1200, 1430 and 1400, 30,000 kip 3-4 hrs. Several of the buses to Ban Nakasang also stop at **Ban Hat Xai Khoune** (the stop off for Don Khong). Make sure that you let the driver know whether you are going to Ban Nakasang or Ban Hat Xai Khoune rather than simply saying the name of the islands.

A more comfortable alternative to Siphandon is to take the minibus service to **Don Deth/Don Khong** which picks you up directly from your hotel and drops you off at either Ban Nakasang or Ban Hat Xai Khoune for 60,000 kip, 2 hrs. This actually works out to be much more cost-effective and time-effective. Most guesthouses can arrange for this minibus service in Pakse, as can Xplore-Asia and Pakse Travel (see Tour operators, above) 60,000 kip 2½ hrs to Ban Hat Xai Khoune, 3 hrs to Ban Nakasang. This is highly recommended as, once you have paid all the fees involved with local transport, it costs roughly the same. It is also a shorter trip, so save yourself the headache.

Khiang Kai, VIP & international bus terminal See Ins and outs, page 227. Near the football stadium and Talaat Lak Song, T031-212228, just off Route 13. VIP buses to **Ubon** (Thailand) leave at 0830 and 1530 55,000 kip, 3 hrs; VIP seat buses leave for **Vientiane** at 2000 arriving in Vientiane at 0600 (stopping in **Thakhek** en route) 150,000 kip. A VIP sleeping bus with comfy beds, duvet, cake, movies and milk thrown in (basically a mobile slumber party) leaves at 0830 arriving in Vientiane at 0600 (stopping en route to Thakhek), 150,000 kip. The beds are double, so unless you book 2 spaces you might end up sleeping next to a stranger. If you're tall, it's best to ask for a bed towards the back of the bus. Make sure you secure your belongings on any of the overnight buses, as some fellow passengers may have sticky fingers.

Buses to **Vietnam** leave via the Bo Y border. To **Danang**, 1900, 18 hrs, 200,000 kip; to **Hué**, 1830, 15½ hrs, 190,000 kip; to Dong Ha, 1800, 14 hrs, 150,000 kip; to Lao Bao, 1700, 11 hrs, 120,000 kip.

Buses to **Cambodia** leave from the adjacent Seangchaolearn terminal. Sorya buses (www.ppsoryatransport.com) leave Pakse for **Stung Treng** at 0730, US$15, 4½ hrs; to **Kratie**, US$15, 6½ hrs; to **Kampong Cham**, 0730, US$15, 9½ hrs; to **Phnom Penh** at 0730, US$30, 13½ hrs.

Warning Note that it is not possible to get to Siem Reap in 1 day from southern Laos. You will need to stay the night in Kampong Cham. Agents who tell you it's possible appear to be operating a scam in southern Laos where they charge

travellers extra to transfer onto a minibus at Kampong Cham to get to Siem Reap well into the night. Sorya is a bit more expensive than most operators, but reliable and recommended.

Motorbike and bicycle hire
The **Lankham Hotel**, near the Xplore Asia office, rents out bicycles (US$1 per day) standard small bikes (US$8 per day) and larger dirt bikes (US$20 per day). Guesthouses and travel agencies are starting to withdraw motorbike hire because of the dangers posed to tourists who have never hired motorbikes before. The death of a US citizen in a motorbike accident in Sekong in 2009 underlined such fears. The Sang Aroun rents bicycles for 30,000 kip.

Tuk-tuk/saamlor
These are the main forms of local transport. A tuk-tuk to the northern bus station should cost 20,000 kip. Shared tuk-tuks to local villages leave from the Daoheung market and from the stop on No 11 Rd near the jetty. Tuk-tuks can also be chartered by the hour. For services to the Thai border, see box, page 228.

Private transport
If you miss public transport, a private *songthaew* from Pakse to **Champasak** (with ferry and tuk-tuk included) will cost you 300,000 kip. A half-day Pakse City tour costs 150,000 kip, full-day 250,000 kip. Ask at **Pakse Hotel** for reliable drivers.

Champasak *p230*
The return boat journey depends on passengers but it usually returns at 1430, 70,000 kip.

Bus/songthaew
To **Pakse** direct at 0630, 0730 and 0800, 15,000 kip 2 hrs (with wait for ferry). A private chartered van to Pakse costs 500,000 kip; to **Paksong**, 700,000 kip; to **Ban Kiet Ngong**, 400,000 kip. A tourist minibus leaves

from the tourist information centre daily at 0800 for **Siphandon**, 70,000 kip. Most of the guesthouses can organize tickets. A chartered *songthaew* to **Wat Phou** is 60,00-80,00 return including waiting time but check the number of hours a driver is prepared to wait. A tuk-tuk from the ferry port to Champasak town is 5000 kip. A tuk-tuk from the ferry port on the other side of the river (Ban Lak Sarm Sip) to the main road at **Ban Muang** is 10,000 kip.

A ferry to **Don Daeng** costs 50,000 kip and can be arranged through the Champasak tourist office. The boat departs from behind the tourist office.

Xe Pian National Protected Area *p235*

Songthaew run to the 4000 Islands or ask a private tourist bus running south to stop at the **Ban Kiet Ngong** junction. There is no waiting transport but **Kingfisher Ecolodge** (see page 238) can arrange transport to the village for 50,000 kip. Call first. A private *songthaew* transport from Pakse direct to **Ban Kiet Ngong**, 250,000 kip; minivan, 350,000 kip.

⊙ Directory

Pakse *p226, map p226*
Banks BCEL Bank, No 11 Rd (beside the river), changes US$ and most currencies (cash) and offers a better commission rate on cash exchange than other banks, also Visa/MasterCard cash advances at 3% commission, Mon-Fri 0830-1530 (with 1 hr lunch break), they have 2 ATMs; **Lao**

Development Bank, No 13 Rd, T031-212168, cash and TCs exchanged. **Embassies and consulates** Vietnam, No 24 Rd, T031-212827, Mon-Fri 0830-1330, 1400-1630, visas for Vietnam cost US$45 and take 4 days to process, so you are better off organizing your Vietnamese visa in Vientiane. **Internet** Expect to pay around 200 kip per min but discounts kick in usually after 1 hr: **SK internet**, No 13 Rd. **Medical services** There is a huge hospital between No 1 Rd and No 46 Rd, T031-212018, but neither their English skills nor medical service will suffice for complex cases; in case of emergencies you are better off going across to Ubon in Thailand; there is a pretty good pharmacy at the hospital which stocks most medications. A new international clinic is under construction. **Police** T031-212641. **Post office** No 1 Rd, overseas telephone calls can also be made from here; express mail service available; note the ashtrays made from defused (one hopes) unexploded shells. **Telephone** Telecommunications office for fax and overseas calls on No 1 Rd, near No 13 Rd; all of the internet cafés have internet-call facilities, and these are by far the cheapest way to phone.

Champasak *p230*
Banks Lao Development Bank, changes cash only Mon-Fri. **Internet** There are 3 internet places including the school and Inthira Hotel.

Bolaven Plateau

The French identified the Bolaven Plateau, in the northeast of Champasak Province, as a prime location for settlement by hardy French farming stock. It is named after the Laven minority group that resides in the area. The soils are rich and the upland position affords some relief from the summer heat of the lowlands. Fortunately, their grand plans came to nought and, although some French families came to live here, they were few in number and all left between the 1950s and 1970s as conditions deteriorated. The area also suffered another setback during the war years, when the major surrounding towns were completely destroyed by US bombing campaigns. Even so, the area was developed as a coffee-, rubber-, tea- and cardamom-growing area. The cool breeze of the plateau, with an average altitude of 600 m, offers much respite from the stifling heat of surrounding lower lands, particularly in April and May. Today it is inhabited by a colourful mix of ethnic groups, such as the Laven, Alak, Tahoy and Suay, many of whom were displaced during the war. There are numerous villages dotted between the small settlement of Tha Teng and Salavan. The premier attraction in the area is the number of roaring falls plunging off the plateau. Today, Tad Lo and Tad Fan are popular tourist destinations. While the grand Tad Yeung makes the perfect picnic destination, the plateau also affords excellent rafting and kayaking trips. A trip to a coffee or tea plantation also provides an interesting insight into the region. ▶▶ *For listings, see pages 255-260.*

Ins and outs

As tourism expands in Laos, so areas like the Bolaven are sure to become more accessible. For the moment, though, the tourist infrastructure is limited. Tour companies, especially in Pakse, 30 km away (see page 240), can organize trips. Alternatively, the best base is Tad Lo (see page 247). Other places near or on the Bolaven are Salavan (see page 248), Sekong (see page 252) and Attapeu (see page 253); guesthouses in these towns can also offer assistance and information on exploring the area. Note that it is not always possible to drive across the Bolaven Plateau from Salavan to Attapeu, as the roads rapidly deteriorate in bad weather. In the wet season, parts of the new road recently constructed from Paksong can be washed away.

Background

The fertile farmland of the Bolaven Plateau has given Salavan Province a strong agricultural base, supporting coffee, tea and cardamom plantations. The road from Paksong to Pakse is known as the Coffee Road. Coffee was introduced to the area by French settlers in the 1920s and 1930s, who then made a quick exit as the bombing escalated in the 1960s. It is mainly exported via Pakse to Thailand, Singapore and, formerly, the USSR. Fair Trade has also catapulted the coffee into the UK and US markets. Tea grown in this area, however, is for local use. The Bolaven also has the perfect climate for durians; villages (particularly on the road from Paksong to Pakse) are liberally dotted with durian trees. The fruit is exceptionally rich and creamy and in the peak season, between May and July, can be bought from roadside stalls for just 1000 kip or so. Thanks to its fertility, the plateau is now rapidly repopulating and new farms are springing up. One can see evidence of the government's relocation policy everywhere on the plateau, where villages have been moved from higher lands to the lower lands, with the end goal of minimizing slash-and-burn agriculture and providing people better access to infrastructure, markets and other facilities. As a result, many new farming practices and produce have been steadily introduced. Towards Salavan, lots of banana plantations are cropping up and, between Paksong and Tha Teng, many small-time village operations are producing cabbage and corn crops, often sold roadside.

During the bombing of the Ho Chi Minh Trail (see box, page 217), to the east, many hilltribes and other ethnic minority groups also migrated to the Bolaven, which consequently has become an ethnographic goldmine with more than 12 obscure minority groups living in the area, including the Katu, Alak, Tahoy, Suay, Ya Houne, Ngai and Suk. Most of the tribes are of Indonesian (or Proto-Malay) stock and have very different facial characteristics from the Lao; they are mainly animist (see page 310).

Paksong (Pakxong) and around → For listings, see pages 255-260. Colour map 3, B3.

→ Phone code: 031.

The main town on the Bolaven Plateau is Paksong, a small market town 50 km east of Pakse. It was originally a French agricultural centre, popular during the colonial era for its cooler temperatures. Paksong was yet another casualty of the war and was virtually destroyed. The area is famous for its fruit and vegetables; even strawberries and raspberries can be cultivated here.

The town occupies a very scenic spot. However, the harsh weather in the rainy season changes rapidly, making it difficult to plan trips around the area. The town consists of little more than a couple of blocks of old shops and a big produce market, which acts as a trading centre for many of the outlying villages of the plateau.

Waterfalls around Paksong

Just 17 km from Paksong are the twin falls of **Tad Mone** and **Tad Meelook**. Once a popular picnic spot for locals, the area is now almost deserted and the swimming holes at the base of the falls are an idyllic place for a dip. To reach the falls take Route 23 northeast of Paksong towards Tha Teng and Salavan, until you reach a signposted turning; follow the road for about 3.5 km to reach the falls.

Not far from Paksong, 1 km off the road to Pakse, is **Tad Fan**, a dramatic 120-m-high waterfall, which is believed to be one of the tallest cascades in the country. The fall splits into two powerful streams roaring over the edge of the cliff and plummeting into the pool below, with mist and vapour shrouding views from above. The fall's name derives from the species of barking deer which formerly surrounded the area and local legends talk of large numbers of the species falling to their death down the falls.

Around 2 km from Tad Fan and 1 km from the main road is **Tad Yeung** (pronounced Tad N'Yeung) ⓘ *entry 5000 kip*. Set amongst beautiful coffee plantations and sprinkled with wooden picnic huts, these falls are possibly the best on the plateau. Packing a picnic in Pakse and bringing it along for an afternoon trip is recommended. The cascades plummet 50 m to a pool at the bottom, which is possible to swim in, in the dry season. During the wet season the waterways create numerous little channels and islands around the cascades. Behind the main falls sits a cave – however it is best to get someone to guide you here. There is a slippery walk-way from the top of the falls to the bottom, where you can swim. The falls can be reached by taking a local bus from Southern bus station in Pakse to Village Km 40 (ask to go to Lak See Sip). The turn-off is on the right from Pakse (and on the left from Paksong). There is a sign on the main road which indicates **Sihom Sabaidy Guesthouse**, follow this road about 700 m to the falls. These falls are a great option if you are trying to avoid the backpacker hoardes.

The falls sit on the edge of the **Dong Hua Sao National Protected Area** and access via the falls is one of the only ways to explore the area. Previously, it was inhabited by a number of rare species now dwindling in number. It is believed that a local population of tigers still resides in the protected area but the chances of spotting one are minimal. Trekking is offered around the waterfall but is quite difficult in the wet season due to slipperiness and leaches, so it's best to hire one of the guides at the **Tad Fan** resort. Take a track to the left off the main road at Ban Lak, Km 38; at the end of the track, a path leads down to a good viewpoint halfway down the horseshoe-shaped gorge. The magnificent falls offer stunning views but if you wish to swim you should trek further along to Tad Gniang, 2 km east of Tad Fan. **Tad Gniang**, named after the wild stags that populate the area, is only recommended for a dip during the dry season (October to the end of March). There is a charge of 2000 kip per person to visit the falls, plus an additional 3000 kip per motorbike. Tours to Tad Fan and Tad Gniang can be organized through most travel agents in Pakse (see page 240).

Thirty-six kilometres northeast of Pakse is **Paseum Waterfall** and **Utayan Bajiang Champasak** ⓘ *T031-251294, 5000 kip entry fee*, a strange ethnic theme park popular with Thai tourists. The large compound features the small cascades, restaurant, model ethnic village, gardens and plenty of trails in between. They have bungalows, a treehouse and rooms available for 1000 baht. To get here from Pakse follow Route 13 towards Paksong and follow the left fork at Km 21 and turn off at the Km 30 mark.

Tha Teng and around → *For listings, see pages 255-260.*

On the Bolaven Plateau, at the junction of Routes 23 and 16 between Salavan (45 km), Sekong (48 km) and Paksong (37 km), is Tha Teng, a village that was levelled during the war. Before that, it was the home of Jean Dauplay, the Frenchman who introduced coffee to Laos from Vietnam in 1920. Today the United Nations Development Programme (UNDP), in a joint venture with a private sector businessman, has set up a small wild honey-processing factory. Villagers are paid for the combs they collect from the jungled hills around Tha Teng. The carefully labelled 'Wild honey from Laos' is exported to European health food shops. There are several ethnic minority villages in the area.

There isn't much to see in the town itself – essentially it's just a big roundabout, affording stunning views. There is, however, an excellent ethnic minority market starting at about 0600 daily, to which villagers come to sell produce from their plots. A convoy of tractors, horses and basket-carrying women puffing on pipes can be seen at day-break approaching the market.

Tad Lo and around → *For listings, see pages 255-260. Colour map 3, B3. Phone code: 031.*

Tad Lo is a popular 'resort' on the edge of the Bolaven Plateau, 30 km from Salavan, and nestled alongside three rolling cascades. There are several places to stay in this idyllic retreat, good hiking, an exhilarating river to frolic in (especially in the wet season) and elephant trekking. In the vicinity of Tad Lo there are also several villages, which can be visited in the company of a local villager. The area has become particularly popular with the backpacker set, many of whom prefer to stay here rather than in Pakse. The LNTA plan to open up one-day trekking routes in the area.

The **Xe Xet** (or Houei Set) flows past Tad Lo, crashing over two sets of cascades nearby: **Tad Hang**, the lower series of waterfalls, is overlooked by the **Tad Lo Lodge** and **Saise**

Hotel (see Sleeping, page 255), while **Tad Lo**, the upper, is a short hike away. The Xe Xet is yet another of the area's rivers that is being dammed to produce hydropower for export to Thailand.

Ins and outs

Getting there The turning for Tad Lo is Ban Houei Set on Route 20 between Pakse and Salavan. Catch a bus or *songthaew* from either town; most drivers know Tad Lo and will stop at Ban Houia Set (2½ hours from Pakse and under an hour from Salavan). There is a sign here indicating the way to Tad Lo – a 1.8-km walk along a dirt track and through the village of Ban Saen Wang. Usually you can get a tuk-tuk to Tad Lo for around 10,000 kip.
▸▸ *See Transport, page 259.*

Tourist information A new **Community Guides** office has been established with trained guides offering 10 treks around the Tad Lo area and to nearby Ngai villages. Elephant treks can also be arranged from the Tad Lo Lodge for 85,000 kip per person for a 90-minute trek through the jungle and river.

Each one of the guesthouses in Tad Lo can arrange guided treks to Ban Khian and Tad Soung for around 90,000 kip per person for a full day's trek.

Around Tad Lo

There are two Alak villages, **Ban Khian** and **Tad Soung**, close to Tad Lo. Tad Soung is approximately 10 km away from the main resort area and are the most panoramic falls in the vicinity. The Alak are an Austro-Indonesian ethno-linguistic group. Their grass-thatched huts, with rounded roofs, are not at all Lao in style and are distinct from those in neighbouring Lao Theung villages. Most fascinating is the Alak's seeming obsession with death. The head of each household carves coffins out of logs for himself and every member of his family (even babies), then stacks them, ready for use, under their rice storage huts. This tradition serves as a reminder that life expectancy in these remote rural areas is around 40 and infant mortality around 100 per 1000 live births; the number one killer here is malaria.

Katou villages such as **Ban Houei Houne** (on the Salavan–Pakse road) are famous for their weaving of a bright cloth used locally as a *pha sinh* (sarong). This village also has an original contraption to pound rice: on the river below the village are several water-wheels which power the rice pounders. The idea originally came from Xam Neua and was brought to this village by a man who had fought with the Pathet Lao.

Salavan (Saravan) and around → *For listings, see pages 255-260. Colour map 3, B3*

→ *Phone code: 034*

The capital of one of the most beautiful provinces in Laos, the old French town of Salavan (also Saravan and Saravane) lies at the northern edge of the Bolaven Plateau and acts as a transport hub and trading centre for the agricultural commodities that are produced on the plateau. The Xe Don river, which enters the Mekong at Pakse, flows along the edge of town. Salavan itself is no beauty, but it is charming, with no pretensions. Pigs and buffalo wander along the roads, children play in the streets and shops sell such practical goods as anvils, bicycle tyres, lengths of wire, transmission parts and brightly coloured functional plastic objects. Tourists are welcomed but not wooed; there are few handicrafts or postcards in sight. In the cool of the evening, when the locals have stopped work and

The fall of Tha Teng: a personal view

In 1968, I read about the fall of Tha Teng to the Pathet Lao. The small article was buried in a back page of the newspaper. Not many Americans really cared about this loss or even knew where Laos was, let alone Tha Teng. In 1969 I was flying over Tha Teng in my Bird Dog – a Cessna 170 – which was used in my work as a Forward Air Controller (Code name, Raven 58) for the United States Air Force. All that was left of this town was about 20 homes on a road on the northern edge of the Bolaven Plateau. The homes were gradually being overrun by heavy vegetation.

What was so important about this town that its loss would be reported in the United States? Tha Teng is strategically located on the northern edge of the Bolaven Plateau. As a military outpost, it could be used to obtain intelligence about enemy activity. So, by occupying Tha Teng, the 'friendlies' – the Royal Lao Government – could, to a certain extent, control the gateway to the Bolaven. With its loss, the Pathet Lao and North Vietnamese could move more easily in their efforts to control the plateau. The significance of the location of Tha Teng was well known to the Pathet Lao. It was rumoured that there was a cave northeast of Tha Teng which could hold a battalion of troops and whose entrance was large enough to walk an elephant through. Elephants were used to haul heavy equipment, ammunition and supplies into the cave. But, from the air, the terrain looked flat. Even the military topological maps did not indicate the possibility of a cave. However, on Thanksgiving Day 1969, I confirmed in fact the existence of that

cave by 'clearing' away the 200-ft trees which protected its entrance. Further, it exposed a large permanent bivouac area in front of the cave entrance which provided facilities for at least a battalion-size unit. This staging area proved successful as the Pathet Lao captured the Bolaven during their campaign of 1970.

The 'war-that-wasn't' in Laos was odd in more than just the sense that it wasn't a war. In Vientiane it was a common sight to see Pathet Lao soldiers coming down out of the mountains in full combat gear, including weapons, to obtain their daily rations. They could shop without concern of being captured and would then return to the mountains to join their combat units. These were the same soldiers that the Royal Lao army, who were also at the market, might be fighting later that same day. Three days each year, the war would stop in southern Laos. Officials from Salavan would get in a truck and head south toward the plateau. At the edge of the Bolavens they would stop to let armed Pathet Lao (PL) get on their truck so they could continue to each village on the plateau. These PL guards would make certain that the officials only went to the villages. As the officials visited each village, they would record the births, deaths and weddings which had taken place during the previous year. War or no war, official government records had to be maintained. Following the three-day yearly truce, the war would resume.

Source: Ken Thompson, Raven 58, who flew as a FAC over Laos and Vietnam from 1968 to 1970.

---

are relaxing, talking, cooking and playing, the town seems – despite the legacy of the war – to epitomize a more innocent past. If you happen to be walking past the market at 1700 or thereabouts, you may even find yourself invited to join the locals in a game of petang. There is a small **tourist office** ① *T034-211528.*

Ins and outs

Getting there Most buses coming from Pakse turn off Route 23 and travel to Salavan via Route 20, a new and comparatively fast road that goes past the turning to Tad Lo (see page 247). They often also stop for a while at the small market town of Ban Lao Ngam on the Houei Tapoung (46 km from Salavan, 79 km from Pakse). Some buses, though, take the longer and rougher route via Paksong (Route 23). ➤➤ *See Transport, page 259.*

History

The area around Salavan was an important Champasak kingdom outpost called Muang Mam and populated by mostly Mon-Khmer ethnic groups. In 1828 the Siamese renamed the area Salawan, which has evolved into the current name.

Salavan changed hands several times during the American war in Indochina, as the Pathet Lao and forces of the Royal Lao Government fought for control of this critical town, which is located on a strategic flank of the Ho Chi Minh Trail. The two sides, with the RLG supported by American air power, bombed and shelled the town in turn as they tried to dislodge one another, and Salavan was all but obliterated. (There is a crude painting of the battle on display in the **Champasak Museum** in Pakse; see page 228.) Until just a few years ago, you would still come across piles of war scrap, including unexploded bombs, shells and mortars in the streets. Now that these have been cleared, reminders of the war are largely confined to the memories of the town's older residents (most of the population is under 30) and the pages of books. The consequences of the shelling and bombing today is that Salavan is a provincial capital with scarcely an ounce of physical beauty and almost no evidence of its French-era origins, with the single exception of the post office.

When US airforce pilots mounted bombing runs in Vietnam, their rules of engagement prohibited airstrikes within 500 m of a temple; in Cambodia, the margins were increased to 1 km. It has been said that in Laos such rules did not apply, but one retired US officer who was based there has written to us saying that "a complex web of rules [was] administered by levels of supervision stretching from the embassy in Vientiane, to Ho Chi Minh City, to Honolulu to the Pentagon, and included consultation with, and on the appropriate occasions approval by, the Lao government." Like Xieng Khouang, another critical town to the north, Salavan had one of the most beautiful temples in the country, **Wat Chom Keoh**, which was destroyed in an air raid in 1968. (The wat was commemorated on a postage stamp in the 1950s.)

Sights

Today all that remains of **Wat Chom Keoh** are two forlorn and shell-pocked corner-posts, one ruined chedi and a dilapidated wat building decaying still further in the grounds of the Salavan general hospital. The daily market in the centre of town is worth a visit, mainly because the only other sight is the handicraft centre. In past years the market was an environmentalist's nightmare: all manner of wild creatures, some endangered, were sold here, either for the cooking pot or for the trade in live wild animals (see page 329). Today the frisson of such sights is, fortunately, no longer on offer. There's the usual array of frogs and fish, and perhaps a wild bird, squirrel or lizard, but not much else.

Ban Nong Boua

Ban Nong Boua, a beautiful lake near the source of the Xe Don, lies 18 km east of Salavan town. It is famed for its crocodiles (although apparently now only two remain), which move into the river in the dry season but usually stay out of sight. The locals have a number of cultural beliefs surrounding the crocodiles, so a donation – perhaps in order to offer a pig to the crocs, which the residents will actually consume themselves – is likely to be expected before they will escort you to the lake. The road to Ban Nong Boua is too rough to be negotiated by tuk-tuk, which means it is necessary to charter a jeep or other sturdy vehicle. There are two river crossings along the way, so any vehicle that won't fit in a small boat or is large enough to brave the waters won't make it there. In the wet season it is advisable to travel by boat.

Ban Nong Boua is also rumoured to be a starting point for climbing **Phou Katae**, the 1588-m-high mountain that looms over Salavan from the south. However, *falangs* aren't welcome to climb it, either because of the American airstrip from the war that is supposedly up there, or because of the logging operations on the other side, which are not entirely legal nor public. Access to both Ban Nong Boua and Phou Katae is very difficult and is only recommended for the tougher independent traveller. There is nowhere to sleep near the mountain but it may be possible to sleep at the nearby temple if you have a mosquito net.

Around Salavan

Tahoy, northeast of Salavan along Route 15, is a major centre of the Tahoy minority ethnic group. There are 30,000 Tahoy spread across the two adjoining provinces but the largest population lives here. Aside from being an interesting cultural insight into the Tahoy culture, the town is also renowned for war junk, as the Ho Chi Minh Trail (see box, page 217) dissected the area. Locals believe that there is a large tiger population in the area and tales are rife of this person or that person being eaten by a tiger. However, it would seem that the tigers aren't very forthcoming, as even tiger specialists have difficulty tracking them.

Toum Lan is a Katong village 46 km north of Salavan, notable for its longhouse and traditional weaving (ask Mr Bousasone at **Saise Guesthouse** for details). They celebrate the Lapup festival, where buffaloes are sacrificed around the full moon in March. During the rainy season it is difficult to access the site. A bus leaves for Toum Lan at 1430 (15,000 kip) and returns at 0700. Accommodation may be possible in the village (10,000 kip).

The **Paseum** waterfall lies 81 km from Salavan on Route 20. It is a beautiful spot but is dominated by the resort that sits on the site. The proprietor has relocated a small ethnic village from their homes to the resort premises in order to make a distinctly dubious 'ethnic museum', where the villagers show tourists their 'traditional way of life'. As tourists approach, the villagers change out of their jeans and into traditional attire before running around, beating drums and playing traditional music.

Coffee Road

Heading south from Salavan, Route 20 reaches Ban Beng after 26 km (4 km from Tad Lo). Turn south (right if coming from Tad Lo or Pakse) on to Route 23 – the 'Coffee Road'. From here the road climbs up to the lower slopes of the Bolaven Plateau. From Ban Beng, the road is poor as far as Tha Teng, although there are indications that upgrading is in the pipeline. From Tha Teng to Sekong, however, the road is paved and very scenic. The area is still largely forested with a sparse population concentrated along the road and mainly cultivating coffee. Buses and trucks usually stop at the local market centre of Ban Tha Teng.

Towards Sekong the land is more intensively cultivated; there is even some irrigated rice. This is also an area of resettlement with a number of new villages carving out a small area of civilized space in the forest. The large logging yard and saw mill at Ban Phon, about 12 km north of Sekong, demonstrates the local economy's dependence on timber.

→ Colour map 3, B4. Phone code: 038.

Sekong (or Xekong) is a new town and capital of the province of the same name. It is located on the Kong River at the eastern edge of the Bolaven Plateau, about 100 km south of Salavan and a similar distance north of Attapeu, and was created comparatively recently from areas formerly part of Attapeu and Salavan. Much of Sekong's population voluntarily moved from Dakchung, close to the Vietnamese border, in the early 1980s, when the government created the new province and established better facilities. There is a small **tourist office** ① *T038-211361*.

For the moment, anyone travelling between Salavan and Attapeu (but probably not vice versa) must stay overnight here as the first bus from Salavan does not arrive until the last Pakse-bound bus for Attapeu has already departed (see Transport, page 260). As roads improve and journey times drop, however, it may become possible to make this trip without spending a night in Sekong.

Those hoping to chance upon an unknown gem of a town will be disappointed. In theory Sekong ought to be a good base to explore the people and scenery of the Bolaven Plateau but there is simply no tourist infrastructure to make that possible. The only reason to come here, other than out of sheer perversity, is to take a boat down the Xe Kong to the much more attractive town of Attapeu (see Transport, page 260). The market, centred on the bus terminal, has some rather pathetic wild animals, such as giant flying squirrels, for sale – more, in fact, than Salavan which has an infamous reputation in this regard. There is a wat behind the market. A reminder of the war is the number of UXO that still litter the area. The UXO office, near the Ministry of Finance, has set up a little exhibition and welcomes tourists.

Health warning Malaria is quite a serious problem in this area, particularly in the wet season, and precautions should be taken to avoid being bitten. Make sure you also take the correct prophylaxis (see page 34). The area is also littered with UXO, so stick to the well-worn path.

Towards Attapeu

Travelling by road to Attapeu, about 25 km south of Sekong near the Alak village of Ban Mun Hua Mung, the Xe Nam Noi crashes over a series of waterfalls: 100 m east of the bridge is **Tad Houakone**, while signposted 4 km downstream is **Tad Phek**; in between are a number of smaller falls. Those tempted to swim in the falls, should dip in the higher pool as the Pa Pao (a nasty piranha-like blowfish) is rumoured to live in the lower pools. A track leads from one to the other; during the dry season you can walk downriver between the two. A tuk-tuk can be hired for a day to see these sights (US$10-15), but you may be better off trying to hire a motorbike from one of the locals.

The road between Sekong and Attapeu, along the eastern edge of the imposing Bolaven Plateau, has finally been completed. The spectacular 120-m-high **Tad Sekatamtok** tumbles from the Xe Nam Noi about 16 km from the junction (Km 52) with the new road towards Paksong and Pakse. Local sources call this the highest waterfall in the country, although it seems that every province will claim their waterfall is Laos' highest. Unlike its closest counterpart, Tad Fan, this fall comprises one giant surge burgeoning over the cliff-top, certainly securing its ranking as one of the country's most spectacular. Along the road to Attapeu are clearings where new villages have been created for the 'upland' Lao. In a bid to resettle these people, the government provided land, aid and resources for building and a space by the banks of the Xe Kong to grow vegetables and other crops to sell.

Eight kilometres from Attapeu is the village of Ban Ta Hin, where locals glaze earthenware pots with a mixture made from black sticky rice and a type of local hardwood, mai seuak. Archaeologists discovered the same glaze used at Angkor.

Attapeu Province → For listings, see pages 255-260. Colour map 3, C4. Phone code: 036.

Attapeu has an altogether different character from the Bolaven Plateau, as the province is predominantly Lao Loum rather than comprised of ethnic minority groups. Attapeu Province was formerly administered under the Lane Xang Kingdom, King Saysetthathirath moved operations in 1571, later dying in the small town. Attapeu suffered greatly between 1964 and 1975, and evidence of this destruction is clear, particularly in the eastern corner along the Ho Chi Minh Trail, where the land is so cratered that some expats refer to it as 'moon-land'.

There are two National Protected Areas in Attapeu the **Dong Ampham Forest** and the eastern portion of the **Xe Pian** (see page 235), covering almost 250,000 ha in total. The NPAs (National Protected Areas) are home to numerous animal and plant species. You'll see giant logging trucks growling along the southern highway, transporting enormous trees, but visitor access to the sites is very difficult and tourism infrastructure is incredibly poor, rendering them almost impossible for a quick visit.

Ins and outs

Tourist information For information on the province, visit the **tourist office** ① *in Attapeu town in the provincial hall, northwest of the town centre, T036-211056.* It has large-scale relief maps of the area, good for hiking on or around the Bolaven Plateau, and informative brochures on all there is to do in Attapeu. If intending to explore the countryside hereabouts, it is best to ask around for a guide.

Health warning Malaria is quite a serious problem in this Attapeu Province and precautions should be taken to avoid being bitten. Make sure you also take the correct prophylaxis (see page 34).

Attapeu town

Attapeu is an attractive, leafy town positioned on a bend in the Xe Kong, at the confluence of the Xe Kaman. Once referred to as the Golden Land for its gold deposits, Attapeu prides itself on the old provincial saying that "Attapeu people traded gold for chickens, while Salavan sold their own elephants to buy fire". According to ML Manich in his *History of Laos*, Attapeu should really be called Itkapü, which translates as 'buffalo dung', due to a misunderstanding between the original population and incoming Lao Loum people. The French, in their turn, transliterated Itkapü as Attapeu. For a pile of dung the town, however, is remarkably picturesque. For those in the ecotourism sector, Attapeu and its surrounding are heralded as the next up-and-coming place in Laos. For now, though, it is relatively free of the tourist hordes.

Apart from an unremarkable monastery, **Wat Luang**, dating from the 1930s, Attapeu is not over-endowed with obvious sights of interest. However, it is a pleasant place to walk around, with traditional wooden Lao houses with verandas and some French buildings. The people are friendly and traffic is limited. Vegetables are grown on the banks of the Xe

The border between Bo Y (Vietnam) and Yalakhuntum (Laos) on the 18B (113 km from Attapeu) is open daily 0800-1600. Lao 30-day visas are issued at the border; Vietnamese visas are not, and must be obtained in advance. Buses leave Attapeu for Play Ku (Pleiku) in Vietnam daily at 0800-0900 (US$10, 12 hours).

Kong. Attapeu was fought over by the Pathet Lao and RLG, so it is a surprise that the town remains as attractive as it is. It was the only capital that was never taken by the RLG and is consequently far more attached to the early years of the Lao PDR than the rest of the country; the local tourism authorities seem more intent on providing patriotic propaganda than real tourist information. Despite being one of the poorest provinces in Laos, Attapeu is developing fast due to improved infrastructure and the 2006 border opening at Bo Y (see right), which has increased both trade and traffic to and from Vietnam.

Nongfa Lake

The real treasure of Attapeu is Nongfa Lake, which was 'discovered' in 1930. The crystal-clear blue lake shares many of its attributes with the beautiful volcanic lake of Yaek Loam in Cambodia. The shores are surrounded by pristine wilderness and mountains and the lake is considered an auspicious site by the local population. Although no conservationists have officially surveyed the lake, the government has done its own survey. Official tourist brochures proclaim, proudly, that the lake is so large that "a shot of an AK47 rifle from one edge of the lake never reaches the other". Most locals can't pinpoint exactly how to get to the lake, so it's best to organize a tour with the tourism authorities. The lake is within the confines of the Dong Ampham National Protected Area, where the provincial tourism authorities run treks. It can also be reached via 4WD. Although trails exist in the area much of the infrastructure remains undeveloped for tourist visits. It may take several days to find this little gem and the trip must not be undertaken without a well-informed guide.

East of Attapeu

The sleepy town of **Xaisetha** (Saisettha), which stretches along the north bank of the Xe Kaman, lies 12 km east of Attapeu along Route 18. There is regular transport from the east bank of the Xe Kong across from Attapeu. A further 18 km along Route 18, 30 km in all from Attapeu, is the Alak village of **Pa-am**, which sits directly on the Ho Chi Minh Trail. War memorabilia freaks might be interested in the Soviet surface-to-air missile launcher (still apparently live), abandoned there by the Vietnamese. It will cost you 5000 kip for a peek through the fence surrounding it.

West of Attapeu

The Lao Loum village of **Ban Mai** lies 50 km southwest of Attapeu. From Ban Mai it's 6 km to Ban Hinlat and, a further 6 km on, is the **Xe Pha** waterfall, which lies on the Se Pian. The falls are around 23 m high and 120 m wide. And another 9 km on from here, on the same river, are the **Xe Pang Lai** falls, the most stunning in the area.

From Ban Mai it is also possible to access the 20-m-wide **Tad Samongphak** on a one-hour boat ride up the Se Pian. You may need a guide between the falls; ask locally, the tourism office is the best starting point. It should be possible to arrange accommodation in either village.

ⓔ Bolaven Plateau listings

For Sleeping and Eating price codes and other relevant information, see pages 23 -24.

ⓔ Sleeping

Paksong and around *p246*
F Borlavan Guesthouse, Route 23 about 2 km north of the market, beyond Paksong town. The new brick and wood building has a cabin feel and is surrounded by coffee trees, corn fields and a flower garden. The simple rooms are clean and bright (with pink floral sheets) with en suite bathrooms but no hot water. The very friendly owner speaks English.

Waterfalls around Paksong *p246*
B-C Tad Fan Resort, T020-5553 1400, www. tadfane.com. Perched on the opposite side of the ravine from the Tad Fane falls, this resort offers a series of wooden bungalows with nicely decorated rooms and en suite bathrooms, with hot-water showers. The 2nd floor of the excellent open-air restaurant offers a distant view of the falls and serves a wide variety of good Lao, Thai and Western food. Great service. Treks to the top of falls and the Dan-Sin-Xay Plain can be arranged.
E Sihom Sabaidy Guesthouse, T020-5667 6186. This is the only operational guesthouse in the vicinity of these falls. There are 8 basic rooms with shared hot-water bathrooms. There is an adjoining restaurant offering basic Lao meals, noodles, eggs and coffee. The guesthouse is on a coffee plantation and tours are available to the waterfall as well as to nearby orchid-growing areas. You can also see how coffee is produced.

Tha Teng *p247*
E Viphavahn Guesthouse, T034-211970, about 1 km east on Route 16 towards Sekong. This is by far the best option in the village. Offers decent, clean, simply

decorated rooms with hot water, fan and Western-style toilet.

Tad Lo and around *p247*
C Tad Lo Lodge, T034-211889, souriyavincente@yahoo.com. The hotel reception is located on the east side of the falls, with chalet-style accommodation, some built right on top of the waterfalls, on the opposite side. (It's a highly inconvenient hike from one to the other for the restaurant.) The location is attractive during the wet season when the falls are full. The accommodation is comfortable, and cane rocking chairs are provided on the balconies overlooking the cascades on the left bank. Rates include breakfast and hot water. The good restaurant serves plenty of Lao and Thai food.
B-F Saise Guesthouse & Resort (aka Sayse Guesthouse), T034-211886. This resort is scattered right across the falls area with varying prices for the accommodation. It is inconvenient to stay in the far-flung buildings (such as the Green and Blue Houses) if the restaurant (at the foot of Tad Hang) is of prime importance. The resort belongs to the Minister of Tourism and his son. It is beneath contempt, therefore, that a government minister houses in his garden 2 caged gibbons, 2 caged macaques, a caged civet and a caged bird. See page 329 for the law on wild animals.

There are now a number of small inexpensive bungalow guesthouses near the bridge on the east side of the river, including the following options.
F Sipaseuth Guesthouse & Restaurant, right next to the bridge, T020-5430 4380. Wooden bungalows right on the riverbank are slightly run down but have fans and en suite bathrooms. Also have concrete rooms set back from the river. Also a restaurant serving decent Lao food. Trekking organized; private transport arranged.

F-G Tim Guesthouse & Restaurant, down the bridge road, T034-211885, soulidet@gmail.com, www.geocities.com/tadlo_net. 5 bungalows and 7 twin and double rooms with shared hot water bathrooms, fans and lock boxes. There is also internet access (500 kip per min with all proceeds going to the local school), international calls, laundry, book exchange, and a substantial music collection. The owner runs a good range of services, including motorbike hire, 80,000 kip per day.

Salavan *p248*

E-F Silsamay 2 Guesthouse, just down the road from **Shai Kham**, T020-55548054. This is a well-run guesthouse offering bright, clean, well-furnished rooms with a/c or just a fan. Bathrooms have hot water and Western toilets. Recommended.

E-G Chindavong, T034-211065. There are 2 types of room on offer here. The cheaper rooms are basic, with fan but no en suite bathroom, the more expensive ones will be beautifully decorated, bamboo-clad, homely twin or double, with a/c, en suite bathroom, writing table, television, and 'chill out' area. Restaurant attached (no menu!). Recommended.

E-G Thiphaphone, T034-211063. Next to the **Chindavong** on the market side. Clean (but somewhat musty) basic rooms with wooden walls and decent mattresses on the beds. Some rooms have a/c, TV and hot water, others only have fans. Spotless bathrooms, some en suite, some communal.

F Saise Hotel, 2.5 km from the bus station on the other side of town near the river (get there by tuk-tuk), T034-211054. This is an attractive guesthouse set in a large garden compound. The newer building has bright a/c rooms of a good standard with hot water; rooms in the older building are large but rather dank with fans and large 'bathrooms' (tank of water and dipper, squat toilet). The management speak English and French and are a useful source of information on the area.

F-G Miss Asam, next to the **Thiphaphone**, T034-211062. This is a tiny little place, with very basic rooms. Not in the least bit customer focused.

There are a couple of other guesthouses on the road to Pakse, about 1 km from the bus station.

Around Salavan *p251*

B-C Utayan Bajiang Champasak, T031-251294. This resort, beside the lovely Paseum waterfall, consists of ethnic-styled bungalows, a treehouse and various other types of accommodation. There's also a restaurant by the water's edge. The resort caters mainly to Thai package tourists and as a result there isn't much transport to get there. You will need to travel independently or organize transport through a Pakse tour operator such as **Sabaidy 2**. There's a fee to enter the compound.

Sekong *p252*

E-F Koky Guesthouse, just off the main road towards the post office, T031-211401. A little house with rooms for rent. Service is very friendly but no English is spoken. Rooms have a/c and TV.

E-F Sackda, between the market and the water tower, T031-211086. Clean and very blue: blue sheets, blue walls, blue curtains, resulting in an overall blue glow. Basic rooms with a/c or a fan. Attached bathrooms have a shower and squat toilet.

E-G Sekong Souksamlane Hotel (aka Sekong Hotel), a block back from the post office, T031-211030, pholsena@laotel.com. Old, but apparently popular with the few local *falangs*, partly due to the attached restaurant, which will cook whatever you want, as long as the food is available at the local market (or just order from the English menu). 16 rooms, with a/c or fan, some with en suite bathrooms, cold shower, very functional and rather worn and dusty but OK for an overnight stop. Also 1 dorm room with 4 beds. The best rooms are upstairs; they have a balcony and get the mountain breeze. One of the rooms is reputedly haunted by some Malaysian UN officials who were drowned while taking a boat downriver to Attapeu. It is said that hey left their bags in their room and come back every so often to retrieve them.

F-G Woman Fever Kosment Center Guesthouse, the block behind the post office, T031-211046. It looks more like a government office or a school than a guesthouse, with cement foundations and a wooden 2nd storey. The large, basic rooms are cheap and have a fan; and the shared bathroom has a *mundi* and squat toilet.

Attapeu *p253*
D-G ATP Palace (formerly the **Hotel Yingchokchay**), T031-212204. Renamed by the current owners, and a favourite with visiting government officials and businessmen, this enormous and slightly decaying building offers a range of good rooms, from ones with fan to suites. The rooms are plain, large and simple, with sweet dream-inducing mattresses and great en suite bathrooms. Breakfast is included in the price. Internet access is also available – when it's working.

F Aloon Sot Sai Guesthouse, 2 doors down from the **Soksomphone**, T031-211250. Small somewhat dingy rooms with fan, TV and en suite bathrooms. Rents motorbikes for US$10 per day.

F Soksomphone Guesthouse, T031-211046. 16 small but well-furnished and airy rooms, some with en suites, some with TVs, others with enormous beds and clean shared bathrooms (*mundi* and squat toilet). Owners are slack but speak some English and French. Tours can be arranged to the surrounding area (but shop around first). Bicycles for hire.

Eating

Paksong and around *p246*
There is a small string of barbecue restaurants, past the market away from

Route 23. The market also has a large restaurant section and there's a row of Vietnamese restaurants along Route 23 near the bank.

♥ **Borravan Plateau**, Route 23 about 1 km from the market towards Tha Teng. Standard selection of Lao dishes in an indoor setting, safe from the weather. The owner is very friendly. Unfortunately there is no menu and no English spoken – so opt for something easy like *feu* or *laap*.

Cafés
Travellers Meeting Point Café, south of Route 23. Coffee tasting, good local advice.

Tad Lo *p247*
There are also a number of small Lao joints along the main road.

♥ **Jom**, friendly with a good range of dishes.
♥ **Tad Lo Lodge**, see Sleeping. A better albeit pricier option serving a variety of Thai Lao and Western dishes.
♥ **Tim Guesthouse**, see Sleeping. This is a popular choice among foreigners. Serves good hearty breakfasts and some generic Western dishes.

Salavan *p248*
Most restaurants in Salavan serve much the same range of dishes. Along the road to Pakse near the handicraft centre are a number of barbecue joints offering whatever parts of a pig can be found, including just the fat. Between the handicraft centre and the market is the **Ladda Café**, a small shop set beneath a few large trees serving ice cream, etc. By the market towards the road to Pakse are a number of restaurants offering Korean grilled meat, the Lao buffet, *khao piak* and *feu*, among other things. The road into town makes a 90° turn to the left; just beyond is a small road on the right heading towards the Xe Don and Sekong. There are a few decent little restaurants here. The 2nd of the 3 is the best, and will make whatever you ask for, if they can understand your Lao.

Vilayvone, on the airstrip side of the market. The only place in town with a written menu – and it's in English. Offers MSG-laden Lao standards; the French fries are Salavan's attempt at Western food.

Sekong *p252*

All of the restaurants close relatively early, so last orders are no later than 2100. There are noodle shops in and around the market.
Khamting Restaurant, next to Phathip. Popular with the locals, but no *falang* options and no English menu.
Phathip Restaurant, opposite the Sekong Hotel. Owned by Nang Tu, a Vietnamese woman with considerable culinary expertise. The huge platters are a treat, especially the Vietnamese options. An amazing range of dishes on offer considering the location. The front of the menu boasts all sorts of information about the area, including dire warnings about both the contamination of Sekong Province with the residue from the Vietnam War, and 'the odd grumpy *falangs* that for one reason or the other seem to be more or less resident in this forgotten corner of Southeast Asia'.
Somview Restaurant, on the other side of the Phathip. Typical Lao food.
Souksamlane Restaurant, attached to Sekong Hotel. Traditional Lao dishes, with some European options also available. Tribal artefacts adorn the walls and are for sale. Not always open.

Attapeu *p253*

Attapeu is a small town and finding an open restaurant after 2100 can be difficult. Most places serve the local breakfast speciality *feu* 0700-0800. Just up from **Souksomphone Guesthouse**, towards the wat, are a few places selling good Lao food in pots. There are also noodle shops in the same area and by the boat jetty on the south side of town.
Sekong River Restaurant, superb location down by the river. The speciality is goat, but fish and other dishes are also available. It's also a good spot for a drink.

Thi Thi Restaurant, between Wat Luang Muang Mai and the bridge, T031-211054. Vietnamese food, with lots of seafood, eel and tortoise, cooked in a variety of ways; sometimes it's best not to ask!

Entertainment

Salavan *p248*

Salavan lacks any sort of discos, clubs or bars but most restaurants serve **Beer Lao**. Apart from these, the closest thing it has to night-time entertainment is the **beer garden** on the road to Pakse across from the Shai Kham and Silsamay Guesthouses. It's popular with locals from about 1600 onwards, but beware that your drink order isn't doubled and come complete with someone to drink it for you.

Festivals and events

Tad Lo *p247*

Buffalo ceremony This Tahoy ceremony takes place in a village near Tad Lo on the first full moon in **Mar. It** is dedicated to the warrior spirit, who is asked for protection. Unfortunately it has become commercialized in recent years.

Shopping

Salavan *p248*

The **handicraft centre** near the market has a selection of locally made textiles, baskets and other products. The shop selling electrical goods also has some allegedly tribal artefacts (probably overpriced and being passed off as antiques). Basketry and traditional textiles can be found in and around the **market**.

Sekong *p252*

Sekong Ethnic Store, a block back from the Sekong Souksamlane Hotel, sells woven basket 'backpacks' and other locally produced items, including Alak and Katu woven textiles.

▲ Activities and tours

To organize **kayaking** and **rafting** trips to the Bolaven Plateau, contact **Green Discovery**, in Pakse, see page 240.

Tad Lo *p247*
Elephant trekking
This is an excellent way to see the area as elephants can go where jeeps cannot. It is also a thrill being on the back of an elephant. The **Tad Lo lodge** organizes treks at 0800, 1000, 1300 and 1500, 85,000 kip per person (2 people per elephant).

Attapeu *p253*
Attapeu Provincial Tourism Office, northwest edge of town, has guides, brochures and maps.
Attapeu Tours & Travel Co Ltd, ATP Palace Hotel, T031-211204, offers trekking, ticketing and car rental service. Aimed at the Viet/Thai tourist crowds.

⊖ Transport

Paksong and around *p246*
Bus
Regular connections to **Pakse**'s southern bus terminal 0830-1530, 1½ hrs, 20,000 kip. For onward journey to **Tad Fan** ask the *songthaew* to stop at Km 38 and follow signs. Also buses to **Attapeu**, daily 0830 and 1200, 3½-4½ hrs.

Tha Teng *p247*
Bus/songthaew
All transport departs from the market. To **Salavan**, 0730 and 0830 daily, 1½ hrs, 10,000 kip; to **Sekong**, 0730, 1 hr, 10,000 kip; to **Pakse**, 0530, 0630, 0730 and 0830 daily, at least 2 hrs (87 km), 20,000 kip. Due to its location many unscheduled buses pass through Tha Teng, running between Pakse, Salavan and Sekong, or Salavan, Paksong and Attapeu. *Songthaew* leave intermittently (mostly in the morning) for various destinations in the vicinity.

Tad Lo *p247*
Bus
There are buses from Ban Houei Set (1.8 km north of Tad Lo) to **Pakse**, hourly 0730-1130 then 1300 and 1400, 20,000 kip; also to **Salavan** (from either Pakse or Lao Ngam), every hr daily 0730-1600, 40 mins. You may also be able to catch the daily service to **Vientiane** on its way north, daily 1600 but you will need to book.

Salavan *p248*
Bus/truck
The bus terminal is 2 km west of the town centre; a tuk-tuk either way costs about 10,000-15,000 kip. Salavan is by no means a tourist hub, which means the reliability of buses is dicey at best; scheduled connection times are as follows: to **Pakse**, 0630, 0730, 0830, 1000, 1215 and 1330 daily, 116 km, 3 hrs, 20,000 kip; to **Sekong**, 0730 and 1300 daily, 98 km, 4 hrs, 18,000 kip; to **Khong Xedon**, 1030 daily, 76 km, 3½ hrs, 17,000 kip, but most Savannakhet-bound buses will pass through as well; to **Lao Ngam** (via **Tad Lo**), 0600, 0815, 0945 and 1200 daily, 1 hr, 10,000 kip; to **Ta Oy**, 1100 daily but departure time varies wildly depending on the season, 84 km, 6 hrs, 28,000 kip; to **Savannakhet**, 0630 daily, 40,000 kip; to **Tha Teng**, 1000 daily, 10,000 kip; to **Vientiane**, 0830 daily, 85,000 kip. There are no buses further north than **Toum Lan**, 1430 daily, 15,000 kip.

Trickier destinations to get to from Salavan include **Attapeu** (you have first to go by bus to Sekong, then find a bus to Attapeu) and **Lao Bao** (the best way to get here is via Savannakhet and then along Route 9).

Sekong *p252*
Boat
Locals do not advise taking a boat along the Xe Kong river from Sekong to Attapeu. The river is dangerous and narrow in parts and the boats are not built for tourist transport. People have died on this stretch.

Bus/truck

The bus station is 2.5 km out of town (tuk-tuk 5000 kip); some also stop on the highway near the hospital. To **Salavan**, 0600 and 1330 daily, 98 km, 3-4 hrs, 20,000 kip; to **Pakse** (via **Paksong**), 0530 and 0600 daily, 4-6 hrs, 25,000 kip. The lone bus to **Attapeu** leaves at 0800 daily, 2-3 hrs, 15,000 kip. This schedule is not set in concrete as buses are passing through.

Attapeu p253
Bicycle

Bikes can be hired from the **Souksomphone Guesthouse** for 20,000 kip.

Boat

An alternative way to get to **Ban Mai** is to charter a boat to Xe Nam Sai and pick up a connection from there.

It is possible to travel upriver from Attapeu to **Sekong**, but it would take much longer than downriver and be quite expensive.

Bus/truck

The main bus station is at the market 3 km northwest of town. It is chaotic and inefficient. Although there are daily connections with the main tourist hubs, departure times are a source of great argument and debate. Prices are more definite. A rough departure schedule follows, but you should check all onward connections on your arrival. To **Pa-am**, 30 km, 12,000 kip (or charter a tuk-tuk, US$15 return); to **Pakse**, from the market, 4 times daily, in the morning, 5-6 hrs, 35,000 kip; to **Sekong**, 1430 daily, 2-3 hrs, 20,000 kip (or you can take the Pakse or Savannakhet bus); to **Vientiane**, 0800 and 1100 daily,

20-24 hrs, 110,000 kip (take warm clothes as it can be chilly and uncomfortable); to **Savannakhet**, 0600 daily, 10-12 hrs, 65,000 kip. To get to **Salavan** you will have to transfer at Tha Teng. There are buses to **Ban Mai**, 0800, 1200 and 1400 daily, 1 hr (returning at 1600) but it is better to rent a tuk-tuk for around US$15 per day.

ⓘ Directory

Salavan p248
Banks Lao Development Bank, near the market, will exchange cash (US$ and Thai baht and TCs, open Mon-Fri. The shop selling electrical goods will also change money.
Post and telephone The post office is in a modern yellow building opposite the market; local calls only from the telephone exchange in the same building. For international calls, go to the **Telecoms** centre, Mon-Sat.

Sekong p252
Banks Lao Development Bank will exchange US$ and Thai baht. **Post and telephone** Post office is in a yellow building not far from the Victory *That*; the **telecommunications centre** is next door, international calls possible.

Attapeu p246
Banks Lao Development Bank, Mon-Fri 0830-1630, reputed to change US$ and Thai baht only, despite what it says. Money changers can be found around the market area; try in the the gold/jewellery shops.
Post and telephone Post office, in town centre, Mon-Fri 0800-1200 and 1300-1600. The **telephone office** is next door, Mon-Sat 0700-1700, international calls.

Islands of the south

→ Phone code: 031. Colour map 3, C2/3.

This area, locally known as Siphandon, 'The 4000 Islands', is an idyllic picture-perfect ending to any trip to Laos. The three main islands offer something for all tourists: the larger Don Khong is great for exploring, take in the stunning vista and the traditional Lao rural life; Don Deth is a backpacker haven and is good if you want to while away the days with a good book in a hammock; and Don Khone is better for those wanting to take in tourist sites such as the Li Phi falls or old colonial ruins. These are just three of the many islands littered across the Mekong right at the southern tip of Laos near the border with Cambodia. Half of the islands are submerged when the Mekong is in flood. Just before the river enters Cambodia it divides into countless channels. The distance between the most westerly and easterly streams is 14 km – the greatest width of the river in its whole 4200-km course. The river's volume is swelled by the Kong, San Srepok and Krieng tributaries, which join just upstream from here. Pakha, or freshwater dolphins, can sometimes be spotted in this area between December and May, when they come upsteam to give birth to their young but they are increasingly endangered. ⏭ *For listings, see pages 269 -276.*

Route 13 to Ban Hat Xai Khoune

The bus journey south from Pakse to Ban Hat Xai Khoune on Route 13 is 120 km and is now surfaced. The trip is worthwhile for the contrast it offers to conditions in northeastern Thailand, just 20 km or so west. Much of the area is still forested (large quantities of Lao timber are trucked to Thailand via Chongmek, west of Pakse; see page 228) and villages are intermittent even on this road, the national artery for north-south communications. Paddy fields sometimes appear to be fighting a losing battle against the encroaching forest and most houses are roofed in thatch rather than zinc. At **Ban Hat Xai Khoune** boats wait to transport passengers across the Mekong to Don Khong and Muang Khong (see below). Further along, at Ban Nakasang, boats shuffle tourists to Don Deth and Don Khone.

Don Khong → *For listings, see pages 269 -276.*

Don Khong is the largest of the Mekong islands at 16 km long and 8 km wide. It's a tremendous place to relax or explore by bicycle. Visitors might be surprised by the smooth asphalt roads, electricity and general standard of amenities that exist on the island but two words explain it all – Khamtai Siphandone – Laos' former president, who has a residence on the island. The island was electrified about five years before the surrounding mainland areas and it is not unusual to see heavily armed personnel cruising around the place. The former president spends much of his time on the island, in his modest quarters near Ban Houa Khong, and ferries back and forth between Vientiane and the island in his private helicopter. According to locals, he has plans to establish some kind of resort on the island.

Ins and outs

Getting there The easiest way to get to all three major Siphandon islands from Pakse is by private minivan, 60,000 kip arranged by **Pakse Travel** and other operators in Pakse. The most luxurious way to get there is aboard the *Vat Phou* (www.vatphou.com), a beautiful boutique river-borne hotel that does a three-day/two-night cruise from Pakse to Champasak and Wat Phou to Don Khong and then back to Pakse.

Songthaew depart Pakse's Southern bus terminal hourly between 0800 and 1200. The occasional bus will also ply the route but *songthaew* are the most common transport option. The journey to Ban Hat Xai Khoune (to catch a boat to Don Khong) should take between four and five hours; in most cases the bus/truck will board the **car ferry** at Ban Hat (1 km south of Ban Hat Xai Khoune) and take you right across to Ban Naa on Don Khong (1 km south of Muang Khong). If your transport doesn't cross, it's 10,000 kip per passenger. Passenger boats run 24 hours but after 1800 the crossing costs 15,000 kip. There are also **motorboats** from Ban Hat Xai Khoune to Muang Khong (20,000 kip). Motorbikes on the car ferry from Ban Hat are charged 5,000 kip. If there is not a bus directly to Don Khong, catch a bus bound for Ban Nakasang (the stop-off for Don Deth and Don Khon) and jump off at Ban Hat Xai Khoune. ➥ *See Transport, page 275.*

Getting around All of the guesthouses can arrange bicycle hire. Some places hire motorbikes too.

Muang Khong

Don Khong's 'capital' is Muang Khong, a small former French settlement. 'Muang' means city but, although Muang Khong is the district's main settlement, it feels more like a village than a town, with only a few thousand inhabitants. Pigs and chickens scrabble for food under the houses and just 50 m inland the houses give way to paddy fields.

There are two wats in the town. **Wat Kan Khong**, also known as Wat Phuang Kaew, is visible from the jetty: a large gold Buddha in the *mudra* of subduing Mara garishly overlooks the Mekong. Much more attractive is **Wat Chom Thong** at the upstream extremity of the village, which may date from the early 19th century but which was much extended during the colonial period. The unusual Khmer-influenced *sim* may be gently decaying but it is doing so with style, and the wat compound, with its carefully tended plants and elegant buildings, is a peaceful and relaxing place. The *naga* heads on the roof of the main *sim* are craftily designed to channel water, which issues from their mouths. The old *sim* to the left of the main entrance is also notable, although it is usually kept locked because of its poor condition.

For early risers the **morning market** in Muang Khong is also worthwhile – if only to see the fish before they are sold to the restaurants here and consigned to the cooking pot. Note that the market only really operates between 0530 and 0730. If you are getting up for the market, it is worth setting the alarm clock even earlier to get onto the banks of the Mekong before 0600, when the sun rises over the hills to the east, picking out the silhouettes of fishermen in their canoes.

Exploring the island

Most people come to Muang Khong as a base for visiting the **Li Phi** and **Khong Phapheng Falls** (see page 268) in the far south of Laos. However, these trips, alongside dolphin-watching trips are much easier to arrange from Don Deth or Don Khone. But the island is a destination in itself, and offers a great insight into Lao rural life without all the hustle and bustle found in more built-up areas. To a certain extent, save electricity, a sprinkling of cars and a couple of internet terminals, time stands still in Dong Khong.

The island is worth exploring by bicycle and deserves more time than most visitors give it. The coastal area is flat (though the interior is hilly) and the roads are quiet, so there is less risk of being mown down by a timber truck than is generally the case, and the villages and countryside offer a glimpse of traditional Laos. Most people take the southern 'loop' around the island, via **Ban Muang Saen Nua**, a distance of about 25 km (two to three hours by bike). The villages south of Ban Muang Saen Nua are wonderfully picturesque with buffalos grazing in the field and farmers tending to their rice crops. Unlike in other parts of Laos the residents here are fiercely protective of their forests and illegal logging incurs very severe penalties.

About 6 km north of Ban Muang Saen Nua is a hilltop wat which is arguably Don Khong's main claim to national fame. **Wat Phou Khao Kaew** (Glass Hill Monastery) is built

Mekong islands

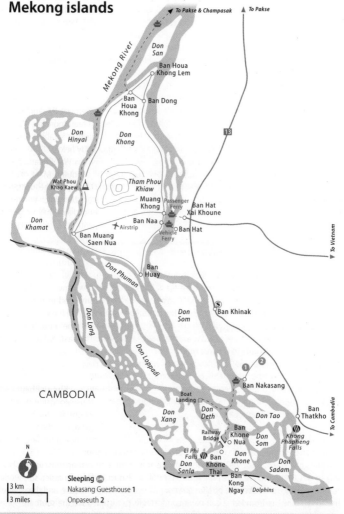

Sleeping 💤
Nakasang Guesthouse **1**
Onpaseuth **2**

on the spot where an entrance leads down to the underground lair of the *nagas*, known as **Muang Nak**. This underground town lies beneath the waters of the Mekong, with several tunnels leading to the surface – another is at That Luang in Vientiane. Lao legend has it that the *nagas* will come to the surface to protect the Lao whenever the country is in danger. (This means, to most Lao, whenever the Thais decide to attack.) Some people believe that the Thais tricked the Lao to build *thats* over the holes to prevent the *nagas* coming to their rescue – the hole at Wat Phou Khao Kaew is covered.

Tham Phou Khiaw is tucked away among the forests of the **Green Mountain** in the centre of the island. It's a small cave, containing earthenware pots. Buddha images and other relics and offerings litter the site. Every Lao New Year (April) townsfolk climb up to the cave to bathe the images. Although it's only 15 minutes' walk from the road, finding the cave is not particularly straightforward except during Lao New Year when it is possible to follow the crowds. Head 1.5 km north from Muang Khong on the road until you come to a banana plantation, with a couple of wooden houses. Take the pathway just before the houses through the banana plantation and at the top, just to the left, is a small gateway through the fence and a fairly well-defined path. Head up and along this path and, after 300 m or so, there is a rocky clearing. The path continues from the top right corner of the clearing for a further 200 m to a rocky mound that rolls up and to the left. Walk across the mound for about 20 m, until it levels out, and then head back to the forest. Keeping the rock immediately to your right, continue round and after 40 m there are two upturned tree trunks marking the entrance to the cave.

On the northern tip of the island is a sandy beach, though swimming is generally not advised due to parasites in the water and potentially strong currents. Word on the ground is that Lao's former President Siphandone is building a resort here. In nearby **Ban Houa Khong**, approximately 13 km north of Muang Khong, is the former President's modest abode set in traditional Lao style.

Don Deth, Don Khone and around → *For listings, see pages 269-276.*

The islands of Don Khone and Don Deth are the pot of gold at the end of the rainbow for most travellers who head to the southern tip of Laos, and it's not hard to see why. After the relative fever and bustle of Pakse, the transport headaches around the Bolaven Plateau and the architectural wonder of Wat Phou, the bamboo huts that stretch along the banks of these two staggeringly beautiful islands are filled with contented travellers in no rush to move on. Don Deth is more of a backpacker haven, not dissimilar to Vang Vieng, while Don Khone has been able to retain a more authentically Lao charm. Travelling by boat in this area is very picturesque: the islands are covered in coconut palms, flame trees, stands of bamboo, kapok trees and hardwoods; the river is riddled with eddies and rapids and it demands a skilled helmsman to negotiate them. In the distance, a few kilometres to the south, are the Khong Hai Mountains, which dominate the skyline and delineate the frontier between Laos and Cambodia.

Ins and outs
Getting there A number of companies run tours to this area, especially from Pakse (see Activities and tours, page 240). Private minivans from Pakse, 60,000 kip, are the quickest way to get there and are worth the few extra dollars. To get to Don Deth or Don Khone independently from Pakse the bus/*songthaew* will need to drop you off at Ban Nakasang. The *songthaew* trip from Pakse can be uncomfortable, particularly if it's raining; aim for a

seat away from the sides of the vehicle if possible. From the road junction, it's not a long haul – perhaps 500 m – but it can be uncomfortable if you're laden with luggage. The 'ticket office' for boats to the islands is located in a little restaurant to the right-hand side of the dock. (You could also ask anyone that's going across to the islands for a lift, at a dramatically reduced rate.) The boats take about 15 to 20 minutes to make the easy trip to the islands and cost around 20,000 kip per person. Prices will be higher if you are travelling on your own.

Getting around A boat between Don Deth and Don Khone costs 30,000 kip; alternatively you can walk between the two islands, paying the 10,000 kip charge to cross the bridge (also used as ticket to see Li Phi Falls). Both islands can easily be navigated by foot or bicycles can be rented from guesthouses for 10,000 kip per day. ▶ *See Transport, page 275.*

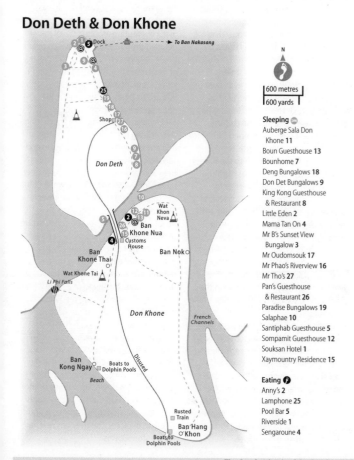

Don Deth & Don Khone

To Ban Nakasang

Don Deth

Don Khone

Wat Khon Neva

Ban Khone Nua

Ban Khone Thai

Wat Khone Tai

Li Phi Falls

Customs House

Ban Nok

French Channels

Diverted

Ban Kong Ngay

Boats to Dolphin Pools

Beach

Rusted Train

Ban Hang Khon

Boats to Dolphin Pools

Shop

N

600 metres
600 yards

Sleeping
Auberge Sala Don Khone **11**
Boun Guesthouse **13**
Bounhome **7**
Deng Bungalows **18**
Don Det Bungalows **9**
King Kong Guesthouse & Restaurant **8**
Little Eden **2**
Mama Tan On **4**
Mr B's Sunset View Bungalow **3**
Mr Oudomsouk **17**
Mr Phao's Riverview **16**
Mr Tho's **27**
Pan's Guesthouse & Restaurant **26**
Paradise Bungalows **19**
Salaphae **10**
Santiphab Guesthouse **5**
Sompamit Guesthouse **12**
Souksan Hotel **1**
Xaymountry Residence **15**

Eating
Anny's **2**
Lamphone **25**
Pool Bar **5**
Riverside **1**
Sengaroune **4**

The Mekong: mother river of Southeast Asia

The Mekong River forms the heart and soul of mainland Southeast Asia, a sinuous thread that binds Vietnam, Cambodia and Laos geographically, historically, culturally and economically.

Its source in eastern Tibet was only pinpointed in 1995. From here the giant river plies 4500 km through six countries, cutting through almost the entire length of Laos, dissecting Cambodia, and plunging into Vietnam's Mekong Delta before emptying into the South China Sea. The river is the 12th longest river in the world and is the 10th largest by volume of water dispersed into the ocean.

French explorer Francis Garnier commented that: "no other river, over such a length, has a more singular or remarkable character". The Mekong has indeed woven itself into the cultural fabric of the region and shaped its history, from the ancient Funan settlement in the Mekong Delta, through to the Khmer Empire, which established its capital at Angkor and relied on the river for transport and agriculture. After several expeditions the French, in the mid-19th century, developed grandiose plans to transform the Mekong into a river highway from China. (The plans were thwarted upon discovering that the Mekong could not be traversed.) The river later played an integral role in the Vietnam War for the transportation of Viet Cong supplies.

The river has been a major purveyor of culture, ushering in various religions, arts and customs and folklore, including colourful boat races and annual water festivals, which celebrate the Mekong and its importance to agriculture. Nor is the river free from superstition or strange phenomena. In Laos thousands of people gather each year to witness *naga* fireballs rising from the river's surface.

Today, the Mekong is instrumental in the region's future prosperity, with more than 60 million people in Southeast Asia dependent on the river and its tributaries for their economic and physical survival. Agriculture, particularly the farming of rice, relies on the river's annual flood-drought cycle. During the monsoon, the river swells to around 30 times its original size, depositing rich fertilizing sediments along the floodplains and riverbanks.

Fish are an important part of the Lao diet, constituting around 80% of many people's protein requirement. The river is home to between 770 and 1300 species of freshwater fish, including the world's largest, a giant 300 kg catfish (the size of a grizzly bear). It also shelters the endangered Irrawaddy dolphin.

However, it is unclear how much longer the Mekong can be relied on to support millions of Vietnamese, Cambodian and Lao people. In the last decade, more than 100 large dam proposals have been tabled for the Mekong Basin, while China, the source of up to 45% of the lower Mekong's water, has embarked on a massive programme for the construction of eight new dams. Two of these have been completed and are already having a detrimental effect, altering the river's natural ebb and flow. Lao also has major dams planned including one mainstream one in the Siphandon region. Whether it goes ahead or not is undecided as opposition to the project is massive. Chainarong Setthachua, director of South East Asia Rivers Network has said that: "Not only is the water the lowest in its history, it is also fluctuating; sometimes up, sometimes down. This comes from dam operations in China." The Mekong River Commission (MRC) agrees, pointing out that, in places, the river has reached rock-bottom levels.

Tourist information The Provincial Tourism Office and Eco Guide Unit in Pakse is responsible for the islands, see page 228. While on the islands, you will need to ask your guesthouse owner or one of the travel operators.

Background

For those who have travelled on the lazy upper reaches of the Mekong, huge roaring waterfalls might seem rather out of character. But here, near the Cambodian border, the geology changes and the river is punctuated by rapids and the Khone Falls. The name Khone is used loosely and there are in fact two impressive cascades in the area: the Li Phi (or Somphamit) Falls and Khong Phapheng Falls – the latter are the largest in Southeast Asia and reputedly the widest in the world. Francis Garnier was impressed when he ascended the Khone cataract in 1860, his boatmen hauling their vessels "through a labyrinth of rocks, submerged trees, and prostrate trunks still clinging to earth by their many roots".

The French envisaged Don Deth and Don Khone as strategic transit points in their grandiose masterplan to create a major Mekong highway from China. In the late 19th century, ports were built at the southern end of Don Khone and at the northern end of Don Deth and a narrow-gauge railway line was constructed across Don Khone in 1897 as an important bypass around the rapids for French cargo boats sailing upriver from Phnom Penh. In 1920, the French built a bridge across to Don Deth and extended the railway line to Don Deth port. This 5-km stretch of railway has the unique distinction of being the only line the French ever built in Laos. Although the lucrative Chinese supply line was never properly realized, the route remained operational until 1940.

A colonial-style customs house still stands in the shadow of the impressive railway bridge on Don Khone. On the southern side of the island lie the rusted corpses of the old locomotive and boiler car. Before pulling into Ban Khone Nua, the main settlement on Don Khone, Don Deth's original 'port' is on the right, with what remains of its steel rail jetty.

Ban Nakasang

Ban Nakasang, the jumping-off point for Don Khone and Don Deth, is not the most pleasant of Lao towns and several travellers have complained about being ripped off here. However, it has a thriving market, where most of the islanders stock up on their goods, so it's worth having a look around before you head off to the islands, particularly if you need to pick up necessities like torches or batteries.

Don Deth

This island has really woken up to tourism in the last couple of years and the riverbank is peppered with cheap-as-chips bamboo huts and restaurants geared to accommodate the growing wave of backpacker travellers that floods south to stop and recoup in this idyllic setting. A good book, hammock and icy beverage are the orders of the day here, but those with a bit more energy should explore the truly stunning surroundings. It's a great location for watching the sunrises and sunsets, for walking through shady palms and frangipani trees and for swimming off the beaches, which attract the hordes in the dry season. Away from the picturesque waterfront, the centre of the island comprises rice paddies and farms; you should take care not to harm crops when exploring the island.

The national tourism authorities have been coordinating with locals to ensure that the beautiful island doesn't become 'Vang Vieng-ified', so you'll find no *Friends* DVDs here, although 'Happy' shakes have started to appear. The islands got 24-hour electricity in November 2009 although not everyone has signed up to the 24-hour connection, there are no cars (except for the odd truck and tourist open-sided buses) and few other modern conveniences. Internet has amazingly made its way to the island, however, and it's still possible to get mobile phone coverage. Most guesthouses run tours to the falls/dolphins. It costs a minimum of 60,000 kip to charter a boat to see the dolphins from Don Khone (a bit more from Don Deth). The dwindling population of dolphins appears between December and May. If you do take a boat out make sure you keep your distance from them. A few entrepreneurial types are starting to promote adventure tourism here. Kayaking and rafting trips can be organized through **Xplore-asia** (near the main port), T031-212893. Several guesthouses also have tubes for rent. The river's current here is probably the strongest in all of Laos, so it is definitely inadvisable to go tubing in the wet season and probably not a good idea at any other time. It is also inadvisable to go by yourself; there are a huge set of falls at the bottom of Laos. Swimming, visiting the falls and other activities all need to be undertaken with the utmost caution as several tourists have drowned here.

Don Khone and Li Phi Falls

From the railway bridge, follow the southwest path through **Ban Khone Thai** and then wind through the paddy fields for 1.7 km (20 minutes' walk) to **Li Phi Falls** ⓘ *aka Somphamit or Khone Yai falls, 10,000 kip entry fee, paid at the bridge*. These are a succession of raging rapids, crashing through a narrow rocky gorge. In the wet season, when the rice is green, the area is beautiful; in the dry season, it is scorching. From the main vantage point on a jagged, rocky outcrop, the falls aren't that impressive, as a large stretch of them are obscured. 'Phi' means ghost, a reference, it is believed, to the bodies that floated down the river from the north during the war.

It's best to visit Li Phi around June or July, when all the fishermen are putting out their bamboo fish traps. Every year Cambodia's Tonlé Sap lake reverses its flow sending millions of fish up the Mekong into Laos. During this time, each fish trap can catch 1000-2000 kg of fish in a day. In theory, enough fish are caught in these two short months to feed half the population of Laos, although most of the catch is exported to Thailand.

Dolphin spotting

The Mekong, south of Don Khone, is one of the few places in the world where it is possible to see freshwater dolphins. They can be spotted from December to May, from the French pier at the end of the island, not far from the village of **Ban Hang Khon**. The walk across Don Khone from the railway bridge is some 4 km and bicycles can be hired. (A much better bicycle route is to head north round the tip and down to Hang Khon, 45 minutes; the disused railway bridge is not a comfortable ride for bikes as it's rocky.) However the dolphins reside in deep-water pools and catching a glimpse of them is more likely if you're in a boat (from **Ban Kong Ngay** or **Ban Hang Khon**; see Activities and tours, page 274). There are thought to be 80-120 dolphins in the lower Mekong area according to the WWF. The Lao-Cambodian border crosses the dolphin pool and the Lao boatmen have to pay US$1 to the Cambodian authorities in order to access the waters in which the dolphins reside; they will ask you on the boat if you want to do this and then you need to pull over at the Cambodia border post to pay the fee. Cambodia gets a bit tetchy about these 'border incursions' and may, on the odd occasion, deny access.

Khong Phapheng Falls

ⓘ *Ban Thatko, 10,000 kip entry fee for foreigners; there are a number of food and drinks stalls. Guesthouses on Don Deth and Don Khone organize trips to the falls for around 60,000 kip* per person (min 4 passengers) and will usually be booked in conjunction with a trip to see the dolphins (this will cost extra). Boats can no longer go direct to the falls, so most tours will include a tuk-tuk ride from Ban Nakasang. There's no public transport to the falls but a motorbike taxi will cost 30,000 kip.

About 36 km south of Ban Hat Xai Khoune at Ban Thatko, a road branches off Route 13 towards Khong Phapheng Falls, which roar around the eastern shore of the Mekong for 13 km. One fork of the road leads to a vantage point, where a large wooden structure on stilts has a fantastic head-on view of the falls. When you see the huge volume of white water boiling and surging over the jagged rocks below, it is hard to imagine that there is another 10 km width of river running through the other channels. A perilous path leads down from the viewpoint to the edge of the water. Be careful here. Unsurprisingly, the river is impassable at this juncture, as an 1860s French expedition led by adventurers Doudart de Lagrée and Francis Garnier discovered. Another road leads down to the bank of the Mekong, 200 m away, just above the lip of the falls; at this deceptively tranquil spot, the river is gathering momentum before it plunges over the edge. It was said that a tongue of rock once extended from the lip of the falls, and the noise of Khong Phapheng – literally 'the voice of the Mekong' – crashing over this outcrop could be heard many miles away. The rock apparently broke off during a flood surge but the cascades still make enough noise to justify their name.

⊙ Islands of the south listings

For Sleeping and Eating price codes and other relevant information, see pages 23-24.

⊙ Sleeping

Don Khong *p261*

Most of the guesthouses in Dong Khong have undergone name changes in recent years due to a change in legislation that requires any guesthouse with 14 or more rooms to be called a hotel and pay double the tax.

A-C Senesothxeune Hotel, 100 m to the left of the main ferry point, T030-526 0577, www.ssxhotel.com. Tastefully designed, modern interpretation of colonial Lao architecture. Beautiful fittings, including carved wooden fish above the entrance of each room and brass chandeliers. Rooms are fitted with mod cons like a/c, TV, hot water and minibar. Superior rooms have fantastic bathtubs. Splurge a little for the superior room, which has a private balcony. The hotel also has a modern internet café (Wi-Fi available) and restaurant. The menu is mainly confined to Asian dishes; the chicken

and vermicelli soup is recommended. Little English is spoken by waiters. This is the island's best accommodation by a long shot although Mr Pon's new hotel will almost certainly give it a run for its money. The hotel is run by the gentle, softly spoken Mr Senesavath and his wife, both former mathematics professors from Don Dok University in Vientiane. Both speak English and French. Recommended.

B-C Pon's Arena Khong Island Hotel, 40 m north of the main strip, T031-253065, pon_arena@hotmail.com. Mr Pon's has opened a handsome new hotel. You'll want one of the rooms with balconies overlooking the river. All tastefully decorated with high ceilings and bathtubs, minibars and TVs; some rooms have tiny 'smoking' balconies. Wi-Fi throughout. Breakfast is served on the upstairs veranda.

B-C Villa Muong Khong Hotel Guesthouse, T031-213 0111, www.xbtravel-vlmkhotel.laopdr.com. This hotel is part chalet, part mock-Tudor, part Lao and part Thai . Despite this, the place is in a perfect location and offers expensive rooms; popular with tour groups. The rooms are large but a little on the spartan side with hot water, bath and a/c. Internet available. Service is a little slow. Also runs **Khong Island Travel Agency**, www.khongislandtravel.com

C-D Auberge Sala Done Khong, T031-212077, www.salalao.com. This traditional wooden house, the former holiday home of the previous regime's foreign minister, was once the best place to stay on Don Khong but, although the exterior is still stunning, the rooms just aren't worth the price. There are 12 large, tastefully decorated rooms with a/c, hot water and en suite bathrooms; some with very lumpy mattresses; the best are in the main building on the first floor where there is an attractive balcony overlooking the Mekong with comfortable deckchairs. Beautiful tilework in shared areas but starting to get a little run down and always seemingly abandoned. A new building is due to open next door under the same management with 15 rooms.

E Pon's Hotel and Restaurant, T031-214037. The large, spotless rooms are very good value, with hot showers, mozzie nets and comfortable beds. For 50,000 kip more you get a/c. Mr Pon, who speaks French and English, is perhaps the most helpful of all accommodation proprietors on the island and can offer an endless supply of tourist information and travel arrangements. Motorbike and bike rental and he can also arrange trips to the Cambodian border, to Don Deth and Don Khon and back to Pakse. In fact, Mr Pon should be your first point of contact for any requirements. Recommended. The restaurant is the most popular on the island.

E-F Souksan Hotel, northern end of town near Wat Chom Thong, T031-212071. The reception is in a homely building at the front, while the main accommodation area is in a block further back. Well-designed a/c rooms with en suite bathrooms and hot water set around a concrete garden. In a separate building, with bizarre river landscape paintings, the rooms are nicely decorated and comfortable with desk, cane chairs, tiled floorboards and hot water. Fan rooms are cheaper and represent good value. They also run one of the most upmarket guesthouses on Don Deth. Friendly management.

E-G Mekong Hotel, T031-213668. Simple, spotless carpeted rooms with fans, some overlooking the Mekong and all with comfortable mattresses. Some rooms (overpriced) have a/c and hot showers with lovely four-poster beds and crisp linen while fan rooms on the ground floor are the same but without the 4-posters and less than half the price. There are even cheaper rooms with shared facilities (equally clean) in a wooden building at the back. Little English is spoken in the restaurant so there's great room for error with orders. Massage service offered daily 1400-2000.

F Villa Khang Kong, set back from the main road, near the ferry point, T031-213539. Fantastic traditional Lao wooden building spruced up with colourful paint, with a great veranda and fab communal lounging area. Spacious clean rooms with or without a/c. No river views.

Don Deth p264, map p265

Many people tend to make their choice of accommodation on the basis of word-of-mouth recommendations from other travellers; this is as good a way to choose as any, as the accommodation is all cheap and much of a muchness. It normally consists of spartan, thread-bare bungalows with bed, mosquito net and hammock, and shared squat toilets (unless otherwise stated). Always opt for a bungalow with a window, as the huts can get very hot. The wooden bungalows don't provide as much ventilation as the rattan equivalents but tend to attract fewer insects. Always check that the bungalow has a mosquito net. Also note that tin-roofed huts will heat up quicker than thatch-roofed ones. Other things to consider is the distance from the toilet to the bungalow (a midnight bolt across a rice paddy isn't much fun), the state of the hammock, whether there is a restaurant attached (more likely than not) and whether 24-hr electricity is now included. Most guesthouses also offer laundry and bike hire.

The accommodation runs along both sides of the island, known as the **Sunset Side** and **Sunrise Side**. There is a large conglomeration of accommodation towards the northern tip, which is a good option for those wishing to socialize and hop between the various establishments' restaurants/bars; this is also the most common drop-off point. As a general rule, if you want peace and quiet, head for the bungalows towards the centre of each coast; ask the boat drivers to drop you off directly at the bungalows as it can be a difficult hike with baggage. There is really very little discernible difference between most of the lodgings on Don Deth, so if you're looking for truly inspirational accommodation pop across to Don Khone.

Sunset Side
D-E Little Eden, Hua Det, T020-7773 9045, www.littleedenguesthouse-dondet.com. Very close to the island tip and a small hike from the main drop-off dock, this place offers the best view of the stunning sunsets. Miss Noy and her husband Mathieu have built the best concrete bungalows on the island: 5 smart and spacious rooms with fan and a/c, mosquito net, hot water and even a bookcase in the rooms. The restaurant, serving top-notch Asian and European dishes (and Belgian fries), is in a prime position. Mathieu is also a good source of local information.
F Souksan Hotel, T020-7937561, Hua Det at the northern tip of the island, at the pinnacle of the Sunset and Sunrise sides. Convenient and very close to the dock. Mrs Khamsone cleared the area which now houses 20 or so twin and double rooms built from wood and bamboo; some with shared shower and toilets. There are also a couple of concrete bungalows that are slightly more expensive

but nice. The beautiful garden is home to hundreds of butterflies, with little paths linking up to the restaurant. This place used to be the best accommodation on the island, now usurped by Little Eden but the rooms and place are still a good bet. It offers electricity 1830-2000 only but this may change.
G Mr B's Sunset View Bungalow, near the northern tip, T020-5418 1171. The bungalows and grounds themselves are a bit lacklustre. However, the river views and the helpful staff make this a good choice. The best options are the well-located 4 riverside rooms. Of the others the rooms without shower are better and bigger than those with a shower.

Sunrise Side
E Don Det Bungalows, T020-7772 1572. Brand-new, mini Khmer wooden bungalows in 2 rows set back from the river. If they can be bothered to show you a room, you will find clean but spartan accommodation without hot water. The riverside bar is a popular hangout.
F-G Deng Bungalows, next to Mr Oudomsouk's. Wooden bungalows on stilts. Very popular with those who want to hang on a hammock overlooking the water. Scenic position.
G Bounhome, T020-2252 1820, close to Bouasone towards the centre of the island. 5 bungalows in either rattan or wood; the 2 rattan ones have inside showers.
G King Kong Guesthouse and Restaurant, riverside, midway along the Sunrise Side, T020-5535 6483. 4 rooms in 1 large house and 2 spartan rattan bungalows and a smallish restaurant serving pizza. Caged animals. Bike hire US$1. Tours and travel services available.
G Mama Tan On, T020-5546 5262. This place changes its name every year but the atmosphere remains unchanged. One of the first bungalows on the island. If you are having trouble finding it also ask for some of its previous incarnations **Mama Rasta**

or **Mama Tanon Rasta**. There is a beautiful view from the communal balcony and the effervescent Mama is good value with her jovial demeanour and back-slapping, cheeky quips. Small library. The place is somewhat down-trodden, with rattan huts and communal facilities, but is popular for hanging out in the hammocks.

G Mr Oudomsouk, north of the old concrete French port, T020-5594 4436. 6 spartan huts, with a couple of newish wooden bungalows. Small restaurant with a few board games and dominoes. Seems to be where the local monks like to chill out.

G Mr Phao's Riverview, on the riverfront, T020-5656 9651. Spanking new 7 wooden bungalows with lovely carved wooden furniture; 2 have inside shower. Mr Phao is one of the friendliest folk on the island and is super helpful. He has a new toilet block with Western loo and squat options. He will take guests across to opposite Aan island where there is a wat (10,000 kip) and will make an ATM run for 120,000 kip return, see Banks, page 276.

G Mr Tho's, T020-5656 7502. Wooden stilt bungalows with good hammocks and views of Don Khone. The staff are friendly. Rooms have unusual names, such as 'sticky rice bungalow' and 'bamboo bungalow'. Restaurant attached. There is also a library.

G Paradise Bungalows, north of the centre. Wooden stilted bungalows in a very enchanting location (the 4 away from the riverfront are cheaper) with a good restaurant (the first to be MSG-free on the island) and reasonable prices. Good book exchange; honesty bar.

G Santiphab Guesthouse, far end of the island next to the bridge, T020-5461 4231, www.santiphab-don-det.com. 7 basic rattan bungalows right beside the bridge, most have the quintessential hammock. Idyllic setting, flanked by the Mekong on one side and rice paddies on the other – a friendly, timeless place. Good for those who want to be secluded and with quick access to Don Khone. Very cheap restaurant serves tasty

fare along with buckets of atmosphere. Very little English spoken.

Ban Nakasang *p267*

Why anyone would want to stay in this town when the islands are 15 mins away is beyond comprehension but in case some kind of catastrophe strikes you can stay at the **Nakasang Guesthouse (F)**, on the main road towards the river, a wooden house with very basic rooms and shared facilities, or the smarter **Onpaseuth**, 1 km from town, T020-5584 1290, onpaseuth@hotmail.com

Don Khone *p268, map p265*

Although Don Deth attracts the vast majority of tourists, Don Khone holds its own by offering some very pleasant accommodation in close proximity to most of the attractions. In general, Don Khone evokes a much friendlier atmosphere.

B Auberge Sala Don Khone, T030-525 6390, www.salalao.com. A former French hospital built in 1927, this is one of the best places to stay on the island with 3 rooms, original tiles and 4-poster beds. In addition, traditional Luang Prabang-style houses have been built in the grounds, with 8 twin rooms, all with en suite hot shower and toilet. Two rooms have paddyfield views. Breakfast is included. The captured gibbon in a cage in the front garden is a disgrace.

B Salaphae, T030-525 6390, www.salalao.com. This is the most unusual accommodation in the whole Siphandon area. 3 rafts (and 6 rooms) are managed by ex-lawyer, Luesak. Rooms have been decorated simply, with all the detailed touches that can make accommodation outstanding. Hot water bathrooms. A wonderful deck, with seating overlooks the stunning river scenery.

D-E Pan's Guesthouse, T030-534 6939. A relative newcomer to Don Khone, these wooden bungalows are exceptionally good value for money. The 6 riverside bungalows with hot water, fan and comfortable mattresses are simple but comfortable and ultra clean. The owner is one of the most helpful hosts in Siphandon. Highly recommended for travellers on a limited budget. New rooms are under construction. Breakfast is included.

G Boun Guesthouse, next door to Auberge Sala Don Khone, T020-2271 0163. Mr Boun has built a couple of cream-painted wooden bungalows, with en suite bathrooms but a private concrete block in the garden obscures the view from some of the rooms.

F Sompamit Guesthouse, across from Boun Guesthouse, on the riverside, T020-5562 6149. Six thatched bungalows with mosquito nets and shared cold-water bathroom facilities. Also a couple of basic rooms with en suite bathrooms. Good location with a patch of garden in the front.

F-G Xaymountry Residence, towards the bridge, T020-5573 5755. This absolutely splendid old wooden villa with polished floorboards does not live up to the potential grandeur of its exterior. Tacky linoleum floor covering but clean en suite bathrooms, some shared. No river views but magnificent old building.

🍴 Eating

Don Khong *p261*

The majority of restaurants only serve fish and chicken. Local fish with coconut milk cooked in banana leaves, *mok pa*, is a truly divine local speciality, which makes a trip to the islands worthwhile in itself. Although many other towns and areas also make the a claim, Don Khong is also renowned for the quality of its *lao-lao* (rice liquor).

†‍† Souksan Chinese Restaurant. An attractive place with a stunning view of the river. Funnily enough, there is an absence of Chinese food but there are other more generic Asian options including good local fish, tasty honeyed chicken and basil pork with chilli.

† Mekong Restaurant, attached to the Mekong Hotel, see Sleeping. This restaurant has a good position near the bank of the

Mekong and provides legendary fare at low prices. Good *feu*. Very little English spoken by the waiting staff, so there's a fair amount of scope for miscommunication.

† Pon's Restaurant, see Pon Hotel and Restaurant, Sleeping, T031-214037. Good atmosphere, excellent food. The fish soup is recommended, as is the *mok pa*, but it must be ordered 2 hrs in advance.

Ban Nakasang *p267*

Two small thatched beachside restaurants serve good chicken *feu*. In the rainy season they move further up the bank. There are also food and drinks stalls on the right as you get off the boat.

Don Deth *p264, map p265*

Most people choose to eat at their guest-houses, all offering similar menus.

†‍† Lamphone. The resident Australian baker cooks up a mean focaccia, and chocolate and banana doughnuts and other delicious freshly baked goodies including carrot cake and lemon sponge. Also burgers in freshly baked buns and other dishes bringing variety to the island's offerings.

†‍† Little Eden, see Sleeping. A large menu with some good Western dishes, such as grilled chicken breast and creamy pepper sauce, as well as salads, sandwiches and soup and lots of catfish dishes (like grilled catfish in a white wine sauce); a change from the rest of the places on the island.

†‍† Mr B's Sunset View Bungalow, see Sleeping. Italian bruschetta, rice pudding and a famous selection of burgers including chicken and pumpkin. Good cocktails.

† The Pool Bar and Restaurant, near the main port. Has a pool table and fantastic Indian and Malay food. Good service. Good book exchange.

Don Khone *p268, map p265*

†† Auberge Sala Don Khone, see Sleeping. There's a beautiful view from the restaurant and some fine options on the menu, such as tuna and orange salad or steak salad.

Unfortunately, the service has deteriorated significantly and is too slow. The lunch menu is sandwich based and not all ingredients may be available.

† **Anny's**, village centre. A new addition to the eating scene, this popular place is offering dishes on smart plates. The fried garlic fish is recommended.

† **Pan's Restaurant**, across from his guest-house (see Sleeping). A fantastic option on the island, serving up a range of excellent home-made meals. The fish served is particularly good.

† **Sengaroune**, near the bridge, T020-5573 5009. This is a huge restaurant with a large deck. Local Lao and Vietnamese-inspired cuisine. Good spring rolls. Very popular with the locals.

⊛ Festivals

Don Khong p261
Dec A 5-day **Boat Racing** festival takes place early in the month, on the river opposite Muang Khong. It coincides with National Day on 2 Dec and is accompanied by a great deal of celebration, feasting and drinking.

⭕ Shopping

Don Deth p264, map p265
There isn't much to buy here. A small grocery store just down from the port has a few essential items and snacks but is not very well stocked . If you're in desperate need of any items, you are better off making a quick trip to Ban Nakasang to pick up things from the market there. Most guesthouse owners go to Ban Nakasang on an almost daily basis and will usually agree to buy things for you if you pay them 5000 kip or so.

▲ Activities and tours

Don Khong p261
All the guesthouses in Don Khong run tours

to Don Deth and Don Khone, taking in the Phaphaeng Falls and dolphin watching. Pon's Hotel charges 150,000 kip per person for a full-day trip. The national tourist authority is due to open an office in Don Khong and plan to run guided treks to the interior of the island.

Don Khone and around p268
For scheduled boat transport, see page 260. Almost every guesthouse can arrange tours, transport and tickets. Tour operators offer trips to Khong Phapheng, 60,000-70,000 kip each, minimum 4 people. From Don Khone, it is possible to hire a boat for the day, to visit the islands including one where the rice pots are made. Ask at Mr Pan's; 2-3 hrs, 150,000 kip for 4 people.

Tour operators
Tour operators offer tickets for transport out of Siphandon down to Cambodia or back up to other parts of Laos. Many people are told they can get to Siem Reap in a day with through transport. However, this is not possible. See the warning under Transport, Pakse, page 243.

Dolphin watching
From **Don Khone**, it is possible to hire a boat from Kong Ngay, 90,000 kip, maximum 3 people to a boat. Further south, at Ban Hang Khon, it's 60,000 kip per boat, maximum 3 people. Tours from Don Deth to the dolphins and Phapheng Falls cost 80,000 kip per person, minimum 6 people. **X-plore Asia** runs tours to the Phapheng tours and dolphin watching for 180,000 per person, minimum 2 people. Costs reduce the larger the group of people. Note that if the dolphins are hanging out across the border in Cambodia, you will be obliged to pay an extra US$1 per person to crisscross the waters.

Fishing and kayaking
Most tour operators would be able to arrange a day out fishing if you asked.

Happy Island Adventure Tour, T020-
2267 7698, happytour_bs@hotmail.com,
runs fishing trips for 120,000 per person,
minimum 5 people. Kayaking is also possible
including trips to the falls and dolphins,
200,000 kip per person, minimum 3 people.

Swimming

There is a sandy beach on **Don Khone**
where many travellers like to take a dip.
However, in the wet season this can
be particularly dangerous as there is a
nasty undercurrent and tourists have
drowned here, so be careful. The other
thing to consider when bathing is the
possibility of picking up the parasite called
schistosomiasis, also known as bilharzia.

⊖ Transport

Don Khong p261
Boat

See also Ins and outs, page 264.
  Pon's Hotel (reliable and recommended)
can arrange boats to **Don Deth** or
Don Khone, 30,000 kip, 1½ hrs. Other
guesthouses also offer this price (including
Don Khong guesthouse) while Villa Muang
Khong and Senesothxeune are a bit more
expensive There are also several boatmen
on the riverfront who are more than happy
to take people for the right price. Fares tend
to fluctuate according to fuel prices but the
rate at the time of publication was 150,000
kip for up to 10 people, one way. Most boats
leave at 0830. Private boat charter to **Pakse**,
US$150.

Bus/truck

Songthaew and buses head to **Pakse** at
0630, 0700, 0800, 0830, 3-4 hrs, from in front
of What Kan Khong, 30,000 kip. Or cross
to Ban Hat Xai Khoune and then try for
transport south.
  The minibus service back to Pakse can be
organized by Mr Pon, it costs 50,000 kip and
includes ferry and drop off at your hotel in
Pakse (2 hrs). Leaves at 1130; drop off at Ban

Muang for **Champasak** possible, 50,000 kip.
Xplore-Asia passes the Don Khong turn-off
at 1230 for the return journey, 50,000 kip.
  Guesthouses also arrange transport to
the Cambodian border and beyond (to
Siem Reap, US$23; to **Phnom Penh**, US$18,
Kratie, US$12, **Stung Treng**, US$8; to the
border US$5. Private transport to anywhere
can also be arranged; sample fares
include transfer to Pakse airport, US$80; to
Kingfisher Ecolodge, US$60.

Motorbike and bicycle

Many of the guesthouses offer motorbikes
(100,000 kip a day at **Senesothxeune**; 80,000
kip with Pon's Hotel) and bicycles (10,000-
20,000 kip).

Don Deth, Don Khone and around
p264, map p265
Boat

To **Ban Nakasang**, 20,000 kip per person.
The first boat is the market boat, leaving
at 0630; before that you will need to pay
40,000 kip.
  There are 2 ways to get to **Don Khong**,
from Ban Nakasang, either by boat,
2 hrs,180,000 kip per boat (bargain hard),
or by bus (see above); motorbike taxis also
make the trip for US$3. Although it's slower
and more expensive, the boat trip is one of
the loveliest in Laos. Boats between Don
Khong and Don Deth cost 30,000 kip.

Ban Nakasang p267
Boat

To **Don Deth** and **Don Khone**, 15-20 mins,
20,000 kip per person. To **Don Khong**, 2 hrs,
180,000 per boat. Between **Don Khone** and
Don Deth, 30,000 kip.

Bus/songthaew

Decent buses depart from Ban Nakasang's
market, hourly 0600-1000 daily, northbound
for **Pakse**, 40,000 kip; some continue
onwards to **Vientiane**; get off at **Ban Hat
Xai Khoune** for the crossing to **Don Khong**.
Xplore-Asia tourist buses go to **Pakse** at

Border essentials: Voen Kham-Don Kralor (Cambodia)

It's easy to get to Cambodia from the islands of Siphandon, although rules and regulations change regularly so it is better to check in advance. Cambodian visas are available on the border and cost US$20 for 30 days. You'll need two passport photographs; for a hefty fee, the Cambodian officials are happy to provide you with some. Lao visas are now available at the border from 2010. The border is officially open daily 0800-1600; however, border officials will process outside of these times for a overtime fee so expect to pay anything between US$3 and US$5 on the Cambodian side and a little less on the Lao side. On both sides of the border, officials will charge US$2-3 to stamp your passport.

Most tour operators can arrange buses from Don Khong, Don Deth and Done Khone to the border and beyond. You will need to change vehicles on the Cambodian side on most transport although Sorya company passes right through. Transport is available to Stung Treng, Phnom Penh and Kampong Cham. See the warning under Pakse, page 243, for through transport to Siem Reap from Laos. Pon's Hotel can also organize transport for visitors from the Cambodian side back to Don Khong.

1100, 50,000 kip including ferry crossing. The same minivan will stop at **Ban Muang** for **Champasak**, 50,000 kip. To get to **Don Kralor** (on the Cambodian border) most guesthouses can organize the trip on a minivan. (There is no public transport now; a motorbike taxi costs 40,000 kip.) Cambodian visas are available on the border and Lao visas are now also available. To **Don Kralor**, the largest town on the other side of the Cambodian border, US$4, 2 hrs. Tickets can also be bought to more distant destinations in Cambodia, to **Stung Treng**, US$6, **Kratie**, US$11, **Kampong Cham,** US$12 or **Phnom Penh**, US$13. The **Siem Reap** bus requires an overnight stop in **Kampong Cham**, US$18. Note that the **Paramount** company requires a change of bus in Cambodia but the **Sorya** company travels on to further destinations. But take heed of the warning under Transport, Pakse, page 243. For the Cambodia border, see box above.

X-plore Asia and other agencies can also arrange bus tickets for destinations further afield such as **Attapeu**, 120,000 kip; **Ubon Ratchathani**, 110,000 kip; **Bangkok**, 250,000 kip; and **Vientiane**, 220,000 kip.

Directory

Don Khong (Muang Khong) p261
Banks There is a Lao Agriculture Promotion bank in town; hours are erratic and it accepts only US$ or Thai baht. Pon's Hotel and Pon's Arena Khong Hotel advance cash against Visa and Mastercard for a 5% fee. **Internet** Guesthouses offer internet at 500-1000 kip a minute. Senesothxeune has Wi-Fi (US$5 a day), as do the two Pon's establishments.

Don Deth, Don Khone and around p264, map p265
Banks There are no banks, but some guesthouses change money. Mr Phao of **Phao's Riverview** on Don Deth will take you by boat to Ban Khinak, north of Ban Nakasang, where there is a Visa and MasterCard ATM, for 120,000 kip return. **Internet** There are internet cafés on Don Deth and Don Khone; minimum 400 kip/minute; calls can also be made, minimum 10 mins. **Telephone** It's cheapest to call via the net. Guesthouses may let you call from their mobiles, at US$4 or more a min.

Contents

Footprint features

Background

History

Scholars of Lao history, efore they even begin, need to decide whether they are writing a history of Laos; a history of the Lao ethnic group; or histories of the various kingdoms and principalities that have, through time, been encompassed by the present boundaries of the Lao People's Democratic Republic. Historians have tended to confront this problem in different ways without, often, acknowledging on what basis their 'history' is built. It is common to see 1365, the date of the foundation of the kingdom of Lane Xang, as marking the beginning of Lao history. But, as Martin Stuart-Fox points out, prior to Lane Xang the principality of Muang Swa, occupying the same geographical space, was headed by a Lao. The following account provides a brief overview of the histories of those peoples who have occupied what is now the territory of the Lao PDR.

Archaeological and historical evidence indicates that most Lao originally migrated south from China. This was followed by an influx of ideas and culture from the Indian subcontinent via Myanmar (Burma), Thailand and Cambodia – something which is reflected in the state religion, Theravada Buddhism.

Being surrounded by large, powerful neighbours, Laos has been repeatedly invaded over the centuries by the Thais (or Siamese) and the Vietnamese – who both thought of Laos as their buffer zone and backyard. They too have both left their mark on Lao culture. In recent history, Laos has been influenced by the French during the colonial era, the Japanese during the Second World War, the Americans during the Indochinese wars and, between 1975 and the early 1990s, by Marxism-Leninism.

It is also worth noting, in introduction, that historians and regimes have axes to grind. The French were anxious to justify their annexation of Laos and so used dubious Vietnamese documents to provide a legal gloss to their actions. Western historians, lumbered with the baggage of Western historiography, ignored indigenous histories. And the Lao People's Revolutionary Party uses history for its own ends too. The official three volume *History of Laos* is being written by Party-approved history hacks. The third volume (chronologically speaking) was published in 1989 and, working back in time, the first and second thereafter. As Martin Stuart-Fox remarks in his *A History of Laos*, "the communist regime is as anxious as was the previous Royal Lao government [pre-1975] to establish that Laos has a long and glorious past and that a continuity exists between the past and the present Lao state". In other words, Laos has not one history, but many. Take your pick.

First kingdom of Laos

Myth, archaeology and history all point to a number of early feudal Lao kingdoms in what is now South China and North Vietnam. External pressures from the Mongols under Kublai Khan and the Han Chinese forced the Tai tribes to migrate south into what had been part of the Khmer Empire. The mountains to the north and east served as a cultural barrier to Vietnam and China, leaving the Lao exposed to influences from India and the West. There are no documentary records of early Lao history (the first date in the Lao chronicles to which historians attach any real veracity is 1271), although it seems probable that parts of present-day Laos were annexed by Lannathai (Chiang Mai) in the 11th century and by the Khmer Empire during the 12th century. But neither of these states held sway over the entire area of Laos. Xieng Khouang, for example, was probably never under Khmer domination. This was followed by strong Siamese influence over the cities of Luang Prabang and Vientiane under the Siamese Sukhothai Dynasty. Laos (the country) in effect did not exist, although the Laos (the people) certainly did.

The downfall of Sukhothai in 1345 and its submission to the new Siamese Dynasty at Ayutthaya (founded in 1349) was the catalyst for the foundation of what is commonly regarded as the first truly independent Lao Kingdom – although there were semi-independent Lao *muang* (city states, sometimes transliterated as *meuang*) existing prior to that date.

Fa Ngum and Lane Xang

The kingdom of Lane Xang (Lan Chang) emerged in 1353 under Fa Ngum, a Lao prince who had grown up in the Khmer court of Angkor. Fa Ngum is clearly an important man – that is, if the amount of space devoted to his exploits in the Lao chronicles is anything to go by. There is more written about him than there is about the following two centuries of Lao history. It is also safe to say that his life is more fiction than fact. Fa Ngum was reputedly born with 33 teeth and was banished to Angkor after his father, Prince Yakfah, was convicted of having an incestuous affair with a wife of King Suvarna Kamphong. In 1353 Fa Ngum led an army to Luang Prabang and confronted his grandfather, King Suvarna Kamphong. Unable to defeat his grandson on the battlefield, the aged king is said to have hanged himself and Fa Ngum was invited to take the throne. Three years later, in 1356, Fa Ngum marched on Vientiane – which he took with ease – and

Kings of Lane Xang

Fa Ngum	1353-1373
Samsenthai	1373-1416
Lan Kamdaeng	1417-1428
Phommathat	1428-1429
Mun Sai	1429-1430
Fa Khai	1430-1433
Khong Kham	1433-1434
Yukhon	1434-1435
Kham Keut	1435-1441
Chaiyachakkapat- Phaenphaeo (aka Sao Tiakaphat)	1441-1478
Suvarna Banlang (aka Theng Kham)	1478-1485
Lahsaenthai Puvanart	1485-1495
Sompou	1497-1500
Visunarat	1500-1520
Pothisarath	1520-1548
Setthathira	1548-1571
Saensurin	1572-1574
Mahaupahat (under Burmese control)	1574-1580
Saensurin	1580-1582
Nakhon Noi (under Burmese control)	1582-1583
Interregnum	1583-1591
Nokeo Koumone	1591-1596
Thammikarath	1596-1622
Upanyuvarat	1622-1623
Pothisarat	1623-1627
Mon Keo	1627
Unstable period	1627-1637
Sulinya Vongsa	1637-1694

then on Vienkam, which proved more of a challenge. He is credited with piecing together Lang Xang – the Land of a Million Elephants (or, if not accented, the Valley of Elephants) – the golden age to which all histories of Laos refer to justify the existence (and greatness) of the country.

In some accounts Lang Xang is portrayed as stretching from China to Cambodia and from the Khorat Plateau in present-day Northeast Thailand to the Annamite mountains in the east. But it would be entirely wrong to envisage the kingdom controlling all these regions. Lane Xang probably only had total control over a comparatively small area of present-day Laos and parts of Northeast Thailand; the bulk of this grand empire would have been contested with other surrounding kingdoms. In addition, the smaller muang and principalities would themselves have played competing powers off, one against another, in an attempt to maximize their own autonomy. It is this 'messiness' which led scholars of Southeast Asian history to suggest that territories as such did not exist, but rather zones of variable control. The historian OW Wolters coined the term *mandala* for "a particular and often unstable political situation in a vaguely defined geographical area without fixed boundaries and where smaller centres tended to look in all directions for security. *Mandalas* would expand and contract in concertina-like fashion. Each one contained several tributary rulers, some of whom would repudiate their vassal status when the opportunity arose and try to build up their own network of vassals".

Legend relates that Fa Ngum was a descendant of Khoum Borom, "a king who came out of the sky from South China". He is said to have succeeded to the throne of Nanchao in 729, aged 31, and died 20 years later, although this historical record is, as they say, exceedingly thin. Khoum Borom is credited with giving birth to the Lao people by slicing open a gourd in Muong Taeng (Dien Bien Phu, Vietnam) and his seven sons established the great Tai kingdoms. He returned to his country with a detachment of Khmer soldiers and united several scattered Lao fiefdoms. In those days, conquered lands were usually razed and the people taken as slaves to build up the population of the conquering group. (This largely explains why today there are far more Lao in northeastern Thailand than in Laos – they were forcibly settled there after King Anou was defeated by King Rama III of Siam in 1827) The kings of Lane Xang were less philistine, demanding only subordination and allegiance as one part of a larger *mandala*.

Luang Prabang became the capital of the kingdom of Lane Xang. The unruly highland tribes of the northeast did not come under the kingdom's control at that time. Fa Ngum made Theravada Buddhism the official religion. He married the Cambodian king's daughter, Princess Keo Kaengkanya, and was given the Pra Bang (a golden statue, the most revered religious symbol of Laos), by the Khmer court.

It is common to read of Lane Xang as the first kingdom of Laos; as encompassing the territory of present-day Laos; and as marking the introduction of Theravada Buddhism to the country. On all counts this portrait is deeply flawed. As noted above, there were Lao states that predated Lane Xang; Lane Xang never controlled Laos as it currently exists; and Buddhism had made an impact on the Lao people before 1365. Fa Ngum did not create a kingdom; rather he brought together various pre-existing *muang* (city states) into a powerful *mandala*. As Martin Stuart-Fox writes, "From this derives his [Fa Ngum's] historical claim to hero status as the founder of the Lao Kingdom." But, as Stuart-Fox goes on to explain, there was no central authority and rulers of individual *muang* had considerable autonomy. As a result the "potential for disintegration was always present".

After Fa Ngum's wife died in 1368, he became so debauched, it is said, that he was deposed in favour of his son, Samsenthai (1373-1416), who was barely 18 when he acceded the throne. He was named after the 1376 census, which concluded that he ruled over 300,000 Tais living in Laos; *samsen* means, literally, 300,000. He set up a new administrative system based on the existing *muang*, nominating governors to each that lasted until it was abolished by the Communist government in 1975. Samsenthai's death was followed by a period of unrest. Under KingChaiyachakkapat-Phaenphaeo (1441-1478), the kingdom came under increasing threat from the Vietnamese. How the Vietnamese came to be peeved with the Lao is another story which smacks of fable more than fact. King Chaiyachakkapat's eldest son, the Prince of Chienglaw, secured a holy white elephant. The emperor of Vietnam, learning of this momentous discovery, asked to be sent some of the beast's hairs. Disliking the Vietnamese, the Prince dispatched a box of its excrement instead, whereupon the Emperor formed an army of an improbably large 550,000 men. The Prince's army numbered 200,000 and 2000 elephants. (Considering that the population of Lane Xang under Samsenthai was said to be 300,000 this beggars statistical belief. Still, it is a good story.) The massive Vietnamese army finally prevailed – two Lao generals were so tired that they fell off their elephants and were hacked to pieces – and entered and sacked Luang Prabang. But shortly thereafter they were driven out by Chaiyachakkapat-Phaenphaeo's son, King Suvarna Banlang (1478-1485). Peace was only fully restored under King Visunarat (1500-1520), who built Wat Visoun in Luang Prabang.

Increased prominence and Burmese incursions Under King Pothisarath (1520-1548) Vientiane became prominent as a trading and religious centre. The king married a Lanna (Chiang Mai) princess, Queen Yotkamtip, and when the Siamese King Ketklao was put to death in 1545, Pothisarath's son claimed the throne at Lanna. He returned to Lane Xang when his father died in 1548. Once again an elephant figured in the event: Pothisarath was demonstrating his prowess in the art of elephant lassoing when he was flung from his mount and fatally crushed. Asserting his right as successor to the throne, he was crowned Setthathirat, in 1548 and ruled until 1571 – the last of the great kings of Lane Xang.

At the same time, the Burmese were expanding East and in 1556 Lanna fell into their hands. Setthathirat gave up his claim to that throne, to a Siamese prince, who ruled under Burmese authority. (He also took the Phra Kaeo – Thailand's famous 'Emerald' Buddha and its most sacred and revered image – with him to Luang Prabang and then to Vientiane. The residents of Chiang Mai are reputed to have pleaded that he leave it in the city, but these cries fell on deaf ears. The Phra Kaeo stayed in Vientiane until 1778 when the Thai general Phya Chakri 'repatriated' it to Thailand.) In 1563 Setthathirat pronounced Vieng Chan (Vientiane) the principal capital of Lane Xang. Seven years later, the Burmese King Bayinnaung launched an unsuccessful attack on Vieng Chan itself.

Setthathirat is revered as one of the great Lao kings, having protected the country from foreign domination. He built Wat Phra Kaeo (see page 53) in Vientiane, in which he placed the famous Emerald Buddha brought from Lanna. Setthathirat mysteriously disappeared during a campaign in the southern province of Attapeu in 1574, which threw the kingdom into crisis. Vientiane fell to invading Burmese the following year and remained under Burmese control for seven years. Finally the anarchic kingdoms of Luang Prabang and Vientiane were reunified under Nokeo Koumane (1591-96) and Thammikarath, king of Lane Xang (1596-1622).

Disputed territory

From the time of the formation of the kingdom of Lane Xang to the arrival of the French, the history of Laos was dominated by the struggle to retain the lands it had conquered. Following King Setthathirat's death, a series of kings came to the throne in quick succession. King Souligna Vongs, crowned in 1633, brought long awaited peace to Laos. The 61 years he was on the throne are regarded as Lane Xang's golden age. Under him, the kingdom's influence spread to Yunnan in South China, the Burmese Shan States, Issan in Northeast Thailand and areas of Vietnam and Cambodia.

Souligna Vongsa was even on friendly terms with the Vietnamese: he married Emperor Le Thanh Ton's daughter and he and the Emperor agreed the borders between the two countries. The frontier was settled in a deterministic – but nonetheless amicable – fashion: those living in houses built on stilts with verandas were considered Lao subjects and those living in houses without piles and verandas owed allegiance to Vietnam.

During his reign, foreigners first visited the country – the Dutch merchant Gerrit van Wuysthoff arrived in 1641 to assess trading prospects – and Jesuit missionaries too. But other than a handful of adventurers, Laos remained on the outer periphery of European concerns and influence in the region.

The three kingdoms After Souligna Vongsa died in 1694, leaving no heir, dynastic quarrels and feudal rivalries once again erupted, undermining the kingdom's cohesion. In 1700 Lane Xang split into three: Luang Prabang under Souligna's grandson, Vientiane under Souligna's nephew and the new kingdom of Champasak was founded in the south 'panhandle'. This weakened the country and allowed the Siamese and Vietnamese to encroach on Lao lands. *Muang*, which previously owed clear allegiance to Lane Xang, began to look towards Vietnam or Siam. Isan muang in present day Northeast Thailand, for example, paid tribute to Bangkok; while Xieng Khouang did the same to Hanoi and, later, to Hué. The three main kingdoms that emerged with the disintegration of Lane Xang leant in different directions: Luang Prabang had close links with China, Vientiane with Vietnam's Hanoi/Hué and Champasak with Siam.

By the mid-1760s Burmese influence once again held sway in Vientiane and Luang Prabang and before the turn of the decade, they sacked Ayutthaya, the capital of Siam. Somehow the Siamese managed to pull themselves together and only two years later in 1778 successfully rampaged through Vientiane. The two sacred Buddhas, the Phra Bang and the Phra Kaeo (Emerald Buddha), were taken as booty back to Bangkok. The Emerald Buddha was never returned and now sits in Bangkok's Wat Phra Kaeo.

King Anou (an abbreviation of Anurutha), was placed on the Vientiane throne by the Siamese. With the death of King Rama II of Siam, King Anou saw his chance of rebellion, asked Vietnam for assistance, formed an army and marched on Bangkok in 1827. In mounting this brave assault, Anou was apparently trying to emulate the great Fa Ngum. Unfortunately, he got no further than the Northeast Thai town of Korat where his forces were driven back. Nonetheless, Anou's rebellion is considered one of the most daring and ruthless rebellions in Siamese history and he was lauded as a war hero back home.

King Anou's brief stab at regional power was to result in catastrophe for Laos – and tragedy for King Anou. The first US arms shipment to Siam allowed the Siamese to sack Vientiane, a task to which they had grown accustomed over the years. (This marks America's first intervention in Southeast Asia.) Lao artisans were frogmarched to Bangkok and many of the inhabitants were resettled in Northeast Siam. Rama III had Chao Anou locked in a cage where he was taunted by the population of Bangkok. He died soon afterwards, at the age of 62. The cause of his death has been variously linked to poison and shame. One of his supporters is said to have taken pity on the king and brought him poison. Other explanations say that he wished himself dead or that he choked to death. Whatever the real cause, before he died, the disconsolate Anou put a curse on Siam's monarchy, promising that the next time a Thai king set foot on Lao soil, he would die. To this day no Thai king has crossed the Mekong River. When the agreement for the supply of hydroelectric power was signed with Thailand in the 1970s, the Thai king was invited to open the Nam Ngum Dam, a feat he managed to achieve from a sandbank in the middle of the Mekong.

Disintegration of the kingdom Over the next 50 years, Anou's Kingdom was destroyed. By the time the French arrived in the late 19th century, the virtually unoccupied city was subsumed into the Siamese sphere of influence. Luang Prabang also became a Siamese vassal state, while Xieng Khouang province was invaded by Chinese rebels – to the chagrin of the Vietnamese, who had always considered the Hmong mountain kingdom (they called it Tran Ninh), to be their exclusive source of slaves. The Chinese had designs on Luang Prabang too and in order to quash their expansionist instincts, Bangkok dispatched an army there in 1885 to pacify the region and ensure the north remained firmly within the Siamese sphere of influence. This period was clearly one of confusion and rapidly shifting allegiances. In James McCarthy's book of his travels in Siam and Laos, *Surveying and Exploring in Siam* (1900), he states that an old chief of Luang Prabang remarked to him that the city had never been a tributary state of Annam (North Vietnam) but had formerly paid tribute to China. He writes:

"The tribute had consisted of four elephants, 41 mules, 533 lbs of nok (metal composed of gold and copper), 25 lbs of rhinoceros' horns, 100 lbs of ivory, 250 pieces of home-spun cloth, one horn, 150 bundles of areca palm nuts [for betel 'nut' chewing], 150 cocoanuts [sic] and 33 bags of roe of the fish *pla buk* [the giant Mekong cat fish]."

The history of Laos during this period becomes, essentially, the history of only a small part of the current territory of the country: namely, the history of Luang Prabang. And because Luang Prabang was a suzerain state of Bangkok, the history of that kingdom is, in turn, sometimes relegated to a mere footnote in the history of Siam.

The French and independence

Following King Anou's death, Laos became the centre of Southeast Asian rivalry between Britain, expanding east from Burma and France, pushing west through Vietnam. In 1868, following the French annexation of South Vietnam and the formation of a protectorate in Cambodia, an expedition set out to explore the Mekong trade route to China. Once central and north Vietnam had come under the influence of the Quai d'Orsay in Paris, the French became increasingly curious about Vietnamese claims to chunks of Laos. Unlike the Siamese, the French – like the British – were concerned with demarcating borders and establishing explicit areas of sovereignty. This seemed extraordinary to most Southeast Asians at the time who could not see the point of spending so much time and effort mapping space when land was so abundant. However, it did not take long for the Siamese king to realize the importance of maintaining his claim to Siamese territories if the French in the east and the British in the south (Malaya) and west (Burma) were not to squeeze Siam to nothing.

However, King Chulalongkorn was not in a position to confront the French militarily and instead he had to play a clever diplomatic game if his kingdom was to survive. The French, for their part, were anxious to continue to press westwards from Vietnam into the Lao lands over which Siam held suzerainty. Martin Stuart-Fox argues that there were four main reasons underlying France's desire to expand West: the lingering hope that the Mekong might still offer a 'back door' into China; the consolidation of Vietnam against attack; the 'rounding out' of their Indochina possessions; and a means of further pressuring Bangkok. In 1886, the French received reluctant Siamese permission to post a vice consul to Luang Prabang and a year later he persuaded the Thais to leave. However, even greater humiliation was to come in 1893 when the French, through crude gunboat diplomacy – the so-called Paknam incident – forced King Chulalongkorn to give up all claim to Laos on the flimsiest of historical pretexts. Despite attempts by Prince Devawongse to manufacture a compromise, the French forced Siam to cede Laos to France and, what's more, to pay compensation. It is said that after this humiliation, King Chulalongkorn retired from public life, broken in spirit and health. So the French colonial era in Laos began.

What is notable about this spat between France and Siam is that Laos – the country over which they were fighting – scarcely figures. As was to happen again in Laos' history, the country was caught between two competing powers who used Laos as a stage on which to fight a wider and to them, more important, conflict.

Union of Indochina In 1893 France occupied the left bank of the Mekong and forced Thailand to recognize the river as the boundary. The French Union of Indochina denied Laos the area which is now Isan, northeast Thailand, and this was the start of 50 years of colonial rule. Laos became a protectorate with a *résident-superieur* in Vientiane and a vice-consul in Luang Prabang. However, as Martin Stuart-Fox points out, Laos could hardly be construed as a 'country' during the colonial period. "Laos existed again", he writes, "but not yet as a political entity in its own right, for no independent centre of Lao political power existed. Laos was but a territorial entity within French Indochina." The French were not interested in establishing an identifiable Lao state; they saw Laos as a resource-rich appendage to Vietnam. Though they had grand plans for the development of Laos, none of them came to anything. Unlike Cambodia to the south, the French did not perceive Laos to have any historical unity or coherence and therefore it could be hacked about and developed or otherwise, according to their whim, as if it were a piece of brie.

In 1904 the Franco-British convention delimited respective zones of influence. Only a few hundred French civil servants were ever in Vientiane at any one time and their attitude to colonial administration – described as 'benign neglect' – was as relaxed as the people they governed. To the displeasure of the Lao, France brought in Vietnamese to run the civil service. But for the most part, the French colonial period was a 50-year siesta for Laos. The king was allowed to stay in Luang Prabang, but had little say in administration. Trade was left to the Chinese and the Vietnamese. A small, French-educated Lao élite did grow up and by the 1940s had become the core of a laid-back Lao nationalist movement.

Japanese coup Towards the end of the Second World War, Japan ousted the French administration in Laos in a coup in March 1945. The eventual surrender of the Japanese in August that year gave impetus to the Lao independence movement. Prince Phetsarath, , hereditary viceroy and premier of the Luang Prabang Kingdom, took over the leadership of the Lao Issara, the Free Laos Movement (originally a resistance movement against the Japanese). They prevented the French from seizing power again and declared Lao independence on 1 September 1945. Two weeks later, the north and south provinces were reunified and in October, Phetsarath formed a Lao Issara government headed by Prince Phaya Khammao, the governor of Vientiane.

France refused to recognize the new state and crushed the Lao resistance. King Sisavang Vong, unimpressed by Prince Phetsarath's move, sided with the French, who had their colony handed back by British forces. He was crowned the constitutional monarch of the new protectorate in 1946. The rebel government took refuge in Bangkok. Historians believe the Issara movement was aided in their resistance to the French by the Viet Minh – Hanoi's Communists.

Independence In response to nationalist pressures, France was obliged to grant Laos ever greater self government and, eventually, formal independence within the framework of the newly reconstructed French Union in July 1949. Meanwhile, in Bangkok, the Issara movement had formed a government-in-exile, headed by Phetsarath and his half-brothers: Prince Souvanna Phouma (see box opposite) and Prince Souphanouvong. Both were refined, French-educated men, with a taste for good wine and cigars. The Issara's military wing was led by Souphanouvong who, even at that stage, was known for his Communist

Prince Souvanna Phouma: architect of independence and helmsman of catastrophe

Prince Souvanna Phouma was Laos' greatest statesman. He was prime minister on no less than eight occasions for a total of 20 years between 1951 and 1975. He dominated mainstream politics from independence until the victory of the Pathet Lao in 1975. But he was never able to preserve the integrity of Laos in the face of much stronger external forces. "Souvanna stands as a tragic figure in modern Lao history," Martin Stuart-Fox writes, a "stubborn symbol of an alternative, neutral, 'middle way'."

He was born in 1901 into a branch of the Luang Prabang royal family. Like many of the Lao elite he was educated abroad, in Hanoi, Paris and Grenoble, and when he returned to Laos he married a woman of mixed French-Lao blood. He was urbane, educated and arrogant. He enjoyed fine wines and cigars, spoke French better than he spoke Lao, and was a Francophile – as well as a nationalist – to the end.

In 1950 Souvanna became a co-founder of the Progressive Party and in the elections of 1951 he headed his first government which negotiated and secured full independence from France.

Souvanna made two key errors of judgement during these early years. First, he ignored the need for nation building in Laos. And, second, he underestimated the threat that the Communists posed to the country. With regard to the first of these misjudgements, he seemed to believe – and it is perhaps no accident that he trained as an engineer and architect – that Laos just needed to be administered efficiently to become a modern state. He appeared either to reject, or to ignore the idea that the government first had to try and inculcate a sense of Lao nationhood. The second misjudgement was his

long-held belief that the Pathet Lao was a nationalist and not a Communist organization. He let the Pathet Lao grow in strength and this, in turn, brought the US into Lao affairs.

By the time the US began to intervene in Lao affairs in the late 1950s, the country already seemed to be heading for catastrophe. But in his struggle to maintain some semblance of independence for his tiny country, he ignored the degree to which Laos was being sucked into the quagmire of Indochina. As Martin Stuart-Fox writes: "He [Souvanna] knew he was being used, and that he had no power to protect his country from the war that increasingly engulfed it. But he was too proud meekly to submit to US demands – even as Laos was subjected to the heaviest bombing in the history of warfare. At least a form of independence had to be maintained."

When the Pathet Lao entered Vientiane in victory in 1975, Souvanna did not flee into exile. He remained to help in the transfer of power. The Pathet Lao, of course, gave him a title and then ignored him as they pursued their Communist manifesto. Again, Martin Stuart-Fox writes: "Souvanna ended his days beside the Mekong. He was to the end a Lao patriot, refusing to go into exile in France. The leaders of the new regime did consult him on occasions. Friends came to play bridge. Journalists sought him out, although he said little and interviews were taped in the presence of Pathet Lao minions. When he died in January 1984, he was accorded a state funeral."

From Martin Stuart-Fox's *Buddhist Kingdom, Marxist State: the Making of Modern Laos* (White Lotus, 1996).

sympathies. This was due to a temporary alliance between the Issara and the Viet Minh, who had the common cause of ridding their respective countries of the French. Within just a few months the so-called Red Prince had been ousted by his half-brothers and joined the Viet Minh where he is said to have been the moving force behind the declaration of the Democratic Republic of Laos by the newly-formed Lao National Assembly. The Lao People's Democratic Republic emerged – albeit in name only – somewhere inside Vietnam, in August 1949. Soon afterwards, the Pathet Lao (the Lao Nation) was born. The Issara movement quickly folded and Souvanna Phouma went back to Vientiane and joined the newly formed Royal Lao Government.

By 1953, Prince Souphanouvong had managed to move his Pathet Lao headquarters inside Laos and with the French losing their grip on the north provinces, the weary colonizers granted the country full independence. Retreating honourably, France signed a treaty of friendship and association with the new royalist government and made the country a French protectorate.

The rise of Communism

French defeat While all this was going on, King Sisavang Vong sat tight in Luang Prabang instead of moving to Vientiane. But within a few months of independence, the ancient royal capital was under threat from the Communist Viet Minh and Pathet Lao. Honouring the terms of the new treaty, French commander General Henri Navarre determined in late 1953 to take the pressure off Luang Prabang by confronting the Viet Minh who controlled the strategic approach to the city at Dien Bien Phu. The French suffered a stunning defeat which presaged their withdrawal from Indochina. The subsequent occupation of two north Lao provinces by the Vietnam-backed Pathet Lao forces, meant the kingdom's days as a Western buffer state were numbered. The Vietnamese, not unlike their previous neighbours, did not respect Laos as a state, but as a extension of their own territory to be utilized for their own strategic purposes during the ensuing war.

With the Geneva Accord in July 1954, following the fall of Dien Bien Phu in May, Ho Chi Minh's government gained control of all territory north of the 17th parallel in neighbouring Vietnam. The Accord guaranteed Laos' freedom and neutrality, but with the Communists on the threshold, the US was not prepared to be a passive spectator: the demise of the French sparked an increasing US involvement. In an operation that was to mirror the much more famous war with Vietnam to the East, Washington soon found itself supplying and paying the salaries of 50,000 royalist troops and their corrupt officers. Clandestine military assistance grew, undercover special forces were mobilized and the CIA began meddling in Lao politics. In 1960 a consignment of weapons was dispatched by the CIA to a major in the Royal Lao Army called Vang Pao – or VP, as he became known – who was destined to become the leader of the Hmong.

US involvement: the domino effect Laos had become the dreaded first domino, which, using the scheme of US President Dwight D Eisenhower's analogy, would trigger the rapid spread of Communism if ever the country fell. The time-trapped little kingdom rapidly became the focus of superpower brinkmanship. At a press conference in March 1961, President Kennedy is said to have been too abashed to tell the American people that US forces might soon become embroiled in conflict in a far-away flashpoint that went by the name of 'Louse'. For three decades Americans have unwittingly mispronounced the country's name as Kennedy decided, euphemistically, to label it 'Lay-os' throughout his national television broadcast.

Coalitions, coups and counter-coups Even though it was headed by the neutralist, Prince Souvanna Phouma, the US-backed Royal Lao Government of independent Laos ruled over a divided country from 1951 to 1954. The US played havoc with Laos' domestic politics, running anti-communist campaigns, backing the royalist army and lending support to political figures on the right (even if they lacked experience or political qualifications). The Communist Pathet Lao, headed by Prince Souphanouvong and overseen and sponsored by North Vietnam's Lao Dong party since 1949, emerged as the only strong opposition. By the mid-1950s, Kaysone Phomvihane, later prime minister of the Lao PDR, began to make a name for himself in the Indochinese Communist Party. Indeed the close association between Laos and Vietnam went deeper than just ideology. Kaysone's father was Vietnamese, while Prince Souphanouvong and Nouhak Phounsavanh both married Vietnamese women.

Government of National Union Elections were held in Vientiane in July 1955 but were boycotted by the Pathet Lao. Souvanna Phouma became prime minister in March 1956. He aimed to try to negotiate the integration of his half-brother's Pathet Lao provinces into a unified administration and coax the Communists into a coalition government. In 1957 the disputed provinces were returned to royal government control under the first coalition government. This coalition government, much to US discontent, contained two Pathet Lao ministers including Souphanouvong and Phoumi Vongvichit. This was one of Souvanna Phouma's achievements in trying to combine the two sides to ensure neutrality, although it was only short-lived. In May 1958 elections were held. This time the Communists' Lao Patriotic Front (Neo Lao Hak Xat) clinched 13 of the 21 seats in the Government of National Union. The Red Prince, Souphanouvong and one of his aides were included in the cabinet and former Pathet Lao members were elected deputies of the National Assembly.

Almost immediately problems which had been beneath the surface emerged to plague the government. The rightists and their US supporters were shaken by the result and the much-vaunted coalition lasted just two months. Driven by Cold War prerogatives, the US could not abide by any government that contained Communist members and withdrew their aid, which the country had become much dependent upon. Between 1955 and 1958 the US had given four times more aid to Laos than the French had done in the prior eight years and it had become the backbone of the Lao economy. If Laos was not so dependent on this aid, it is quite plausible that the coalition government may have survived. The National Union fell apart in July 1958 and Souvanna Phouma was forced out of power. Pathet Lao leaders were jailed and the right-wing Phoui Sananikone came to power. With anti-Communists in control, Pathet Lao forces withdrew to the Plain of Jars in Xieng Khouang province. A three-way civil war ensued, between the rightists (backed by the US), the Communists (backed by North Vietnam) and the neutralists (led by Souvanna Phouma, who wanted to maintain independence from both the US and Communist countries).

Civil war CIA-backed strongman General Phoumi Nosavan thought Phoui's politics rather tame and with a nod from Washington he stepped into the breach in January 1959, eventually overthrowing Phoui in a coup in December and placing Prince Boun Oum in power. Pathet Lao leaders were imprisoned without trial. Confusion over Phoumas, Phouis and Phoumis led one American official to comment that it all "could have been a significant event or a typographical error".

Within a year, the rightist regime was overthrown by a neutralist *coup d'état* led by General Kong Lae and Prince Souvanna Phouma was recalled from exile in Cambodia to become prime minister of the first National Union. Souvanna Phouma incurred American wrath by inviting a Soviet ambassador to Vientiane in October. With US support, Nosavan staged yet another armed rebellion in December and sparked a new civil war. In the 1960 general elections, provincial authorities were threatened with military action if they did not support the right-wing groups and were rigged to ensure no Pathet Lao cadres could obtain a seat in office. In August 1960 paratroop neutralist Kong Le staged a successful coup d'état; however, with US funding, the rightists were able to assemble formidable troops in Savannakhet and marched to Vientiane, retaking the capital in mid-December. Kong Lae backed down, Souvanna Phouma shuffled back to Phnom Penh and a new rightwing government was set up under Boun Oum. By this stage, the Pathet Lao had consolidated considerable forces in the region surrounding the Plain of Jars and, with support from the Vietnamese, had been able to expand their territorial control in the north. This represented a major crisis to the incoming Kennedy administration that Stuart Martin-Fox (1996) describes as "second only to Cuba".

Zurich talks and the Geneva Accord The new prime minister, the old one and his Marxist half-brother finally sat down to talks in Zurich in June 1961, but any hope of an agreement was overshadowed by escalating tensions between the superpowers. In 1962, an international agreement on Laos was hammered out in Geneva by 14 participating nations and accords were signed, once again guaranteeing Lao neutrality.

By implication, the Geneva Accord denied the Viet Minh access to the Ho Chi Minh Trail. But aware of the reality of constant North Vietnamese infiltration through Laos into South Vietnam, the head of the American mission concluded that the agreement was "a good bad deal".

Another coalition government of National Union was formed under the determined neutralist Prince Souvanna Phouma (as prime minister), with Prince Souphanouvong for the Pathet Lao and Prince Boun Oum representing the right. A number of political assassinations derailed the process of reconciliation. Moreover, antagonisms between the left and the right, both backed financially by their respective allies, made it impossible for the unfunded neutralists to balance the two sided into any form of neutrality. It was no surprise when the coalition government collapsed within a few months and fighting resumed. This time the international community just shrugged and watched Laos sink back into the vortex of civil war. Unbeknown to the outside world, the conflict was rapidly degenerating into a war between the CIA and North Vietnamese jungle guerrillas.

Secret War

The war that wasn't In the aftermath of the Geneva Accord, the North Vietnamese, rather than reducing their forces in Laos, continued to increase their manpower on the ground. With the Viet Minh denying the existence of the Ho Chi Minh Trail, while at the same time enlarging it, Kennedy dispatched an undercover force of CIA men, green berets and US-trained Thai mercenaries to command 9000 Lao soldiers. By 1963, these American forces had grown to 30,000 men. Historian Roger Warner believes that by 1965 "word spread among a select circle of congressmen and senators about this exotic program run by Lone Star rednecks and Asian hillbillies that was better and cheaper than anything the Pentagon was doing in South Vietnam." To the north, the US also supplied Vang Pao's force of Hmong guerrillas, dubbed 'Mobile Strike Forces'. With the cooperation of Prince Souvanna Phouma, the CIA's commercial airline, Air America, ferried men and equipment into Laos from Thailand (and opium out, it is believed). Caught between Cold

War antagonisms it was impossible to maintain a modicum of neutrality as even the most staunch neutralist, Souvanna Phouma, began to become entangled. As Robbins argues, by the early 1960s, Sovanna Phouma – trying to reinforce the middle way – had given permission "for every clandestine manoeuvre the United States made to match the North Vietnamese. In turn Souvanna demanded that his complicity in such arrangements be kept secret, lest his position in the country become untenable." Owing to the clandestine nature of the military intervention in Laos, the rest of the world – believing that the Geneva settlement had solved the foreign interventionist problem – was oblivious as to what was happening on the ground. Right up until 1970, Washington never admitted to any activity in Laos beyond 'armed reconnaissance' flights over northern provinces. Richard Nixon, for example, claimed that "there are no American ground combat troops in Laos".

Meanwhile the North Vietnamese were fulfilling their two strategic priorities in the country: continued use of the Ho Chi Minh trail (by this stage the majority of North Vietnamese munitions and personnel for the Viet Cong was being shuffled along the trail) and ensuring that the Plain of Jars did not fall under the control of the right, where the US could launch attacks on North Vietnam. This latter goal amounted to supporting the Pathet Lao in their aim to hold onto as much territory as possible in the north. The Pathet Lao, in turn, were dependent on the North Vietnamese for supplies – both material and manpower. As Martin Stuart-Fox (1996) argues, "Pathet Lao leaders were not in a position after 1964 to reach any settlement that might have disadvantaged their Vietnamese mentors. Genuine Lao neutrality was out of the question for the Pathet Lao. It had to be subverted for the sake of the Vietnamese revolution." With both the US bankrolling the Royalist right and the Vietnamese puppeteering the Pathet Lao, within the country any pretence of maintaining a balance in the face of Cold War hostilities was shattered for neutralists like Souvanna Phouma.

Souvanna Phouma referred to it as 'the forgotten war' and it is often termed now the 'non-attributable war'. The willingness on the part of the Americans to dump millions of tonnes of ordnance on a country which was ostensibly neutral may have been made easier by the fact that some people in the administration did not believe Laos to be a country at all. Bernard Fall wrote that Laos at the time was "neither a geographical nor an ethnic or social entity, but merely a political convenience", while a Rand Corporation report written in 1970 described Laos as "hardly a country except in the legal sense". More colourfully, Secretary of State Dean Rusk described it as a "wart on the hog of Vietnam". Perhaps those in Washington could feel a touch better about bombing the hell out of a country which, in their view, occupied a sort of political never-never land – or which they could liken to an unfortunate skin complaint.

Not everyone agrees with this view that Laos never existed until the French wished it into existence. Scholar of Laos Arthur Dommen, for example, traces a true and coherent Lao identity back to Fa Ngum and his creation of the kingdom of Lane Xang in 1353, writing that it was "a state in the true sense of the term, delineated by borders clearly defined and consecrated by treaty" for 350 years. He goes on:

"Lao historians see a positive proof of the existence of a distinct Lao race (*sua sat Lao*), a Lao nation (*sat Lao*), a Lao country (*muong Lao*) and a Lao state (*pathet Lao*). In view of these facts, we may safely reject the notion, fashionable among apologists for a colonial enterprise of a later day, that Laos was a creation of French colonial policy and administration".

American bombing of the North Vietnamese Army's supply lines through Laos to South Vietnam along the Ho Chi Minh Trail in East Laos (see box, page 217) started in

Vietnam War

NORTH VIETNAM

CHINA

o Dien Bien Phu

Haiphong

HANOI □

LAOS

Xam Neua o

Gulf of Tonkin

o Luang Prabang

Phonsavanh o

Plain of Jars

Mekong River

□

VIENTIANE

Ho Chi Minh Trail

Demilitarized Zone (22-7-54)

THAILAND

Khe Sanh □

o Quang Tri

Hamburger Hill

Hué

Danang

Pakse o

Boloven Plateau

My Lai o

Kontum

o Pleiku

Ia Drang Valley

Qui Nhon

CAMBODIA

SOUTH VIETNAM

Mekong River

Ho Chi Minh Trail

o Dalat

Cam Ranh Bay

PHNOM PENH □

Tay Ninh o

Cu Chi o

Bien Hoa

SAIGON □

Vung Tao

Sihanoukville o

Can Tho o

Ap Bac

South China Sea

Gulf of Thailand

Ca Mau o

N

100 km

100 miles

1964 and fuelled the conflict between the Royalist Vientiane government and the Pathet Lao. The neutralists had been forced into alliance with the Royalists to avoid defeat in Xieng Kouang province. US bombers crossed Laos on bombing runs to Hanoi from air bases in Thailand and gradually the war in Laos escalated. In his book *The Ravens* (1987), Christopher Robbins sets the scene:

"Apparently, there was another war even nastier than the one in Vietnam and so secret that the location of the country in which it was being fought was classified. The cognoscenti simply referred to it as 'the Other Theater'. The men who chose to fight in it were hand-picked volunteers and anyone accepted for a tour seemed to disappear as if from the face of the earth."

America's side of the secret war was conducted from a one-room shack at the US base in Udon Thani, 'across the fence' in Thailand. This was the CIA's Air America operations room and in the same compound was stationed the 4802 Joint Liaison Detachment – or the CIA logistics office. In Vientiane, US pilots supporting Hmong General Vang Pao's rag-tag army, were given a new identity as rangers for the US Agency for International Development; they reported directly to the air attaché at the US embassy (see box, page 292). Robbins writes that they "were military men, but flew into battle in civilian clothes – denim cutoffs, T-shirts, cowboy hats and dark glasses ... Their job was to fly as the winged artillery of some fearsome warlord, who led an army of stone age mercenaries in the pay of the CIA and they operated out of a secret city hidden in the mountains of a jungle kingdom ..." He adds that CIA station chiefs and field agents "behaved like warlords in their own private fiefdoms."

The most notorious of the CIA's unsavoury operatives was Anthony Posepny – known as Tony Poe, on whom the character of Kurtz, the crazy colonel played by Marlon Brando in the film *Apocalypse Now*, was based. Originally, Poe had worked as Vang Pao's case officer; he then moved to North Laos and operated for years, on his own, in Burmese and Chinese border territories, offering his tribal recruits one US dollar for each set of Communist ears they brought back. Many of the spies and pilots of this secret war later re-emerged in covert and illegal arms-smuggling rackets to Libya, Iran and the Nicaraguan Contras.

By contrast, the Royalist forces were reluctant warriors: despite the fact that civil war was an ingrained tradition in Laos, the Lao went to great lengths to avoid fighting each other. One foreign journalist, reporting from Luang Prabang in the latter stages of the war, related how Royalist and Pathet Lao troops, encamped on opposite banks of the Nam Ou, agreed an informal ceasefire over Pi Mai (Lao New Year), to celebrate the king's visit to the sacred Pak Ou Caves (see page 115). Most Lao did not want to fight. Correspondents who covered the war noted that without the goading of their respective US and North Vietnamese masters, many would have gone home. Prior to the war, one military strategist described the Lao forces as one of the worst armies ever seen, adding that they made the [poorly regarded] "South Vietnamese Army look like Storm Troopers". "The troops lack the basic will to fight. They do not take initiative. A typical characteristic of the Laotian Army is to leave an escape route. US technicians attached to the various training institutions have not been able to overcome Lao apathy". (Ratnam, P, *Laos and the Superpowers*, 1980.)

Air Force planes were often used to carry passengers for money – or to smuggle opium out of the Golden Triangle. In the field, soldiers of the Royal Lao Army regularly fled when faced with a frontal assault by the Vietnam People's Army (NVA). The officer corps was uncommitted, lazy and corrupt; many ran opium-smuggling rackets and saw the war as a ticket to get rich quick. In the south, the Americans considered Royal Lao Air Force pilots unreliable because they were loath to bomb their own people and cultural heritage.

Raven 58, crossing the Fence

'Raven' was the call sign used by Forward Air Controllers (FACs) in Laos. It came to designate, however, a special breed of FAC – someone who was highly motivated, aggressive, decisive, daring and exceptionally skilled and professional in their work. The mystique was heightened by the secrecy of the assignment. Pilots would set off from Vietnam and then seemingly disappear.

To understand the importance of a Raven's mission, it is first necessary to understand the mission of an FAC. An FAC had three responsibilities: to conduct air reconnaissance to obtain first-hand information concerning enemy locations, activity and threats; to control and direct Air Force or Navy aircraft bombers or Army artillery on enemy targets; and to control, direct and coordinate air strikes with ground troops for close air support.

As a Raven Forward Air Controller (Raven FAC), I had the privilege of belonging to an elite group of pilots who flew covert operations in Laos in support of the Royal Laotian Army or the CIA Special Guerrilla Units (SGUs).

SGUs were trained by CIA Country Team members. They were an elite fighting force designed to interdict movement of the North Vietnamese along the Ho Chi Minh Trail in the south or in areas around the Plain of Jars in the north. When they operated along the trail or in other forward locations, their supplies would be flown in by a Porter aircraft, piloted by Continental Air Service or Air America pilots. The advantage of this aircraft was that it could land and take off on a very short 'runway' – about 30.5 m long.

Normally, I would support the SGUs from the air, providing reconnaissance or fighter aircraft support. However, on one day they returned the favour. My airplane

crashed in a rice paddy south of Attapeu. Nine North Vietnamese were across the paddy as I made a judicious move toward the opposite side. I knew that the SGUs were in the area near Attapeu, as I headed in that direction. As I came upon them, I recognized that they were friendly and shortly thereafter I was picked up by an Air America helicopter and flown to a nearby Lima Site (PS-38) for the night.

During the time of the Ravens, 1966 to 1975, there were only 191 pilots. Very few Americans actually ever went into Laos, except along the Ho Chi Minh Trail. My time in Laos was quite enjoyable. Officially, I was a forest ranger working for the Lao government. In fact, I worked for the American ambassador and provided visual reconnaissance and direct air support for the Royal Laotian Army and the CIA SGUs.

And there was much to discourage volunteers. The casualty rate was said to be 50%. The conditions were more harsh. And, then there were the drug dealers and gold dealers. (At that time it was illegal to trade in gold in the United States. One could only buy 'jewellery'. For that reason, contracted CIA pilots from Air America and Continental Air Service would be seen wearing heavy gold bracelets which were not much more than gold bars formed into a bracelet.)

But I had volunteered to join the Air Force for the specific purpose of going to Vietnam and Laos. I had been a student at Ohio State University and was exempt from the draft. I was 26 years old when I joined the Air Force – just under the 26½ age limit required of Air Force pilots. Having never flown before in my life I became a '90-day Wonder' as I received my commission as a second Lieutenant at Lackland Air Force Base in San Antonio, Texas. From Lackland I went to Laredo,

Texas for Undergraduate Pilot Training. I completed my training in 1968, followed by 0-1 (Bird Dog) Special Operations Training, POW training and then on to the Philippines for Jungle Survival Training.

In Vietnam I was stationed at the Tuy Hoa MACV (Military Assistance Command Vietnam) compound where I flew in support of the Vietnamese Army. I volunteered for the Steve Canyon Program soon after arriving at Tuy Hoa. The Steve Canyon Program was named after the adventurist comic strip character. As I departed Bien Hoa Air Force Base near Saigon for Laos, I learned why it had been called Steve Canyon. The colonel who drove me to the airplane which would take me to my first stop in Thailand said: "Well, now all you have to look forward to is ... glory, money and medals!"

Ravens were a breed apart. They would wear what they wanted when flying – shorts and T-shirts, homemade flying suits or cowboy outfits. They would disregard the Air Force standards for flying time and clock as much as 150 to 200 hours a month.

The monetary rewards were appealing. While not the income a true 'mercenary' could receive – US$50,000 or US$100,000 for flying certain cargo in Southeast Asia or the Middle East – the extra per diem income, free in addition to being paid for board and room, maids and cooks, and combat pay, was welcome. It could amount to an extra US$1000 per month.

Arriving at Udon Air Force Base in Northeast Thailand, I was directed to a remote area of the base called 'Det-1'. The commander didn't know much about what I would be doing, but he had to maintain my Air Force records, since when I went into Laos, I would be a 'civilian'. Flying into Laos was quite different from flying into other countries. To protect my destination, when I crossed the border I would radio: "Raven 58, crossing the fence." 'Laos' would never be mentioned.

Along with the AOC (Air Operations Center) commander, a radio operator, two airplane mechanics and a medic, I lived in the town of Pakse, in a large colonial villa. The living conditions were excellent. After flying out into the war zone each day and returning, I would go down town to a movie or to the Mekong Bar for dancing and music, or to a sidewalk café for dinner.

I believed that the Lao knew who I was. But, I found out that many did not. While trying to make a call to Vietnam to speak with my future Vietnamese wife, Kim Chi, a new Air Force Lieutenant received the call and became inquisitive as to why I referred to myself as "Mister Thompson" rather than "Captain". Even military personnel in Vietnam, including Air Force Forward Air Controllers, did not know about the clandestine operations of the Ravens.

Adapted from text written by Ken Thompson, or Raven 58, who flew as a FAC in Vietnam and Laos for over 26 months between 1968 and 1970. He was awarded two Distinguished Flying Crosses and a Bronze Star for valour.

(Footprint managed to contact Ken and is pleased to report the following update. Ken's eldest daughter Mai has since married and has three children. Ken and Kim Chi returned to Vietnam in 1998 with their youngest daughter. Ken writes: "In 1998 while I was at our home, this older gentleman came riding in on his bicycle. He knew I was there and wanted to come and see me. We sat down and had some tea as my wife translated for him. He was the former VC general whose troops I had bombed and who had tried to capture my wife during the war. We sat and talked and had a good time together.")

The air war The clandestine bombing of the Ho Chi Minh Trail (see box, page 217) caused many civilian casualties – so-called collateral damage – and displaced much of the population in Laos' eastern provinces. A whole gamut of military devices and defoliants were used to destroy Lao territory and, although there are not really any official casualty figures in circulation, it is estimated that between a sixth and a tenth of the population were killed. By 1973, when the bombing stopped, the US had dropped more than two million tonnes of bombs on Laos – equivalent to some 700 kg of explosives for every man, woman and child in the country. It is reported that up to 70% of all B-52 strikes in Indochina were targeted at Laos. To pulverize the country to this degree 580,994 bombing sorties were flown.

The bombing intensified during the Nixon administration: up to 1969 less than 500,000 tonnes of bombs had been dropped on Laos; from then on nearly that amount was dropped each year. In the 1960s and early 1970s, more bombs rained on Laos than were dropped during the Second World War – the equivalent of a plane load of bombs every eight minutes for nine years. This campaign cost Americans more than US$2 million a day but the cost to Laos was incalculable. The activist Fred Branfman, quoted by Roger Warner in *Shooting at the Moon*, wrote: "Nine years of bombing, two million tons of bombs, whole rural societies wiped off the map, hundreds of thousands of peasants treated like herds of animals in a Clockwork Orange fantasy of an aerial African Hunting safari."

The war was not restricted to bombing missions – once potential Pathet Lao strongholds had been identified, fighters, using rockets, were sent to attempt to destroy them. Such was the intensity of the bombing campaign that villagers in Pathet Lao-controlled areas are said to have turned to planting and harvesting their rice at night. Few of those living in Xieng Khouang province, the Bolovan Plateau or along the Ho Chi Minh Trail had any idea of who was bombing them or why. The consequences were often tragic, as in the case of Tham Phiu Cave (see page 174).

In *The Ravens*, Robbins tells of how a fighter pilot's inauspicious dream would lead the commander to cancel a mission; bomber pilots hated dropping bombs and when they did, aluminium canisters were brought back and sold as scrap. After the war, the collection and sale of war debris turned into an industry for tribes' people in Xieng Khouang province and along the Ho Chi Minh Trail. Bomb casings, aircraft fuel tanks and other bits and pieces that were not sold to Thailand have been put to every conceivable use in rural Laos. They are used as cattle troughs, fence posts, flower pots, stilts for houses, water carriers, temple bells, knives and ploughs. The bomb craters are often turned into fish ponds.

But the bombing campaign has also left a more deadly legacy – of unexploded bombs and anti-personnel mines. Today, over 30 years after the air war finally ended, over 500,000 tonnes of deadly unexploded ordnance (UXO) is believed to still be scattered throughout nine of Laos' 13 provinces. Most casualties are caused by cluster bombs, or 'bombis' as they have become known. Cluster bombs are carried in large canisters called Cluster Bomb Units (CBUs), which open in mid-air, releasing around 670 tennis ball-sized bomblets. Upon detonation, the bombie propels around 200,000 pieces of shrapnel over an area the size of several football fields. This UXO contamination inhibits long-term development, especially in Xieng Khouang Province (see page165), making farming in this part a Laos a highly dangerous occupation was simply one of those 'accidents' of war.

The land war Within Laos, the war focused on the strategic Plain of Jars in Xieng Khouang province (see page 169) and was co-ordinated from the town of Long Tien (the secret city), tucked into the limestone hills to the southwest of the plain. Known as the most secret spot on earth, it was not marked on maps and was populated by the CIA, the Ravens (the air controllers who flew spotter planes and called in air strikes) and the Hmong.

The Pathet Lao were headquartered in caves in Xam Neua province, to the north of the plain. Their base was equipped with a hotel cave (for visiting dignitaries), a hospital cave, embassy caves and even a theatre cave.

The Plain of Jars (known as the PDJ, after the French Plaine de Jarres), was the scene of some of the heaviest fighting and changed hands countless times, the Royalist and Hmong forces occupying it during the wet season, the Pathet Lao in the dry. During this period in the conflict Long Tien, known as one of the country's 'alternate' bases to keep nosy journalists away (the word 'alternate' was meant to indicate that it was unimportant), grew to such an extent that it became Laos' second city. James Parker in his book *Codename Mule* claims that the air base was so busy that at its peak it was handling more daily flights than Chicago's O'Hare airport. Others claim that it was the busiest airport in the world. There was also fighting around Luang Prabang and the Bolovan Plateau to the south.

The end of the war Although the origins of the war in Laos were distinct from those in Vietnam, the two wars had effectively merged by the early 1970s and it became inevitable that the fate of the Americans to the east would determine the outcome in Laos. By 1970 it was no longer possible for the US administration to shroud the war in secrecy: a flood of refugees had arrived in Vientiane in an effort to escape the conflict.

During the dying days of the US-backed regime in Vientiane, CIA agents and Ravens lived in quarters south of the capital, known as KM-6 – because it was 6 km from town. Another compound in downtown Vientiane was known as 'Silver City' and reputedly also sometimes housed CIA agents. On the departure of the Americans and the arrival of the new regime in 1975, the Communists' secret police made Silver City their new home. Today, Lao people still call military intelligence officers 'Silvers'.

A ceasefire was agreed in February 1973, a month after Washington and Hanoi struck a similar deal in Paris. Power was transferred in April 1974 to yet another coalition government set up under the premiership of Souvanna Phouma. The neutralist prince once again had a Communist deputy and foreign affairs minister. The Red Prince, Souphanouvong, headed the Joint National Political Council. Foreign troops were given two months to leave. The North Vietnamese were allowed to remain along the Ho Chi Minh Trail, for although US forces had withdrawn from South Vietnam, the war there was not over.

The communists' victories over Saigon (and Phnom Penh) in April 1975 were a catalyst for the Pathet Lao, who advanced on Vientiane. It is widely hailed as the 'bloodless' takeover. Due to the country's mixed loyalties the Pathet Lao government undertook a gradual process of eroding away loyalties to the Royalist government. As the end drew near and the Pathet Lao advanced out of the mountains and towards the more populated Mekong valley – the heartland of the Royalist government – province after province fell with scarcely a shot fired. The mere arrival of a small contingent of Pathet Lao soldiers was sufficient to secure victory – even though these soldiers arrived at Wattay Airport on Chinese transport planes to be greeted by representatives of the Royal Lao government.

Administration of Vientiane by the People's Revolutionary Committee was secured on 18 August. The atmosphere was very different from that which accompanied the Communist's occupation of Saigon in Vietnam the same year. In Vientiane peaceful crowds turned out to hear speeches by Pathet Lao cadres. The King remained unharmed in his palace and while a coffin representing 'dead American imperialism' was burned this was done in a 'carnival' atmosphere. Vientiane was declared 'officially liberated' on 23 August

1975. The coalition government was dismissed and Souvanna Phouma resigned for the last time. All communications with the outside world were cut.

While August 1975 represents a watershed in the history of Laos, scholars are left with something of a problem: explaining why the Pathet Lao prevailed. According to Martin Stuart-Fox, the Lao revolutionary movement "had not mobilized an exploited peasantry with promises of land reform, for most of the country was underpopulated and peasant families generally owned sufficient land for their subsistence needs. The appeal of the Pathet Lao to their lowland Lao compatriots was in terms of nationalism and independence and the preservation of Lao culture from the corrosive American influence; but no urban uprising occurred until the very last minute when effective government had virtually ceased to exist … The small Lao intelligentsia, though critical of the Royal Lao government, did not desert it entirely and their recruitment to the Pathet Lao was minimal. Neither the monarchy, still less Buddhism, lost legitimacy." Stuart-Fox concludes that it was external factors, and in particular the intervention of outside powers, which led to the victory of the Pathet Lao. Without the Vietnamese and Americans, the Pathet Lao would not have won. For the great mass of Laos' population before 1975, Communism meant nothing. This was not a mass uprising but a victory secured by a small ideologically committed elite and forged in the furnace of the war in Indochina.

As the Pathet Lao seized power, rightist ministers, ranking civil servants, doctors, much of the intelligentsia and around 30,000 Hmong crossed the Mekong and escaped into Thailand, fearing that they would face persecution. Although the initial exodus was large, most refugees fled in the next few years up until 1980 as the Lao government introduced new reforms aimed at wiping out decadence and reforming the economic system.

The refugee camps By the late 1980s, a total of 340,000 people – 10% of the population and mostly middle class – had fled the country. At least half of the refugees were Hmong, the US's key allies during the war, who feared reprisals and persecution. From 1988, refugees who had made it across the border began to head back across the Mekong from camps in Thailand and to asylum in the US and France. More than 2000 refugees were also repatriated from Yunnan Province in China. The government offered to return confiscated property so long as they stayed for at least six months and become Lao citizens once again.

Nonetheless, many lived for years in refugee camps, while the better connected secured US, Australian and French passports. For Laos, a large proportion of its human capital drained westwards, creating a vacuum of skilled personnel that would hamper – and still does – reconstruction. But a significant number who had aligned themselves with the Royalists decided to help build a new Laos; they saw themselves as Lao patriots and their duty was to stay.

Laos under Communism

The People's Democratic Republic of Laos was proclaimed in December 1975 with Prince Souphanouvong as president and Kaysone Phomvihane as secretary-general of the Lao People's Revolutionary Party (a post he had held since its formation in 1955). The king's abdication was accepted and the ancient Lao monarchy was abolished, together with King Samsenthai's 600-year-old system of village autonomy. But instead of executing their vanquished foes, the LPRP installed Souvanna and the ex-king, Savang Vatthana, as 'special advisers' to the politburo. On Souvanna's death in 1984, he was accorded a full state funeral. The king did not fare so well: he later died ignominiously while in detention after his alleged involvement in a counter-revolutionary plot (see below).

Surprisingly, the first actions of the new revolutionary government was not to build a new revolutionary economy and society, but to stamp out unsavoury behaviour. Dress and hairstyles, dancing and singing, even the food served at family celebrations, were all subject to scrutiny by 'Investigation Cadres'. If a person was found not to match up to the Party's standards of good taste they were bundled off to re-education camps.

Relations with Thailand, which in the immediate wake of the revolution remained cordial, deteriorated in late 1976. A military coup in Bangkok led to rumours that the Thai military, backed by the CIA, was supporting Hmong and other right-wing Lao rebels. The regime feared that Thailand would be used as a springboard for a royalist coup attempt. This prompted the arrest of King Savang Vatthana, together with his family and Crown Prince Vongsavang, who were dispatched to a re-education camp in Sam Neua province, never to be heard from again. In December 1989 Kaysone Phomvihane admitted in Paris that the king had died of malaria in 1984 and that the queen had also died "of natural causes" – no mention was made of Vongsavang.

Re-education camps Between 30,000 and 40,000 reactionaries who had been unable to flee the country were interned in remote camps for 're-education'. These camps referred to as Samanaya took their name from the Western word, seminar. The reluctant scholars were forced into slave labour in jungle conditions and subjected to political propaganda for anything from a few months up to 15 years.

By 1978, the re-education policy starting to wind down, although, in 1986, Amnesty International released a report on the forgotten inhabitants of the re-education camps, claiming that 6000-7000 were still being held. By that time incarceration behind barbed wire had ended and internees were 'arbitrarily restricted' rather than imprisoned. They were assigned to road construction and other public works. Nonetheless, conditions for these victims of the war in Indochina suffered from malnutrition, disease and many died prematurely in captivity. It is unclear how many died, but at least 15,000 have been freed. Officials of the old regime, ex-government ministers and former Royalist air force and army officers, together with thousands of others unlucky enough to have been on the wrong side, were released from the camps, largely during the mid to late 1980s. Most of the surviving political prisoners have now been reintegrated into society. Some work in the tourism industry and one, a former colonel in the Royal Lao Army, jointly owns the **Asian Pavilion Hotel** (formerly the **Vieng Vilai**) on Samsenthai Road in downtown Vientiane.

The Lao, as scores of books like this one keep reminding their readers, are a gentle people and it is hard not to leave the country without that view being reinforced. Even the Lao People's Revolutionary Party seems quaintly inept and it is hard to equate it with its more brutal sister parties in Vietnam, Cambodia, China or the former Soviet Union. Yet five students who meekly called for greater political freedom in 1999 were whisked off by the police and have not been heard of since. So much for soggy ineptness.

Reflecting on 10 years of 'reconstruction' Laos' recent political and economic history is covered under Modern Laos (see below). But it is worth ending this account of the country's history by noting the brevity of Laos' experiment with full-blown Communism. Just 10 years after the Pathet Lao took control of Vientiane, the leadership were on the brink of far-reaching economic reforms. By the mid-1980s it was widely acknowledged that Marxism-Leninism had failed the country. The population was still dreadfully poor; the ideology of Communism had failed to entice more than a handful into serious and enthusiastic support for the party and its ways; and graft and nepotism were on the rise.

Modern Laos

Politics

President Kaysone Phomvihane died in November 1992, aged 71. (His right-hand man, Prince Souphanouvong – the so-called Red Prince – died just over two years later, on 9 January 1995.) As one obituary put it, Kaysone was older than he seemed, both historically and ideologically. He had been chairman of the LPRP since the mid-1950s and had been a protégé and comrade of Ho Chi Minh, who led the Vietnamese struggle for independence from the French. After leading the Lao Resistance Government – or Pathet Lao – from caves in Xam Neua province in the north, Kaysone assumed the premiership on the abolition of the monarchy in 1975. But under his leadership – and following the example of his mentors in Hanoi – Kaysone became the driving force behind the market-orientated reforms. The year before he died, he gave up the post of prime minister for that of president.

His death didn't change much, as other members of the old guard stepped into the breach. Nouhak Phounsavanh – a sprightly 78-year-old former truck driver and hardline Communist – succeeded him as president, but in February 1998 was replaced by 75-year-old General Khamtai Siphandon – the outgoing prime minister and head of the LPRP. Khamtai represents the last of the revolutionary Pathet Lao leaders who fought the Royalists and the Americans. In April 2006, Siphandon, the last of the old guard from the caves in Vieng Xai, was replaced as president by Choummaly Sayasone.

Recent years

With the introduction of the New Economic Mechanism in 1986 there were hopes that economic liberalization would be matched by political *glasnost*. So far, however, the monolithic Party shows few signs of equating capitalism with democracy. While the Lao brand of Communism has always been seen as relatively tame, it remains a far cry from political pluralism. Laos' first constitution since the Communists came to power in 1975 was approved in 1991. The country's political system is referred to as a popular democracy, yet it has rejected any significant moves towards multi-party reforms.

Take the elections to the 108-seat National Assembly on 24 February 2002. All of the candidates standing for election had been approved by the LPRP's mass organization, the Lao Front for National Construction. While it is not necessary for a candidate to be a member of the LPRP to stand, they are closely vetted and have to demonstrate that they have a 'sufficient level of knowledge of party policy'. As with the previous elections to the National Assembly at the end of 1997, only one of the 108 deputies elected was not a member of the Lao People's Revolutionary Party. This pattern of party cadres maintaining political seats was repeated in the National Assembly elections held in April 2006, where LPRP members won 114 out of 115 parliamentary seats.

On the dreamy streets of Vientiane, the chances of a Tiananmen-style uprising are remote. But the events of the late 1980s and early 1990s in Eastern Europe and Moscow did alarm hardliners – just as they did in Beijing and Hanoi. They can be reasonably confident, however, that in their impoverished nation, most people are more worried about where their next meal is going to come from than they are about the allure of multi-party democracy. Day-to-day politics aren't on the radar of most Lao citizens and many would find it hard to name the president and prime minister.

The greatest concern for the Lao leadership is what effect westernization is having upon the population. The economic reforms, or so the authorities would seem to believe, have brought not only foreign investment and new consumer goods, but also greed, corruption, consumerism and various social ills from drugs to prostitution.

In 2010, the politburo still largely controlled the country and, for now, sweeping changes are unlikely. Most of the country's leaders are well into their 60s and were educated in communist countries like Russia and Vietnam. However, the younger Lao people (particularly those that have studied abroad in Japan, Australia, UK or the US) are starting to embrace new political and economic ideas. The government takes inspiration from Vietnam's success and is more likely to follow the lead of its neighbour rather than adopting any Western model of government.

Foreign relations

Laos is rapidly becoming a keystone in mainland Southeast Asia and sees its future in linking in with its more powerful and richer neighbours. To this end Laos joined the Association of Southeast Asian Nations (ASEAN) on 23 July 1997, becoming the group's second Communist member (Vietnam joined in July 1995). By joining, Vientiane hoped to be in a better position to trade off the interests of the various powers in the region, thereby giving it greater room for manoeuvre. It was also hoped that Laos would be able to develop on the coat tails of Southeast Asia's economic 'tigers'.

One of Laos' strategies for further integration into the Asian economy is to establish itself as a regional transit point, with new highways dissecting the country at 100 km intervals. Construction of one major highway started in 2005, connecting Thailand's northernmost province of Chiang Rai to Kunming in China via the Lao provinces of Bokeo and Luang Namtha. The 700-km-long highway (of which 228 km is in Laos) could generate more income for the landlocked country. However, it also poses a major threat in terms of increased transmission of HIV from transient workers and truckers. To add considerable insult to injury, China is building a huge truck-stop near Boten in northwest Laos (see page 148), which is likely to wipe out a large proportion of the income Laos might have earned from transit vehicles.

Laos is the only landlocked country in Southeast Asia and Vientiane is keen to pursue a cooperative 'equilibrium policy' with its neighbours. There is a widely held view that Laos – a small, poor, weak and landlocked country – is best served by having multiple friends in international circles. It has often been referred to as a 'buffer' state, which exists to ensure that none of the surrounding countries have to border each other. The leadership in Vientiane is in the tricky situation of having to play off China's military might, Thailand's commercial aggressiveness and Vietnam's population pressures, while keeping everyone happy. The answer, in many people's minds, is to promote a policy of interdependence in mainland Southeast Asia.

Relations with Thailand From the 1980s the government took steps to improve its foreign relations – and Thailand has been the main beneficiary. Historically, Thailand has always been the main route for international access to landlocked Laos. Survival instincts told the Vientiane regime that reopening its front door was of paramount importance. The border disputes with Thailand have now been settled and the bloody clashes of 1987 and 1988, when thousands on both sides lost their lives, are history. Thailand is Laos' largest investor and the success of the market reforms depend more on Thailand than any other country. Economic pragmatism, then, has forced Vientiane to cosy up to Bangkok. This does not mean that relations are warm. Indeed, Vientiane is suspicious of Thai intentions, a suspicion born of a history of conflict.

Thailand is Vientiane's lifeline to the outside world. In 1994 the two old foes agreed to build the Mittaphab – or Friendship – bridge across the Mekong linking Vientiane with Nong Khai in Northeast Thailand. The bridge was built with Australian assistance and opened in 1994 (see box, page 80).

Thais have emerged as one of the main sources of foreign investment in Laos. A number of Thai commercial banks have set up in Laos, along with businesspeople, consultants and loggers. Young Lao, who once attended universities in the old Soviet bloc, are now dispatched to Thai universities. The warming of relations between Bangkok and Vientiane has raised some eyebrows: sceptics say Laos' wealth of unexploited natural resources is a tempting reward for patching things up. Thailand is also the most important player in the Nam Theun II hydropower project (see box, page 196). But to its credit, Thailand has prioritized aid to Laos and has signed joint ventures in almost every sector – from science and technology to trade, banking and agriculture. Thai businesspeople have partially taken over the state beer and brewery and the Thai conglomerate Shinawatra (owned by the former disgraced Thai prime minister) has been given telecommunications concessions. Nonetheless, Thai diplomats are only too aware of the poor reputation that their businessmen have in Vientiane. They are regarded as overbearing and superior in their attitude to the Lao and rapacious, predatory and mercenary in their business dealings. The Thai government has even run courses to try and improve business behaviour.

The sleeping giant awakens: relations with China In 1988 China and Laos normalized relations and this was followed by a defence co-operation agreement signed in 1993. Recently, Beijing has taken a particular interest in developing Laos' infrastructure, more out of self-interest than altruism. As China continues to develop at a breakneck speed, its interest in Laos' natural resources is expected to escalate, particularly in the areas of timber, iron ore, copper, gold, and gemstones. China is now Laos' second largest trading partner and foreign investor. The Asian Development Bank (ADB) reported that Lao-China trade grew from US$33.1 million in 1990 to US$118.3 million in 2003 and to US$250 million in 2007, for the most part, in China's favour. Over the last few years the economic giant has secured a deal to build numerous roads in Laos pro bono, in exchange for logging the areas around the roads.

China's now gives more than US$280 million annually to Laos in development aid. It is also building the highway that will eventually link Yunnan province to Thailand via Laos. Between 2001 to August 2007, Chinese foreign direct investment amounted to US$1.1 billion and by 2009 at more than US$2 billion. They are the second largest foreign investment country after Thailand. Of the $4313 million investment approved in 2009, the greatest number of projects were Chinese, at 324.

Chinese companies are investing heavily in Lao's natural resources, including mining, rubber plantations and hydropower (the largest sector), as well as telecommunications, construction materials and hotels and restaurants. Alongside this economic investment, there has been an increase in Chinese migration. The number of Chinese officially living in Laos is 30,000, though the unofficial number is estimated to be 10 times that. Nonetheless, not a bad word is to be whispered about Beijing in the political corridors of Vientiane.

Laos' ever-tightening relationship with China could jeopardize ties with the country's closest ally, Vietnam, which shares a 1300-km-long border with Laos and historically has had poor relations with China.

Relations with Vietnam The Lao government has a special relationship with Vietnam, as it was Hanoi that helped the LPRP achieve power. Vietnam is also Laos' biggest trading partner. However, as Laos has turned to the West, Japan and Thailand for economic help, the government has become more critical of its closest Communist ally, Vietnam. Following Vietnam's invasion of Cambodia in December 1978, thousands of Vietnamese moved into northern Laos as permanent colonizers and by 1978 there were an estimated 40,000 Vietnamese regulars in Laos but, in 1987, 50,000 Vietnamese troops withdrew. In 1990 a Vientiane census found 15,000 Vietnamese living illegally in the capital, most of whom were promptly deported. With the death of President Kaysone Phomvihane in November 1992, another historical link with Vietnam was cut. He was half-Vietnamese and most of his cabinet owed their education and their posts to Hanoi's succour during the war years. As the old men of the Lao Communist Party die off, so their replacements are looking elsewhere for investment and political support. They do not have such deep fraternal links with their brothers in Hanoi and are keen to diversify their international relations.

Relations with the USA Laos is the only country in Indochina to have maintained relations with the US since 1975, despite the fact that, 30 years since the illegal bombing campaign of Laos subsided, the US has neither offered a substantial sum of money for reparations nor helped to clear the tonnes of unexploded ordnance littering the eastern side of the country. Washington even expected the Lao government to allocate funds to help locate the bodies of US pilots shot down in the war. At a meeting between the Foreign Affairs Minister, General Phoune Sipaseuth, and the US Secretary of State, James Baker, in October 1990, Vientiane pledged to co-operate with the US over the narcotics trade and to step up the search for the 530 American MIAs still listed as missing in the Lao jungle. In 1993, trilateral talks between Laos, Vietnam and the US allowed for greater cooperation in the search for MIAs, many of whom are thought to have been airmen, shot down over the Ho Chi Minh Trail. The MIA charity, based in Vientiane, has since assumed quite a high profile. In 1992, America's diplomatic presence in Laos was upgraded to ambassadorial status from chargé d'affaires and, at the end of 1997, a high-level US mission to Laos promised greater support in the country's bomb-defusing work. However, until 2004, Laos remained one of the few countries to be denied normal trade relations with the US, the others being North Korea, Cuba and Myanmar (Burma).

Under pressure from the US (a dangling carrot perhaps?) Laos has all but eradicated opium, at huge cost to the country socially and economically. Since 1989, the US government has handed over US$38 million for drug control to the Lao government but this hasn't stretched far enough to ensure that former opium producers aren't left starving.

But relations between the two countries have improved. This is driven by the US desire to counterbalance growing Chinese influence in the region. Most mainland Southeast Asian countries are reaping the rewards by simultaneously playing off the two superpowers and securing as much aid and trade as possible from both. In February 2005, a Bilateral Trade Agreement between the US and Laos entered into force, leading to a rise in bilateral trade from US$15.7 million in 2006, to US$8.9 million in 2003 and to US$63.8 million in 2009.

Relations with other countries Fortunately Laos is unwilling to put all its eggs in one basket. Japan is now Laos' biggest aid donor and Vientiane has also courted other Western countries, particularly Sweden (a long-time ally), France, Germany and Australia, who have donated significant sums of aid. Lao's former lifeline with Moscow is now of scant importance to Laos' economic future.

Economy

Twenty years ago, if the world's financial markets crashed and international trade and commerce collapsed overnight, Laos would have been blissfully immune from the catastrophe. It would be 'farming as usual' the next morning. Since the mid-1980s, though, the government has gradually begun cautiously to tread the free market path, veering off the old command system. Farms have been privatized and the state has to compete for produce with market traders at market prices. Many of the unprofitable state-owned businesses and factories have been leased or sold off.

Centuries of war and 15 years of Communism had little impact on the self-reliant villages of rural Laos. After the 1975 takeover, the Lao government, reliant on aid from Vietnam, decided to assuage this dependency by expanding on their existing economic base – agriculture. To this end, in March 1978 the government launched an agricultural cooperativization scheme – a plan to collectivize agriculture through the development of village-based cooperatives. The government's attempts at cooperativization proved unpopular and unworkable. Just before the cooperativization programme was abruptly suspended in mid-1979 there were 2800 cooperatives accounting for perhaps 25% of farming families. But even these figures overestimate the role of cooperatives at that time, for many were scarcely functioning.

The little work that has been undertaken on agriculture during this period has shown that even when cooperatives were functioning, their members were reluctant participants and there was a good amount of petty obstructionism. The reasons why cooperatives were such a failure are numerous. To begin with and unlike China and Vietnam, there were almost no large landlords, there was little tenancy and there was abundant land. The inequalities that were so obvious in neighbouring countries simply did not exist in Laos. Second, most farmers were subsistence cultivators; capitalism had barely made inroads into the Lao countryside and the forces of commercialization were largely absent. Further and third, the LPRP provided little support either of a technical or financial kind. As a result, farmers – largely uneducated and bound to their traditional methods of production – saw little incentive to change. In some areas it was not so much a lack of interest in cooperatives, but a positive dislike of them. There were reports of farmers slaughtering their cattle, burning their fields and eating their poultry, rather than handing their livestock or crops over to the Party. By mid-1979, when the policy was suspended, the leadership in Vientiane had concluded that their attempts at cooperativization had been a disaster.

After the policy was suspended, the government returned to a free enterprise system in the countryside. Farmers now effectively own their land and, since a new land law was approved by the National Assembly in 1997, they can pass it on to their children and use it as collateral to get a bank loan. They can produce whatever crops they like and can sell these on what has become virtually a free market. Lao farmers, though they may be poor and though technology may be antiquated, are in essence no different in terms of the ways they work than their kinsfolk over the Mekong in Thailand.

Laos made the jump from a sleepy agrarian economy hidden behind a facade of socialism to a reforming economy like China and Vietnam in the 1980s. In English this change is rather blandly named the New Economic Mechanism (NEM). Locally, the more evocative terms *chin thanakan mai* (new thinking) and *kanpatihup setthakit* (reform economy) are used. The origins of the NEM can be traced back to 1982 when the possibility of fundamental reform of the economy was first entertained by a small group within the leadership. The logic for economic reform and the integration of Laos into the regional –

and world – economies was pretty compelling. During the decade of command planning from 1975 through to 1985 the economy grew at just 2.9% per year, barely sufficient to meet the needs of a growing population and not enough to fuel the desire for a better standard of living. The government's fear was that, like other communist countries, the failure to bring the Lao people a better standard of living might challenge the supremacy of the Lao People's Revolutionary Party. The decision to opt for reform seemed to be borne out as the economy picked up steam. For the next three or four years the debate continued within this small circle and it was not until 1985 that the NEM was actually pilot-tested in the Vientiane area, making Laos one of the very first countries to embrace 'perestroika'. As late General Secretary Kaysone Phomvihane stated at the Fourth Party Congress in 1986:

"In all economic activities, we must know how to apply objective laws and take into account socio-economic efficiency. At the present time, our country is still at the first stage of the transition period. Hence the system of economic laws now being applied to our country is very complicated. It includes not only the specific laws of socialism but also the laws of commodity production. Reality indicates that if we only apply the specific economic laws of socialism alone and defy the general laws pertaining to commodity production, or vice versa, we will make serious mistakes in our economic undertaking during this transition period" (General Secretary Kaysone Phomvihane, Fourth Party Congress 1986; quoted in Lao PDR 1989).

Under the horrified gaze of Marx and Lenin – their portraits still dominate the plenary hall – it was announced that the state motto had changed from "Peace, Independence, Unity and Socialism" to "Peace, Independence, Democracy, Unity and Prosperity". The last part is largely wishful thinking for one of the poorest countries in Southeast Asia, but it reflected the realization that unless Laos turned off the socialist road fast, it would have had great difficulty digging itself out of the economic quagmire that 15 years' adherence to Marxism had created.

The success of the reforms there led to the NEM being presented at – and adopted by – the critical Fourth Party Congress of 1986. The NEM encompasses a range of reformist policies, much like those adopted in other countries from Russia to Vietnam: a move to a market determination of prices and resource allocation; a shift away from central planning to 'guidance' planning; a decentralization of control to industries and lower levels of government and the encouragement of the private sector; the encouragement of foreign investment and the promulgation of a new investment law allowing more relaxed foreign ownership and 'tax holidays'; a lifting of barriers to internal and external trade.

What Laos was able to achieve by introducing the NEM was a very rapid reorientation of its economy. But the question to be asked is: 'what exactly was being reformed?' The assumption is that Laos, as a so-called transitional economy, was making – is making – the transition from communism to capitalism, from state to market. This, though, misses the point that in 1986 there was remarkably little in Laos to reform. The great majority of the population were poor farmers (and still are) and the country's industrial base was almost non-existent. There were almost no communes to break up and there was no large state industrial sector to dismember. It all meant that the task of the Lao leadership has been comparatively easy when compared with, say, Vietnam. In a sense, Laos was never socialist except in name and so the shift to a market economy involved not a move from socialism to capitalism, but from subsistence to capitalism.

This doesn't mean that reform has been easy, because although Laos may not have had to undo years of socialist reconstruction and development, there was also little that the leadership could build on to promote modernization. There were few skilled workers, low levels of infrastructure, large slices of the country are almost impossible to reach and few entrepreneurs and even fewer people with the money to invest in new ventures. In other words, Laos was short of most of the elements that constitute a modern economy.

To introduce the sweeping reforms former President Kaysone Phomvihane shouldered much of the blame for the miserable state of the economy, admitting that the Party had made mistakes. Laos underwent the political equivalent of an earth tremor in March 1991 at the Fifth Congress of the Lao People's Revolutionary Party (LPRP). Pro-market reforms were embraced and the politburo and central committee got a much-needed transfusion of new blood. At the same time, the hammer and sickle motif was quietly removed from the state emblem and enlightened sub-editors set to work on the national credo, which is emblazoned on all official documents. In August 1991, at the opening of the People's Supreme Assembly, Kaysone Phomvihane, the late President, said: "Socialism is still our objective, but it is a distant one. Very distant." With that statement, Kaysone embraced – somewhat reluctantly, it must be said – the country's market-orientated policy, Chin Thanakan Mai or 'New Thinking'.

At the Congress in 1991 he set the new national agenda: Laos had to step up its exports, encourage more foreign investment, promote tourism and rural development, entice its shifting cultivators into proper jobs and revamp the financial system. In doing so he prioritized the problems but offered no solutions bar the loosening of state control and the promotion of private enterprise.

The first task for the government was to stabilize the value of the local currency, the kip, and introduce market 'discipline' so as to eliminate a booming currency black market. So from 1986, when economic reforms were first introduced, Laos eliminated six of its seven official exchange rates to create a unified market-related rate. By the early 1990s the kip had stabilized at around 700 to the US dollar. The once-booming black market all but disappeared. Although still a non-convertible currency, the kip was as much in demand in Laos as the US dollar and Thai baht. This helped put Laos on a more competitive footing. Unfortunately for supporters of economic reform, the collapse of the Thai baht and the consequent fall in the value of the kip encouraged the Lao government to reintroduce currency controls (see the section below).

During the early years of reform, between 1986 and 1990, the economy grew and from 1991-1995 increased again to 6.5% per year. However economic liberalization also has its risks. The collapse of the Thai baht at the beginning of July 1997 also dragged down the Lao kip while Thailand's fall from economic grace caused Thai investment in Laos to evaporate (Thailand is Laos' largest foreign investor). 1998 saw zero growth and inflation escalated to nearly 100% as the government rather ineptly tried to control events. Since then the economy has stabilized.

Reform in a period of economic crisis

While Laos might be poor it was not insulated from the effects of Asia's economic crisis. Indeed, it is the reforms of the years since 1986 which has made the country vulnerable to developments beyond its borders. The Lao kip was dragged down by the depreciation of the Thai baht and lost value from US$1 = 978 kip in December 1996 to US$1 = 1780 kip in November 1997. Since then, it has sunk further and when this book went to press, there were 8265 kip to the US dollar. In fact there is no currency in Southeast Asia, with the exception of the Burmese kyat, which has lost more value.

As the currency lost value the government lost its nerve and slapped on currency controls and rounded up the private money changers who have been operating for years in Vientiane. The governor of the Lao central bank blamed "speculative attempts by opportunists" for the Kip's collapse. The trade deficit widened and eight state-owned banks became effectively insolvent. Inflation during 1997 rose and in 1998 continued to escalate to reach 100% by the end of the year. There was also a sharp downturn in investment (remember, Thailand is Laos' largest foreign investor).

The leadership held very different views on how to deal with the crisis. The so-styled conservatives in the politburo wanted the Lao government take a step back from the market and emphasize domestic resources. Reformists wanted further liberalization – à la IMF – and to extricate the country from the economic mess by integrating still more rapidly into the regional and world economies. The outcome of this debate, in typically Lao style, was a bit of both. The leadership took their foot off the pedal of economic reform but did not substantially reverse what was already in place. It also seems that they may have realized the futility of trying to rein back trade with neighbouring Thailand and China given their lack of economic control in many areas.

What was perhaps most surprising about Laos' economic malaise was the absence of any public disturbances. With the economy contracting, inflation running at more than 100%, banks broke, foreign investment evaporating and the government apparently clueless and helpless as to what to do, one might have expected just a little more public debate and criticism. After all, Thailand and South Korea both saw a change of government, Malaysia the trial and imprisonment of Deputy Prime Minister Anwar Ibrahim and Indonesia the violent dumping of Suharto, president of more than three decades. Laos may be renowned for the relaxed and forgiving ways of its people, but it is hard not to wonder, 'for how much longer?'

Building up the economy

Laos, as books constantly reiterate, is poor. While it is tempting to mouth those favourite words 'poor but happy', there can be little doubt that the major challenge facing the country is how to promote development. There are few people – whether government ministers or shifting cultivators, businessmen or hawkers – who do not fervently hope that their children will be better off than they. And 'better off' means richer. As Houmpheng Souralay of the Foreign Investment Management Committee said to Singapore's *Sunday Times*, "We want to catch up with our neighbours like Thailand, Cambodia and Vietnam." But, he significantly added, only if those "investments are wholesome and do not erode our cultural identity".

Traditionally, one of Laos' most important sources of foreign exchange was receipts from over-flight rights as the Bolovan Plateau lies on the flight path from Bangkok to Hong Kong and Tokyo. Nearly 100 international flights traverse Lao airspace every day and in the mid-1990s the government was receiving payment for each one. But, today, most of the Laos' foreign exchange is reaped from their natural resources.

The country and its foreign strategists look to four distinct areas for future income. The first concentrates on mining and energy. Mining rights to some of Laos' huge lignite reserves have been sold to Thai investors, while hydropower projects are plentiful. Other untapped mineral resources include reserves of gold, gemstones and iron ore, while foreign companies have undertaken preliminary searches for oil. The second area of interest is agriculture and forestry. Investors are looking at growing feed grains like soya beans and maize for export to Thailand. Raw timber exports are being replaced by processed wood industries. More enlightened analysts also see Laos as a potential large exporter of organic agricultural products – after all, agriculture in the country has never had to rely on biochemical inputs or genetically engineered seeds. The third potential area for ongoing development is tourism, which continues to grow at the rate of knots but the government is wary of Laos going the same way as Thailand. The fourth and final strategy – and the most ambitious – is for Laos to become the service centre between China, Vietnam, Cambodia and Thailand.

In 2010 Lao was still amending policy and legislation in order to prepare for accession to the World Trade Organization. Laos' stated aim is to graduate from LDC (least developed country) status by 2020.

Major development constraints in Laos are the shortage of skilled workers and capital, an undeveloped communication system, poor educational and health resources, rugged terrain and low population density. Add to this a patchwork of cultures and different languages and it is easy to see why the country is difficult to manage. Even with large amounts of public expenditure going into infrastructure, the challenge of linking people to the market and the state remains supremely important. Without roads and transport farmers cannot obtain inputs for agriculture, market any surplus production or increase their incomes.

In an effort to make the business climate more attractive, the state bank now supplies credit to all sectors of the economy. Provincial banks have been told to operate as autonomous commercial banks. State enterprises have been warned that if their bottom line does not show a profit they are out of business. Provinces are free to conclude their own trading agreements with private companies and neighbouring countries – which generally means Thailand.

Tens of thousands of people work for the government in a top-heavy and often corrupt bureaucracy. Working for the Laos government is considered a job for life. Civil servants are paid the equivalent of US$20-40 per month while domestic servants working for expatriate families receive double this figure, or more. No wonder official corruption and profiteering are on the increase. The main financial incentive available to civil servants are the perks offered by NGOs – such as use of a car, per diems for trips away and scholarships to foreign universities. Admirably, most people who work for the civil service in Laos do so for prestige and personal pride; there is little other incentive as the lure of long-term gains, in the form of corruption, usually take years to accrue.

In 2010, and in conjunction with Korea Exchange, Laos opened its own stock market in Vientiane to invigorate the economy in the downturn. In June 2010 Prime Minster Bouasone Bouphavanh told the World Economic Forum on East Asia that Laos is aiming for 'no less than' 8% annual economic growth until 2015. Bouphavanh also told the conference that it wants to elevate its status out of underdevelopment by 2020.

Hydropower

The country's greatest economic potential lies in its natural resources – timber, gold, precious stones, coal and iron – and hydropower. Laos has been dubbed the 'battery' or 'Kuwait' of Southeast Asia and the government has signed various deals with Thailand, China and Vietnam to sell electricity.

It has been estimated that only 1% of the country's hydropower potential of some 18,000 MW has so far been exploited and myriad schemes are being discussed. The largest is Nam Theun II (see page 196). The huge dam is expected to generate up to US$150 million revenue a year for Laos or approximately US$2 billion over a 25-year period. The hydropower project will involve exporting 95% of the electricity to Thailand; the rest will be used domestically.

A few years ago these grand hydropower plans all seemed eminently sensible: energy-hungry Thailand's economy was rapidly growing and Laos was well placed to meet its needs. But there were two issues that the Lao government and its international advisers failed to take sufficiently into account: the international environmental lobby and an economic slowdown. The Nam Theun II dam, for example, was delayed by the discoveries of rare bats and birds, with financial backing from agencies like the World Bank and the Asian Development Bank held up for years. The World Bank, now all too conscious that its environmental credentials have been tarnished by dam developments in India and elsewhere, went out of its way to ensure that all the required environmental and other studies were undertaken.

But the Nam Theun II dam is not quite the open-and-shut case it might appear, with the international environmental lobby on the side of local people and animals and the dastardly World Bank supporting shadowy businessmen and the interests of international capital. When local people were asked their views of the dam, many welcomed the proposal. Even some environmentalists argued that having the dam might be preferable to having the forests logged. For without the money that can be earned from selling electricity to Thailand one of the few alternatives is selling wood. With the dam newly running, the results are yet to be determined. The majority of villagers seem happy with relocation efforts, while conservationists argue that the environmental damage is yet to be properly evaluated. Plans are underway to further exploit the potential of the Mekong and its tributaries, with over 60 projects slated for development over the next decade.

Mining and logging

Mining is also providing large revenue for the country. In the years leading up to 2007, more than 140 mining concessions were allocated, many to Chinese looking for gold, copper, iron, potassium and bauxite. Australia's ORD Rivers Resources in collaboration with China's Nonferrous Metals International Mining Company (CNMIM) plans to develop a 727-sq-km concession on the Bolovan Plateau in southern Laos into one of the world's largest bauxite mines.

The symbol of southern Laos should be the timber truck, gargantuan beasts loaded with decades-old trees dwarfing the small roads. Malaysian, Taiwanese, Chinese and Thai firms have been awarded timber concessions in the country, many of them working in collaboration with the Lao military, which has become an important economic player.

Agriculture

This remains the mainstay of the Lao economy, accounting for just under half of the country's GDP. Around 80% of Lao citizens are employed in some kind of subsistence agriculture, which they depend on for their survival. Rice is the staple food crop, cultivated by the majority of the population, and nearly three-quarters of Laos' farmers grow enough to sell or barter some of their crop. It is believed that rice accounts for a quarter of the country's GDP. Other primary agricultural products include coffee, corn, sugarcane, vegetables, tobacco, ginger, water buffalo, pigs, cattle, poultry, sweet potatoes, cotton, tea and peanuts.

While Laos may be land rich, this does not mean that everyone necessarily has enough to eat, and the achievement of food security is one of the government's priority. National self-sufficiency does not equate with local food security. Food deficits are common, resulting in many households experiencing both chronic and acute malnutrition. There is also intra-regional variation. For example, Sekong in the south is traditionally a rice deficit province, as is Xieng Khouang in the centre. Further down the scale, from national to regional, provincial, district and village, there are likely to be variations in food security. Even households that are in production surplus may face a consumption deficit due to their having to sell a portion of production to meet demands for cash or to pay off debts.

The growing population poses a challenge to rice farmers. Laos' population is increasing at 2.5% per annum – from 4.25 million in 1990 to 6.8 million in 2009. This means that in the last 20 years Laos has had to feed 50% more people. Luckily, during the same period it increased rice production by 70% (one million tonnes a year). However, the challenge for Lao farmers is whether they will be able to increase the level of rice production as the population demand increases. As Laos' population is expected to grow to 8.8 million by the year 2020, the demand for rice is expected to exceed an additional million tons of rice.

The main agricultural areas are on the Mekong's floodplains, especially around Vientiane and Savannakhet. The government has been successful in expanding the area capable of producing two rice crops a year by developing the country's irrigation infrastructure. Cotton, coffee, maize and tobacco are the other main crops and the production of these and other 'industrial' crops such as soya and mung beans has increased in recent years.

While shifting cultivators continue to pose a 'problem' to the government, their numbers have dropped substantially since 1985 as the land allocation programme has been enthusiastically implemented. This is reflected by the fact that they are now said to cut down 100,000 ha of forest a year, compared with 300,000 in the early 1980s. The situation has improved dramatically since the mid-1970s when Hmong General Vang Pao complained to a *National Geographic* reporter that "In one year a single family will chop down and burn trees worth US$6000 and grow a rice crop worth US$240."

Dependency on aid and development aims
Laos depends heavily on imports – everything from agricultural machinery and cars to petrol products, textiles and pharmaceuticals – which are heavily financed by foreign aid. Western bilateral donors are enthusiastically filling the aid gap left by the Socialist bloc. In June 2003, Russia agreed to write off 70% of the loans from the Cold War period.

Countries and private donors are falling over each other to fund projects, particularly anything that involves government reform; NGOs are homing in and development banks are offering soft loans and structural adjustment programmes. As Laos' foreign debt is mostly on highly concessional terms, it is not crippled by repayment schedules, though there is a reasonably hefty bill awaiting them. But with development banks accelerating their project-funding, fears are mounting that Laos is teetering on the edge of a debt trap. Laos' annual debt service repayments, as a proportion of GDP is almost double the government's expenditure on health.

The share of foreign assistance to GDP has nearly tripled since the mid-1980s. In 2005, Laos' Foreign Minister Somsavat Lengsavat said that the country had received more than US$2.4 billion from foreign donors between 1991 and 2005. Economists based in Vientiane suggest that ODA (Official Development Assistance) accounts for roughly 60-70% of Laos' annual public expenditure budget. Official statistics put ODA at 16% of the country's annual GDP.

Poverty
As in neighbouring Vietnam, the economic reforms are beginning to widen inequalities. Most of those who are doing well live in towns or at least close to one of the country's main roads. This means that off-road communities, and especially those in remote rural

areas, are finding that – at least in relative terms – they are becoming poorer. In addition, because it is mostly minority Lao Soung and Lao Theung who live in these marginal areas, the economic reforms are widening inequalities between ethnic groups. One foreign aid worker was quoted in the Far Eastern Economic Review saying: "When they come down to Vientiane, where the lowland Lao [the Lao Loum] live, it's like Hong Kong to them. Here's money, here's development. In their own villages, there's nothing." As in Vietnam, the need to ensure that the economic reforms bring benefits to all and not just a few, is a key political question. The leadership are acutely aware that widening inequalities could fuel discontent and this is perhaps one reason why the government seems so intent on increasing the number of members of the National Assembly from ethnic minorities

The average annual income in 2006 was US$572 and U$878 in 2009. Laos was ranked 133 out of 182 countries in the 2009 Human Development report but coming just before Cambodia, ranked 137. Just over 1 in 5 of people aged 15-24 is illiterate. Around 15% of children still don't go to primary school and a further 60% are not enrolled in secondary school. Only 63% of students who started grade one were still in school by grade 5.

A fifth of the population is undernourished, 40% of children are underweight and only half the population has access to safe drinking water. Almost one in 10 children dies before the age of five, usually from communicable and preventable diseases such as acute respiratory infections, diarrhoea, malaria, measles, dengue fever and meningitis. Maternal mortality is also dangerously high, with around 530 maternal deaths per 100,000 births, probably due to the fact that only 17% of pregnant women have their baby delivered by a trained doctor.

The keystone of mainland Southeast Asia

In what sceptics might view as an ultimately futile effort, the leadership in Vientiane have chanced upon an economic future for their country: as the 'keystone' or 'crossroads' of Southeast Asia. Nor is it just Laos' leaders who are drumming up enthusiasm for this notion. The Asian Development Bank (the Asian arm of the World Bank) is at the forefront of developing – and funding – what has become known as the Greater Mekong Sub-region or GMS. This will link southwest China, Thailand, Myanmar (Burma), Cambodia, Vietnam and Laos. And within this scenario, Laos is the crucial pivotal country through which most transport links will have to pass. There is talk of a 'Golden Quadrangle' (as opposed to the infamous Golden Triangle) – even of a Golden Land. This reference draws on ancient Indian texts which talked of 'Suvarnaphum' – a Golden Land – which encompassed modern-day Thailand, Laos, Myanmar and probably Peninsular Malaysia and parts of Indonesia too.

Culture

People

Laos has a population of 6.8 million people, with an estimated annual growth rate of 2.3%, one of the highest in Southeast Asia. Savannakhet has the biggest population among provinces, with around 721,500 people. Vientiane is second with around 695,473 people, while Champasak province is in third place, with 603,880 people.

Ethnic groups

Laos is less a nation state than a collection of different tribes and languages. Its enormous ethnic diversity has long been an impediment to national integration. In total there are more than 60 ethnic groups which are often described as living in isolated, self-sufficient communities. Although communication and intercourse may have been difficult – and remains so – there has always been communication, trade and inter-marriage between the different Lao 'worlds' and today, with even greater interaction, the walls between them are becoming more permeable still.

Laos' ethnically diverse population is usually – and rather simplistically – divided by ecological zone into three groups: the wet rice cultivating, Buddhist Lao Loum of the lowlands, who are politically and numerically dominant, constituting just under half of the total population; the Lao Theung who occupy the mountain slopes and make up about a quarter of the population; and the Lao Soung, or upland Lao, who live in the high mountains and practise shifting cultivation and who represent less than a fifth of Laos' total population. Overall, in Laos the ethnic majority, Lao Loum, are in the minority. The terms were brought into general usage by the Pathet Lao who wished to emphasize that all of Laos' inhabitants were 'Lao' and to avoid the more derogatory terms that had been used in the past – such as the Thai word *kha*, (slave), to describe the Mon-Khmer Lao Theung like the Khmu and Lamet. Stereotypical representations of each category are depicted on the 1000 kip note.

Although the words have a geographical connotation, they should be viewed more as contrasting pairs of terms: loum and *theung* mean 'below' and 'above' (rather than hillsides and lowland), while *soung* is paired with *tam*, meaning 'high' and 'low'. These two pairs of oppositions were then brought together by the Pathet Lao into one three-fold division. Thus, the Lao Theung in one area may, in practice, occupy a higher location than Lao Soung in another area. In addition, economic change, greater interaction between the groups and the settlement of lowland peoples in hill areas means that it is possible to find Lao Loum villages in upland areas, where the inhabitants practise swidden, not wet rice, agriculture. So, although it is possible to characterize the hills as inhabited by shifting cultivating Lao Theung of Mon-Khmer descent, in practice the neat delimitation of people into discrete spatial units breaks down and as the years go by is becoming untenable.

Lao Loum

It has been noted that the Lao who have reaped the rewards of reform are the Lao Loum of T'ai stock – not the Lao Theung who are of Mon-Khmer descent or the ethnic Lao Soung, such as the Hmong but also Akha and Lahu. Ing-Britt Trankell, in her book *On the Road in Laos: an Anthropological Study of Road Construction and Rural Communities* (1993), writes

Population by ethnic group

Group population	Official category	% of total
Tai	Lao Loum	55
Mon-Khmer	Lao Theung	35
Tibeto-Burman	Lao Soung	10.

that the Lao Loum's "sense of [cultural and moral] superiority is often manifested in both a patronizing and contemptuous attitude toward the Lao Theung and Lao Sung, who are thought of as backward and less susceptible to socio-economic development because they are still governed by their archaic cultural traditions". This attitude is still prevalent today, where Lao Loum sneer at the cultural practices of other ethnic groups, such as the Akha, as being unmodern. As a result many of these groups are ashamed to wear their traditional clothes in wider society, as there is s a stigma attached.

During the sixth and seventh centuries the Lao Loum arrived from the southern provinces of China. They occupied the valleys along the Mekong and its tributaries and drove the Lao Theung to more mountainous areas. The Lao Loum, who are ethnically almost indistinguishable from the Thais of the Isan region (the Northeast of Thailand), came under the influence of the Khmer and Indonesian cultures and sometime before the emergence of Lane Xang in the 14th century embraced Theravada Buddhism. The majority of Lao are Buddhist but retain many of their animist beliefs. Remote Lao Loum communities still usually have a *mor du* (a doctor who 'sees') or medium. The medium's job description is demanding: he must concoct love potions, heal the sick, devise and design protective charms and read the future.

Today, the Lao Loum are the principal ethnic group, accounting for nearly half the population, and Lao is their mother tongue. As the lowland Lao, they occupy the ricelands of the Mekong and its main tributary valleys. Their houses are made of wood and are built on stilts with thatched roofs – although tin roofs and Thai concrete houses are popular these days. The extended family is spread throughout several houses in one compound.

There are also several tribal sub-groups of this main Thai-Lao group; they are conveniently colour-coded and readily identifiable by their sartorial traits. There are, for example, the Red Tai, the White Tai and the Black Tai – who live in the upland valley areas in Xieng Khouang and Hua Phan provinces. That they live in the hills suggests they are Lao Theung, but ethnically and culturally they are closer to the Lao Loum.

Lao Theung

The Lao Theung, consisting of 45 different sub-groups, are the descendants of the oldest inhabitants of the country and are of Mon-Khmer descent. They are sometimes called Kha (slave), as they were used as labourers by the Thai and Lao kings and are still poorer than the Lao Loum. Traditionally, the Lao Theung were semi-nomadic and they still live mainly on the mountain slopes of the interior, along the whole length of the Annamite Chain from South China. There are concentrations of Akha, Alak and Ta-Oy on the Bolaven Plateau in the south (see page 245) and Khmu in the north.

The Lao Theung's reliance on slash-and-burn, or shifting, agriculture is slowly being phased out. Traditionally, they would burn a small area of forest, cultivate it for a few years and then, when the soil was exhausted, abandon the land and moved on to a new area until the vegetation had regenerated and replenished the soil. Some groups merely shifted fields in a 10-15 year rotation; others not only shifted fields but also their villages, relocating in a fresh area of forest when the land had become depleted of nutrients. To obtain salt, metal implements and other goods that could not be made or obtained in the hills, the tribal peoples would trade resins and animal skins with the settled lowland Lao. Some groups, mainly those living closer to the towns, have converted to Buddhism but many are still animist.

The social and religious beliefs of the Lao Theung and their general outlook on health and happiness are governed by their belief in spirits. The shaman is a key personality in any village. The Alak, from the Bolovan Plateau (see page 245) test the prospects of a marriage by killing a chicken: the manner in which it bleeds will determine whether the marriage will be propitious. Buffalo sacrifices are also common in Lao Theung villages and it is not unusual for a community to slaughter all its livestock to appease the spirits.

Viet Minh guerrillas and American B-52s made life difficult for many of the Lao Theung tribes living in East Laos, who were forced to move away from the Ho Chi Minh Trail. By leaving their birth places the Lao Theung left their protecting spirits, forcing them to find new and unfamiliar ones.

Lao Soung

The Lao Soung began migrating to Laos from South China, Tibet and Burma, in the early 18th century, settling high in the mountains (some up to 2500 m). The Hmong (formerly known as the Meo) and Yao (also called the Mien) are the principal Lao Soung groups.

Yao (or Mien)

The Yao mainly live around Nam Tha – deep inside the Golden Triangle, near the borders with Thailand, Myanmar (Burma) and China. They are known as craftspeople – the men make knives, crossbows, rifles and high-quality, elaborately designed silver jewellery, which is worn by the women. Silver is a symbol of wealth among the Yao and Hmong.

The Mien or Yao are unique among the hilltribes in that they have a tradition of writing based on Chinese characters. Mien legend has it that they came from 'across the sea' during the 14th century, although it is generally thought that their roots are in South China where they originated about 2000 years ago.

The Mien village is not enclosed and is usually found on sloping ground. The houses are large, wooden and need to accommodate an extended family of 20 or more. They are built on the ground, not on stilts and have one large living area and four or more bedrooms. As with other tribes, the construction of the house must be undertaken carefully. The house needs to be orientated appropriately, so that the spirits are not disturbed and the ancestral altar installed on an auspicious day.

The Mien combine two religious beliefs: on the one hand they pay their dues to spirits and ancestors (informing them of family developments); and on the other, they follow Taoism as it was practised in China in the 13th and 14th centuries. The Taoist rituals are expensive and the Mien spend a great deal of their lives struggling to save enough money to afford life cycle ceremonies such as weddings and death ceremonies. Their economy is based upon the cultivation of dry rice, maize and small quantities of opium poppy.

Material culture The Mien women dress distinctively, with black turbans and red-ruffed tunics, making them easy to distinguish from the other hilltribes. All their clothes are made

Lao, Laos and Laotians

Most Lao are not Laotians. And not all Laotians are Lao. Lao tends to be used to describe people of Lao stock. There are, in fact, several times more Lao in northeastern Thailand (Issan) – roughly 20 million – than there are in Laos, with a total population of some 5 million, of whom perhaps a little over a half are ethnic Lao. At the same time not all Laotians – people who are nationals of Laos – are ethnic Lao. There are also significant minority populations including Chinese, Vietnamese, the Mon-Khmer Lao Theung and the many tribal groups comprising the Lao Soung. After a few too many *lao-lao* it is easy to get confused.

of black or indigo-dyed homespun cotton, which is then embroidered using distinctive cross-stitching. Their trousers are the most elaborate garments. Unusually, they sew from the back of the cloth and cannot see the pattern they are making. The children wear embroidered caps with red pompoms on the top and by the ears. The men's dress is a simple indigo-dyed jacket and trousers, with little embroidery. They have been dubbed "the most elegantly dressed but worst-housed people in the world".

Akha (or Kaw)

The Akha, also called as the Ikho, Kho or Kha, have their origins in Yunnan, southern China, and from there spread into Burma (where there are nearly 200,000) and Laos and rather later into Thailand. There are three different Akha groups in northern Laos: the Akha Pouli, the Akha Pen and the Akha Jijaw. Around Muang Sing (see page 148) they constitute 22% of the population. They traditionally speak a Tibeto-Burmese language, which is believed to be represented in nine different written forms.

The Akha are shifting cultivators, growing primarily dry rice on mountainsides but also a wide variety of vegetables. The cultivation of rice is bound up with myths and rituals: the rice plant is regarded as a sentient being and the selection of the swidden, its clearance, the planting of the rice seed, the care of the growing plants and the harvest of the rice, must all be done according to the Akha Way. Any offence to the rice soul must be rectified by ceremonies. The Akha have no word for religion but believe in the 'Akha Way'. They are able to recite the names of all their male ancestors (60 names or more) and they keep an ancestral altar in their homes, at which food is offered up at important festivals and after the rice harvest. The two most important Akha festivals are the four-day Swinging Ceremony, celebrated during August, and New Year, when festivities also extend over four days. When someone dies they are wrapped in cloth, poor people in a white cloth, and rich people in a black cloth. They are kept in a wooden coffin, with a lid similar to a xylophone, for up to a month. A usual ritual *baci* will follow.

Akha villages are identified by their gates, a village swing and high-roofed houses on posts. At the upper and lower ends of the village are gates which are renewed every year. Visitors should walk through them to rid themselves of the spirit of the jungle. The gates are sacred and must not be defiled. Visitors must not touch them and should avoid going through them if they do not intend to enter a house in the village. A pair of wooden male and female carved figures are placed inside the entrance to signify that this is the realm of human beings. The female and male parts of the house are divided and the house has two doorways – one the entrance and the other the exit. ▶▶ *For information on how to behave in an Akha village, see Visiting an Akha village, page 144.*

The Akha are relatively sexually liberal. Each village usually has a small courting house, where young men and women can rendezvous privately. Women will generally have a number of partners before settling into marriage and pregnancy prior to marriage is seen as a sign of fecundity. Sexual abstinence is often used as punishment for those who commit offences. Marriage is monogamous; however, the rich and powerful are entitled to additional wives if their first wives can't conceive. Women adopt the husband's lineage upon marriage and move into or close to her partner's family home. Divorce exists but is not common, due to the financial pressures of raising children. A midwife generally delivers babies and men are not allowed in the house when the woman is in labour. Historically, twins born in villages were regarded as a very bad omen and were killed but this practice has now been outlawed and the children are put up for adoption.

Today the Akha are finding it difficult to follow the 'Akha Way'. Their complex rituals set them apart from both the lowland Lao and from the other hilltribes. The conflicts and pressures which the Akha face and their inability to reconcile the old with the new is claimed by some to explain the high incidence of opium addiction.

Material culture Akha clothing is made of homespun blue-black cloth (dyed from indigo), which is appliquéd for decoration. The basic clothing of an Akha woman is a headdress, a jacket, a short skirt worn on the hips, with a sash and leggings worn from the ankle to below the knee, though many are starting to wear more mainstream clothing, as they are self-conscious of their traditional dress. They wear their jewellery as an integral part of their clothing, mostly sewn to their head dresses. This is the most characteristic item of Akha clothing and is adorned with jewellery and coins. The coins are made of pure silver and are used as currency (the small coins are worth about 15,000 kip and the large are worth about 50,000 kip). Girls wear similar clothing to the women, except that they sport caps rather than the elaborate headdress of the mature women. The change from girl's clothes to women's clothes occurs through four stages during adolescence. Unmarried girls can be identified by the small gourds tied to their waist and headdress. Men's clothing is much less elaborate. They wear loose-fitting Chinese-style black pants and a black jacket which may be embroidered. Both men and women use cloth shoulder bags.

Hmong

Origins The Hmong are probably the best-known tribe in Laos. In the 19th century, Chinese opium farmers drove many thousands of Hmong off their poppy fields and forced them south into the mountains of Laos. The Hmong did not have a written language before contact with Europeans and Americans and their heritage is mainly preserved through oral tradition. Hmong mythology relates how they flew in from South China on magic carpets. Village storytellers like to propagate the notion that the Hmong are werewolves, who happily devour the livers of their victims. This warrior tribe now mainly inhabits the mountain areas of Luang Prabang, Xieng Khouang and Xam Neua provinces where they practise shifting cultivation.

Economy and society Until a few years ago, other Lao and the rest of the world knew the Hmong as the Meo. Unbeknown to anyone except the Hmong, 'Meo' was a Chinese insult meaning 'barbarian' – conferred on them several millennia ago by Chinese who developed an intense disliking for the tribe. Returning from university in France in the mid-1970s, the Hmong's first highly qualified academic decided it was time to educate the world. Due to his prompting, the tribe was rechristened Hmong, their word for 'mankind'. This change has not stopped the Hmong from referring to the Chinese as 'sons of dogs'. Nor has it stopped the Lao Loum from regarding the Hmong as their cultural inferiors. But, again, the feelings are reciprocated: the Hmong have an inherent mistrust of the lowland Lao – exacerbated by many years of war – and Lao Loum guides are relectant to enter Hmong villages.

The Hmong value their independence and tend to live at high altitudes, away from other tribes. This independence in addition to their former association with poppy cultivation and their siding with the US during the war has meant that of all the hilltribes, it is the Hmong who have been most persecuted. They have, in recent history, been perceived as a threat to state security, a group that needs to be controlled and carefully watched.

Hmong villages tend not to be fenced, while their houses are built of wood or bamboo at ground level. Each house has a main living area and two or three sleeping rooms. The extended family is headed by the oldest male; he settles family disputes and has authority over family affairs. Like the Karen, the Hmong too are spirit worshippers and believe in household spirits. Every house has an altar, where protection for the household is sought.

As animists, the Hmong believe everything from mountains and opium poppies to cluster bombs, has a spirit – or *phi* – some bad, some good. Shamans – or witchdoctors – play a central role in village life and decision making. The *phi* need to be placated incessantly to ward off sickness and catastrophe. It is the shaman's job to exorcise the bad *phi* from his patients. Until modern medicine arrived in Laos along with the Americans, opium was the Hmong's only palliative drug. Due to their lack of resistance to pharmaceuticals, the Hmong responded miraculously to the smallest doses of penicillin. Even plasters were revered as they were thought to contain magical powers which drew out bad *phi*.

Material culture The Hmong are the only tribe in Laos who make batik; indigo-dyed batik makes up the main panel of their skirts, with appliqué and embroidery added to it. The women traditionally wore black leggings from their knees to their ankles, black jackets (with embroidery) and a black panel or 'apron', held in place with a cummerbund. Even the youngest children wore clothes of intricate design. Traditionally the cloth would have been woven by hand on a foot-treddle/back-strap loom; today it is increasingly purchased from markets and often made of synthetic fabrics. Most Hmong today tend to wear Western-style clothes except for on auspicious occasions, such as Hmong New Year.

The White Hmong tend to wear less elaborate clothing from day to day, saving it for special occasions only. Hmong men wear loose-fitting black trousers, black jackets (sometimes embroidered) and coloured or embroidered sashes.

The Hmong particularly value silver jewellery; it signifies wealth and a good life. Men, women and children wear silver – tiers of neck rings, heavy silver chains with lock-shaped pendants, earrings and pointed rings on every finger. Through their life the Hmong will collect these heavy bands and lock them together with a spirit lock, which holds in their 32 souls. All the family jewellery is brought out at New Year.

Hmong fighters in the 20th century In the dying days of the French colonial administration, thousands of Hmong were recruited to help fight the Vietnamese Communists. Vang Pao – known as VP – who would later command 30,000 Hmong mercenaries in the US-backed war against the Pathet Lao, was first picked out by a French colonel in charge of these *maquisards* (native movements). Later, the Hmong were recruited and paid by the CIA to fight the Pathet Lao. Under General VP, remote mountain villagers with no education were trained to fly T-28 fighter-bombers.

At its peak, VP's army consisted of 250,000 fighters, the majority of whom were Hmong. Around 30,000 Hmong lost their life in the war, over a tenth of the Hmong population at the time. Even after the Pathet Lao's 'liberation' of Vientiane in 1975, Hmong refugees, encamped in hills to the south of the Plain of Jars, were flushed out by Vietnamese troops.

When the war ended in 1975 there was a mass exodus of Hmong from Laos, especially to Thailand. Many ended up in Thai refugee camps, where they lived in terrible conditions, for many years, sometimes decades.

Today more than 100,000 Hmong live in the US – mostly on the west coast and in Minnesota – where they regularly lobby politicians. They are a powerful pressure group but they are increasingly out of touch with the situation in Laos. Where the US-based Hmong remain important, however, is in the money they remit to their relatives in Laos.

Hmong insurgency In Laos, Hmong insurgents have been staging reasonably regular attacks for years. A spate of bombings in Vientiane in 2000 was linked to the Hmong resistance and in 2004-2005 at least 15 civilians were killed by Hmong insurgents in the north of the country. The Hmong claim to be fighting for democracy and freedom but most are living in terrible conditions and starving, so robbery seems a more likely motivation.

The Lao government tends publicly to sidestep the issue, saying there is no official policy towards the Hmong. However, the eradication of opium and the related resettlement programme has had a negative impact on the Hmong and there is evidence of human rights violations against the Hmong by the Lao government. In 2004, video footage was smuggled out of Laos showing the carnage of a military attack on a Hmong rebel group that had taken place; the victims were children. On the other hand, the Lao government has appointed Hmong as governors of Phonsavanh, Xam Neua and Sayaboury provinces.

Between 2004 and 2006 several groups of hundreds of Hmong insurgents surrendered. In December 2006 alone more than 400 members of the Hmong ethnic insurgents and their families came out of the jungle and surrendered to the authorities.

In 2007 American officials in the US arrested Vang Pao, the 77-year-old former CIA-backed general of the Royal Army in Laos, on a conspiracy to stage a coup in Vientiane. The criminal complaint said Vang Pao and the other Hmong defendants formed a committee "to evaluate the feasibility of conducting a military expedition or enterprise to engage in the overthrow of the existing government of Laos by violent means, including murder, assaults on both military and civilian officials of Laos and destruction of buildings and property." This included charges of inspecting shipments of military equipment that were to be shipped to Thailand. That equipment included machine guns, ammunition, rocket-propelled grenade launchers, anti-tank rockets, stinger missiles, mines and C-4 explosives.

In 2009, the US dropped the charges against Vang Pao. He made plans to return to Laos but the government communicated that he would be executed if he did. In late 2009 more than 4000 Hmong refugees living in Thailand were forcibly repatriated to Laos.

Other communities

The largest non-Lao groups in Laos are the Chinese and Vietnamese in the main cities. Many of the Vietnamese were brought in by the French to run the country and stayed. The Chinese have been migrating to Laos for centuries, where they are traders, restaurateurs and shop owners. Chinese immigration has increased in recent years, and with the relaxation in Communist policies there has been an influx of Thais, many in business. In Vientiane there is a small community of Indians running restaurants, jewellery and tailors' shops. Most Europeans are NGO, embassy or mining company staff.

Architecture

The architecture of Laos reflects its turbulent history and has strong Siamese/Thai, Burmese and Khmer influences. Philip Rawson, in his book *The Art of Southeast Asia*, goes so far as to state that "The art of Laos is a provincial version of the art of Siam." This is unjustified in so far as art and architecture in Laos, though it may show many links with that of Siam/Thailand, also has elements which are unique to it. Unfortunately, little has survived because many of the older structures were built of wood and were ransacked by the Siamese/Thais, Chinese and Vietnamese and then bombed by the Americans. Religious buildings best exhibit the originality of Lao art and architecture.

Like Thailand and Myanmar (Burma), the stupa is the most dominant architectural form in Laos. In its classic Indian form, it is a voluptuous half round – a hemisphere – very like the upturned begging bowl that it is supposed to symbolize. This is surmounted by a shaft representing the Buddha's staff and a stepped pediment symbolizing his folded cloak. In Thailand the stupa has become elongated while in Laos it is also more angular, with four distinct sides. They are referred to as *that* (rather than *chedi*, as in Thailand).

In addition to the *that*, a Lao monastery or *wat* (*vat*) will also have a number of other buildings of which the most important is the *sim* or ordination hall (in Thai, *bot* or *ubosoth*). See box, page 319, for a short rundown on the structures found in an orthodox Lao wat.

Architectural styles

Lao wats are generally less ornate and grand than those in Thailand, although the temples of Luang Prabang are stunning, with their layered roofs that sweep elegantly towards the ground. There are three main styles of temple architecture in Laos: Luang Prabang, Vientiane and Xieng Khouang. The last of these was almost lost forever because of the destruction wrought on the city of Xieng Khouang during the war.

The Vientiane style is influenced by the central Thai style, with its high, pointed and layered roofs. Most of the main sanctuaries are rectangular and some, such as Wat Phra Kaeo in Vientiane, have a veranda around the entire building – a stylistic feature imported from Bangkok. Most of the larger *sim* have a veranda at the back as well as at the front. Vientiane's wats have higher roofs than those in Luang Prabang, the buildings are taller and the entrances more prominent. The steps leading up to the main entrance are often guarded by *nagas* or *nyaks*, while the doorways themselves are usually flanked by pillars and topped with intricately carved porticoes. That Luang, in Vientiane, historically provided a template for most Lao stupas and its unique shape is found only in Laos and some areas of North and Northeast Thailand. As in other Buddhist countries, many of the stupas contain sacred relics – bones or hairs of the Buddha, or the ashes of kings.

The Luang Prabang architectural style has been influenced by North Thai temples. The roofs of the main sanctuaries almost touch the ground – best exemplified by Wat Xieng Thong in Luang Prabang. The pillars narrow towards the top, as tree trunks were originally used for columns and this form was copied when they started to be made of stuccoed brick. The wats often have a veranda at the back and the front. The most famous wats in Luang Prabang and Vientiane were built with royal patronage. But most wats in Laos were and are built with donations from the local community. Royal wats can be identified by the number of *dok sofa*: more than 10 'flowers' signifies that the wat was built by a king.

The Xieng Khouang style appears to be an amalgam of Vientiane and Luang Prabang influences. The *sim* is raised on a multi-level pediment, as with Vientiane-style *sim*, while the low, sweeping roofs are similar to *sim* in Luang Prabang.

The Lao wat

There is no English equivalent of the Lao word wat or vat. It is usually translated as either monastery or temple, although neither is correct. A wat is the focus of a village or town; it serves as places of worship, education, meeting and healing. Without a wat, a village was not, and is not, a 'complete' community.

The wat is a relatively new innovation. Originally, there were no wats, as monks were wandering ascetics. Although the word was in use in the 14th century, it probably referred to shrines. By the late 18th century, the wat had metamorphosed into a monastery. Although wats vary in complexity, most conform to a traditional layout.

Wats are usually separated from the secular world by two walls. Between these walls are the monks' quarters (*kutis*), perhaps a drum or bell tower (*hor kong*), used to toll the hours and to warn of danger, and in larger complexes schools and other buildings. Traditionally the *kutis* were placed on the south side of the wat. It was believed that if the monks slept

Generalized plan of a wat

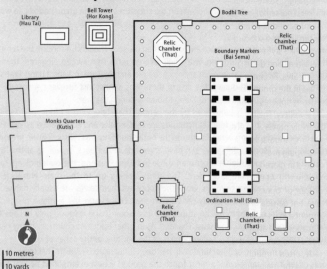

Library (Hau Tai)

Bell Tower (Hor Kong)

Bodhi Tree

Relic Chamber (That)

Boundary Markers (Bai Sema)

Relic Chamber (That)

Monks Quarters (Kutis)

N

Relic Chamber (That)

Ordination Hall (Sim)

Relic Chambers (That)

10 metres
10 yards

Arts and crafts

Lao art is well known for its wealth of ornamentation. As in other neighbouring Buddhist countries, the focus has been primarily religious in nature. Temple murals and bas-reliefs usually tell the story of the Buddha's life: the jataka tales. However, there has never been the range of art in Laos that there is in Thailand, as the country has been constantly dominated and influenced by foreign powers. Much of Laos's artistic heritage was destroyed or in front of the main Buddha image they would die young; if they slept to the left they would become ill; and if they slept behind it there would be discord in the community of monks.

The inner wall, which in bigger wats may take the form of a gallery or cloister (*phra rabieng*) lined with Buddha images, represents the division between the worldly and the holy, the sacred and the profane. It is used as a quiet place for meditation. Within the inner courtyard, the holiest building is the ordination hall or sim, reserved for monks only. This is built on consecrated ground, and has a ring of eight stone tablets or boundary markers (*bai sema*), sometimes contained in mini-pavilions, arranged around it at the cardinal and subcardinal points and shaped like stylized leaves of the bodhi tree, often carved with representations of Vishnu, Siva, Brahma or Indra, or of *nagas*. Buried in the ground beneath the bai sema are stone spheres – and sometimes gold and jewellery. The *bai sema* mark the limit of earthly power. The ordination hall is a large, rectangular building with high walls and sloping roofs (always odd in number) covered in glazed clay tiles (or wood tiles, in the north). At each end of the roof are *dok sofa*, or 'bunches of flowers', which represent garuda grasping two *nagas* (serpents) in its talons. *Chao faa*, flame-like protrusions are attached to the extreme edge of the downward slope of the roofs. Inside, often through carved and inlaid doors, is the main Buddha image. There may also be subsidiary images. The inside walls of the sim may be decorated with murals depicting the Jataka tales or scenes from Buddhist and Hindu cosmology. Like the Buddha, these murals are meant to serve as meditation aids. Many complexes have secondary chapels, or *hor song phra* attached to the main *sim*.

Also in the inner courtyard may be a number of other structures. Among the more common are *that* (chedis), tower-like relic chambers which in Laos and parts of northeastern Thailand take the lotus bud form. These can be massive (such as That Luang in Vientiane, see page 49), and contain holy relics of the Buddha. More often, *thats* are smaller and contain the ashes of royalty, monks or pious lay people.

Another rarer feature is the library or scripture repository (*hau tai*), usually a small, tall-sided building where the Buddhist scriptures can be stored high off the ground. *Salas* are open-sided rest pavilions found anywhere in the wat compound; the *sala long tham* (study hall) is the most impressive of these and is almost like a *sim* or *viharn* without walls. Here the monks say their prayers at noon. In villages wats often consist only of a *sala*, or meeting hall.

It seems that wats are often short-lived. Even great wats, if they lose their patronage, are deserted by their monks and fall into ruin. Unlike churches, they depend on constant support from the laity; the wat owns no land or wealth, and must depend on gifts of food to feed the monks and money for repairs.

disappeared over the centuries, as invading neighbours ransacked towns and cities and plundered the finest work. The *Ramayana*, the Hindu epic from India, known in Laos as the *Phra Lak Phra Lam* (see box, page 321) is highly influential and has become part of the Lao cultural heritage. Many of the most elaborate doors and windows of temples are engraved with scenes from this story, depicting the struggle between good and evil. The most outstanding examples of this art form are the huge teak shutters at Wat Xieng Thong in Luang Prabang.

Sculpture

Sculpture in Laos is more distinctive in style; the best pieces originate from the 16th to 18th centuries. Characteristic of Lao Buddha images is a nose like an eagle's beak, flat, extended earlobes and tightly curled hair. The best examples are in Wat Phra Kaeo and Wat Sisaket in Vientiane.

The 'Calling for Rain' mudra (the Buddha standing with hands pointing towards the ground, arms slightly away from the torso) is distinctively Lao (see page 324). The 'Contemplating the Tree of Enlightenment' mudra is also uniquely Lao – it depicts a standing Buddha with hands crossed in front of the body. There are many examples in the Pak Ou Caves, on the Mekong, 25 km upstream from Luang Prabang (see page 115).

Textiles

Weaving is a craft almost entirely performed by women. Traditionally, a girl was not considered fit for marriage until she had mastered the art of weaving and the Lao Loum women were expected to weave a corsage for their wedding day. Today these traditions are inevitably less strictly adhered to and there are also a handful of fine male weavers. Even so, a skilled weaver is held in high regard and enjoys a position of respect. Cloth is woven from silk, cotton, hemp and a variety of synthetic materials (mostly polyester) – or in some combination of these.

The finest weaving comes from the north. Around Xam Neua (and especially near Xam Tai), the Lao Neua produce some outstanding pieces. These were handed down through a family as heirlooms, stored in lidded stone jars to protect them from insects, moisture and sunlight and only worn on special occasions. But the recent history of this area forced people to sell their treasured textiles and few remain in situ. Indeed it was feared that the art of traditional weaving had been lost in the area. Only the work of some NGOs and committed supporters has resuscitated high quality weaving in the area (and in Vientiane where some of the best weavers live and work).

Lao Neua textiles are usually woven with a cotton warp and a silk weft and pieces include *pha sinh* (sarong), *pha baeng* (shawl) and blankets. Various methods are employed including *ikat* – where cotton is used (see page 69), as the Lao Neua consider that indigo dye does not take well on silk – and supplementary weft techniques. Pieces show bold bands of design and colour and the *pha sinh* is usually finished with a separate handwoven border. Among the designs are swastika motifs, *hong* (geese), diamond shapes, *nyak* (snake) heads, lions and elephants.

The Lao Loum of the Luang Prabang area also have a fine weaving tradition. *Pha sinh* produced here tend to have narrow vertical stripes, often alternating between dark and light. Silk tends to be used throughout on the finer pieces, although the yarn may be imported rather than locally produced and it is coloured using chemical dyes. Motifs include zigzags, flowers and some designs that are French in inspiration.

Around Pakse in the south and also in central Laos around Savannakhet and Thakhek designs are influenced by the Khmer and closest to those produced in the Isan region of northeast Thailand. *Matmii* ikat-woven cotton cloth is most characteristic. Designs, handed down by mothers to their daughters, are invariably geometric and encompass a broad range from simple *sai fon* (falling rain) designs where random sections of weft are tied, to the more complex *mee gung* and *poom som*. The less common *pha kit* is a supplementary weft *ikat*, although designs are similar to those in *matmii*. *Pha fai* is a cotton cloth, in blue or white and sometimes simply decorated, for everyday use and also used as part of the burial ceremony, when a white length of *pha fai* is draped over the coffin.

The Lao Ramayana: the *Phra Lak Phra Lam*

The *Phra Lak Phra Lam* is an adaptation of the Indian Hindu classic, the *Ramayana*, written by the poet Valmiki about 2000 years ago. This 48,000 line epic odyssey, likened to the works of Homer, was introduced into mainland Southeast Asia in the early centuries of the first millennium. The heroes were transposed to a mythical Southeast Asian landscape.

The Lao, and Thai, versions of the *Ramayana* follow that of the original Indian story. They tell of the life of Ram (Rama), the King of Ayodhia. In the first part of the story, Ram renounces his throne following a long and convoluted court intrigue and flees into exile. With his wife Seeda (Sita) and trusted companion Hanuman (the monkey god), they undertake a long and arduous journey.

In the second part, his wife Seeda is abducted by the evil king Ravana, forcing Ram to wage battle against the demons of Langka Island (Sri Lanka). He defeats the demons with the help of Hanuman and his monkey army and recovers his wife. In the third and final part of the story – and here it diverges sharply from the Indian original – Seeda and Ram are reunited and reconciled with the help of the gods (in the Indian version there is no such reconciliation). There are also numerous sub-plots which are original to the *Phra Lak Phra Lam*, many building upon local myth. In tone and issues of morality, the Lao and Thai versions are less puritanical than the Indian original. There are also, of course, differences in dress, ecology, location and custom.

Literature

Lao literature is similar to Thai and is likewise also influenced by the Indian epic the *Ramayana*, which in Laos is known as the *Phra Lak Phra Lam* (see box). Scenes from the *Phra Lak Phram Lam* can often be seen depicted in temple murals. The first 10 jataka tales, recounting the last 10 lives of the Gautama Buddha (the historic Buddha), have also been a major inspiration for Lao literature. The versions that are in use in Laos are thought to have been introduced from Lanna Thai (northern Thailand, Chiang Mai) in the 16th century, or perhaps from the Mon area of present day Myanmar and Thailand. In these 10 tales, known as the *Vesantara Jataka*, the Buddha renounces all his earthly possessions, even his wife and children. Although the jataka tales in Laos are linked with Buddhism and therefore with India, the stories have little in common with the Indian originals. They draw heavily on local legends and folklore, animist tales provided with a Buddhist gloss.

Traditionally texts were recorded on palm leaves, the letters were inscribed with a stylus and the grooves darkened with oil. A palm leaf manuscript kept under good conditions in a well-maintained *hau tai* or library can last 100 years or more.

With the incorporation of Laos into French Indochina in the late 19th century, the Lao elite renounced traditional Lao literature in favour of the French language and artistic traditions. Many of the Lao elite received a French-style education. Lao literature came to be looked down upon as simplistic and most scholars wrote instead in French.

In 1778 the Thais plundered Laos and along with the two most sacred Buddha images – the Phra Bang and the Phra Kaeo (Emerald Buddha) – they pillaged Lao religious literature and historical documents. Most Lao manuscripts – or *kampi* – are 40-50 cm long, pierced with two holes and threaded together with cord. A bundle of 20 leaves forms a *phuk* and these are grouped together into *mat*, which is then wrapped in a piece of cloth.

Language

The official language is Lao, the language of the ethnic majority. Lao is basically a monosyllabic, tonal language. It contains many polysyllabic words borrowed from Pali and Sanskrit (ancient Indian dialects) as well as words borrowed from Khmer. It has six tones, 33 consonants and 28 vowels. It is also spoken in Northeast Thailand and North Cambodia, which was originally part of the kingdom of Lane Xang. Lao and Thai, particularly the Northeast dialect, are mutually intelligible. French is still spoken in towns – particularly by the older generation – and is often used in government, but English is on the increase.

Lao script is similar to Thai. One of the kings of the Sukhothai Dynasty, Ramkhamhaeng, devised the Thai alphabet in 1283 and introduced the Thai system of writing. Modelled on this early Thai script, Lao is written from left to right with no spacing between the words.

The leadership in the Lao PDR has attempted to make Lao the national language, in fact as well as in rhetoric. Because it is so similar to Thai, there has also been an attempt to maintain a difference between the two countries' languages. To do this it was necessary to establish an national version of spoken Lao which could be taught in schools, promoted in the media, and used in government. This effort at language engineering can be dated from the 1930s, and saw further refinements in the 1940s-1950s, 1970s and 1990s. While this has been successful in that Lao remains significantly different from Thai, the major influence on the Lao language today remains that of Thai. ▸▸ *See also Language, page 334*.

Dance, drama and music

Lao music, songs and dances have much in common with those of Thailand. Instruments include bamboo flutes, drums, gongs, cymbals and pinched or bowed string instruments shaped like banjos. The national instrument is the *kaen*, a hand-held pipe organ made from bamboo, similar to the South American pan pipes. Percussion is an important part of a Lao orchestra and two of the most common instruments are the *nang nat*, a xylophone and the *knong vony*, a series of bronze cymbals suspended from a wooden frame. The *seb noi* orchestra – a consortium of these instruments – is used to introduce or conclude vocal recitals. The *seb gnai* orchestra includes two big drums and a Lao-style clarinet.

Despite the lack of written notation, many epic poems and legends have survived to the present day as songs, passed, with the composition itself, from generation to generation. Early minstrels took their inspiration from folklore, enriched by Indian myths. Traditional Lao music can now only be heard during performances of the *Phra Lak Phra Lam* (see box, page 321), the Lao version of the Indian epic the Ramayana. Many monasteries have experts on percussion who play every Buddhist sabbath. There is also a strong tradition of Lao folk music, which differs between tribal groups.

Secular songs, drawing on Lao literature for inspiration, are known as *mau lam* and can be heard at festivals not just in Laos but also in Northeast Thailand (where they are known as *mor lam*), which is also, culturally, 'Lao'. Indeed, some of the best performers are based there, and it is also a good place to pick up music of famous *mor lam/mau lam* singers.

In Vientiane and the provincial capitals, younger Lao tend to opt for Western-style pop. The Communist leadership , increasingly concerned at this invasion of Western and Thai culture, has dictated that only a certain proportion of songs can be non-Lao. Cultural police occasionally check that these rules are being observed.

Classical Lao theatre and dance have Indian origins, probably imported from the Cambodian royal courts in the 14th century. Thai influence has also crept in over the years.

Religion

Theravada Buddhism

Theravada Buddhism, from the Pali word *thera* (elders), means the 'way of the elders' and is distinct from the dominant Buddhism practised in India, Mahayana Buddhism or the 'Greater Vehicle'. The sacred language of Theravada Buddhism is Pali rather than Sanskrit, Bodhisattvas (future Buddhas) are not given much attention and emphasis is placed upon a precise and 'fundamental' interpretation of the Buddha's teachings, as they were originally recorded. By the 15th century, Theravada Buddhism was the dominant religion in Laos – as it was in neighbouring Siam (Thailand), Myanmar and Cambodia. Buddhism shares the belief, in common with Hinduism, in rebirth. A person goes through countless lives and the experience of one life is conditioned by the acts in a previous one. This is the Law of Karma (act or deed, from Pali *kamma*), the law of cause and effect. But, it is not, as commonly thought in the West, equivalent to fate.

For most people, nirvana is a distant goal and they merely aim to accumulate merit by living good lives and performing good deeds such as giving alms to monks. In this way the layman embarks on the Path to Heaven. It is also common for a layman to become ordained, at some point in his life (usually as a young man), for a three month period during the Buddhist Rains Retreat. An equally important reason for a man to become ordained is so that he can accumulate merit for his family, particularly for his mother, who as a woman cannot become ordained

Monks should endeavour to lead stringently ascetic lives. They must refrain from murder, theft, sexual intercourse, untruths, eating after noon, alcohol, entertainment, ornament, comfortable beds and wealth. They are allowed to own only a begging bowl, three pieces of clothing, a razor, needle, belt and water filter. They can only eat food that they have received through begging. Anyone who is male, over 20 and not a criminal can become a monk. The 'Way of the Elders', is believed to be closest to Buddhist as it developed in India. It is often referred to by the term 'Hinayana' (Lesser Vehicle), a disparaging name foisted onto Theravadans by Mahayanists. This form of Buddhism is the dominant religion in the mainland Southeast Asian countries of Laos, Thailand, Cambodia and Myanmar (Burma).

In Theravadan Buddhism, the historic Buddha, Sakyamuni, is revered above all else and most images of the Buddha are of Sakyamuni. Importantly and unlike Mahayana Buddhism, the Buddha image is only meant to serve as a meditation aid; it does not embody supernatural powers and is not supposed to be worshipped. However, the popular need for objects of veneration has meant that most images are worshipped. Pilgrims bring flowers and incense and prostrate themselves in front of the image. This is a Mahayanist influence which has been embraced by Theravadans.

Buddhism in Laos

The Lao often maintain that the Vientiane area converted to Buddhism at the time of the Moghul emperor Asoka. This seems suspiciously early and is probably untrue. The original stupa at That Luang, so it is claimed, was built to encase a piece of the Buddha's breastbone provided by Asoka. Buddhism was undoubtedly practised before Fa Ngum united Lane Xang and created a Buddhist Kingdom in the mid-14th century. He was known as the Great Protector of the Faith and brought the Phra Bang, the famous golden statue – the symbol of Buddhism in Laos – from Angkor in Cambodia to Laos.

Mudras and the Buddha image

Artists producing images of the Buddha are trying to be faithful to a tradition which can be traced back over centuries, creating not merely a work of art but an object of and for worship. Sanskrit poetry even sets down the characteristics of the Buddha: legs like a deer, arms like an elephant's trunk, a chin like a mango stone and hair like the stings of scorpions. The Pali texts of Theravada Buddhism add the 108 auspicious signs, long toes and fingers of equal length, body like a banyan tree and eyelashes like a cow's. The Buddha can be represented either sitting, lying (indicating paranirvana), or standing, and (in Thailand) occasionally walking. He is often represented standing on an open lotus flower: the Buddha was born into an impure world, and likewise the lotus germinates in mud but rises above the filth to flower. Each image is represented in a particular mudra or 'attitude', of which there are 40. The most common are:

Abhayamudra – dispelling fear or giving protection; right hand (sometimes both hands) raised, palm outwards, usually with the Buddha in a standing position.

Varamudra – giving blessing or charity; the right hand pointing downwards, the palm facing outwards, with the Buddha either seated or standing.

Vitarkamudra – preaching mudra; the ends of the thumb and index finger of the right hand touch to form a circle, symbolizing the Wheel of Law. The Buddha can either be seated or standing.

Dharmacakramudra – 'spinning the Wheel of Law'; a preaching mudra symbolizing the teaching of the first sermon. The hands are held in front of the chest, thumbs and index fingers of both joined, one facing inwards and one outwards.

Bhumisparcamudra – 'calling the earth goddess to witness' or 'touching the earth'; the right hand rests on the right knee with the tips of the fingers 'touching ground', thus calling the earth goddess Dharani/Thoranee to witness his enlightenment and victory over Mara, the king of demons. The Buddha is always seated.

Dhyanamudra – meditation; both hands resting open, palms upwards, in the lap, right over left.

Other points of note:
Vajrasana – yogic posture of meditation; cross-legged, both soles of the feet visible.
Virasana – yogic posture of meditation; cross-legged, but with the right leg on top of the left, covering the left foot (also known as paryankasana).
Buddha under Naga – the Buddha is shown in an attitude of meditation with a cobra rearing up over his head. This refers to an episode in the Buddha's life when he was meditating; a rain storm broke and Nagaraja, the king of the *nagas* (snakes), curled up under the Buddha (seven coils) and then used his seven-headed hood to protect the Holy One from the falling rain.
Buddha calling for rain – the Buddha is depicted standing, both arms held stiffly at the side of the body, fingers pointing downwards.

Bhumisparcamudra – calling the earth goddess to witness. Sukhothai period, 13th-14th century.

Dhyanamudra – meditation. Sukhothai period, 13th-14th century.

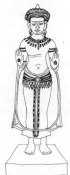

Abhayamudra – dispelling fear or giving protection. Lopburi Buddha, Khmer style 12th century.

Vitarkamudra – preaching, "spinning the Wheel of Law". Dvaravati Buddha, 7th-8th century, seated in the "European" manner.

Abhayamudra – dispelling fear or giving protection; subduing Mara position. Lopburi Buddha, Khmer style 13th century.

The Buddha 'Calling for rain'.

Buddhism was gradually accepted among the lowland Lao but many of the highland tribes remain animist. Even where Buddhism has been practised for centuries, it is usually interwoven with the superstitions and rituals of animist beliefs. Appeasing the spirits and gaining merit are integral features of life. Most highlanders are animists and the worship of *phi* or spirits was central to village life throughout the revolutionary years, despite being officially banned by the government. Similarly, the baci ceremony – when strings representing guardian spirits are tied around the wrists of guests – is still practised in Laos.

In the late 1500s, King Setthathirat promoted Buddhism and built many monasteries or wats. Buddhism was first taught in schools in the 17th century and prospered until the Thai and Ho invasions of the 18th and 19th centuries when many wats were destroyed. With the introduction of socialism in 1975 Buddhism was banned from primary schools and the giving alms to monks was prohibited. With the increasing religious tolerance of the regime Buddhism is undergoing a revival and wats are being restored. .

In line with Buddhist tradition, materialism and the accumulation of personal wealth is generally frowned on in Laos. Poverty is admired as a form of spirituality. This belief proved rather convenient for the Communist regime, when it was taken to extremes.

It is important to draw a distinction between 'academic' Buddhism, as it tends to be understood in the West and 'popular' Buddhism, as it is practised in Laos. In Laos, Buddhism is a syncretic religion: it incorporates elements of Brahmanism, animism and ancestor worship. Amulets are worn to protect against harm and are often sold in temple compounds. In the countryside, farmers have what they consider a regard for the spirits (*phi*) and demons that inhabit the rivers, trees and forests. Astrologers are widely consulted by urban and rural dwellers alike. These aspects of Lao Buddhism are perceived to be complementary, not in contradiction, with Buddhist teachings.

Buddhism under Communism

Buddhism's relationship with Communism has been complex and usually ambivalent. As the Pathet Lao began their revolutionary mission they saw in the country's monks a useful means by which to spread their message. Many monks were conscious of the inequalities in society and the impoverished conditions in which many people lived. Indeed most of them came from poor rural backgrounds. In addition many saw themselves as the guardians of Lao culture and as the US became more closely involved in the country so they increasingly felt that it was their job to protect the people against the spread of an alien culture. Therefore, right from the start, monks had a natural sympathy with the ideals of the Pathet Lao. Indeed, significant numbers renounced their vows and joined the revolution.

The Pathet Lao, for their part, saw the monks as a legitimizing force which would assist in their revolutionary efforts. Monks were often the most respected individuals in society and if the Pathet Lao could somehow piggy-back on this respect then they too, it was reasoned, would gain in credibility and respect. The Rightist government also tried to do the same, but with notably less success.

With the victory of the Pathet Lao in 1975, their view of the *sangha* (monkhood) changed. No longer were monks a useful vehicle in building revolution; overnight they became a potential threat. Monks were forced to attend re-education seminars where they were instructed that they could no longer teach about merit or *karma*, two central pillars of Buddhism. Their sermons were taped by Pathet Lao cadres to be scrutinized for subversive propaganda and a stream of disillusioned monks began to flee to Thailand. So the *sangha* was emasculated as an independent force. Monks were forced to follow the directives of the Lao People's Revolutionary Party and the *sangha* came under strict Party control. Monasteries were expected to become mini-cooperatives so that they did not have to depend on the laity for alms, and they were paid a small salary by the state for undertaking teaching and health work.

The success of the Pathet Lao's policy of marginalization can be seen in the number of monks in the country. In 1975 there were 20,000 monks. By 1979 this had shrunk to 1700.

However, before the *sangha* could sink into obscurity and irrelevance, the government eased its policy in 1979 and began to allow monks and the *sangha* greater latitude. In addition and perhaps more importantly, the leadership embraced certain aspects of Lao culture, one of which was Theravada Buddhism. The memorial to the revolutionary struggle in Vientiane, for example, was designed as a Buddhist *that* (stupa) and government ministers enthusiastically join in the celebration of Buddhist festivals.

Animism

While the majority of the population (about 60-65%) follow Theravada Buddhism, Animism is practised by about 30% of the population. The term Animism derives from the Latin word 'anima', meaning mind or soul. At a very basic level, Animism refers to a belief in spirits. Animism is particularly common among Lao Theung and Lao Soung groups minority groups but elements of Animism have also infiltrated or been grafted onto Buddhism and Lao culture at a broader level. Most people believe in *phi*, spirits, which are seen as fundamental to their relationship with nature and the community. The word *phi* has even been adopted into Lao language to mean ghost, while *phi-baa* means crazy. Many Lao people believe that spiritual forces need to be placated, usually through a *baci* ceremony (see page 28), as they can cause illness, disease or bad luck. Inexplicable events – including strange behaviour by foreign visitors – are often attributed to 'ghosts'. Buddhist monks are often called upon to exorcize bad spirits and most wats have a small spirit house in the grounds. Animists generally suffer little discrimination from the government; however, some practises are discouraged for health and security reasons.

Christianity in post-1975 Laos

The smallest religious group in Laos are Christians, including Roman Catholics, who account for around 2% of the population. There are 30,000 to 40,000 Catholics in the country, many of them ethnic Vietnamese, concentrated in urban centres along the Mekong River.

Following the revolution, many churches were turned into community centres. Vientiane's Evangelical Church has held a Sunday service ever since 1979 but it is only in recent years that Christians have felt free to worship openly. In 1989 the first consultation between the country's Christian leaders (Protestant and Roman Catholic) was authorized by the government; it was the first such meeting since 'liberation' and was also attended by government representatives and two Hmong leaders of the Buddhist Federation.

It's illegal for foreigners to proselytize in Laos; persons found guilty can be subject to arrest and deportation. Foreign missionaries were ejected from Laos in 1975 and, today, foreign NGOs affiliated with religious organizations are only allowed to work in the country on the condition that they don't try to spread their religion. Not many Buddhists have converted to Christianity but it seems to be growing among the animist hilltribes. The US Bible Society has published a modern translation of the Bible into Lao but tribal-language editions do not yet exist.

Land and environment

Geography

Laos stretches about 1000 km from north to south, while distances from east to west range from 140 to 500 km. The country covers 236,800 sq km – less than half the size of France and just a third of the size of Texas. Only 24% of the population lives in towns. The country has the lowest population density in Asia, with 22 people per sq km.

Rugged mountains cover more than three-quarters of the country and with few all-weather roads (there are just 4000 km of sealed roads), rivers remain important communication routes. Historically, the Mekong River was the country's economic artery. On its banks nestle Laos' most important cities: in the north the small, colourful former royal capital of Luang Prabang, further south the administrative and political capital of Vientiane and farther south still the regional centres of Thakhek, Savannakhet and Pakse.

The lowlands of the Mekong valley form the principal agricultural areas, especially around Vientiane and Savannakhet and these are home to the lowland Lao. The Mekong has three main tributaries: the Nam Ou and Nam Tha from the north and the Nam Ngum, which flows into Vientiane province.

Much of the northern half of Laos is 1500 m or more above sea level and its karst limestone outcrops are dissected by steep-sided river valleys. Further south, the Annamite chain has an average height of 1200 m. Heavily forested, rugged mountains form a natural barrier between Laos and Vietnam. Most of the country is a mixture of mountains and high plateau. There are four main plateau: the Xieng Khouang plateau, better known as the Plain of Jars, in the north, the Nakai and the limestone Khammuoane plateau in the centre and the 10,000 sq km Bolovan Plateau to the south. The highest peak is the 2800 m Bia Mountain, which rises above the Xieng Khouang plateau to the northeast.

Climate

The rainy season is from May through to September-October; the tropical lowlands receive an annual average rainfall of 1250 mm a year. Temperatures during these months are between 30 and 40°C. In mountainous Xieng Khoung Province, it is cooler and temperatures can drop to freezing point in December and January. The first half of the dry season, from November to April, is cool, with temperatures between 10 and 20°C. This gives way to a hot, dry season from March to June when temperatures soar and are often in excess of 35°C. Average rainfall in Vientiane is 1700 mm, although in North Laos and the highlands it is much wetter, with more than 3000 mm each year.

Vegetation

Much of Laos is forested. The vegetation is rich and diverse: a mix of tropical and subtropical species. Grassy savannah predominates on plateau areas such as the Plain of Jars. In the forests, some hardwoods tower to over 30 m, while tropical palms and mango are found in the lowlands and large stands of pine in the remote northern hills.

Rural people rely heavily on the Mekong River and its watershed for everything from transport to rice production and fishing. It is estimated that 80% of the country is located near the Mekong, its tributaries or in the watershed. Over half of all protein consumed in rural areas comes from fish, frogs and other river creatures. Agriculture is of utmost importance, with about 80% of the population engaged in subsistence farming.

In the mid-20th century over 70% of the country was covered with forest. Today, this has been reduced to around 40% and of this only 17% remains old growth tropical forest. The rattan, cardamom, mushrooms, orchids and wild meat gathered from these forests are essential to rural livelihoods. The Lao government has established 20 National Protected Areas or NPAs, plus two corridor areas, covering 14.3% of the country. Although this is a step forward, illegal hunting and logging is still rife in most areas.

Logging provides a large slice of Laos's export earnings. Officially, around 450,000 cu m of forest are felled each year for commercial purposes but this is probably an underestimate owing to the activities of illegal loggers, many of whom are Chinese, Vietnamese and Thai. In addition, shifting cultivators clear around 100,000 ha of forest a year.

Wildlife

Mammals include everything from wildcats, leopards and tigers to bears, wild cattle and small barking deer. Laos is also home to the large Asian elk, rhinoceros, elephants, monkeys, gibbons and ubiquitous rabbits and squirrels. There is an abundant reptilian population, including cobras, kraits, crocodiles and lizards. The lower reaches of the Mekong River, marking the border between Cambodia and Laos, is the last place in Indochina where the rare Irrawaddy dolphin is to be found. However, dynamite fishing is decimating the population and today there are probably under 20 left.

Another rare denizen of the Mekong is the *pa buk* (*Pangasianodon gigas*) which weighs up to 340 kg. This riverbed-dwelling fish is a delicacy and has been for many years – its roe was paid as tribute to China in the late 19th century. By the 1980s the numbers of *pa buk* had become severely depleted. However, a breeding programme is having some success and *pa buk* fingerlings are now being released into the Mekong.

In 2004, the Lao government joined CITES, the world's foremost conservation treaty regulating the global trade in endangered species. In spite of this, there is an enormous problem of smuggling rare animals out of Laos, mainly to South Korea and China. Poachers peddle animals across the country's borders; and the authors of 'Wildlife Trade in Laos: the End of the Game', published in 2001, suspected that trade in wildlife was the second-largest source of income (after fishing) in Lao villages, worth around US$35 million per year. A damning report in the *Guardian* in 2010 suggested that little has changed.

Regardless, Laos is still home to a diverse range of wildlife with some 800 bird and 100 mammal species. New species are popping up on an almost annual basis. The degree to which Laos' flora and fauna are under-researched was illustrated in 1999 when it was announced that an unknown species of striped rabbit had been discovered nibbling the grass in the mountains dividing Laos from Vietnam. This area of Indochina has proved a cornucopia of unknown animals. During the 1990s scientists discovered one antelope, several species of deer, an ox and even a remnant herd of Javan rhinoceros, a species previously thought to be confined to a small corner of West Java.

Birds

Laos is nowhere near as popular a destination for birdwatchers as neighbouring Vietnam and Cambodia but there has been a flurry of interest in the birding community since the discovery of a bizarre-looking bald-headed bird in 2009. The bare-faced bulbul is the first new species of Asian bulbul to be discovered in more than 100 years. It inhabits a remote area of rugged limestone karsts in Kammouane Province, 250 km south of Vientiane. Two other scarce inhabitants of limestone karst forest in the region, the sooty babbler and red-collared woodpecker is also found here. See www.vietnambirding.com for information. •

Books

Art and culture

Dakin, Brett (2003) *Another Quiet American*, Asia Books. Dakin's experiences of working in Laos, with some interesting cultural insights.

Evans, Grant (1999) *Laos: Culture and Society*, Chiang Mai, Thailand: Silkworm Books. Edited volume written by assorted scholars of Laos. Highly informed; for those who really want to know about the country.

Fay, Kim (2005) *To Asia with Love: A Connoisseur's Guide to Cambodia, Laos, Thailand Vietnam*, Global Directions Inc/Things Asian Press. Great anthology of ideas, inspirations and experiences of Southeast Asia from the people who live there.

Phia Sing (1995) *Traditional Recipes of Laos*, Totnes, Devon, UK: Prospect Books. The best Lao cookbook available. The recipes were collected by the chief chef at the Royal Palace in Luang Prabang, Phia Sing, in the 1960s. They have been translated into English and made more user-friendly by replacing some of the more esoteric ingredients with ones available in the West.

Economics, politics and development

Dommen, Arthur J (1985) *Laos: Keystone of Indochina*, Boulder: Westview Press. Out of date but a reasonable overview.

Evans, Grant (1990) *Lao Peasants under Socialism*, New Haven: Yale University Press. The definitive account of farmers in modern Laos. A new edition published by Silkworm Books in Chiang Mai (Thailand) takes into account economic changes brought about by the New Economic Mechanism.

Stuart-Fox, Martin (1982) *Contemporary Laos*, St Lucia: Queensland University Press. A useful overview of Laos up to 1980.

Stuart-Fox, Martin (1986) *Laos – Politics, Economics and Society*, London: Francis Pinter. Out of date but a good single volume summary of the country providing historical and cultural background.

Stuart-Fox, Martin (1996) *Buddhist Kingdom, Marxist State: the Making of Modern Laos*, Bangkok: White Lotus. A collection of Stuart-Fox's various papers published over the years and brought up to date. Especially good on recent history.

Zasloff, J J and Unger, L (1991) (eds) *Laos: Beyond the Revolution*, Macmillan, Basingstoke. Edited volume with a mixed collection of papers; the chapters on the country's economics and politics are already rather dated.

History

Kremmer, Christopher, *Bamboo Palace*, HarperCollins Australia. Traces Kremmer's attempts to unravel the mystery surrounding the Lao royal family.

Stuart-Fox, Martin and Kooyman, Mary (1992), *Historical Dictionary of Laos*, New York: the Scarecrow Press. Takes a dictionary approach to Laos' history which is fine if you are looking up a fact or two, but doesn't really lend itself to telling a narrative.

Stuart-Fox, Martin (1997), *A History of Laos*, CUP: Cambridge. Concentrates on the modern period.

Language

Higbie, James, *Lao-English/English-Lao Dictionary and Phrasebook*, Hippocrene Books, Inc.

Marcus, Russell (1983) *Lao-English/ English- Lao Dictionary*, Charles E Tuttle Co, USA. Perhaps the best dictionary available; US$16.95 from www.worldlanguage.com

Phone Bouaravong, *Learning Lao for Everyone*. Locally produced, with tapes.

Werner, Klaus *Learning and Speaking Lao*. Useful and cheaper guide to the Lao language than Marcus Russell's.

Laos and the Indochina War

Castle, Timothy (1993) *A War in the Shadow of Vietnam: US Military Aid to the Royal Lao*

Government 1955-1975, New York: Columbia University Press.

Evans, Grant and Rowley, Kelvin (1990) *Red Brotherhood at War, Vietnam Cambodia & Laos since 1975*, Verso.

Evans, Grant (1983) *Yellow Rainmakers: Are Chemical Weapons Being Used in Southeast Asia*, Verso.

McCoy, Alfred W (1991) *The Politics of Heroin: CIA Complicity in the Global Drugs Trade*, Lawrence Hill/Chicago Review Press. Originally published at the beginning of the 1970s, the classic study of the politics of drugs in mainland Southeast Asia.

Parker, James (1995) *Codename Mule: Fighting the Secret War in Laos for the CIA*, Annapolis, Maryland: Naval Institute Press. Personal story of Americans fighting in Laos. Much of it deals with fighting on the Plain of Jars.

Pyle and Faas (2003) *Lost Over Laos*, De Capo Press. The story of 4 photographers who died in Laos in 1971 and the search, years later, to recover the crash site.

Ratnam, P (1980) *Laos and the Superpowers*, Tulsi Publishing, India.

Robbins, Christopher (1979) *Air America: the Story of the CIS's Secret Airlines*, New York: Putnam Books. The earlier of Robbins' 2 books on the secret war. Made into a film of the same name starring Mel Gibson.

Robbins, Christopher (1989) *The Ravens: Pilots of the Secret War of Laos*, New York: Bantam Press. The best known of all the books on America's secret war in Laos. The story it tells seems almost too incredible to be true.

Warner, Roger (1995) *Back Fire: the CIA's Secret War in Laos and its Link to the War in Vietnam*, New York: Simon and Schuster. The best of the more recent books recounting the experiences of US servicemen in Laos. Excellent, engaging read. Also published as Shooting at the Moon.

Travel and geography

De Carne, Louis (1872) *Travels in Indochina and the Chinese Empire*, London: Chapman Hall. Recounts De Carne's experiences in Laos in 1872, some years before the country was colonized by the French.

Dooley, Tom (1958) *The Edge of Tomorrow*, Farrar, Strauss & Cudahy.

Du Pont De Bie, Natacha (2004) *Ant Egg Soup: The Adventures of a Food Tourist in Laos*, Sceptre. A wonderful portrait of Lao culture and food through the eyes of a food tourist.

Garstin, Crosbie (1928), *The Voyage from London to Indochina*, Heinemann. Hilarious, irreverent journey through Indochina.

Hoskins, John (1991), *The Mekong*, Bangkok: Post Publishing. This is a large format coffee table book with excellent glossy photographs and a modest text. Widely available in Bangkok.

Lewis, Norman (1951), *A Dragon Apparent: Travels in Cambodia, Laos and Vietnam*. One of the finest travel books; reprinted by Eland Books but also available second-hand from many bookshops.

Maugham, Somerset (1930) *The Gentlemen in the Parlour: a Record of a Journey from Rangoon to Haiphong*, Heinemann: London. An account of Maugham's journey through Southeast Asia, in classic limpid prose.

McCarthy, James (1994) *Surveying and Exploring in Siam with Descriptions of Laos Dependencies and of Battles against the Chinese Haws*, White Lotus: Bangkok. First published in 1900. An interesting account by Englishman James McCarthy, who was employed by the government of Siam as a surveyor and adviser.

Mouhot, Henri (1986) *Travels in Indochina*, Bangkok: White Lotus. An account of Laos by France's most famous explorer of Southeast Asia. He tried to discover a 'back door' into China by travelling up the Mekong, but died of Malaria in Luang Prabang in 1860. The book has been republished by White Lotus and is easily available in Bangkok; there is also a more expensive reprint available from OUP (Kuala Lumpur).

Murphy, Dervla (1999) *One Foot in Laos*, John Murphy Publisher. This is an interesting, off-the-beaten-track travelogue of adventures and mishaps during a journey through Laos.

Stewart, Lucretia (1998), *Tiger Balm: Travels in Laos, Cambodia and Vietnam*, London: Chatto and Windus.

Books on Southeast Asia

White Lotus, www.thailine.com/lotus, is a Bangkok-based publisher specializing in English language books (with many reprints of old books) on the region.

Dingwall, Alastair (1994) *Traveller's Literary Companion to Southeast Asia*, In Print: Brighton. Extracts from books by Western and regional writers on Southeast Asia. A good overview of what is available.

Dumareay, Jacques (1991) *The Palaces of South-East Asia: Architecture and Customs*, OUP: Singapore. A broad summary of palace art and architecture in Southeast Asia.

Fraser-Lu, Sylvia (1988) *Handwoven Textiles of South-East Asia*, OUP: Singapore. Large well-illustrated book with informative text.

Higham, Charles (1989) *The Archaeology of Mainland Southeast Asia from 10,000 BC to the Fall of Angkor*, CUP: Cambridge. Best summary of changing views of the archaeology of the mainland.

Reid, Anthony (1988) *Southeast Asia in the Age of Commerce 1450-1680: the Lands below the Winds*, Yale University Press: New Haven. Perhaps the best history of everyday life in Southeast Asia, looking at such themes as physical wellbeing, material culture and social organization. Also Volume 2 (1993) *Southeast Asia in the Age of Commerce 1450-1680: Expansion and Crisis*, Yale University Press: New Haven.

Rigg, Jonathan (1997) *Southeast Asia: the Human Landscape of Modernization and Development*, London: Routledge. Focuses on how people have responded to the challenges and tensions of modernization.

SarDesai, DR (1989) *Southeast Asia: Past and Present*, Macmillan: London. Skillful but at times frustratingly thin history of the region from the 1st century to the withdrawal of US forces from Vietnam.

Steinberg, DJ et al (1987) *In Search of Southeast Asia: a Modern History*, University of Hawaii Press: Honolulu. The best standard history of the region.

Tarling, Nicholars (1992) (edit) *Cambridge History of Southeast Asia*, CUP: Cambridge. 2-volume edited study by theme and region, with contributions from most of the leading historians of the region. The history is fairly conventional.

Contents

Footnotes

Useful words and phrases

Greetings

yes/no men/baw
thank you/ kop jai
no thank you baw, kop jai
hello/goodbye suh-bye-dee/lah-gohn
What is your name? Chow seu yang?
My name is... Koi seu....
Excuse me, sorry Ko toat
Can/do you speak Koy pahk pah-sah
English? Anhg-geet?
A little, a bit Noi, hoi
Where? You-sigh?
How much is...? Tow-dai?
It doesn't matter Baw penh yang
Pardon? Kow toat?
I don't understand Kow baw cow-chi
How are you? Chao suh-bye-dee-baw?
not very well baw suh-bye

Getting around

Where is the Sa ta ni lot
train/bus station? phai/mee yu sai?
How much to go to...? Khit la ka taw dai...?
That's expensive Pheng-lie
Will you go for...kip? Chow ja pai...kip?
What time does the bus/train leave for...?
Lot mea oak jay mong...?
Is it far? Kai baw?
Turn left/turn right Leo sai/leo qua
Go straight on Pai leuy
River xe/se, houei/houai
Town muang/mouang
Mountain phou

Sleeping

What is the charge Kit laka van nuang
each night? taw dai?
Is the room air conditioned? Hong me ai
yen baw
Can I see the room first, please? Koi ko
beunghong dea?

Does the room have hot water? Hong me
nam hawn baw?
Does the room have a bathroom? Me
hang ap nam baw?
**Can I have the bill,
please?** Koi ton han bai hap

Eating

Can I see a menu? Kho beung lay kan
arhan?
Can I have...? Khoy tong kan...?
I am hungry Koy heo kao
I am thirsty Koy heo nahm
I want to eat Koh yahk kin kao
Where is a restaurant? Lahn ah hai you-
sigh?
breakfast arhan sao
lunch arhan athieng
It costs....kip Lah-kah ahn-nee...kip

Time

in the morning muh-sao
in the afternoon thon-by
in the evening muh-leng
today muh-nee
tomorrow muh-ouhn
yesterday muh van-nee
Monday Van Chanh
Tuesday Van Ang Khan
Wednesday Van Pud
Thursday Van Pa Had
Friday Van Sook
Saturday Van Sao
Sunday Van Arthid

Numbers

1 nung
2 song
3 sahm
4 see
5 hah

6 hoke
7 chet
8 pet
9 cow
10 sip
11 sip-et
12 sip-song
20 sao
21 sao-et
22 sao-song
30 sahn-sip
100 hoy
101 hoy-nung
150 hoy-hah-sip
200 song-hoy
1000 phan
10,000 sip-phan
100,000 muun
1,000,000 laan

Basic vocabulary

airport deune yonh
bank had xay
bathroom hong nam
beach heva
beautiful ngam
bicycle loht teep
big nyai
boat quoi loth bath
bus loht-buht
bus station hon kay ya
buy sue
chemist han kay ya
clean sa ard
closed arte
cold jenh
day vanh (or) mua

delicious sehb
dirty soka pox
doctor than mah
eat kinh
embassy Satan Tood
excellent dee leuth
expensive pheng
food ah-han
fruit mak-mai
hospital hong moh
hot (temp) hawn
hotel hong
island koh (or) hath
market ta lath
medicine ya pua payad
open peud
petrol nahm-mahn-eh-sahng
police lam louad
police station poam lam louad
post office hong kana pai sa nee
restaurant han arhane
road tha nonh
room hong
shop hanh
sick (ill) bo sabay
silk mai
small noy
stop yoot
taxi loht doy-sanh
that nahn
this nee, ahn-nee
ticket (air) pee yonh
ticket (bus) pee lot mea
toilet hong nam
town nai mouang
very lai-lai
water nam (or) nah
what men-nyung

Glossary

Amitabha the Buddha of the Past

Amulet protective medallion

Arhat one who has perfected himself

Avadana Buddhist narrative, telling of the deeds of saintly souls

Avalokitsvara also known as Amitabha and Lokeshvara, the name means 'World Lord'; he is the compassionate male Bodhisattva, saviour of Mahayana Buddhism. Represents the central force of creation in the universe

Bai sema boundary stones marking consecrated ground around a bot

Ban village; shortened from muban

Bhikku Buddhist monk

Bodhi the tree under which the Buddha achieved enlightenment (*Ficus religiosa*)

Bodhisattva a future Buddha. In Mahayana Buddhism, someone who has attained enlightenment, but postpones nirvana to help others reach it

Boun Lao festival

Brahma the Creator, one of the gods of the Hindu trinity, usually represented with four faces, and often mounted on a hamsa

Brahmin a Hindu priest

Bun to make merit

Caryatid elephants, often used as buttressing decorations

Champa rival empire of the Khmers, of Hindu culture, based in present day Vietnam

Chao title for Lao kings

Charn animist priest who conducts the *basi* ceremony in Laos

Chat honorific umbrella or royal parasol

Chedi religious monument containing relics of the Buddha or other holy remains

Chenla Chinese name for Cambodia before the Khmer era

Deva a Hindu-derived male god

Devata a Hindu-derived goddess

Dharma the Buddhist law

Dok sofa frond-like construction surmounting temple roofs in Laos. Over 10 flowers means the wat was built by a king

Dtin sin decorative border on a skirt

Funan the oldest Indianised state of Indochina and precursor to Chenla

Ganesh elephant-headed son of Siva

Garuda divine bird, with predatory beak and claws, and human body; the king of birds, enemy of naga and mount of Vishnu

Gautama the historic Buddha

Geomancy divination by lines and figures

Gopura crowned or covered gate, entrance to a religious area

Hamsa sacred goose, Brahma's mount; in Buddhism it represents the flight of doctrine

Hinayana 'Lesser Vehicle', major Buddhist sect, usually termed Theravada Buddhism

Hor kong a pavilion built on stilts where the temple drum is kept

Hor song phra secondary chapel

Hor takang bell tower

Hor tray/trai library where manuscripts are stored in a Lao or Thai temple

Hor vay offering temple

Indra the Vedic god of the heavens, weather and war

Jataka(s) the birth stories of the Buddha; they normally number 547; the last 10 are the most important

Kala (makara) a demon ordered to consume itself; often sculpted with grinning face and bulging eyes over entrances

Kathin/krathin a month period during the 8th lunar month when lay people present robes and gifts to monks

Ketumula flame-like motif above the Buddha head

Kinaree half-human, half-bird, usually depicted as a heavenly musician

Kirtamukha see kala

Krishna incarnation of Vishnu

Kuti living quarters of monks in a temple

Laterite bright red tropical soil/stone commonly used in Khmer monuments

Linga phallic symbol and one of the forms of Siva. Embedded in a pedestal shaped to allow drainage of lustral water poured over it. Typically has a succession of cross

Lokeshvara see Avalokitsvara

Mahabharata a Hindu epic text

Mahayana 'Greater Vehicle', major Buddhist sect

Maitreya the future Buddha

Makara mythological aquatic reptile often found with the kala framing doorways

Mandala a focus for meditation; a representation of the cosmos

Mara personification of evil and tempter of the Buddha

Meru sacred mountain at the centre of the world in Hindu-Buddhist cosmology

Mondop Cube-shaped building, often topped with a conical structure. Contains an object of worship like a footprint of the Buddha

Muang administrative unit

Mudra gesture of the hands of the Buddha

Nak Lao river dragon, a mythical guardian creature (see naga)

Naga benevolent mythical water serpent, enemy of Garuda

Naga makara fusion of naga and makara

Nalagiri the elephant let loose to attack the Buddha, who calmed him

Nandi/nandin bull, mount of Siva

Nirvana release from the cycle of suffering in Buddhist belief; 'enlightenment'

Nyak mythical water serpent (see naga)

Pa kama Lao men's all-purpose cloth

paddy/padi unhulled rice

Pali sacred language of Theravada Buddhism

Parvati consort of Siva

Pathet Lao Communist party based in the northeastern provinces of Laos until they came to power in 1975

Pha biang shawl worn by women in Laos

Pha sin piece of cloth, similar to sarong

Phi spirit

Phra sinh see *pha sin*

Pra Lam Lao version of the Ramayana

Pradaksina pilgrims' clockwise circumambulation of holy structure

The trinity of Brahma, Vishnu and Siva. sections: from square at the base through octagonal to round. These symbolize, in order, the trinity of Brahma, Vishnu and Siva.

Prah sacred

Prang form of stupa built in Khmer style, shaped like a corn cob

Prasada stepped pyramid (see prasat)

Prasat residence of a king or of the gods (sanctuary tower), from the Indian *prasada*

Rama incarnation of Vishnu, hero of the Indian epic, the Ramayana

Ramakien Lao version of the Ramayana

Ramayana Hindu romantic epic

Sakyamuni the historic Buddha

Sal the Indian sal tree (*Shorea robusta*), under which the historic Buddha was born

Sangha the Buddhist order of monks

Sim/sima main sanctuary and ordination hall in a Lao temple complex

Singha mythical guardian lion

Siva the Destroyer, one of the 3 gods of the Hindu trinity; the sacred linga was worshipped as a symbol of Siva

Sofa see *dok sofa*

Sravasti the miracle at Sravasti when the Buddha subdues the heretics

Stupa chedi

Tavatimsa heaven of the 33 gods at the summit of Mount Meru

Thanon street

That shrine housing Buddhist relics, a spire or dome-like edifice commemorating the Buddha's life or a funerary temple for royalty

Theravada 'Way of the Elders'; major Buddhist sect also known as Hinayana Buddhism ('Lesser Vehicle')

Traiphum the 3 worlds of Buddhist cosmology – heaven, hell and earth

Trimurti the Hindu trinity of gods: Brahma, the Creator, Vishnu the Preserver and Siva the Destroyer

Tripitaka Theravada Buddhism's Pali canon

Ubosoth see bot

Urna dot or curl on the Buddha's forehead

Usnisa the Buddha's top knot or 'wisdom bump'

Vahana 'vehicle', a beast, upon which a *deva* or god rides

Viharn assembly hall in a monastery

Vishnu the Protector, one of the gods of the Hindu trinity

Index → *Entries in bold refer to maps.*

Advertisers' index

Credits

Footprint credits

Project Editor: Jo Williams
Layout and production: Angus Dawson, Dorothy Stannard
Colour section: Pepi Bluck
Maps: Kevin Feeney
Proofreader: Dorothy Stannard

Managing Director: Andy Riddle
Commercial Director: Patrick Dawson
Publisher: Alan Murphy
Publishing Managers: Jo Williams, Felicity Laughton, Jen Haddington
Marketing and PR: Liz Harper
Sales: Diane McEntee
Advertising: Renu Sibal
Finance and administration: Elizabeth Taylor

Photography credits

Front cover: Tibor Bognar/Alamy
Back cover: Philippe Body/hemis.fr
Colour section: Page 1: Bruno Morandi/hemis.fr. Page 2: Neil Emmerson/Robert Harding World Imagery. Page 6: Romain Cintract/hemis.fr, Micah Hanson/Alamy, Pisit Jiropas/photolibrary.com, Ian Trower/Alamy, Frank Waldecker/photolibrary.com.
Page 7: Thomas Maresca, Terry Whittaker/Alamy, Andrew McConnell/Alamy, Christophe Boisvieux/hemis.fr.
Page 8: Pisit Jiropas/photolibrary.com

Printed in India by Nutech Print Services.

Footprint feedback

We try as hard as we can to make each Footprint guide as up to date as possible but, of course, things always change. If you want to let us know about your experiences – good, bad or ugly – then don't delay, go to www.**footprinttravelguides.com** and send in your comments.

Publishing information

Footprint Laos
6th edition
© Footprint Handbooks Ltd
November 2010

ISBN: 978 1 907263 11 8
CIP DATA: A catalogue record for this book is available from the British Library

® Footprint Handbooks and the Footprint mark are a registered trademark of Footprint Handbooks Ltd

Published by Footprint
6 Riverside Court
Lower Bristol Road
Bath BA2 3DZ, UK
T +44 (0)1225 469141
F +44 (0)1225 469461
footprinttravelguides.com

Distributed in the USA by Globe Pequot Press, Guilford, Connecticut

Every effort has been made to ensure that the facts in this guidebook are accurate. However, travellers should still obtain advice from consulates, airlines, etc about travel and visa requirements before travelling. The authors and publishers cannot accept responsibility for any loss, injury or inconvenience however caused.

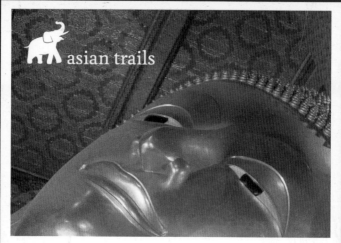

Journey through lost kingdoms and discover the hidden history of Asia to let Asian Trails be your guide!

CAMBODIA
Asian Trails Ltd. (Phnom Penh Office)
No. 22, Street 294, Sangkat Boeng Keng Kong I
Khan Chamkarmorn, P.O. Box 621, Phnom Penh, Cambodia
Tel: (855 23) 216 555 Fax: (855 23) 216 591
E-mail: res@asiantrails.com.kh

CHINA
Asian Trails China
Rm. 1001, Scitech Tower, No. 22 Jianguomenwai Avenue
Beijing 100004, P.R. China
Tel: (86 10) 6515 9259 & 9279 & 9260 Fax: (86 10) 6515 9293
E-mail: kris.vangoethem@asiantrailschina.com

INDONESIA
P.T. Asian Trails Indonesia
Jl. By Pass Ngurah Rai No. 260 Sanur
Denpasar 80228, Bali, Indonesia
Tel: (62 361) 285 771 Fax: (62 361) 281 515
E-mail: info@asiantrailsbali.com

LAO P.D.R.
Asian Trails Laos (AT Lao Co., Ltd.)
P.O. Box 5422, Unit 10, Ban Khounta Thong
Sikhottabong District, Vientiane, Lao P.D.R.
Tel: (856 21) 263 936 Fax: (856 21) 262 956
E-mail: vte@asiantrails.laopdr.com

MALAYSIA
Asian Trails (M) Sdn. Bhd.
11-2-B Jalan Manau off Jalan Kg. Attap 50460
Kuala Lumpur, Malaysia
Tel: (60 3) 2274 9488 Fax: (60 3) 2274 9588
E-mail: res@asiantrails.com.my

MYANMAR
Asian Trails Tour Ltd.
73 Pyay Road, Dagon Township, Yangon, Myanmar
Tel: (95 1) 211 212, 223 262 Fax: (95 1) 211 670
E-mail: res@asiantrails.com.mn

THAILAND
Asian Trails Ltd.
9th Floor, SG Tower, 161/1 Soi Mahadlek Luang 3, Rajdamri Road
Lumpini, Pathumwan, Bangkok 10330
Tel: (66 2) 626 2000 Fax: (66 2) 651 8111
E-mail: res@asiantrails.org

VIETNAM
Asian Trails Co., Ltd.
5th Floor, 21 Nguyen Trung Ngan Street, District 1
Ho Chi Minh City, Vietnam
Tel: (84 8) 3 910 2871 Fax: (84 8) 3 910 2874
E-mail: vietnam@asiantrails.com.vn

CONTACT
Contact us for our brochure or log into
www.asiantrails.info   www.asiantrails.net   www.asiantrails.com   www.asiantrails.travel